Software Engineering

(A Lifecycle Approach)

AF656372

Software Engineering

(A Lifecycle Approach)

Pratap K.J. Mohapatra
Professor
Department of Industrial Engineering & Management
Indian Institute of Technology, Kharagpur
Kharagpur, West Bengal

PUBLISHING FOR ONE WORLD

NEW AGE INTERNATIONAL (P) LIMITED, PUBLISHERS
New Delhi • Bangalore • Chennai • Cochin • Guwahati • Hyderabad
Jalandhar • Kolkata • Lucknow • Mumbai • Ranchi
Visit us at **www.newagepublishers.com**

Copyright © 2010, New Age International (P) Ltd., Publishers
Published by New Age International (P) Ltd., Publishers
First Edition: 2010
Reprint: 2010

All rights reserved.
No part of this book may be reproduced in any form, by photostat, microfilm, xerography, or any other means, or incorporated into any information retrieval system, electronic or mechanical, without the written permission of the copyright owner.

Branches:
- No. 37/10, 8th Cross (Near Hanuman Temple), Azad Nagar, Chamrajpet, **Bangalore**- 560 018. Tel.: (080) 26756823, Telefax: 26756820, E-mail: bangalore@newagepublishers.com
- 26, Damodaran Street, T. Nagar, **Chennai**- 600 017. Tel.: (044) 24353401, Telefax: 24351463 E-mail: chennai@newagepublishers.com
- CC-39/1016, Carrier Station Road, Ernakulam South, **Cochin**- 682 016. Tel.: (0484) 2377004, Telefax: 4051303 E-mail: cochin@newagepublishers.com
- Hemsen Complex, Mohd. Shah Road, Paltan Bazar, Near Starline Hotel, **Guwahati**- 781 008.Tel.: (0361) 2513881 Telefax: 2543669, E-mail: guwahati@newagepublishers.com
- No. 105, 1st Floor, Madhiray Kaveri Tower, 3-2-19, Azam Jahi Road, Nimboliadda, **Hyderabad**- 500 027. Tel.: (040) 24652456, Telefax: 24652457, E-mail:hyderabad@newagepublishers.com
- RDB Chambers (Formerly Lotus Cinema)106A, 1st Floor, S.N. Banerjee Road, **Kolkata**- 700 014. Tel.: (033) 22273773, Telefax: 22275247, E-mail:kolkata@newagepublishers.com
- 16-A, Jopling Road, **Lucknow**- 226 001. Tel.: (0522) 2209578, 4045297, Telefax: 2204098 E-mail: lucknow@newagepublishers.com
- 142C, Victor House, Ground Floor, N.M. Joshi Marg, Lower Parel, **Mumbai**- 400 013. Tel.: (022) 24927869 Telefax: 24915415, E-mail: mumbai@newagepublishers.com
- 22, Golden House, Daryaganj, **New Delhi**- 110 002. Tel.: (011) 23262370, 23262368, Telefax: 43551305 E-mail: sales@newagepublishers.com

ISBN : 978-81-224-2721-9

Rs. 260.00

C-10-06-4763

Printed in India at Ajit Printers, Delhi.
Typeset at Monu Printographics, Delhi.

PUBLISHING FOR ONE WORLD
NEW AGE INTERNATIONAL (P) LIMITED, PUBLISHERS
4835/24, Ansari Road, Daryaganj, New Delhi-110002
Visit us at **www.newagepublishers.com**

Preface

With the growth of computer-based information systems in all walks of life, software engineering discipline has undergone amazing changes and has spurred unprecedented interest among individuals — both old and new to the disciplines. New concepts in software engineering discipline are emerging very fast, both enveloping and replacing the old ones. Books on the subject are many and their sizes are getting bigger and bigger everyday.

A few trends are visible. Software engineering books used to contain a few chapters on software project management. Today, with new concepts on software project management evolving, the newly published books on software engineering try to cover topics of software project management, some topics such as requirements analysis, central to software engineering, get less priority, and the coverage of details of software tools is less than adequate. Further, many topics of historical importance, such as Jackson and Wariner-Orr approach, do not find place, or find only passing reference, in the books.

The book on Software Engineering — The Development Process is the first of a two-volume series planned to cover the entire gamut of areas in the broad discipline of software engineering and management. The book encompasses the approaches and tools required only in the software development process and does not cover topics of software project management. It focuses on the core software development life cycle processes and the associated tools. The book divides itself into five parts:

- Part 1 consists of two chapters in which it gives an historical overview and an introduction to the field of software engineering, elaborating on different software development life cycles.
- Part 2 consists of eight chapters covering various facets of requirements analysis. Highlighting the importance and difficulty in requirements elicitation process, it covers a wide variety of approaches spanning from the document flow chart to Petri nets.
- Part 3 consists of seven chapters dealing with the approaches and tools for software design. It covers the most fundamental design approach of top-down design and the most advanced approach of design patterns and software architecture. For convenience, we have included a chapter on coding in this part.
- Part 4 consists of six chapters on coding and unit testing. Keeping the phenomenal growth of object-oriented approaches in mind, we have also included here a chapter on object-oriented testing.
- Part 5 contains a chapter on integration testing.

Written on the basis of two decades of experience of teaching the subject, this book, we hope, will enthuse teachers, students, and professionals in the field of software engineering to get better insights into the historical and current perspectives of the subject.

Pratap K. J. Mohapatra

Acknowledgement

The book is a result of thirty-five years of teaching and learning the subject and ten years of effort at compiling the work. My knowledge of the subject has grown with the evolution of the area of Software Engineering. The subjects I introduced in the M. Tech. curricula from time to time are: Business Data Processing in the seventies, Management Information System in the eighties, System Analysis and Design in the early nineties, Software Engineering in the late nineties, and Software Project Management in the current decade. I acknowledge the inspiration I drew from my philosopher guide Professor Kailas Chandra Sahu who as Head of the Department always favoured introduction of new subjects in the curricula. I owe my learning the subject from numerous books and journals. The students in my class had gone through the same pains and pleasures of learning the subject as I. I acknowledge their inquisitiveness in the class and their painstaking effort of doing their home tasks at late nights.

The effort of writing the book would not have succeeded without the encouraging words from my wife, Budhi, and without the innocent inquiries regarding the progress in the book front from our daughter, Roni. I dedicate the book to them.

Pratap K. J. Mohapatra

Contents

THE BASICS

1 Introduction

We are living in an *information society* where most people are engaged in activities connected with either producing or collecting data, or organising, processing and storing data, and retrieving and disseminating stored information, or using such information for decision-making. Great developments have taken place in computer hardware technology, but the key to make this technology useful to humans lies with the software technology. In recent years software industry is exhibiting the highest growth rate throughout the world, India being no exception.

This book on software engineering is devoted to a presentation of concepts, tools and techniques used during the various phases of software development. In order to prepare a setting for the subject, in this introductory chapter, we give a historical overview of the subject of software engineering.

1.1 HISTORY OF SOFTWARE ENGINEERING

1.1.1 The Term 'Software Engineering'

While documenting the history of software engineering, we have to start with IBM 360 computer system in 1964 that combined, for the first time, the features of scientific and business applications. This computer system encouraged people to try to develop software for large and complex physical and management systems, which invariably resulted in large software systems. The need for a disciplined approach to software development was felt strongly when time and cost overruns, persisting quality problems, and high maintenance costs, etc., rose tremendously, giving rise to what was then widely termed as the "Software Crisis."

In a letter to Dr. Richard Thayer, the first editor of the IEEE Computer Society Publication on Software Engineering, Bauer (2003) who is credited to have coined the term "Software Engineering", narrates his experience of the origin of software engineering.

In the NATO Science Committee Dr. I. I. Rabi, the renowned Nobel laureate and physicist gave vent to this crisis and to the fact that the progress in software did not match the progress in hardware. The Committee set up a Study Group on Computer Science in the year 1967 with members drawn from a number of countries to assess the entire field of computer science. In its first meeting members discussed various promising scientific projects but they fell far short of a common unifying theme wanted by the Study Group. In a sudden mood of anger, Professor (Dr.) Fritz Bauer of Munich, the member from West Germany, said, "The whole trouble comes from the fact that there is so much tinkering with software. It is not made in a clean fabrication process. What we need is software engineering." The remark shocked, but got stuck in the minds of the members of the group (Bauer 2003). On the recommendation of the Group, a Working Conference on Software Engineering was held in Garmish, West Germany, during October 7–10, 1968 with Bauer as Chairman to discuss various issues and problems surrounding the development of large software systems. Among the 50 or so participants were P. Naur, J. N. Buxton, and Dijkstra, each of whom made significant contribution to the growth of software engineering in later years.

The report on this Conference published a year later (Naur and Randell, 1969) credited Bauer to have coined the term "Software Engineering." NATO Science Committee held its second conference at Rome, Italy in 1969 and named it the "Software Engineering Conference."

The first International Conference on Software Engineering was held in 1973. Institute of Electronics and Electrical Engineers (IEEE) started its journal "IEEE Transactions on Software Engineering" in 1975. In 1976, IEEE Transactions on Computers celebrated its 25th anniversary. To that special issue, Boehm contributed his now-famous paper entitled, Software Engineering (Boehm 1976), that clearly defined the scope of software engineering.

In 1975, Brooks (1975), who directed the development of IBM 360 operating system software over a period of ten years involving more than 100 man-months wrote his epoch-making book, "The Mythical Man-Month" where he brought out many problems associated with the development of large software programs in a multi-person environment.

In 1981, Boehm (1981) brought out his outstanding book entitled "Software Engineering Economics" where many managerial issues including the time and cost estimate of software development were highlighted.

Slowly and steadily software engineering grew into a discipline that not only recommended technical but also managerial solutions to various issues of software development.

1.1.2 Development of Tools and Techniques of Software Engineering

Seventies saw the development of a wide variety of engineering concepts, tools, and techniques that provided the foundation for the growth of the field. Royce (1970) introduced the phases of the software development life cycle. Wirth (1971) suggested stepwise refinement as method of program development. Hoare *et al.* (1972) gave the concepts of structured programming and stressed the need for doing away with GOTO statements. Parnas (1972) highlighted the virtues of modules and gave their specifications.

Endres (1975) made an analysis of errors and their causes in computer programs. Fagan (1976) forwarded a formal method of code inspection to reduce programming errors. McCabe (1976) developed flow graph representation of computer programs and their complexity measures that helped in testing. Halstead (1977) introduced a new term "Software Science" where he gave novel ideas for using information on number of unique operators and operands in a program to estimate its size and complexity. Gilb (1977) wrote the first book on software metrics. Jones (1978) highlighted misconceptions surrounding software quality and productivity and suggested various quality and productivity measures. DeMarco (1978) introduced the concept of data flow diagrams for structured analysis. Constantine and Yourdon (1979) gave the principles of structured design.

Eighties saw the consolidation of the ideas on software engineering. Boehm (1981) presented the COCOMO model for software estimation. Albrecht and Gaffney (1983) formalised the concepts of "function point" as a measure of software size. Ideas proliferated during this decade in areas such as process models, tools for analysis, design and testing. New concepts surfaced in the areas of measurement, reliability, estimation, reusability and project management.

This decade witnessed also the publication of an important book entitled, "Managing the Software Process" by Humprey (1989), where the foundation of the capability maturity models was laid.

Nineties saw a plethora of activities in the area of software quality, in particular, in the area of quality systems. Paulk *et al.* (1993) and Paulk (1995) developed the capability maturity model. Gamma *et al.* (1995) gave the concepts of "design patterns." This decade also saw publications of many good text books on software engineering (Pressman 1992, Sommerville 1996). This decade has also seen the introduction of many new ideas such as software architecture (Shaw and Garlan, 1996) and component-based software engineering (Pree 1997). Another development in this decade is the object-oriented analysis and design and unified modeling language (Rumbaugh *et al.* 1998 and Booch *et al.* 1999).

The initial years of the twenty-first century have seen the consolidation of the field of design patterns, software architecture, and component-based software engineering.

We have stated above that the many problems encountered in developing large software systems were bundled into the term software crisis and the principal reason for founding the discipline of software engineering was to defuse the software crisis. In the next section we shall see more clearly the factors that constituted the software crisis.

1.2 SOFTWARE CRISIS

During the late 1960s and 1970s, there was an outcry over an impending "software crisis." The symptoms of such a crisis surfaced then and are present even today. The symptoms are the following:

1. Software cost has shown a rising trend, outstripping the hardware cost. Boehm (1976, 1981) indicated that since the fifties, the percentage of total cost of computation attributable to hardware has dramatically reduced and that attributable to software has correspondingly increased (Fig. 1.1). Whereas software cost was only a little over 20% in the 1950's, it was nearly 60% in the 1970's, and about 80% in the 1980's. Today, the computer system that we buy as 'hardware' has generally cost the vendor about three times as much for the software as it has for the hardware (Pressman 1992).

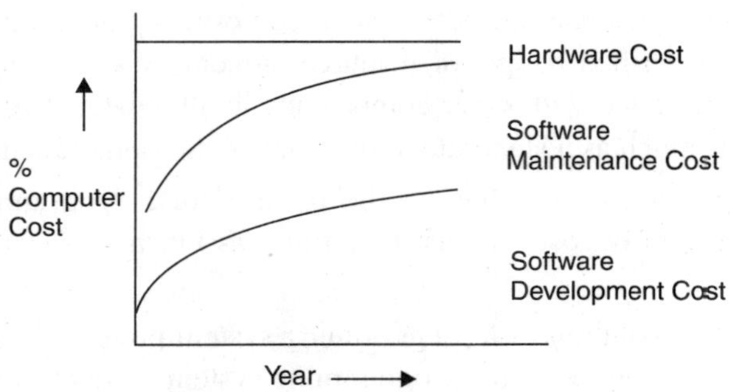

Fig. 1.1. Hardware and software costs

2. Software maintenance cost has been rising and has surpassed the development cost. Boehm (1981) has shown that the bulk of the software cost is due to its maintenance rather than its development (Fig. 1.1).
3. Software is almost always delivered late and exceeds the budgeted cost, indicating time and cost overruns.
4. It lacks transparency and is difficult to maintain.
5. Software quality is often less than adequate.
6. It often does not satisfy the customers.
7. Productivity of software people has not kept pace with the demand of their services.
8. Progress on software development is difficult to measure.
9. Very little real-world data is available on the software development process. Therefore, it has not been possible to set realistic standards.
10. How the persons work during the software development has not been properly understood.

One of the earliest works that explained to a great extent the causes of software crisis is by Brooks (1972). We shall get in the next section a glimpse of the work of Brooks.

1.3 EVOLUTION OF A PROGRAMMING SYSTEM PRODUCT

In his book 'The Mythical Man-Month' Brooks (1975) narrates his experience on the development of the IBM 360 operating system software. Among his many significant observations, one that is relevant at this stage is his observation on the effect of multiple users and multiple developers on the software development time. He distinguishes a program written by a person for his (her) use from a programming product, a programming system, and from a programming systems product.

A *program* is complete in itself, run by the author himself (herself), and is run on the machine on which it is developed. A *programming product* is a program that is written in a generalised fashion such that it can be run, tested, repaired, and extended by anybody. It means that the program must be tested, range and form of input explored, and these are well-recorded through documentation. A program, when converted into a programming product, costs, as a rule of thumb, three times as much as itself.

A *programming system* is a collection of interacting programs, coordinated in function and disciplined in format, so that the assemblage constitutes an entire facility for large tasks. In a programming system component, inputs and outputs must conform in syntax and semantics with precisely defined interfaces, use a prescribed budget of resources—memory space, input-output devices, and computer time, and must be tested with other components in all expected combinations. It generally costs at least three times as much as a stand-alone program of the same function.

A *programming system product* has all the features of a programming product and of a programming system. It generally costs at least nine times as much as a stand-alone program of the same function.

Figure 1.2 shows the evolution of a programming system product. It shows how product cost rises as a program is slowly converted into a programming system product. This discussion by Brooks is meant to bring home the point that developing software containing a set of interacting programs for the use by persons other than the developers requires much more time and effort than those required for developing a program for use by the developer. Since most software today is used by persons other than the developers, the cost of software development is surely going to be prohibitive. Software engineering methods, tools, and procedures help in streamlining the development activity so that the software is developed with high quality and productivity and with low cost.

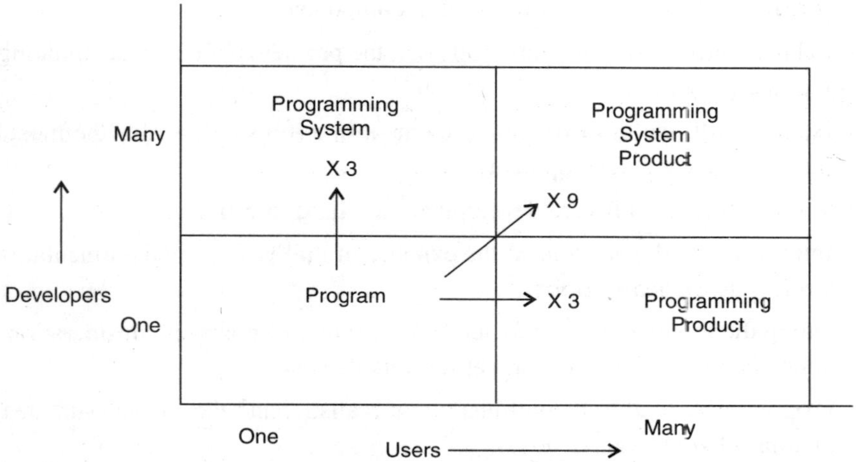

Fig. 1.2. Levels of programming

Some of the major reasons for this multiplying effect of multiple users and developers on software development time and, in general, the genesis of the software crisis can be better appreciated if we understand the characteristics of software and the ways they are different from those in the manufacturing environment.

1.4 CHARACTERISTICS OF SOFTWARE

Software is a logical rather than a physical system element. Therefore, software has characteristics that are considerably different from those of hardware (Wolverton 1974, and Pressman 1992). Some of the major differences are the following:

1. Software is developed or engineered, it is not manufactured.
   - The concept of 'raw material' is non-existent here. It is better visualised as a process, rather than a product (Jensen and Tonies, 1979).
   - The 'human element' is extremely high in software development, compared to manufacturing.
   - The development productivity is highly uncertain, even with standard products, varying greatly with skill of the developers.
   - The development tools, techniques, standards, and procedures vary widely across and within an organisation.

- Quality problems in software development are very different from those in manufacturing. Whereas the manufacturing quality characteristics can be objectively specified and easily measured, those in the software engineering environment are rather elusive.

2. Software development presents a job-shop environment.
   - Here each product is custom-built and hence unique.
   - It cannot be assembled from existing components.
   - All the complexities of a job shop (*viz.*, the problems of design, estimating, and scheduling) are present here.
   - Human skill, the most important element in a job shop, is also the most important element in software development.
3. Time and effort for software development are hard to estimate.
   - Interesting work gets done at the expense of dull work, and documentation, being a dull work, gets the least priority.
   - Doing the job in a clever way tends to be a more important consideration than getting it done adequately, on time, and at reasonable cost.
   - Programmers tend to be optimistic, not realistic, and their time estimates for task completion reflect this tendency.
   - Programmers have trouble communicating.
4. User requirements are often not conceived well enough; therefore a piece of software undergoes many modifications before it is implemented satisfactorily.
5. There are virtually no objective standards or measures by which to evaluate the progress of software development.
6. Testing a software is extremely difficult, because even a modest-sized program (< 5,000 executable statements) can contain enough executable paths (*i.e.*, ways to get from the beginning of the program to the end) so that the process of testing each path though the program can be prohibitively expensive.
7. Software does not wear out.
   - Software normally does not lose its functionality with use.
   - It may lose its functionality in time, however, as the user requirements change.
   - When defects are encountered, they are removed by rewriting the relevant code, not by replacing it with available code. That means that the concept of replacing the defective code by spare code is very unusual in software development.
   - When defects are removed, there is likelihood that new defects are introduced.
8. Hardware has physical models to use in evaluating design decisions. Software design evaluation, on the other hand, rests on judgment and intuition.
9. Hardware, because of its physical limitations, has practical bound on complexity because every hardware design must be realised as a physical implementation. Software, on the other hand, can be highly complex while still conforming to almost any set of needs.

10. There are major differences between the management of hardware and software projects. Traditional controls for hardware projects may be counterproductive in software projects. For example, reporting percent completed in terms of Lines of Code can be highly misleading.

It is now time to give a few definitions. The next section does this.

1.5 DEFINITIONS

Software

According to Webster's New Intercollegiate Dictionary, 1979,

"Software is the entire set of programs, procedures and related documentation associated with a system and especially a computer system."

The New Webster's Dictionary, 1981, reworded the definition, orienting it completely to computers:

"Software is the programs and programming support necessary to put a computer through its assigned tasks, as distinguished from the actual machine."

A more restrictive but functional definition is given by Blum (1992):

"Software is the detailed instructions that control the operation of a computer system. Its functions are to (1) manage the computer resources of the organisation, (2) provide tools for human beings to take advantage of these resources, and (3) act as an intermediary between organisations and stored information."

Gilb (1977) defines two principal components of software:

1. *Logicware*, the logical sequence of active instructions controlling the execution sequence (sequence of processing of the data) done by the hardware, and
2. *Dataware*, the physical form in which all (passive) information, including logicware, appears to the hardware, and which is processed as a result of the logic of the logicware.

Figure 1.3 (Gilb 1977) shows not only these two elements of a software system, but it also shows the other components as well.

There are eight levels of software that separate a user form the hardware. Following Gilb (1977) and Blum (1992), we show these levels in Fig. 1.4.

A. Hardware Logic	1. Machine Micrologic
B. System Software	2. Supervisor or Executive
	3. Operating System
	4. Language Translators
	5. Utility Programs

C. Application Software	6. Inquiry, File, and Database Software
	7. Programming and Assembly Languages and Programs
D. End-user Software	8. Fourth-Generation Languages and User Programs, such as SPSS, dbase-IV, and Lotus 1-2-3, SQL, etc.

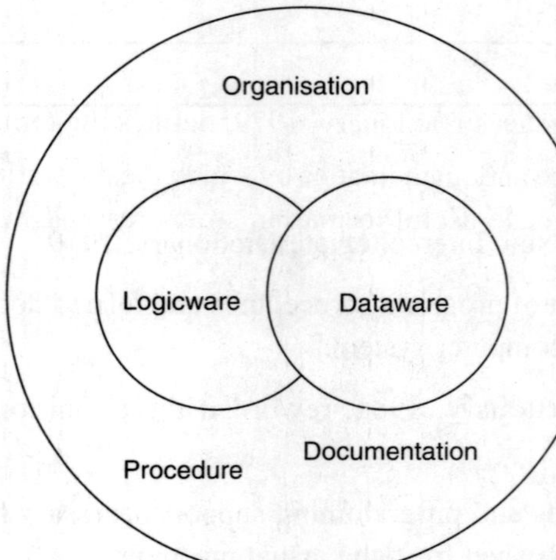

Fig. 1.3. Components of software systems

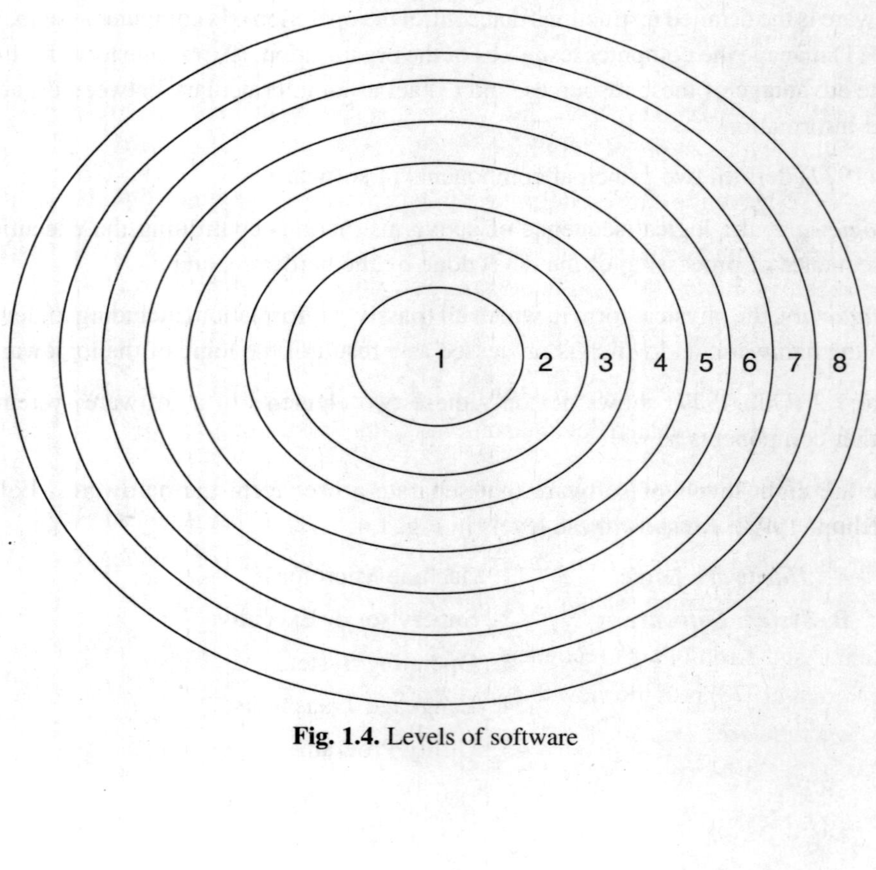

Fig. 1.4. Levels of software

What it is important to note here is that, contrary to popular belief, software includes not only the *programs* but also the *procedures* and the *related documentation*. Also important to note is that the word *software* is a collective noun just as the word *information* is; so the letter *s* should not be used after it. While referring to a number of packages, one should use the term *software packages*. Similarly, one should use the terms *software products*, *pieces of software*, and so on, and not the word *softwares*.

Engineering

New Intercollegiate Webster's Dictionary, 1979, defines the term *engineering* as

"the application of science and mathematics by which the properties of matter and the sources of energy in nature are made useful to man in structures, machines, products, systems and processes."

Thus, engineering denotes the application of scientific knowledge for practical *problem solving*.

Software Engineering

Naur (Naur and Randell 1969) who co-edited the report on the famous NATO conference at Garnish also co-authored one of the earliest books on the subject (Naur *et al.* 1976). In this book, the ideas behind *software engineering* were given as the following:

- Developing large software products is far more complex than developing stand-alone programs.
- The principles of engineering design should be applied to the task of developing large software products.

There are as many definitions of "Software Engineering" as there are authors. We attempt to glimpse through a sample of definitions given by exponents in the field.

Bauer (1972) gave the earliest definition for software engineering (Bauer 1972, p. 530):

"… the establishment and use of sound engineering principles (methods) in order to obtain economically software that is reliable and works on real machines."

According to Boehm (1976), software engineering is

"… the practical application of scientific knowledge in the design and construction of computer programs and the associated documentation required to develop, operate and maintain them."

Boehm (1976) expanded his idea by emphasising that the most pressing software development problems are in the area of requirements analysis, design, test, and maintenance of application software by technicians in an *economics-driven context* rather than in the area of detailed design and coding of system software by experts in a relatively *economics-independent* context.

DeRemer and Kron (1976) recognise *software engineering* to deal with *programming-in-the-large*, while Parnas (1978) is of the view that *software engineering* deals with '*multi-person construction of multi-version software*.'

Sommerville (1992) summarises the common factors involving software engineering:

1. Software systems are built by teams rather than individuals.
2. It uses engineering principles in the development of these systems that include both technical and non-technical aspects.

A more recent definition by Wang and King (2000) considers software engineering as a discipline and makes the engineering principles and product attributes more explicit:

"Software engineering is a discipline that adopts engineering approaches such as established methodologies, process, tools, standards, organisation methods, management methods, quality assurance systems, and the like to develop large-scale software with high productivity, low cost, controllable quality, and measurement development schedules."

Conventional Engineering and Software Engineering: Similarities and Differences

It is obvious from some of the above-stated definitions that software engineering shares quite a few things common with the principles of conventional engineering. Here we outline these similarities and a few differences between the two disciplines.

Jensen and Tonies (1979) consider software engineering to be related to the design of software or data processing products and to belong to its *problem solving* domain, encompassing the class of problems related to software and data processing. They expand their idea by drawing analogy from the methods that are generally used in engineering. According to them, just as the celebrated *scientific method* is used in the field of scientific research, the steps of *engineering design process* are used in the process of problem solving in the field of engineering. These steps, which are mostly iterative, are: (1) Problem formulation, (2) Problem analysis, (3) Search for alternatives, (4) Decision, (5) Specification, and (6) Implementation. Jenson and Tonies suggest that these steps are applicable to the field of software engineering as well.

Pressman (1992) considers software engineering as an outgrowth of hardware and systems engineering, encompassing a set of three key elements—methods, tools and procedures which enable the manager to control the process of software development. According to Pressman, *methods* provide the technical "how to's" for building software; *tools* provide automated or semi-automated support for methods; and *procedures* define the sequence of applying the methods, the deliverables, the controls, and the milestones.

Wang and King (2000) have highlighted the philosophical foundations of software engineering. Compared to traditional engineering disciplines, software engineering shows a few remarkable differences:

- In conventional engineering, one moves from an abstract design to a concrete product. In contrast, in software engineering, one moves from design to coding (that can be considered as abstract).

Software Engineering:	Abstract Design	⟶	More Abstract Code
Manufacturing Engineering:	Abstract Design	⟶	Concrete Products

- The problem domains of software engineering can be almost anything, from word processing to real-time control and from games to robotics. Compared to any other engineering discipline, it is thus much wider in scope and thus offers greater challenges.

- Traditional manufacturing engineering that normally emphasises mass production is loaded with production features. Thus, it is highly *production intensive*. Software engineering, on the other hand, is inherently *design intensive*.
- *Product standardisation* helps in cost reduction in manufacturing, whereas such a possibility is remote in software engineering. The possibility of *process standardisation*, however, is very high in the latter.
- Unlimited number of domain- and application-specific notions prevails in engineering disciplines. Software engineering, on the other hand, uses a limited, but universal, number of concepts, for example, standard logical structures of sequence, condition, and repetition.

1.6 NO SILVER BULLETS

In a widely-referred paper, Brooks, Jr. (1986) draws analogy of software projects with werewolves in the American folklore. Just as the werewolves transform unexpectedly from the familiar into horrors and require bullets made of silver to magically lay them to rest, the software projects, appearing simple and without problem, can transform into error-prone projects with high time and cost overruns. There is no silver bullet to ameliorate this problem, however.

According to Brooks, the *essence* of difficulties associated with software engineering lies with specification, design, and testing of the conceptual constructs while the error during representation are *accidents*. Software engineering must address the *essence*, and not the *accidents*.

The properties of essence of modern software systems, according to Brooks, Jr. (1986) are the following:

1. Complexity: No two parts of a software product are alike.
2. Conformity: Unlike natural laws in the physical systems, there does not seem to be a unifying theory for software systems.
3. Changeability: While manufactured products do not change very frequently, software products change, particularly with user requirements changing.
4. Invisibility: No really geometric representation, unlike a plan for a building or a drawing of the design of a machine, can represent the design of a software program.

Brooks, Jr. is of the opinion that the past breakthroughs, like high-level languages, time-sharing facility, and unifying programming environments (such as Unix), have attacked only the accidental problems of software engineering, not the essential ones. He is also skeptical about the ability of such developments as advances in other high-level languages, object-oriented programming, artificial intelligence, expert systems, automatic programming, program verification, programming environments and tools, and workstations in solving the essential problems of software engineering.

Brooks, Jr. suggests that the following developments have high potential in addressing the essential problems of software engineering:

1. *Buy rather than build.* Tested components already developed and in use are the best candidates to be reused in new software products. They will be error free. However, the

components have to be selected and they have to be properly integrated with the new software being developed.

2. *Requirements refinement and rapid prototyping.* Prototyping is a very useful method to elicit user information requirement. It helps to find out core requirements which are then refined when new prototypes are displayed to the users.
3. *Incremental development.* Developing the core functional requirements and then incrementally adding other functions hold the key to developing error-free software products.
4. *Creative designers.* The software firms should retain the best and the most skilled designers because they hold the key to bring out quality software products.

We end this chapter by stating a few myths surrounding development of software systems.

1.7 SOFTWARE MYTHS

Pressman (1992) has compiled the following myths that prevail in the software industry:

A. Management Myths:

- We already have a book that's full of standards and procedures for building software. Won't that provide my people with everything they need to know?
- My people do have state-of-the-art software development tools; after all, we buy them the newest computers.
- If we get behind schedule, we can add more men and catch up.

B. Customer's Myths:

- A general statement of objectives is sufficient to begin writing programs—we can fill in the details later.
- Project requirements continually change, but change can be easily accommodated because software is flexible.

C. Practitioner's Myths:

- Once we write the program and get it to work, our job is done.
- Until I get the program "running," I really have no way of assessing its quality.
- The only deliverable for a successful project is the working program.

As software engineering tools and techniques are developed and practiced, these myths have given way to genuine concern for new development tools and to a strong desire to know them. The following chapters elucidate them with examples and with reference to their development from the past to the present.

REFERENCES

Albrecht A. J. and J. E. Gaffney (1983), Software Function, Lines of Code and Development Effort Prediction: A Software Science Validation, IEEE Transactions on Software Engineering, vol. 9, no. 6, pp. 639–647.

Bauer, F. L. (1972), Software Engineering, Information Processing 71, North-Holland Publishing Co., Amsterdam.

Bauer, F. L. (1976), Software Engineering, in Ralston, A. and Mek, C. L. (eds.), Encyclopaedia of Computer Science, Petrocelli/charter, New York.

Bauer, F. L. (2003), The Origin of Software Engineering—Letter to Dr. Richard Thayer in Software Engineering, by Thayer, R. H. and M. Dorfman (eds.) (2003), pp. 7–8, John Wiley & Sons, Inc., N.J.

Blum, B. I. (1992), Software Engineering: A Holistic View, Oxford University Press, New York.

Boehm, B. W. (1976), Software Engineering, IEEE Transactions on Computers, vol. 25, no. 12, pp. 1226–1241.

Boehm B. W. (1981), Software Engineering Economics, Englewood Cliffs, NJ: Prentice Hall, Inc.

Booch, G., J. Rumbaugh, and I. Jacobson (1999), The Unified Modeling Language User Guide, Addison-Wesley Longman, Singapore Pte. Ltd.

Brooks, F. (1975), The Mythical Man-Month, Reading, MA: Addison-Wesley Publishing Co.

Brooks, F. P., Jr. (1986), No Silver Bullet: Essence and Accidents of Software Engineering, Information Processing '86, H. J. Kugler (ed.), Elsevier Science Publishers, North Holland, IFIP 1986.

DeMarco. T. (1978), Structured Analysis and System Specification, Yourdon Press, New York.

DeRemer, F. and H. Kron, (1976), Programming-in-the-Large versus Programming-in-the-Small, IEEE Transactions on Software Engineering, vol. 2, no. 2, pp. 80–86.

Endres, A. (1975), An Analysis of Errors and Their Causes in System Programs, IEEE Transactions on Software Engineering, vol. 1, no. 2, pp. 140–149.

Fagan, M. E. (1976), Design and Code Inspections to Reduce Errors in Program Development, IBM Systems J., vol. 15, no. 3, pp. 182–211.

Gamma, E., R. Helm, R. Johnson, and J. Vlissides (1995), Design Patterns: Elements of Reusable Object-Oriented Software, MA: Addison-Wesley Publishing Company, International Student Edition.

Ghezzi C., M. Jazayeri, and D. Mandrioli (1994), Fundamentals of Software Engineering, Prentice-Hall of India Private Limited, New Delhi.

Gilb, T. (1977), Software Metrics, Cambridge, Mass: Winthrop Publishers, Inc.

Halstead, M. H. (1977), Elements of Software Science, North Holland, Amsterdam.

Hoare, C. A. R., E-W, Dijkstra, and O-J. Dahl (1972), Structured Programming, Academic Press, New York.

Humphrey, W.S. (1989), Managing the Software Process, Reading MA: Addison-Wesley.

Jensen, R. W. and C. C. Tonies (1979), Software Engineering, Englewood Cliffs, NJ: Prentice Hall, Inc.

Jones, T. C. (1978), Measuring Programming Quality and Productivity, IBM Systems J., vol. 17, no. 1, pp. 39–63.

McCabe, T. J. (1976), A Complexity Measure, IEEE Transactions on Software Engineering, vol. 2, no. 4, pp. 308–320.

McDermid, J. A., ed. (1991), Software Engineering Study Book, Butterworth-Heinemann Ltd., Oxford, UK.

Naur, P. and Randell, B. (eds.) (1969), Software Engineering: A Report on a Conference Sponsored by the NATO Science Committee, NATO.

Naur, P., B. Randell, and J. Buxton (eds.) (1976), Software Engineering: Concepts and Techniques, Petrocelli/Charter, New York.

Parnas, D. L. (1972), A Technique for Module Specification with Examples, Communications of the ACM, vol. 15, no. 5, pp. 330–336.

Parnas, D. L. (1978), Some Software Engineering Principles, in Structured Analysis and Design, State of the Art Report, INFOTECH International, pp. 237–247.

Paulk, M. C. Curtis, B., Chrissis, M. B. and Weber, C. V. (1993), Capability Maturity Model, Version 1-1, IEEE Software, vol. 10, no. 4, pp. 18–27.

Paulk, M. C. (1995), How ISO 9001 Compares with the CMM, IEEE Software, January, pp. 74–83.

Pree, W. (1997), Component-Based Software Development—A New Paradigm in Software Engineering, Software Engineering Conference, ASPEC 1997 and ICSC 1997, Proceedings of Software Engineering Conference 1997, 2–5 December 1997, pp. 523-524.

Pressman, R. S. (1992), Software Engineering: A Practitioner's Approach, McGraw-Hill International Editions, Third Edition, Singapore.

Royce, W. W. (1970), Managing of the Development of Large Software Systems, in Proceedings of WESTCON, San Francisco, CA.

Rumbaugh, J., Jacobson, I., and Booch, G. (1998), The Unified Modeling Language Reference Manual, ACM Press, New York.

Shaw, M. and D. Garlan (1996), Software Architecture: Perspectives on an Emerging Discipline, Prentice-Hall.

Sommerville, I. (1996), Software Engineering (Fifth edition), Addison-Wesley, Reading MA.

Wang, Y. and G. King (2000), Software Engineering Process: Principles and Applications, CRC Press, New York.

Wang, Y., Bryant, A., and Wickberg, H. (1998), A Perspective on Education of the Foundations of Software Engineering, Proceedings of 1st International Software Engineering Education Symposium (SEE'98), Scientific Publishers OWN, Poznars, pp. 194–204.

Wirth, N. (1971), Program Development by Stepwise Refinement, Communications of the ACM, vol. 14, no. 4, pp. 221–227.

Wolverton, R. W. (1974), The Cost of Developing Large-scale Software, IEEE Transactions on Computers, June, pp. 282–303.

2 Software Development Life Cycles

We may define a cycle as 'a succession of events repeated regularly within a given period of time' or 'a round of years or recurring period of time, in which certain events repeat themselves'. 'Life cycle' is a sequence of events or patterns that reveal themselves in the lifetime of an organism. Software products are seen to display such a sequence of pattern in their lifetimes. In this chapter, we are going to discuss a generalized pattern that is generally observed in the lifetime of a software product. Recognition of such a software development life cycle holds the key to successful software development.

2.1 SOFTWARE DEVELOPMENT PROCESS

The process of software development has taken different routes at different times in the past. One can discern the following idealized models of software development process:

1. The code-and-fix model
2. The waterfall model
3. The evolutionary model
4. The spiral model

2.2 THE CODE-AND-FIX MODEL

During the early years of software development (the fifties and the sixties), the software development was a single-person task, characterized by the following:

1. It was a science or an engineering application.
2. The developer was also the user of the software.
3. The requirements were fully known.
4. The development of a software product primarily involved coding and fixing bugs, if any.

Ghezzi *et al.* (1994) call this type of development process the code-and-fix model.

As years rolled by, however, this type of process model was found to be highly inadequate because of many changes that took place in the software development environment. The changes that had highly significant effect on the development process were the following:

1. Computers started becoming popular and its application domain extended considerably, from science and engineering to business, industry, service, military, and government.
2. Developers became different from users. A piece of software was developed either in response to a request from a specific customer or targeted towards the general need of a class of users in the marketplace.
3. Developers spent considerable time and effort to understand user requirements. Developers changed their codes several times, sometimes even after they thought they had completed the development of the software, in order to incorporate the user requirements.
4. Applications often became so complex and large that the software had to be developed by a group of persons, rather than a single person, requiring considerable amount of planning for the division of the work, coordination for their smooth execution, and control so that the software was developed within the stipulated time.
5. Large software products and their development by a group of persons invariably led to frequent malfunctioning of the software products during testing (by the developers) and use (at the user sites). Identifying the defects and correcting them became increasingly difficult. Large turnover of software developers accentuated this problem. Quality assurance and maintenance, thus, needed disciplined design and coding. It also needed careful documentation. Testing at various levels assumed great significance. Maintenance of a piece of software became an inevitable adjunct of the development process.
6. The changing requirements of a customer often called for modification and enhancement of an existing piece of software. Coupled with the opportunities provided by new hardware and software, such modification and enhancement sometimes led to discarding the old software and paved the way for a new piece of software.

These changes led to a more systematic way to developing software products.

2.3 THE WATERFALL MODEL

For a long time the software industry was in a quandary as to what guidelines to follow during the software development process. Influenced by the development process followed in the famous air defense software project called SAGE (Semi-Automated Ground Environment) and by concepts forwarded by Bennington (1956) and Rosove (1976), Royce (1970) proposed the celebrated 'Waterfall Model' of the software development process (Fig. 2.1). This model became popular and provided the much-needed practical guidelines for developing a piece of software. Boehm had been a strong proponent of the waterfall model. He provided an economic rationale behind this model (Boehm 1976) and proposed various refinements therein (Boehm 1981).

Closely associated with the waterfall model was the concept of the 'software development life cycle'. Software was conceived as a living being with clearly defined sequence of development phases, starting from the conceptualization of the problem (the birth of an idea—the first phase) to the discarding of the software (the death of the software—the last phase).

The waterfall model derives its name from the structural (geometric) similarity of a software development process with a waterfall. The model makes the following major assumptions:

1. The software development process consists of a number of phases in sequence, so that only after a phase is complete, work on the next phase can start. It, thus, presupposes a unidirectional flow of control among the phases.
2. From the first phase (the problem conceptualization) to the last phase (the retirement), there is a downward flow of primary information and development effort (Sage 1995).
3. Work can be divided, according to phases, among different classes of specialists.

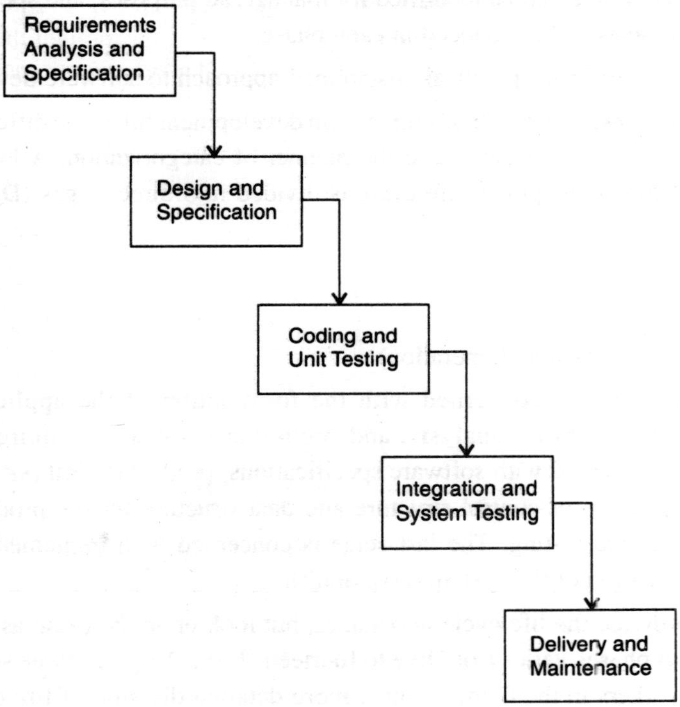

Fig. 2.1. The waterfall model of Royce (1970)

4. It is possible to associate a goal for each phase and accordingly plan the deliverables (the exit condition or the output) of each phase.
5. The output of one phase becomes the input (*i.e.,* the starting point) to the next phase.
6. Before the output of one phase is used as the input to the next phase, it is subjected to various types of review and verification and validation testing. The test results provide a feedback information upward that is used for reworking and providing the correct output. Thus, although the overall strategy of development favours unidirectional (or sequential) flow, it also allows limited iterative flow from the immediately succeeding phases.
7. Normally, the output is frozen, and the output documents are signed off by the staff of the producing phase, and these become the essential documents with the help of which the

work in the receiver phase starts. Such an output forms a *baseline*, a 'frozen' product from a life-cycle phase, that provides a check point or a stable point of reference and is not changed without the agreement of all interested parties. A definitive version of this output is normally made available to the controller of the configuration management process (the Project Librarian).

8. It is possible to develop different development tools suitable to the requirements of each phase.
9. The phases provide a basis for management and control because they define segments of the flow of work, which can be identified for managerial purposes, and specify the documents or other deliverables to be produced in each phase.

The model thus provides a practical, disciplined approach to software development.

Different writers describe the phases for system development life cycle differently. The difference is primarily due to the amount of detail and the manner of categorization. A less detailed and broad categorization is that the development life cycle is divided into three stages (Davis and Olson 1985, Sage 1995).

Definition,

Development, and

Deployment (installation and operation)

The definition stage is concerned with the formulation of the application problem, user requirements analysis, feasibility analysis, and preliminary software requirements analysis. The development stage is concerned with software specifications, product design (*i.e.,* design of hardware-software architecture, design of control structure and data structure for the product), detailed design, coding, and integrating and testing. The last stage is concerned with implementation, operation and maintenance, and evoluation of the system (post-audit).

Others do not divide the life cycle into stages, but look upon the cycle as consisting of various phases. The number of phases varies from five to fourteen. Table 2.1 gives three sequences of phases as detailed by various workers in the field. A much more detailed division of life cycle into phases and sub-phases is given by Jones (1986, p. 118) and is given in Table 2.2.

According to New Webster's Dictionary, a *stage* is 'a single step or degree in process; a particular period in a course of progress, action or development; a level in a series of levels'. A *phase,* on the other hand, is 'any of the appearances or aspects in which a thing of varying models or conditions manifests itself to the eye or mind; a stage of change or development'. *We take a stage to consist of a number of phases.*

Figures 2.1 and 2.2 show, respectively, the waterfall model by Royce and the modified waterfall model by Boehm. Note that the original model by Royce was a feed-forward model without any feedback, whereas the Boehm's model provided a feedback to the immediately preceding phase. Further, the Boehm's model required verification and validation before a phase's output was frozen.

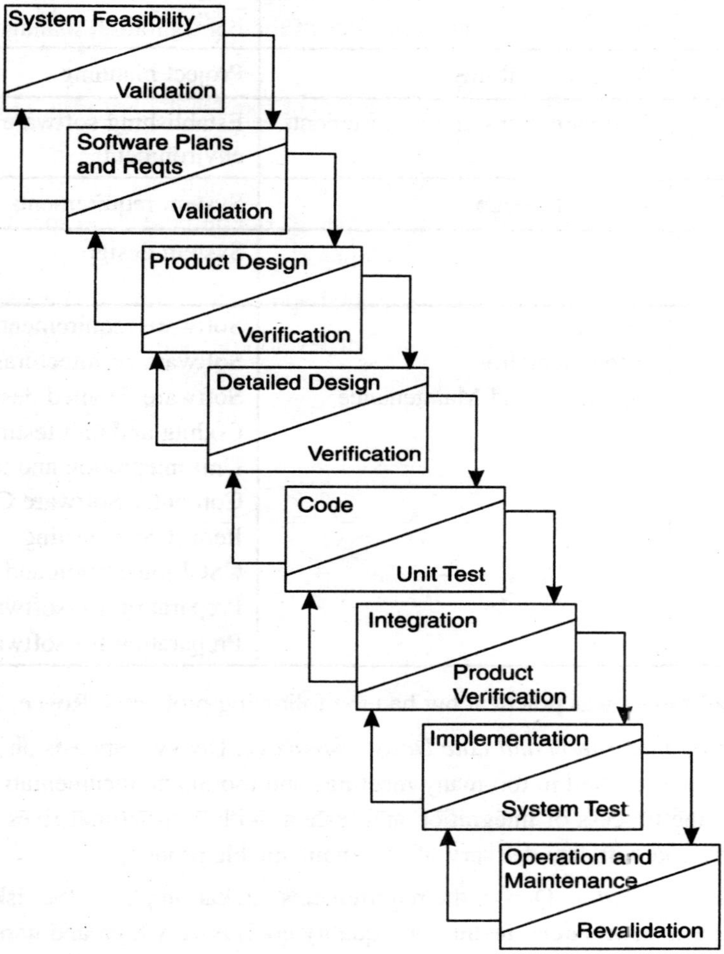

Fig. 2.2. The waterfall model of Boehm (1981)

Table 2.1: Life Cycle Phases by Various Authors

Thibodeau and Dodson (1985)	Boehm (1981)	Sage (1995)
Analysis	System feasibility	Project planning
Design	Software plans and requirements	Establishing software development environment
Coding	Detailed design	System requirements analysis
Test and Integration	Code	System design
Operation and Maintenance	Integration Implementation Operation and Maintenance	Software requirements analysis Software architectural design Software detailed design Coding and unit testing Unit integration and testing Computer Software Configuration Item (CSCI) testing CSCI integration and testing Preparation for software use and support Preparation for software delivery

The waterfall model was practical but had the following problems (Royce, 2000):

1. *Protracted Integration and Late Design Breakage.* Heavy emphasis on perfect analysis and design often resulted in too many meetings and too much documentation and substantially delayed the process of integration and testing, with non-optimal fixes, very little time for redesign, and with late delivery of non-maintainable products.
2. *Late Risk Resolution.* During the requirements elicitation phase, the risk (the probability of missing a cost, schedule, feature or a quality goal) is very high and unpredictable. Through various phases, the risk gets stabilized (design and coding phase), resolved (integration phase) and controlled (testing phase). The late resolution of risks result in the late design changes and, consequently, in code with low maintainability.
3. *Requirements-Driven Functional Decomposition.* The waterfall model requires specifying requirements completely and unambiguously. But it also assumes that all the requirements are equally important, and they do not change over the development phases. The first assumption is responsible for wasting away many person-days of effort while the second assumption may make the software engineering useless to the ultimate user. In most waterfall model-based developments, requirements are decomposed and allocated to functions of the program. Such decomposition and allocation are not possible in object-oriented developments that are the order of the day.

Table 2.2: Phases and Sub-Phases of Software Life Cycle

Phase I	Problem definition	Problem analysis Technology selection Skills inventory
Phase II	Requirements	Requirements exploration Requirements documentation Requirements analysis
Phase III	Implementation planning	Make-or-buy decisions Tool selection Project planning
Phase IV	High-level design	Basic data analysis Basic function analysis Basic structure analysis Inspection, repair and rework
Phase V	Detailed design	Functional specifications Logic specifications System prototype
Phase VI	Implementation	Reusable code acquisition New code development Customization
Phase VII	Integration and test	Inspection, repair and rework Local and component integration Test environment construction Full integration and test repair, rework
Phase VIII	Customer acceptance	Defect removal efficiency Defect removal calibration Packaging and delivery On-site assistance
Phase IX	Maintenance (Defect repairs)	Defect reporting Defect analysis Defect repairs
Phase X	Functional enhancements	Customer-originated enhancements Technically-originated enhancements

4. *Adversarial Stakeholder Relationships.* As already discussed, every document is signed off by two parties at the end of the phase and before the start of the succeeding phase. Such a document thus provides a contractual relationship for both parties. Such a relationship can degenerate into mistrust, particularly between a customer and a contractor.

2.3.1 Performance of Conventional Software Process in Practice

Boehm (1987) presents a list of ten rules of thumb that characterize the conventional software process as it is practiced during the past three decades.

1. Finding and fixing software problem after delivery costs 100 times more than finding and fixing the problem in early design phases.
2. One can compress software developments schedules 25% of nominal, but no more.
3. For every US $1 one spends on development, he/she will spend $2 on maintenance.
4. Software development and maintenance costs are primarily a function of the number of source lines of code.
5. Variations among people account for the biggest differences in software productivity.
6. The overall ratio of software to hardware costs is still growing. In 1955 it was 15:85; in 1985, it is 85:15.
7. Only about 15% of software development effort is devoted to programming.
8. Software systems and products typically cost 3 times as much per SLOC (Source Lines of Code) as individual software programs. Software system products cost 3 times as much.
9. Walk-throughs catch 60% of the errors.
10. 80% of the contribution comes from 20% of the contributions.

Boehm (1976, 1981) gives the following economic rationale behind the phases and their sequential ordering:

1. *All the phases and their associated goals are necessary.* It may be possible, as in the code-and-fix models, for highly simple, structured, and familiar applications to straight away write a code without going through the earlier phases. But this informal practice has almost always led to serious deficiencies, particularly in large and complex problems.
2. *Any different ordering of the phases will produce a less successful software product.* Many studies (for example, Boehm 1973, 1976, 1981; Myers 1976 and Fagan 1976) have shown that the cost incurred to fix an error increases geometrically if it is detected late. As an example, fixing an error can be 100 times more expensive in the maintenance phase than in the requirements phase (Boehm 1981). Thus, there is a very high premium on the value of analysis and design phases preceding the coding phase.

Davis *et al*. (1988) cite the following uses of a waterfall model:

1. The model encourages one to specify what the system is supposed to do (*i.e.,* defining the requirements) before building the system (*i.e.,* designing).
2. It encourages one to plan how components are going to interact (*i.e.,* designing before coding).
3. It enables project managers to track progress more accurately and to uncover possible slippages early.
4. It demands that the development process generates a series of documents that can be utilized later to test and maintain the system.

5. It reduces development and maintenance costs due to all of the above-mentioned reasons.
6. It enables the organization that will develop the system to be more structured and manageable.

2.3.2 A Critique of the Waterfall Model

The waterfall model has provided the much-needed guidelines for a disciplined approach to software development. But it is not without problems.

1. *The waterfall model is rigid.* The phase rigidity, that the results of each phase are to be frozen before the next phase can begin, is very strong.
2. *It is monolithic.* The planning is oriented to a single delivery date. If any error occurs in the analysis phase, then it will be known only when the software is delivered to the user. In case the user requirements are not properly elicited or if user requirements change during design, coding and testing phases, then the waterfall model results in inadequate software products.
3. *The model is heavily document driven to the point of being bureaucratic.*

To get over these difficulties, two broad approaches have been advanced in the form of refinements of the waterfall model:

1. The evolutionary model.
2. The spiral model.

2.4 THE EVOLUTIONARY MODEL

The waterfall model is a pure level-by-level, top-down approach. Therefore, the customer does not get to know anything about the software until the very end of the development life cycle. In an evolutionary approach, by constrast, working models of the software are developed and presented to the customer for his/her feedback, for incorporation in and delivery of the final software.

The evolutionary approach can be implemented in two forms:

1. Incremental implementation.
2. Prototyping.

2.5 THE INCREMENTAL IMPLEMENTATION (BOEHM 1981, GILB 1988)

Here the software is developed in increments of functional capability; *i.e.,* the development is in steps, with parts of some stages postponed in order to produce useful working functions earlier in the development of the project. Other functions are slowly added later as increments. Thus, while analysis and design are done following the waterfall process model, coding, integration and testing are done in an incremental manner.

As an example, IGRASP, the Interactive Graphic Simulation Package, was developed in three steps, one kernel and two increments (Fig. 2.3). Initially, the *kernel* included the routines written to

1. Error-check and manually sort inputted program statements,
2. Include functions and subroutines, and
3. Make the computations and provide tabular outputs.

Increment 1 added the features of

1. Icon-based diagrammatic input,
2. Automatic code generation, and
3. Graphic output.

Increment 2 provided the facilities of

1. Output animation and
2. Gaming.

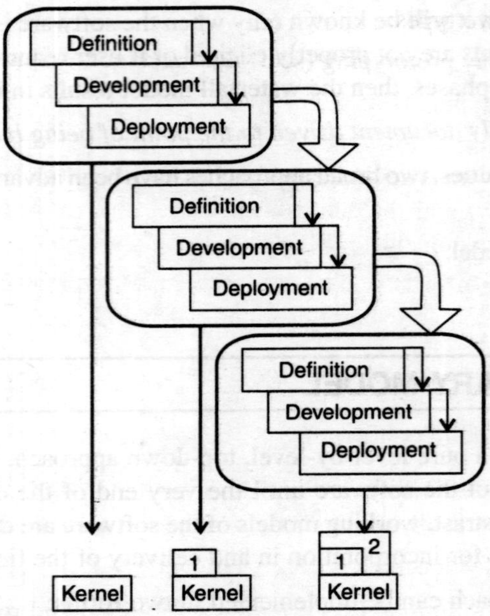

Fig. 2.3. Incremental development of IGRASP

The incremental approach has got many advantages:

1. Users can give suggestions on the parts to be delivered at later points of time.
2. The developers engage themselves in developing the most fundamental functional features of the software in its first increment. Thus, these features get the maximum, and the most concentrated, attention from the developers. Therefore, there is great likelihood that the programs are error-free.
3. The time to show some results to the users is considerably reduced. User reactions, if any, can threfore be incorporated in the software with great ease.
4. Testing, error detection, and error correction become relatively easy tasks.

Certain problems, generally associated with incremental development of software, are the following:

1. The overall architectural framework of the product must be established in the beginning and all increments must fit into this framework.
2. A customer-developer contract oriented towards incremental development is not very usual.

2.6 PROTOTYPING

This method is based on an experimental procedure whereby a working prototype of the software is given to the user for comments and feedback. It helps the user to express his requirements in more definitive and concrete terms.

Prototype can be of two types:

1. The rapid throwaway prototyping (scaffolding) (Fig. 2.4) and
2. Evolutionary prototyping (Fig. 2.5)

Throwaway prototyping follows the 'do it twice' principle advocated by Brooks (1975). Here, the initial version of the software is developed only temporarily to elicit information requirements of the user. It is then thrown away, and the second version is developed following the waterfall model, culminating in full-scale development.

In case of evolutionary prototyping, the initial prototype is not thrown away. Instead, it is progressively transformed into the final application.

2.6.1 Evolutionary vs. Throwaway Prototyping

Characteristics of both the prototyping methods are given below:

- Both types of prototyping assume that at the outset some abstract, incomplete set of requirements have been identified.
- Both allow user feedback.
- An evolutionary prototype is continuously modified and refined in the light of streams of user beedback till the user is satisfied. At that stage, the software product is delivered to the customer.
- A throwaway prototype, on the other hand, allows the users to give feedback, and thus provides a basis for clearly specifying a complete set of requirements specifications. These specifications are used to start *de novo* developing another piece of software following the usual stages of software development life cycle.

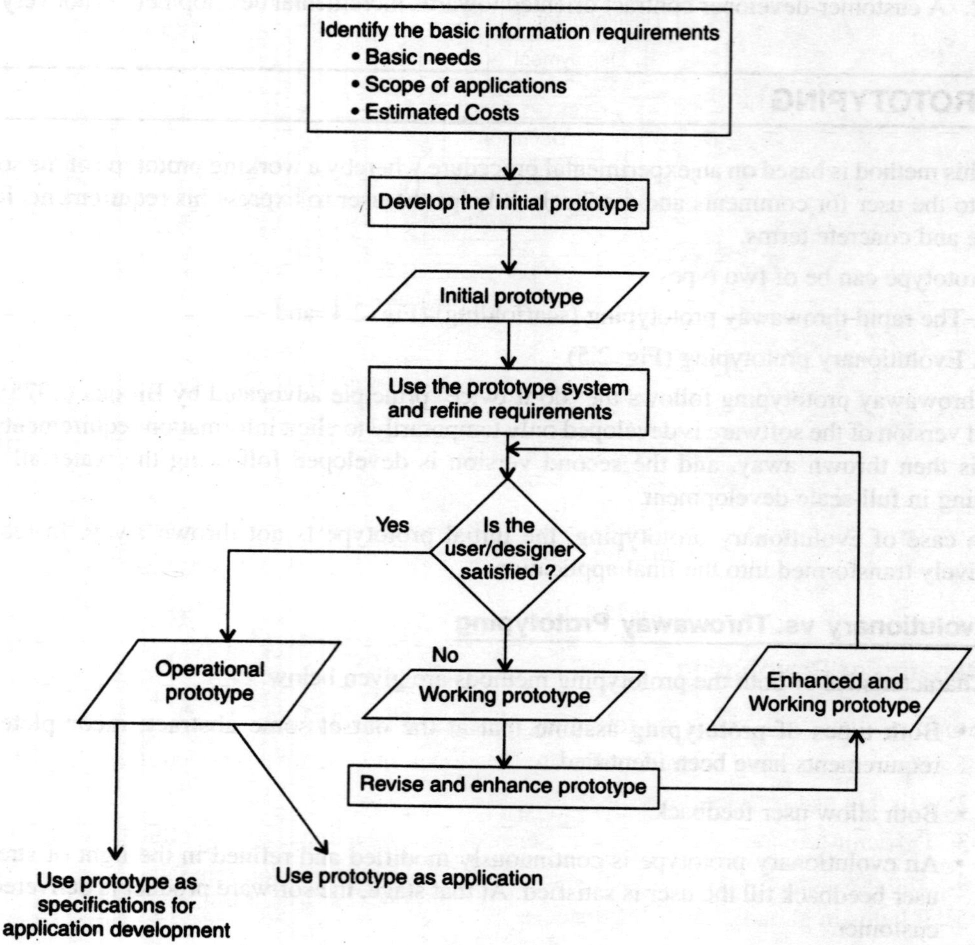

Fig. 2.4. Application system prototype development model
(Adapted from Davis and Olson, 1985)

- **Various revisions carried out an evolutionary prototype usually result in bad program structure and make it quite bad from the maintainability point of view.**
- **A throwaway prototype is usually unsuitable for testing non-functional requirements and the mode of the use of this prototype may not correspond with the actual implementation environment of the final software product.**

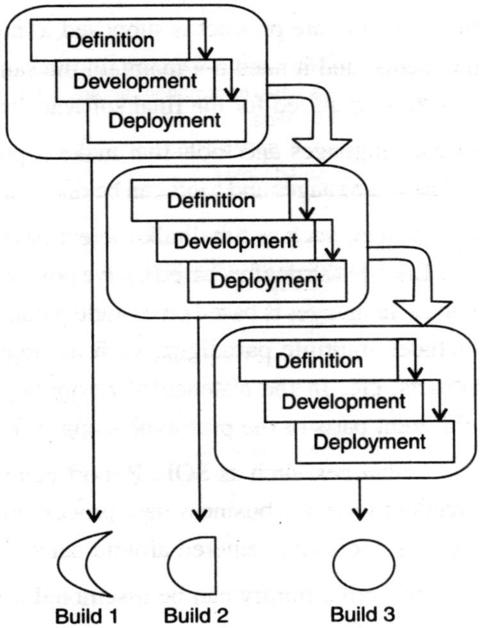

Fig. 2.5. Evolutionary prototyping

2.6.2 Benefits of Prototyping

Sommerville (1999) states the following benefits of prototyping:

1. Misunderstanding between software developer and user may be identified.
2. Missing user services may be detected.
3. Difficult-to-use or confusing user services may be identified and refined.
4. The developers may find incomplete and/or inconsistent requirements.
5. It helps in gaining user confidence.
6. It helps in writing the specification.
7. Correct specification of requirements reduces requirements-related errors and therefore the overall development cost.
8. It can be used for training users before the final system is delivered.
9. Test cases for prototype can be used for the final software product (back-to-back testing). In case the results are the same, there is no need for any tedious manual checking.

The last two benefits cited are due to Ince and Hekmatpour (1987).

2.6.3 Guidelines for Developing Prototypes

The following guidelines are available for developing prototypes:

1. The objectives of a prototype must be explicit so that the users are clearly aware of them. They may be to develop the user interface, validate functional requirements, or achieve a similar kind of specific objective.

2. Prototyping requires additional cost. Thus a prototype should be developed for a subset of the functions that the final software product is supposed to have. It should therefore ignore non-functional requirements, and it need not maintain the same error-handling, quality and reliability standards as those required for the final software product.
3. The developers must use languages and tools that make it possible to develop a prototype fast and at a low cost. These languages and tools can be one or a combination of the following:
   (*a*) *Very high-level languages,* such as Smalltalk (object based), Prolog (logic based), APL (vector based), and Lisp (list structures based), have powerful data management facilities. Whereas each of these languages is based on a single paradigm, Loops is a wide-spectrum language that includes multiple paradigms such as objects, logic programming, and imperative constructs, etc. In the absence of Loops, one can use a mixed-language approach, with different parts of the prototype using different languages.
   (*b*) *Fourth-generation languages,* such as SQL, Report generator, spreadsheet, and screen generator, are excellent tools for business data processing applications. They are often used along with CASE tools and centered around database applications.
   (*c*) *Reusable components* from a library can be assembled to quickly develop a prototype. However, since the specification of the components and of the requirements may not match, these components may be useful for throwaway prototyping.
   (*d*) An *executable specification language,* such as Z, can be used to develop a prototype if the requirements are specified in a formal, mathematical language. Functional languages, such as Miranda and ML, may be used instead, along with graphic user interface libraries to allow rapid prototype development.

Summerville (1999) summarizes the languages, their types, and their application domains (Table 2.3).

Table 2.3: Languages for Rapid prototyping

Language	Type	Application Domain
Smalltalk	Object-oriented	Interactive Systems
Loops	Wide-spectrum	Interactive Systems
Prolog	Logic	Symbolic Processing
Lisp	List-base	Symbolic Processing
Miranda	Functional	Symbolic Processing
SETL	Set-based	Symbolic Processing
APL	Mathematical	Scientific Systems
4GLs	Database	Business Data Processing
CASE tools	Graphical	Business Data Processing

2.7 THE SPIRAL MODEL

Boehm (1988) has advanced the spiral model of software development. The model integrates the characteristics of the waterfall model, the incremental implementation, and the evolutionary prototyping approach. In this sense, it is a *metamodel* (Ghezzi *et al.* 1994). The model has the following features:

1. The process of the software development can be depicted in the form of a spiral that moves in a clockwise fashion (Fig. 2.6).
2. Each cycle of the spiral depicts a particular phase of software development life cycle. Thus the innermost cycle may deal with requirements analysis, the next cycle with design, and so on. The model does not pre-assume any fixed phases. The management decides on the phases; thus the number of cycles in the spiral model may vary from one organization to another, from one project to another, or even from one project to another in the same organization.

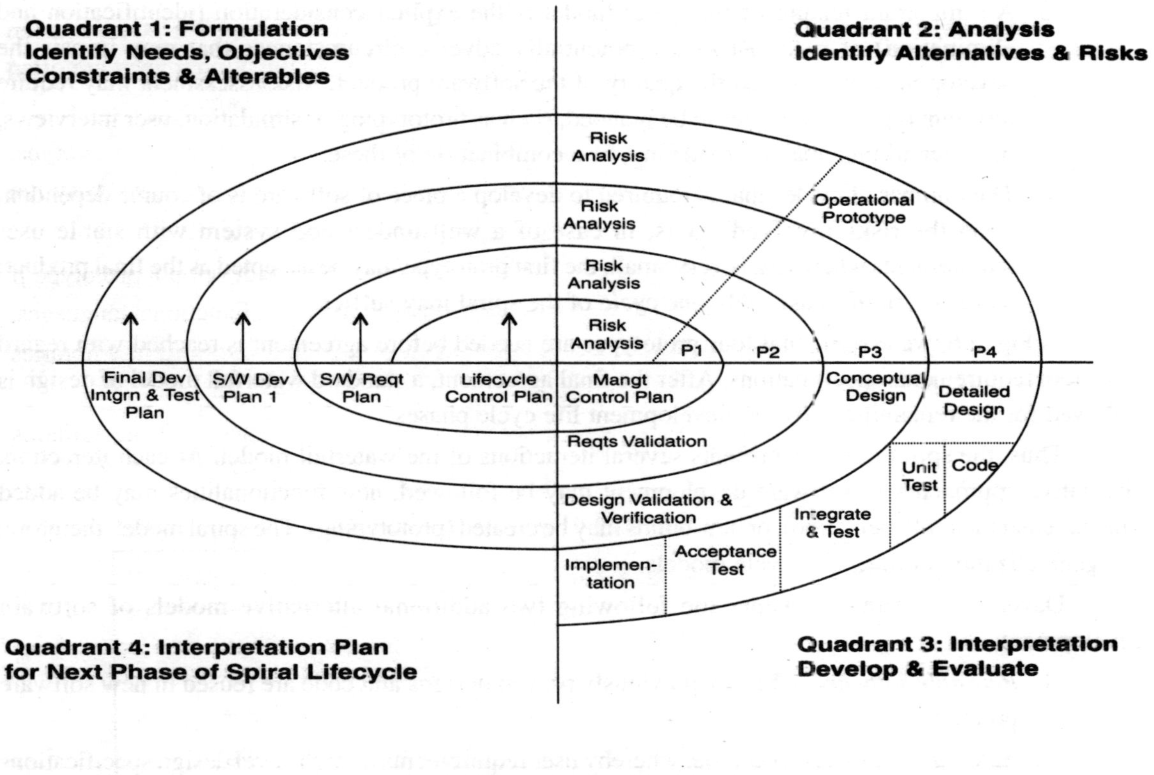

Fig. 2.6. The spiral model by Boehm

3. Each quadrant of the spiral corresponds to a particular set of activities for all phases. The four sets of activities are the following:

   (*a*) ***Determine objectives, alternatives and constraints.*** For each phase of software development, objectives are set, constraints on the process and the product are determined, and alternative strategies are planned to meet the objectives in the face of the constraints.

(*b*) *Evaluate alternatives and identify and resolve risks with the help of prototypes.* An analysis is carried out to identify risks associated with each alternative. Prototyping is adopted to resolve them.

(*c*) *Develop and verify next-level product, and evaluate.* Here the dominant development model is selected. It can be evolutionary prototyping, incremental, or waterfall. The results are then subjected to verification and validation tests.

(*d*) *Plan next phases.* The progress is reviewed and a decision is taken as to whether to proceed or not. If the decision is in favour of continuation, then plans are drawn up for the next phases of the product.

4. The radius of the spiral (Fig. 2.6) represents the cummulative cost of development; the angular dimension represents the progress; the number of cycles represents the phase of software development; and the quadrant represents the set of activities being carried out on the software development at a particular point of time.
5. An important feature of the spiral model is the explicit consideration (identification and elimination) of risks. Risks are potentially adverse circumstances that may impair the development process and the quality of the software product. Risk assessment may require different types of activities to be planned, such as prototyping or simulation, user interviews, benchamarking, analytic modeling, or a combination of these.
6. The number of cycles that is required to develop a piece of software is of course dependent upon the risks involved. Thus, in case of a well-understood system with stable user requirements where risk is very small, the first prototype may be accepted as the final product; therefore, in this case, only one cycle of the spiral may suffice.

In Fig. 2.6, we assume that four prototypes are needed before agreement is reached with regard to system requirements specifications. After the final agreement, a standard waterfall model of design is followed for the remaining software development life cycle phases.

Thus, the spiral model represents several iteractions of the waterfall model. At each iteraction, alternative approaches to software development may be followed, new functionalities may be added (the incremental implementation), or new builds may be created (prototyping). The spiral model, therefore, is a generalization of other life-cycle models.

Davis *et al.* (1988) consider the following two additional alternative models of software development:

1. *Reusable software*, whereby previously proven designs and code are reused in new software products,
2. *Automated software synthesis*, whereby user requirements or high-level design specifications are automatically transformed into operational code by either algorithmic or knowledge-based techniques using very high-level languages (VHLL).

Reusability helps to shorten development time and achieve high reliability. However, institutional efforts are often lacking in software firms to store, catalogue, locate, and retrieve reusable components. Automatic software synthesis involves automatic programming and is a highly technical discipline in its own right.

2.8 SOFTWARE REUSE

Many software firms develop, in course of time, libraries of generic reusable software components that can be assembled to give shape to new software products. Not only codes, but designs and specifications can also be reused. Components that can be reused may be (1) a whole application system, (2) major subsystems of an application, (3) modules or objects, or (4) functions.

Advantages accruing from software reuse are many (Sommerville 1999):

1. Increased system reliability.
2. Reduced overall project risk due to less uncertainty in cost estimates.
3. Effective use of specialists in developing generic components than in a wide array of variety of products.
4. Embodiment of organizational standards in reusable components, such as menus in user interface and error handling procedures.
5. Reduction in software development time.

The steps for developing a piece of software with reusable components are depicted in Fig. 2.7.

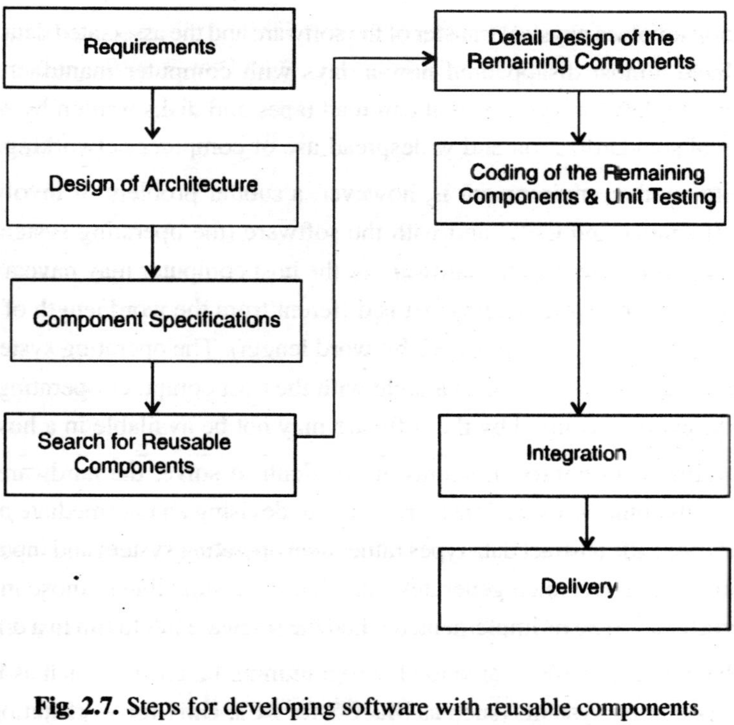

Fig. 2.7. Steps for developing software with reusable components

The following guidelines should be used to make a software component reusable:

1. The software component should be generalized by way of generalizing names, operations, and exceptions.
2. Complete documentation should be available for a reusable component.

3. Test cases for such a component must be available to, and used by, a reuser while integrating it with the remaining developed components.

With object-oriented programming becoming popular, the concept of reusability has gained momentum. Objects encapsulate data and functions, making them self-contained. The inheritance facility available in object-oriented programming facilitates invoking these objects for reusability. But extra effort is required to generalize even these objects/object classes. The organization should be ready to meet this short-term cost for potential long-term gain.

The most common form of reuse is at the level of whole application system. Two types of difficulties are faced during this form of reuse:

A. Portability

B. Customization.

A. Portability

Whenever a piece of software is developed in one computer environment but is used in another environment, portability problems can be encountered. The problems may be one of (1) transportation or (2) adaptation.

Transportation involves physical transfer of the software and the associated data. The transportation-related problems have almost disappeared now-a-days with computer manufacturers forced, under commercial pressure, to develop systems that can read tapes and disks written by other machine types and with international standardization and widespread use of computer networking.

Adaptation to another environment is, however, a subtler problem. It involves communication with the hardware (memory and CPU) and with the software (the operating system, libraries, and the language run-time support system). The hardware of the host computer may have a data representation scheme (for example, a 16-bit word length) that is different from the word length of the machine where the software was developed (for example, a 32-bit word length). The operating system calls used by the software for certain facilities may not be available with the host computer operating system. Similarly, run-time and library features required by the software may not be available in a host computer.

Whereas run-time and library problems are difficult to solve, the hardware and the operating system related problems could be overcome by recourse to devising an intermediate portability interface. The application software calls abstract data types rather than operating system and input-output procedures directly. The portability interface then generates calls that are compatible to those in the host computer. Naturally, this interface has to be re-implemented when the software has to run in a different architecture.

With the advent of standards related to (1) programming languages (such as Pascal, COBOL, C, C++, and Ada), (2) operating systems (such as MacOS for PCs, Unix for workstations), (3) networking (such as TCP/IP protocols), and (4) windows systems (such as Microsoft Windows for the PCs and X-window system for graphic user interface for workstations), the portability problems have reduced significantly in recent days.

At the end of this phase, one has the detailed system objectives and scope, the chosen architecture, the mitigation of major risks, and a decision to go ahead (or otherwise).

Construction

In this phase, a number of iterations are made to incrementally develop the software product. This includes coding, testing, integrating, and preparing documentation and manuals, etc., so that the product can be made operational.

Transition

Starting with the beta release of the system, this phase includes doing additional development in order to correct previously undetected errors and add to some postponed features.

Boehm, *et al.* (2000) have defined certain anchor-point milestones (Fig. 2.25) defined at the end points of these phases. These anchor-point milestones are explained below:

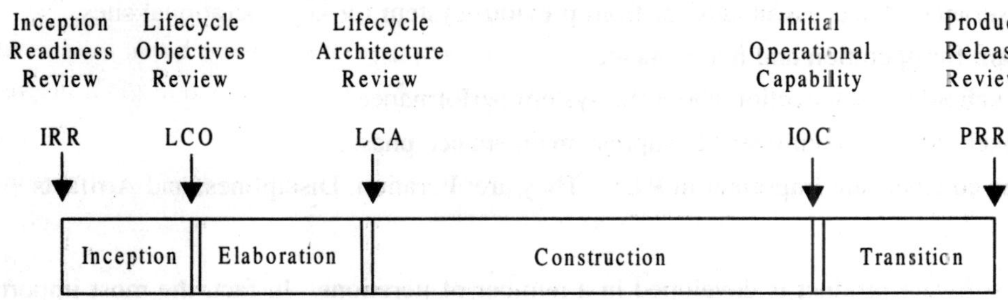

Fig. 2.25. Milestones in the RUP model

Inception Readiness Review (IRR)

- Candidate system objectives, scope, and boundary: Key stakeholders.
- Support to inception phase: Commitment to achieve successful LCO package.

Life-Cycle Objectives (LCO) Review

- LCO package: System objectives and scope, system boundary, environmental parameters and assumptions, current system shortfalls, key nominal scenarios, stakeholder roles and responsibilities, key usage scenarios, requirements, prototypes, priorities, stakeholders' concurrence on essentials, software architecture, physical and logical elements and relationships, COTS and reusable components, life-cycle stakeholders and life-cycle process model.
- Feasibility assured for at least one architecture: Assurance of consistency.
- Feasibility validated by a Review Board: Accepted by a Review Board, stakeholders' concurrence on essentials, and commit to support elaboration phase.
- Resources committed to achieve successful LCA package.

Life-Cycle Architecture (LCO) Review

- LCA package: Elaboration of system objectives and scope by increment, key off-nominal scenarios, usage scenarios, resolution of outstanding risks, design of functions and interfaces, architecture, physical and logical components, COTS and reuse choices, to-be-done (TBD) list for future increments, and assurance of consistency.
- Feasibility assured for selected architecture.

- Feasibility validated by the Review Board.
- Resources Committed to achieve Initial Operational Capability

Initial Operational Capability (IOC)

- Software preparation: Operational and support software with commentary and documentation, initial data preparation or conversion, necessary licenses and rights for COTS and reused software, and appropriate readiness testing.
- Site preparation: Initial facilities, equipment, supplies, and COTS vendor support arrangements.
- Initial user, operator and maintainer preparation: team building, training, familiarization with usage, operations, and maintenance.
- Transition Readiness Review: Plans for conversion, installation, training, and operational cutover, and stakeholders' commitment to support transition and maintenance phases.

Product Release Review (PRR)

- Assurance of successful cutover from previous system for key operational sites.
- Team for operation and maintenance.
- Stakeholders' satisfaction about the system performance.
- Stakeholders' commitment to support maintenance phase.

Three concepts are important in RUP. They are: Iteration, Disciplines, and Artifacts.

Iteration

The software product is developed in a number of iterations. In fact, the most important idea underlying RUP is the iterative and incremental development of the software. An iteration is a complete development cycle, starting from requirements to testing that results in an executable product, constituting a subset of the final product under development. Each iteration is time-boxed (i.e. of fixed time length), the time being usually small.

Disciplines

Known previously as workflows, the Unified Process model defines nine disciplines one or more of which occur within each iteration. The nine disciplines are: Business Modelling, Requirements, Design, Implementation, Test, Deployment, Configuration and Change Management, Project Management, and Environment.

Artifacts

A discipline consists of a set of activities and tasks of conceptualizing, implementing, and reviewing and a set of artifacts (related document or executable that is produced, manipulated, or consumed). Artifacts are work products (such as code, text documents, diagrams, models, etc.) that are generated as contractual deliverables (outputs) of discipline activities and used as baselines (or references) for, and inputs to, subsequent activities.

Models are the most important form of artifact used in the RUP. Nine types of models are available in the RUP: Business model, Domain model, Use case model, Analysis model, Design model, Process model, Deployment model, Implementation model, and Test model. The Analysis and Process models are optional.

2.14.3 Win-Win Spiral Model

Boehm and Ross (1989) extended the original spiral model by including considerations related to stakeholders. The win-win spiral model uses the theory W management approach, which requires that for a project to be a success, the system's key stakeholders must all be winners. The way to achieve this win-win condition is to use the negotiation-based approach to define a number of additional steps of the normal spiral development cycle. The additional steps are the following (Fig. 2.26):

- Identify next-level stakeholders.
- Identify stakeholders' win conditions.
- Reconcile win conditions.
- Establish next-level objectives, constraints, and alternatives.
- Evaluate product and process alternatives.
- Resolve risks.
- Define the next-level of product and process, including partitions.
- Validate product and process definitions.
- Review and commit.

The advantages from a win-win spiral model is the collaborative involvement of stakeholders that results in less rework and maintenance, early exploration of alternative architecture plans, faster development, and greater stakeholder satisfaction upfront.

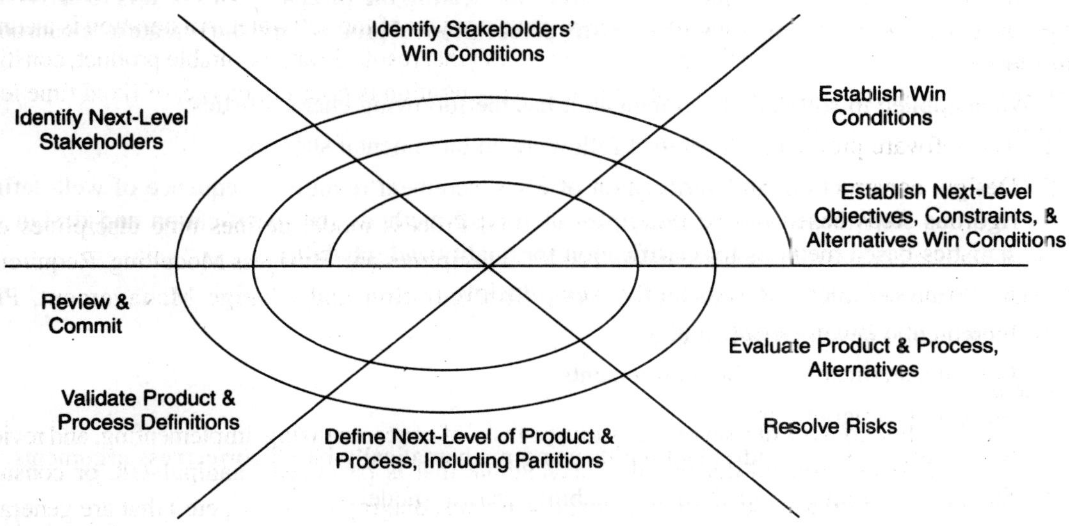

Fig. 2.26. The Win-Win Spiral Model

2.14.4 Rapid Application Development (RAD) Model

IBM's response to the deficiencies of the waterfall model was the rapid application development (RAD) model (Martin, 1991). The features of this model are the following:

1. The user is involved in all phases of life cycles—from requirements to final delivery. Development of GUI tools made it possible.
2. Prototypes are reviewed with the customer, discovering requirements, if any. The development of each integrated delivery is time-boxed (say, two months).
3. Phases of this model are the following:
   - Requirements Planning with the help of Requirements Workshop (Joint Requirements Planning, JRP)—structured discussions of business problems.
   - User Description with the help of joint application design (JAD) technique to get user involvement, where automated tools are used to capture user information.
   - Construction ("do until done") that combines detailed design, coding and testing, and release to the customer within a time-box. Heavy use of code generators, screen generators, and other productivity tools are made.
   - Cutover that includes acceptance testing, system installation, and user training.

2.14.5 Cleanroom Software Engineering

Originally proposed by Mills, *et al.* (1987) and practiced at IBM, cleanroom philosophy has its origin in the hardware fabrication. In fact, the term "Cleanroom" was used by drawing analogy with semiconductor fabrication units (clean rooms) in which defects are avoided by manufacturing in an ultra-clean atmosphere. The "hardware" approach to hardware fabrication requires that, instead of making a complete product and then trying to find and remove defects, one should use rigorous methods to remove errors in specification and design before fabricating the product. The idea is to arrive at a final product that does not require rework or costly defect removal process, and thus create a "cleanroom" environment.

When applied to software development, it has the following characteristics:

1. The software product is developed following an incremental strategy.
2. Design, construction, and verification of each increment requires a sequence of well-defined rigorous steps based on the principles of formal methods for specification and design and statistics-based methods for certification for quality and reliability.

The cleanroom approach rests on five key principles:

1. Incremental development strategy.
2. Formal specification of the requirements.
3. Structured programming.
4. Static verification of individual builds using mathematically based correctness arguments.
5. Statistical testing with the help of reliability growth models.

The cleanroom approach makes use of box-structure specification. A "box" is analogous to a module in a hierarchy chart or an object in a collaboration diagram. Each box defines a function to be carried out by receiving a set of inputs and producing a set of outputs. Boxes are so defined that when they are connected, they together define the delivered software functions.

Boxes can be of three types in increasing order of their refinement: Black Box, State Box, and Clear Box. A black box defines the inputs and the desired outputs. A state box defines, using concepts of state transition diagrams, data and operations required to use inputs to produce desired outputs. A clear box defines a structured programming procedure based on stepwise refinement principles that defines how the inputs are used to produce outputs.

Formal verification is an integral part of clearnroom approach. The entire development team, not just the testing team, is involved in the verification process. The underlying principle of formal verification is to ensure that for correct input, the transformation carried out by a box produces correct output. Thus, entry and exit conditions of a box are specified first. Since the transformation function is based on structured programming, one expects to have sequence, selection, and iteration structures. One develops simple verification rules for each such structure. It may be noted that the formal methods, introduced in Chapter 7, are also used for more complex systems involving interconnected multiple-logic systems.

2.14.6 Concurrent Engineering (Concurrent Process Model)

In software projects, especially when they are large, one finds that at any point of time, activities belonging to different phases are being carried out concurrently (simultaneously). Furthermore, various activities can be in various states. Keeping track of the status of each activity is quite difficult. Events generated within an activity or elsewhere can cause a transition of the activity from one state to another. For example, unit test case development activity may be in such states as *not started, being developed, being reviewed, being revised,* and *developed*. Receipt of detailed design, start of test case design, and end of test case design, etc., are events that trigger change of states.

A concurrent process model defines activities, tasks, associated states, and events that should trigger state transitions (Davis and Sitaram, 1994). Principles of this model are used in client-server development environment where system- and server (component)-level activities take place simultaneously.

2.14.7 Agile Development Process

To comply with the changing user requirements, the software development process should be agile. Agile development process follows a different development sequence (Fig. 2.27).

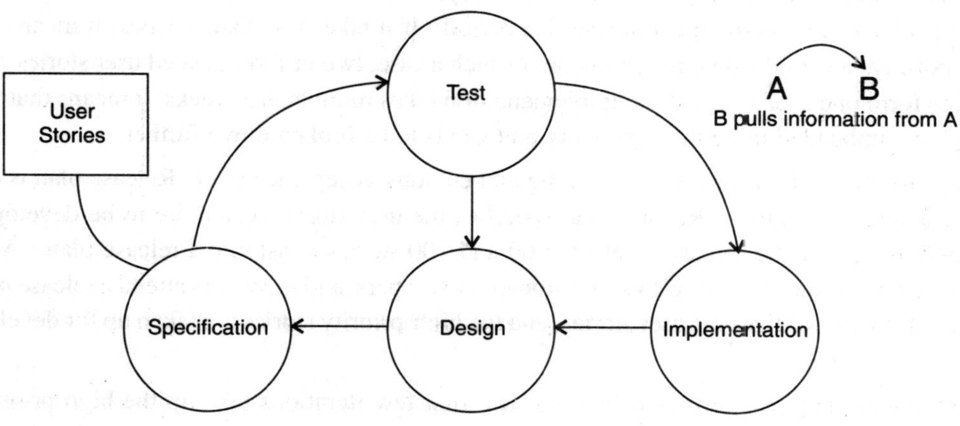

Fig. 2.27. The Agile Development Process

Agile processes are preferred where requirements change rapidly. At the beginning of each development scenario, system functionalities are recorded in the form of *user stories*. Customer and development team derive the test situations from the specifications. Developers design programming interface to match the tests' needs and they write the code to match the tests and the interface. They refine the design to match the code.

Extreme Programming (XP) is one of the most mature and the best-known agile processes. Beck (2000) and Beck and Fowler (2000) give details on XP-based agile processes. SCRUM is another popular agile process. We discuss below their approach to agile development in some detail.

Figure 2.28 shows the agile process in some more detail. User stories are descriptions of the functionalities the system is expected to do. The customer writes a user story about each functionality in no more than three sentences in his/her own words. User stories are different from use cases in that they do not merely describe the user interfaces. They are different from traditional requirement specifications in that they are not so elaborate; they do not provide any screen layout, database layout, specific algorithm, or even specific technology. They just provide enough details to be able to make low-risk time estimate to develop and implement. At the time of implementation, the developers collect additional requirements by talking to the customer face to face.

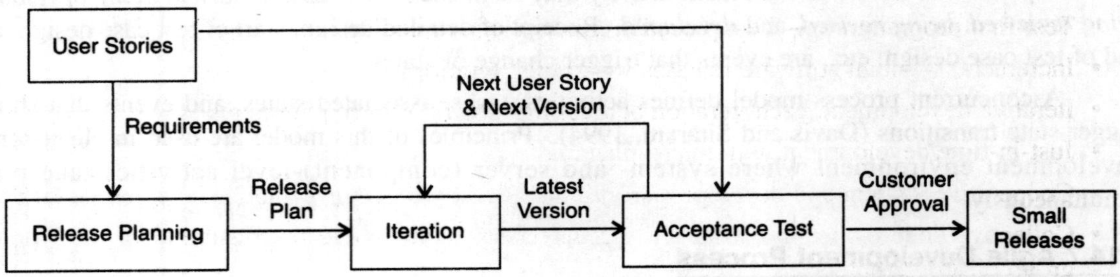

Fig. 2.28. Extreme programming–simplified process

User stories are used to make time estimates for implementing a solution. Each story ideally takes between 1 to 3 weeks to implement if the developers are totally engaged in its development, with no overtime or any other assignment during this period. If it takes less than 1 week, it means that the user story portrays a very detailed requirement. In such a case, two or three related user stories could be combined to form one user story. If the implementation takes more than 3 weeks, it means that the user story may have imbedded more than one story and needs to be broken down further.

User stories are used for release planning and creating acceptance tests. Release plan is decided in a release planning meeting. Release plan specifies the user stories which are to be developed and implemented in a particular release. Between 60 and 100 stories constitute a release plan. A release plan also specifies the date for the release. Customer, developers, and managers attend a release planning meeting. Customer prioritizes the user stories, and the high-priority stories are taken up for development first.

Each release requires several *iterations*. The first few iterations take up the high-priority user stories. These user stories are then translated into programming tasks that are assigned to a group of programmers. The user stories to be taken up and the time to develop them in one iteration are decided in an iteration planning meeting.

User stories are also used to plan acceptance tests. Extreme programming expects that at least one automated acceptance test is created to verify that the user stories are correctly implemented.

Each iteration has a defined set of user stories and a defined set of acceptance tests. Usually, an iteration should not take less than 2 weeks or more than 3 weeks. Iteration planning meeting takes place before the next iteration is due to start. A maximum of dozen iterations are usually done for a release plan.

Spike solutions are often created to tackle tough design problems that are also associated with uncertain time estimates. A spike solution is a simple throwaway program to explore potential solutions and make a more reliable time estimate. Usually, 1 or 2 weeks are spent in developing spike solutions.

Coding required for a user story is usually done by two programmers. Unit tests are carried out to ensure that each unit is 100% bug free. Programmers focus on the current iteration and completely disregard any consideration outside of this iteration. The code is group owned, meaning that any code not working is the responsibility of the whole group and not merely of the programmer writing the code.

When the project velocity is high, meaning that the speed with which the project progresses is very good, the next release planning meeting is usually convened to plan the next release.

The characteristics of agile development are the following:

- Test-first programming—Test precedes either design or coding.
- Incremental—small software releases with rapid iterations.
- Iterative development, each iteration addressing specific user requirements.
- Just-in-time development with micro-planning taking place for each iteration
- Cooperative—client and developers working constantly together with close communication.
- Collective code ownership, with writing defect-free code as the responsibility of the whole group of programmers.
- Straightforward—the model itself is easy to learn and to modify and is well-documented.
- Adaptive—last-minute changes can be made.
- Intensive user involvement in specifying requirements, prioritizing them, making release plans, and creating acceptance tests.

SCRUM is similar to extreme programming that comprises a set of project management principles based on small cross-functional self-managed teams (Scrum teams). The teams work on a 30-day iteration (sprint) with a 40-hour work week. Each iteration ends with a sprint review. A marketing man acts a product owner and determines the features that must be implemented in a release to satisfy the immediate customer needs. A Scrum master coaches the team through the process and removes any obstacles. In a 15-minute stand-up meeting, the team members take stock every morning and speak out the obstacles and the daily plans.

Fowler (2000) has divided the spectrum of development processes as heavy or light and predictive or adaptive. Heavy processes are characterized by rigidity, bureaucracy, and long-term planning. Predictive processes are characterized by prediction of user requirements at the beginning of the development phase and detailed planning of activities and resources over long time spans, and usually follow sequential development processes. Agile processes are both light and adaptive.

2.15 DIFFERING CONCEPTS OF 'LIFE CYCLE'

Jones (1986, pp. 117–120), in his foreword on programming life cycle analysis, feels that the phrase 'life cycle' is ambiguous and conveys three different concepts when analyzed closely. The first of these concepts relates to the conventional birth-to-death sequence of events of a single, new programming system.

The second concept underlying the phrase 'life cycle' is ''more global in scope and refers to the growth of programming and data-processing activities within an enterprise. The items of interest are such things as the magnitude of applications that are backlogged, the relative proportion of personnel working in new system development vis-a-vis working in maintenance, the gradual trends in software quality and productivity throughout the enterprise ... and the slowly (or rapidly in some cases) growing set of system and application programs that the enterprise will run to fulfill its data processing needs'' (Jones 1986, pp. 117–118).

The third concept deals with the people that are employed by an enterprise to work on programs and data processing activities. The items of interest here are the career progression of software practitioners from entry through retirement, the training need at various levels, and the like.

This chapter has discussed different forms of software development life cycle. The remaining chapters of the book give the details of various phases of this life cycle.

REFERENCES

Beck, K. (2000), Extreme Programming Explained–Embrace Change, Reading, MA: Addison-Wesley.

Beck, K. and M. Fowler (2000), Planning Extreme Programming, Reading, MA: Addison-Wesley.

Bennington, H.D. (1956), Production of Large Computer Programs, ONR Symposium on Advanced Programming Methods for Digital Computers, June 1956.

Boehm, B.W. (1973), Software and Its Impact: A Quantitative Assessment, Datamation, pp. 48–59.

Boehm, B.W. (1976), Software Engineering, IEEE Trans. Computers, pp. 1226–1241.

Boehm, R.W. (1981), Software Engineering Economics, Prentice-Hall, Englewood Cliffs, N.J.

Boehm, B.W. (1987), Industrial Software Metrics Top 10 List, IEEE Software, Vol. 4, No. 5, September, pp. 84–85.

Boehm, B.W. (1988), A Spiral Model of Software Development and Enhancement, IEEE Computer, Vol. 21, No. 5, 61–72.

Boehm, B.W. and R. Ross (1988), Theory W Software Project Management Principles and Examples, IEEE Transactions on Software Engineering, Vol. 15, No. 7, pp. 902–916.

Boehm, B.W., C. Abts, W. Brown, S. Chulani, B. K. Clark, E. Horowitz, R. Madachy, D.J. Reifer and B. Steece (2000), Software Cost Estimation with COCOMO II, New Jersey: Prentice-Hall, Inc.

Booch, G.J. Rumbaugh and I. Jacobson (2000), The Unified Modeling Language User Guide, Addison Wesley Longman (Singapore) Pte. Ltd., Low Price Edition.

Brooks, F. (1975), The Mythical Man-Month, Reading, MA : Addision-Wesley Publishing Co.

Brown, A. and K. Wallnau (1996), Engineering of Component-Based Systems Proceedings, of the 2nd Int. Conf. on Engineering of Complex Computer Systems.

Capretz, L. F., M. A. M. Carpretz and D. Li (2001), Component-Based Software Development, IECON '01: The 27th Annual Conference of the IEEE Industrial Electronics Society.

Cox, P. T. and B. Song (2001), A Formal Model for Component-Based Software, Proceedings of IEEE Symposium on Human-Centric Computing Languages and Environments, 5–7 September '01, pp. 304–311.

Davis, A.M.E.H. Bersoff and E.R. Comer (1988), A Strategy for Comparing Alternative Software Development Life Cycle Models, IEEE Trans. On Software Engineering, Vol. 14, No. 10, 1453–1461.

Davis, G.B. and M.H. Olson (1985), Management Information Systems: Conceptual Foundations, Structure, and Development, Singapore: McGraw-Hill Book Company, International Student Edition.

Davis, A. and P. Sitaram (1994), A Concurrent Process Model for Software Development, Software Engineering Notes, ACM Press, Vol. 19, No. 2, pp. 38–51.

D'Souza and A. C. Wills (1997), Objects, Components, and Frameworks with UML – The Catalysis Approach, Addison-Wesley, Reading, Mass.

Fagan, M.E. (1976), Design and Code Inspections to Reduce Errors in Program Development, IBM System J. Vol. 15, No. 3, 182–211.

Fowler, M. (2000), Put Your Process on a Diet, Software Development, December, CMP Media.

Ghezzi, C., M. Jazaueri and D. Mandrioli (1994), Fundamentals of Software Engineering, Prentice-Hall of India Private Limited, New Delhi.

Gilb, T. (1988), Principles of Software Engineering and Management, Reading, Mass: Addison-Wesley.

Herzum, P. and Sims, O. (2000), Business Component Factory: A Comprehensive Overview of Component-Based Development for the Enterprise, New York: Wiley.

Ince, D.C. and Hekmatpour, S. (1987), Software Prototyping — Progress and Prospects, Information and Software Technology, Vol. 29, No. 1, pp. 8–14.

Jones, C. (ed.) (1986), Programming Productivity, Washington: IEEE Computers Society Press, Second Edition.

Kruchten, P. (2000), The Rational Unified Process: An Introduction, Reading, MA. Addison-Wesley.

Larman, C. (2002), Applying UML and Patterns: An Introduction to Object-Oriented Analysis and Design and the Unified Process, Pearson Education (Singapore) Pte. Ltd., Indian Branch, Delhi, 2nd Edition.

Martin, J. (1991), Rapid Application Development, NY: Macmillan, 1st Edition.

Mills, H. D., Dyer, M. and Linger, R. (1987), Cleanroom Software Engineering, IEEE Software, Vol. 4, no. 5, pp. 19–25.

Myers, G.H. (1976), Software Reliability, John Wiley & Sons, Inc, New York.

Naumann, J.D., G.B. Davis and J.D. McKeen (1980), Determining Information Requirements: A Contingency Method for Selection of a Requirements Assurance Strategy, Journal of Systems and Software, Vol. 1, p. 277.

Nordon, P.V. (1970), Useful Tools for Project Management, in Management of Production, M.K. Starr, Ed. Baltimore, MD: Penguin, 1970, pp. 71–101.

Ould, M.A. (1990), Strategies for Software Engineering: The Management of Risk and Quality, John Wiley & Sons, Chichester, U.K.

Pour, D. (1998), Moving Toward Component-Based Software Development Approach, Proceedings of Technology of Object-Oriented Languages, Tools 26, 3–7 August 1998, pp. 296–300.

Pree, W. (1997), Component-Based Software Development – A New Paradigm in Software Engineering, Software Engineering Conference, ASPEC '97 and ICSC '97 Proceedings of Software Engineering Conference 1997, 2-5 December 1997, pp. 523–524.

Putnam, L.H. (1978), A General Empirical Solution to the Macro Software Sizing and Estimation Problem, IEEE Transactions in Software Engineering, Vol. SE-4, No. 4, pp. 345–360.

Rosove, P.E. (1976), Developing Computer-Based Information Systems, John Wiley & Sons, Englewood Cliffs, NJ : Prentice-Hall, Inc.

Royce, W.W. (1970), Managing the Developing of Large Software Systems: Concepts and Techniques, Proceedings of IEEE WESCON, August 1970, pp.1–9.

Royce, W.W. (2000), Software Project Management: A Unified Framework, Addison–Wesley, Second Indian Reprint.

Sage, A.P. (1995), Systems Management for Information Technology and Software Engineering, John Wiley & Sons, New York.

Sommerville, I. (1999), Software Engineering, Addison-Wesley, Fifth Edition, Second ISE Reprint.

Szyperki, C. (1998), Component Software, Beyond Object-Oriented Programming, ACM Press, Addison-Wesley, New Jersey.

Thiboudeau, R. and E.N. Dodson (1985), Life Cycle Phase Interrelationships in Jones (1986), pp. 198–206.

Vitharana, P., H. Jain and F. M. Zahedi (2004), Strategy Based Design of Reusable Business Components, IEEE Trans. On System, Man and Cybernetics – Part C: Applications and Reviews, vol. 34, no. 4, November, pp. 460–476.

Wolverton, R.W. (1974), The Cost of Developing Large-Scale Software, IEEE Trans. on Computer, pp. 282–303.

REQUIREMENTS

3 Requirements Analysis

3.1 IMPORTANCE OF REQUIREMENTS ANALYSIS

Requirements are the things that a software developer should discover before starting to build a software product. Without a clear specification of a set of valid user requirements, a software product cannot be developed and the effort expended on the development will be a waste. The functions of a software product must match the user requirements. Many computer-based information systems have failed because of their inability to capture correctly the user requirements. And when a completed software product is modified to incorporate lately understood user requirements, the effort spent, and consequently, the cost are extremely high.

A study by The Standish Group (1994) noted that the three most commonly cited root causes of project failures, responsible for more than a third of the projects running into problems, are the following:

- Lack of user input: 13% of all projects.
- Incomplete requirements and specifications: 12% of all projects.
- Changing requirements and specifications: 12% of all projects.

Davis (1993) suggests that requirements error can be very costly to repair if detected late in the development cycle. Figure 3.1 plots the relative cost to repair a requirement error in a log scale and indicates how it varies when detected at various development phases. Here the cost is normalized to 1 when error is detected and corrected during coding. This figure indicates that unless detected early in the development cycle, the cost to repair the error increases almost exponentially. This phenomenon emphasizes the importance of ascertaining the user requirements very carefully in the requirements analysis phase only.

3.2 USER NEEDS, SOFTWARE FEATURES, AND SOFTWARE REQUIREMENTS

Leffingwell and Widrig (2000) suggest that *software requirements* reflects specific *features* of the *user needs*. The user needs arise when business or technical problems are faced. They lie in the *problem domain*. They are expressed in the language of the user. Leffingwell and Widrig define *software requirement* as:

- A software capability needed by the user to solve a problem to achieve an objective.
- A software capability that must be met or possessed by a system or system component to satisfy a contract, standard, specification, or other formally imposed documentation.

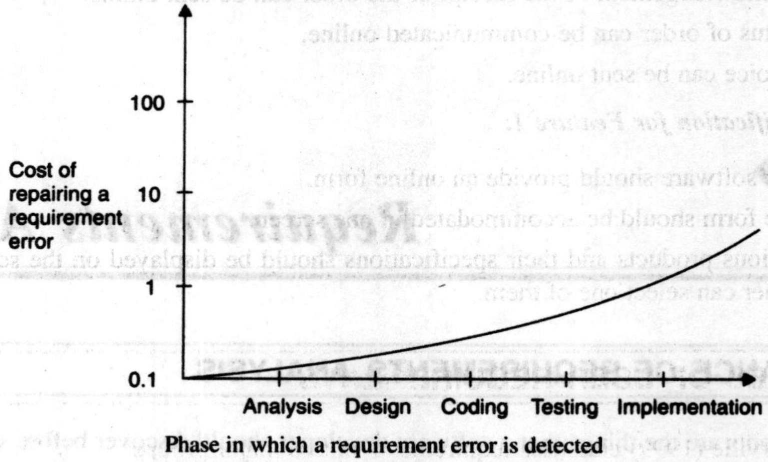

Fig. 3.1. Relative cost to repair a requirement error.

A *feature* is a service that the system provides to fulfill one or more stakeholder needs. Thus while user needs lie in the problem domain, features and software requirements lie in the *solution domain*. Figure 3.2 shows, in a pyramidal form, the needs, the features, and the software requirements. More efforts are required to translate the user's needs to software requirements—shown by the wider part in the bottom of the pyramid.

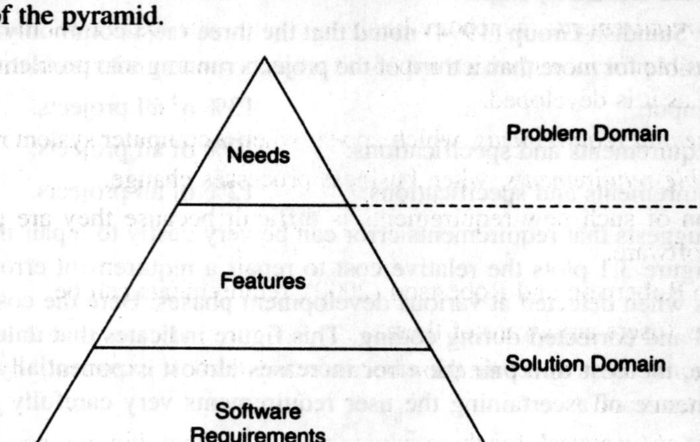

Fig. 3.2. Needs, features and software requirements

(Adapted from Leffinwell & Widrig 2000)

An example is given below to illustrate the difference between user needs, features, and software requirements.

User Need:

The delay to process a customer order be reduced.

Features:

1. Customers can send their orders online.
2. Acknowledgement of the receipt of the order can be sent online.
3. Status of order can be communicated online.
4. Invoice can be sent online.

Software Specification for Feature 1:

1. The software should provide an online form.
2. The form should be accommodated in one screen.
3. Various products and their specifications should be displayed on the screen so that a customer can select one of them.

3.3 CLASSES OF USER REQUIREMENTS

Sommerville (1999) classifies requirements in two major groups:

1. Enduring requirements
2. Volatile requirements

Enduring requirements are the core and stable requirements of the users whereas *volatile requirements* change during the development of, or operation with the software. These volatile requirements can take one of the following four forms:

1. *Mutable requirements,* which are likely to change due to changes in environment.
2. *Emergent requirements,* which appear as users begin to understand the functionalities of the software as it is developed.
3. *Consequential requirements,* which appear when a computer system replaces a manual one.
4. *Compatible requirements,* when business processes change.

The evolution of such new requirements is difficult because they are difficult to gauge and incorporate in the software.

According to Robertson and Robertson (2000), requirements can be

(*a*) *conscious* (users are aware of them),

(*b*) *unconscious* (users don't mention because they think it is natural, so they assume everyone knows them) and

(*c*) *undreamt of* (users ask for them when they realize that they are possible).

Thus, we see that user requirements can be of various classes. They emerge at different points of time and in fact, change with time. We shall now see how other factors also affect the user requirements.

3.4 SUB-PHASES OF REQUIREMENTS PHASE

The *requirements analysis* phase of system development life cycle, commonly called the *Analysis phase,* can be seen to consist of two sub-phases (Fig. 3.3):

(1) Requirements gathering and
(2) Systems analysis.

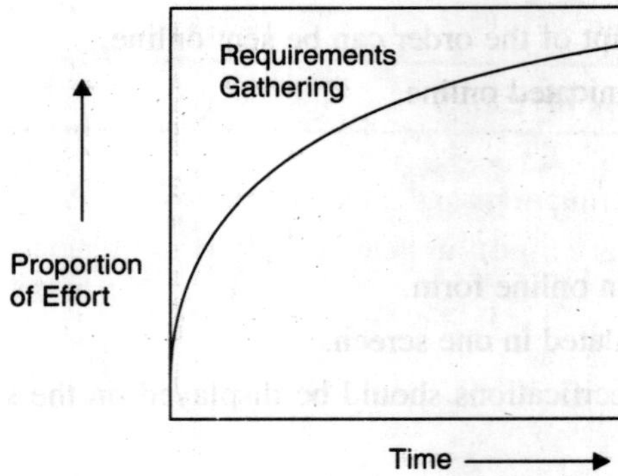

Fig. 3.3. Sub-phases of requirements analysis

Requirements gathering process studies the work in order to devise the best possible software product to help with that work. It discovers the business goals, the stakeholders, the product scope, the constraints, the interfaces, what the product has to do, and the qualities it must have.

Systems analysis develops working models of the functions and data needed by the product as its specification. These models help in proving that the functionality and the data will work together correctly to provide the outcome that the client expects.

In the remaining portion of this chapter we shall discuss the various aspects of the requirements gathering phase, while the details of the systems analysis pahse will be discussed in the next two chapters.

3.5 BARRIERS TO ELICITING USER REQUIREMENTS

3.5.1 Endemic Syndromes in Requirements Elicitation Process

Leffingwell and Widrig (2000) suggest three endemic syndromes that complicate the requirement elicitation process:

- The 'Yes, But' syndrome.
- The 'Undiscovered Ruins' sydrome.
- The 'User and the Developer' syndrome.

When the user experiences the software for the first time, the 'Yest, But' syndrome is observed. While the user may accept a number of incorporated software functionalities, he may have reservations about many others. In the waterfall model of development, this form of syndrome occurs commonly.

Search for requirements is like a search for undiscovered ruins: The more that are found, the more remain unknown. The essence of the 'Undiscovered Ruins' syndrome is that the more the number and variety of stakeholders, the more are the undiscovered requirements.

The 'User and the Developer' syndrome stems from the fact that they belong to two different worlds—the former in a real world who would face the consequences at all times and the latter in a virtual world who most likely escapes the severest consequences, both brought up in different cultures and speaking different languages.

B. Customization

Now-a-days it has become customary to develop generalized software packages and then customize such a package to satisfy the needs of a particular user.

2.9 AUTOMATIC SOFTWARE SYNTHESIS

Program generators for stereotypical functions and code generators in CASE tools are examples of automatic software synthesis. They are very useful in generating codes for such functions as

- Creating screens,
- Editing input data,
- Preparing reports,
- Processing transactions, and
- Updating database.

Obviously, these generators are not very generalized and need deep understanding of the features of application domains.

2.10 COMPARING ALTERNATIVE SOFTWARE DEVELOPMENT LIFE CYCLE MODELS

From the discussions made above, we note the following distinctive features of the life cycle models:

1. The waterfall model looks upon the life cycle of a software development as consisting of a sequence of phases, with limited feedback and interactions between the phases. The prototype model allows a number of iterations between the developer and the user with a view to receiving feedback on partially built, incomplete software systems that can be improved and rebuilt. The incremental development allows addition of functionality on an initially built kernel to build the final system. The spiral model reflects a generalized approach to software development where either an incremental strategy or a prototyping strategy is followed to identify and eliminate risks and to establish user requirements and detailed software design, before undertaking final coding, testing, and implementing in the line of the waterfall model.
2. The waterfall model is document based, the evolutionary approach is user based, and spiral model is risk based.
3. Ould (1990) compares the characteristics of the different life cycle models with the help of the following process views:
    - The V process view (Fig. 2.8) of the waterfall model,
    - The VP process view (Fig. 2.9) of the initial spiral life cycle model,

- The evolutionary process (successive build) view (Fig. 2.10, which is a repetition of Fig. 2.5) of the prototyping model, and
- The iterative process view (Fig. 2.11) of the incremental development approach.

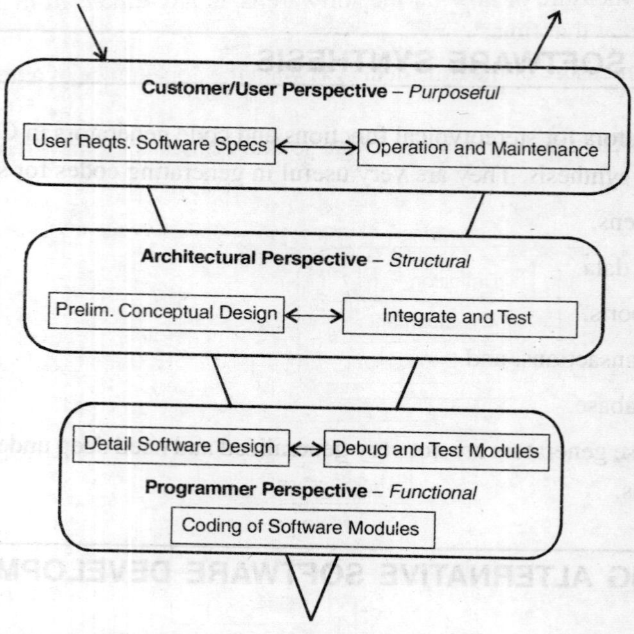

Fig. 2.8. The V-process view of the waterfall model

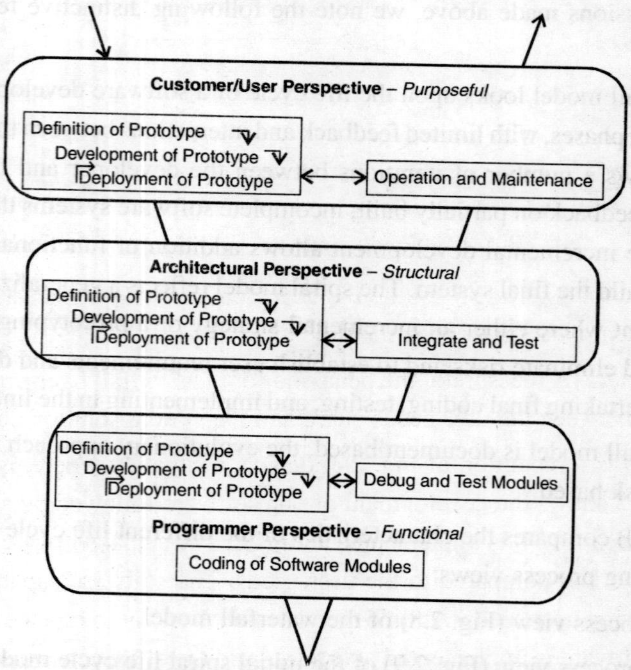

Fig. 2.9. The VP-process view of the initial spiral model

Davis *et al.* (1988) suggest a strategy for comparing alternative software development life cycle models. They define the following five software development metrics for this purpose:

1. *Shortfall.* A measure of how far the software is, at any time *t*, from meeting the actual user requirements at that time.
2. *Lateness.* A measure of the time delay between the appearance of a new requirements and its satisfaction.
3. *Adaptability.* The rate at which a software solution can adapt to new requirements, as measured by the slope of the solution curve.

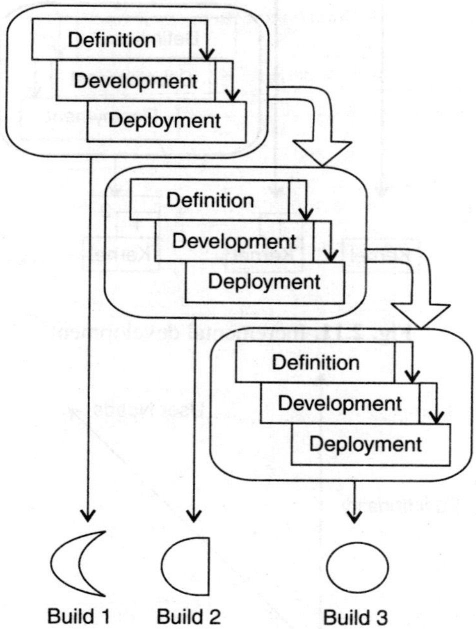

Fig. 2.10. Evolutionary prototyping

4. *Longevity.* The time a system solution is adaptable to change and remains viable, *i.e.*, the time from system creation through the time it is replaced.
5. *Inappropriateness.* A measure of the behaviour of the shortfall over time, as depicted by the area bounded between the user needs curve and the system solution curve.

Figure 2.12, which is a repetition of Fig. 2.3, depicts a situation where user needs continue to evolve in time. Figure 2.13 shows the development of one software followed by another. The software development work starts at time t_0. It is implemented at time t_1. The actual software capability (indicated by the vertical line at t_1) is less compared to the user needs. The software capability continues to be enhanced to meet the growing user needs. At time t_3, a decision is takent to replace the existing software by a new one. The new software is implemented at time t_4. And the cycle continues. All the five metrics are illustrated in Fig. 2.14.

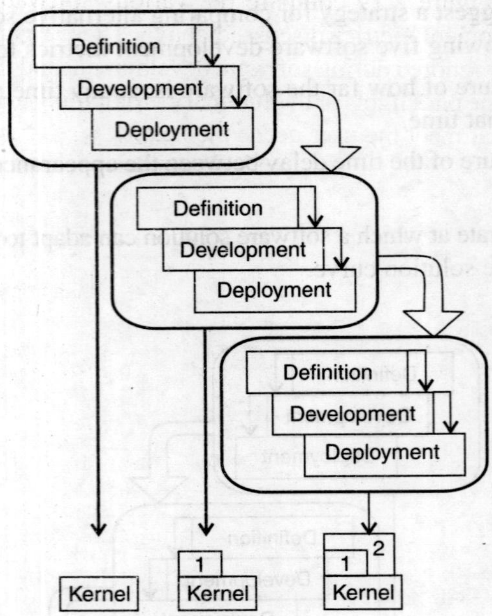

Fig. 2.11. Incremental development

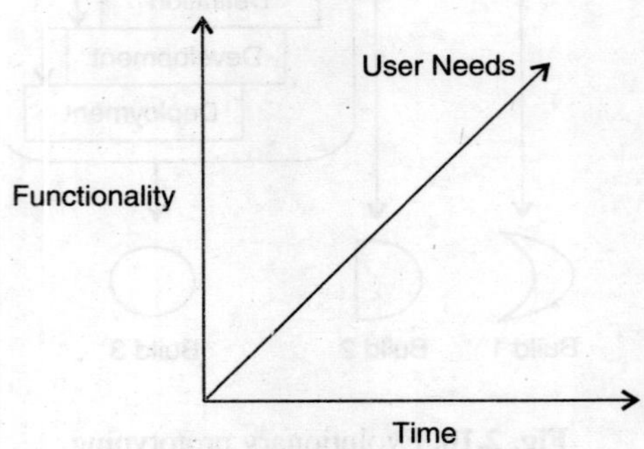

Fig. 2.12. Constantly evolving user needs

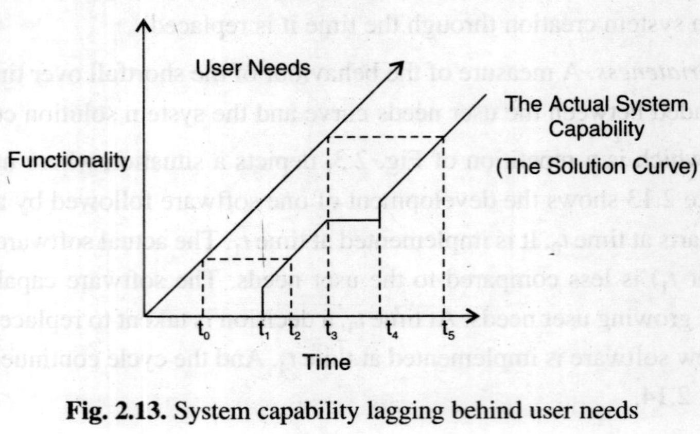

Fig. 2.13. System capability lagging behind user needs

Figure 2.15 through Figure 2.19 compare the various software development models in the framework of the five development metrics discussed above. These figures show that evolution of user requirements is fundamentally ignored during software development and that in such situation of dynamic change in user requirements, the paradigms of evolutionary prototyping and automated software synthesis result in software products that meet the user needs the best.

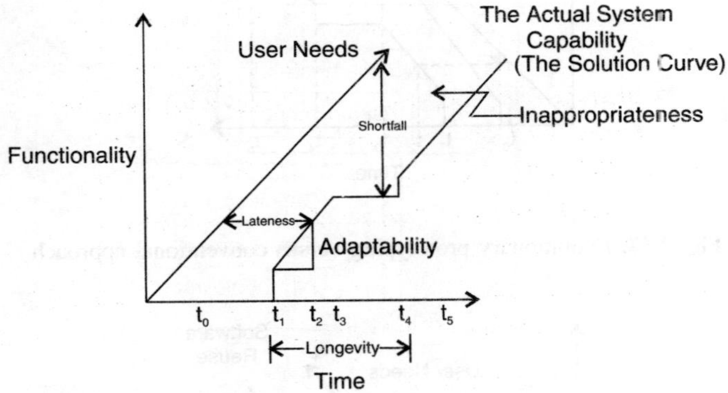

Fig. 2.14. Software productivity metrics

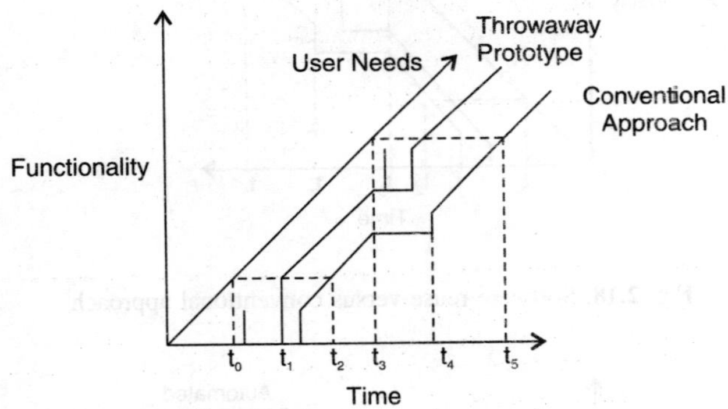

Fig. 2.15. System capability lagging behind user needs

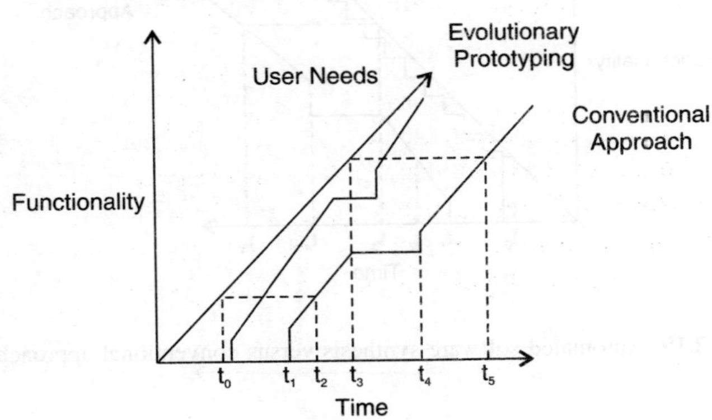

Fig. 2.16. Incremental versus conventional approach

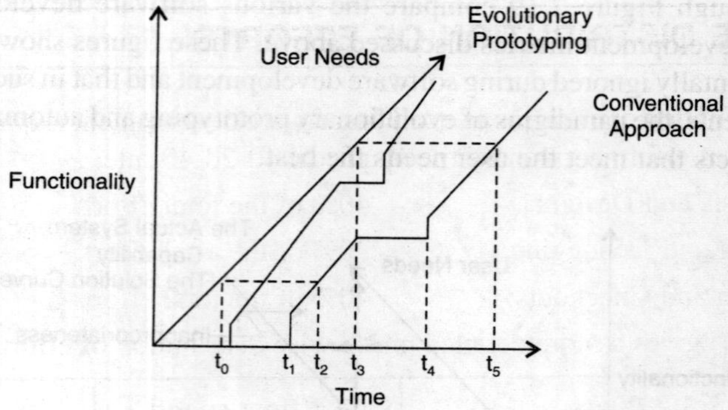

Fig. 2.17. Evolutionary prototyping versus conventional approach

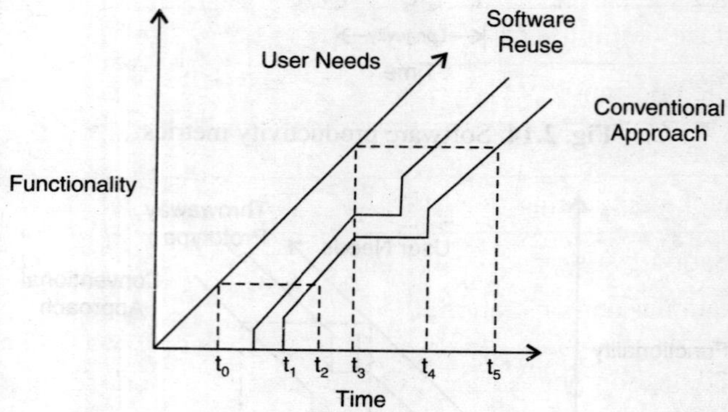

Fig. 2.18. Software reuse versus conventional approach

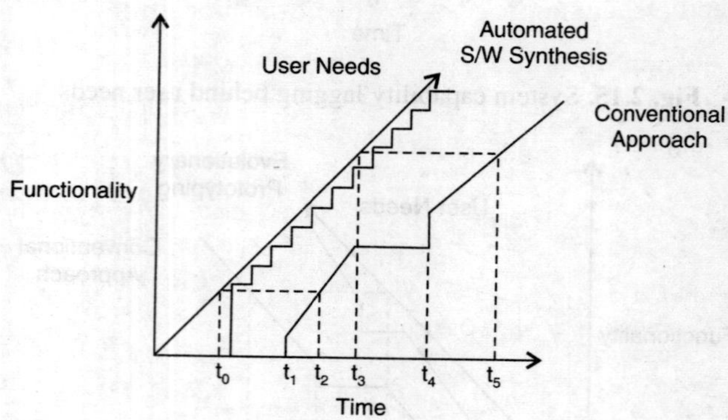

Fig. 2.19. Automated software synthesis versus conventional approach

2.11 PHASEWISE DISTRIBUTION OF EFFORTS

Phase-wise distribution of efforts expended in software development is quite revealing. A popular phase-wise distribution of effort is given by the empirical 40-20-40 rule:

Analysis and Design: 40% of the total effort
Coding and Debugging: 20% of the total effort
Testing and Checkouts: 40% of the total effort

Wolverton (1974) gives a more detailed phase-wise distribution of efforts as:

Phase	% Effort spend	
Requirements analysis	8	
Preliminary design	18	46%
Interface definition	4	
Detailed design	16	
Code and debug	20	20%
Development testing	21	
Validation testing and Operational demonstration	13	34%

Based on published data on phase-wise effort spent in eleven projects and on those reported by twelve authors and companies, Thibodeau and Dodson (1985) report that average effort spent in various phases are the following:

Analysis and Design: 37% of the total effort
Coding and Debugging: 20% of the total effort
Testing and Checkout: 43% of the total effort

Fagan (1976) suggests a *snail*-shaped curve (Fig. 2.20) to indicate the number of persons who are normally associated with each life cycle phase.

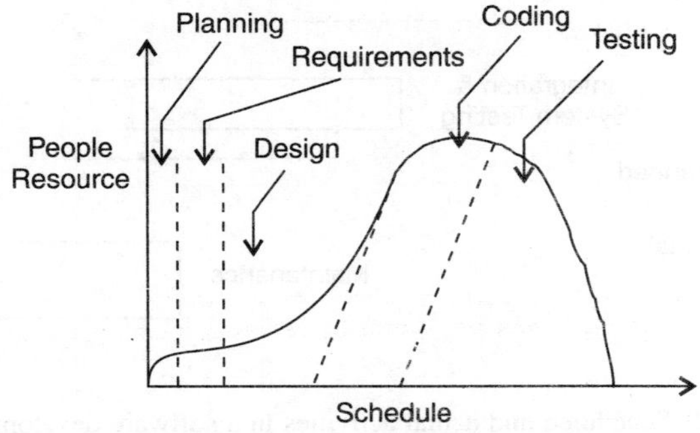

Fig. 2.20. Development people resource and schedule (Fagan 1986)

Thus, we see that the 40-20-40 rule more or less matches with the empirically found phase-wise distribution of efforts.

2.12 LIFE CYCLE INTERRELATIONSHIPS

Phase relationships can be often visualized clearly with the use of a progress chart (Thibodeau and Dodson, 1985). A progress chart shows the planned and the actual values of start and end of activities related to each phase and of resource (person-hour) loading for each phase.

Figure 2.21 shows such a *progress chart.* The horizontal axis of the chart indicates 'time' and the vertical axis the resource (person-hour) loading. The solid lines indicate the planned values and the dotted lines the actual values. The length of a rectangle indicates the start, the end, the time span of the phase, and the breadth the resource deployed. The chart indicates that analysis used less resource and took more time than their planned values; design activities started later and ended earlier but used more resources than planned; coding started and ended later but used more resources than planned, which were the cases with testing as well. The chart also illustrates significant amount of time overlap between phases (particularly adjacent phases). It is thus possible to hypothesize that delay in completion of activities in one phase has substantial influence on the resource deployed in, and the time schedule of, the immediately following phase (and of the other subsequent phases too).

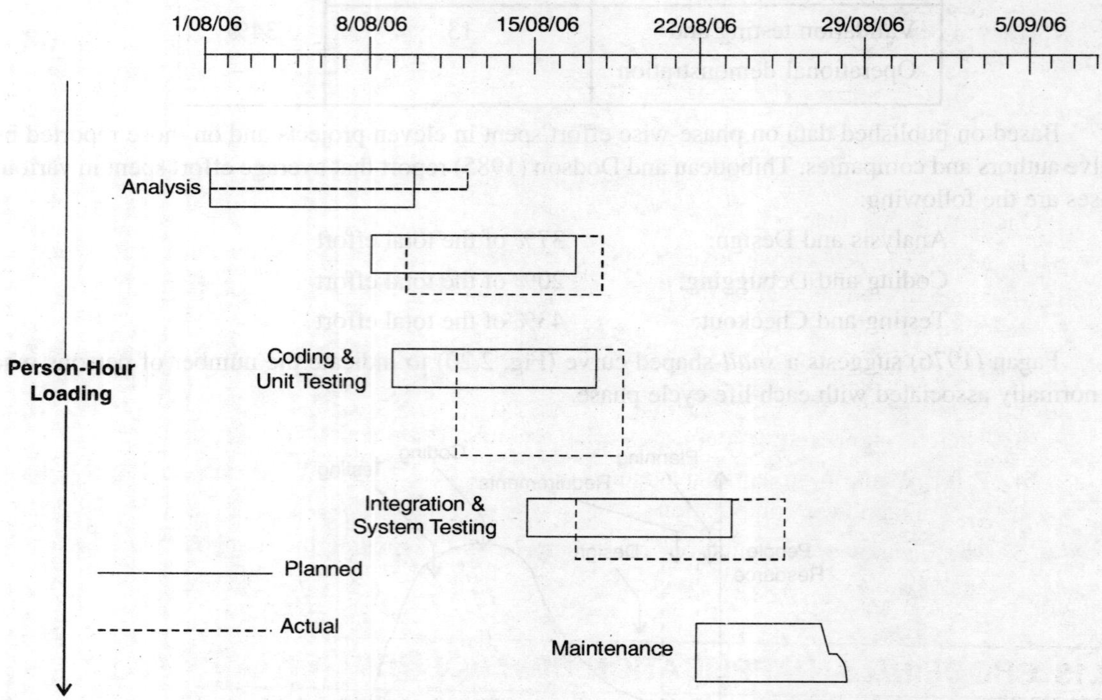

Fig. 2.21. Scheduled and actual activities in a software development

Based on the above observations, Thibodeau and Dodson hypothesized and observed that for software with a given size, over some range, a trade-off is possible between the resources in a phase and the resources in its succeeding phases (or the preceding phases). Figure 2.21, for example, shows that if the effort given to design is reduced (increased), then more (less) effort will be required in coding. Thibodeau and Dodson, however, could not conclusively support this hypothesis, because the projects (whose data they used) had extremely small range of efforts spent in various phases.

Based on the work of Nordon (1970) and on the study of the data on about 150 other systems reported by various authors, Putnam (1978) suggests that the profile of the effort generally deployed on a software per year (termed the *project curve*) or the (overall *life-cycle manpower curve*) is produced by adding the ordinates of the manpower curves for the individual phases. Figure 2.22 shows the individual manpower curve and the project curve.

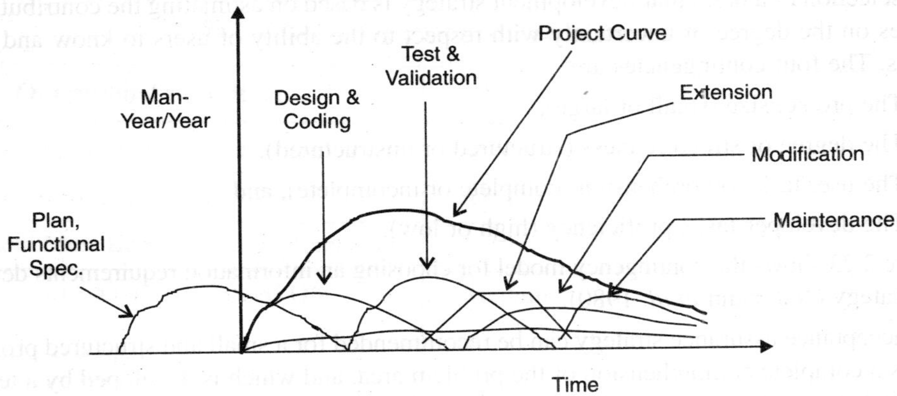

Fig. 2.22. The project curve

One may notice that

1. Most sub-cycle curves (except that for extension) have continuously varying rates and have long tails indicating that the final 10% of each phase of effort takes a relatively long time to complete.
2. The project curve has a set of similar characteristics as those of its constituent sub-cycles: a rise, peaking, and exponential tail off.
3. There is significant amount of overlap among phases.
4. Effort spent on project management (although small, only 10%) is also included in the life cycle manpower computation.
5. The manpower computation, made here, does not include the manpower requirement for analysis.

2.13 CHOOSING AN APPLICATION DEVELOPMENT STRATEGY

In the earlier sections we discussed the different strategies of software development. In real life, the developer has to choose a specific development strategy before embarking on the task of development. Two approaches are recommended for this choice:

Phases of RUP

The Rational Unified Process defines four development phases (Table 2.5) that can be grouped under two broad categories:

Engineering:

1. Inception: Requirements
2. Elaboration: Analysis and Design

Production:

3. Construction: Code and Test
4. Transition: Deployment

Inception

Spanning over a relatively short period of about one week or so, this phase is concerned with forming an opinion about the purpose and feasibility of the new system and to decide whether it is worthwhile investing time and resource on developing the product. Answers to the following questions are sought in this phase (Larman, 2002):

- What are the product scope, vision, and the business case?
- Is it feasible?
- Should it be bought or made?
- What is the order of magnitude of a rough estimate?
- Is it worthwhile to go ahead with the project?

As can be seen, inception is not a requirement phase; it is a more like a feasibility phase.

Table 2.5: Phase-wise Description of the Unified Process

Phase	Activities	Anchor-point milestone	Deliverables
Inception	Overview and feasibility study	Life-Cycle Objectives (LCO) Review	Overview and feasibility report
Elaboration	Detailed system objectives and scope	Life-Cycle Architecture (LCO) Review	Architecture
Construction	Coding, testing, and integration	Initial Operational Capability (IOC) Review	Tested software
Transition	Conversion planning and user training	Product Release Review (PRR)	Deployed software

Elaboration

Consisting of up to four iterations and each iteration spanning a maximum of six weeks, this phase clarifies most of the requirements, tackles the high-risk issues, develops (programs and tests) the core architecture in the first iteration and increments in subsequent iterations. This is not a design phase and does not create throw-away prototypes; the final product of this phase is an executable architecture or architectural baseline.

3.5.2 Difficulty in Understanding User Information Requirements

Eliciting user information requirements is one of the most difficult tasks a system analyst faces. There are four major reasons:

1. Constraints on humans as specifiers of information requirements—the limited rationality of human mind.
2. The variety and complexity of information requirements.
3. The complex patterns of interaction among users and analysts in defining requirements.
4. Unwillingness of some users to provide requirements (for political or behavioural reasons).

The first reason cited is discussed at length later. We discuss the last three reasons first. Software normally serves a variety of users, each obsessed with different issues associated with the overall problem addressed by the software. Each has a separate view of the problem. The objective of one set of users may be in direct conflict with that of another user set (The classic tussle of objectives between the production and marketing departments is a good example). All these practical problems give rise to a wild variety and complexity of information requirements that make determining user requirements very difficult.

Lack of communication between the system analyst and the user hinders the process of elicitation of user information requirement. A system analyst's previous knowledge and experience in the field of application is very important. But equally or even more important is the analyst's behavioural patterns—the *interpersonal skills and the personality traits.* Oftentimes a user may consider an analyst as intruding into his time. The analyst's lack of knowledge about the problem domain during the initial phase of the inquiry may give the impression to the user that the former is not competent in tackling his problem. The user is likely to ignore the analyst and may not cooperate.

Users do not like to disclose information requirement for purely personal reasons also:

1. Information is generally considered as power; nobody likes to part with it.
2. Sometimes a user may apprehend that his freedom and power to act may be curtailed due to the business process reengineering that is normally associated with the implementation of a new system.
3. Oftentimes a user may not be convinced of a need for a new system; therefore he may not be a willing partner in the process for change to a new system.

In spite of the barriers cited above, it may be mentioned that a most unwilling user can turn out to be the most vocal supporter of the new system if the analyst can provide solutions that improve the situation. In addition to the behavioural reasons discussed above, there are also natural, intrinsic psychological reasons associated inherently with the human brain that create barriers to eliciting user information requirements.

Limited Rationality of Human Mind

One of the methods for understanding user information requirements is talking to users and asking them for their requirements. This method is unlikely to be effective at all times. Two reasons may be cited for this:

1. Humans are not very good information processors.
2. There is inherently a bias in the selection and use of data.

Simon (1980) has extensively worked to show that there are limits on the information processing capability of humans. The following limitations of the human mind were pointed out by him:

- The human brain is incapable of assimilating all the information inputs for decision making and in judging their usefulness or relevance in the context of a particular decision-making situation. This assimilation process is even much less effective when time for assimilation is less, say in emergency situations. This inability is referred to as the *limited rationality of human mind.*
- There are inherent *limits on human short-term memory.*

Psychologists have studied human bias in the selection and use of data extensively. These studies point to the following types of human bias (Davis and Olson, 1985):

1. *Anchoring and Adjustment.* Humans generally use past standards and use them as anchors around which adjustments are made. They thus create bias in information assimilation and decision making.
2. *Concreteness.* For decision making, humans use whatever information is available, and in whatever form it is available, not always waiting for the most relevant information.
3. *Recency.* Human mind normally places higher weight to recent information than to historical information that was available in the past.
4. *Intuitive Statistical Analysis.* Humans usually draw doubtful conclusions based on small samples.
5. *Placing Value on Unused Data.* Humans often ask for information that may not be required immediately but just in case it is required in the future.

Thus, while information requirements at the operating level management may be fully comprehensible (because the information requirements tend to be historical, structured, and repetitive), they may be beyond comprehension at the top level.

We shall now discuss the broad strategies that a system analyst can adopt to gather user information requirements.

3.6 STRATEGIES FOR DETERMINING INFORMATION REQUIREMENTS

3.6.1 The Strategies

Davis and Olson (1985) have identified four strategies for determining user information requirements:

1. Asking
2. Deriving from an existing information system
3. Synthesizing from the characteristics of the utilizing system
4. Discovering from experimentation with an evolving information system.

In practice, a combination of these strategies is used.

Asking

Asking consists of the following methods:

• Interviewing each user separately

• Group meetings

• Questionnaire survey and its variants (like Delphi).

Interviewing each user separately helps in getting everybody's point of view without getting biased by other viewpoints.

Group meetings help in collectively agreeing to certain points about which there may be differences in opinion. However, group meetings may be marred by *dominant personalities* and by a *bandwagon effect* where a particular viewpoint often gathers momentum in a rather unusual way.

Questionnaire surveys help in accessing large number of users placed at distant and dispersed places. *Delphi studies* involve many rounds of questionnaires and are designed to allow feedback of group responses to the respondents after every round as well as to allow them to change their opinions in the light of the group response.

The *mehods of asking* is

- *a necessary adjunct* to whichever method may be used for information elicitation.
- *good only for stable systems* for which structures are well established by law, regulation or prevailing standards.

Deriving from an Existing Information System

An existing information system is a rich source of determining the user information requirements. Such an information system may reside in four forms:

1. Information system (whether manual or computerized) that will be replaced by a new system.
2. System that is in operation in another, similar organization.
3. System is standardized and it exists in a package that will be adopted or customized.
4. System that is described in textbooks, handbooks, and the like.

This method uses the principle of *'anchoring and adjustment'* in system development. The structure of the existing information system is used as an anchor and it is appropriately adjusted to develop the new information system.

This method of deriving information requirements from an existing system, if used in isolation, is appropriate if the information system is performing standard operations and providing standard information and if the requirements are stable. Examples are: *transaction processing and accounting systems.*

Synthesis from the Characteristics of the Utilizing Systems

Information systems generate information that is used by other systems. A study of characteristics of these information-utilizing systems helps the process of eliciting the user information requirements. Davis and Olson discuss several methods that can help this process:

1. Normative Analysis
2. Strategy Set Transformation
3. Critical Factors Analysis
4. Process Analysis
5. Ends-Means Analysis
6. Decision Analysis
7. Input-Process-Output Analysis.

Normative analysis is useful where standard procedures (norms) are used in carrying out operations such as calling tenders, comparing quotations, placing purchase orders, preparing slipping notes and invoices, etc.

Strategy set transformation requires one to first identify the corporate strategies that the management has adopted and then to design the information systems so that these strategies can be implemented.

Critical factors analysis consists of (*i*) eliciting critical success factors for the organization and (*ii*) deriving information requirements focusing on achieving the target values of these factors.

Process analysis deals with understanding the key elements of the business processes. These elements are the groups of decisions and activities required to manage the resources of the organization. Knowing what problems the organization faces and what decisions they take help in finding out the needed information.

Ends-means analysis defines the outputs and works backwards to find the inputs required to produce these outputs and, of course, defines the processing requirements.

Decision analysis emphasizes the major decisions taken and works backward to find the best way of reaching the decisions. In the process, the information base is also specified.

Input-process-output analysis is a top-down, data-oriented approach where not only the major data flows from and to the outside entities are recognized, but the data flows and the data transformations that take place internally in the organization are also recognized.

Discovering from Experimentation with an Evolving Information System

This method is same as prototyping that has been discussed at great length in Chapter 2. Hence we do not discuss it any longer.

3.6.2 Selecting an Appropriate Strategy

Davis and Olson (1985) have suggested a *contingency approach* for selecting a strategy appropriate for determining information requirements. This approach considers the factors that affect the uncertainties with regard to information determination:

1. Characteristics of the utilizing system
2. Complexity of information system or application system
3. Ability of users to specify requirements
4. Ability of analysts to elicit and evaluate requirements.

Some examples of characteristics of utilizing system that contribute to the uncertainty in information determination are:

1. Existence of large number of users engaged in differing activities.
2. Non-programmed activities that lack structures and change with change in user personnel.
3. Lack of a well-understood model of the utilizing system, leading to confused objectives and poorly defined operating procedures.
4. Lack of stability in structure and operation of the utilizing system.

Two examples of uncertainty arising out of the complexity of information system or application system are:

1. Information system to support decisions at the top-level management.
2. Information system that interacts with many other information systems.

A few examples of uncertainty about the inability of users to specify requirements are:

1. Lack of user experience in the utilizing system.
2. A complex utilizing system.
3. Instability in the utilizing system.
4. Lack of user conceptual model of the utilizing system, *i.e.,* lack of a structure for activity or decision being supported.
5. Varied and large user base that does not own the responsibility of specifying requirements.
6. Vested interest of users leading to nonparticipation.

Examples of uncertainty regarding the ability of the analyst:

1. Prior experience with similar projects may be absent.
2. Time allotted for requirements analysis may be too small.
3. Training of the analyst to deal with complex issues may be poor.

The contingency approach to selecting the appropriate strategy requires an estimation of the overall requirements process uncertainty based on the evaluation of the above-mentioned factors in a particular situation and then using this esimate to select the appropriate development strategy (Fig. 3.4). When the level of uncertainty is low, *asking* will be the best strategy. If the uncertainty level is deemed medium, *deriving from the existing system* should be the best strategy. As the uncertainty level grows from medium to high, *synthesizing from the characteristics of the utilizing system* should be the best strategy, whereas when the uncertainty level is very high, *prototyping* should be adopted as the main strategy.

3.7 THE REQUIREMENTS GATHERING SUB-PHASE

The main activities in the Requirements Gathering phase are depicted in Figure 3.5 (Robertson, and Robertson, 2000). The main activities are indicated by the elliptical symbols and the major documents created are indicated by the rectangles. The major activities are:

1. Set the project scope.
2. Trawl for requirements.

3. Write the requirements.
4. Verify and validate requirements.
5. Review the requirements specifications.
6. Prototype the requirements
7. Reuse requirements.

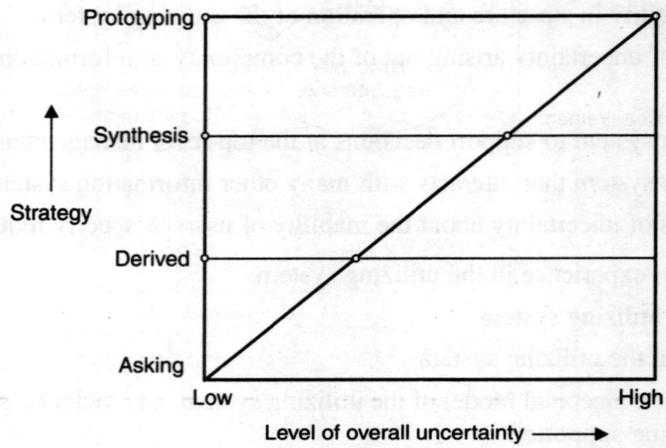

Fig. 3.4. Selection of strategy for information elicitation

1. Set the Project Scope

The various steps in this activity are

A. Recognize the stakeholders of the project. They are:

- The *client* who pays for the development of the product.
- The *customer* who is going to buy the product.
- The *user* who is going to operate the product.
- *Management* – the functional manager, the project sponsor, and the project leaders.
- *Domain analysts* – business consultants and analysts who have some specialized knowledge of the business subject.
- *Developers* – system analysts, product designers, programmers, testers, database designers, and technical writers.
- *Marketing personnel* (relevant if the product is for sale).
- *Legal personnel* – lawyers and police.
- *Opposition* – people who do not want the product.
- *Professional bodies* who have set guidelines and norms.

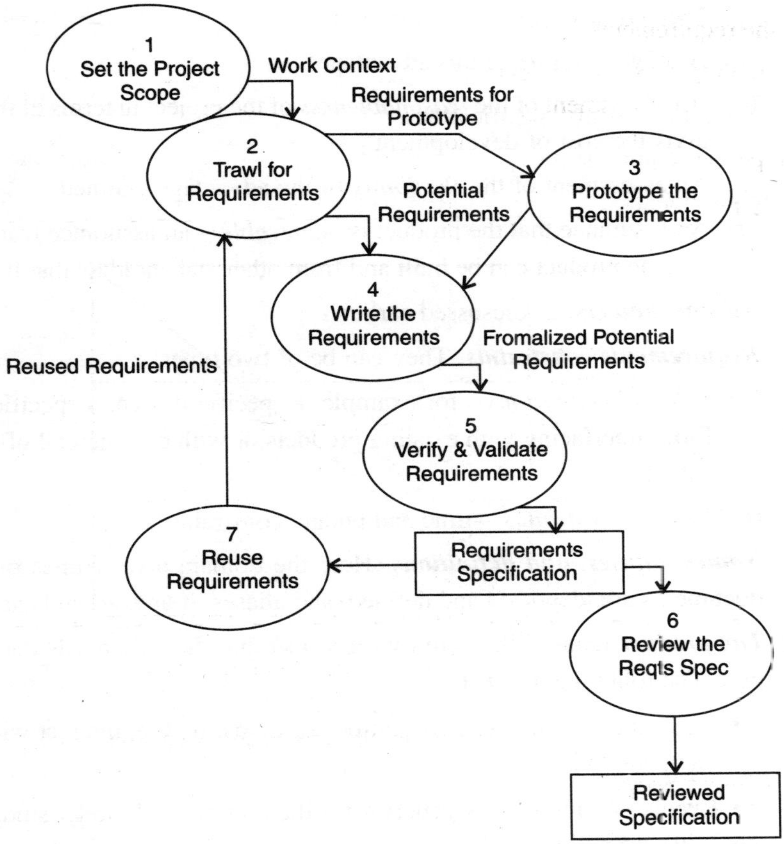

Fig. 3.5. Activities in the requirements gathering sub-phase (adopted from Robertson and Robertson, 2000)

- *Public* (if the user group of the product is the general public, such as for railway and airlines reservation system, banking system, etc.)
- *Government agencies* (if some information passes from or to the government).
- *Special interest groups* – environment groups, affected groups like workers, aged and women, or religious, ethnic or political groups.
- *Technical experts* – hardware and software experts.

B. Brainstorm the appropriate stakeholders in one or more group meetings where the analyst works as a facilitator. The main principle underlying brainstorming is to withhold commenting on opinions expressed by others in the initial round. Subsequently though, opinions are rationalized and are analyzed in a decreasing order of importance. Web-based brainstorming is also a possibility.

C. Determine the work context and the product scope in the brainstorming sessions. The specific items to be identified are the following:

(*i*) ***Product purpose.*** It has several attributes:

(*a*) A *statement of purpose*.

(*b*) The *business advantage* it provides.

(*c*) A rough *measure* of this advantage.

(*d*) An assessment of the *reasonableness* of the project in terms of the advantage vis-à-vis the cost of development.

(*e*) An assessment of the *feasibility* of the advantage claimed.

(*f*) An assurance that the product is *achievable* – an assurance from the developers that the product can be built and from other stakeholders that it can be operated.

(*ii*) ***All stakeholders,*** as dicsussed earlier.

(*iii*) ***Requirements constraints.*** They can be of two types:

(*a*) *Solution constraints*—for example, a specific design, a specific hardware platform, interfacing with existing products or with commercial off-the-shelf applications.

(*b*) *Project constraints* – time and budget constraints.

(*iv*) ***Names, aliases, and definitions.*** Here the domain-level names of processes, and documents are identified and defined, and aliases, if any, are indicated.

(*v*) ***The product scope*** – the activity (or work) that the user needs the product to support. The following is a list:

- Adjacent external systems (entities or domains) that interact with the system in its operation,
- Events (stimulus) they generate for the unit or work under study, and
- Response of the system under study to such events.

The part of the response that is done by the product is a *use case.* The use cases are explained in detail later in a separate chapter on object-oritented analysis.

D. Preliminary estimates of project time, cost, and risks involved. An estimate of time and cost required to complete the project, however rough it may be, is desirable even at this preliminary stage. Also important is an estimate of risks associated with the availability of skilled manpower, software and hardware facility, during the development of the project.

E. Go/no go decision as to whether to continue with the project.

2. Trawl for Requirements

Users, customers, and clients, together with the analysts, trawl for these requirements. Trawling requires various approaches:

Understand how the work responses are generated**:** Basically it means understanding the various *functions* that have to be done and the files and the *data stores* that are to be accessed. It calls for a first-level breakdown of the work into more deseggregated functions with attendant data files and interconnecting *data flows.* This calls for drawing first-level data flow diagrams.

***Be an apprentice*:** The analyst sits with the user to learn the job by observation, asking questions, and doing some work under the user's supervision.

***Observe abstract repeating patterns*:** Various people may be engaged in these functions and various technologies may be used to carry out these functions. If these implementation details are ignored, the similar patterns in their abstract forms become visible. Such patterns, once recognized, help in understanding a new requirement very fast.

***Interview the users*:** Although an art, interviewing process can be quite structured. The important points in the interviewing process are: fixing prior appointments, preparing an item-wise list of specific questions, allowing more time to the interviewee, taking down notes, and providing the interviewee with a summary of the points after the interview.

***Get the essence of the system*:** When the implementation details are ignored, the logical structures of the functions and data flows become more apparent. The outcome of such analysis is a logical data flow diagram.

***Conduct business event workshops*:** Every business event is handled by an *'owner'* who is the organization's expert to handle that event. This expert and the analyst together participate in a workshop. Here the expert describes or enacts the work that is normally done in response to that event. Such a workshop helps the analyst to know a number of things:

(*a*) the business event and the desired outcome,

(*b*) the series of actions (scenarios) of the work done,

(*c*) 'what-if' scenarios when things go wrong,

(*d*) the business rules,

(*e*) part of the work to be done by the product,

(*f*) the likely users, and

(*g*) candidate requirements for prototyping.

***Conduct requirements workshops*:** In a requirements workshop the key stakeholders meet and discuss the issue of requirements threadbare. A facilitator helps the requirements elicitation process. Normally, some warm-up materials giving brief details of project-specific information and the points to be discussed are distributed among the participants before the meeting.

***Brainstorm*:** In a brainstorming session, the participating stakeholders come out with their point of view without any inhibition. These views are discussed, rationalized, and finalized.

***Study existing documents*:** This is a rich source of information for eliciting requirements.

***Resort to video taping*:** This helps to analyze the process operations later, off-line.

Use electronic media to gather opinion and information requirements of unknown users for developing commercial off-the-shelf software.

***Use storyboards*:** Storyboards are used to obtain user's reaction early on almost any facet of an application—understand data visualization, define and understand new business rules desired to be implemented, define algorithms to be excecuted in the system, and demonstrate reports and hardcopy outputs. Storyboarding can be:

Passive: Screen shots, Business rules, and Output reports.

Active: Slide show, Animation, and Simulation.

Interactive: Live demonstration and Interactive presentation.

Develop scenario models: Used commonly in theatres and cartoons, a scenario is a number of scenes or episodes that tell a story of a specific situation. These models can be used effectively in eliciting requirements. Scenario models for this purpose can be text based, picture based, or a mixture of both. Let us take the example of a bank counter for withdrawals. Three scenes (episodes) can constitute this scenario:

(*a*) No customer at the counter.

(*b*) Two customers on an average at any time at the counter.

(*c*) Nine customers on average at the counter at any time.

A picture-based scenario model of these three situations is given in Fig. 3.6(*a*) – (*c*). When there are more than one teller counter, the bank may decide to close the counter for the day in case of episode 1. On the other hand, in case of episode 3, the bank may decide to open a new counter, or investigate as to whether the bank officer is inefficient (a newly recruited person), or if (*s*) he is not on the seat most of the time, or the like.

The above situations are depicted in picture form, often called ***storyboards***. They can be very powerful in discovering requirements.

Develop use cases. Use cases, developed by Jacobson, *et al.* (1992), help to identify user needs by textually describing them through stories.

3. Prototype the Requirements

Before the requirements are written, it is often useful to develop prototypes of requirements for a face-to-face discussion with the users to know from them whether their needs are well captured. Examples of prototypes are: drawings on paper, clip-charts, white boards, or a use case on paper, white board or clip-charts, with its attendant adjacent external system event, and the major task the product is supposed to do. A user is then initiated into an intensely involved discussion on what the product should provide in order to accomplish the task and respond to that event most satisfactorily.

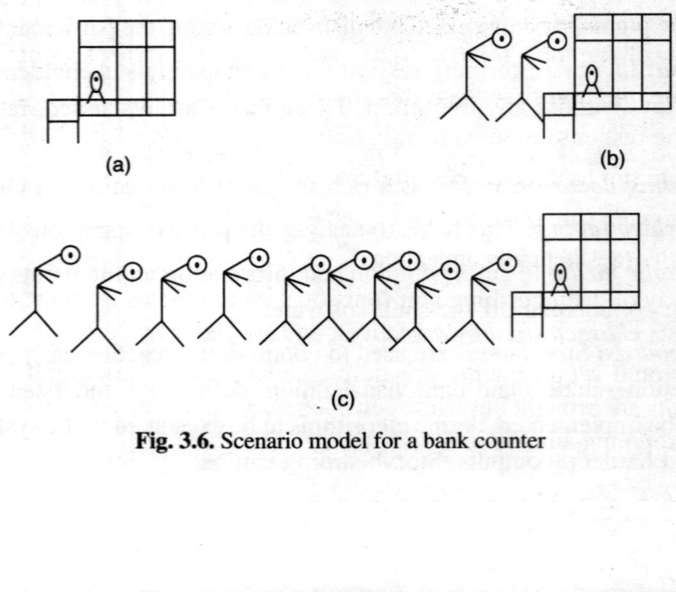

(a) (b) (c)

Fig. 3.6. Scenario model for a bank counter

4. Write the Requirements

The requirements gathered during the process of trawling are now described in a written form, in a ***requirements template.*** Such a written document forms the basis for a contract between the developer and the client. Therefore, these written requirements must be clear, complete, and testable.

A requirements template has four major divisions:

- product contraints,
- functional requirements,
- non-functional requirements, and
- project issues.

We have already dicussed earlier the elements of product constraints in the form of solution constraints. We now discuss the remaining three divisions.

Functional requirements

Functional requirements specify what the product must do in order to satisfy the basic reason for its existence. They are:

- Specifications of the product's functionality.
- Actions the product must take – check, compute, record, and retrieve.
- Derived from the basic purpose of the product.
- Normally business-oriented, rather than technical.
- Not the technical solution constraints that are often referred as the 'system requirements'. System requirements are discussed later in this chapter.
- Derived mostly from the use case scenarios.
- Not a quality.
- Not measurable or testable at this stage.
- To be free from ambiguities.

Non-functional requirements

Non-functional requirements are *properties, characteristics, or qualities* that a software product must have for it to do a task (a functional requirement) well.

For example, the user may want that the product be

- *fast* (the response time be less than a specified time),
- *accurate* (up to three places after decimal),
- *user friendly* (the input screen be self explanatory),
- *attractive* (aesthetically appealing).

A useful way of distinguishing non-functional requirements from the functional ones is that the *former is characterized by adjectives,* and *the latter by verbs.*

Non-functional requirements are delineated for each functional requirements. These requirements are brought out while considering use case scenarios for each adjacent system, during prototyping, and by interviewing the stakeholders.

Look and feel requirements are meant to make the product attractive for the intended audience by making it

- Colourful, animated, exciting, and artistic,
- Highly readable,
- Interactive, and
- Professional looking.

Usability requirements describe the appropriate level of usability, given the intended users of the product. Some examples are:

- The product can be used by users from non-English-speaking countries.
- The product can be used by children.
- The product shall be easy to learn.
- The product can be used easily by people with no previous experience with computers.

Performance requirements describe various facets of the product such as

- speed,
- accuracy,
- safety,
- range of allowable values, and
- throughput such as the rate of transactions, efficiency of resource usage, and reliability.

Some examples of performance requirements are:

- The product shall switch on the motor within 2 seconds.
- The speed of the athletes will be measured in seconds up to four places after decimal.
- The product will actuate a siren as soon as the pressure rises up to its safety limit.
- The product will allow monetary units such as US dollar, Indian rupees, pound sterling, mark, and yen.
- A maximum of 5,000 transactions will be handled within an hour.
- The program will occupy 20 MB of space of hard disk.
- Software failures will not exceed one in a month.

Operational requirements describe the environment in which the product is to be used. The environment can be recognized from the context diagram or the use case diagram by finding out the needs and conditions of each of the adjacent systems or actors. These requirements relate to

- *physical environment* (*e.g.*, freezing temperature, poor lighting).
- *condition of the user* (*e.g.,* user on wheelchair or aircraft seat),
- *interfacing systems* (*e.g.*, access to database of another system), and
- *portability* (*e.g.,* ability to work in both Windows and Unix environment).

Maintainability requirements can be described, although too early to predict. For example, requirements can be delineated with regard to the maintenance of a product arising out of certain foreseeable changes. These can be changes in

1. *Business rules* (*e.g.*, advance payment must be made before a product can be delivered to a customer; credit card facility will not be extended to a particular class of customers).

2. *Location of the product* (*e.g.*, the software will handle international business across many countries and have to be commensurate with new conditions).
3. *Environment* (*e.g.*, the product shall be readily portable to Linux operating system).

Security requirements describe three features:

- *Confidentiality* (protects the product from unauthorized users),
- *Integrity* (ensures that the product's data are the same as those obtained from the source or authority of the data), and
- *Availability* ensures that the authorized users have access to data and get them without the security delaying the access.

Cultural and political requirements are important considerations when a software product is sold to organizations with different cultural setting. A functionality may appear irrational to a person with a different cultural background. For example, the function of maintaining an optimum inventory may appear irrational to an organization that practices JIT for a long time.

Legal requirements should be understood and incorporated to avoid major risks for commercial software. Conforming to ISO certification, displaying copyright notices, giving statutory warnings, and following laws with regard to privacy, guarantees, consumer credit, and right to information are some examples of legal requirements that a software developer should consider.

Project Issues

Project issues are not requirements, but they are highlighted because they help to understand the requirements. There are many forms of project issues:

- ***Open issues*** are those that remained unresolved. Examples could be that a firm decision had not been taken on whether to buy or make a graphic software package, or that the business rules regarding credit sales are being changed.
- ***Off-the-shelf solutions*** are the available software packages that can support certain functions of the product.
- ***New problems*** created by the introduction of the product include new ways of doing work, fresh work distribution among employees, new types of documents, etc., about which the client should be alert.
- ***Tasks*** are the major steps the delivering organizations will take to build/buy/assemble and install the product.
- ***Cutover*** is the set of tasks that have to be done at the time of installing/implementing the new product while changing over from the old product. They may include conversion of an old data file, collection of new data, installation of a new data input scheme, and so on.
- ***Risks*** are unforeseen events that may occur and adversely affect the project execution. The major risks need to be highlighted here to alert both the client and the developers.
- ***Costs*** should be estimated in terms of person-months of work to build the product.
- The ***user documentation*** section will specify the type of help, such as an implementation manual, a user manual, and on-line help, that will be provided to the user.
- The ***waiting room*** section includes all the requirements that could not be included in the initial version of a software, but which are recognized and stored for use in the future expansion, if any, of the product.

5. Verify and Validate Requirements

Every potential requirements listed in the Requirements Template must be examined/tested to decide whether it should be included in the Requirements Specifications. This examination process has got two steps:

1. *Establish fit criteria* (measurement scales) for each requirement.
2. *Test each requirement* for completeness, relevance, and viability.

Establishing Fit Criteria

Establishing a *fit criterion* to a requirement basically means quantifying the requirement. Such quantification makes the requirement credible and testable, and induces the users to expect it to happen and the developers to match the user's expectation. Fit criteria can be of two types:

- Functional Fit Criteria
- Non-functional Fit Criteria

Functional fit criteria require that all terms be defined. They may, for example, take the following forms:

- The recorded data shall match the input data.
- The reviewed data shall match the input data.
- The computed value shall agree with the specified scheme approved by the authority.
- The response shall match every point raised in the inquiry.
- A downtime report of an equipment shall give downtime value for each equipment costing more than 100 thousand rupees; so the number of such equipment should match with the actual number in the plant.

Non-functional fit criteria are also to be defined in terms of their fit criteria. A few examples are the following:

Description:	The product shall be colourful and attractive to children.
Fit Criteria:	Nine out of 10 children in the age group of 8–10 years will spend a minimum of five minutes in their first encounter with the product.
Description:	The product shall be easy to use.
Fit Criteria:	New users shall generate 10 output screens.
Description:	The product shall generate all the supporting reports well before the Board Meeting.
Fit Criteria:	The product shall generate all the supporting reports at least two days before the Board Meeting.
Description:	The product shall not be offensive to Japanese.
Fit Critertia:	No output screen will contain a picture or a cartoon that can be offensive to Japanese. It will be certified by the Department of Japanese Studies of JNU, New Delhi.

In addition to developing fit criteria for each functional and non-functional requirement, it is also useful to develop them for each use case and each constraint. A fit crterion for a use case has to be aggregative in character. An example of a fit criterion for a use case is:

Description : Generate a master production schedule.

Fit Criteria : The schedule will be made for a year and will be made for the refrigerator division and air conditioning division only.

An example of a solution constraint is:

Description : The product will run in the Windows operating system.

Fit Criteria : The product will run in the Windows 2000 operating system.

Testing Requirements

A number of requirement tests have been suggested to accept the requirements from the list of potential ones. The tests are carried out for checking for (*a*) completeness, (*b*) traceability, (*c*) use of consistent terminology, (*d*) relevance, (*e*) viability, (*f*) solution boundedness (*g*) gold-plating, (*h*) creep, (*i*) conflict, and (*j*) ambiguity. Only the appropriate test has to be used. We discuss the requirement tests.

A. Completeness

To ensure completeness,

- There should be no missing component in the requirements set.
- Every requirement should be written as clearly and unambiguously as possible.

To find *missing requirements,* one must review the adjacent external agencies, the events and the use cases. At this stage it may be necessary to develop

(1) ***data models*** (like bottom-level data flow diagrams, entity-relationship diagrams, class diagrams, etc.) to show event-response data models, and

(2) ***object life history (or state) diagrams*** to show all the states of an entity and the transitions caused by the events.

These diagrams will be discussed in the latter chapters.

B. Traceability

Whenever a requirement changes and such a change is accommodated it is important to know which parts of the product are affected by that change. To help traceability, the requirement should have

1. A unique indentifier.
2. An indicator of the type of requirement or constraint.
3. References to all business events and use cases that contain it.
4. References to dependent requirements.
5. References to conflicting requirements.

C. Consistent Terminology

It is required that

1. The terms are defined.
2. Every requirement uses a term in a manner consistent with its specified meaning.
3. The analyst should expect inconsistent terminology and therefore should look for it consciously.

D. Relevance

Every requirement must be immediately relevant to the purpose of the product. Users often ask for much more than necessary. Also unnecessary external agencies are considered or superfluous constraints are identified, while setting the work context. These cases give rise to irrelevancy that should be avoided.

E. Viability

Each requirement must be viable within the specified constraints of time, cost, available technology, development skills, input data sources, user expectation, and stakeholder interactions.

F. Solution Boundedness

A requirement should not be described in terms of a solution. To provide a password to be able the access the system is a solution whereas the real requirement is to allow authorized users the access to confidential information. Similarly, to prepare an annual report on projects is a solution whereas the real requirement may be to provide information on time and cost overrun.

G. Gold Plating

Giving more than necessary is gold plating. A user may like to have an additional piece of information, but the cost of providing this piece of information may outweigh its value to the user. Instances of gold plating include:

- Giving names of all customers in an annual sales report
- Giving names of all executives associated with each project in a quarterly review report on projects.

H. Creep

Many times, after the requirements process is complete, *new requirements* are discovered not because of genuine systemic or environmental changes, but because they were left out due to an incomplete requirements process arising out of low budget, less permitted time, unplanned requirements elicitation process, and low skills of the analysts.

Extra information in the form of leakage may also enter the requirements specification due to the fault of the analyst. Proper investigation may not have been made and therefore nobody may own them, and no explanation can be given as to how they were derived.

To carry out requirements testing, a *four-stage review process* is recommended:

1. Each individual developer reviews against a checklist.
2. A peer review by another member of the team examines the requirements related to a particular use case.
3. Requirements that fail the tests should be reviewed by a team that includes users and customers.
4. A management review considers a summary of the requirements tests.

I. Conflicting

When two requirements are conflicting, they are difficult or impossible to be implemented.

For example, one requirement may ask for a one-page summary of transactions within a month, whereas another requirement may ask for details of daily transactions, both for the same purpose to be provided to the same person.

To detect *conflicting requirements,* one should search for requirements that

- use the same data,
- are of the same type, and
- use the same fit criteria.

If we prepare a matrix where each row and each column represents a requirement, then we can examine if a row and a column requirement are in conflict. If they are, then we can tick the corresponding cell. The result is an upper-triangular matrix where some cells are ticked because the corresponding row and column requirements are conflicting.

The requirements analyst has to meet each user separately in a group and resolve the issue by consensus or compromise.

J. Ambiguity

Specifications should be so written that two persons should not make different interpretations out of it. Ambiguity is introduced due to bad way of writing specifications. The following conditions increase the likelihood of presence of ambiguity.

1. Not defining terms,
2. Not using the terms consistently,
3. Using the word 'should',
4. Using unqualified adjectives or adverbs, and
5. Not applying fit criteria.

The validated requirements are now ready to be put in the Requirements Specification document. All the items discussed above are included in the Requirements Specification document and each requirement is qualified by establishing functional and non-functional fit criteria and tested for completeness, relevance, etc.

6. Reviewing the Requirements Specifications

The resulting requirements specifications are now reviewed by the customers, the users, the analysts, and the project team members, both individually and jointly. Any doubt or misgiving must be mitigated and the change incorporated in the requirement specifications. The document resulting from the reviewing process is the *User Requirements Specification (URS).*

7. Reusing Requirements

Although every problem area is unique in some way, in many ways it may have a pattern that can be found in many other problem areas. For example, customer order processing involves procedures and steps that are fairly common across companies. Similar is the situation for financial accounting, material requirement planning, and several transaction processing systems.

To reuse requirements, one must have a *library of generic requirements.* To build this library, one has to first develop generic, abstract requirements, and maintain them. The advent of object orientation with its attendant advantage of encapsulation of functions and parameters has boosted the prospect of reusability in recent days.

3.8 REQUIREMENTS ENGINEERING

What started as requirements analysis has now grown into the field of requirements engineering that demands a systematic use of verifiable principles, methods, languages, and tools in the analysis and description of user needs and the description of the behavioral and non-behavioral features of a software system satisfying the user needs (Peters and Pedrycz, 2000). Requirements engineering is generally discussed from the point of view of the whole system – the *system requirements engineering* – and the software that is a part of the system – the *software requirements engineering*—(Thayer and Dorfman 1997). Whereas a *system* is a conglomeration of hardware, software, data, facilities, and procedures to achieve a common goal, a *software system* is a conglomeration of software programs to provide certain desired functionalities.

System requirements engineering involves transforming operational needs into a system description, systems performance parameters, and a system configuration by a process of allocation of the needs into its different components. The output of the system requirements engineering process is either the System Requirements Specification (SyRS) or the Concept of Operations (ConOps) document. Software requirements engineering, on the other hand, uses the system requirements to produce Software Requirements Specification (SRS). Figure 3.7 shows their relationships.

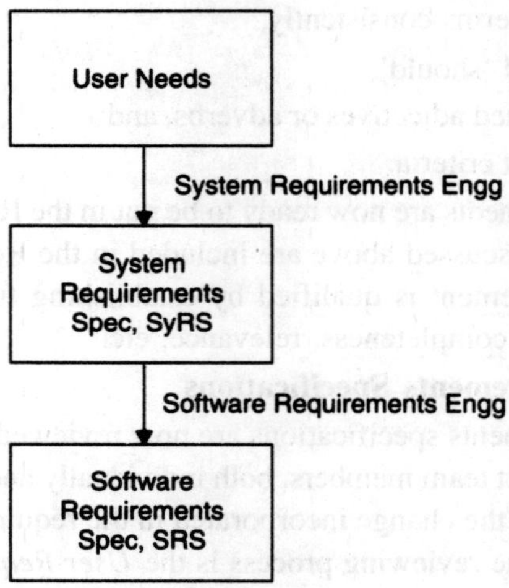

Fig. 3.7. System and Software Requirements Engineering

Software must be compatible with its operational environment for its successful installation. Software, together with its environment, constitutes the system. Knowledge of system engineering and system requirements engineering therefore becomes quite important.

3.8.1 System Engineering

Software is part of a larger system that satisfies the requirements of users. User requirements are satisfied not merely by designing the software entities, it requires the design of a product or a system of which the software is only a part. The other parts are (1) the necessary hardware, (2) the people to operate the hardware and the software, (3) the subsystems that contain elements of hardware, software, and people, and (4) the interfaces among these subsystems. The design process that takes a holistic view of the user requirements in order to evolve a product or a system is called *system engineering*. In the context of manufacturing, this design process is called *product engineering*, while this is called *information engineering* in the context of a business enterprise. Excellent software, developed with a myopic view, may soon become out-of-date because the system-level requirements were not fully understood.

Many concepts surround the word 'system'. Chief among them are the concepts of environment, subsystems, and hierarchy. Anything that is not considered a part of a system is the environment to the system. Forces emanating from the environment and affecting the system function are called exogenous, while those emanating from within are called endogenous. For development of an information system it is necessary that the analyst knows which elements are within the system and which are not. The latter set of elements lies in the environment. Because the environmental forces can impair the effectiveness of an information system, a system engineering viewpoint requires that great care be taken to project environmental changes that include change in business policies, hardware and software interfaces, and user requirements, etc.

A way to break down systemic complexity is by forming a hierarchy of subsystems. The functions of the system are decomposed and allotted to various subsystems. The function of each subsystem, in turn, is decomposed and allotted to sub-subsystems, and this process of decomposition may continue, thus forming a hierarchy (Pressman 1997). The *world view*, defining the overall business objective and scope and the particular domain of interest, appears on the top while the *detailed view*, defining the construction and integration of components, appears on the bottom of the hierarchy. The *domain view* (analysis of the concerned domain of interest) and the *element view* (design of concerned hardware, software, data, and people) separate these two. Figure 3.8 shows schematically the hierarchy of the views.

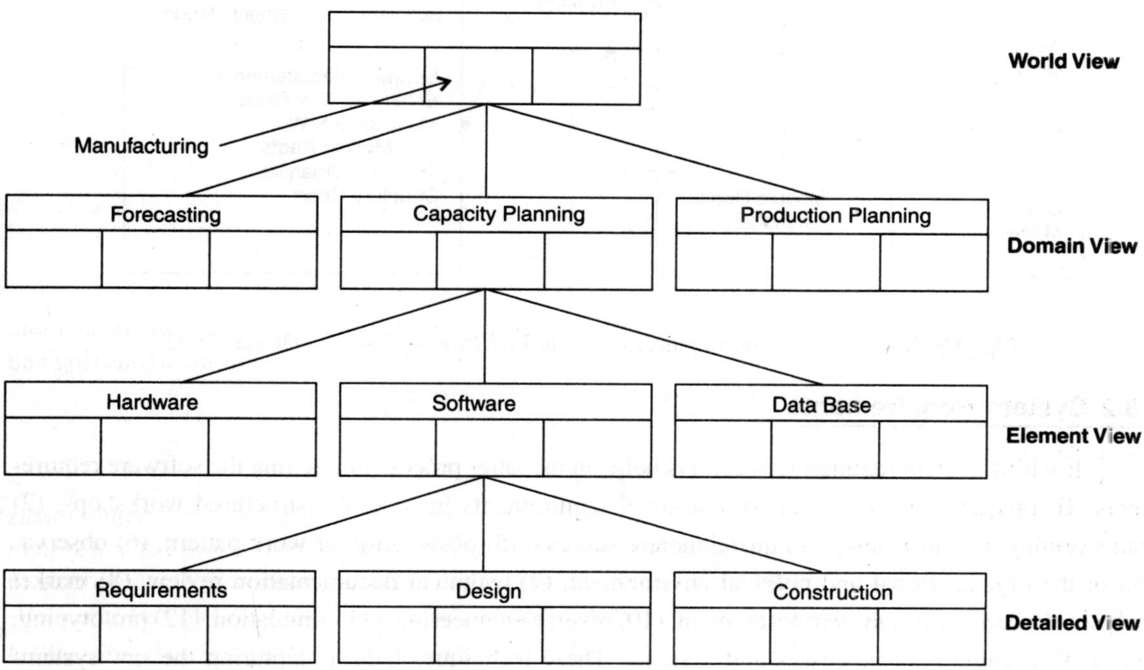

Fig. 3.8. The hierarchy of subsystems

Software engineering is relevant in the element and the detailed view. It is however important to consider the top views in the hierarchy in order to align the software goal with the business goal. Today when information systems are developed for business areas rather than isolated business functions, a system engineering perspective helps to understand the constraints and preferences in the higher levels of the hierarchy imposed by the business strategy.

Futrell, *et al.* (2002) present a classical systems engineering model that integrates the system requirements with the hardware and the software requirements (Fig. 3.9). In a very interesting paper, Thayer (2002) distinguishes between system engineering, software system engineering, and software engineering. Figure 3.10 shows the distinctions graphically.

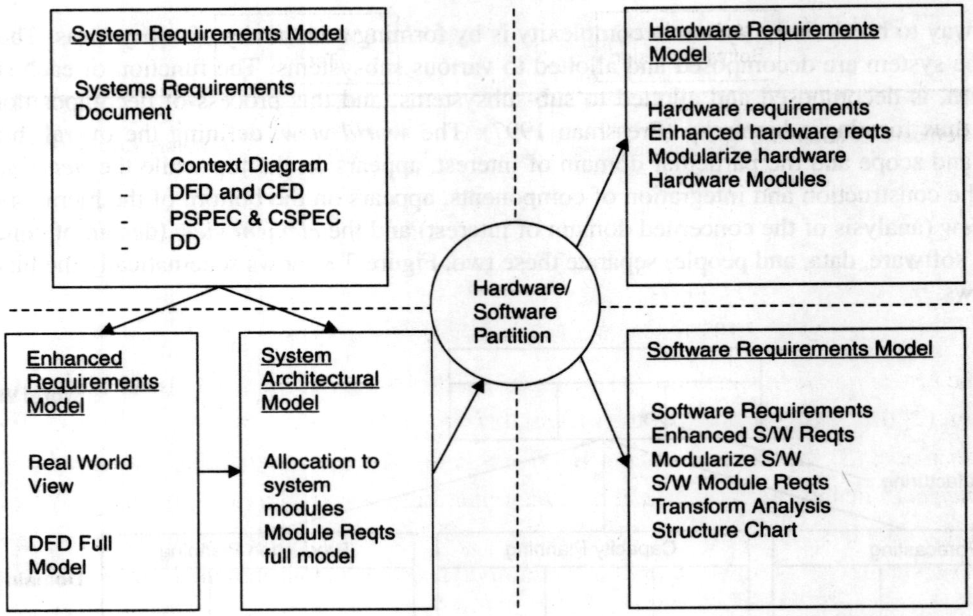

Fig. 3.9. Classical Systems Engineering Front-End Process Model, (Thayer, 2002)

3.8.2 System Requirements

Eliciting system requirements always helps in the latter process of eliciting the software requirements. Techniques for identifying system-level requirements include: (1) structured workshops, (2) brainstorming, (3) interviews, (4) questionnaire surveys, (5) observation of work pattern, (6) observation of the organizational and political environment, (7) technical documentation review, (8) market analysis, (9) competitive system assessment, (10) reverse engineering, (11) simulation, (12) prototyping, and (13) benchmarking processes and systems. These techniques help in capturing the raw system-level requirements that are imprecise and unstructured. In this text, we shall not discuss the individual techniques; we shall, instead, emphasize on the system-level requirements.

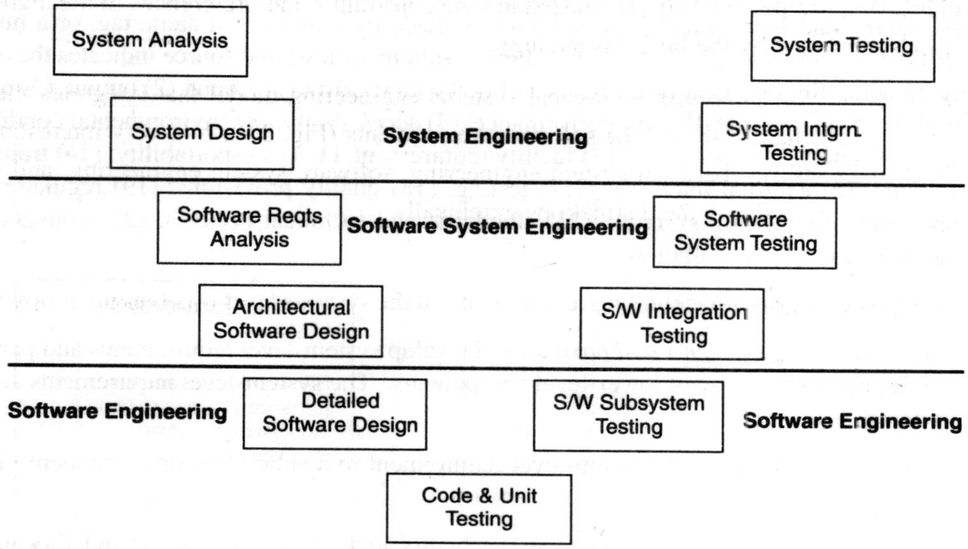

Fig. 3.10. System and Software Relationship (Thayer, 2002)

The *raw requirements* include: (1) the goals, objectives, and the desired capabilities of the potential system, (2) the unique features of the system that provide it an edge over the competing systems in the market place, (3) the external system interfaces, and (4) the environmental influences. *External system interfaces* include all the data and hardware interfaces that can be (a) computer-to-computer, (b) electrical, (c) data links and protocol, (d) telecommunication links, (e) device to system and system to device, (f) computer to system and system to computer, and (g) environmental sense and control.

The environmental influences can be categorized as (1) political or governmental laws and regulations with regard to zoning, environmental hazards, wastes, recycling, safety, and health, (2) market influences that consider (a) matching of customer needs to the systems, (b) distribution and accessibility of the system, and (c) competitive variables such as functionality, price, reliability, durability, performance, maintenance, and system safety and security, (3) technical policies influence that consider standards and guidelines with regard to system consistency, safety, reliability, and maintainability, (4) cultural influence, (5) organizational policies with regard to development and marketing, (6) physical factors such as temperature, humidity, radiation, pressure, and chemical.

It is necessary to transform the raw requirements to *well-formed requirements*. A well-formed requirement is a statement of (1) *system functionality* (that represents the features of functions of the system (system capabilities) needed or desired by the customer) and (2) the conditions and the constraints that constitute the attributes of these requirements. Conditions are measurable qualitative or quantitative attributes that are stipulated for a system functionality thus allowing the functionality to be verified and validated. Constraints are requirements that are imposed on the solution by circumstance, force or compulsion and that restrict the solution space.

Well-formed requirements should be categorized by their identification, priority, criticality, feasibility, risk, source and type. Identification could be made by a number, a name tag, or a mnemonic; priority, criticality, and feasibility may each be high, medium, or low; and source indicates the originator of the requirement. Requirement types can be defined with regard to (1) input, (2) output, (3) reliability, (4) availability, (5) maintainability, (6) performance, (7) accessibility, (8) environmental conditions, (9) ergonomic, (10) safety, (11) security, (12) facility requirement, (13) transportability, (14) training, (15) documentation, (16) external interfaces, (17) testing, (18) quality provisions, (19) regulatory policy, (20) compatibility to existing systems, (21) standards and technical policies, (22) conversion, (23) growth capacity, and (24) installation.

Dorfman (1997) says that eliciting requirements at the systems level involves the following steps:

1. *System-level requirements and partitions.* Develop system-level requirements and partition the system into a hierarchy of lower-level components. The system-level requirements are general in nature.
2. *Allocation.* Allocate each system-level requirement to a subsystem or component of the system.
3. *Breakdown.* Breakdown (or flowdown) each allocated set of requirements and allocate them to smaller sub-subsystems. These allocated requirements are very specific.
4. *Traceability.* When the number of requirements becomes high, keep track of each of one them and the component with which they are associated.
5. *Interfaces.* Recognize the external interfaces and internal interfaces. External interfaces define the subsystems that actually interface with the outside world, while internal interfaces define the subsystem-to-subsystem interfaces.

System requirements are specified in either the SyRS document or Concept of Operations (ConOps) document

3.8.3 System Requirements Specification

A system requirement specification (*SyRS*) is a document that communicates the requirements of the customer to the technical community to specify and build the system. The customer includes the person/section/organization buying the system, the agency funding the system development, the acceptor who will sign-off delivery, and the managers who will oversee the implementation, operation, and maintenance of the system. The technical community includes analysts, estimators, designers, quality assurance officers, certifiers, developers, engineers, integrators, testers, maintainers, and manufacturers. The document describes what the system should do in terms of the system's interaction or interfaces with the external environment, other systems, and people. Thus, the document describes the system behavior as seen from outside. Prepared mostly by system engineers with limited software knowledge, the document can be interpreted by customers, non-technical users, as well as analysts and designers.

IEEE has developed a guide for developing the system requirement specification (IEEE P1233/D3). Table 3.1 gives an outline recommended by IEEE.

Table 3.1: An SyRS Outline

Table of Contents

List of Figures

List of Tables

1. INTRODUCTION

1.1 System Purpose
1.2 System Scope
1.3 Definitions, Acronyms, and Abbreviations
1.4 References
1.5 System Overview

2. GENERAL SYSTEM DESCRIPTION

2.1 System Context
2.2 System Modes and States
2.3 Major System Capabilities
2.4 Major System Conditions
2.5 Major System Constraints
2.6 User Characteristics
2.7 Assumptions and Dependencies
2.8 Operational Scenarios

3. SYSTEM CAPABILITIES, CONDITIONS, AND CONSTRAINTS

(Note: System behaviour, exception handling, manufacturability, and deployment should be covered under each capability, condition, and constraint.)

3.1 Physical
- 3.1.1 Construction
- 3.1.2 Durability
- 3.1.3 Adaptability
- 3.1.4 Environmental Conditions

3.2 System Performance Characteristics
3.3 System Security
3.4 Information Management
3.5 System Operations
- 3.5.1 System Human Factors
- 3.5.2 System Maintainability
- 3.5.3 System Reliability

3.6 Policy and Regulation

3.7 System Life Cycle Sustainment

4. SYSTEM INTERFACE

3.8.4 The Concept of Operations (ConOps) Document

Conceived by many scientists of US defense organizations, *Concept of Operations* (known also as *ConOps*) document has been projected as a useful artifact for describing a system's characteristics from the user's operational viewpoint. Written in the user's language and in a narrative prose with the help of graphs, diagrams and storyboards, it acts as a bridge – a means of communication between the users and the developers. The document can be developed by a buyer, a user, or even a developer, right at the beginning or in the middle of the development of the software, but it must always reflect the viewpoint of, and be approved by, the user community.

The traditional development process stresses functionality and does not concern with how the functionality will be used. *Concept analysis*, on the other hand, is the process of analyzing a problem domain and an operational environment for the purpose of specifying the characteristics of a proposed system from the users' perspective (Fairley and Thayer, 2002). It is the first step in the system development process. It identifies various classes of users, their needs and desires (both desirable and optional), and their priorities. It also identifies various modes of operations that include diagnostic mode, maintenance mode, degraded mode, emergency mode, and backup mode.

A ConOps document unifies diverse user viewpoints, quantifies vague and immeasurable requirements ("fast response", "reliable response", etc., are quantified), and provides a bridge between the user's operational needs and the developer's technical requirement document.

An outline of ConOps document is given below (Fairley and Thayer, 2002).

1. Scope

1.1 Identification

1.2 System Overview

1.3 Document Overview

2. Referenced Documents

3. The Current System or Situation

3.1 Background, Objectives, and Scope of the Current System or Situation

3.2 Operational Policies and Constraints for the Current System or Situation

3.3 Description of the Current System or Situation

3.4 Modes of Operation for the Current System

3.5 User Classes for the Current System

3.5.1 Organizational Structure

3.5.2 Profiles of User Classes

3.5.3 Interactions Among User Classes

3.6 Other Involved Personnel

3.7 Support Environment for the Current System

4. Justification for and Nature of Proposed Changes/New Features

4.1 Justification for Changes and New Features

4.2 Description of Needed Changes and New Features

4.3 Priorities Among Changes and New Features

4.4 Changes and New Features Considered but not Included

4.5 Assumptions and Constraints

5. Concepts of Operations for the Proposed System

5.1 Background, Objectives, and Scope for the New or Modified System

5.2 Operational Policies and Constraints

5.3 Description of the Proposed System

5.4 Modes of Operation of the Proposed System

5.5 User Classes for the Proposed System

5.5.1 Organizational Structure

5.5.2 Profiles of User Classes

5.5.3 Interactions Among User Classes

5.6 Other Involved Personnel

5.7 Support Environment for the Proposed System

6. Operational Scenarios for the Proposed System

7. Summary of Impacts

7.1 Operational Impacts

7.2 Organizational Impacts

7.3 Impacts During Development

8. Analysis of the Proposed System

8.1 Summary of Improvements

8.2 Disadvantages and Limitations

8.3 Alternatives and Trade-offs Considered

9. Notes

Appendices

Glossary

This chapter brings out the essential features of requirements analysis. In the next seven chapters, we present the tools of requirements analysis and the elements of software requirements specification.

sanction is available, the Department invites Quotations from Suppliers. On receiving the Quotations, it prepares a Comparative Statement. It then sends the Deputy Director's Sanction Letter, the Quotations received from the Suppliers, and the Comparative Statement to the Deputy Registrar (Finance & Accounts) for booking funds. Thereafter it sends the same set of three documents to the Purchase Department for it to place the Purchase Requisition with the identified Supplier.

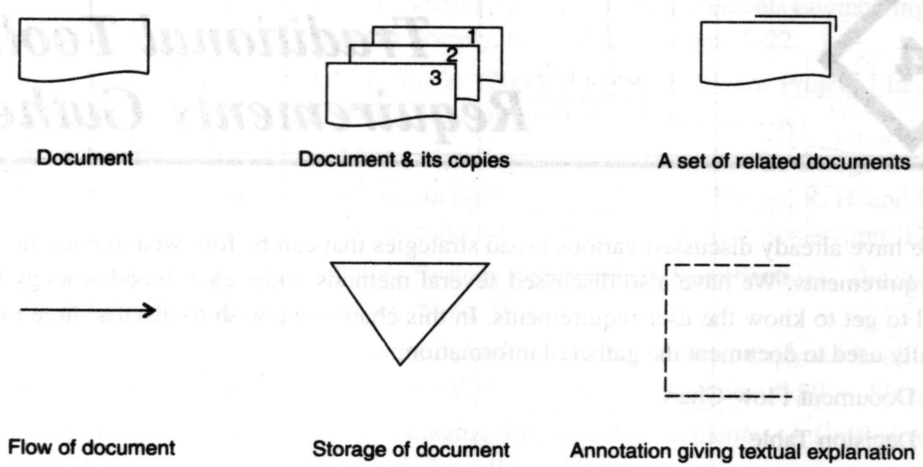

Fig. 4.1. Symbols used in a document flow chart

A document flow chart indicates the flow of documents from one department (or person) to another. It brings to light the following:

- The number of copies of a document.
- The place (and/or person) of origin of the document.
- The places (and/or persons) where the document is sent.
- The decisions and actions taken at various places (or by various persons) where the document is sent.

A document flow chart is very useful for an analyst in

- Documenting the existing information system in an organization. It is particularly very useful in documenting a manual information system.
- Understanding the existing procedure of decision making in an organization.
- Convincing the client that he has fully understood the existing procedures in the organization.
- Analyzing the good and bad points of the existing information system. For example, an examination of the flow chart helps in identifying (*a*) unnecessary movement of documents and (*b*) wasteful and time-consuming procedure and in suggesting new procedures.

Because the major flows take place horizontally, this chart is also called a ***horizontal flow chart.***

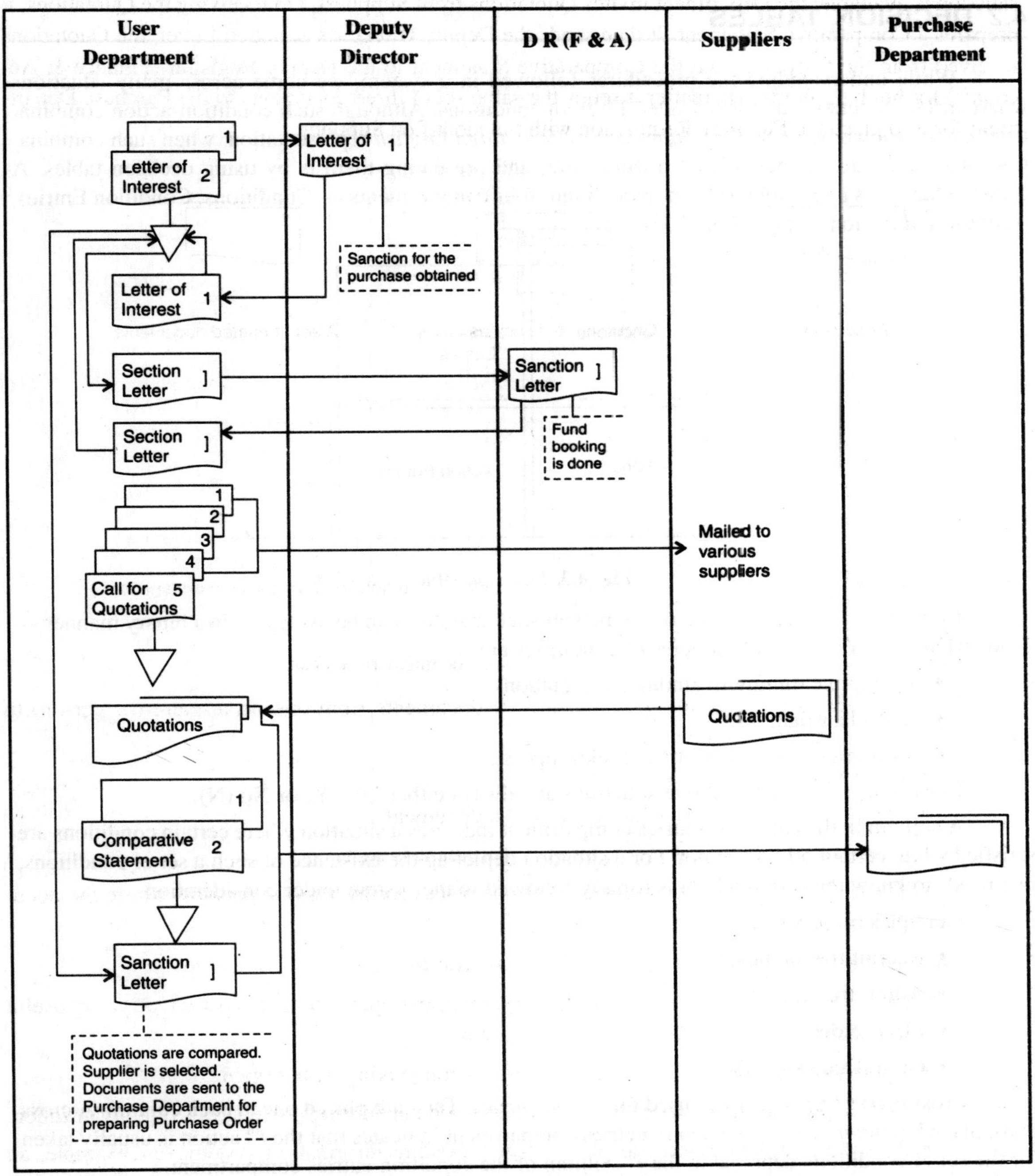

Fig. 4.2. Partial document flow chart for placing purchase requisition

4.2 DECISION TABLES

While understanding the procedures followed in a system, we come across many situations where different actions are taken under different conditions. Although such condition-action combinations can be shown by *logic flow charts* and by *Structured English* representation, when such combinations are many, a compact way of documenting and presenting them is by using decision tables. A decision table has a rectangular form divided into four compartments — Conditions, Condition Entries, Actions, and Action Entries (Fig. 4.3).

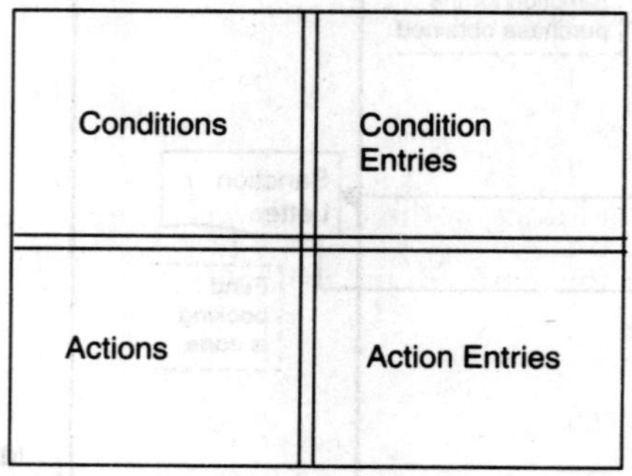

Fig. 4.3. Decision table

Conditions are usually defined in a manner such that they can be expressed in a binary manner — True or False, or Yes or No. Examples of conditions are:

- Is the price minimum among all quotations?
- Is age less than 40?
- Is taxable income more than 4 lakh rupees?

Condition entries in the above situations are always either Yes (Y) or No (N).

A column in the condition entries compartment indicates a situation where certain conditions are satisfied while certain others are not. For a situation depicting the existence of such a set of conditions, one needs to know the action which is usually followed in the system under consideration.

Examples of *actions* are:

- Recruit the applicant.
- Admit the student.
- Place order.
- Go to Decision Table 2.

Cross marks (X) are always used for *action entries*. They are placed one in each column. A cross mark placed in the ij^{th} cell of the action entries compartment indicates that the ith action is usually taken for the set of conditions depicted in the jth column of the condition entries compartment.

A condition-action combination defines a *decision rule*. The columns spanning the decision entries and the action entries compartments are the various decision rules. Usually the decision entries compartment is partitioned to create a small compartment for decision rules. Further, the decision rules are numbered.

4.2.1 An Example of Library Requisition

The Head of the Department (HOD) recommends books to be bought by the Library. If funds are available, then the books are bought. In case funds don't permit, a textbook is kept waitlisted for purchase on a priority basis during the next year, whereas the Library returns the requisitions for all other books to the Head of the Department. A familiar logic chart representation of this situation is given in Fig. 4.4. A Structured English representation of the same problem is given in Fig. 4.5. And, a decision table representation of the same case is given in Fig. 4.6.

Note that for this case there are two conditions:

1. Is it a Textbook?
2. Are funds available?

One writes down these conditions in the Conditions compartment of the Decision Table.

Three possible actions for this case are the following:

1. Buy the book.
2. Waitlist for the next year.
3. Return the recommendation to the Head of the Department.

One also writes down the actions in the Action compartment of the Decision Table.

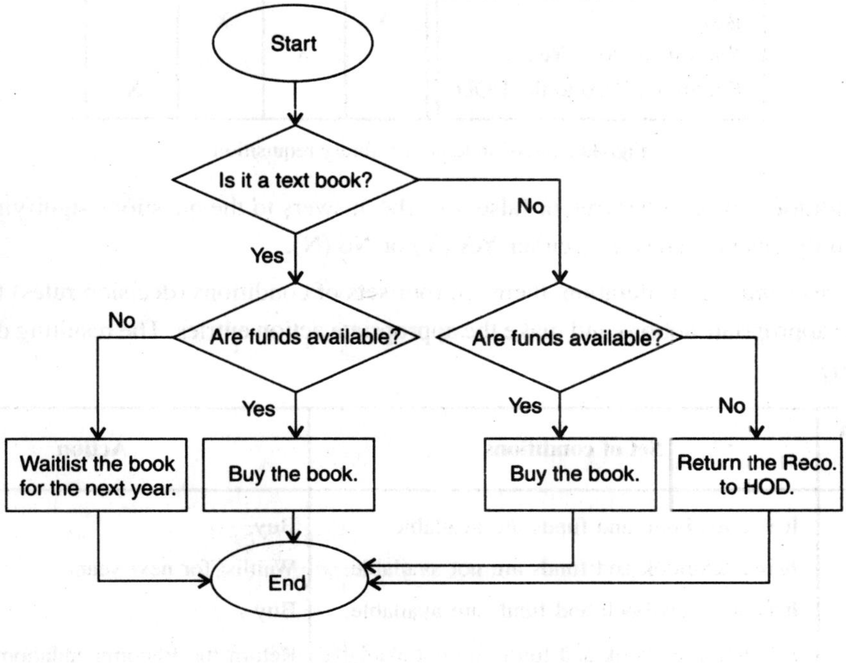

Fig. 4.4. A logic chart representation

```
If the book is a textbook
    then if funds are available
        then buy the book
        else waitlist the book for the next year
      endif
    else if funds are available
        then buy the book
        else return the recommendation to the HOD
      endif
endif
```

Fig. 4.5. A structured English representation

Conditions	Decision rules			
	1	2	3	4
Textbook?	Y	Y	N	N
Funds Available?	Y	N	Y	N
Actions				
Buy	X		X	
Waitlist for Next Year.		X		
Return the Reco to the HOD.				X

Fig. 4.6. Decision table for library requisition

The condition can be either true or false, *i.e.,* the answers to the questions signifying the conditions can take only binary values, *i.e.,* either Yes (Y) or No (N).

For the case under consideration, there are four sets of conditions (decision rules) for which we have to find the appropriate actions and make the appropriate action entries. The resulting decision rules are the following:

Decision rule	Set of conditions	Action
1.	It is a textbook and funds are available.	Buy.
2.	It is a textbook and funds are not available.	Waitlist for next year.
3.	It is not a textbook and funds are available.	Buy.
4.	It is not a textbook and funds are not available.	Return the Recommendation to HOD.

4.2.2 Exhaustive Generation of Decision Rules

Sometimes it may be a very tedious job having to exhaustibly generate all sets of conditions. In general, if there are c conditions, then the number of decision rules is 2^c. In the Library requisition case, the number of conditions $c = 2$. Thus the number of decision rules $= 2^2 = 4$.

We can generate these decision rules exhaustively if we follow the following scheme:

1. Determine the total number of decision rules $= 2^c$.
2. For the first condition, write Y, 2^{c-1} number of times and follow it by writing N, 2^{c-1} number of times.
3. For the second condition, write Y, 2^{c-2} number of times, follow it up by writing N, 2^{c-2} number of times, and alternate like this, till all the decision rules are covered.
4. Continue to alternate Y's and N's till one reaches the last condition where Y and N alternate after occurring only once.

4.2.3 Removing Redundancies

Often the number of decision rules, therefore the size of a decision table, can be reduced by identifying redundancies and removing them. For example, if we consider the conditions for decision rules 1 and 3, we notice that as long as funds are available the book will be bought whether or not it is a textbook. So we can merge these two rules into one. The resulting decision rule is given in Fig. 4.7. Note that we have placed a dash (—) for the first condition and for decision rules 1 and 3. That is, the action is Buy the Book as long as funds are available, no matter whether the requisition is for a textbook or not.

Conditions	Decision rules		
	1 and 3	2	3
Textbook?	—	Y	N
Funds Available?	Y	N	Y
Actions			
Buy	X		
Waitlist for Next Year.		X	
Return the Reco to the HOD.			X

Fig. 4.7. Decision table for library requisition

To identify redundancies and merge the decision rules, the following steps are followed:

1. Consider two decision rules that have the same action.
2. If they differ in their condition entries in only one row, then one of the them can be treated as redundant.
3. These decision rules can be merged into one, by placing a dash (—) in the place of the corresponding condition entry.

4.2.4 Identifying Misspecifications

A decision table helps in highlighting ambiguities, if any. It also indicates absence of specific actions if no such action is indicated for a particular case. *More than one cross mark for a decision rule* clearly indicates an ambiguity. Presence of more than one cross mark indicates more than one action for a set of conditions. In such a case either the organization does not follow any strict action plan or it has left the action plan to the subjective evaluation by its employees so that two different action plans are contemplated at different times or by different persons. All these situations suggest bad or no management. Such a situation warrants management attention and the ambiguity needs to be resolved.

No cross mark for a decision rule, on the other hand, indicates either that proper investigation has not been carried out or that such a case had not arisen in the past, and the organization had not contemplated any action plan for that case. Such a case also needs to be brought to the attention of management so that it decides on an action for the existence of such a set of conditions.

The two misspecifications of a decision table are shown in Fig. 4.8.

C_1	Y	Y	N	N
C_2	Y	N	Y	N
A_1	X			
A_2		X		
A_3	X		X	

Action missing (rule N, N)
Ambiguity (rule Y, Y)

Fig. 4.8. Misspecifications in decision tables

4.2.5 Decision Table Hierarchy

When the number of conditions (c) is large, the number of decision rules (2^c) becomes very large. For example, if c equals 3, the number of decision rules is 8; when c equals 4, it is 16; and so on. In such situations, it is better to construct more than one decision table — a main table and one or more branch tables. Here, going to a branch table becomes an action in the main table. We give an example.

An Example of Giving Discounts on Sale of Products

A company has two divisions in one location — one producing refrigerators and the other air conditioners. The company has a policy of giving discounts to wholesalers. If the total order quantity for refrigerators exceeds 10 and the delivery time wanted exceeds 2 weeks, then the company gives a 20 percent discount on all units. But the order quantity remaining same, if the delivery time is equal to or less than 2 weeks, it gives a 10 percent discount. If the order quantity does not exceed 10, then no discount is offered. In case of air conditioners, the company gives a discount of 10% on all units if the order quantity exceeds 5 and delivery time exceeds 4 weeks. Order quantity remaining same, if the delivery time is less than 4 weeks, the company gives a 5% discount. No discount is given in the remaining cases.

If we construct one decision table, then we have four conditions:

1. Product is refrigerator and order quantity > 10.
2. Product is refrigerator and delivery time > 2 weeks.
3. Product is air conditioner and order quantity > 5.
4. Product is refrigerator and order delivery time > 4 weeks.

The number of decision rules to be considered is $2^4 = 16$. We may, instead, decide to have three decision tables as shown in Fig. 4.9. Note that the third column in each branch table has actually merged a redundant decision rule (containing the entry N).

A decision table has merits over a logic chart and the Structured English representation, because a decision table can check if all the decision rules are specified in a systematic manner while the other two techniques do not automatically check this.

Condition	Decision rules	
Product is refrigerator?	Y	N
Go to refrigerator table.	X	
Go to air conditioner table.		X

Conditions	Decision rules		
Order quality > 10?	Y	Y	N
Delivery time > 2 weeks?	Y	N	–
Give 20% discount.	X		
Give 10% discount.		X	
Do not give a discount.			X

Conditions	Decision rules		
Order quality > 5?	Y	Y	N
Delivery time > 4 weeks?	Y	N	–
Give 10% discount.	X		
Give 5% discount.		X	
Do not give a discount.			X

Fig. 4.9. A decision table branching out to other decision tables

4.2.6 Decision Table vis-a-vis Logic Chart

An Example of Student Admission

Consider a flow chart (Fig. 4.10) that shows the rules relevant to admission of students into a course. In this flow chart, it is unclear as to what will happen if a student fails in either of the subjects but secures more than 80% total marks. Further, the flow chart has a redundancy—testing one condition: whether physics mark is greater than 90, twice. Further, checking if we have considered all sets of conditions is quite difficult.

A decision table forces the analyst to input actions for all possible decision rules, thus leaving no room for doubt. We leave this as an exercise for the reader.

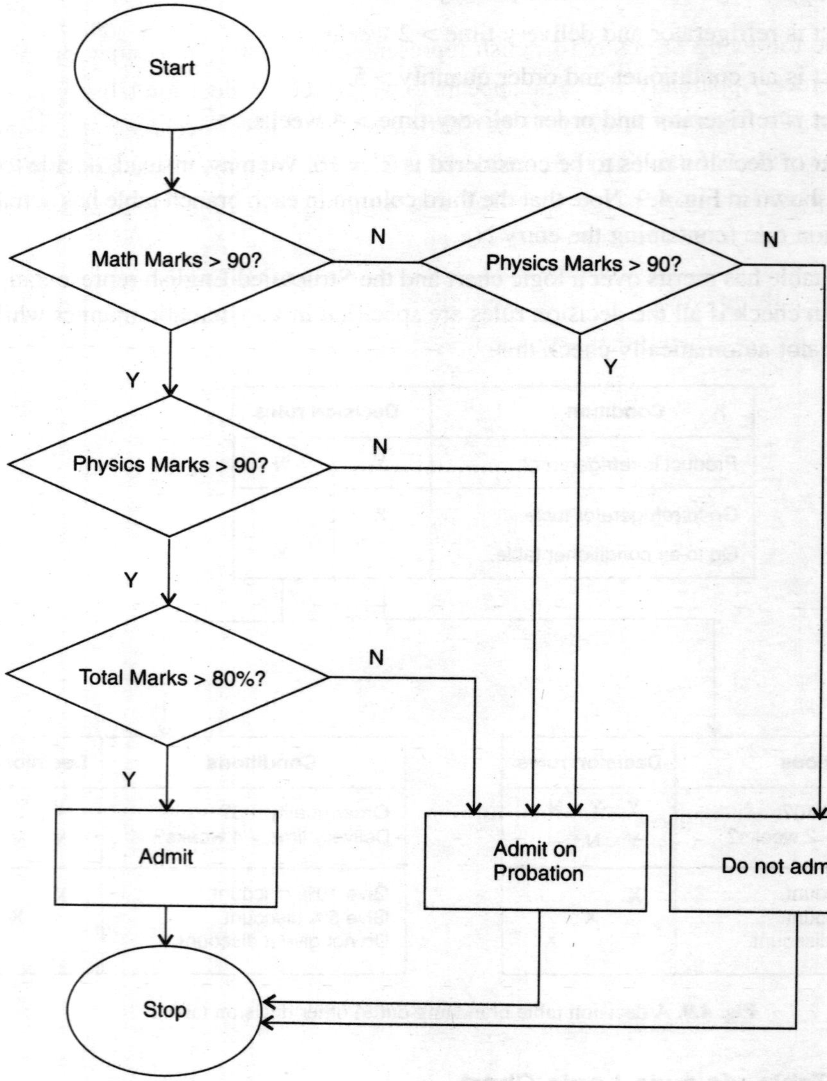

Fig. 4.10. Flow chart for admission procedure

4.2.7 Decision Table vis-a-vis Structured English Representation of Decision Situation

Structured English is a means of presenting a case with the help of natural English which is arranged using the basic structured programming constructs of Sequence, Selection, and Iteration. In the following example, we show the use of Structured English in documenting a decision situation and compare it with its decision-table representation.

A Case of Order Supply

Consider the following Structured English representation of a decision situation (Fig. 4.11) of supplying against order. Apparently, the logic appears to be in order. A decision table representation of this situation (Fig. 4.12), however, brings to light a deficiency. Action for decision rules 5 and 6 appear to be illogical because even if the item is nonstandard it is available in the stock. So the logical action should be Supply from Inventory rather than Buy and Supply. This illogical situation could not be identified clearly in a Structured English representation.

```
If the order is for a standard item
        then if the item is in inventory
                then supply the item from inventory
                else place production order
            endif
        else if the item can be purchased from a subcontractor
                then place purchase order
                else refuse order
            endif
endif
```

Fig. 4.11. Structured English representation of order supply

Conditions	Decision rules							
	1	2	3	4	5	6	7	8
Order for a standard item?	Y	Y	Y	Y	N	N	N	N
Item in stock?	Y	Y	N	N	Y	Y	N	N
Item available with a subcontractor?	Y	N	Y	N	Y	N	Y	N
Supply from inventory.	X	X						
Make and supply.			X	X				
Buy and supply.					X		X	
Refuse.						X		X

Fig. 4.12. Decision table for order supply

Structured English often uses a large number of words and clumsy notations because the analyst has the freedom to use them as (s) he pleases. If these clumsy words and notations are thrown away and the text reflects a precise and complete analysis, then it is said to be written in *Tight English.*

4.3 DECISION TREES

Decision trees provide a very useful way of showing combinations of conditions and resulting action for each such combination. A decision tree starts from a root node, with braches showing conditions. We show in Fig. 4.13 a decision tree for the Textbook problem that was taken up earlier.

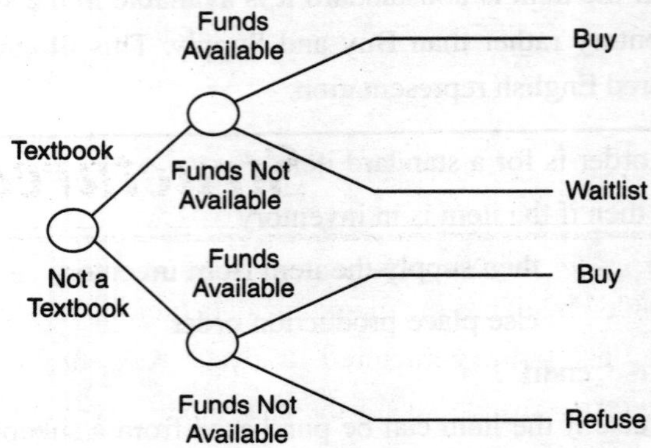

Fig. 4.13. Decision tree

Gane and Sarson (1979) give the following when-to-use guidelines for Decision Trees, Decision Tables, Structured English, and Tight English:

- Decision Trees are best used for logic verification or moderately complex decisions which result in up to 10–15 actions. It is also useful for presenting the logic of a decision table to users.
- Decision Tables are best used for problems involving complex combinations up to 5–6 conditions. They can handle any number of actions; large number of combinations of conditions can make them unwieldy.
- Structured English is best used wherever the problem involves combining sequences of actions in the decisions or loops.
- Tight English is best suited for presenting moderately complex logic once the analyst is sure that no ambiguities can arise.

In this chapter, we have discussed various traditionally used tools for documenting gathered information during the requirement gathering sub-phase. They are quite useful. However, alone, they cannot effectively depict the complexities of real-life information-processing needs. In the next chapter, we shall discuss evolution of data flow diagrams that led to a structured way of analyzing requirements of real systems.

REFERENCE

Gane, C. and T. Sarson (1979), Structured Systems Analysis: Tools and Techniques, Prentice-Hall, Inc., Englewood Cliffs, NJ.

5 Structured Analysis

Requirements analysis aided by data flow diagrams, data dictionaries, and structured English is often called *structured analysis*. The term, 'Structured Analysis' was introduced by DeMarco (1978) following the popularity of the term 'structured' in the structured programming approach to writing computer codes. The use of the structured analysis tools results in a disciplined approach to analyzing the present system and in knowing the user requirements.

5.1 DATA FLOW DIAGRAMS (DFD)

A way to understand how an information system operates in a real system is by understanding how data flow and get transformed and stored. Following notations similar to the ones given by Martin and Estrin (1967) for representing programs in the form of program graphs and taking ideas from Ross and Shooman (1977) who described a very general graphical approach to systems analysis which comprehended data flow as one of its aspects, DeMarco (1978) proposed data flow diagramming, a graphical technique, to facilitate that understanding. Yourdon and Constantine (1979) used similar notations while using the data flow approach to structured design of programs. Gane and Sarson (1979) recognized the data flow diagram at the logical level as the key to understand the system of any complexity and refined the notations to make it an extremely useful tool of system analysis.

A data flow diagram uses four symbols (Fig. 5.1), one each for data flow, process (or data transform), data store, and external entity (data originator or data receiver).

A *data flow* is either an input to or an output of a process. The input data flow may be in the form of a document, a record, a control signal transmitted by a transducer, a packet of information transmitted on a network link, a voluminous data file retrieved from secondary storage, or even a series of numbers keyed by a human operator. The output data flow may be a signal that actuates a light-emitting diode or a 200-page report. The arrowhead of the symbol indicates the direction of flow of the data. A data flow may occur from outside the bounds of the system under consideration and may go out of the bounds of the system.

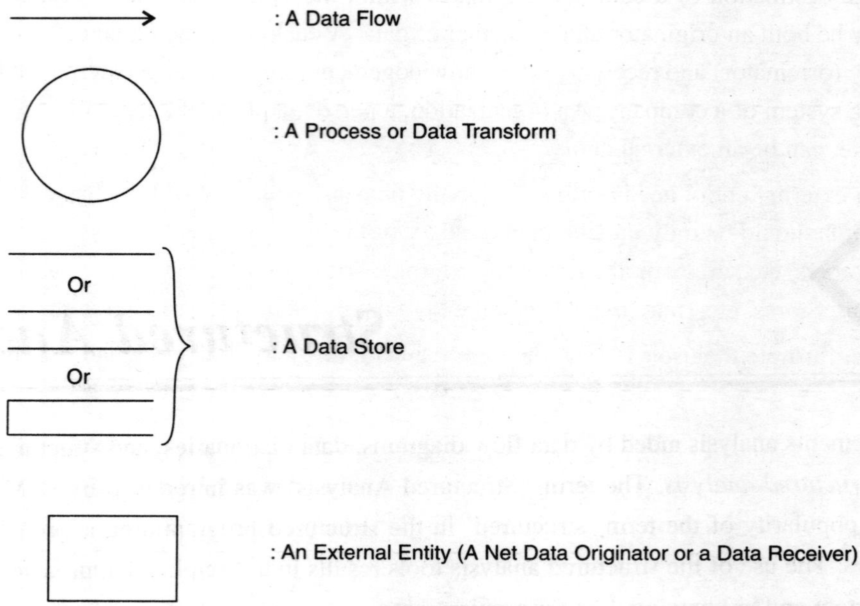

Fig. 5.1. The four symbols used in data flow diagrams

A *data transform* (or a *process*) receives data as input and transforms it to produce output data. However, it may not always involve a physical transformation; it may involve, instead, a filtration or distribution of data. For example, the Purchase Department of a company, upon scrutinizing a purchase registration raised by a Department, returns the incomplete requisition back to the Department. As another example, the Head of a Department sends the list of students to his office for storing it in a file. The transformation process may involve arithmetic, logical, or other operations involving complex numerical algorithm, or even a rule-inference approach of an expert system. A process may bring in the following simple changes to the input data flows:

1. It can only add certain information. For example, it adds an annotation to an invoice.
2. It can bring in a change in the data form. For example, it computes total.
3. It can change the status. For example, it indicates approval of purchase requisition, changing the status of purchase requisition to approved purchase requisition.
4. It can reorganize the data. For example, it can arrange the transactions in a sorted manner.

The operations in a process can be carried out with the help of hardware, software, or even by human elements. The processes reside within the bounds of the system under consideration.

A *data store* represents a repository of data that is stored for use as input to one or more processes. It can be a computer database or a manually operated file.

An *external entity* lies outside the boundary of the system under consideration. It may be the origin of certain data that flows into the system boundary thus providing an input to the system, or it may be the destination of a data that originates within the system boundary. Frequently, an external entity may be both an originator and a receiver of data. A customer placing an order for a product with a company (originator) and receiving an acknowledgement (receiver) is an external entity for the Order Processing system of a company. An organization, a person, a piece of hardware, a computer program, and the like, can be an external entity.

An external entity need not be outside the physical boundary of the physical system of the organization; it should be only outside the boundary of the system under consideration. Thus while vendors, customers, etc., are natural choices for external entities for the organization as a whole, Marketing Department, Stores, etc., may be considered external entities for the Production Department.

We illustrate the use of these four symbols with the help of a very small example.

Example 1

Customer places order with the sales department of a company. A clerk verifies the order, stores the order in a customer order file, and sends an acknowledgement to the customer.

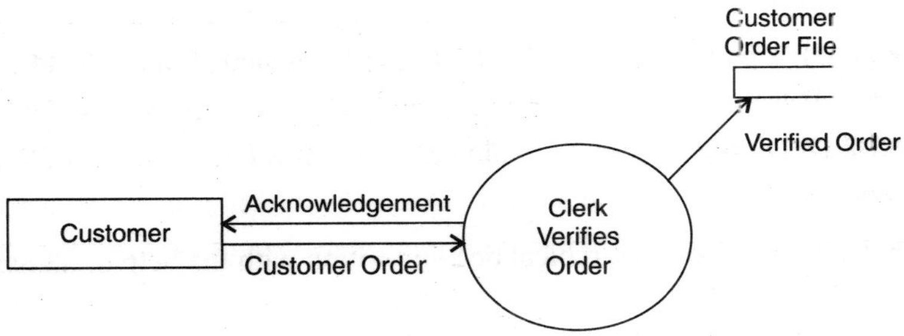

Fig. 5.2. DFD for customer order receipt

Figure 5.2 is the data flow diagram (DFD) of the situation described in the example. This example has only one external entity (Customer), one process (Clerk Verifies Order), one data store (Customer Order File), and three data flows (Customer Order, Acknowledgement, and Verified Order). Note that Customer Order is the input data flow into the process and Acknowledgement and Verified Order are the data flows out of the process. A Verified Order is stored in the data store Customer Order File.

5.1.1 Hierarchical Organization of Data Flow Diagrams

Any real-life situation with even moderate complexity will have a large number of processes, data flows, and data stores. It is not desirable to show all of them in one data flow diagram. Instead, for better comprehension, we normally organize them in more than one data flow diagram and arrange them in a hierarchical fashion:

Context Diagram

Overview Diagram

Exploded Bottom-Level Diagrams

A *Context Diagram* identifies the external entities and the major data flows across the boundary separating the system from the external entities, and thus defines the context in which the system operates. A context diagram normally has only one process bearing the name of the task done by the system.

An *Overview Diagram* is an explosion of the task in the Context Diagram. It gives an overview of the major functions that the system carries out. The diagram shows the external entities, major data flows across the system boundary, and a number of aggregate processes that together define the process shown in the Context Diagram. These processes are numbered consecutively as 1, 2, 3, ..., and so on. The Overview Diagram is also called the Level-Zero (or Zero-Level) Diagram. A Level-Zero Diagram may also show the major data stores used in the system.

Depending on the need, any process in an overview diagram can now be exploded into a lower level diagram (Level-1 Diagram). Suppose, for example, process 2 is exploded into a level-1 data flow diagram, then the processes in this diagram are numbered 2.1, 2.2, ..., and so on, and the diagram is called a *Level-1 Data Flow Diagram for Process 2*. Similarly, level-1 data flow diagrams can be created for processes 1, 3, and so on.

Whenever required, a process of a level-1 DFD can be exploded into a level-2 DFD. A *level-2 DFD for process 2.4* will have processes numbered as 2.4.1, 2.4.2, and so on. In a similar fashion, process 2.4.2, a level-2 DFD process, can be exploded into a *Level-3 Data Flow Diagram* with processes bearing numbers 2.4.2.1, 2.4.2.2, and so on.

We illustrate the principle of hierarchical decomposition with the help of an example.

Example 2

When a student takes admission in an academic programme of an Institute, he (she) has to undergo a process of academic registration. Each student pays semester registration fee at the cash counter by filling in a pay-in slip and paying the required amount. On production of the Cash Receipt, a clerk of the Academic Section gives him/her two copies of Registration Card and a copy of Curricula Registration Record. The student meets the Faculty Advisor and, with his/her advice, fills in the Registration Cards and the Curricula Registration Record with names of the subjects along with other details that he/she will take as credit subjects during the semester. The Faculty Advisor signs the Registration Card and the Curricula Registration Record and collects one copy of the Registration Cards. Later, he deposits all the Registration Cards of all the students at the Department Office. The Office Clerk sends all the Registration Cards together with a Forwarding Note signed by the Faculty Advisor to the Academic Section. When the student attends the classes, he (she) gets the signatures of the subject teachers on his (her) copy of the Registration Card and on the Curricula Registration Record. When signatures of all the teachers are collected, the student submits the Registration Card to the Department Office for its record.

Figure 5.3 is a context diagram for the above-described situation. Here, Student is considered to be the external entity. The details of the registration process are not shown here. Registration Process is depicted only as one process of the system. The data flowing between the Student and the Registration

Process are: (*i*) the Pay-in Slip—a data flow from the Student to the Registration Process, (*ii*) the Cash Receipt, (*iii*) the Registration Card, and (*iv*) the Curricula Registration Record—a data flow from the Registration Process to the Student. Both the Cash Receipt and the Registration Card are the data flows from the Student to the Registration Process and from the Student to the Registration Process.

Note here that the student pays a semester registration fee. The fee is an amount and not a piece of data. Therefore the fee is not shown as a flow of data. The Pay-in Slip that is used to deposit the amount is considered as a data flow, instead.

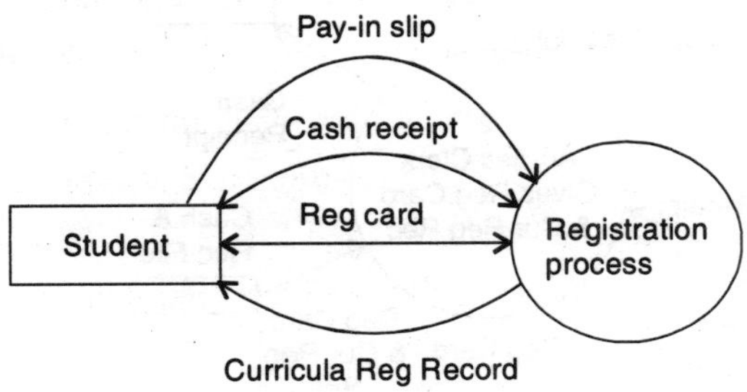

Fig. 5.3. Context diagram for the academic registration

Figure 5.4 shows the overview diagram for the academic registration of the students. There are six processes and four data stores involved in the registration process. The six main processes of this system are the following:

1. Cash Counter gives Cash Receipt.
2. Academic Section Clerk gives Registration Card and Curricula Registration Record.
3. Faculty Advisor approves the subjects.
4. Teacher admits Students in the Class.
5. Department Office sends Cards to Accounts Section and Stores a Copy.
6. Accounts Section stores the Registration Card.

Note that the single process in the context diagram has been expanded into six processes in the level-zero diagram. Also note that the data flows from and to the Student in the overview diagram are the same as those in the context diagram.

Suppose it is required to depict the detailed activities done at the Academic Section (shown in Process 2 in Fig. 5.4). Then process 2 has to be exploded further. Figure 5.5*a* shows how the process 2 has to be exploded. However it is not a data flow diagram. Figure 5.5*b* is the level-1 data flow diagram for process 2. Note the process numbers 2.1 and 2.2 in Fig. 5.5*a* and Fig. 5.5*b*.

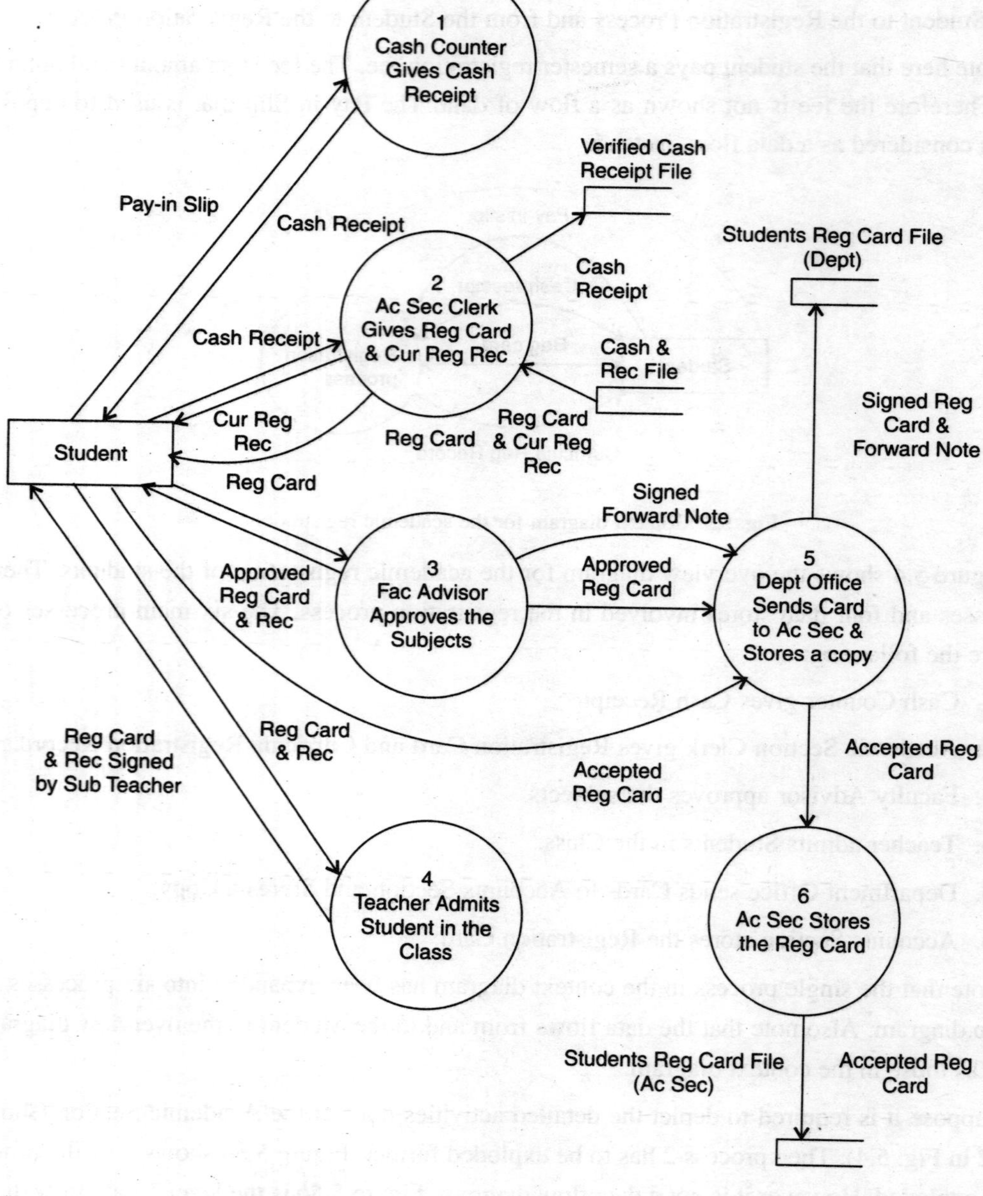

Fig. 5.4. Overview diagram (Level-Zero DFD) for academic registration

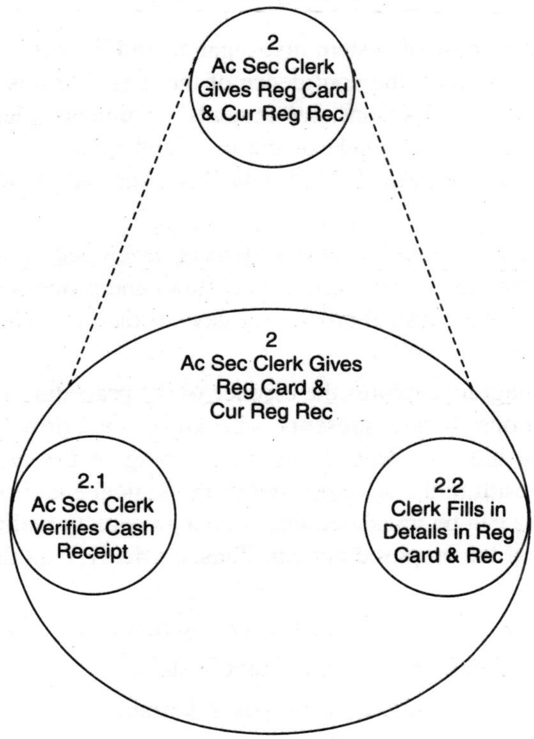

Fig. 5.5*a*. Explosion of process 2

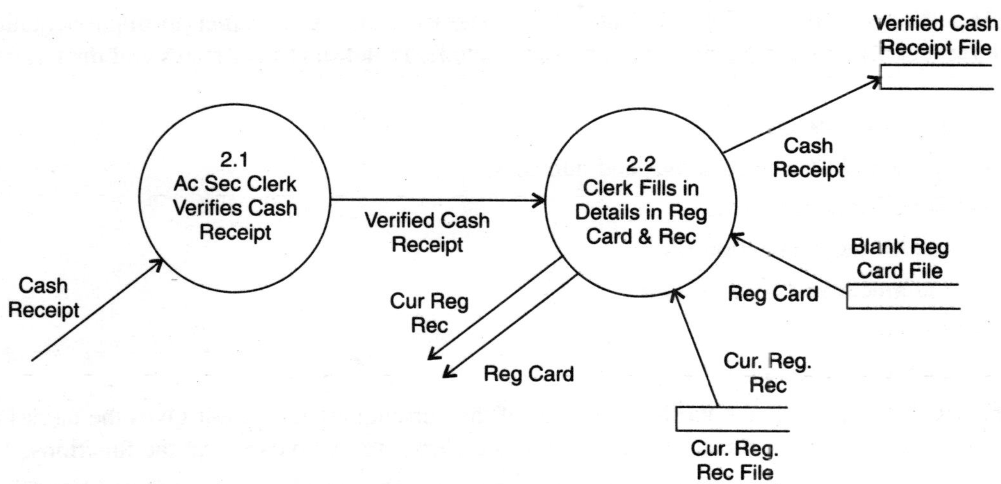

Fig. 5.5*b*. Level-1 DFD for process 2

5.1.2 Physical and Logical Data Flow Diagrams

It is essential, for the purpose of system investigation and improvement, that the system analyst fully understands the system and gets the confidence of the user. For this purpose, he/she has to first develop the DFD using the names of persons, departments, documents, files, locations, procedures and hardware so that he/she speaks the language of the user, and the user is convinced that the system analyst has fully understood the system. Such a data flow diagram is called a *Physical Data Flow Diagram.*

Once a physical data flow diagram of a system is developed, a simplified logical data flow diagram is derived to represent the logic of various data flows and processes. This diagram is devoid of names of persons, sections, or the physical processing devices that may have been used in the physical data flow diagram.

A logical data flow diagram captures the essence of the procedure and the logic of information flow and decisions and actions. It thus presents a backdrop for critical assessment of the current system and for carrying out improvements in the functioning of the system. Improvements in the logic of system operations result in the development of the logical data flow diagram of the proposed system. These improvements can be translated later into a physically realizable system, resulting in a physical data flow diagram of the proposed system. Thus, normally, data flow diagrams are developed in four stages:

1. Physical Data Flow Diagrams of the Current System.
2. Logical Data Flow Diagrams of the Current System.
3. Logical Data Flow Diagrams of the Proposed System.
4. Physical Data Flow Diagrams of the Proposed System.

The first two diagrams are meant for analysis of the current system while the next two diagrams are meant for the improvement and design of the new, proposed system.

As indicated above, a Physical Data Flow Diagram is meant to depict an implementation-dependent view of the system. Such a diagram may include, in defining data flows and data stores, the following:

— names of persons
— forms and document names and numbers
— names of departments
— master and transaction files
— equipment and devices used
— locations
— names of procedures

Figure 5.4 is a physical data flow diagram of the current system since it gives the names of the subjects (such as the faculty, the academic section, the clerk, etc.) who carry out the functions.

A *Logical Data Flow Diagram* abstracts the logical tasks out of a Physical Data Flow Diagram. Thus it is an implementation-independent view of a system, without regard to the specific devices, locations, or persons in the system. Further, many unnecessary processes are removed. Such unnecessary processes to be removed are routing, copying, storing, or even device-dependent data preparation activity.

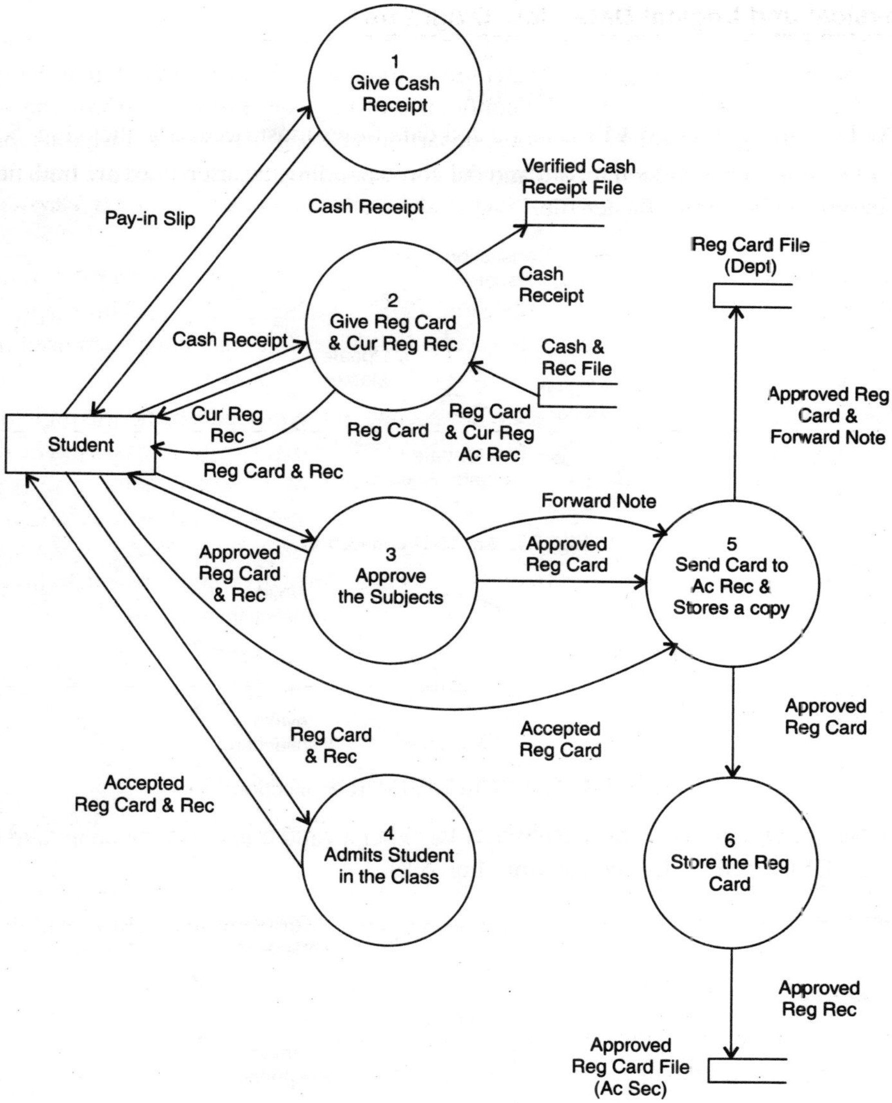

Fig. 5.6. Overview diagram (Zero-Level DFD) for academic registration — the logical DFD for the current system

Figure 5.6 is a logical data flow diagram of the current system for Fig. 5.4 — the physical data flow diagram for the academic registration of the students.

5.1.3 Logical Associations Among Data Flows

In general, a process may receive and produce multiple data flows. The multiple data inflows, as also the multiple data outflows, may have some logical operational associations among them. In the bottom-level data flow diagrams we sometimes show these associations with the help of additional symbols. The symbols used are:

* AND connection

⊕ EXCLUSIVE-OR connection

○ INCLUSIVE-OR connection

An AND connection implies that the related data flows must occur together (Fig. 5.7).

In this example, a transaction record and the corresponding master record are both necessary (an AND connection) to update the master file.

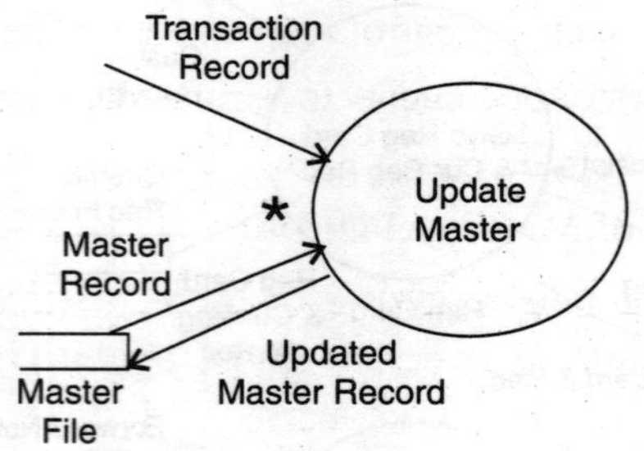

Fig. 5.7. An AND connection

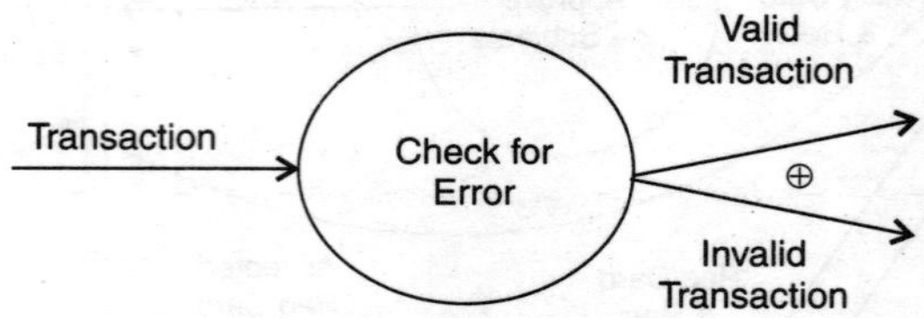

Fig. 5.8. An EXCLUSIVE-OR connection

When checked for errors, a transaction may be either a valid transaction or an invalid transaction, but not both (an EXCLUSIVE-OR connection, Fig. 5.8).

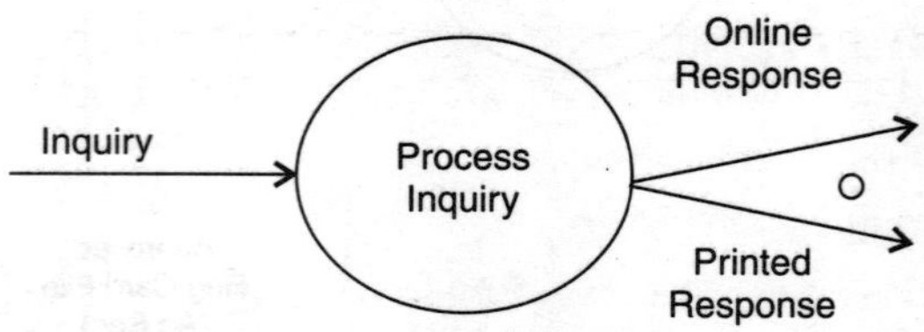

Fig. 5.9. An INCLUSIVE-OR connection

An inquiry can be processed to produce either an online response or a printed response or both (an INCLUSIVE-OR connection, Fig. 5.9).

5.1.4 Guidelines for Drawing Data Flow Diagrams

Senn (1985) has offered the following guidelines for drawing data flow diagrams:

A. General Guidelines

1. Identify all inputs and outputs.
2. Work your way from inputs to outputs, outputs to inputs, or from the middle out to the physical input and output origins.

3. Label all data flows carefully and descriptively.
4. Label all transforms by means of a specific transitive verb of non-plural object.
5. Classify the association of data streams to a transform in detailed DFDs by clearly indicating the appropriate logical AND and OR connections.
6. Ignore initialization and termination.
7. Omit the details of error paths in generalized levels of DFD.
8. Don't show control logic such as control loop and associated decision making.
9. Don't show flow of copies of documents to various departments for information.
10. Use levels of DFDs, if required.

B. Guidelines in the Creation of Multilevel DFDs

1. Number each process within the overview DFD.
2. Identify any process within the overview DFD (Parent Diagram) that requires a more detailed breakdown of function.
3. Draw a level-2 DFD (Child Diagram); number it.
4. Make sure inputs and outputs are matched between parent and associated child diagrams, except for error paths that may be present in the child but absent in the parent diagram.
5. Repeat the procedure for every process in the DFD.

C. Guidelines for Deriving Logical DFD from Physical DFD

1. Show actual data in a process, not the documents that contain them.
2. Remove routing information, *i.e.*, show the flow between procedures, not between people, offices, or locations.
3. Remove tools and devices (for example, file cabinets or folders, etc.).
4. Consolidate redundant data stores.
5. Remove unnecessary processes (for example, routing, storing, or copying) that do not change the data or data flows or are device-dependent data preparation or data entry activities, or duplicate other processes.

D. Guidelines for Drawing Logical DFDs

1. Only data needed to perform a process should be an input to the process.
2. Any data leaving a process must be based on data inputted to the process.

E. Guidelines for Explosions

1. Explode a process for more detail. The process of explosion may proceed to an extent that ensures that a process in the lowest level DFD has only one outflow.
2. Maintain consistency between processes. New inputs or outputs that were not identified in a higher level may be introduced in a lower level.
3. Data stores and data flows that are relevant only to the inside of a process are concealed until that process is exploded into greater detail.
4. Add control on lower-level diagrams only.
   - Handling errors and exceptions should be done in lower level diagrams only.
   - Avoid document copy description (such as: copy 1, copy 2, etc.).

– Avoid time description of logic or control description (such as: Do on Monday).

– Avoid procedure control descriptions. (such as: Find, review, and annotate the record).

5. Assign meaningful labels

   – Dataflow naming

   - Name should reflect the data, not the document. Online processing has only data.
   - Data flowing into a process should undergo a change; so outbound data flow is named differently from the inbound one.

   – Process naming

   - Names should contain transitive verbs and non-plural objects.
   - Name should fully describe the process. Thus if a process both edits and validates invoice data, it should not be labeled as EDIT INVOICE.
   - Names should explain linkage between inflows and outflows.
   - Avoid vague names, such as PROCESS, REVIEW, ASSEMBLE, HANDLE, or ORGANIZE.
   - Lower-level processes should be much more specific and descriptive than the higher-level ones.
   - Names must be unique to the activity they describe.

F. Evaluate DFD for Correctness

Data Flow Diagrams should be free from errors, omissions, and inconsistencies. The following checklist can be used to evaluate a DFD for correctness:

1. Unnamed components?
2. Any processes that do not receive input?
3. Any processes that do not produce output?
4. Any processes that serve multiple purposes? If so, explode them into multiple processes.
5. Is the inflow of data adequate to perform the process and give the output data flows?
6. Is the inflow of data into a process too much for the output that is produced?
7. Any data stores that are never referenced?
8. Is there storage of excessive data in a data store (more than the necessary details)?
9. Are aliases introduced in the system description?
10. Is each process independent of other processes and dependent only on data it receives as input?

5.1.5 Common Mistakes in Drawing Data Flow Diagrams

Hawryszkeiwycz (1989) gives the following additional guidelines:

1. A DFD should not include flowchart structures.
2. A process in a DFD should conserve data.
3. The DFD must follow good naming conventions.

Exclusion of Flowchart Structures

A DFD should have no

1. data flows that split up into a number of other data flows (Fig. 5.10).
2. data flows depicting logic (Fig. 5.11).
3. loops of control elements (Fig. 5.12).
4. data flows that act as signals to activate processes (Fig. 5.13). Thus showing day-of-week triggers, such as Process Transactions on Last Working Day of the Month or Reinstall the Attendance Software on Monday, are not permitted.

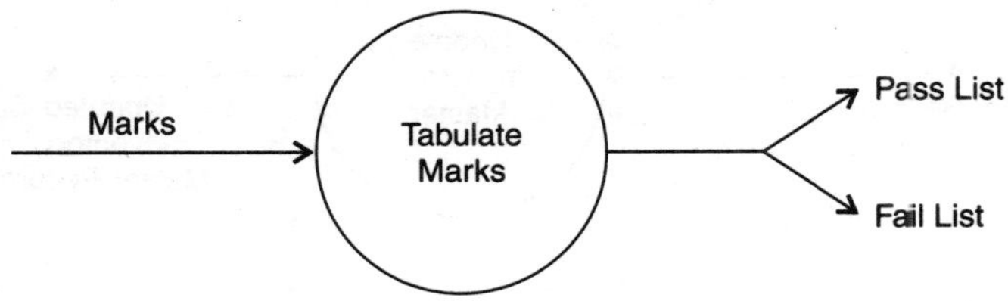

Fig. 5.10. Splitting of data flows

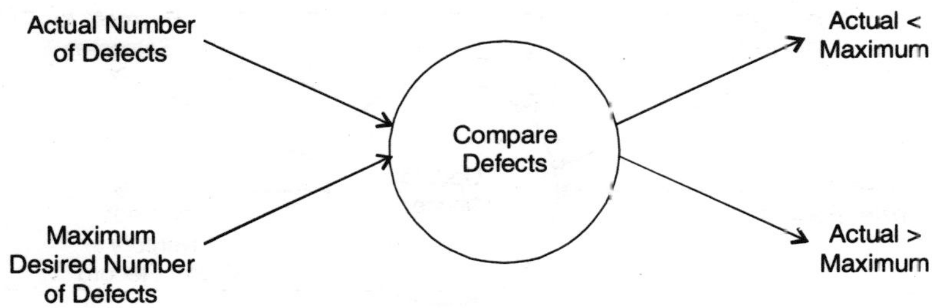

Fig. 5.11. Control signals from a process

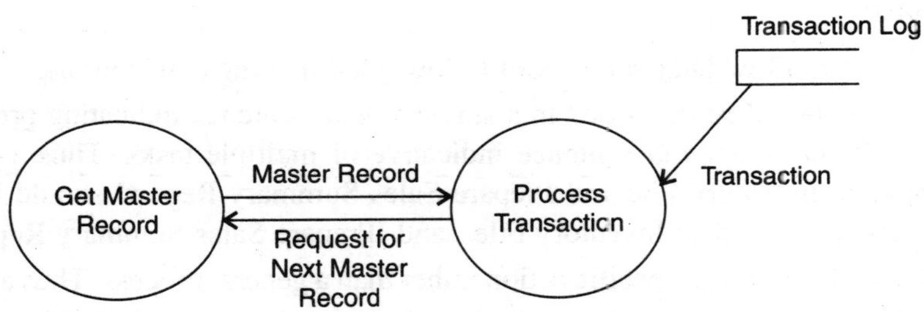

Fig. 5.12. Loop

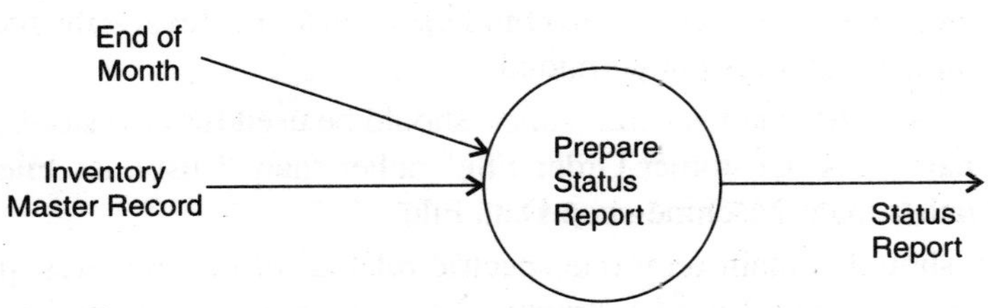

Fig. 5.13. Input signal to activate a process

Conservation of Data

A process should conserve data. That is, the input data flows of a process should be both necessary and sufficient to produce the output data flows. Thus, the following two situations are illegal:

1. Information inputted is not used in the process (Fig. 5.14).
2. The process creates information that cannot be justified by the data inflows (Fig. 5.15).

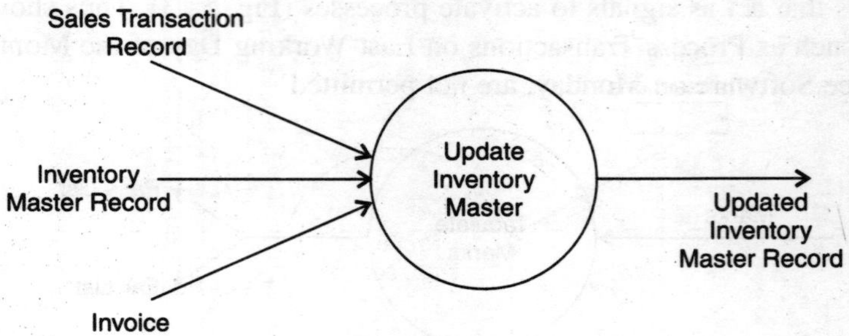

Fig. 5.14. Data input not used in a process

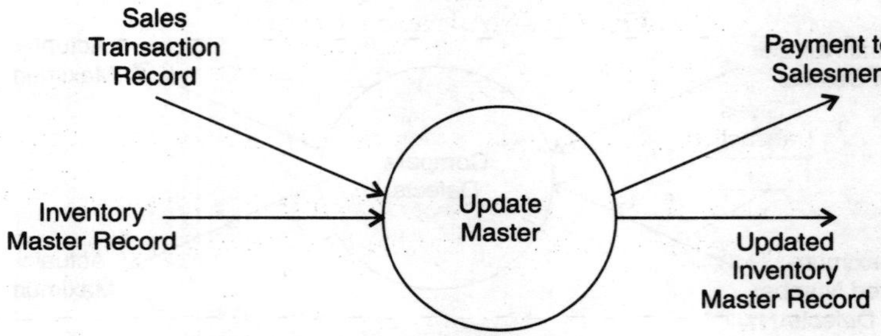

Fig. 5.15. Data output not justified by the input

Naming Conventions

A bottom-level Data Flow Diagram should follow good naming conventions:

(*a*) Each process should be described in a single *simple* sentence indicating processing of one task, rather than *compound* sentence indicative of multiple tasks. Thus a process with a name 'Update Inventory File and Prepare Sales Summary Report' should be divided into two processes — 'Update Inventory File', and 'Prepare Sales Summary Report'.

(*b*) A process should define a specific action rather than a general process. Thus a process should be named as 'Prepare Sales Summary Report' and not 'Prepare Report', or as 'Edit Sales Transactions' and not 'Edit Transactions'.

(*c*) Showing procedural steps, such as: (*a*) Find the record, (*b*) Review the record, and (*c*) Write comments on the record, is not permitted.

(*d*) Specific names, rather than general names, should be used for data stores. Thus, a data store should be named as 'Customer-Order File' rather than 'Customer File', or as 'Machine Schedule' rather than 'Machine-shop Data File'.

(*e*) Data stores should contain only one specific related set of structures, not unrelated ones. Thus, a data store should not be structured as 'Customer and Supplier File'; instead they should be divided into two different data stores — 'Customer File' and 'Supplier File'.

(*f*) Data flows that carry the whole data store record between a process and a data store may not be labelled (Fig. 5.16).

(*g*) However, if a process uses only part of a data store record, the data store must be labelled to indicate only the referenced part. In this case the data flow is labelled by the names in capitals of the accessed data store items (Fig. 5.17).

(*h*) Data flows may be bi-directional (Fig. 5.17).

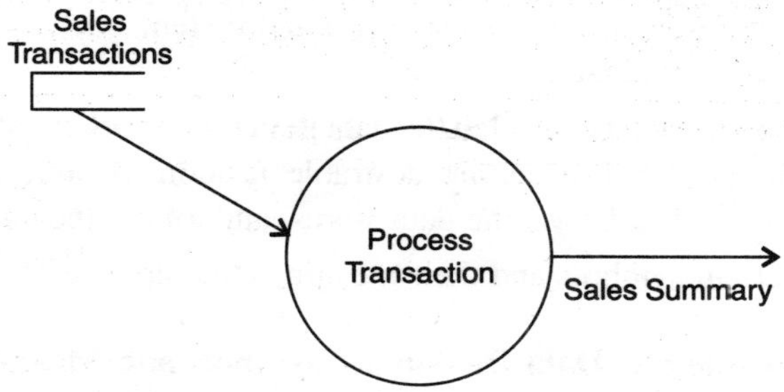

Fig. 5.16. Non-labelled data flow

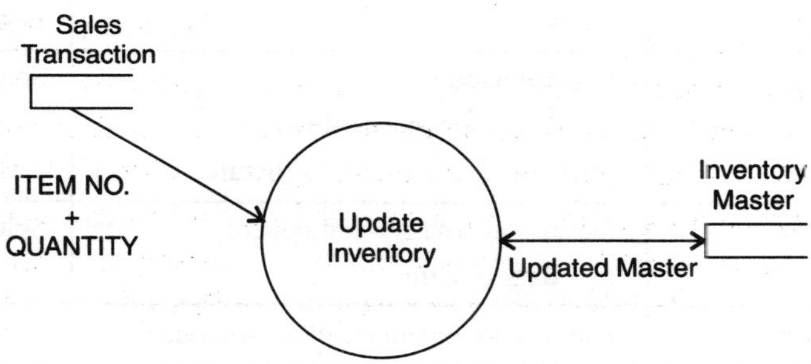

Fig. 5.17. Specific fields used in a process and bi-directional data flows

5.1.6 Weaknesses of Data Flow Diagrams

There are many weaknesses of data flow diagrams (Ghezzi, *et al.* 1994):

1. They lack precise meaning. Whereas their syntax, *i.e.*, the way of composing the processes, arrows, and boxes, is sometimes defined precisely, their semantics is not. Thus, for example, a process, Handle Record, does not make much meaning. Although such poor semantic is a common flaw in this diagram, there is no full-proof method of ensuring that such a poor diagram is not developed.
2. They do not define the control aspects. For example, if a particular process will be executed only upon satisfaction of a condition, it cannot be depicted on the diagram; it can however be specified in the data dictionary details of the process.
3. As a consequence of (1) and (2) above, one cannot test whether the specifications reflect a user's expectations (for example, by simulation). Thus a traditional data flow diagram is a semiformal notation.

5.2 DATA DICTIONARY

Data dictionary (DD) keeps details (data) about various components of a data flow diagram. It serves multiple purposes:

1. It documents the details about the system components—data flows, data stores, and processes.
2. It gives a common meaning to each system component.
3. It helps identifying errors and omissions in the system, such as those that were discussed in describing data flow diagrams.

The elementary form of a data is called the data item (or data element). Data flows and data stores consist of data elements structured in certain desirable fashion. Among other things data dictionary specifies the structures of the data flows, the data stores, and, often, the data elements.

Table 5.1 gives certain symbols and their meanings that are used to specify the data structures.

Table 5.1: Data Dictionary Symbols and Meanings

Symbols	Meaning	Explanation	Type of relationship
=	Is equivalent to	Alias	Equivalent relationship
+	And	Concatenation Defines components always included in a particular structure	Sequential relationship
[ ]	Either/or	Defines alternative component of a data structure	Selection relationship
{ }	Iterations of	Defines the repetition of a component	Iteration relationship
( )	Optional	Defines iteration that occurs only 0 or 1 time.	Optional relationship
* *	Comment	Enclose annotation	—
|	Separator	Separates alternatives	—

We present the use of these symbols in defining structural relationships among various components with the help of a few examples.

Name consists of the first name, the middle name, and the last name:

NAME = FIRST_NAME + MIDDLE_NAME + LAST_NAME

Name consists of the first name and the last name, but the middle name is not mandatory:

NAME = FIRST_NAME + (MIDDLE_NAME) + LAST_NAME

The first name is a string of up to 20 alphabetic characters:

FIRST_NAME = $\{\text{Alphabetic Characters}\}_1^{20}$

Another form is the following:

FIRST_NAME = 1 {Alphabetic Characters} 20

Payment can be either cash, cheque or draft (where postdated cheque is not allowed):

PAYMENT = [CASH | CHEQUE | DRAFT]* Postdated cheque is not permitted.*

Recording Data Description in Data Dictionaries

Certain standards are maintained while recording the description of various forms of data in data dictionaries. Table 5.2 and Table 5.3 respectively define the way data on data flows and data stores are recorded.

Table 5.2: Define Data Flows

Data flow name
Description
From process/data stores/ext. entity
From process/data store/ext. entity
To process/data stores/ext. entity
Data structure

Table 5.3: Defining Data Stores

Data Store name
Description
Inbound data flows
Outbound data flows
Data structure
Volume
Access

The symbols introduced earlier in defining the structural relationship among data are used while defining the data structures of both data flows and data stores. Often individual data items are described in some detail giving the range of values for the same, typical values expected, and even list of specific values.

Table 5.4 gives the way the process details are recorded in data dictionaries.

Table 5.4: Defining Processes

Process
Description
Input
Output
Logic Summary

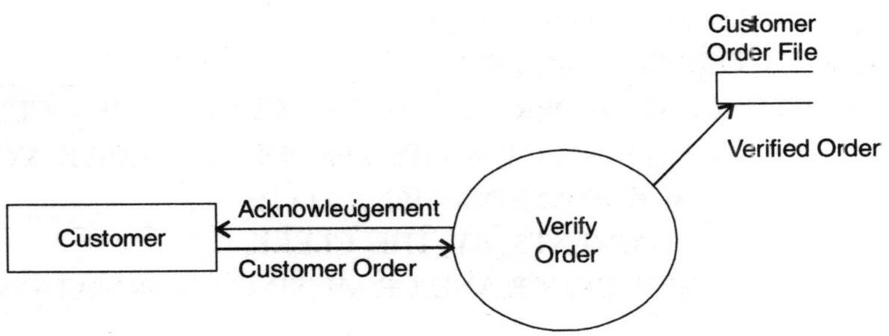

Fig. 5.18. DFD for customer order receipt

We now present data dictionary details of the example given in Fig. 5.2 (which is reproduced here in Fig. 5.18).

Customer Order

Name:	Customer Order
Description:	It is a form that gives various details about the customer, and the products he wants, and their specifications.
From:	The external entity, Customer.
To:	Process 1
Data Structure:	CUSTOMER_ORDER = CUST_ORDER_NO + DATE + CUST_NAME + CUST_ADDRESS + 1 {PRODUCT_NAME + PRODUCT_SPECIFICATION} n + (Delivery Conditions)

Acknowledgement

Name:	Acknowledgement
Description:	It is an acknowledgement of the receipt of the purchase order sent by the customer.
From:	Process 1.
To:	The external entity, Customer
Data Structure:	ACKNOWLEDGEMENT = CUST_ORDER_NO + DATE + CUST_NAME + CUST_ADDRESS + ACK_DATE + 1 {PRODUCT_NAME + PRODUCT_SPECIFICATION _ PRICE} n

Verified Order

Name:	Verified Order
Description:	The purchase order received from the customer along with all its original contents plus comments from the clerk as to whether there is any missing information. Also the verified order contains the date on which the order is received.
From:	Process 1
To:	The external entity, Customer
Data Structure:	VERIFIED ORDER = CUST_ORDER_NO + DATE + CUST_NAME + CUST_ADDRESS + 1 {PRODUCT_NAME + PRODUCT_SPECIFICATION + PRICE} n + ACKNOWLEDGEMENT_DATE + COMMENTS_BY_THE_CLERK * NEW ORDER AND/OR MISSING INFORMATION*

Verify Order

Name:	Verify Order
Description:	The customer order is verified for its completeness and the date of its receipt is written on the top of the order. Furthermore, an acknowledgement is sent to the customer.

Input: Customer Order
Output: Acknowledgement and Verified Order
Logic Summary: Check the contents of the 'Customer Order'
Write the DATE OF RECEIPT of the order on the order itself.
If some information is missing or incomplete
Then prepare a list of missing information
Send 'acknowledgement' asking for these missing information.
Else send 'acknowledgement' thanking the customer order.
Endif.

Customer Order File

Data Store: Customer Order File
Description: It stores details about the Customer Order
Inbound data flows: Verified Order
Outbound data flows: None
Data Structure: CUSTOMER ORDER FILE
= 1{CUST_ORDER_NO + DATE + CUST_NAME + CUST_ADDRESS
+ 1 {PRODUCT_NAME + PRODUCT_SPECIFICATION _ PRICE} n
+ ACKNOWLEDGEMENT_DATE
+ COMMENTS_BY_THE_CLERK
* NEW ORDER AND/OR MISSING INFORMATION*} m
Volume: Nearly 100 customer orders are received daily and growing 10% annually.
Access: As and when required for processing.

5.3 STRUCTURED ENGLISH

In the previous chapter we had used structured English representation of the logic of decision rules. We discuss here the basic features of structured English in detail. Basically, structured English is natural English written in a structured programming fashion. It is well known that structured programming requires and makes it possible to write programs using three basic constructs: (1) Sequence, (2) Selection, and (3) Repetition. Structured English uses these constructs for specifying the logic of a process in data flow diagrams. The logic summary of the Verify Order Process for the data flow diagram given in Fig. 5.18, as written in its data dictionary details in the previous section, is written in Structured English.

Guidelines for writing the process logic in structured English are the following:

(*a*) Since the logic of a process consists of various executable instructions, the structured English sentences mostly take the form of imperative statements. An imperative sentence usually consists of an imperative verb followed by the contents of one or more data stores on which the verb operates.

(*b*) Unclear verbs, such as 'process', 'handle', or 'operate' should not be used.

(*c*) Adjectives having no precise meaning, such as 'some', or 'few' should not be used.

(*d*) Data flow names are written in lower case letter within quotes.

(*e*) Data store names are written in capital letters.

(*f*) Specific data items in either data flows or data stores are in capital letters.

(*g*) Arithmetic and Boolean symbols may be used to indicate arithmetic and logical operations:

Boolean	
and	
or	
not	
greater than	(>)
less than	(<)
less than or equal to	(≤)
greater than or equal to	(≥)
equals	=
not equal to	(≠)

(*h*) Certain keywords are used in structured English that allow program-like representation of process logic. They are:

BEGIN	REPEAT	IF
END	UNTIL	THEN
CASE	WHILE	ELSE
OF	DO	FOR

(*i*) The keywords BEGIN and END are used to group a *sequence* of imperative statements. Figure 5.19 is a data flow diagram for updating a master file when a sale takes place. The structured English representation for the logic of the updaing process is as under:

```
BEGIN
        Receive 'sales transaction record'.
        Get ITEM NUMBER in the 'sales transaction record'.
        Read SALES in the 'sales transaction record'.
        Get 'inventory master record' from INVENTORY MASTER.
        QUANTITY_ON_HAND = QUANTITY_ON_HAND – SALES
        Write 'inventory master record'.
END
```

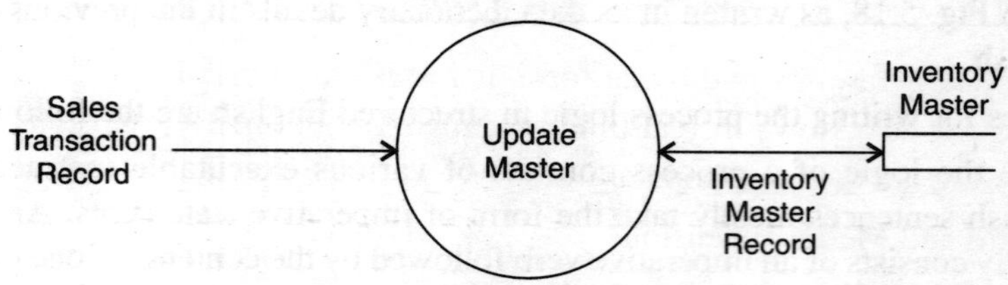

Fig. 5.19. Updating inventory master

(*j*) The keywords IF, THEN, and ELSE are used to denote *decisions*.

(*k*) The keywords FOR, WHILE ... DO, and REPEAT ... UNTIL are used to denote *repetitions*.

Features of Structured English

- Structured English is a subset of natural English with limited vocabulary and limited format for expression.
- It is easily understandable by managers and thus is often used to denote procedures and decision situations in problem domains.

In software engineering, structured English is used to write the logic of a process in data flow diagram — a requirement analysis tool.

5.4 DATA FLOW DIAGRAMS FOR REAL-TIME SYSTEMS

Real-time systems are software systems that produce responses to stimuli within acceptable time durations. They are characterized by the following:

1. Data are gathered or produced on a continuous-time basis.
2. Real-time systems respond to events that represent some aspect of system controls that are exercised on the satisfaction of predefined conditions. An event, thus, is data in Boolean from — on or off, true or false, yes or no.
3. In fact, many real-time systems process as much or even more control-oriented information than data.
4. Multiple instances of the same transformation occur in multitasking situations.
5. As time progresses, a system occupies various states with transitions triggered by satisfaction of predefined conditions.

Real-time software for temperature control, for example, carries out three operations:

1. It measures temperature continuously.
2. It actuates the heating system when temperature goes beyond the set temperature limits.
3. It switches on the heating system when temperature goes below the lower temperature limit (T_L) and switches off the system when the temperature goes above the higher temperature limit (T_H), and allows the physical system to occupy three states: (*i*) Temperature > T_H, (*ii*) Temperature < T_L, and (*iii*) $T_L \leq$ Temperature $\leq T_H$.

5.4.1 Extensions of DFD Symbols to Handle Real-Time Systems

A data flow diagram, in its traditional form, is forbidden to handle control-oriented data and is inadequate to represent data flows in real-time systems. Among many extensions of the basic DFD notations, the following are the most popular ones:

1. The Ward and Mellor Extension
2. The Hatley and Pirbhai Extension

The Ward and Mellor Extension

Ward and Mellor propose the following additional symbols to handle control-oriented information (Table 5.5):

Table 5.5: Ward and Mellor Extension of DFD Notations

Symbol	Name	Description
	Quasi-Continuous Data Flow:	A data object that is input to or output from a process on a 'continuous' basis.
	Control Process:	A transformer of control or 'events' that accepts control as input and produces control as output.
	Control Item:	A control item or event that takes on a Boolean or discrete value.
	Control Stores:	A repository of control items that are to be stored for use by one or more processes.
	Process:	Multiple equivalent instances of the same processes; used when multiple processes are created in multitasking system.

Ward and Mellor recommended one consolidated data flow diagram that contains both data and control-oriented information. Thus, for example, the temperature control process can be depicted as in Fig. 5.20. In this figure, the measured temperature can take continuous values, the flag is a control item that can take three values: –1 if measured temperature is less than T_L, +1 if it is more than T_H, and 0 if it is neither. Actuating the heating system on the basis of the flag value is a control process.

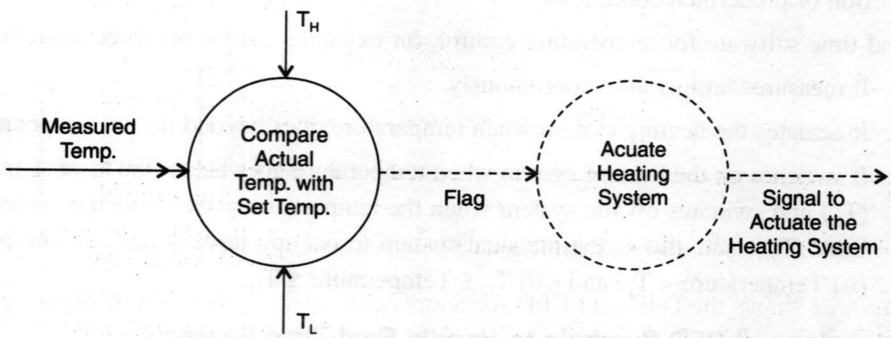

Fig. 5.20. Data flow diagram for temperature control

The Hatley and Pirbhai Extension

Hatley and Pirbhai instead proposed the following symbols to handle control-oriented information (Table 5.6):

Table 5.6: Hatley and Pirbhai Extension of DFD Notations

Symbol	Meaning
	A control item or event that takes on a Boolean or discrete value
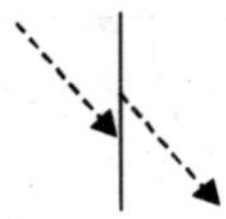	The vertical bar is a reference to a control specification (CSPEC) that defines how a process is activated as a consequence of events.

Hatley and Pirbhai recommended that in addition to drawing a DFD that shows the flow of data, one should draw a Control Flow Diagram (CFD) that shows the flow of control. The process in the CFD is the same as the one in the DFD. A vertical bar gives a reference to the control specification that indicates how the process is activated based on the event passed on to it.

The DFD and CFD mutually feed each other. The process specification (PSPEC) in the DFD gives the logic of the process and shows the data condition it generates, whereas the control specification (CSPEC) gives the process activate on the basis of this data condition. This process activate is the input to the process in the CFD (Fig. 5.21).

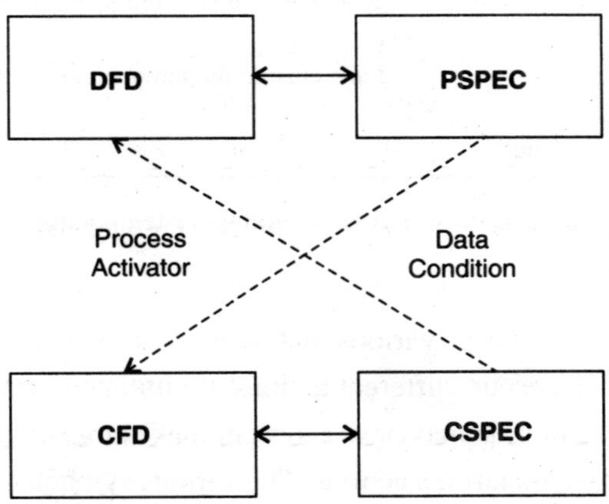

Fig. 5.21. DFD and CFD and their relationship

Figure 5.22 shows the DFD and CFD for temperature control. The specification of the process defined in the DFD is also given in Fig. 5.22. The specification of the control depicted in the CFD is however not shown in Fig. 5.22. Control specifications are usually given in *state transition diagrams* and/or *process activation tables.*

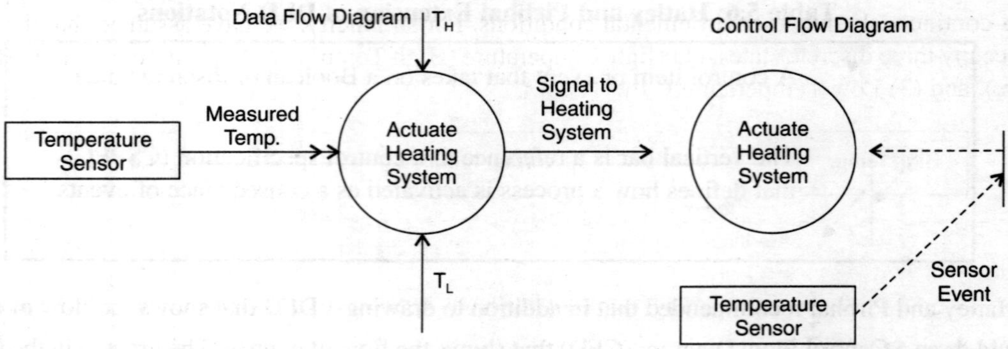

PROCESS SPECIFICATION

```
PSPEC
  if Measured Temp. < T_L
    then
      increase the temperature setting
    else
      if Measured Temp. > T_H
        then
          reduce the temperature setting
        else
          don't change the temperature setting
      endif
  endif
```

Fig. 5.22. Data and control flow diagrams for temperature control

State Transition Diagram

A system can be thought to be in various states, each signifying a specific mode of system behaviour. As different conditions occur, different actions are initiated bringing in changes in the system states. A state transition diagram depicts how a system makes transition from one state to another responding to different events and predefined actions. The various symbols and their meanings in a state transition diagram are given in Table 5.7. In Table 5.7, X is an event that indicates that the system must move from the present state to another state and Y is the action, consequent to the occurrence of the event, which initiates the transition.

Table 5.7: Symbols in a State Transition Diagram

Symbol		Meaning
[...] (box)	⇨	A system state
$\xrightarrow[Y]{X}$	⇨	A transition from one state to another

Figure 5.23 shows the state transition diagram for the temperature control system. Temperature varies continuously due to environmental conditions. For simplicity, we have assumed that the system can occupy three discrete states: (1) High Temperature (High Temp.), (2) Normal Temperature (Normal Temp.), and (3) Low Temperature (Low Temp.).

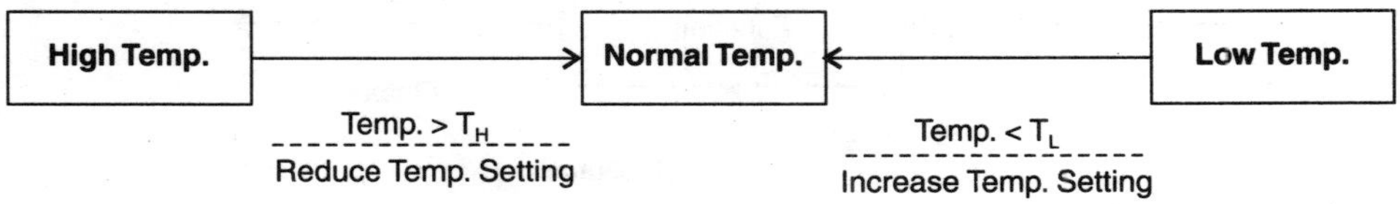

Fig. 5.23. State transition diagram for temperature control

Process Activation Table

The process activation table is another way to specify system behaviour. Instead of defining the transition taking place from one state to another, it defines the conditions that excite a process in a control flow diagram. The temperature control is very simple, so in its process activation table (Table 5.8), we have only one process that gets activated (1) when the sensor event is on (1) and the output of the process, change in the temperature setting, is also on (1). In all other cases the entries in the process activation table are zero.

Table 5.8: Process Activation Table for Temperature Control

Input Event Sensor Event	0 1
Output Change in Temp. Setting	0 1
Process Activation Actuate Heating System	0 1

5.5 OTHER STRUCTURED ANALYSIS APPROACHES

Any discussion on structured analysis is incomplete without a mention of the structured analysis and design technique (SADT) developed by Ross and Shooman (1977) and the structured systems analysis and design method (SSADM) developed in 1981 in UK (Ashworth, 1988). As the names indicate, the two techniques are useful in both the analysis and the design phase. Both have a number of automatic tools to support their use.

SADT adds control flow (required in the design step) to the data flow (required in the analysis phase). Figure 5.24 shows the basic atomic structure of the technique. Using this atomic structure, it constructs *actigram* (for activities) and *datagram* (for data) separately. Like DFD, leveling of an SADT diagrams can be drawn in more than one level, with the context diagram that can be exploded into low-level diagrams. For details, see Marca and McGowan (1988).

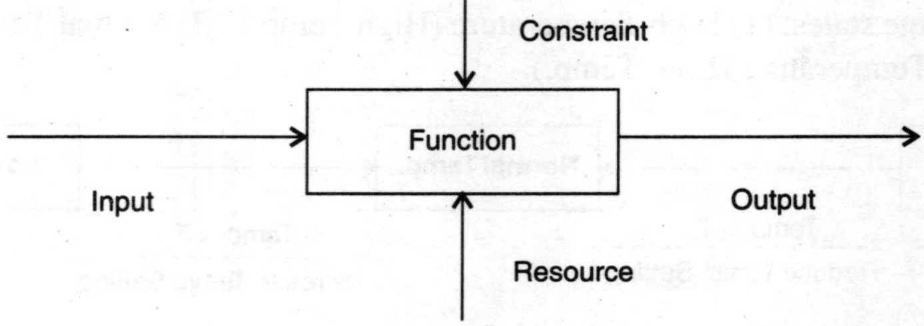

Fig. 5.24. Basic notation in SADT diagram

The method SSADM integrates various structured techniques for analysis and design. For example, it uses DFD for process analysis, entity-relationship approach for data modeling, entity life history technique, and top-down approach for analysis and design. For details, see Longworth and Nichols (1987).

REFERENCES

Ashworth, C. M. (1988), Structured Systems Analysis and Design Method (SSADM), Information and Software Technology, Vol. 30, No. 3, pp. 153–163.

DeMarco, T. (1978), Structured Analysis and System Specification, Yourdon, New York.

Gane, C. and T. Sarson (1979), Structured Systems Analysis: Tools and Techniques, Prentice-Hall, Inc., Englewood Cliffs, NJ.

Ghezzi, C., M. Jazayeri, and D. Mandrioli (1994), Fundamentals of Software Engineering, Prentice-Hall of India Private Limited, New Delhi.

Hawryszkeiwycz, I. T. (1989), Introduction to System Analysis and Design, Prentice-Hall of India, New Delhi.

Longworth, G. and D. Nichols (1987), The SSADM Manual, National Computer Centre, Manchester, UK.

Marca and D. A. and C. L. McGowan (1988), SADT–Structured Analysis and Design Technique, McGraw-Hill, New York.

Martin, D. and G. Estrin (1967), Models of Computations and Systems – Evaluations of Vertex Probabilities in Graph Models of Computations, J. of ACM, Vol. 14, No. 2, April, pp. 181–199.

Ross, D. and K. Shooman (1977), Structured Analysis for Requirements Definition, IEEE Trans. on Software Engineering, Vol. SE-3, No. 1, pp. 6–65.

Senn, J.A. (1985), Analysis and Design of Information Systems, McGraw-Hill, Singapore.

Yourdon, E. and L. Constantine (1979), Structured Design, Englewood Cliffs, NJ: Prentice Hall, Inc.

6 Other Requirements Analysis Tools

So far we have discussed various popular tools that are used in the requirements analysis phase. In this chapter, we are going to briefly discuss three advanced requirements analysis tools. These tools have the ability to model both concurrent and asynchronous information flows. Furthermore, these tools also pave the way for formalizing information requirements and for validating them in an objective way. The tools we are going to discuss here are the following:

1. Finite State Machines
2. Statecharts
3. Petri Nets

6.1 FINITE STATE MACHINES

Finite State Machines (FSM), introduced by Alan Turing in 1936 and used by McCulloch and Pitts (1943) to model neurological activities of the brain, are often used for specification of processes and controls and for modeling and analysis of system behaviour. An FSM is like a state-transition diagram (discussed in the previous chapter). It is basically a graph with nodes and arrows. *Nodes* define various states of a system, and *arrows* define the transitions from a given node (state) to the same or another node (state). Arrows are labeled to indicate the conditions or events (also called external inputs) under which transitions occur. Four symbols are mainly used here (Fig. 6.1).

We illustrate the use of finite state machines with the help of an example of a customer order placed with a company. The company scrutinizes the customer order for its validity (with respect to the customer details, item specifications, and item availability, etc.). If the customer order is not in order (*i.e.*, incomplete, erroneous, or invalid), it is returned to the customer. A valid customer order is processed for delivery. In case, stock of items demanded is adequate, the order is complied; otherwise the company initiates production order and delivers the items when items are produced in adequate quantity.

We are interested in depicting the states of the customer order and the state transitions. Figure 6.2 shows the finite state machine for the problem.

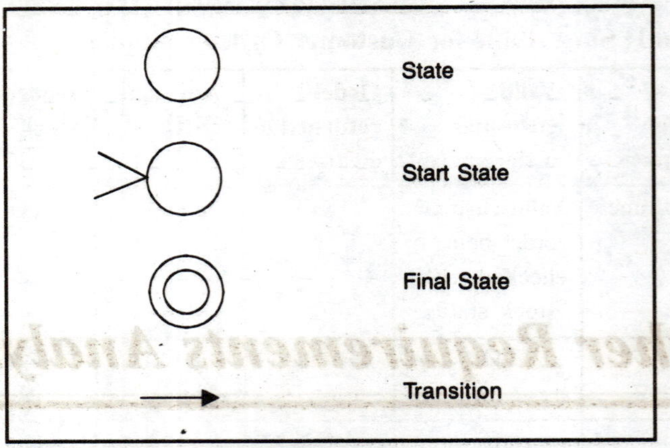

Fig. 6.1. Symbols used in FSM

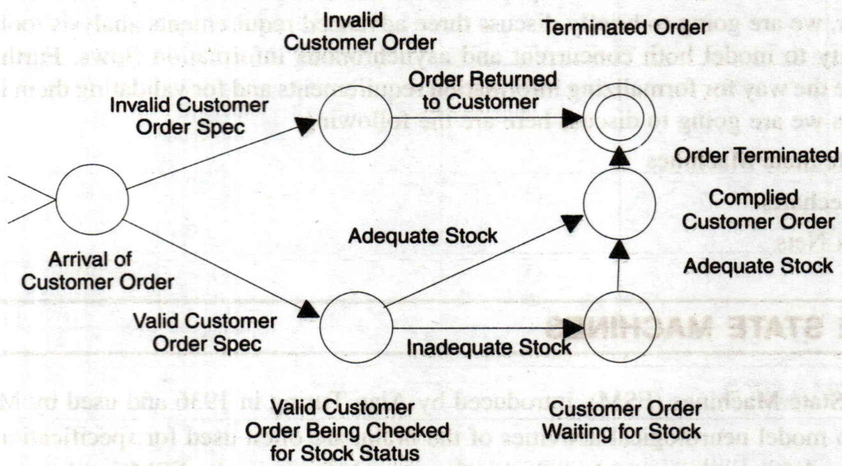

Fig. 6.2. Finite state machines for customer order

Often state transitions are defined in a state table. It shows various states in the first column and various conditions (considered inputs) in the first row. The ij^{th} entry in the state table indicates the node to which a transition will take place from the ith state if it gets the jth input. A *state table* is like the process activation table discussed earlier. The state table for the problem of customer order is shown in Table 6.1. Suppose the state *Valid Customer Order Being Checked with Stock Status* is occupied and the input is *Inadequate Stock*, then a transition will take place to *Customer Order Waiting for Stock*. The symbol Ø in the ij^{th} cell of the table indicates a non-accepting state of an FSM, *i.e.*, it indicates that the condition defined in the jth column is not applicable when the state is occupied.

Finite state machines have been a popular method of representing system states and transitions that result in response to environmental inputs. An underlying assumption in this method is that the system can reside in only one state at any point of time. This requirement does not allow the use of the method to represent real time systems that are characterized by simultaneous state occupancies and concurrent operations. Statecharts extend the FSM concepts to handle these additional requirements.

Table 6.1: State Table for Customer Order Compliance

Condition / State	Invalid customer order space	Valid customer order space	Order returned to customer	Adequate stock	Inadequate stock	Order terminated
Arrival of customer order (start state)	Invalid customer order	Valid customer order being checked with stock status	Ø	Ø	Ø	Ø
Invalid customer order	Ø	Ø	Terminated order	Ø	Ø	Ø
Valid customer order being checked for stock status	Ø	Ø	Ø	Complied customer order	Customer order waiting for stock	Ø
Customer order waiting for stock	Ø	Ø	Ø	Complied customer order	Ø	Ø
Complied customer order	Ø	Ø	Ø	Ø	Ø	Terminated order
Terminated order	Ø	Ø	Ø	Ø	Ø	Ø

6.2 STATECHARTS

The concepts of finite state machines have been extended by Harel (1987, 1988), Harel and, Naamad (1996), and Harel and Grey (1997) to develop statecharts. The extensions are basically twofold:

1. A transition is not only a function of an external stimulus but also of the truth of a particular *condition*.
2. States with common transitions can be aggregated to form a *superstate*. Such a superstate can be decomposed into subordinate states. Harel introduced *or* and *and* functions. If, when a superstate is occupied, only one of the subordinate functions is occupied, then it is a case of an *or* function. On the other hand, if, when a stimulus is received by the superstate, transitions are made to all its subordinate states simultaneously, it is a case of an *and* function. Further refinement of the subordinate states of superstate is possible with their defined transitions and stimulus conditions. Thus it is possible that a particular stimulus results in transitions in states within a subordinate state and not in the states of other subordinate states. This property of independence among the subordinate states is called *orthogonality* by Harel.

Table 6.2 gives the notations used for drawing the statecharts. Notice that we place two subordinate states, one above the other, to indicate an *or* function, whereas we partition a box by a dashed line to indicate an *and* function.

Table 6.2: Notations for Statechart

Notation	Meaning
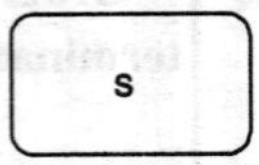	State
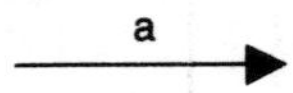	Transition taking place in the event of stimulus *a*.
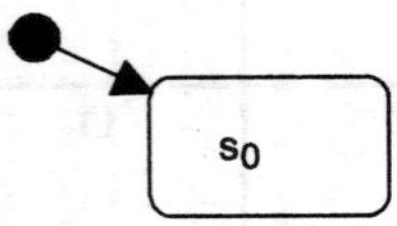	A start state s_0.
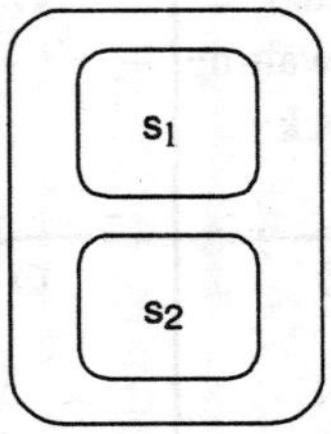	A superstate with two subordinate states s_1 and s_2 with no transition between them. We enter both states s_1 and s_2 whenever a transition takes place to superstate.
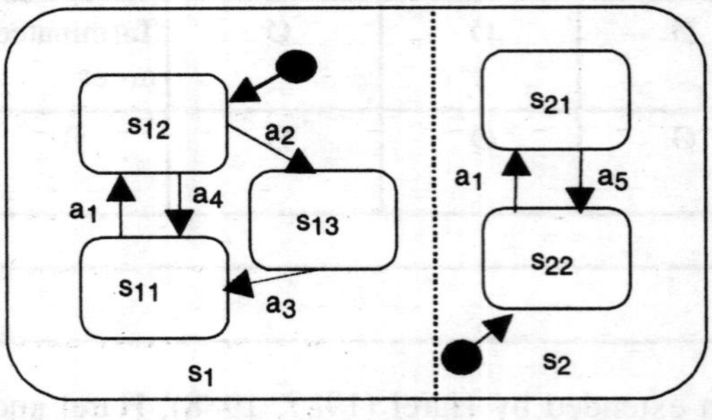	Concurrent statecharts that are refinements of states s_1 and s_2. On receipt of a stimulus, we enter states s_{12} and s_{22} (marked with the arrows). When a stimulus a_2 or a_4 occurs, transition takes place from state s_{12} to s_{13} or to s_{11} respectively. Stimulus a_1 or a_3 does not lead to any transition when the states s_{21} and s_{11} are occupied.

In Fig. 6.3, we show a context-level statechart of the process of dispatch of material via truck against receipt of customer order. Figure 6.4 and Fig. 6.5 show decompositions of the states in the context-level diagram into various subordinate states. Figure 6.4 shows a case of orthogonality where receipt of customer order leads simultaneously to preparation of dispatch order and invoice for the materials to be sent to the customer. In Fig. 6.5, the material dispatched state in the context-level statechart is decomposed into various substates.

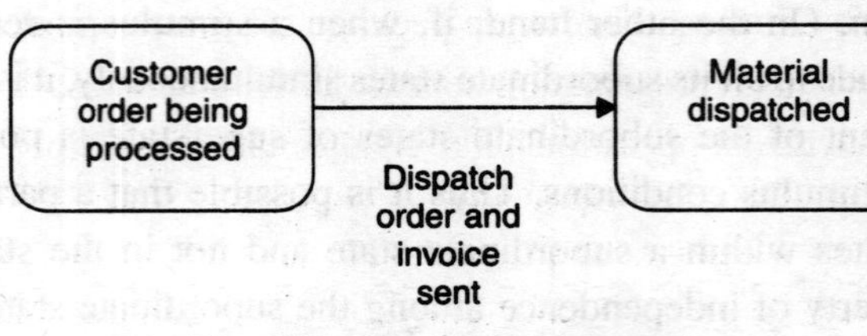

Fig. 6.3. Context-level statechart

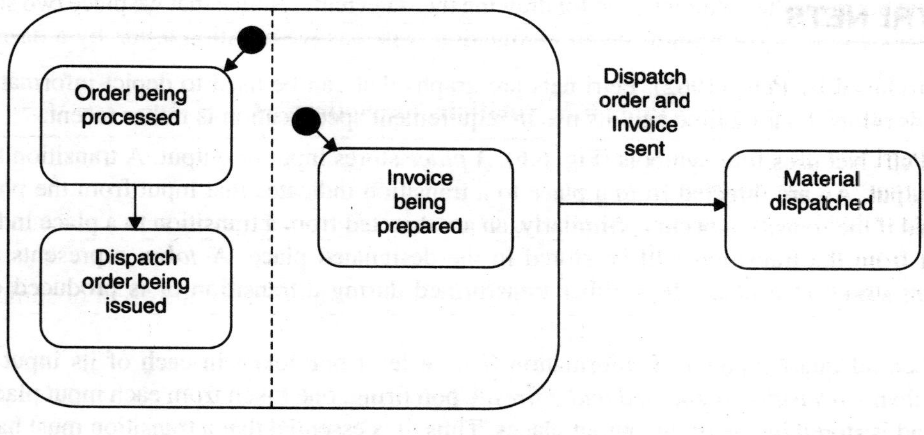

Fig. 6.4. Decomposition of a state with orthogonality

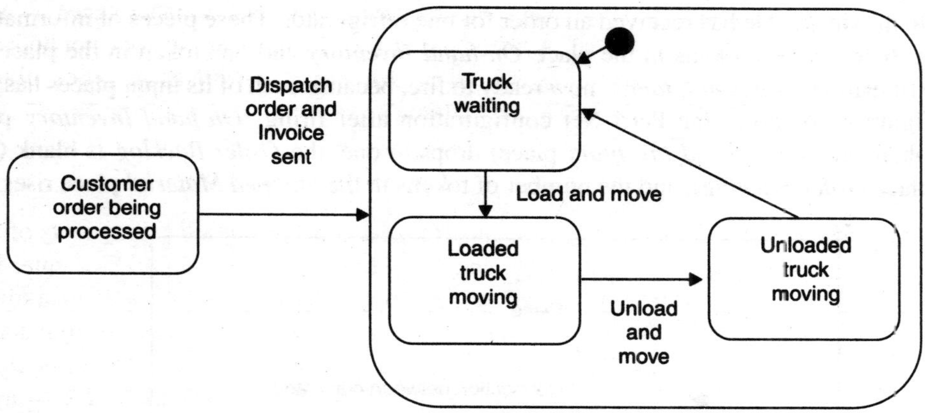

Fig. 6.5. Decomposition of the material dispatch state

We thus see that statecharts allow hierarchical representation of state structure and *broadcast communication* of information on occurrence of events that can trigger simultaneous state transitions in more than one subordinate state. According to Peters and Pedrycz (2000), a statechart combines four important representational configurations:

Statechart = state diagram + hierarchy + orthogonality + broadcast communication

A natural extension to FSM, statecharts are quite suitable to specify behaviour of real-time systems. It is also supported by Statemate software package for system modeling and simulation (Harel and Naamad, 1996). However, its representation scheme lacks precision. Petri nets are a step forward in this direction. It allows concurrent operations, like a statechart and defines the conditions and actions without any ambiguity.

6.3 PETRI NETS

Introduced by Petri (1962), Petri nets are graphs that can be used to depict information flows. Although developed a long time ago, its use in requirement specification is rather recent.

A Petri Net uses four symbols (Fig. 6.6). *A place* stores input or output. A transition transforms input to output. An arc directed from a place to a transition indicates that input from the place can be transformed if the transition occurs. Similarly, an arc directed from a transition to a place indicates that the output from the transition will be stored in the designated place. A *token* represents a piece of information stored in a place. It is either transformed during a transition or is produced during the transition.

When adequate amount of information (*i.e.*, at least one token in each of its input places) is available, then *a transition is enabled and it fires*. Upon firing, one token from each input place changes its place and is stored in one of the output places. Thus, it is essential that a transition must have at least one token in each of its input places in order to fire.

We take an example to illustrate the use of Petri Nets. Assume that a retailer has only two refrigerators in his stores. He has received an order for one refrigerator. These pieces of information are shown, in Fig. 6.7*a*, by two tokens in the place *On-hand Inventory* and one token in the place *Order Backlog*. The transition *Shipment Order* is now ready to fire, because each of its input places has at least one token. Figure 6.7*b* shows the Petri Net configuration after firing. *On-hand Inventory* position (number of tokens in the *On-hand Inventory* place) drops to one, the *Order Backlog* is blank (*i.e.*, no token in the place *Order Backlog*), and the number of tokens in the *Shipped Material* place rises to one.

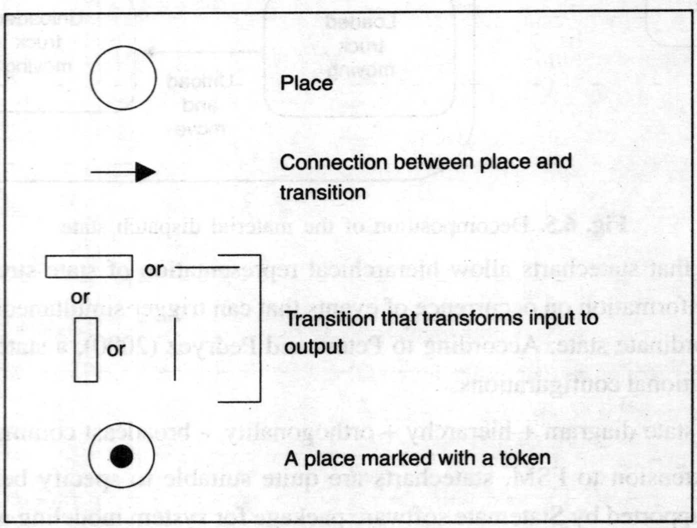

Fig. 6.6. Symbols used in Petri Nets

Often the Petri net configurations are defined. The Petri net configurations in Figs. 6.7*a* and 6.7*b* are defined as under:

Fig. 6.7*a*: I (Shipment Order) = {Order Backlog, On-hand Inventory}

Fig. 6.7*b*: O (Shipment Order) = {Shipped Material}

Here the inputs to and the outputs from the transition *Shipment Order* are defined.

This simple example illustrates how Petri Nets model *concurrency* with ease; shipping order simultaneously reduces both *On-hand Inventory* level and *Order Backlog*.

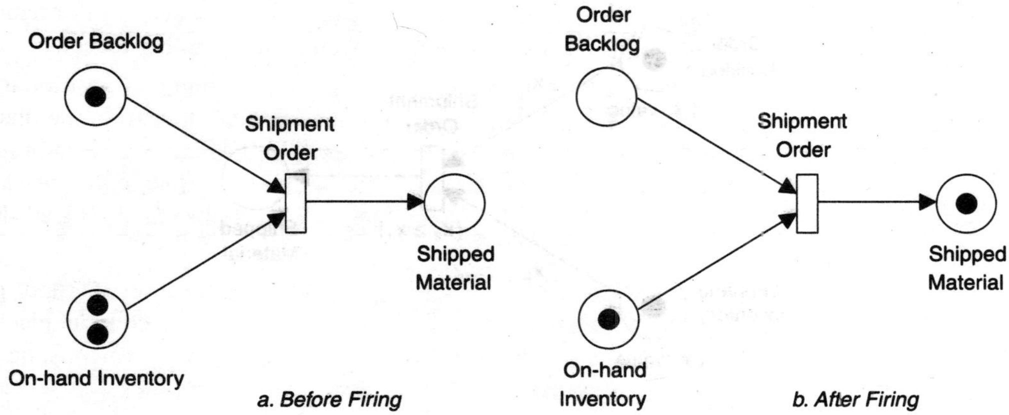

Fig. 6.7. Petri net configurations

6.3.1 Coloured Petri Nets

A significant extension of the basic Petri net is the *coloured Petri net*. Coloured Petri Nets allow modeling of complicated conditions (*guards*) for firing the transitions. For proper specification of the guards, it also allows naming, data typing, and assigning values to tokens. We give the same example of 'Order Compliance' shown earlier in Fig. 6.7. But we now model the more general case where shipment takes place only when the number of items in stock exceeds the number of items demanded. The Petri net for this model is shown in Fig. 6.8. In Fig. 6.8, 1'x_1-value indicates that only one token is available in place *Order Backlog* and that it is assigned an x_1 value. Similar is the explanation for 1'x_2-value. x_1 indicates the value of the token in the place *Order Backlog*. It means that the number of items demanded by the customer is x_1. Similarly, x_2 indicates the value of the token in the place *On-hand Inventory*. It means that it is the amount of on-hand inventory. Naturally, only when the condition $x_2 \geq x_1$ is satisfied, the transition *Shipment Order* will fire.

Several tokens can be defined in a place, each having several names (x_{11}, x_{12}, ..., x_{1m}), several types (real, integer, etc.), and several values ($x_{11} \in [0, \infty)$, $x_{12} \in [0, 1]$, ..., and so on). And, several conditions can be defined for firing.

Consider the case of a dealer of refrigerators (x_1) and TV sets (x_2). Assume that he has a stock of 20 refrigerators and 10 TV sets with him. Further, assume that he has received orders (x_1) of 14 refrigerators and 3 TV sets from various retailers residing in a town which is about 15 km away from his stockyard. So he needs a truck to carry and deliver the goods to the customer. He has only one truck (x_3).

To reduce transportation charges, the dealer wishes to have a minimum of 10 units of products (either or both types to deliver). The truck can carry a maximum of 15 units. After the units are delivered, the truck returns to the dealer's stockyard.

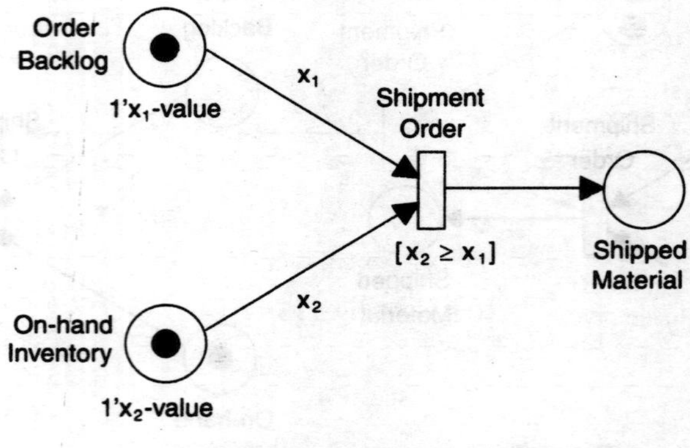

Fig. 6.8. Coloured Petri net

We define the following:

x_{11} : number of refrigerators ordered

x_{12} : number of TVs ordered

x_{21} : number of refrigerators in the inventory

x_{22} : number of TVs in the inventory

Figure 6.9 shows a Petri Net when the order for refrigerator is 14 and that for TV sets is 3. Notice that in Fig. 6.9 we define two types of tokens in the places for *Order Backlog* and *On-hand Inventory*. The initial conditions, therefore, are the following:

$$x_{11} = 14,\ x_{12} = 3,\ x_{21} = 20,\ x_{22} = 10$$
$$x_3 = 1$$

Conditions for firing are the following:

$x_{21} \geq x_{11}$ (Number of refrigerators in the inventory must exceed or equal that demanded)

$x_{22} \geq x_{12}$ (Number of TV sets in the inventory must exceed or equal that demanded)

$10 \leq x_{11} + x_{12} \leq 15$ (The truck must carry a minimum of 10 and a maximum of 15 units)

For the initial conditions stated above, the transition will fire.

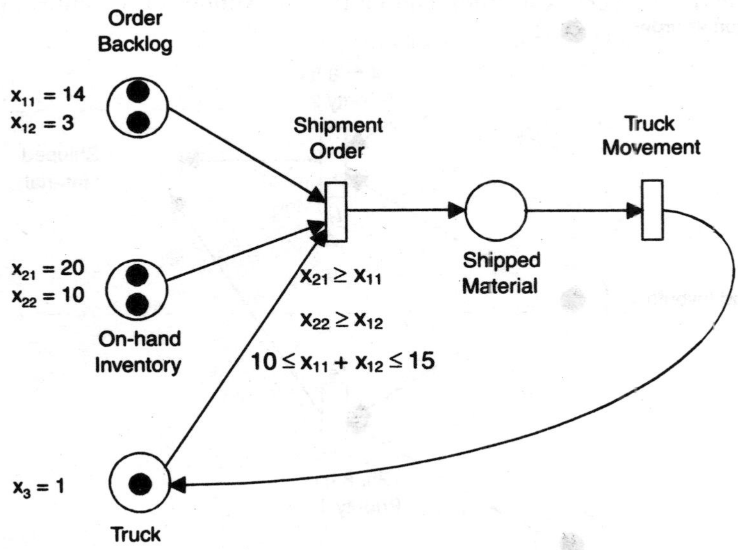

Fig. 6.9. Petri net with multiple tokens and conditions

6.3.2 Timed Petri Nets

Another extension of the basic Petri net is often done by assigning a pair $<t_{min}, t_{max}>$ to each transition. When such an assignment is made to a transition and the transition is enabled, then it must wait for at least t_{min} time before it can fire, and it must fire before t_{max} time elapses.

Often priorities are also assigned to transitions. Thus, when two transitions are enabled and both have passed t_{min} time after getting enabled, then the one with higher priority will fire first.

We take the example of a retailer who has single refrigerator with him. He gets an order for a refrigerator from a customer, but before he could dispatch the unit, he gets another order from a customer whom he values more. He assigns higher priority to the second customer and dispatches the unit to him. Figure 6.10 depicts the situation. In Fig. 6.10, we have defined two transitions t_1 and t_2. The transitions are timed <4 h, 8 h> for the ordinary *Customer Order* and <2 h, 8 h> for the *Valued Customer Order*. Further, a higher priority is assigned to transition t_2.

Notice that when the transitions are neither timed nor prioritized, then they are in *conflict* when their input places are marked. But by defining the timing restrictions and by prioritizing, one can resolve the conflict. Thus, if the customer order is not dispatched within 4 hours and if at this time a valued customer order is received, then the latter gets a priority and the corresponding transition t_2 is fired following the timing constraints. But with no item left in *On-hand Inventory*, the transition t_1 cannot fire, *i.e.*, the ordinary customer order cannot be dispatched unless the on-hand inventory position improves. But, if by that time another valued customer order arrives at the retailer, then again transition t_2 will fire and again the customer order will wait. If such a thing continues perpetually and there is no policy to resolve this situation, the process is said to suffer from *starvation* for want of the needed resource.

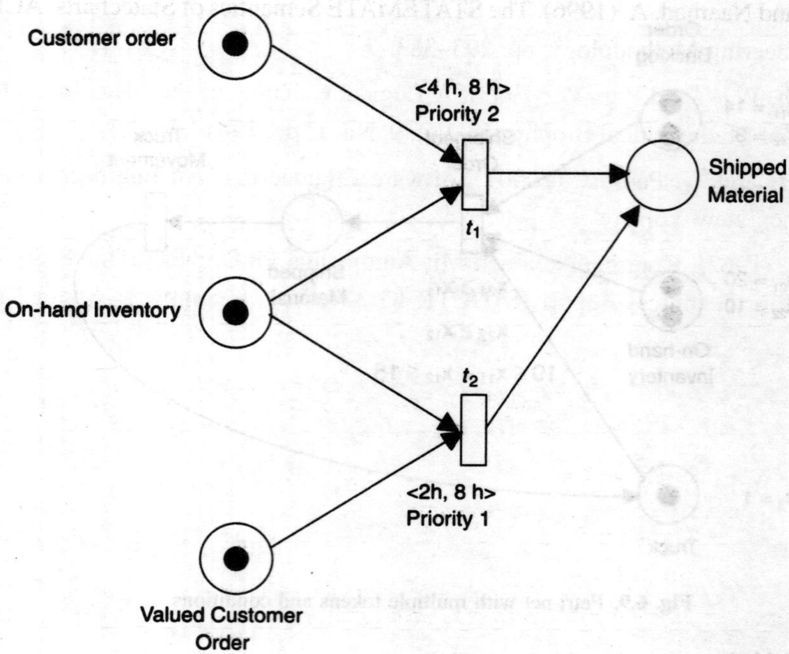

Fig. 6.10. Timed Petri Net

Often a *firing sequence* is predefined for the transitions. Thus, in Fig. 6.10, if the times and priorities were absent, we could define a firing sequence $<t_2, t_1>$, where t_1 and t_2 are the transitions. By so defining the firing sequence, the valued customer is once again given the priority and the item demanded by him is dispatched to him first. The potential problem of starvation therefore remains with this method.

A problem that a Petri net approach can identify is the problem of *deadlock*. A deadlock situation occurs when, after a succession of firing, conditions are not satisfied any more for any transition to fire.

With the provision of precisely defining conditions and actions, Petri nets are a step forward toward formal requirement specification—the subject of the next chapter.

REFERENCES

Harel, D. (1987), Statecharts: A Visual Formalism for Complex Systems, Science of Computer Programming, Vol. 8, pp. 231–274.

Harel, D. (1988), On Visual Formalism, Communications of the ACM, pp. 514–530.

Harel, D. and E. Grey (1997), Executable Object Modeling with Statecharts, IEEE Computer, Vol. 30, No. 7, pp. 31–42.

Harel, D. and Naamad, A. (1996), The STATEMATE Semantics of Statecharts, ACM Transactions of Software Engineering Methodology, pp. 293–383.

McCulloch, W.W. and Pitts W. (1943), A Logical Calculus of the Ideas Immanent in Nervous Activity, Bulletin of Mathematical Biophysics, Vol. 9, No. 1, pp. 39–47.

Peters, J. F. and W. Pedrycz (2000), Software Engineering: An Engineering Approach, John Wiley & Sons, Inc., New York.

Petri, C.A. (1962), Kommunikationen Mit Automaten, Ph.D. thesis, University of Bonn, 1962, English Translation: Technical Report RADCTR-65-377, Vol. 1, Suppl. 1, Applied Data Research, Princeton, N.J.

7 Formal Specifications

Often we experience cases of new software installations which fail to deliver the requirements specified. One of the reasons for such deficiency is that the specified requirements are not feasible to attain. Formal methods of requirements specification make it possible to verify before design work starts if the stated requirements are incomplete, inconsistent, or infeasible. When the requirements are expressed in natural textual language, which is usually the case, there is ample room for the requirements to remain fuzzy. Although specifications of non-functional requirements help to reduce this problem, still a large amount of imprecision continues to stay in the requirements specifications. By using the language of discrete mathematics (particularly set theory and logic), formal methods remove the imprecision and help testing the pre- and post-conditions for each requirement.

There have been many proponents and opponents of the formal methods. Sommerville (1996) nicely summarizes the viewpoints of both. Arguments forwarded in favour of formal methods include, in addition to those given in the previous paragraph, the possibility of automatic program development and testing. Unfortunately, the success stories are much too less, the techniques of logic and discrete mathematics used are not widely known, and the additional cost of developing formal specifications is considered an overhead, not worthy of undertaking. Providing a middle path, Sommerville (1996) suggests using this approach to (*i*) interactive systems, (*ii*) systems where quality, reliability and safety are critical, and to (*iii*) the development of standards.

Although today formal methods are very advanced, the graphical techniques of finite state machines, statecharts, and Petri Nets were the first to ignite the imagination of the software engineers to develop formal methods. In the current chapter, we highlight the basic features of the formal methods to requirement specifications.

There have been a number of approaches to the development of formal methods. They all use the concept of *functions, pre-conditions,* and *post-conditions* while specifying the requirements. But they differ in the mathematical notations in defining them. Three notations are prominent:

1. The Vienna Development Method (VDM)
2. The Z-Specification Language
3. The Larch Notation

The first two were developed by IBM. They adopted notations used in set theory and first-order theory of logic and defined certain specialized symbols. The third uses mnemonic notation that is compatible to a standard keyboard. Sommerville calls the first two methods as *model-based* and calls the Larch notation *algebraic*. All the three of them are, however, abstract data type specification languages, which define formal properties of a data type without defining implementation features. We use the model-based Z-specification language in this chapter to highlight the basic features of formal methods.

7.1 NOTATIONS USED IN FORMAL METHODS

Notations used in formal methods are usually borrowed from those in discrete mathematics. Discrete mathematics deals with discrete elements and operations defined on them, rather than continuous mathematics that deal with differentiation and integration. Pressman (1997) gives a number of basic notations that are used in formal methods. We discuss below a few of these notations.

Specification of Sets

A set is a collection of unique (non-repeating) elements. There are two ways to specify a set:

1. By enumeration.
2. By creating a constructive set specification.

When enumerated, a set is specified as under:

A = {1, 3, 2, 4, 5}; B = {1, 9, 4, 16, 25}; C = {Ram, Gopal, Hari}; D = {(1, 4), (3, 6), (5, 8)}.

Separated by commas, the elements of a set are written within braces and the order of their appearance is immaterial.

When the elements of a set are constructed, a set is specified as under:

$E = \{n: N \mid n < 6\}$; $F = \{m: N \mid m < 6 . m^2\}$; $G = \{n: N \mid n < 4 . (2n - 1, 2n + 2)\}$.

Here E is defined as a set of natural numbers (N) the elements of which are less than six. We see that the sets A (defined earlier by enumeration) and E (defined now by constructive set specification) are same. F is defined as the set of squares of natural numbers that are less than 6. When enumerated, F = {1, 4, 9, 16, 25}. We see that B = F. We can also check that G = D.

The general form of a *constructive set specification* is

{*signature/predicate.term*}

Signature specifies the range of values when forming a set. *Predicate* is a Boolean expression which can take the value either *true* or *false* and defines how the set is to be constructed. *Term* gives the general form of each element in the set.

The cardinality of a set is the number of elements in the set expressed by using the # operator:

{1, 3, 2, 4, 5} = 5; # $\{n: N \mid n < 6\}$ = 5; # F = 5 (where F is the set defined earlier).

Here the # operator returns the number of elements in the set.

The symbol ∅ indicates a null set that contains no element. It is equivalent to zero in number theory. Other useful symbols that are generally used in set theory are the following:

I : Set of integers, ..., – 2, – 1, 0, 1, 2, ...

N : Set of natural numbers, 1, 2, ...

R : Set of all real numbers—both negative and positive integers and fractional values (lying on the real line)

R^+ : Set of all real numbers greater than zero

Set Operators

A number of operators are used to manipulate sets. They are tabulated in Table 7.1 with examples.

Table 7.1: The Set Operators

Operator	Expression	Example	Returns
$\in$	$x \in A$	Ram $\in$ {Gopal, Ram, Hari}	True
$\notin$	$x \notin A$	Sita $\notin$ {Gopal, Ram, Hari}	True
$\subseteq$	$A \subseteq B$	{Hari, Ram} $\subset$ {Gopal, Ram, Hari}	True
$\subset$	$A \subset B$	{Hari, Gopal, Ram} $\subseteq$ {Gopal, Ram, Hari}	False (Since the sets are the same)
$\cup$	$A \cup B$	$\{2, 4\} \cup \{1, 4\}$	$\{1, 2, 4\}$
$\cap$	$A \cap B$	$\{2, 4\} \cap \{1, 4\}$ $\{2, 4\} \cap \{1, 3\}$	$\{4\}$ $\varnothing$
$\backslash$	$A \backslash B$	$\{1, 2, 4\} \backslash \{1, 4\}$	$\{2\}$
$\times$	$A \times B$	$\{2, 4\} \times \{1, 4\}$	$\{(2, 1), (2, 4), (4, 1), (4, 4)\}$
P (Power set)	*P* A	*P* {1, 3, 5}	$\{\varnothing, \{1\}, \{3\}, \{1, 3\}, \{5\}, \{1, 5\}, \{3, 5\}, \{1, 3, 5\}\}$

Logic Operators

The logic operators commonly used in formal methods are given in Table 7.2.

Table 7.2: The Logic Operators

Operator	Meaning	Example	Explanation
$\vee$	and	*if* Inventory > 0 $\vee$ Order > 0 *then* Order_Fill = min (Inventory, Order)	If both customer order and inventory are positive, then the order filled is equal to the minimum of the two
$\wedge$	or	*if* Inventory = 0 $\wedge$ Order = 0 *then* Order_Fill = 0	If either inventory or order is zero, then order filled is zero
$\neg$	not	*If* $\neg$Rain *then* no umbrella	If there is no rain then no umbrella is carried
$\Rightarrow$	implies	Queue is empty $\Rightarrow$ Server is idle	An empty queue implies that the server at the counter is idling
$\forall$	for all	$\forall$ i $\in$ N, $i^2 \in$ N	For all values of i which are natural numbers, their squares are also natural numbers
$\Leftrightarrow$	if and only if	Vacant Room $\Leftrightarrow$ Switch Off	If the room is vacant it implies that the switch is off; and if the switch is off, it implies that the room is vacant

The various operators applied to sequences are given in Table 7.3.

Sequences

Sequence is a set of pairs of elements whose first elements are numbered in the sequence 1, 2, …, and so on:

{(1, Record 1), (2, Record 2), {(3, Record 3)}

This may be also written using angular brackets as under:

<Record 1, Record 2, Record 3>

Unlike a set, a sequence may contain duplication:

<Record 1, Record 2, Record 1>

Since the order of elements in the sequence is important, the following two sets are different although they contain the same elements:

<Record 1, Record 2, Record 3> ≠ <Record 1, Record 3, Record 2>

An empty sequence is denoted as <>.

Table 7.3: The Sequence Operators

Operator	Example	Return
Catenation	<1, 2, 3> <1, 4, 5>	<1, 2, 3, 1, 4, 5>
Head	Head <1, 2, 3>	1
Tail	Tail <1, 2, 3>	<2, 3>
Last	Last <1, 2, 3>	3
Front	Front <1, 2, 3>	<1, 2>

A sequence is denoted by using the keyword *seq*:

Recordlist : *seq* Records

When the number of elements in a sequence is just two, then the sequence is called an *ordered pair*. Thus <x, y> is an ordered pair. When generalized, the sequence is called an *ordered n-tuple*: <x_1, x_2, …, x_n>.

Binary Relations

A *binary relation* (or simply a *relation*) is any set of ordered pairs that defines a binary relation, R. It is represented in many ways:

<*x*, *y*> ∈ R

x R *y* (read as '*x* is in relation R to *y*').

R = {(*x*, *y*) | predicate}

Domain of a set of ordered pairs S, D(S), is the set of all objects *x* for which *x* R *y* holds (or for which <*x*, *y*> ∈ S). *Range* of S, R(S), is the set of all objects *y* such that for some *x*, <*x*, *y*> ∈ S). Thus, if

S = {<1, 5>, <2, 9>, <3, 13>},

then

D (S) = {1, 2, 3} and R (S) = {5, 9, 13}.

Operations on Relations

Since a relation is a set of ordered pairs, the set operations can be applied to relations. Thus, if S_1 and S_2 are defined as under:

$$S_1 = \{<1, 5>, <2, 9>, <3, 13>\} \text{ and } S_2 = \{<5, 1>, <2, 9>\}$$

then

$$S_1 \cup S_2 = \{<1, 5>, <2, 9>, <3, 13>, \{<5, 1>\}$$

and $S_1 \cap S_2 = \{<2, 9>\}$.

Functions

Functions are a special class of relations. A relation f from a set X to another set Y is called a function if for every $x \in$ X, there is a unique $y \in$ Y such that $<x, y> \in f$. The notation used to denote a function f is the following:

$$f\!: X \rightarrow Y$$

The *domain* of f is the whole set X:

$$D_f = X$$

That is, every $x \in$ X must be related to some $y \in$ Y.

The *range* of f, however, may be a subset Y:

$$R_f \subseteq Y$$

Note that if for some $x \in$ X, the mapping to the set Y results in more than one point, the uniqueness of mapping is lost; hence this relation is not a function.

It is customary to write a function in one of the following forms:

$$y = f(x)$$

$$f\!: x \rightarrow y$$

Here x is called the *argument* and the corresponding y is called the *image* of x under f.

A mapping f: X → Y is called *onto* (surjective, a surjection) if R_f = Y; otherwise it is called *into*. A mapping f: X → Y is called *one-to-one* (injective, or 1–1) if distinct elements of X are mapped into distinct elements of Y. A mapping f: X → Y is called *one-to-one* onto (bijective) if it is both one-to-one and onto. Such a mapping is also called a *one-to-one correspondence* between X and Y. Examples of such functions are given below:

Onto function:	f: N → {0,1}, $f(j)$ equals 0 if j is odd and equals 1 if j is even.
Into function:	f: N → N, $f(j)$ equals 0 if j is odd and equals 1 if j is even.
One-to-one function:	f: X → Y, X = {1, 2, 3, 4, 5} and Y = {1, 4, 9, 16, 25, 36}
Bijective:	f: X → Y, X = {1, 2, 3, 4, 5} and Y = {1, 4, 9, 16, 25}

A function f is called *number-theoretic* if the arguments $x \in$ X and values $y \in$ Y are natural numbers. Such a function is depicted as $f(x_1, x_2, \ldots, x_n)$.

A function f: $N^n \rightarrow N$ is called *total* because it is defined for every n-tuple in the power set N^n. For example, if $g(x_1, x_2) = x_1 - x_2$, where $x_1, x_2 \in \{1, 2, 3, 4, 5\}$, then g has values for all of the following cases:

{{5,1}, {5,2}, {5,3}, {5,4}, {5,5},{4,1}, {4,2}, {4,3}, {4,4}, {4,5},{3,1}, {3,2}, {3,3}, {3,4}, {3,5}, {2,1}, {2,2}, {2,3}, {2,4}, {2,5}, {1,1), {1,2}, {1,3}, {1,4}, {1,5}}.

On the other hand, if f: $D^n \rightarrow N$ where $D \subseteq N^n$, then f is called *partial*. For example, if $g(x_1, x_2) = x_1 - x_2$, where $x_1 > x_2$ and $x_1, x_2 \in \{1, 2, 3, 4, 5\}$, then g has values only for the cases:

{{5,1}, {5,2}, {5,3}, {5,4}, {4,1}, {4,2}, {4,3}, {3,1}, {3,2}, {2,1}}.

7.2 THE Z-SPECIFICATION LANGUAGE

The main building block of a Z-specification language is a two-dimensional graphical structure called a *schema*. A schema is analogous to a subroutine or procedure of a programming language. It represents the static aspects (the states) and the dynamics aspects (the operations on the states) of a system. Schemas can also be expressed in terms of other schemas. Figure 7.1 shows the basic structure of a schema.

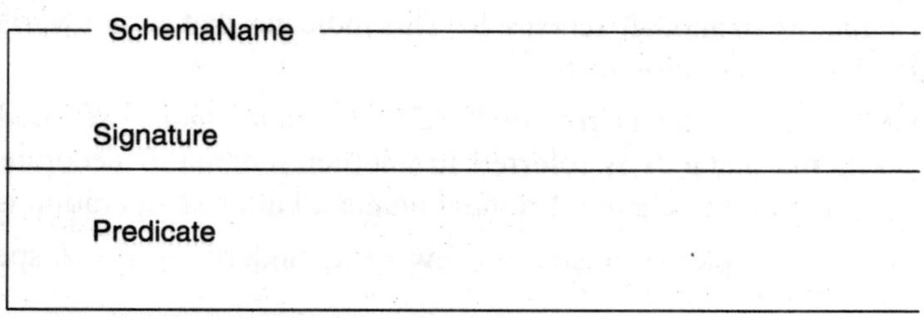

Fig. 7.1. A Z Schema

The *schema name* should be meaningful. This name can be used by another schema for reference. The *signature* declares the names and types of the entities (*the state variables*) that define the system state. The *predicate* defines relationships among the state variables by means of expressions which must always be true (*data invariant*). Predicates can specify initial values of variables, constraints on variables, or other invariant relationships among the variables. When there are more than one predicate, they are either written on the same line separated by the *and* operator $\wedge$ or written on separate lines (as if separated by an implicit $\wedge$).

Predicates may also be specifications of *operations* that change the values of state variables. Operations define the relationship between the old values of the variables and the operation parameters to result in the changed values of the variables. Operations are specified by specifying pre-conditions and post-conditions. Pre-conditions are conditions that must be satisfied for the operation to be initiated. Post-conditions are the results that accrue after the operation is complete.

The specification of a function that reflects the action of an operation using pre-conditions and post-conditions involves the following steps (Sommerville, 1996):

1. Establish the input parameters over which the function should behave correctly. Specify the input parameter constraint as a predicate (pre-condition).

2. Specify a predicate (post-condition) defining a condition which must hold on the output of the function if it behaves correctly.
3. Combine the above two for the function.

Various types of decorations are used to specify operations:

- *Decoration with an apostrophe* ('). A state variable name followed by ' indicates the value of the state variable after an operation. Thus *StVar'* is the new value of *StVar* after an operation is complete. A scheme name followed by ' attaches apostrophe to values of all names defined in the schema together with the invariant applying to these values. Thus, if a schema *SchemaName* defines two state variables *StVar1* and *StVar2* and defines a predicate that uses these two state variable names, then a new schema *SchemaName'* will automatically define *StVar1'* and *StVar2'* in its signature and predicate.
- *Decoration with an exclamation mark* (!). A variable name followed by ! indicates that it is an output; for example, *report*!.
- *Decoration with a question mark* (?). A variable name followed by ? indicates that it is an input; for example, *quantity_sold* ?.
- *Decoration with Greek character Delta* (Δ). A schema name *A* preceded by Δ, Δ*A*, can be used as a signature in another schema *B*. This indicates that certain variable values of A will be changed by the operation in *B*.
- *Decoration with the Greek character Xi* (Ξ). A schema name preceded by Ξ indicates that when the schema name *A* is referred in another schema *B* decorated with Ξ, then the variables defined in the schema *A* remain unaltered after an operation is carried out in *B*.

We give below an example to illustrate a few ideas underlying the Z specification language mentioned above.

Figure 7.2 shows a schema for a regular polygon. The schema name is *Regular Polygon*. The signature section defines four variables denoting the number of sides, length, perimeter, and area of the polygon. Whereas the number of sides has to be a natural number, the other three variables may take any positive real value. In the predicate section, the invariants are given. The first shows that a polygon must have at least three sides. The second and the third are relations that define perimeter and area.

```
── Regular Polygon ──────────────────────────
 noofsides : N
 length : R+
 perimeter : R+
 area : R+
─────────────────────────────────────────────
 noofsides > 2
 perimeter = noofsides × length
 area = noofsides × [1/4 length² tan ((n–2)/2n) π]
─────────────────────────────────────────────
```

Fig. 7.2. Schema for regular polygon

Steps to Develop Z Language Specifications

Saiedian (1997) has suggested the following steps to develop the Z language specifications for software requirements:

1. Present the given, user-defined, and global definitions.
2. Define an abstract state.
3. Define the initial state.
4. Present the state transition operations.

We take a sample of requirements for the circulation system of a library adapted from Saiedian (1997).

7.3 Z LANGUAGE SPECIFICATION FOR LIBRARY REQUIREMENTS — AN ILLUSTRATION

We consider the following requirements for LibCirSys — the information system for the circulation section of a library:

1. A user can borrow a book if the book is available in the library and if he/she has already borrowed less than ten books. A message 'OK' shall appear on the screen after the checkout operation. If, however, the book is already borrowed by another user or if the book has been declared lost, then messages 'Sorry, the book is already issued' and 'Sorry, the book is lost' shall appear on the screen.
2. A user can return a book that he/she had borrowed. After this successful check-in operation a message 'The book is returned.' shall appear on the screen.
3. The *LibCirSystem* can be queried to find out the titles and the number of books borrowed by a user at any time.
4. If a book is neither available in the library nor borrowed by any user for a period of one year, it is declared lost and a message 'The book is now included in the list of lost books.' shall appear on the screen. One is interested to know the number of lost books.

We follow the four steps of developing the Z specifications.

Step 1: Present the Given, User-Defined, and Global Definitions

Given Sets

Whenever the details of a given set (type) are not needed, we assume that the set is given. For the library circulation system we assume BOOK and USER as given sets. We represent the given sets in all upper-case letters, separated by semicolons, within brackets. For the library circulation system the given sets are:

$$[BOOK;\ USER]$$

User-Defined Sets

When the details of a set are required, we define the elements explicitly using enumeration or construction techniques described earlier. For the library circulation system, the user-defined sets are enumerated as under:

MESSAGE = {'OK', 'Sorry, the book is already issued.', 'Sorry, it is a lost book.',
'The book is returned', 'The book is now included in the list of lost books.'}

Step 2: Define an Abstract State

We define the state of a book in the library circulation system as composed of three variables: 'available', 'borrowed', and 'lost'. The variable 'available' indicates the set of books that are available on the shelf of the library and can be borrowed by users. The variable 'borrowed' indicates the set of books that the users have borrowed. And the variable 'lost' indicates the set of books that are declared lost; these are books that are neither available nor borrowed and have not been located for at least a year. We use a Z schema to represent the states (Fig. 7.3). The term *dom* in Fig. 7.3 stands for domain.

LibCirSys

available : *P BOOK*
lost : *P BOOK*
borrowed : *BOOK* ⇸ *USER*

---

available $\cup$ *dom borrowed* $\cup$ *lost* = *BOOK*
available $\cap$ *dom borrowed* $\cap$ *lost* = $\varnothing$
available $\cap$ *dom borrowed* = $\varnothing$

Fig. 7.3. Schema for LibCirSys

The signature of this schema defines three variables: *available, lost*, and *borrowed.* The variable *available* (as also the variable *lost*) belongs to the power set of all books (denoted by the power set symbol *P*) and is of type *BOOK.* That means that suppose the library has only three books, {A, B, C}. The variable *available* can take any value in the power set [∅, {A}, {B}, {AB}, {C}, {AC}, {BC}, {ABC}], ∅ indicating that no book is available on the shelf (they are all issued out or lost) and {ABC} indicating that all books are on the shelf (no book is issued out or lost). The variable *borrowed* is basically a many-to-many relation from BOOK to USER. The symbol ⇸ indicates a partial function that says that while all books can be borrowed, certain books may not be actually borrowed at all, because no user is interested in them.

The predicates state the following:

1. The union of available books, borrowed books, and lost books represents all books owned by the library (the first predicate).
2. A book is either available, or borrowed, or lost (the next two predicates).

Step 3: Define the Initial State

We assume that initially all the books belonging to the library are available in the library with no book either borrowed or lost. Figure 7.4 shows the schema for this case. Note that the schema *LibCirSys* is decorated with an apostrophe in the signature section, and so the variables belonging to this schema and appearing in the predicate section are also each decorated with an apostrophe.

Step 4: Present the State Transition Operations

These operations reflect the requirements of the software stated earlier.

```
┌─ InitialLibCirSys ──────────────────────────
│ LibCirSys'
├──────────────────
│ available' = BOOK
│ borrowed ' = ∅
│ lost ' = ∅
└─────────────────────────────────────────────
```

Fig. 7.4. Schema for LibCirSys

Operation 1: A user borrows a book

Figure 7.5 shows a schema for this case. Here a reference to *LibCirSys* is made because the variables *available* and *borrowed* are to be updated in this operation. So a Δ-decoration is added and the variables in *LibCirSys* whose values are updated are each decorated with an apostrophe in the predicate section. Another schema *BooksBorrowedByAUser* (to be discussed later) decorated with a Ξ symbol is introduced here. One of its signatures *booksborrowed* is used here to specify a precondition. But in the execution of this operation, its value is not being changed. In the signature section, the input variables *user* and *book* are each decorated with ? and the output variable *reply* decorated with !

```
┌──── BorrowABook ────────────────────────────
│ Δ LibCirSys
│ Ξ BooksBorrowedByAUser
│ user? : USER
│ book? : BOOK
│ reply! : MESSAGE
├──────────────────
│ book ? ∈ available
│ booksborrowed ? < 10
│ available ' = available\{book?}
│ borrowed' = borrowed ∪ { book? ↦ user?}
│ reply! = 'OK'
└─────────────────────────────────────────────
```

Fig. 7.5. Schema for LibCirSys

The first expression in the predicate section is a pre-condition that checks if the book to be borrowed is available. The second expression is another pre-condition that checks if the number of books already borrowed by the user is less than 10. The next three expressions are all post-conditions that specify what happens when the specified pre-condition is satisfied. The new value of variable *available* is now a set that does not contain the book issued out (checked out), the new value of variable *borrowed* is now the set that includes the book borrowed, and an 'OK' message is outputted. The symbol $\mapsto$ shows the mapping or association between the elements of a relation.

Request for a Book by the users may not be fulfilled if the book is either not available or lost. Figure 7.6 is a schema for this situation.

The Ξ operator is used in the signature section of this schema to indicate that the schema *LibCirSys* is used here but its variable values will remain unaltered after the operation. In the predicate section, we see two sets of expressions separated by an 'or' (∨) operator. It means that if the book is already borrowed by another user or if the book is a lost book, then appropriate messages appear and the user request is not fulfilled.

```
—— UnfilledUserRequest ——————————————————
  Ξ LibCirSys
  book? : BOOK
  reply! : MESSAGE
  ————————————————————
  book? ∈ borrowed
  reply! = 'Sorry, the book is already issued.'
  ∨
  book? ∈ lost
  reply! = 'Sorry, it is a lost book.'
——————————————————————————————
```

Fig. 7.6. Schema for unfilled user request

Operation 2: The user returns a book

Figure 7.7 shows the schema for the return of a book. The predicate section shows the pre-condition to check if the book is already borrowed by the user. The post-condition actions are to update the available set of books, reduce the set of borrowed books by the user, and output a message that the book is returned.

```
—— ReturnABook ——————————————————
  Δ LibCirSys
  user? : USER
  book? : BOOK
  reply! : MESSAGE
  ————————————————————
  (book? ⟼ user?) ∈ borrowed
  available'  = available ∪   {book?}
  borrowed'   = borrowed \    {book?} ⟼ User?}
  reply!  =  'The book is returned.'
——————————————————————————————
```

Fig. 7.7. Schema for book return

Operation 3: Find the number and titles of books borrowed by a user

Figure 7.8 shows a schema for this case. Here a new output variable *booksborrowed* is defined in the signature section to take values that lie in the set of integers. The predicate section gives the names and the number of books borrowed by the user. It uses a *range restriction operator* $\rhd$ to produce a new set of books containing those entries in the *borrowed* relation that have *user*? as a range value. The *dom* operator produces the books titles and the size operator # gives the size.

Operation 4: Update the list of lost books and find the number of lost books

If a book is neither available nor borrowed and is not traceable for more than one year, then it is declared lost and the book is included in the lost list. The first expression in the predicate section in Fig. 7.9 writes the pre-condition and second expression updates the list of lost books. The third expression uses the # operator to count the number of elements in the lost book set. Because a signature of LibCirSys schema is being changed, the delta operator is used in the signature section.

```
 ── BooksBorrowedByAUser ─────────────────────
| Ξ LibCirSys
| user? : USER
| books! : P BOOKS
| booksborrowed! : N
|─────────────────
| book! = dom (borrowed ▷ {user?})
| booksborrowed! = # (borrowed▷ {user?})
 ─────────────────────────────────────────────
```

Fig. 7.8. Schema for books borrowed by a user

```
 ── BookIsLost ───────────────────────────────
| Δ LibCirSys
| book? : BOOKS
| searchtime? : R+
| numlost! : N
| reply! : MESSAGE
|─────────────────
| book? ∉ dom borrowed ∧ book? ∉ available ∧
| searchtime ? > 1
| lost' = lost ∪ book?
| numlost ! = # lost'
| reply ! = 'The book is now included in the list of lost books.'
 ─────────────────────────────────────────────
```

Fig. 7.9. Schema for lost books

Formal methods help in precisely specifying requirements and in validating them. Based on the basics of discrete mathematics and aided by such specification languages like Z and its associated automated tools such as ZTC, FUZZ, and CADiZ (Saiedian, 1997), formal methods have helped lifting requirements analysis to the status of requirements engineering—a strong, emerging sub-discipline of the general field of software engineering.

Despite the great promise shown, formal methods have not been very popular in industry mainly due to their mathematical sophistication. Considering the additional effort required for applying the formal methods, they should be applied to specifying (1) critical system components that are required to be absolutely correct (such as safety-critical systems that can lead to major catastrophes including loss of human lives) and (2) reusable components which, unless absolutely correct, can infuse errors in many host programs.

REFERENCES

Pressman, R.S. (1997), Software Engineering: A Practitioner's Approach, McGraw-Hill, 4th Edition, International Editions, New York.

Saiedian, H. (1997), Formal Methods in Information Systems Engineering, In Software Requirements Engineering, R.H. Thayer and M. Dorfman (Eds.), IEEE Computer Society, 2nd Edition, pp. 336–349, Washington.

Sommerville, I. (1996), Addison-Wesley, Reading, 5th Edition.

8 Object-Oriented Concepts

In the past decade, requirements analysis is increasingly being done in the framework of object-oriented analysis. Object orientation is based on a completely different paradigm. The present and the next chapter discuss requirements analysis based on the conceptual framework provided by object orientation. While the current chapter discusses the dominant concepts underlying object orientation and the various Unified Modeling Language notations for graphical representation of these modeling concepts, the next chapter uses them to delineate the user requirements.

8.1 POPULARITY OF OBJECT-ORIENTED TECHNOLOGY

Object-oriented approach to system analysis and design is becoming increasingly popular. The following reasons are cited for this popularity (Yourdon 1994):

1. It helps in rapid program development. This has become possible due to (*a*) the facility of reusability of libraries of classes and objects and (*b*) easy development of prototypes.
2. It helps developing high-quality and highly maintainable programs. It becomes possible principally due to the property of encapsulation in objects that ensures less number of defects in code and allows easy replacement of an object with a new implementation.
3. As a result of the above two, software productivity improves when an object-oriented approach is adopted.
4. Today, software systems tend to be large and complex and require rapid development. Older methodologies that separated process models from data models are not as effective as the object-oriented methodology for such systems.

8.2 EMERGENCE OF OBJECT-ORIENTED CONCEPTS

Object-oriented concepts have emerged gradually over a period of time with contributions originating from various sources:

A. Contributions from diverse disciplines
B. Contributions from computer scientists

8.2.1 Contributions from Diverse Disciplines

The term 'object' independently emerged in different fields of computer science in the seventies:

1. Advances in computer architecture
2. Developments of object-oriented operating systems
3. Advances in programming languages
4. Development of entity-relationship approach to data modeling
5. Development in knowledge representation in artificial intelligence
6. Development in the model of intelligence.

We follow Booch (1994) to discuss the contribution of each of the above.

1. *Advances in computer architecture*

In the Von Neumann architecture that marked the beginning of digital computers, executable object code in machine language resided in the computer memory. The low-level abstraction of the object code differed greatly from the high-level abstraction of the source code. Development of such computers as Burroughs 5000, Intel 432, IBM/38, etc., represented a break from this classical architecture, and significantly closed the gap. In the architecture of these computers, various characteristics of the object code started appearing in the source code itself.

2. *Development of object-oriented operating system*

Many object-oriented operating systems were developed based on: (1) Dijkstra's development of the multiprogramming system that introduced the concept of building systems as *layered state machines* (Dijkstra 1968), (2) the idea of *information hiding* introduced by Parnas (1972), (3) the idea of abstract *data-type mechanisms* introduced by Liskov and Zilles (1974) and Guttag (1977), and (4) the idea of theory of types and subclasses introduced by Hoare (1974). Two such object-oriented operating systems are the following:

1. CALTSS for the CDC 6400
2. iMAX for the Intel 432

3. *Advances in programming languages*

Programming languages may be thought to be belonging to different generations, depending on the way a program is structured and the way data and program are connected.

First-Generation Languages (*1954–1958*). These first-generation languages (Fortan I, ALGOL 58) have the following features (Fig. 8.1):

1. Subprograms were seen as more labour-saving devices.
2. Data were globally defined.

Second-Generation Languages (*1959–1961*). To this generation belong such languages as Fortran II, Algol 60, COBOL and LISP. They have the following features (Fig. 8.2):

A. Nesting of subprograms was allowed.
B. Various methods were used for passing parameters from one subprogram to another.
C. Structured programming constructs were used.

Third-Generation Languages (*1962–1970*). The languages belonging to this generation are PL/1, ALGOL 68, PASCAL, and Simula. The features of these languages are as under (Fig. 8.3):

- Programming-in-the-large
- Separately compiled modules
- Presence of data types

The Generation Gap (*1970–1990*). A plethora of languages developed during the seventies.

Object-Based and Object-Oriented Programming Languages (*1990–*). These languages (Ada, Smalltalk, C++, Object PASCAL, Eiffel, CLOS, etc.) have the following features (Fig. 8.4):

1. Data-driven design methods were used.
2. Theory of data typing emerged.
3. Little or no global data was present.
4. Physical structure of an application appears like a graph, rather than a tree.

Table 8.1 gives the evolution of generation of languages.

Table 8.1: Evolution of Generation of Languages

1st Generation	2nd Generation	3rd Generation	Generation Gap (1970–1990)	Object-based & 00-Generation 1990–
Fortran I	Fortran II	PL/1		
ALGOL 58	ALGOL 60	ALGOL 68		Ada (Contribn. from Alphard CLU)
	COBOL	PASCAL		Object PASCAL, Eiffel Smalltalk
	LISP	SIMULA		C ++ (Contribn. from C) CLOS (Contribution from LOOPS+ & Flavors)

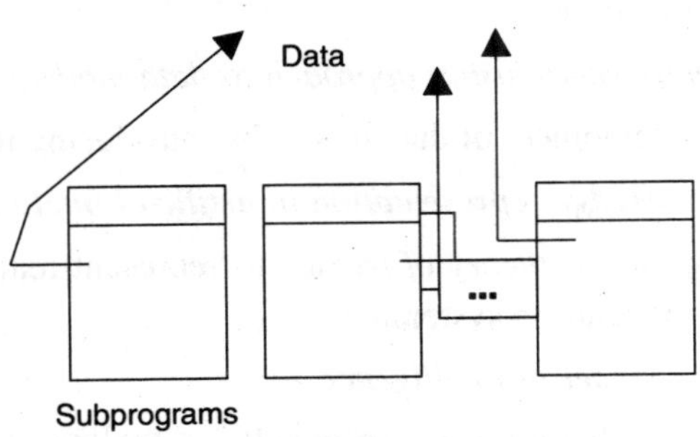

Fig. 8.1. First-generation languages

Simula-80 had the fundamental ideas of *classes* and *objects*. Alphard, CLU, Euclid, Gypsy, Mesa and Modula supported the idea of *data abstraction*. Use of object-oriented concepts led the development of C to C++; Pascal to Object Pascal, Eiffel, and Ada; LISP to Flavors, LOOPS, and to Common LISP Object System (CLOS).

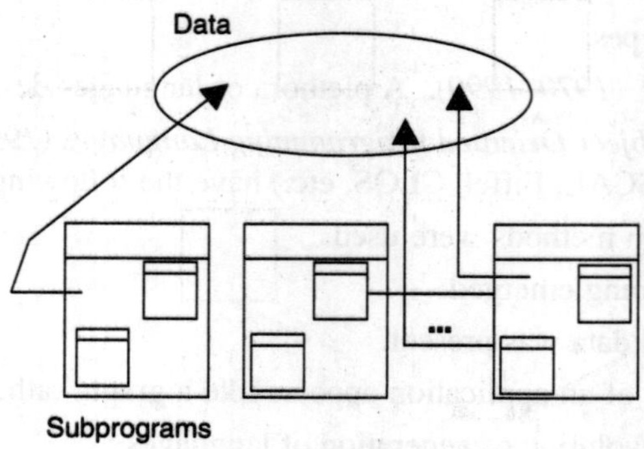

Fig. 8.2. Second-generation languages

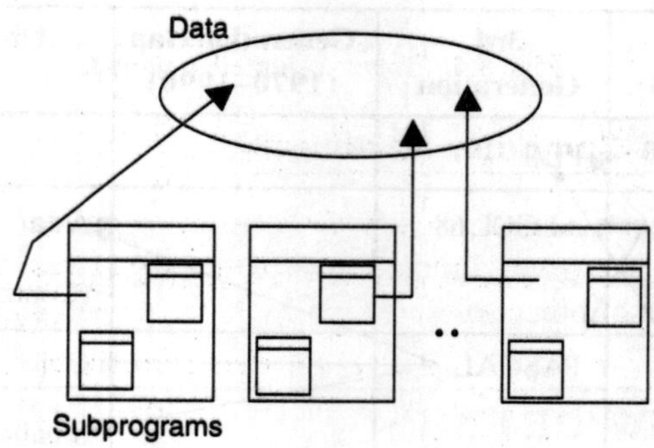

Fig. 8.3. Third-generation languages

One way to distinguish a procedure-oriented language from an object-oriented language is that the former is organized around procedures and functions (verbs) whereas the latter is organized around pieces of data (nouns). Thus, in a procedure-oriented program based design, a module represents a major function, such as 'Read a Master Record', whereas in an object-oriented program based software design, 'Master Record' is a module.

4. *Development of entity-relationship approach to data modeling*

Chen pioneered the development of data model by introducing the *entity-relationship diagrams.*

5. *Development in knowledge representation in artificial intelligence*

In 1975, Minsky proposed *a theory of frames* to represent real-world objects as perceived by image and natural language recognition system.

6. *Development of the model of intelligence*

Minsky (1986) observed that mind is organized as a society of mindless objects and that only through the cooperative behaviour of these *agents* do we find what we call intelligence.

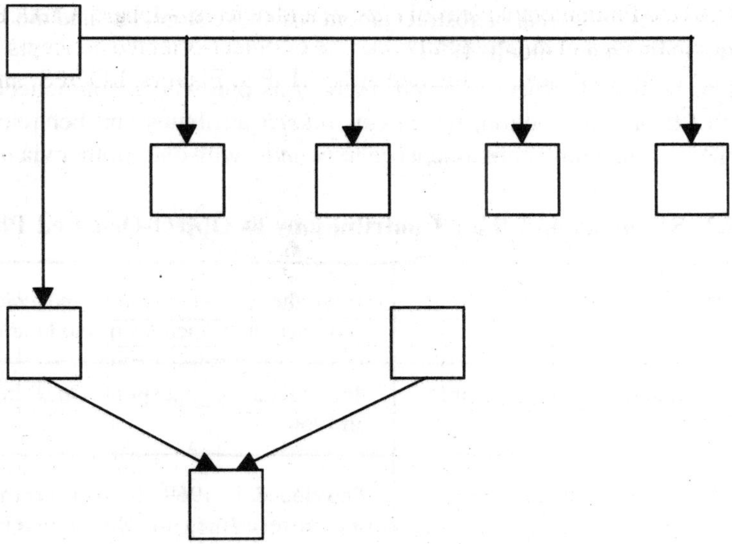

Fig. 8.4. Object-oriented languages

8.2.2 Contributions from Computer Scientists

The concepts of object orientation came from many computer scientists working in different areas of computer science. We give, almost chronologically, a list of prominent scientists whose contributions to development of object-oriented concepts have been significant (Table 8.2).

8.3 INTRODUCTION TO 'OBJECT'

According to New Webster's Dictionary (1981), an object is:

- some visible or tangible thing;
- that toward which the mind is directed in any of its states or activities;
- that to which efforts are directed.

Thus an object refers to a thing, such as a chair, a customer, a university, a painting, a plan, or a mathematical model. The first four of these examples are *real-world objects*, while the last two are *conceptual or abstract objects*. Software engineers build abstract objects that represent real-world objects which are of interest to a user.

In the context of object-oriented methodologies, the second dictionary definition is more appropriate:

> "An object is anything, real or abstract, which is characterized by the *state* it occupies and by the *activities* defined on that object that can bring about changes in the state."

The state of an object indicates the information the object stores within itself at any point of time, and that the activities are the operations that can change the information content or the state of the object.

Two other definitions are worth mentioning:

1. An object is anything, real or abstract, about which we store data and methods that manipulate the data. (Martin and Odell, 1992).
2. A system built with object-oriented methods is one whose components are *encapsulated* chunks of data and function, which can *inherit* attributes and behaviour from other such components, and whose components *communicate* with one another via messages. (Yourdon, 1994).

Table 8.2: Scientists and their Contributions to Object-Oriented Philosophy

1.	Larry Constantine	Gave the idea of *coupling* and *cohesion* in 1960s that provided the principles of modular design of programs.
2.	K. Nygaard and O. J. Dahl (1981)	Introduced the concept of '*class*' in the language *Simula* in 1966.
3.	Adele Goldberg and Allan Kay (1976)	Developed, in 1969, the first incarnation of *Smalltalk*—*the* purest form of object orientation where they introduced the concepts of *inheritance, message*, and *dynamic binding*.
4.	Edsger Dijkstra (1968)	Gave the idea of semantically separated layers of abstraction during software building, which is the central concept of *encapsulation*.
5.	Barbara Liskov (1974)	Developed the *theory of Abstract Data Type* (ADT) and also developed, in 1970s, *the CLU Language* that supported the notion of *hidden internal data representation*.
6.	David Parnas (1972)	Forwarded the *principle of information hiding* in 1972.
7.	Jean Ichbiah and others	Developed ADA that had, for the first time, the features of *genericity* and *package*.
8.	Bjarne Stroustrup (1991)	Grafted object orientation on C, in 1991, to develop C++ that is portable across many machines and operating systems due to its foundation on C.
9.	Bertrand Meyer (1988)	Combined the best idea of computer science with the best idea of object orientation, in 1995, to develop *Eiffel*.
10.	Grady Booch (1994), Ivar Jacobson *et al.* (1992), and Jim Rumbaugh *et al.* (1991)	Developed, in the late 1990s, the Unified Modeling Language (UML) that has the power of graphically depicting the object-oriented concepts.

8.4 CENTRAL CONCEPTS UNDERLYING OBJECT ORIENTATION

Various authors have suggested various concepts that, they think, are central to object orientation. We give below some of the oft-repeated concepts:

Encapsulation	Object identity	Inheritance
State retention	Message	Polymorphism
Information hiding	Classes	Genericity

Encapsulation

Encapsulation means enclosing related components within a capsule. The capsule can be referred to by a single name. In the object-oriented methodology, the components within this capsule are (1) the attributes and (2) the operations.

Attributes store information about the object. *Operations* can change the values of the attributes and help accessing them.

State Retention

The idea of encapsulation is not unique to object orientation. Subroutines in early high-level languages had already used the idea of encapsulation. Modules in structured design also represent encapsulation. There is however a difference between encapsulation represented in modules and that represented in objects. After a module completes its tasks, the module returns back to its original state. In contrast, after an operation is performed on an object, the object does not return to its original state; instead it continues to retain its final state till it is changed when another operation is performed on it.

Information Hiding

One result of encapsulation is that details of what takes place when an operation is performed on an object are suppressed from public view. Only the operations that can be performed on an object are visible to an outsider. It has two major benefits:

1. It localizes design decisions. Private design decisions (within an object) can be made and changed with minimal impact upon the system as a whole.
2. It decouples the content of information from its form.

Once again the idea of information hiding is not new. This idea was forwarded by Parnas (1972) and was used in the modular design of programs in structured design.

Object Identity

Every object is unique and is identified by an *object reference* or an *object handle*. A programmer can refer to the object with the help of such a reference (or handle) and can manipulate it. Thus a program statement

var cust-rec1: customer := Customer.new

defines a variable *cust-rec1* and causes this variable to hold the handle of the object *customer*, created newly. This object belongs to the class *Customer*. The assignment operator (:=) directs the class *Customer* to create (through the operator *new*) an instance (*customer*) of its own.

Message

An object *obj1* requests another object *obj2*, via a *message*, to carry out an activity using one of the operations of *obj2*. Thus *obj1* should

1. Store the handle of *obj2* in one of its variables.
2. Know the operation of *obj2* that it wishes to execute.
3. Pass any supplementary information, in the form of arguments, which may be required by *obj2* to carry out the operation.

Further, *obj2* may pass back the result of the operation to *obj1*.

The structure of a message is defined as under:

paymentOK := customer.addPayment (cashTendered)

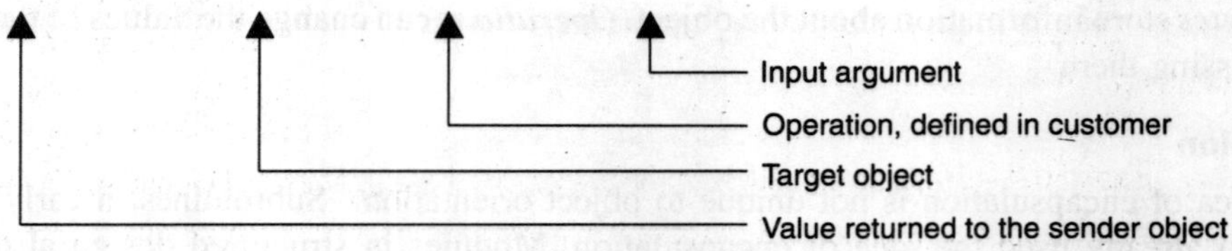

The UML representation of the message is given in Fig. 8.5. (We discuss about UML towards the end of this chapter.)

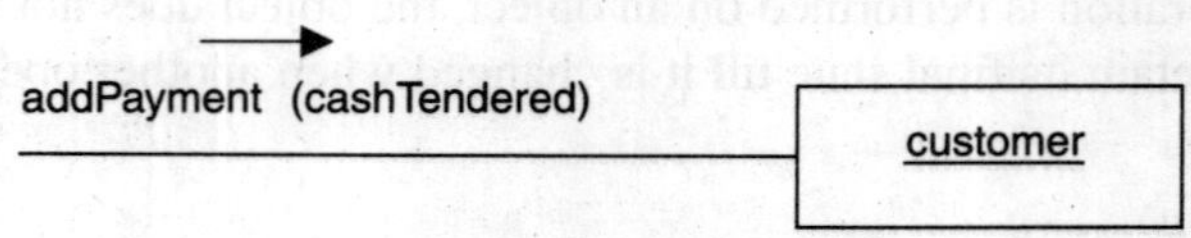

Fig. 8.5. Message sent to an object

The input arguments are generally parameter values defined in (or available at) *obj1*. But they can also be other objects as well. In fact, in the programming language Smalltalk, there is no need for any data; objects point to other objects (via variables) and communicate with one another by passing back and forth handles of other objects.

Messages can be of three types:

1. Informative (past-oriented, update, forward, or push)
2. Interrogative (present-oriented, real, backward, or pull)
3. Imperative (future-oriented, force, or action)

An *informative message* provides the target object information on what has taken place elsewhere in order to update itself:

employee.updateAddress (address: Address)

Here *Address* is the type declaration for the input argument *address* for the operation *updateAddress* defined on the object *employee*.

An *interrogative message* requests the target object for some current information about itself:

inventory.getStatus

An *imperative message* asks the object to take some action in the immediate future on itself, another object, or even on the environment around the system.

payment.computeAmount (quantity, price)

Class

A class is a stencil from which objects are created (instantiated); that is, instances of a class are objects. Thus *customer1, customer2*, and so on, are objects of the class *Customer*; and *product1, product2*, …, and so on are objects of the class *Product*.

The UML definition of a *class* is "a description of a set of objects that share the same attributes, operations, methods, relationships, and semantics". It does not include concrete software implementation such as a Java class; thus it includes all specifications that precede implementation. In the UML, an implemented software class is called an *implementation class*.

Oftentimes a term *type* is used to describe a set of objects with the same attributes and objects. Its difference from a *class* is that the former does not include any methods. A *method* is the implementation of an operation, specifying the operation's algorithm or procedure.

Although objects of a class are structurally identical, each object

1. has a separate handle or reference and
2. can be in different states.

Normally, operations and attributes are defined at the object level, but they can be defined at the level of a class as well. Thus, creating a new customer is a *class-level operation*:

Customer.new

new is a class operation that creates a new customer.

Similarly, *noOfCustomersCreated* that keeps a count of the number of Customer objects created by the class *Customer* is a *class-level attribute*:

noOfCustomersCreated:Integer

noOfCustomersCreated is an integer-type class attribute the value of which is incremented by 1 each time the operation *new* is executed.

The UML notation of a class, an instance of a class, and an instance of a class with a specific name are as under:

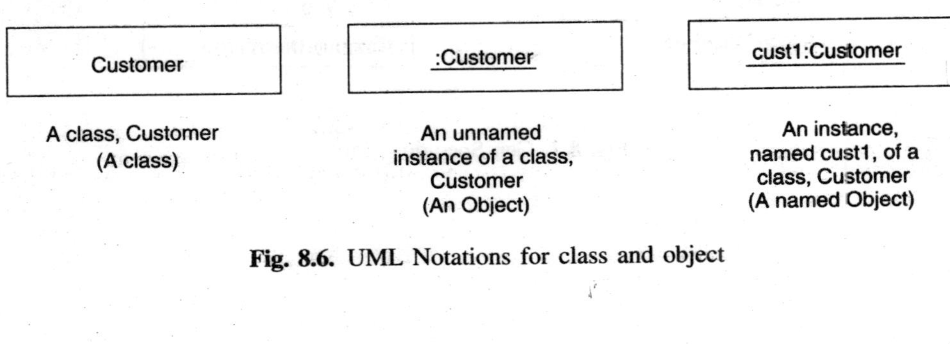

Fig. 8.6. UML Notations for class and object

Inheritance

Inheritance (by D from C) is a facility by which a *subtype* D implicitly defines upon it all the attributes and operations of a *supertype* C, as if those attributes and operations had been defined upon D itself.

Note that we have used the terms *subtypes* and *supertypes* instead of the terms subclasses and superclasses (although the latter two terms are popularly used in this context) because we talk of only operations (and attributes), and not methods.

The classes *Manager* and *Worker* are both *Employee*. So we define attributes such as *Name*, *Address*, and *EmployeeNo*, and define operations such as *transfer*, *promote*, and *retire* in the supertype *Employee*. These attributes and operations are valid for, and can be used by, the subtypes, *Manager* and *Worker*, without separately defining them for these subtypes. In addition, these subtypes can define attributes and operations that are local to them. For example, an attribute *OfficeRoom* and operation *attachOfficeRoom* can be defined on the *Manager*, and an attribute *DailyWage* and an operation *computeDailyWage* can be defined on *Worker*.

Inheritance is best depicted in the form of a *Gen-Spec* (*Generalization-Specialization*) diagram. The example of *Manager* and *Worker* inheriting from *Employee* is depicted below in the form of a Gen-Spec diagram Fig. 8.7. Here, *Employee* is a generalized class and *Manager* and *Worker* are specialized classes.

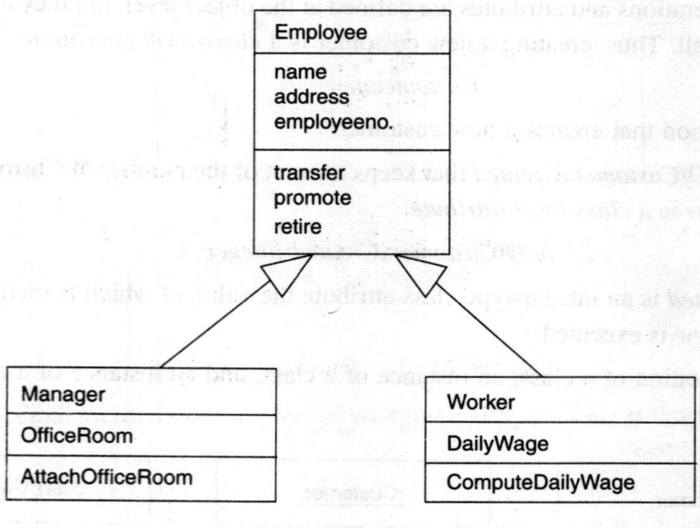

Fig. 8.7. Gen-Spec diagram

To define a correct subtype, two rules are to be satisfied:

1. The *100% Rule*. The subtype conforms to 100% of the supertype's attributes and operations.
2. The *Is-a Rule*. The subtype is a member of the supertype.

The Gen-spec diagram is often called an '*Is-a*' diagram.
An alternative UML notation is given in Fig. 8.8.

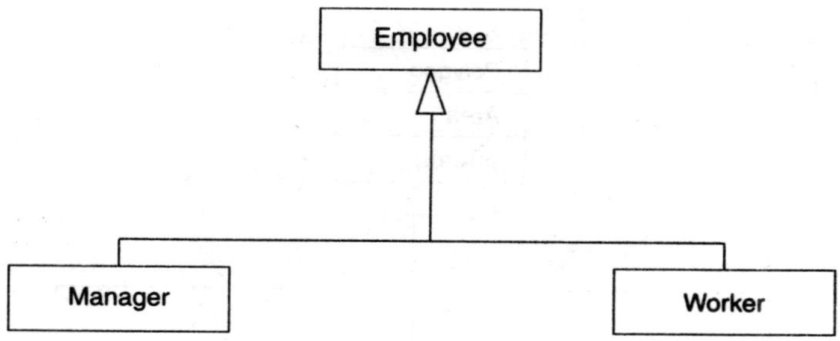

Fig. 8.8. Alternative form of Gen-Spec diagram

Often a subtype can inherit attributes and operations from two supertypes. Thus a *Manager* can be both an *Employee* and a *Shareholder* of a company. This is a case of *multiple inheritance* (Fig. 8.9).

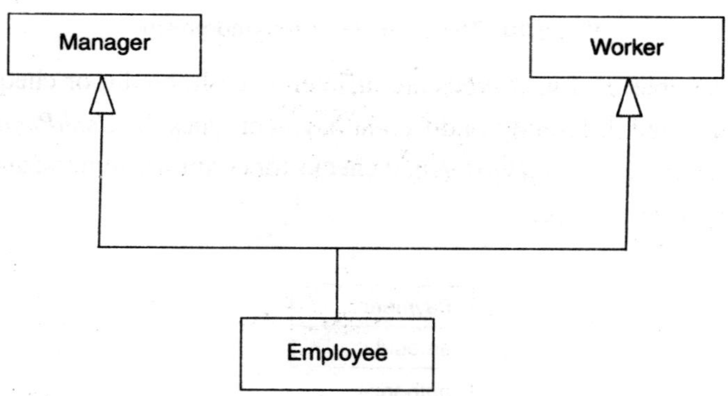

Fig. 8.9. Multiple inheritance

While languages such as C++ and Eiffel support this feature, Java and Smalltalk do not. Multiple inheritance leads to problems of

1. Name-clash
2. Incomprehensibility of structures

Polymorphism

Polymorphism is a Greek word, with *poly* meaning 'many' and *morph* meaning 'form'. Polymorphism allows the same name to be given to services in different objects, when the services are similar or related. Usually, different object types are related in a hierarchy with a common supertype, but this is not necessary (especially in dynamic binding languages, such as Smalltalk, or languages that support interface, such as Java). Two examples are shown in Fig. 8.10 and Fig. 8.11 to illustrate the use of polymorphism.

In the first example, *getArea* is an operation in the supertype *Hexagon* that specifies a general method of calculating the area of a *Polygon.* The subtype *Hexagon* inherits this operation, and therefore the method of calculating its area. But if *Polygon* happens to be *Triangle,* the same operation *getArea* would mean calculating area by simpler methods such as ½ × (product of base and the height); while if it is *Rectangle*, then *getArea* will be computed by the product of two adjacent sides.

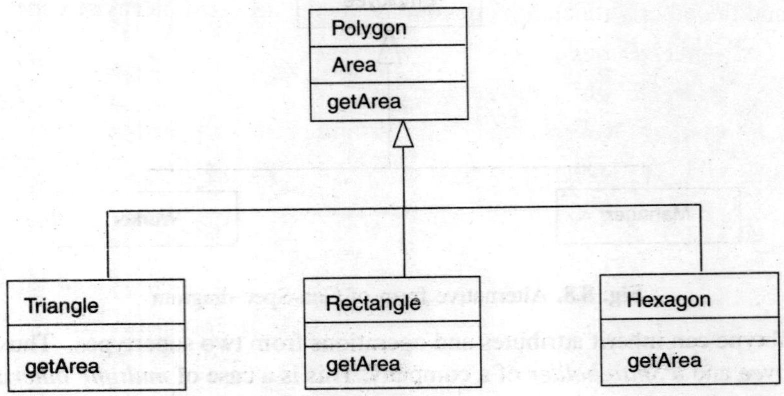

Fig. 8.10. The example of polymorphism

In the second example, *Payment* types are different—cash, credit, or cheque. The same operation *authorize* is implemented differently in different payment types. In *CashPayment*, *authorize* looks for counterfeit paper currency; in *CreditPayment*, it checks for credit worthiness; and in *ChequePayment*, it examines the validity of the cheque.

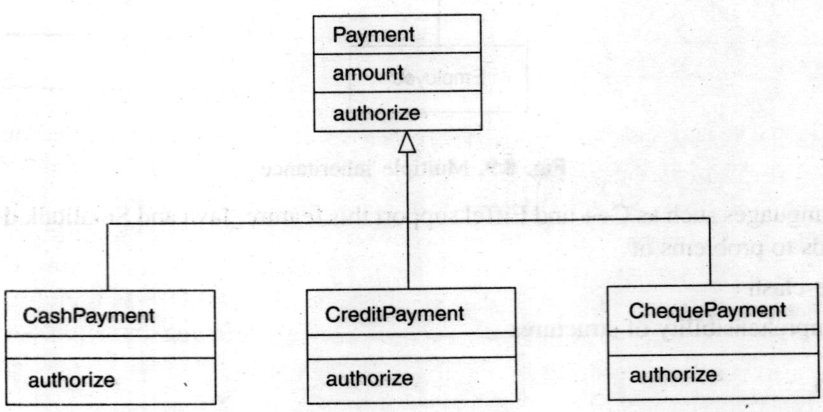

Fig. 8.11. A second example of polymorphism

In these two examples, the concept of *overriding* has been used. The operations *getArea* and *authorize* defined on the supertype are overridden in the subtypes, where different methods are used.

Polymorphism is often implemented through *dynamic binding*. Also called *run-time binding* or *late binding*, it is a technique by which the exact piece of code to be executed is determined only at run-time (as opposed to compile-time), when the message is sent.

While polymorphism allows the same operation name to be defined differently across different classes, a concept called *overloading* allows the same operation name to be defined differently several times within the same class. Such overloaded operations are distinguished by the *signature* of the message, *i.e.*, by the number and/or class of the arguments. For example, two operations, one without an argument and the other with an argument, may invoke different pieces of code:

giveDiscount

giveDiscount (*percentage*)

The first operation invokes a general discounting scheme allowing a standard discount percentage, while the second operation allows a percentage discount that is specified in the argument of the operation.

Genericity

Genericity allows defining a class such that one or more of the classes that it uses internally is supplied only at run time, at the time an object of this class is instantiated. Such a class is known as a *parameterized class*. In C++ it is known as a *template class*. To use this facility, one has to define parameterized class argument while defining the class. In run time, when we desire to instantiate a particular class of items, we have to pass the required argument value. Thus, for example, we may define a parameterized class

class Product < Product Type>;

while instantiating a new object of this class, we supply a real class name as an argument:

var product 1: product : = Product. new <Gear>

or

var product 2: product : = Product. new <Pump>

8.5 UNIFIED MODELING LANGUAGE (UML)

Various object-oriented analysis and design approaches were forwarded during the 1970s and 1980s, prominent among them being Booch's method (Booch 1994) at Rational Software Corporation, Object-Oriented Software Engineering (OOSE) by Jacobson (Jacobson *et al.* 1992) at Objectory, and Object Modeling Technique (OMT) by Rumbaugh at General Electric (Rumbaugh *et al.* 1991). While the Booch's method was directed mostly at the design and construction phases, OOSE supported the requirements and high-level design phases the maximum, and OMT was useful for analysis and data-intensive informative systems. Although the approaches were different, the similarities were conspicuous. There was also clearly a need felt by the user community to have one comprehensive approach that unifies all other approaches.

With both Rumbaugh and Jacobson joining Rational in 1994 and 1995 respectively, the effort at unification of the various approaches began. Various versions of UML (Unified Modeling Language) were made after incorporating suggestions from the user community. A UML consortium with partners from such leading software giants as Digital Equipment Corporation, Hewlett-Packard, IBM, Microsoft, Oracle, and Texas Instrument was formed. The resulting modeling language UML 1.0 was submitted to the Object Management Group (OMG) during 1997. Incorporation of the feedback from the Group led to UML 1.1 that was accepted by OMG in late 1997. The OMG Revision Task Fore has released UML 1.2 and UML 1.3 in 1998. Information on UML is available at *www.rational.com, www.omg.org,* and at *uml.shl.com*.

Unified Modeling Language (UML) is defined as "a standard language for writing software blueprints" (Booch, *et al.* 2000, p. 13). The language is graphical. It has its vocabulary and rules to represent structural and behavioral aspects of software systems. The representation can take the form of

- Visualizing the details of a piece of code for understanding and communicating,
- Specifying precisely and completely the system structure and behavior,
- Constructing code from the UML model of the system (forward engineering) and reconstructing a UML model from a piece of code (reverse engineering), and
- Documenting artifacts of the system requirements, design, code, tests, and so on.

UML is independent of the particular software development life cycle process in which the software product is being designed, but it is most effective when the process is case driven, architecture-centric, iterative, and incremental.

For a full understanding of the software architecture, one can take five views:

1. The use case view – exposing the requirements of the system.
2. The design view – capturing the vocabulary of the problem and solution space.
3. The process view – modeling the distribution of the system's processes and threads.
4. The implementation view – addressing the physical realization of the system.
5. The deployment view – focusing on the system engineering issues.

Whereas all views are pertinent to any software system, certain views may be dominant depending on the characteristics of a specific software system. For example, a use case view is dominant in a GUI-intensive system, a design view is dominant in a data-intensive system, a process view is dominant in complex interconnected system, and implementation and deployment views are important in a Web-intensive system. UML is useful irrespective of the type of architectural view one takes.

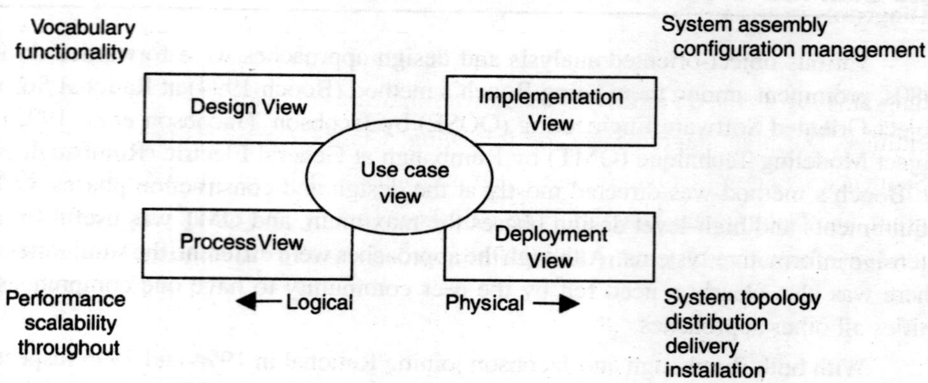

Fig. 8.12. Five views of system architecture

8.5.1 Building Blocks in UML

There are three types of building blocks in UML. They are: (1) Entities, (2) Relationships among the entities, and (3) Diagrams that depict the relationships among the entities.

UML Entities

Entities can be structural, behavioral, grouping, or annotational. Table 8.3 gives the names of the various entities. Table 8.4 briefly describes the entities, and shows their UML symbols.

Table 8.3: The Entities in UML

Structural entity		Behavioral entity	Grouping entity	Annotational entity
Conceptual	**Physical**			
Class Interface Collaboration Use Case Active Class	Component Node	Interaction State machine	Package	Note

Relationships among Entities

A relationship is defined between two entities to build a model. It can be of four types:

1. Dependency (A semantic relationship)
2. Association (A structural relationship)
3. Generalization (A generalization/specialization relationship)
4. Realization (A semantic relationship)

Table 8.5 gives the description of the relationships and their UML symbols.

Diagrams in the UML

UML specifies nine diagrams to visualize relationships among the entities of a system. The diagrams are directed graphs in which nodes indicate entities and arcs indicate relationships among the entities. The nine diagrams are the following: Class Diagram, Object Diagram, Use Case Diagram, Sequence Diagram, Collaboration Diagram, Statechart Diagram, Activity Diagram, Component Diagram, and Deployment Diagram. These diagrams are described later in the text. For the present, Table 8.6 indicates which diagrams are useful in which view of the software architecture.

Table 8.4: Entity Descriptions and Their UML Symbols

Entity	Description	UML symbol
Class	A template for a set of objects.	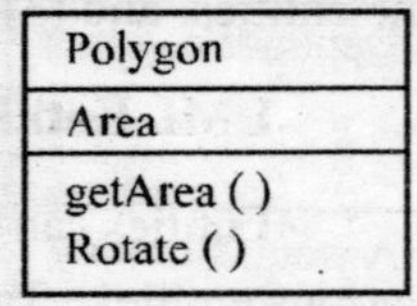
Interface	A set of operations specifying a service of a class or component.	
Collaboration	Interaction among entities to provide a service.	
Use Case	A set of sequence of actions that an actor and the system do.	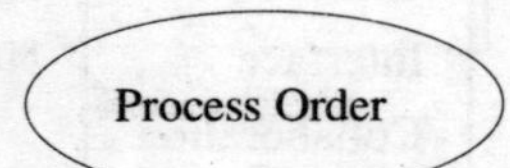
Active Class	A class whose objects own processes or threads and hence can initiate a control activity required in concurrent systems.	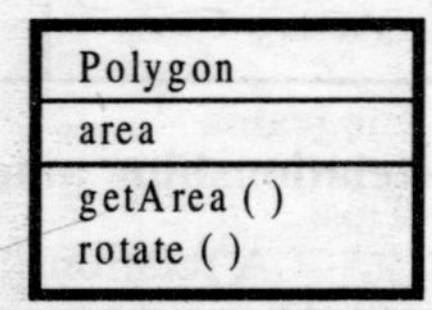
Component	A replaceable entity—packaging classes, interfaces, collaborations, and standard deployment components—which conforms to and provides the realization of a set of interfaces.	
Node	An element that exists at run time, executes components, and is a computational resource (with some memory and processing capability).	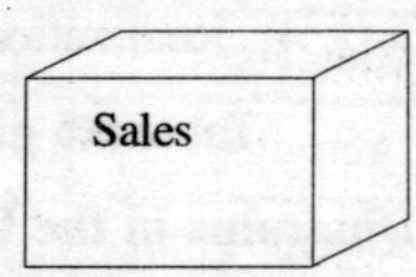
Interaction	A set of messages exchanged among a set of objects.	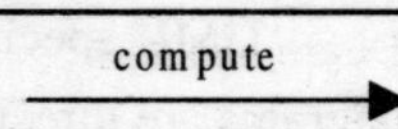
State Machine	Sequences of states an object or an interaction goes through during its lifetime in response to events.	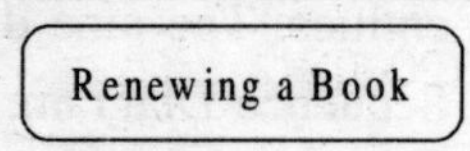
Package	A mechanism for organizing elements of structural, behavioural, and grouping entities into a set.	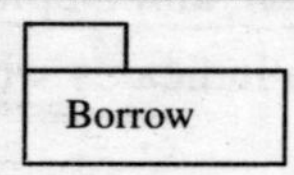
Note	Comments and constraints attached to an element or a collection of elements of a UML model.	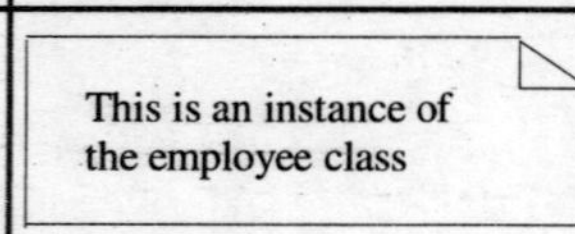

Table 8.5: Relationship Description and Their UML Symbols

Relationship	Description	UML symbol
Dependency	A semantic relationship between an independent entity and a dependent entity—a change in the former causes a semantic change in the latter.	------------>
Association	A structural relationship describing a set of links—a set of connections—among objects	1 ———— * teacher student
Generalization	A generalization/specialization relationship in which objects of a child inherit the structure and behaviour of a parent.	————▷
Realization	A semantic relationship between classifiers (*i.e.*, between interfaces and classes and between use cases and their collaborations) so that a contract specified by one is carried out by the other.	-------------▷

Table 8.6: Use of Diagrams in the Architectural Views of Software Systems

Architectural view	**Use case**		**Design**		**Process**		**Implementation**		**Deployment**	
Diagrams	Static	Dynamic	Static	Dynamic	Static	Dynamic	Static	Dynamic	Static	Dynamic
Class			x		x					
Object			x		x					
Use Case	x									
Sequence		x		x		x		x		x
Collaboration		x		x		x		x		x
Statechart		x		x		x		x		x
Activity		x		x		x		x		x
Component							x			
Deployment									x	

In the following sections we give various UML guidelines following the work of Booch, *et al.* (2000).

8.5.2 Class-Related UML Guidelines

UML guidelines on defining a class name are as follows:

— A class name may have any number of letters, numbers and punctuation marks (excepting colon) and may continue over several lines.

— Typically they are short nouns or noun phrases.

— The first letter and the first letter of every word in the name are capitalized.

— Sometimes one specifies the path name where the class name is prefixed by the package in which it lives.

UML guidelines with regard to the attributes are as follows:

— A class may have any number of attributes or no attribute at all.

— It is described as a text.

— The first letter is always a small letter whereas every other word in the attribute name starts with a capital letter.

— The type of an attribute may be specified and even a default initial value may be set:

result: Boolean = Pass

Here *Boolean* is the type of the attribute *result*, and *Pass* is the default value.

UML guidelines with regard to an operation are as under:

— It is the implementation of service that can be requested from any object of the class to affect behaviour.

— A class may have any number of operations or no operation at all.

— Operation name is normally a short verb or verb phrase.

— The first letter of every word is capitalized except the first letter.

— One can specify the signature of an operation by specifying its name, type, and default values of all parameters, and a return type (in case of functions).

— Sometimes operations may be grouped and are indicated by headers.

UML guidelines with regard to responsibilities are as under:

— They should be distributed as evenly as possible among the classes with each class having at least one responsibility and not many.

— Tiny classes with trivial responsibilities may be collapsed into larger ones while a large class with too many responsibilities may be broken down into many classes.

8.5.3 Class-Related Symbolic Notations

Class

The normal symbol used for a class is given in Fig. 8.13. Here the topmost compartment defines the name of the class, the second compartment defines the attributes, the third compartment defines the operations, and the fourth compartment defines the responsibilities.

Often, when one does not have to define the attributes, the operations, and the responsibilities, only the top portion of the symbol is retained to denote a class (Fig. 8.14). Also, as stated in the previous paragraph, very rarely one uses the fourth, bottommost compartment.

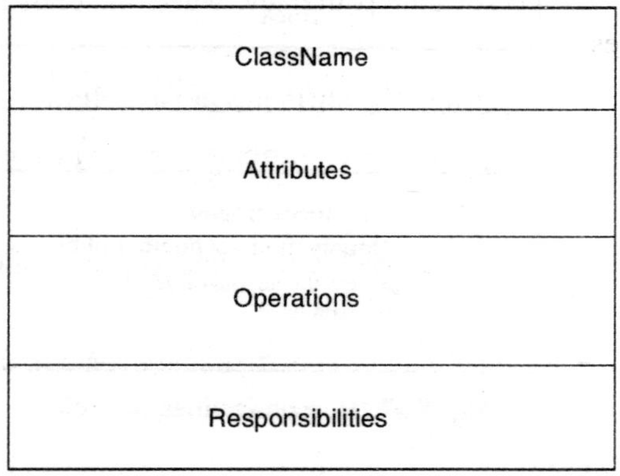

Fig. 8.13. Notation for a class

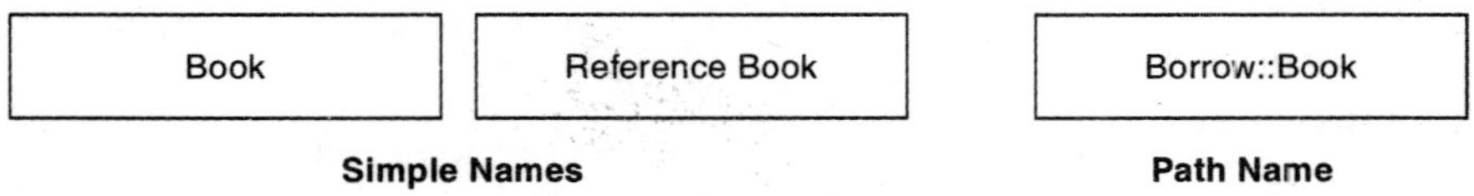

Fig. 8.14. Alternative notations for a class

The attributes occupy the second (from top) compartment (Fig. 8.15).

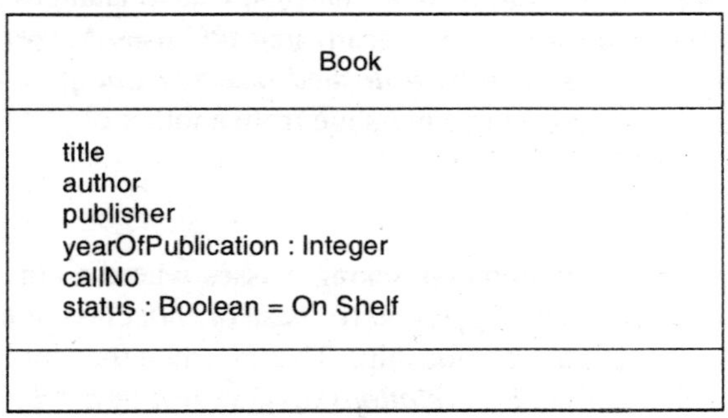

Fig. 8.15. Alternative of a class

Operations occupy the third (from top) compartment (Fig. 8.16)

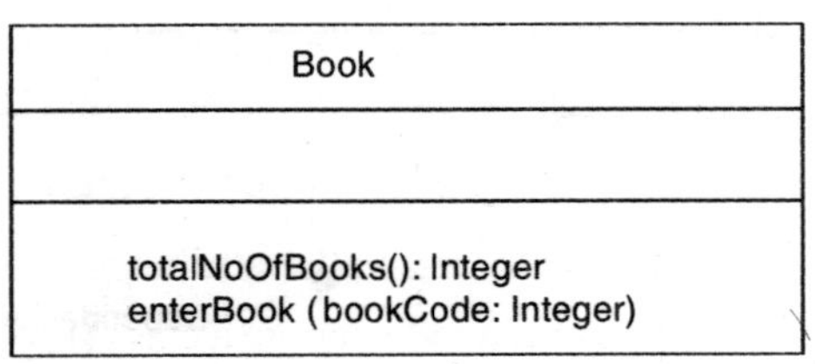

Fig. 8.16. Class operations

Responsibility occupies the fourth compartment (Fig. 8.17).

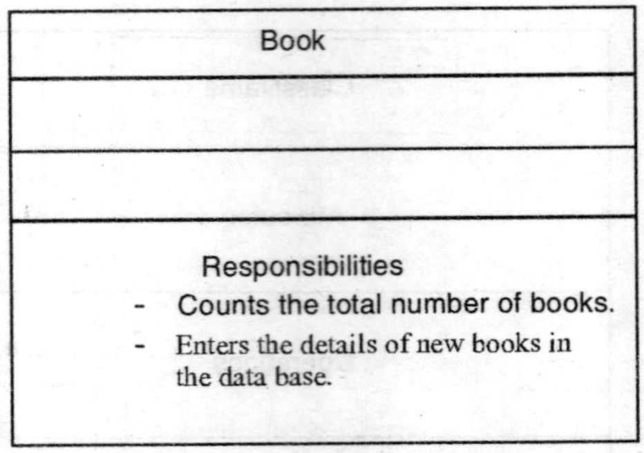

Fig. 8.17. Responsibilities of a class

Relationships among Classes

Relationship indicates a connection among classes. It can be of four types:

1. Dependency
2. Generalization
3. Association
4. Realization

Dependency

Quite often, a class C uses another class A as an argument in the signature of one of its operations. Then C is dependent on A. That is, if A changes, C also changes. It indicates a 'using' relationship. It is also a one-way relationship. That means that if C uses A, then A has no knowledge about it. *The dependency relationship is shown by a dashed directed line pointed from C to A.* Usually, the operation of C is invoked upon receiving a message from another object B. Figure 8.18 shows a collaboration diagram.

Generalization

It depicts a hierarchical relationship among classes where a *child* (or a *leaf* class or a subtype) inherits the attributes and operations of a *parent* (or *base* or *root* class or the supertype). It depicts an 'is-a' relationship. It is also a one-way relationship. That is, when the child uses the features of the parent, the parent has no knowledge of this. *This relationship is shown by a solid directed line with a large open arrowhead pointed to the parent* (Fig. 8.19). Figure 8.19 shows a *Generalization-Specialization* (*Gen-Spec*) diagram or an '*is-a*' diagram.

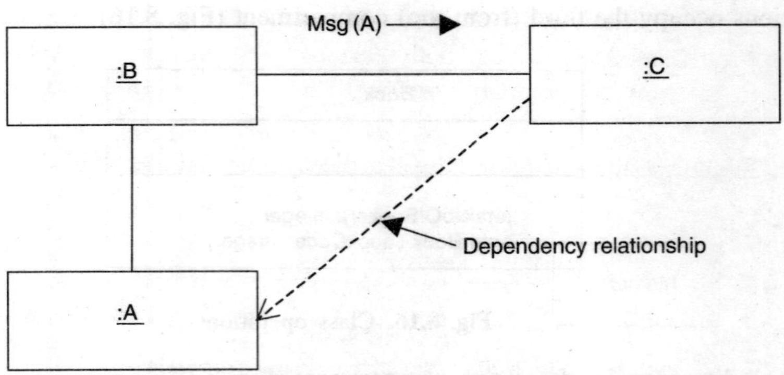

Fig. 8.18. Dependency relationship among C and A

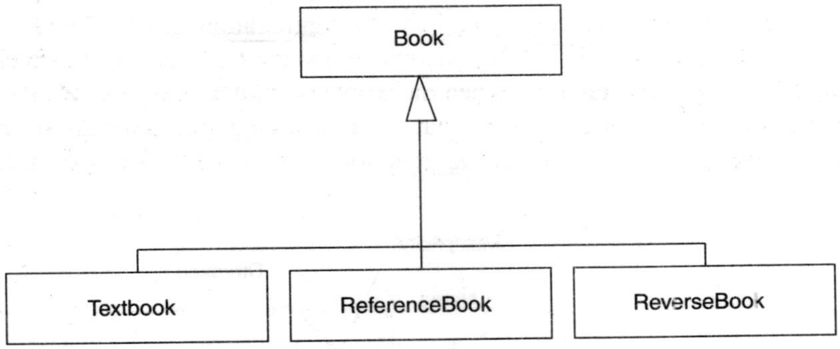

Fig. 8.19. Generalization relationship

The child can inherit all the attributes and operations defined in the parent class; it can additionally have its own set of attributes and operations.

In a Gen-Spec diagram every subtype is always a supertype. But the reverse may not be always true. For example, an instance of a book may not always be either or textbook or a reference book or a reserve book; because there may be another book type such as *Book Received on Donation*. If, however, an instance of a supertype is always an instance of one of its subtypes, then it is unnecessary to have an instance of the supertype. It means this supertype is an *abstract type* having no instance of its own.

Association

It is a structural relationship between peers, such as classes that are conceptually at the same level, no one more important than the other. These relationships are shown among objects of the classes. Thus one can navigate from an object of one class to an object of another class or to another object of the same class. If there is an association between A and B, then one can navigate in either direction.

An association can have four adornments:

— Name

— Role

— Multiplicity

— Aggregation

Name of an association is optional. Often one puts a direction to make the meaning clear. *Role* indicates one end of the association. Thus both the ends will have one role each. *Multiplicity* indicates the one-to-one, one-to-many, or the many-to-many relationships. *Aggregation* indicates a 'has-a' relationship.

Figure 8.20 shows an association between the mother and the child. Figure 8.21 explains the adornments.

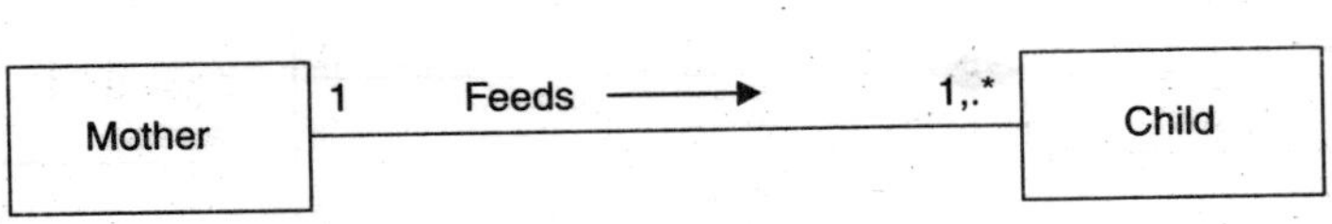

Fig. 8.20. Association between two classes

Aggregation shows a whole-part or a '*has-a*' relationship which is shown by an association adorned with a diamond appearing at the whole end. An aggregation can be simple (or shared) or composite. In a *simple aggregation* (Fig. 8.22a), the whole and the parts can be separately created and destroyed while in a *composite aggregation*, when the whole is created or destroyed, the part is simultaneously created or destroyed (Fig. 8.22b). Note that a shared aggregation is a many-to-many relationship with an open diamond, while the composite aggregation is a lifetime (one-to-one) relationship with a filled diamond.

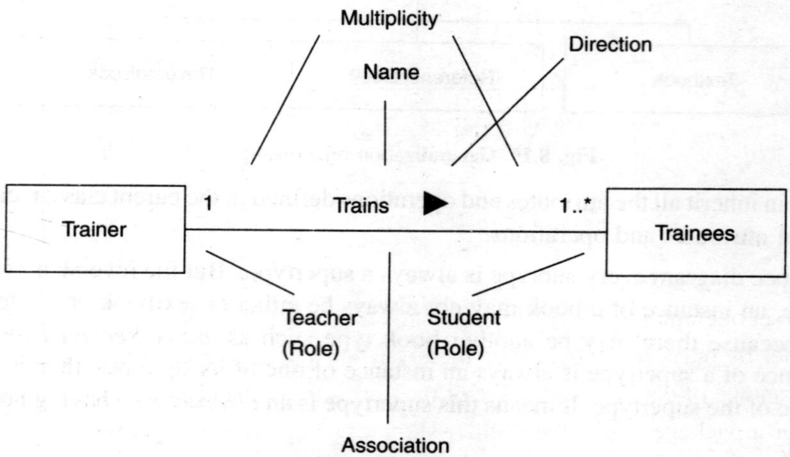

Fig. 8.21. Adornments of an association

We skip the discussion on "Realization" – the fourth type of relationship among classes.

Mechanisms

UML allows the use of certain mechanisms to build the system. We shall present two of these mechanisms: (1) Notes and (2) Constraints. Notes are graphical symbols (Fig. 8.23) giving more information, in the form of comments or even graphs on requirements, reviews, link to or embed other documents, constraints, or even live URL. They are attached to the relevant elements using dependencies.

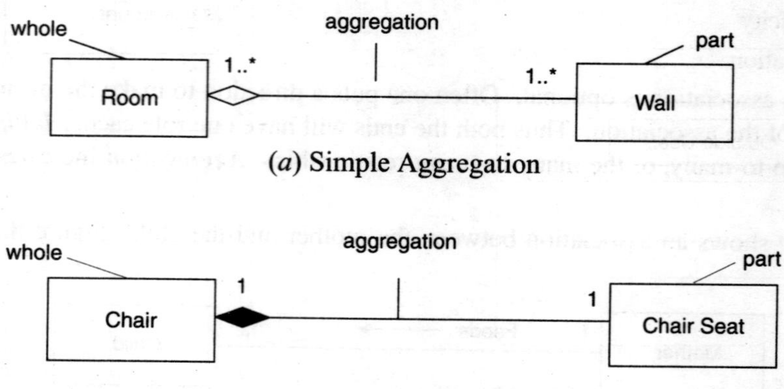

(*a*) Simple Aggregation

(*b*) Composite Aggregation

Fig. 8.22. Aggregation

Constraints allow new rules or modify existing ones. They specify conditions that must be held true for the model to be well-formed. They are rendered as a string enclosed by brackets ({ }) and are placed near the associated elements (Fig. 8.24).

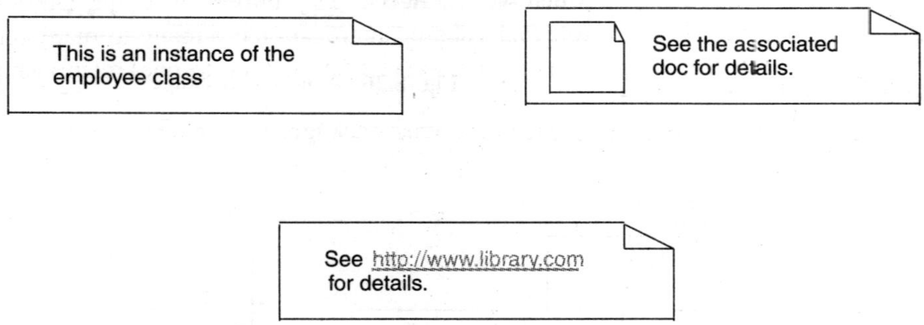

Fig. 8.23. Notes

Packages

A *package* is a set of elements that together provide highly related services. The elements should be closely related either by purpose, or by a type hierarchy, or in a use case, or in a conceptual model. Thus there can be a package of classes, a package of use cases, or a package of collaboration diagrams. The UML notation for a package is a tabbed folder shown in Fig. 8.25. Packages can be nested (Fig. 8.26). Note that if the package is shown without its internal composition, then the label for the package is shown in the middle of the lower rectangle. If, on the other hand, the internal details of the package are shown, then the label for the package is shown in the upper rectangle.

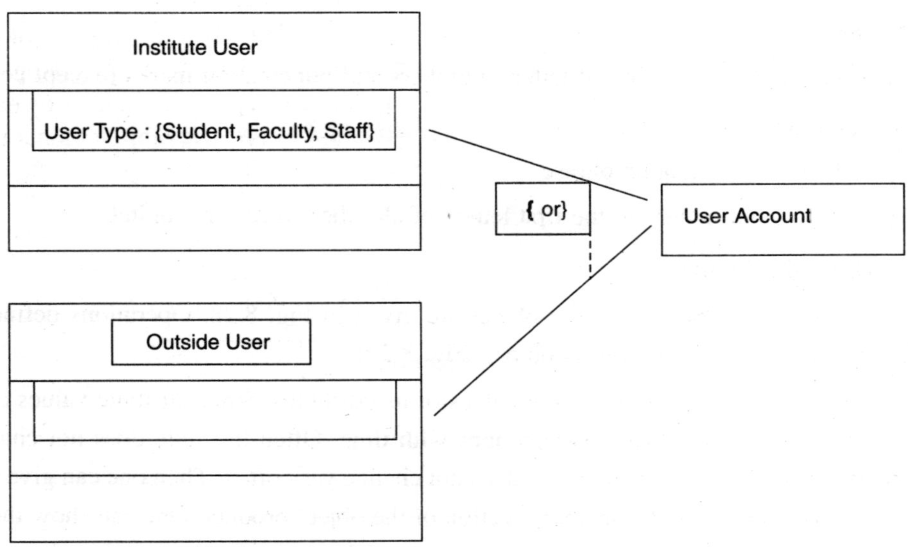

Fig. 8.24. Constraints

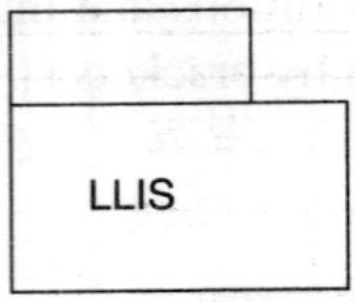

Fig. 8.25. A package

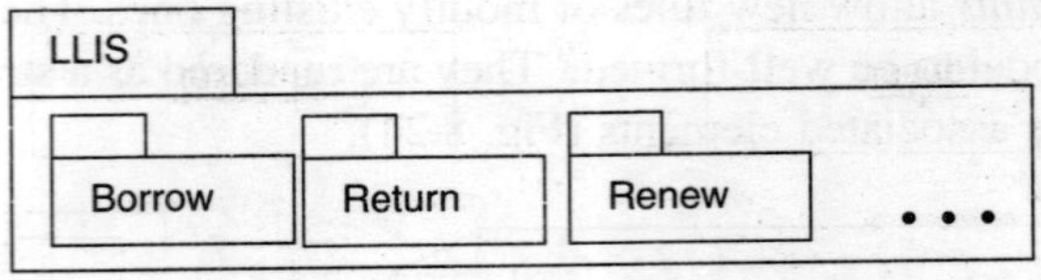

Fig. 8.26. A nested package

An element in a package can be referenced by other packages (Fig. 8.27)

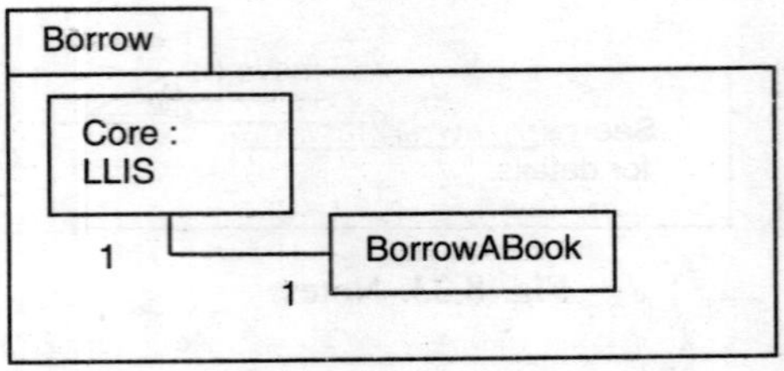

Fig. 8.27. A package referencing another package

Since the internal constituent elements of a package serve highly related services, they are highly coupled; but the package, as a whole, is a highly cohesive unit.

8.5.4 Object-related Guidelines

The terms objects and instances are used synonymously. An instance of a class is an object. Not all instances are objects, however. For example, an instance of an association is not an object; it is just an instance, also called a *link*.

The Object Name

- It is a textual string consisting of letters, numbers and punctuation marks (except colon).
- It may continue over several lines.
- It is usually a noun or a noun phrase.
- It starts with a small letter but the first letters of all other words are capital.

Symbolic Notations of an Object

Alternative symbolic notations of an object are given in Fig. 8.28. Operations defined in the abstraction (class) can be performed on its object (Fig. 8.29).

An object has a *state*, depending on the values of its attributes. Since attribute values change as time progresses, the state of an object also changes with time. Often the state does not change very frequently. For example, the price of a product does not change very often. Then one can give the value of the product price (Fig. 8.30) in the attribute section of the object product. One can show the state of the object, particularly for event-driven systems or when modeling the lifetime of a class, by associating a state machine with a class. Here the state of the object at a particular time can also be shown (Fig. 8.31).

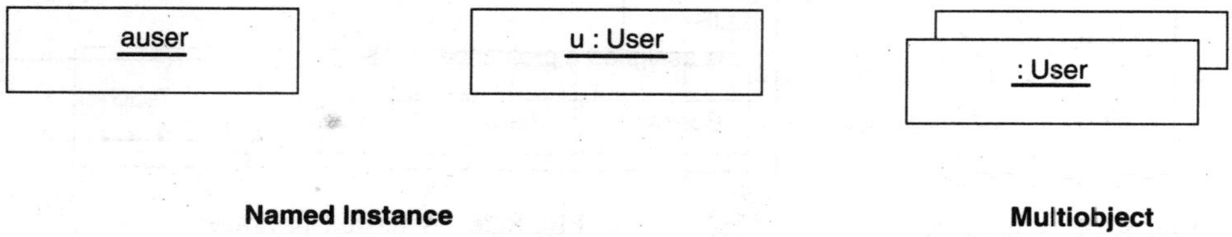

Fig. 8.28. Alternative symbolic notations of an object

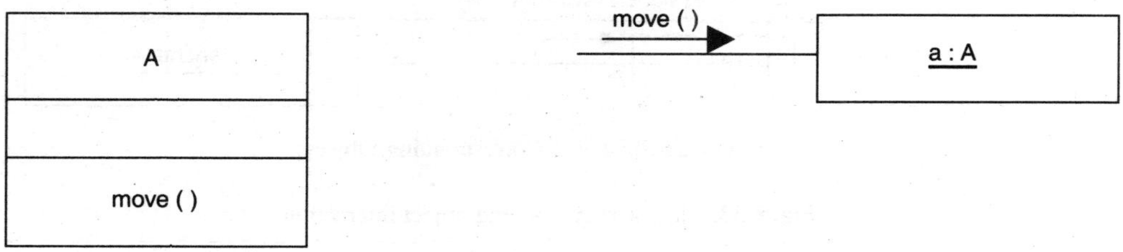

Fig. 8.29. An operation

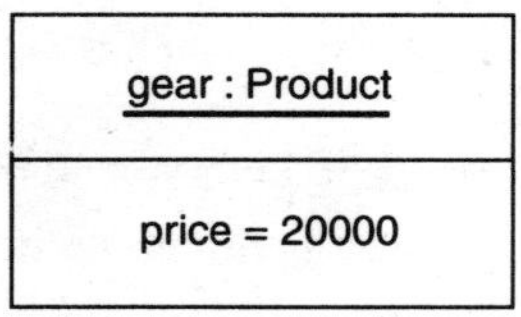

Fig. 8.30. Object state with defined attribute values

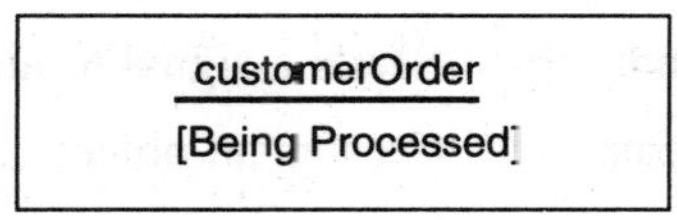

Fig. 8.31. Object state with a state machine

Object Interactions

Whenever a class has an association with another class, a link exists between their instances. Whenever there is a link, an object can send a message to the other. Thus, objects are connected by links and a link is an instance of association. An interaction is a behaviour that comprises a set of messages exchanged among a set of objects within a context to accomplish a purpose.

A link between two objects is rendered as a line joining the two objects. Figure 8.32 shows an association between two classes *Student* and *Teacher* (Fig. 8.32*a*) and the links between their corresponding instances (Fig. 8.32*b*).

The sending object sends a message to a receiving object. The receipt of the message is an event. It results in an action (executable statement is invoked). The action changes the state of the object.

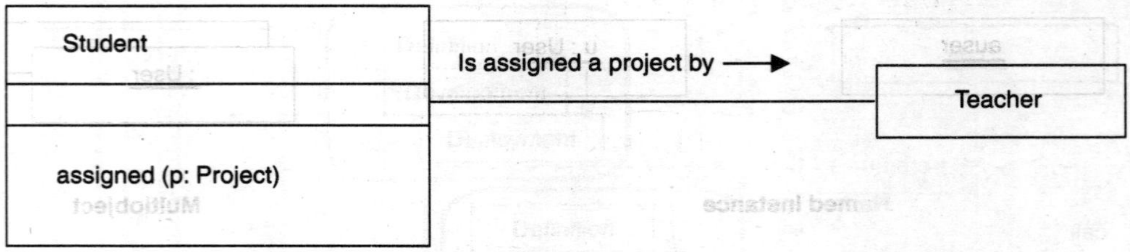

(*a*) Association between Classes

(*b*) Interaction between Corresponding Objects

Fig. 8.32. Class association and object interaction

Actions can be of various types:

Call:	Invokes operation on another object or on itself.
Return:	Returns value to the caller.
Send:	Sends a signal to another object (notify).
Create:	Creates an object.
Destroy:	Destroys an object (Commits suicide).

Interactions are represented by either sequence diagrams or collaboration diagrams. *Sequence diagrams* emphasize: (1) time ordering of messages and (2) modeling the lifeline of an object from creation to destruction. *Collaboration diagrams* emphasize structural organization of objects that send and receive messages.

Figure 8.33 shows a sequence diagram of an example for calculating the total price of a product where all the action types (messages) are used. Figure 8.34 shows an equivalent collaboration diagram of depicting the passage of messages. Notice that in this diagram the actions *create* and *destroy* are not shown because they are considered trivial.

The sequence of the streams of messages can be specified by using numbers 1, 2, 3, …, and so on. Often a particular message, say message 2, to be fully executed, requires other messages. Such nesting of messages can be specified by numbers like 2.1, 2.2, and so on. Notice that Fig. 8.34 specifies the implementation sequence of all the messages.

A message specified as

2.1 : unitPrice := getUnitPrice (productCode)

indicates that this message is the first message nested in the second message.

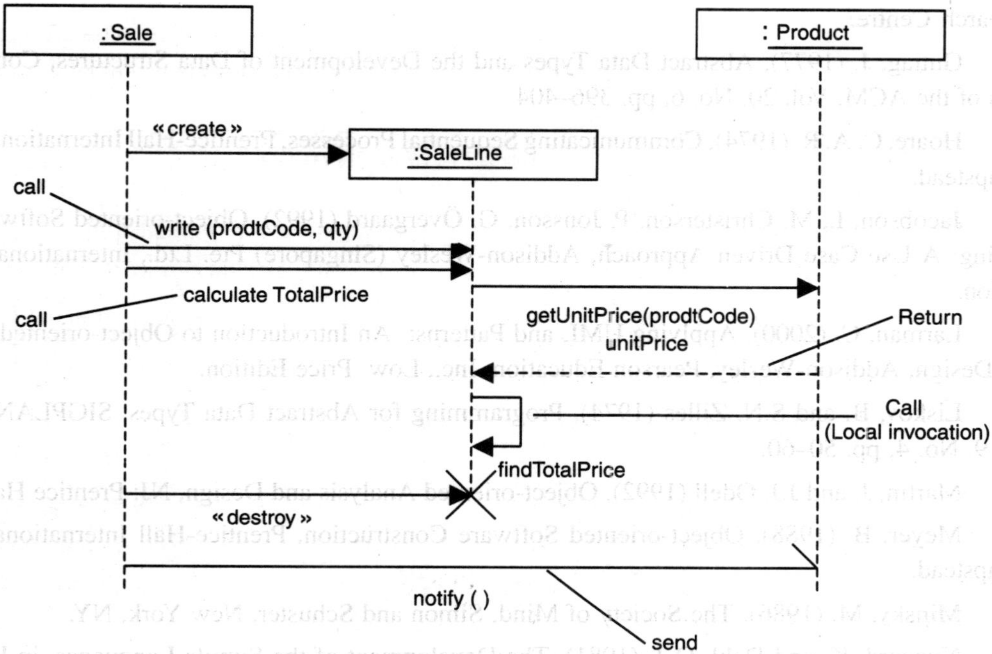

Fig. 8.33. Messages in a sequence diagram

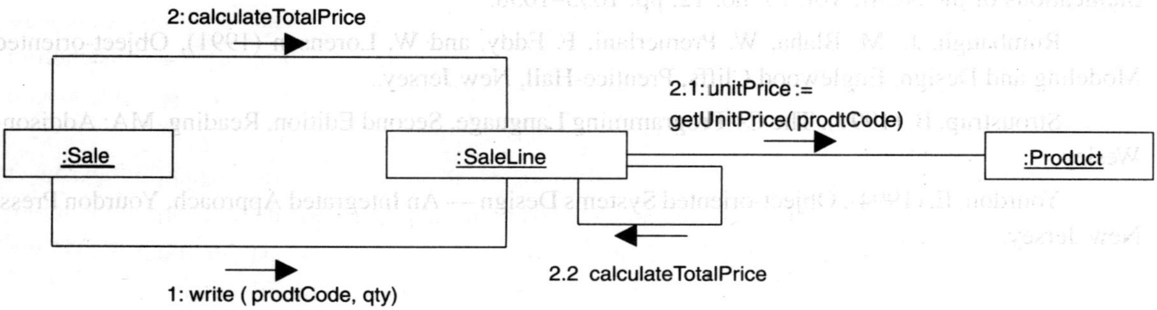

Fig. 8.34. Message in a collaboration diagram

REFERENCES

Booch, G. (1994), Object-oriented Analysis and Design with Applications, Addison-Wesley, Reading, Mass, 2nd Edition.

Booch, G. J. Rumbaugh, and I. Jacobson (2000), The Unified Modeling Language User detail Guide, Addison-Wesley Longman (Singapore) Pte. Ltd., Low Price Edition.

Dijkstra, E.W. (1968), The Structure of the Multiprogramming System, Communications of the ACM, Vol. 11, No. 5, pp. 341–346.

Goldberg, A. and A. Kay (1976), Smalltalk 72 Instruction Manual, Pal Alto, CA: Xerox Palo Alto Research Centre.

Guttag, J. (1977), Abstract Data Types and the Development of Data Structures, Communications of the ACM, Vol. 20, No. 6, pp. 396–404.

Hoare, C. A. R. (1974), Communicating Sequential Processes, Prentice-Hall International, Hemel Hempstead.

Jacobson, I., M. Christerson, P. Jonsson, G. Övergaard (1992), Object-oriented Software Engineering: A Use Case Driven Approach, Addison-Wesley (Singapore) Pte. Ltd., International Student Edition.

Larman, C. (2000), Applying UML and Patterns: An Introduction to Object-oriented Analysis and Design, Addison-Wesley, Pearson Education, Inc., Low Price Edition.

Liskov, B. and S.N. Zilles (1974), Programming for Abstract Data Types, SIGPLAN Notices, Vol. 9, No. 4, pp. 50–60.

Martin, J. and J.J. Odell (1992), Object-oriented Analysis and Design, NJ: Prentice Hall.

Meyer, B. (1988), Object-oriented Software Construction, Prentice-Hall International, Hemel Hempstead.

Minsky, M. (1986), The Society of Mind, Simon and Schuster, New York, NY.

Nygaard, K. and Dahl, O-J. (1981), The Development of the Simula Languages, in History of Programming Languages, Computer Society Press, New York, NY.

Parnas, D.L. (1972), On the Criteria to be Used in Decomposing Systems into Modules, Communications of the ACM, Vol. 15, no. 12, pp. 1053–1058.

Rumbaugh, J., M. Blaha, W. Premerlani, F. Eddy, and W. Lorensen (1991), Object-oriented Modeling and Design, Englewood Cliffs, Prentice-Hall, New Jersey.

Stroustrup, B. (1991), The C+ Programming Language, Second Edition, Reading, MA: Addison-Wesley.

Yourdon, E. (1994), Object-oriented Systems Design — An Integrated Approach, Yourdon Press, New Jersey.

9 Object-Oriented Analysis

9.1 STEPS IN OBJECT-ORIENTED ANALYSIS

Object-oriented analysis is a method of analysis that examines requirements from the perspective of the classes and objects found in the vocabulary of the problem domain (Booch 1994). Here the emphasis is on finding and describing the objects (or concepts) in the problem domain (Larman 2000). Input-process-output view, process-orientation, top-down decomposition, and end-to-end processing sequence, which form the principal features of structured analysis are conspicuously absent in object-oriented analysis (Pressman 1997).

Various approaches to object oriented analysis have been proposed in the literature (*e.g.*, Booch 1994, Coad and Yourdon 1991, Jacobson, *et al.* 1992, and Rumbaugh, *et al.* 1991, Pressman 1997, Larman 2000). The Coad and Yourdon method is the simplest and the most straightforward. It demands defining classes and objects, class hierarchies, and attributes and services (operations) as part of the object-oriented analysis. The Rambaugh method is the most elaborate. In addition to defining the classes, the class hierarchies, and their properties (the object model), it also demands defining the dynamic aspects of objects (the object behaviour—the dynamic model) and modeling it with the high-level DFD-like representation flow (the functional model). Jacobson introduced the concept of "*use case*" that has now become very popular as a necessary tool for object-oriented analysis. Pressman synthesizes the concepts of object-oriented analysis by suggesting various generic steps. Larman suggests various steps and illustrates them with an example.

We follow Pressman and Larman in suggesting the steps for object-oriented analysis. The steps (and sub-steps) of carrying out object-oriented analysis are mentioned in Table 9.1. Table 9.1 also gives the dominant tools used for each step.

Table 9.1: Steps and Tools in Object-Oriented Analysis

Sl. No.	Major steps/Substeps of OOA	Useful tools/Approaches for the step
1	Get user requirements.	Use Case — the narrative description of domain processes
2	Build the structure of an object model: Identify objects. Identify relationships between objects. Identify attributes.	 CRC method and diverse perspectives Static structure diagram (Class and Object diagrams) Various judgment-based guidelines
3.	Model system behaviour — I: Identify system events & system operations. Write contracts for each operation.	Various judgment-based guidelines System sequence diagrams. Examine pre- and post-condition state changes.
4.	Review and change if necessary: Add new functionality. Relate use cases. Extend the object model.	 Revisit use cases Use *includes* relationships. Develop the real use cases
5.	Find generalized class relationships	Gen-Spec diagram
6.	Find associations between classes	Whole-Part and other associations
7.	Organize the object model into packages	Package diagram
8.	Model system behaviour — II: Model state changes. Depict workflows.	 Statechart diagram Activity diagram

9.2 USE CASE — THE TOOL TO GET USER REQUIREMENTS

First introduced by Jacobson, *et al.* (1992), *use cases* have gained popularity as an analysis tool among not only those who use object-oriented approach for system development but also those who do not adopt this approach. A use case is a narrative description of the domain process. It describes a story or a case of how an external entity (actor) initiates events and how the system responds to them. Thus it specifies the interactions between an actor and the system, describing the sequence of transactions they undertake to achieve system functionality. Together, all the use cases specify all the existing ways of using the system. We define below the key terms.

An *actor* resides outside the system boundary and interacts with the system in either providing input events to which the system responds or receiving certain system responses. An actor may be the end user — a *primary actor* — of the system, or he may only be participating in the functioning of the system — a *secondary actor*. Thus a Customer is a primary actor for Sales Accounting system, whereas a Sales Person, an Accountant, the Materials Management system, or the Production Planning System is a secondary (or participating) actor. Not only human beings, but also electro-mechanical devices such as electrical, mechanical, and computer systems qualify as actors.

A *process* describes, form start to finish, a sequence of events, actions, and transactions required to produce or complete something of value to an organization or actor (Larman, 2000).

As described above, use cases describe business processes and requirements thereof in a textual descriptive form. They are stories or *cases* of *using* a system. A use case is a document that describes the sequence of events of an actor (an external agent) using a software-hardware system to complete a process.

It is a normal practice to start the name of a use case with a transitive verb followed by an object (*e.g.*, Pay Cash, Update Database, and Prepare Summary Report), like process naming pattern in the top-level data flow diagram.

Use cases are usually of black-box type, meaning that they describe what the software system is expected to do (i.e., what responsibilities the system is expected to discharge) rather than how it does it.

A particular sequence (or path) of events and responses indicates a use case instance (or a scenario). If it meets the user goal, it is a success scenario (or main flow). Thus, for example, successfully issuing General Books is a success scenario of a Borrow Books use case. There can be many alternative scenarios. For example, issuing Reserved Books, which has restrictions and requires specific permission from the Librarian, could be an alternative scenario (alternative flow).

Use cases can be identified in two ways: (1) actor-based and (2) event-based. The sequence of activities to identify the use cases are as under:

1. Actor-based use cases
   (*a*) Identify the actors.
   (*b*) Trace the processes each actor initiates or participates in.
2. Event-based use cases
   (*a*) Identify the external events that the system must respond to.
   (*b*) Trace the actors and processes that are relevant to these events.

Use cases can be classified in different ways:

1. On the basis of degree of details shown
   (*a*) High level (Brief or Casual)
   (*b*) Expanded level (Fully dressed)
2. On the basis of importance of the process it represents
   (*a*) Primary
   (*b*) Secondary
   (*c*) Optional
3. On the basis of degree of or implementation details shown
   (*a*) Essential (or Abstract)
   (*b*) Real (Concrete)

A *high-level use case* is a brief narrative statement of the process, usually in two or three sentences, to quickly understand the degree of complexity of the process requirements at the initial requirements and scoping phase. It can be either a *brief use case* or a *casual use case*. A brief use case could be just a one-paragraph write-up on the main responsibility or the main success scenario of the system. A casual use case informally covers the main and the alternative scenarios in separate paragraphs. An *expanded use case* or *fully dressed case* provides typical course of events that describes, in a sequential form, the actor actions and the system responses for the main flow. The alternative flows are written separetely with conditions stated in the main flow to branch off to the alternative flows.

Various formats for the fully dressed use cases, including the one-column format, are available but the one available at *www.usecases.org* is very popular. This format is given as under:

Use case

Primary Actor: ... Stakeholders and Interests: ... Preconditions: ... Postconditions: ... Main Success Scenario (Basic Flow) ... Extensions (Alternative Flows) ... Special Requirements ... Technology & Data Variation List ... Frequency of Occurrence ... Open Issues ...

Primary use cases describe major processes, important for successful running of the organization, such as Buy Items, Update Stock, and Make Payment. *Secondary use cases* represent minor processes that help achieving better quality of service that the organization renders, such as Prepare Stock Status Report. *Optional use cases* represent processes, such as Start, Log in, and Exit, that may not be considered at all.

Essential use cases are built on abstract design, without committing to any specific technology or implementation details. *Real use cases* are built on real design with commitments to specific technologies and implementation details. When user interface is involved, they often show screen layouts and describe interaction with the widgets.

9.2.1 Development of Use Cases

Development of use cases follows a top-down approach. To start with, one follows a highly aggregative view of the system where a use-case diagram showing only the actors and the major system functions are spelt out (almost like a top-level data flow diagram), but soon one resorts to writing the details of the various activities that are done in order to respond to the actor-initiated event.

Use case development requires the following steps:

1. Define the system boundary and identify actors and use cases.
2. Draw a use case diagram.
3. Write all use cases in high-level format.
4. Write only the most critical use cases in expanded format in the analysis phase, so as to judge the complexity of the task.
5. Illustrate relationships among multiple use cases in the use case diagram with "*includes*" associations.
6. Write real use cases if it is a design phase of the development. Write them also in the analysis phase if the clients demand for it or if concrete descriptions are considered necessary to fully comprehend the system.

Larman (2000) suggests that the task of defining use cases can be made easy by first identifying the user goals (*i.e.*, the goals of the primary actor), and then defining a use case for each goal. A requirements workshop brings out the goals specific to each user type. It is therefore easy to visualize and construct a hierarchy of goals. For example, to borrow a book is a high-level goal, whereas to authenticate a user is a low-level goal. The high-level goals are candidates for defining the use cases.

9.2.2 Use Case Diagrams

A use case diagram for a system shows, in a pictorial form using UML notations, the use cases, the actors, and their relations. The boundary that separates the system from its environment is shown by a rectangle that shows the use cases inside its boundary and actors outside it. Straight lines are drawn between a use case and the actors that take part in the use case. An actor can initiate more than one use case in the system.

The UML notations used in a use case diagram are shown in Fig. 9.1. Notice in Fig. 9.2 the use of a rectangle with a stereotype «non-human actor» to indicate an alternative form of representing a non-human actor.

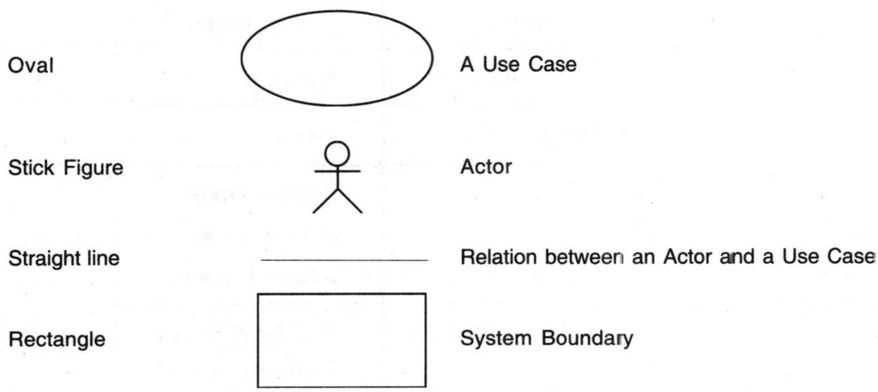

Fig. 9.1. Use case notations

9.2.3 Writing a Use Case

Certain guidelines used in describing use cases are given below:

- While writing an expanded use case, it should start with an Actor action to be written in the following format:

  This use case begins when <Actor> <initiates an event>.

- Often, in an expanded use case, it may be necessary to branch out to Alternative Sections to depict decision points or alternatives.

9.2.4 Example of a Library Lending Information System (LLIS)

A library lending information system is a simple example to record books issued to and returned by the users. It is used at the gate of a library. It includes a computer, a bar code scanner, and software to run the system. We shall focus on the issues relevant to software development.

Step 1: Define System Boundary and Identify Actors and Use Cases

For the library lending information system, the system boundary will include the computer, the bar code scanner, and the software. A first list of actors and the use cases is given in Table 9.2.

Step 2: Draw a Use Case Diagram

We use the use case notations used in Fig. 9.1 to draw the use case diagram (Fig. 9.2) for the library lending information system.

Step 3: Write All Use Cases in High-level Format

A sample high-level use case is given below:

Use Case: Borrow Books.
Actors: User, Library Assistant
Type: Primary
Description: A User arrives at the lending counter with books to borrow. The Library Assistant records the books in the User's name. The User leaves the counter with the books and gate pass.

Table 9.2: Actors and Use Cases in LLIS

Actors	Use cases
System Manager	Start Up
Library Assistant	Log in
User	Borrow Books Return Books Renew Books
Assistant Librarian	Add New Users Terminate Users

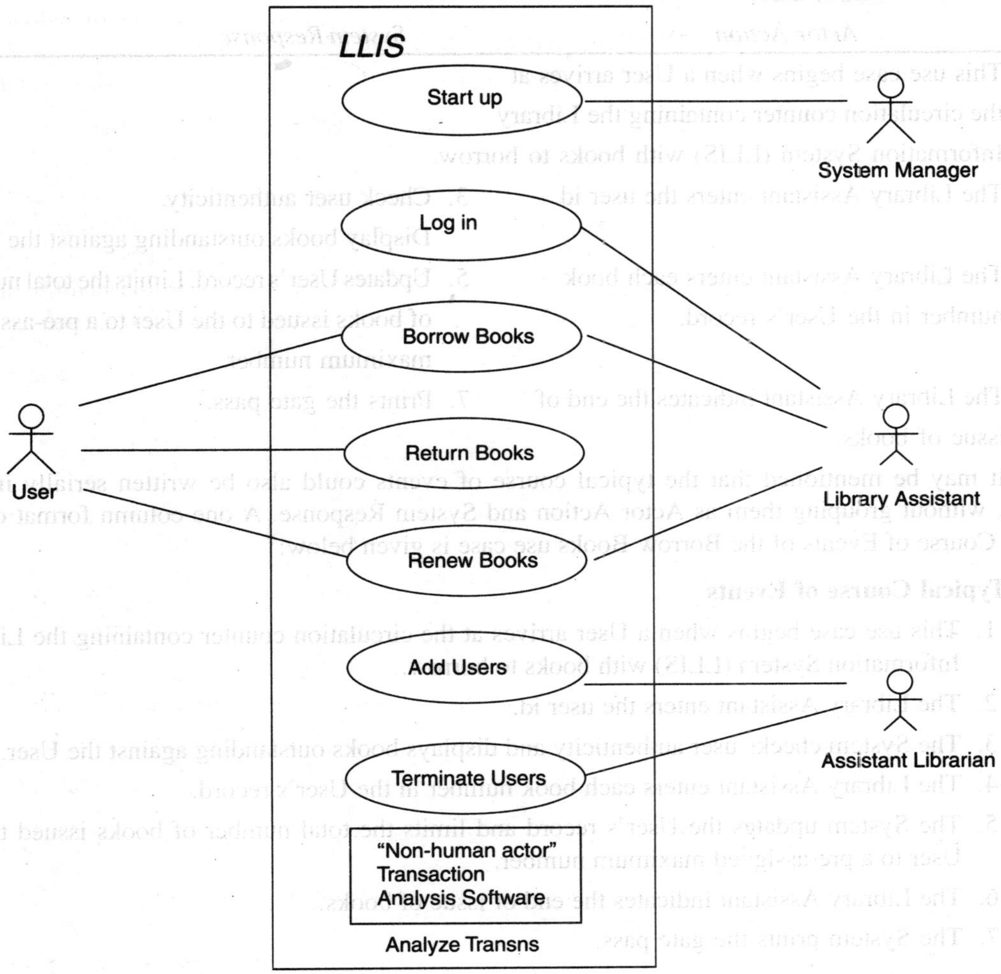

Fig. 9.2. Use case diagram for the library lending information system

Step 4: Write the Most Critical Use Cases in Expanded Format

A sample expanded use case is given below:

Use Case:	Borrow Books
Section:	Main
Actors:	User (initiator), Library Assistant
Purpose:	Record books borrowed by a User.
Overview:	Same as 'Descriptions' in the high-level format.
Type:	Primary and essential.
Cross References:	The Library Assistant must have completed the 'log in' use case.

Typical Course of Events

Actor Action	*System Response*
1. This use case begins when a User arrives at the circulation counter containing the Library Information System (LLIS) with books to borrow.	
2. The Library Assistant enters the user id.	3. Check user authenticity. Display books outstanding against the User.
4. The Library Assistant enters each book number in the User's record.	5. Updates User's record. Limits the total number of books issued to the User to a pre-assigned maximum number.
6. The Library Assistant indicates the end of issue of books.	7. Prints the gate pass.

It may be mentioned that the typical course of events could also be written serially in one column, without grouping them as Actor Action and System Response. A one-column format of the Typical Course of Events of the Borrow Books use case is given below:

Typical Course of Events

1. This use case begins when a User arrives at the circulation counter containing the Library Information System (LLIS) with books to borrow.
2. The Library Assistant enters the user id.
3. The System checks user authenticity and displays books outstanding against the User.
4. The Library Assistant enters each book number in the User's record.
5. The System updates the User's record and limits the total number of books issued to the User to a pre-assigned maximum number.
6. The Library Assistant indicates the end of issue of books.
7. The System prints the gate pass.

Before ending this section, we wish to mention the following:

- Unlike the waterfall model, it is not necessary to identify all use cases at the start of software development. Since object-oriented development should ideally follow the iterative unified process model discussed in Chapter 2, requirements are captured in an incremental manner through the development of use cases. Thus, at the beginning, only the most basic use cases are developed; the other use cases are developed at the end of various elaboration iterations. The process of requirement capture is similar here to that in the agile development process.
- Adopted as an inception phase artifact of the Rational Unified Process approach to software development, use cases can be used to extract requirements whether or not an object-oriented solution approach is followed. However, whereas the followers of object-oriented and agile philosophy are always the first to adopt it, others are slow to adopt it as a requirements phase artifact.
- Use cases are alternatively called "user stories". Agile development, for example, rarely uses the term "use cases", but always refers to "user stories".

9.3 IDENTIFY OBJECTS

9.3.1 Object Identification Perspectives

Identifying objects is one of the first steps in object-oriented analysis of systems. Various perspectives can be taken to identify objects:

A. The Data Perspective

B. The Functional Perspective

C. The Behavioural Perspective

D. The Scenario Perspective

The Data Perspective

This perspective takes a view similar to finding entities in data-modeling methodologies. One looks for *nouns* or *noun clauses* in a textual description (processing narrative) of the problem. It is similar to looking around oneself and seeing the physical objects. The difference, however, is that in a problem space, objects are difficult to comprehend.

A *Common Noun* is often a class of objects, such as 'Person'. A *Proper Noun* can be an instance of a class, such as 'Gopal'. An *Abstract Noun* is the name an activity, a quantity, or a measure, such as 'Crowd', which is a collection of proper nouns within the class implied as the common noun 'Person'.

The objects in the problem space that appear as nouns or noun clauses can take the following forms:

- *External entities* (*terminators*). They produce or consume information. Examples are *people*, *devices* and *systems* that are outside the boundary of the system under consideration.
- *Physical devices* (*or things*). They are part of the information domain of the problem. Examples are *reports, documents, signals,* and *displays*.
- *Events to be recorded and remembered.* They occur in the context of the system operations. Examples are: *arrival of an order, occurrence of stock-out, and shipment of backlogged order.*
- *Roles played by people.* People interact with the system taking the roles of *supplier, customer, manager, salesperson, engineer,* and *accountant*, etc.
- *Physical and geographical locations*. Examples are: *shop floor, shipyard, stores,* and *foundry.*
- *Organizational units*, such as *division, team, committee,* and *group*.
- *Structures*. They define a class of objects or related classes of objects. Examples are: *computer, car,* and *crane*. Strictly speaking, *structures* are aggregates or composites.

The Functional Perspective

This perspective emphasizes on 'what an object does'. A person is not "height-weight-name-age, etc.", but what he/she does. A method to identify an object is to write answers to three questions on a CRC (Class-Responsibility-Communication) card. The three questions are:

1. What class does it belong to?
2. What responsibility does it have?

3. How does it communicate with other objects?

More about CRC cards is discussed in the next section.

The Behavioural Perspective

This perspective emphasizes the operational aspect of the object. The analyst tries to understand the overall behaviour of the system. Then he/she assigns the various behaviours to different parts of the system and tries to understand who initiates and participates in these behaviours. Participants who play significant roles are recognized as objects. Answers are sought to the following questions:

How do objects communicate?

With whom?

How do they respond to messages, signals, interrupts, or other forms of communication?

The Scenario Perspective

Jacobsen, *et al.* (1992) suggest identifying and analyzing various scenarios of system use (the use-case method). As each scenario is analyzed, the team responsible for analysis identifies the required objects and their attributes and operations.

We next discuss the CRC model — the dominant tool for object identification.

9.3.2 The Class-Responsibility-Collaboration (CRC) Modelling

Developed by Beck and Cunningham (1989), a CRC model provides a novel way of defining a class, its function, the attributes and the operations required to carry out the function, and the other classes whose assistance it needs to carry out the function. The model is operationalized by having a number of *class index cards*. Usually, each card has three separate zones, the top zone for 'Class Name', the left hand side of the bottom zone for 'Responsibilities', and the right hand side of the bottom zone for 'Collaborators' (Fig. 9.3). On each card one writes down a specific class name and its associated features — the responsibilities and the collaborators.

A responsibility includes a function that the class performs, the attributes required to perform the function, and the operation that carries out that function. In case the class is unable to perform the responsibility with the help of attributes and operations defined on itself, it collaborates with other classes to perform the responsibility.

Class Name	
Responsibility	Collaborators
…	…

Fig. 9.3. A CRC class index card

Normally, the team developing the model brainstorms and writes down a list of potential classes. The class names are written down on the class index cards — one for each class. A team member picks up a card bearing the name of a class and writes down the responsibilities of the class on the left hand side of the bottom zone of the card. He then considers each responsibility separately and makes a judgment as to whether the class can discharge this responsibility on its own. In case he thinks that the class cannot discharge this responsibility without collaborating with other classes, he writes down, along-side the responsibility, the names of the collaborating classes on the card on the right hand side of the bottom zone of the card. The team members thus write down the name, responsibilities, and collaborating classes for each class.

After a CRC model is developed it is a usual practice for the system analysis team to walk-through the model (often with the direct participation of the customer):

1. Cards describing collaborating classes are distributed among different persons.
2. The leader of the walk-through reads out each use case narrative.
3. While reading whenever he comes across an object, the person holding the corresponding class index card reads out the responsibility and the collaborating class names.
4. Immediately thereafter, another person holding the named collaborating class index card reads out its responsibility.
5. The walk-through team then determines whether the responsibilities and the collaborations mentioned on the index card satisfy the use case requirements. If not, then the new classes are defined or responsibilities and the collaborators for the existing classes are revised.

Werfs-Brock, *et al.* (1990) suggest the following guidelines for defining the responsibilities and the collaborators:

Responsibilities:

1. Responsibilities should be as evenly distributed among the classes as possible.
2. Each responsibility (both attributes and operations) should be stated as generally as possible to enable them to reside high in the class hierarchy. Polymorphism should automatically allow the lower-level subclasses to define their specific required operations.
3. Data and operations required to manipulate the data to perform a responsibility should reside within the same class.
4. In general, the responsibility for storing and manipulating a specific data type should rest on one class only. However, when appropriate, a responsibility can be shared among related classes. For example, the responsibility 'display error message' could be shared among other classes also.

Collaborators:

Classes may have three types of relationships among them:

1. 'Has-a' or a 'Whole-Part' relationship. A class (say, *Refill*) is a part of another class (say, *Pen*).
2. 'Is-a' or a 'Gen-Spec' relationship. Here a class (say, *Chair*) may be a specific case of another class (say, *Furniture*).
3. 'Dependency' relationship. A class may depend on another class to carry out its function.

9.3.3 Criteria for Evaluating Candidate Objects

Six criteria can be set to judge the goodness of the candidate objects. They are described below:

1. *Necessary Remembrance* (*Retained Information*). Every object must have certain data that it must store and remember. Data storing is done with the help of attributes.
2. *More than one attribute*. If an object has only one attribute, perhaps it is not an object; it is an attribute of another object.
3. *Needed functionality*. The object must have some operations to perform, so that it can change the value of its attributes.
4. *Common functionality*. All the operations of the proposed class should apply to each of the instances of the class.
5. *Essential functionality*. External entities are always objects. The identified functionality should be relevant and necessary irrespective of the hardware or software technology to be used to implement the system.
6. *Common attributes*. All the attributes of the proposed class should apply to each of the instances of the class.

9.3.4 Categories of Objects

Larman (2000) has given an exhaustive list of categories of objects (Table 9.3). This table gives practical guidance to select objects of interest in any context.

Table 9.3: Object Categories & Examples

Object categories	Examples
Physical and Tangible Objects	Product
Specifications, Designs, or Description of Things	Product Specification
Places	Store, Shop, Factory
Transactions	Sale, Buy, Payment, Receipt Sales Line Item
Transaction Line Items	Sales Line Item
Roles of People	Sales Manager, Accountant
Containers of Other Things	Bin, Packet
Things in a Container	Item
Computers/Devices External to Our System	Inventory Control, Production Planning
Abstract Nouns	Theft, Loss, Failure
Organizations	Factory, Sales Department
Events	Meeting, Inauguration
Processes (often not considered as an object)	Buying A Product
Rules and Policies	Recruitment Policy, Promotion Policy
Catalogs	Product Catalog, Train Time Table
Records of Finance, Work, Contracts, Legal Matters	Ledger, Log Book, Attendance Registrar
Financial Instruments and Services	Credit, Share
Manuals/Books	User Manual, Maintenance Manual

9.4 IDENTIFY RELATIONSHIPS BETWEEN OBJECTS

Once the objects are identified, even if they are not exhaustive, one should develop the relationships among them. Recall that relationships include dependency, generalization, association, and realization. Dependency and realization are low-level constructs and should be relegated to a later stage of model development. At the initial stage, one should develop a domain model by drawing *static structure diagram* (or also known as *class diagram*) showing the middle two types of relationships among the classes. Of course, the association type of relationship is commonly used at the beginning of model development. As the model is refined, other forms of relationships are added.

At the time of developing the static structure diagram one can also define the attributes for each object. At this stage it does not matter even if it is not an exhaustive set of attributes. The attributes occupy the second compartment in the symbol for a class.

Before ending this section we wish to mention that at the initial *inception* phase of software development, the classes (objects) are *domain-level classes* (objects) which are also called *conceptual* or *domain classes*. In the design and construction phases, more classes are defined. They are *software classes* which are also called *design classes* or *implementation classes*, depending on the phase in which they are defined and used.

9.5 IDENTIFY ATTRIBUTES

Recall that attributes have the following characteristics:

- Attributes describe *data-related information* hidden inside the class and the object.
- They clarify the meaning of an object in the context of the problem space.
- An analyst can select, as attributes, those things from the processing narrative of the problem, that reasonably 'belong' to an object.
- They can be manipulated by the *operations* defined in the class and the object.
- Attributes define the *state* of an object.
- They also describe an object with non-state variables; and they are typically used as the means of implementing the object connections, in the form of pointers.

The following strategies can be followed to discover attributes:

1. Try to set an answer to the following question: What data items (composite and/or elementary) fully define this object in the context of the problem at hand?
2. Study the application, interview the users, and learn as much as possible about the true nature of each class and object.
3. Investigate each class and object from a 'first-person' perspective, *i.e.*, pretend that you are the object and try to answer questions of the following types:
   - How am I to be described?
   - What states can I be in?
   - How am I going to be affected by an operation?

Guidelines for defining attributes are as under:

- Attributes should be placed as high as possible in a class diagram, so that their definition is carried down to all subclasses below them automatically.
- The attributes in a conceptual model should preferably be *simple attributes* or *pure data values*.
- Objects should be related with associations, not with attributes (Fig. 9.4).
- The type of an attribute (such as *Product Code, Address, and Quantity*) may be described as non-primitive data type, whereas each of them could have been defined as an object.

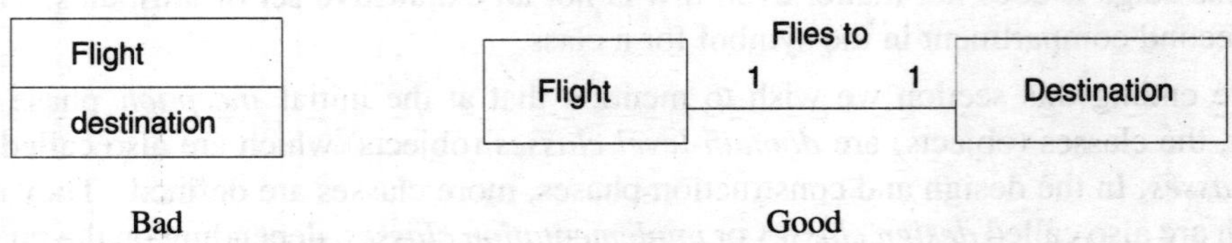

Fig. 9.4. Bad and good examples of objects

9.6 IDENTIFY SYSTEM EVENTS AND SYSTEM OPERATIONS

A *system event* is an external event generated by an actor to the system whereas a *system operation* is an operation of the system that is initiated and executed in response to the occurrence of the system event. System events are identified from the consideration of typical course of events in each use case. Every such event leads to the execution of a system operation. Thus at this stage we define a class *System* which is associated with system operations. Although each such system operation would lead to a number of operations, at this stage, we do not take those operations into account.

The system sequence diagram shows, in a diagrammatic form, the actors, the system, and the sequence of operations the events generate. Usually, the events and the operations have the same name. Whereas the former is a stimulus, the latter is the response. Although ideally one should define the parameters associated with each operation, at this stage the parameters may be omitted.

Figure 9.5 shows a system sequence diagram for a *Buy Items* use case that is relevant in a shop where the sale and payment are handled by computerized software at the counter. Here the counter person (namely the operator) is the actor. She enters the item numbers and the number of items of each type bought by a customer. After the entry of the relevant sale information for a customer, she presses the *End Sale* button. Thus she generates two system events — *enterProduct and endSale*. In turn, two system operations — *enterProduct and endSale* operations — are executed.

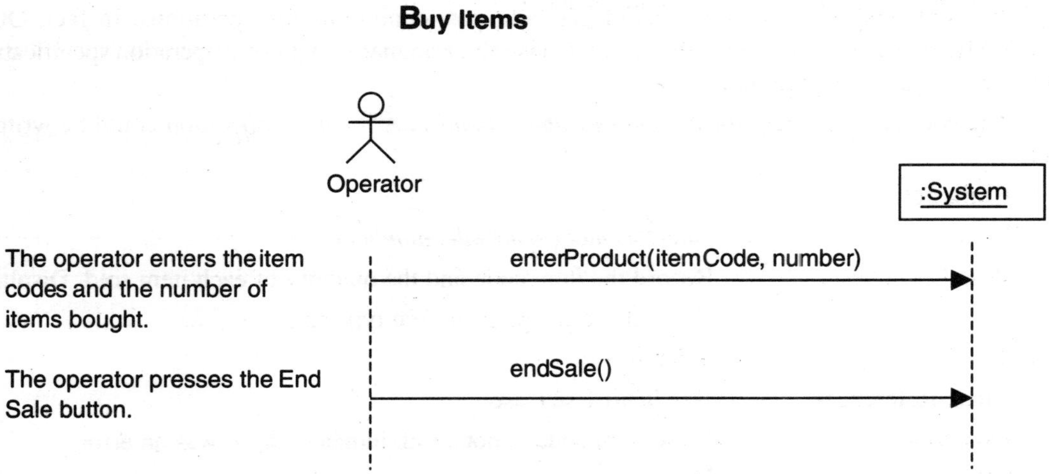

Fig. 9.5. System sequence diagram for the buy items use case

9.7 WRITE CONTRACTS FOR EACH OPERATION

When a system is stimulated by an outside event to execute an operation, certain *pre-conditions* are to be satisfied. Thus, for example, if the *enterProduct* (*itemCode, number*) operation has to be executed, it is necessary that the system data base should have the item code and other detailed information (such as price) about the item. Upon execution of the operation, certain changes in the system states are apt to occur. The desired changes in the system states are the *post-conditions* that the operations are expected to bring in when they are executed. Thus, when the *enterProduct* (*itemCode, number*) operation is executed, we would expect that a *Sale* object and a *SaleLine* object will be created, and an association between the two along with an association between the *SaleLine* object and the *ProductSpecification* object (to facilitate the transfer of information on price) will be formed.

Three categories of post-conditions can be visualized:

1. Instance creation and deletion.
2. Attribute modification.
3. Associations (with other objects) formed and broken.

A *contract* document describes the pre- and post-conditions and also other details for an operation. To write the contract, it is first necessary to write down the *responsibilities* (or the purpose) of the operation. The post-conditions are the next important section of a contract document. The post-conditions are normally comprehended with the help of a static structure diagram. To emphasize that they are not actions but state changes, they are written in a declarative, passive, past tense form. The pre-conditions are the next most important section of a contract document. They indicate the states of the system that help execute the operation. The sections of a contract document include notes, type, cross-references, and exceptions.

UML does not use the term "contract". But it requires specifying operations that indirectly refers to writing contracts with specifications of pre- and post-conditions for operations. In fact, OCL, a formal UML-based language called the Object Constraint Language, expresses operation specification in terms of pre- and post-conditions.

The contract document for the *enterProduct* (*itemCode, number*) operation could be written as under:

Contract

Name:	*enterProduct* (*itemCode, number*)
Responsibilities:	Record the item code and the quantity of each item sold. Display the total sales price of each item type sold.
Type:	System
Cross References:	*Buy Items* Use Case
Exceptions:	If the item code is not valid, indicate that it was an error.
Output:	Nil
Pre-Conditions:	The item code is known to the system.
Post-Conditions:	– If a new sale, a *Sale* was created (instance created). – An instance of a *SaleLine* was created (instance created). – An association was formed between *Sale* and *SaleLine* (association formed). – An association was formed between *SaleLine* and *ProductSpecification* (association formed).

At this stage we digress from the theoretical approach that we had taken so far. We now present an application of whatever we have learnt so far.

9.8 AN EXAMPLE OF ISSUE OF LIBRARY BOOKS

In the Use Case section we had considered the *Library Lending Information System*. One of the use cases considered there was *Borrow Books*. Here we consider the *Borrow Books* use case in greater depth. First we give here a narration of what happens when books are issued out to a user.

The Library has a set of registered users who borrow books whenever they require. When a user comes to the Library Assistant sitting at the circulation counter of the Library with books to borrow, the Library Assistant checks the user_id for his authenticity, verifies the number of books the user has already issued, continues to enter each book in the user's record while ensuring the number of books issued to him does not exceed a pre-assigned limit, prints a gate pass for each book issued, and gives the books and the gate pass back to the user. The books are then shown in the LLIS software to have been issued to the user.

9.8.1 Identification of Objects

The main nouns and noun clauses that appear in the Typical Course of Events in the Extended Format of the Borrow Books use case and those that appear in the text of the example given above are the following:

LLIS	Issue of Books
Book	Gate Pass
User	User's Record
Library Assistant	Number of Books Issued

9.8.2 The Static Structure Diagram

A *static structure diagram* (or *class diagram*) shows the domain-level classes and their associations. Wherever possible, attributes defined on each class are also highlighted, even if it is an early stage of model development. However, no attempt is made to define the operations at this stage.

We had discussed various types of relationships between two classes in Chapter 8. Recall that an *association* (along with the adornments) between two classes indicates the relationship that exists between them. Usually, one considers an association if the knowledge of the relationship needs to be preserved for some time ('need-to-know' association). It is shown on a static diagram by a straight line joining the classes. An association should be so named that it should read like a sentence when read with the class names, from left to right or from top to bottom. Often, one also shows the *multiplicity of association* by putting number(s) near the two ends of the association line.

A static structure diagram cannot be complete so early in the development stage. To start with, therefore, one develops only a partial model. A partial static diagram is now developed for the Library Lending Information System (Fig. 9.6).

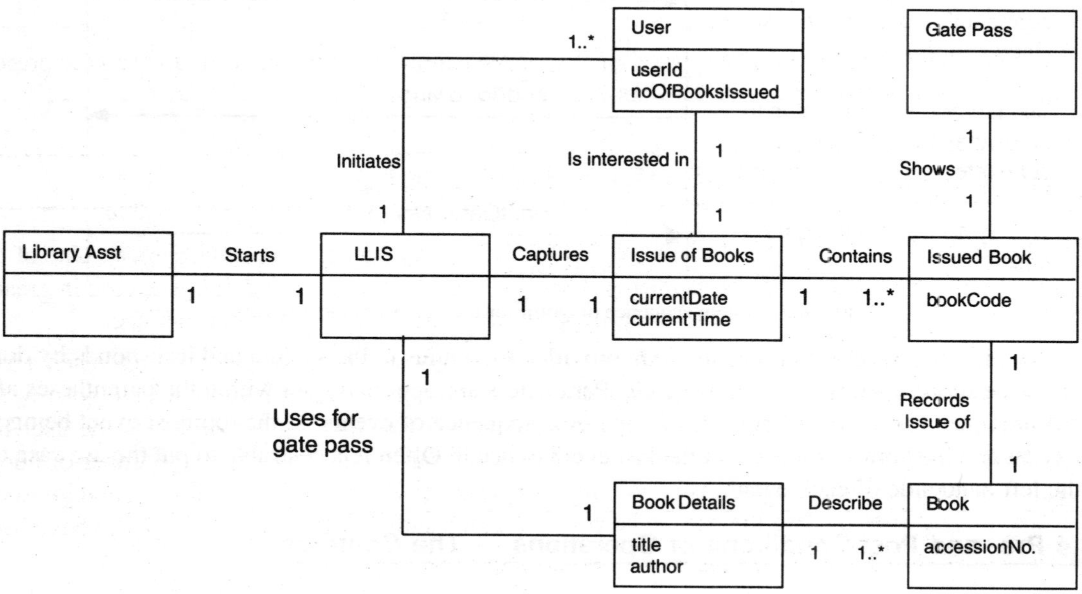

Fig. 9.6. Partial static structure (class) diagram for *Issue of Books*

9.8.3 System Sequence Diagram

A *system sequence diagram* illustrates events that are initiated by the actors and incident on to the system in course of a particular use case. The system responds to these events by doing certain operations. The diagram thus shows what a system does, and not how it does it. The diagram also shows the time sequence of occurrence of the events.

We take the example of *Borrow Books* use case to illustrate the drawing of its system sequence diagram (Fig. 9.7).

Borrow Books

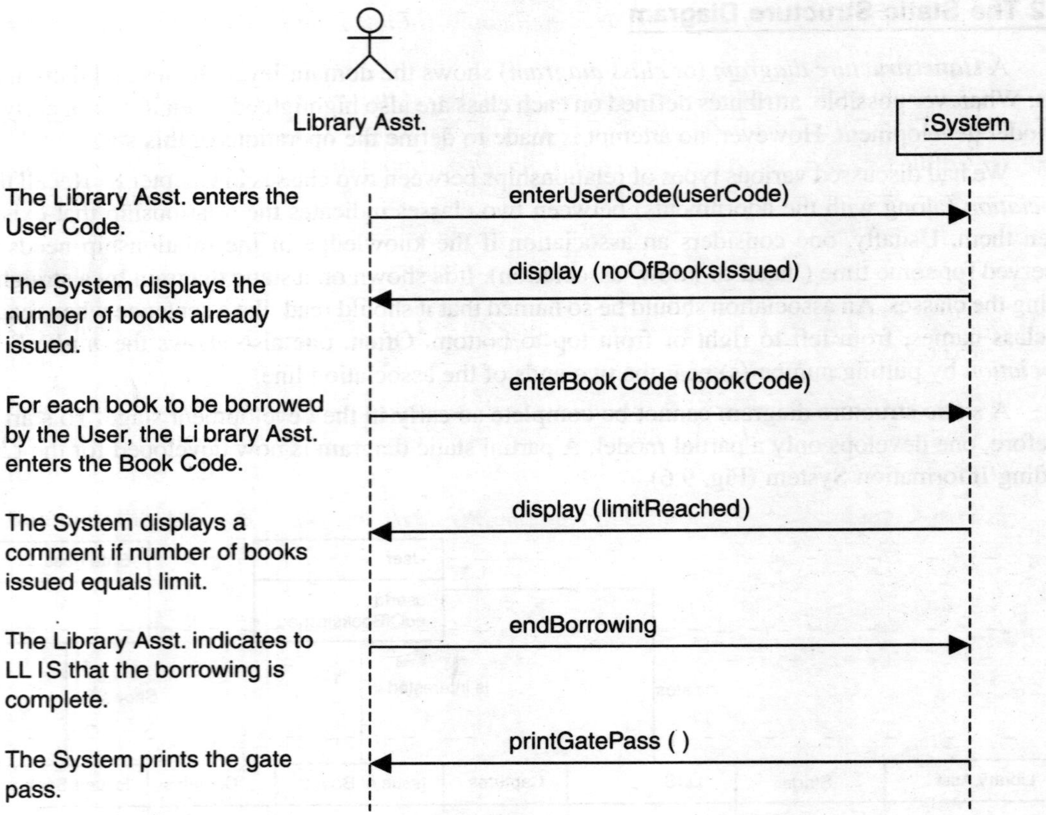

Fig. 9.7. System sequence diagram for the borrow books use case

In Fig. 9.7, the event *enterUserCode* provides a stimulus to the system and it responds by doing the likewise-name operation *enterUserCode*. Parameters are optionally put within the parentheses after the event name. The vertical lines indicate the time sequence of events — the topmost event being the first event and the bottom-most event the last event to occur. Often it is desirable to put the use case text on the left hand side of each event.

9.8.4 Pre- and Post-Conditions of Operations — The Contracts

We illustrate a contract document for the *enterUserCode* operation.

Contract

Name:	*enterUserCode* (*userCode*)
Responsibilities:	Record the User Code. Display the books outstanding with the User.
Type:	System

Cross References: Borrow Books Use Case
Exceptions: If User Code is not valid, it was an error.
Output: Displays the number of books already issued.
Pre-Conditions: The User Code is known to the system.
Post-Conditions: – If a new user, an instance of User was created (instance created).
– An association was formed with LLIS (association formed).

Contract

Name: *enterBookCode* (*bookCode*)
Responsibilities: Record the Book Code. Check the number of books outstanding with the maximum limit. Update the books issued to the User. Change the status of books in the Library to 'Issued Out'.
Type: System
Cross References: Borrow Books Use Case
Exceptions: If it is a Reserve or a Reference Book, then the issue was denied. Also if the limit of number of books is reached, then no book was issued.
Output: Displays the total number of books issued till the end of last transaction.
Pre-Conditions: The User Code is known to the system.
Post-Conditions: – An instance of Issue of Books was created (instance created).
– User was associated with Issue of Books (association formed).
– An instance of Issued Book was created (instance created).
– Issue of Book was associated with Issued Book (association formed).
– An instance of Book was created (instance created).
– Issued Book was associated with Book (association formed).

Contract

Name: *endBorrowing* ()
Responsibilities: Print Gate Pass
Type: System
Cross References: Borrow Books Use Case
Exceptions: Nil
Output: Print Gate Pass
Pre-Conditions: The User Code is known to the system
Post-Conditions: – An instance of Book Details was created (instance created).
– Book was associated with Book Details (association formed).
– Book Details was associated with LLIS (association formed).

Now that we have illustrated various essential steps required for object-oriented analysis given in Table 9.1, we are now in a position to carry out some higher-level steps required for the analysis.

9.9 RELATING MULTIPLE USE CASES

Normally, in a typical library certain books are kept reserved for reading in the Library only. Issue facilities are extended for these books only in exceptional situations with permission obtained from officers in charge. Similarly, reference books, that include handbooks and dictionaries, are usually not lent out. However, with permission from in-charge of the Reference Section, such books may be lent out. Thus, borrowing books includes borrowing not only textbooks, but also books that belong to reserve and reference sections. So we can have four use cases, a general use case and three separate use cases, one each for textbooks, reserve books, and reference books. Such use cases are related to one another through the use of the generalization relationship. Figure 9.8 shows a use case diagram involving multiple use cases.

While writing about the typical course of events followed in the description of *BorrowBook* use case, one must write about the initiation of the other three use cases, depending on the type of the book to be borrowed.

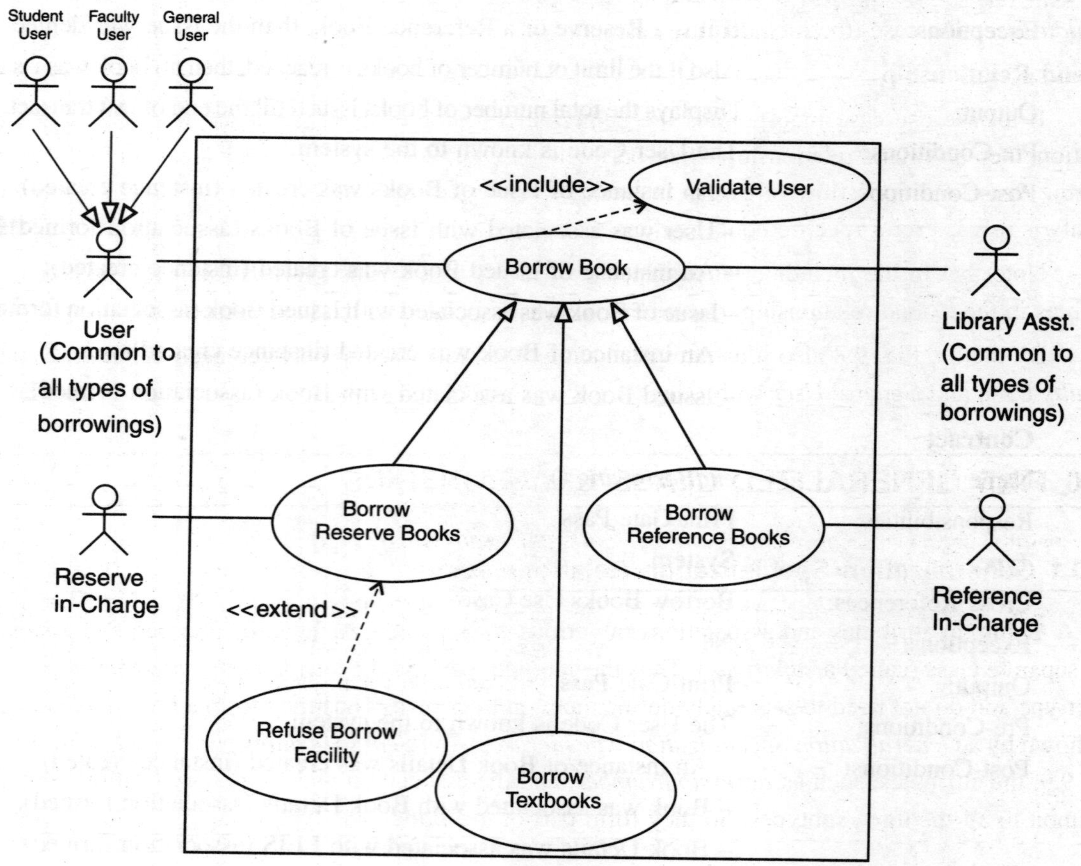

Fig. 9.8. Relating multiple use cases using '*includes*' clause

In fact, use cases can be related in three ways:

1. Generalization relationship
2. Include relationship
3. Extend relationship

Generalization Relationship

Like classes, use cases may have gen-spec relationships among them, where a child use case inherits the behaviour and meaning of a parent use case and adds or overrides the behaviour of its parent. In Fig. 9.8, we show this relationship between each of *Borrow Reserve Books, Borrow Text-books,* and *Borrow Reference Books* with *Borrow Books.*

Include Relationship

When several use cases (base use cases) have certain common flow of events then the common flow of events can be put as a responsibility of a separate use case (the included use case). It is shown as a dependency. In Fig. 9.8, *Borrow Books* use case (the base use case) includes the flow of events of *Validate User* use case (the included use case).

Extend Relationship

If a base use case incorporates the behaviour of another use case at an indirectly specified location, then an extend relationship exists between the two. Denoted by a dependency, in Fig. 9.8, the *Borrow Reserve Books*' flow of events is extended to *Refuse Borrow Facility* use case if borrowing facility is refused for a specific book (optional behaviour).

Note that in the include relationship, the base use case points towards the included use case, whereas in the extend relationship, the extending use case points to the base use case.

By the by, Fig. 9.8 also illustrates a generalization relationship between each of *Student User*, *Faculty User,* and *General User* with *User.*

9.10 FIND GENERALIZED CLASS RELATIONSHIPS

9.10.1 Generalization Specialization Relationships

Common attributes and associations in various classes (*subtypes*) can be grouped and assigned to a separate class (called a *supertype*). Thus the subtypes can use the attributes and associations of the supertype and do not need to separately define them on their own. Thus they form a hierarchy and can be shown by a *Generalization Specialization type hierarchy* (or *Gen-Spec diagram* or *Is-a Diagram*). In Fig. 9.9, the attributes, such as *accessionNumber*, and the association with *BookDetails* (Fig. 9.6), are common to all the three subtypes. So they form part of the *Book* supertype.

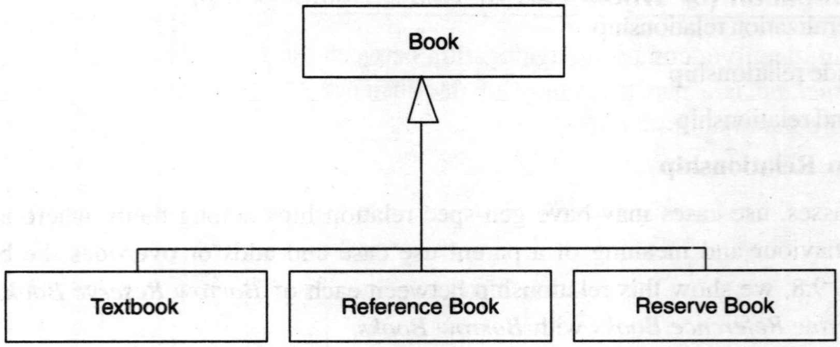

Fig. 9.9. Gen-Spec diagram

9.10.2 Find Associations between Classes

There are cases when an attribute of a class A can take multiple values, depending on the association it has with another class B. In such a case, the attribute depends on the association and the association should be considered as a class in its own right — an *Association Class*. As an example, when a book is borrowed by a user, they have an association. The date and time of borrowing depends on the particular association (*Transaction*) created between the *Book* and the *User* classes (Fig. 9.10). Here *Transaction* is a class. Notice in Fig. 9.10 that the *Transaction* can have its own child classes — *IssueTransaction* and *ReturnTransaction* classes.

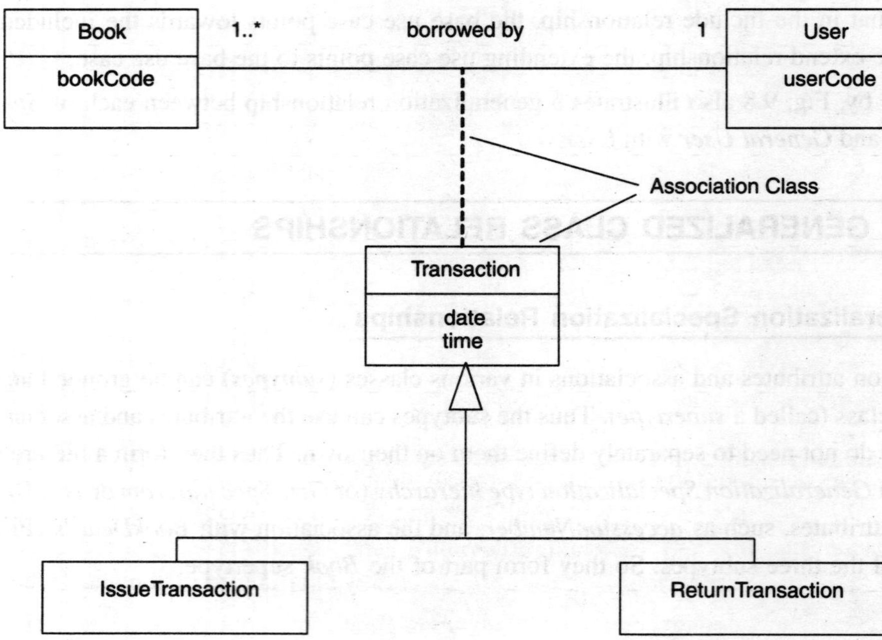

Fig. 9.10. Association class

9.10.3 Aggregation (or Whole-Part or Has-a Relationship)

We can identify a composite aggregation between the *IssueOfBook* and *IssueLine* classes (Fig. 9.11). An *IssueLine* is a part of at most of one instance of *IssueOfBook* whereas *IssueOfBook* may consist of more than one *IssueLine*.

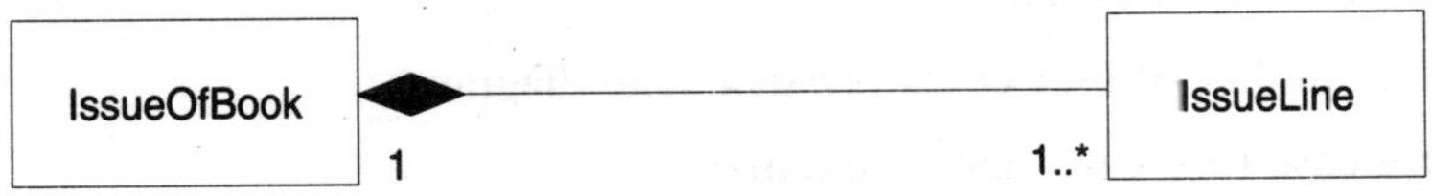

Fig. 9.11. Composite aggregation

9.11 ORGANIZE THE OBJECT MODEL INTO PACKAGES

Recall that a package is a set of elements that together provide highly related services. The elements are closely related. We can define a nested package for the Library Lending Information System (Fig. 9.12).

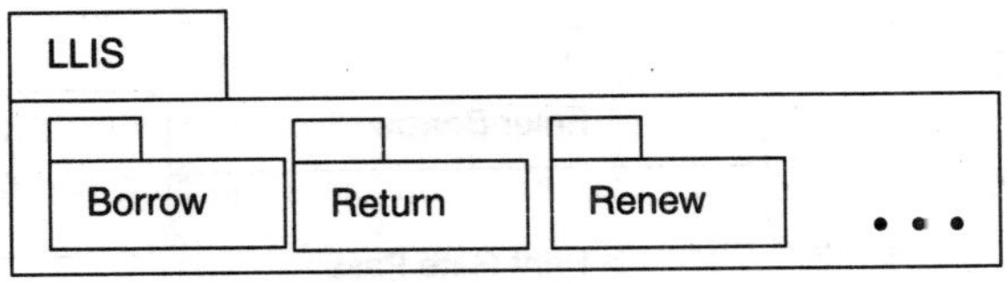

Fig. 9.12. A nested package

9.12 MODELLING SYSTEM BEHAVIOUR

System behaviour is a dynamic phenomenon and is usually addressed in the design phase. However, even at the analysis phase one may take up the high-level behavioural issues. We shall take up here the modelling of system behaviour with the help of state diagrams and activity diagrams. In this section we take up state diagrams while the activity diagram is the subject of the next section.

System behaviour is usually modelled with the help of *state (or state chart) diagrams*. State diagrams show how the objects change their states in response to various external and temporal events. Since collaboration diagrams show object responses to internal events, often state diagrams are not drawn for internal events.

A *state* is the condition of an object at a moment in time. It is quantified by assigning values to the attributes of the object. An event is a significant and noteworthy occurrence. Events can be of three types: External, Internal, and Temporal. *External events* (or system events) are caused by an actor outside the system boundary. *Internal events* are caused inside the system boundary when an operation is invoked in an object upon receiving a message. *Temporal events* are caused after the passage of some specific time or on a specific date and time; for example, automatic notification a week before the due date of return of a book, or automatic listing of transactions at 10.00 PM everyday.

State diagrams use rounded rectangles to indicate the states of the object and use arrows to indicate the events. A filled small circle indicates the initial state of the object. The state of the object changes as an event occurs. Often an arrow is labelled not only by the event name but also by the condition that causes the occurrence of the event.

State diagrams can be drawn at various levels:

- system of a number of user cases (system state diagram)
- specific use case (use case state diagram)
- classes and types (class or type state diagram)

We show the system state diagrams for library lending information system (Fig. 9.13) and for *Borrow Book* use case (Fig. 9.14).

The statechart diagrams are simple to understand. However, UML allows statecharts to depict more complicated interactions between its constituent parts.

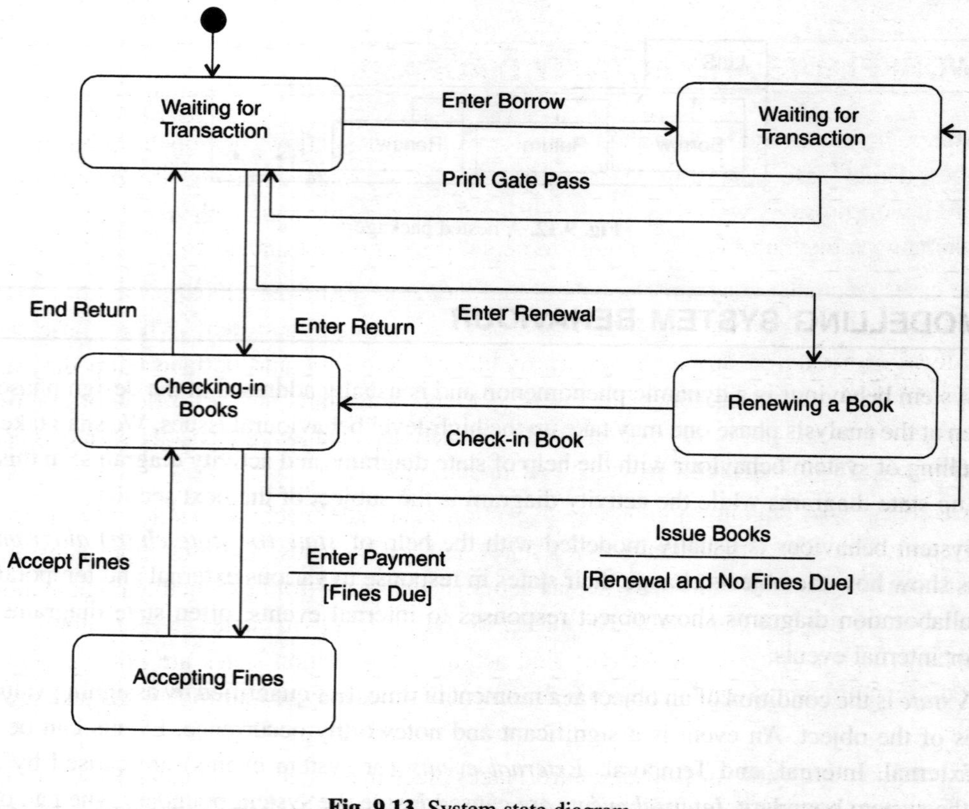

Fig. 9.13. System state diagram

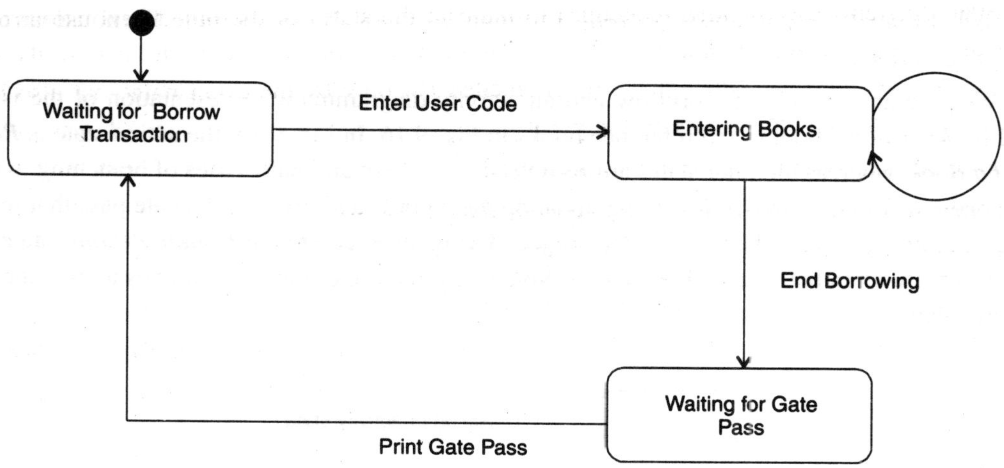

Fig. 9.14. Borrow book use case state (or statechart) diagram

9.13 WORKFLOWS AND ACTIVITY DIAGRAMS

Business processes can be described in the form of high-level flows of work and objects. Activity diagrams best depict these *workflows*. Usually, these diagrams are developed for important workflows, and not for all workflows. A workflow starts with an initial state and ends with an exit state. Although used for workflows, they are flexible enough to depict system operations as well.

Use cases, sequence diagrams, collaboration diagrams (to be described in the chapter dealing with object-oriented design), and statecharts model the dynamics of a system. Whereas use cases are very high-level artifacts for depicting system dynamics, sequence and collaboration diagrams are concerned with flow of control from object to object, and statecharts deal with flow of control from state to state of a system, use case, or of an object. An activity diagram is a special case of statecharts in which flow of control is depicted from activity to activity.

An activity is an ongoing non-atomic execution of a state machine. An activity diagram is a directed graph where nodes represent activity states and action states, and arcs represent transitions from state to state or flows of control. Whereas action states result from executable computations and are atomic in nature not being amenable for further breakdown, activity states are non-atomic that can be decomposed further into a set of activity and action states. Action states are not interrupted and generally take insignificant execution time whereas activity states may be interrupted and take some time to complete.

The common transition (or flow of control) takes place in a sequential manner. However, *activity diagrams* can also depict more realistic transitions involving *branching* and *concurrency*. Modelling concurrency requires *forking* and *joining*. Details of these are given below with the help of an example. Activity diagrams are often extended to include flow of objects showing change in state and attribute

REFERENCES

Beck, K. and W. Cunningham (1989), A Laboratory for Object-oriented Thinking, Proceedings of OOPSLA 1989, SIGPLAN Notices. Vol. 24, No.10.

Booch, G. (1994), Object-oriented Analysis and Design with Applications, Addison-Wesley, Reading, Mass, 2nd Edition.

Booch, G., J. Rumbaugh and I. Jacobson (2000), The Unified Modeling Language User Guide, Addison-Wesley Longman (Singapore) Pte. Ltd., Low Price Edition.

Coad, P. and E. Yourdon, (1991), Object-oriented Analysis, Second Edition, Englewood Cliffs, Yourdon Press, New Jersey.

Jacobson, I., M. Christerson, P. Jonsson and G. Övergaard (1992), Object-oriented Software Engineering: A Use Case Driven Approach, Addison-Wesley (Singapore) Pte. Ltd., International Student Edition.

Larman, C. (2000), Applying UML and Patterns: An Introduction to Object-oriented Analysis and Design, Addison-Wesley, Pearson Education, Inc., Low Price Edition.

Pressman, R.S. (1997), Software Engineering: A Practitioner's Approach, McGraw-Hill, International Editions.

Rumbaugh, J., M. Blaha, W. Premerlani, F. Eddy and W. Lorensen (1991), Object-oriented Modeling and Design, Englewood Cliffs, Prentice-Hall, New Jersey.

Wirfs-Brock, R., B. Wilkerson and L. Wiener (1990), Designing Object-oriented Software, Englewood Cliffs, Prentice Hall, New Jersey.

10 Software Requirements Specification

A specification is a detailed itemized description of dimensions, plans, materials, and other requirements. When applied to software engineering, it indicates an agreement between a consumer of a service and a producer of a service, or between a user and an implementer (Ghezzi, *et al.* 1991). Thus it can be requirements specification (agreement between user and developer), design specification (agreement between designer and implementer of the design), or module specification (agreement between the designer writing the detail design and the programmer).

10.1 PROPERTIES OF AN SRS

Software requirements specification (SRS) documents the user needs. Its functions are to:

1. Formalize the developer's concepts and express them effectively and succinctly.
2. Communicate this understanding to the sponsor and get it validated.
3. Have a baseline against which the software is implemented and maintained.

The desirable properties of an SRS are the following:

1. It should *cover only the essential features* of the system that are fixed, known, and agreed to be delivered.
2. It should *cover what to deliver, not how to deliver them*. Thus the implementation details are to be taken up during the design stage only.
3. It should use a *vocabulary that the client understands.*
4. It should be *correct.* For example, it may say that it will process 50,000 documents in an hour, whereas in practice it may not be able to process beyond 20,000 documents — a case of incorrect specification.
5. It should be *precise*. For example, merely saying that a large number of documents can be processed or that it will take very small time to process a document is imprecise.
6. It should be *unambiguous, i.e.*, a statement should convey only one meaning. Lack of written communication skill can make a statement ambiguous. Use of formal specification helps in unambiguously expressing a statement. But this makes the statement less understandable, however. As an example, consider the following specification of a software requirement:

Send a request to the Guesthouse Manager whenever a Head of the Department invites an outside person. Such a request has to be ratified by the Director of the Institute.

The first statement gives the Head of the Department the sole authority; the second sentence imposes a condition, however. It does not say anything about whether the Director's approval should accompany the invitation. Therefore two interpretations are possible:

I. Ignore the invitation if the Director's approval is available.

II. Generate a request on the basis of invitation, and confirm/cancel it later, depending on whether Director's approval comes.

7. It should be *complete*. The statement "the database should be updated if a transaction is 'buy-type' " is incomplete; it must indicate the type of action to be taken if the transaction is not 'buy-type'.
8. It should be *verifiable*. Once a system is designed and implemented, it should be possible to verify that the system design/implementation satisfies the original requirements (using analytical or formal methods).
9. It should be *validatable*. The user should be able to read/understand requirements specification and indicate the degree to which the requirements reflect his/her ideas.
10. It should be *consistent*. A statement in one place of an SRS may say that an error message will appear and the transaction will not be processed if the inventory becomes negative; in another place of the SRS another statement may say that the quantity needed to bring the inventory to the desired level will be calculated for all transactions even though a transaction could make the inventory negative.
11. It should be *modifiable*. The structure and style of an SRS should be such that any necessary changes to the requirements can be made easily, completely, and consistently. Thus it requires a clear and precise table of contents, a cross reference, an index, and a glossary.
12. It must be *traceable*. The requirements should allow referencing between aspects of the design/implementation and the aspects of the requirements.

10.2 CONTENTS OF AN SRS

An SRS should have the following contents:

- Functionality
- Environment Description and System Objectives
- Project Management
- System Delivery and Installation Requirements
- Functional Constraints
- Design Constraints
- Data and Communication Protocol Requirements

Functionality

It indicates the services provided by a software system required by the customers and users. They thus form the heart and soul of an SRS.

In addition to including the requirements delineated by the users and the customers, these functional requirements include description of

- Procedures for starting up and closing down the system.
- Self-test procedures.
- Operation under normal conditions.
- Operation under abnormal conditions.
- Procedures for controlling the mode of operation.
- Recovery procedures.
- Procedures for continuing under reduced functionality.

Environment Description and System Objectives

- Physical attributes of the environment: size, shape, and locality.
- Organizational attributes: office applications, military applications.
- Models of potential users
- Safety/security/hazards

Project Management

Life Cycle Requirements: How system development will proceed (system documentation, standards, procedures for model testing and integration, procedures for controlling change, assumptions/expected changes).

System Delivery and Installation Requirements

Examples of these requirements are: Deliverables, deadlines, acceptance criteria, quality assurance, document structure/standards/ training/manuals/support and maintenance.

Functional Constraints

They describe the necessary properties of the system behaviour described in the functional requirements. Examples of these properties are: Performance, efficiency, response times, safety, security, reliability, quality, and dependability.

Design Constraints

The user may want that the software satisfy certain additional conditions. These conditions are: hardware and software standards, particular libraries and operating systems to be used, and compatibility issues.

Data and Communication Protocol Requirements

They are: inputs, outputs, interfaces, and communication protocols between system and environment.

10.3 WHAT AN SRS SHOULD NOT INCLUDE

An SRS should give what the software is required to do, not how to do them. Thus the SRS should not address any design issues such as: (*a*) partitioning of the software into modules, (*b*) assigning functions to modules, (*c*) describing flow of information and control between modules, and (*d*) choosing data structures. However there are special cases where certain design considerations such as compliance to standards, performance standards, etc., are to be specified in the SRS as design constraints.

Also, an SRS should not include project requirements information such as project cost, delivery schedule, reporting procedures, software development methods, quality assurance, validation and verification criteria, and acceptance procedures. They are generally specified in other documents such as software development plan, software quality assurance plan, and statement of work.

10.4 STRUCTURE OF AN SRS

IEEE Std. 830-1993 defines a format for an SRS. The format is not prescriptive; it is only representative. In fact, it presents the basic format and its many versions. Whatever the format may be, the document has three main sections, each divided into many subsections and sub-subsections. The document has three supporting information — table of contents, appendices, and index -- the first appearing in the beginning and the other two appearing at the end of the document.

An outline of the IEEE Std. 830-1993 format is given below. While an SRS need not adhere exactly to the outline nor use the exact names used in this outline, it should contain the basic information given in this outline.

1. **Introduction**
   - **1.1 Purpose**
   - **1.2 Scope**
   - **1.3 Definitions, Acronyms, and Abbreviations.**
   - **1.4 References**
   - **1.5 Overview**
2. **General Description**
   - **2.1 Product perspective**
   - **2.2 Product Functions**
   - **2.3 User Characteristics**
   - **2.4 Constraints**
   - **2.5 Assumptions and Dependencies**
3. **Specific Requirements**

Appendices

Index

There are a number of variants for Section 3. This section can be organized according to (*a*) mode, (*b*) user class, (*c*) object, (*d*) feature, (*e*) stimulus, (*f*) functional hierarchy, and (*g*) multiple organizations. We give below the templates for each such variant.

Template of SRS Section 3 Organized by Mode: Version 1

3. **Specific Requirements**
   - **3.1 External Interface Requirements**
     - **3.1.1 User Interfaces**
     - **3.1.2 Hardware Interfaces**
     - **3.1.3 Software Interfaces**
     - **3.1.4 Communication Interfaces**

3.2 Functional Requirements
3.2.1 Mode 1
3.2.1.1 Functional Requirement 1.1
...
3.2.1.n Functional Requirement 1.n
3.2.2 Mode 2
...
3.2.m Mode m
Functional Requirement m.1
...
Functional Requirement m.n
3.3 Performance Requirements
3.4 Design Constraints
3.5 Software System Attributes
3.6 Other Requirements

Template of SRS Section 3 Organized by Mode: Version 2

3. Specific Requirements
3.1 Functional Requirements
3.1.1 Mode 1
3.1.1.1 External Interfaces
3.1.1.1.1 User Interfaces
3.1.1.1.2 Hardware Interfaces
3.1.1.1.3 Software Interfaces
3.1.1.1.4 Communication Interfaces
3.1.1.2 Functional Requirements
3.1.1.2.1 Functional Requirement 1.1
...
3.1.1.2.n Functional Requirement 1.n
3.1.1.3 Performance
3.1.2 Mode 2
...
3.1.m Mode m
3.2 Design Constraints
3.3 Software System Attributes
3.4 Other Requirements

Template of SRS Section 3 Organized by User Class

3. Specific Requirements
3.1 External Interface Requirements
3.1.1 User Interfaces
3.1.2 Hardware Interfaces

3.1.3 Software Interfaces
3.1.4 Communication Interfaces
3.2 Functional Requirements
3.2.1 User Class 1
3.2.1.1 Functional Requirement 1.1
...
3.2.1.n Functional Requirement 1.n
3.2.2 User Class 2
...
3.2.m User Class m
Functional Requirement m.1
...
Functional Requirement m.n
3.3 Performance Requirements
3.4 Design Constraints
3.5 Software System Attributes
3.6 Other Requirements

Template of SRS Section 3 Organized by Object

3. Specific Requirements
3.1 External Interface Requirements
3.1.1 User Interfaces
3.1.2 Hardware Interfaces
3.1.3 Software Interfaces
3.1.4 Communication Interfaces
3.2 Classes/Objects
3.2.1 Class/Object 1
3.2.1.1 Attributes (direct or inherited)
3.2.1.1.1 Attribute 1
...
3.2.1.1.n Attribute n
3.2.1.2 Functions (services, methods, direct or inherited)
3.2.1.2.1 Functional requirement 1.1
...
3.2.1.2.n Functional requirement 1.n
3.2.2 Class/Object 2
...
3.2.p Class/Object p
3.3 Performance Requirements
3.4 Design Constraints
3.5 Software System Attributes

3.6 Other Requirements

Template of SRS Section 3 Organized by Feature

3. Specific Requirements
    3.1 External Interface Requirements
        3.1.1 User Interfaces
        3.1.2 Hardware Interfaces
        3.1.3 Software Interfaces
        3.1.4 Communication Interfaces
    3.2 System features
        3.2.1 System feature 1
            3.2.1.1 Introduction/Purpose of Feature
            3.2.1.2 Stimulus/Response Sequence
            3.2.1.3 Associated functional requirements
                3.2.1.3.1 Functional requirement 1.1
                …
                3.2.1.2.n Functional requirement 1.n
        3.2.2 System feature 2
        …
        3.2.m System feature p
    3.3 Performance Requirements
    3.4 Design Constraints
    3.5 Software System Attributes
    3.6 Other Requirements

Template of SRS Section 3 Organized by Stimulus

3. Specific Requirements
    3.1 External Interface Requirements
        3.1.1 User Interfaces
        3.1.2 Hardware Interfaces
        3.1.3 Software Interfaces
        3.1.4 Communication Interfaces
    3.2 Functional requirements
        3.2.1 Stimulus 1
            3.2.1.1 Functional requirement 1.1
            …
            3.2.1.n Functional requirement 1.n
        3.2.2 Stimulus 2
        …
        3.2.m Stimulus m

3.2.m.1 Functional requirement m.1

...

3.2.m.n Functional requirement m.n

3.3 Performance Requirements

3.4 Design Constraints

3.5 Software System Attributes

3.6 Other Requirements

Template of SRS Section 3 Organized by Functional Hierarchy

3. Specific Requirements

3.1 External Interface Requirements

3.1.1 User Interfaces

3.1.2 Hardware Interfaces

3.1.3 Software Interfaces

3.1.4 Communication Interfaces

3.2 Functional requirements

3.2.1 Information Flows

3.2.1.1 Data flow diagram 1

3.2.1.1.1 Data entities

3.2.1.1.2 Pertinent processes

3.2.1.1.3 Topology

3.2.1.2 Data flow diagram 2

3.2.1.2.1 Data entities

3.2.1.2.2 Pertinent processes

3.2.1.2.3 Topology

...

3.2.1.n Data flow diagram n

3.2.1.n.1 Data entities

3.2.1.n.2 Pertinent processes

3.2.1.n.3 Topology

3.2.2 Process Descriptions

3.2.2.1 Process 1

3.2.2.1.1 Input data entities

3.2.2.1.2 Algorithm or formula of processes

3.2.2.1.3 Affected data entities

...

3.2.2.1 Process m

3.2.2.m.1 Input data entities

3.2.2.m.2 Algorithm or formula of processes

3.2.2.m.3 Affected data entities

3.2.3 Data construct specifications
  3.2.3.1 Construct
    3.2.3.1.1 Record type
    3.2.3.1.2 Constituent fields
  ...
  3.2.3.p Construct
    3.2.3.p.1 Record type
    3.2.3.p.2 Constituent fields
3.2.4 Data dictionary
  3.2.4.1 Data element 1
    3.2.4.1.1 Name
    3.2.4.1.2 Representation
    3.2.4.1.3 Units/Format
    3.2.4.1.4 Precision/Accuracy
    3.2.4.1.5 Range
  ...
  3.2.4.q Data element 1
    3.2.4.q.1 Name
    3.2.4.q.2 Representation
    3.2.4.q.3 Units/Format
    3.2.4.q.4 Precision/Accuracy
    3.2.4.q.5 Range

3.3 Performance Requirements

3.4 Design Constraints

3.5 Software System Attributes

3.6 Other Requirements

Template of SRS Section 3 Showing Multiple Organizations

3. Specific Requirements
  3.1 External Interface Requirements
    3.1.1 User Interfaces
    3.1.2 Hardware Interfaces
    3.1.3 Software Interfaces
    3.1.4 Communication Interfaces
  3.2 Functional requirements
    3.2.1 User class 1
      3.2.1.1 Feature 1.1
        3.2.1.1.1 Introduction/Purpose of feature
        3.2.1.1.2 Stimulus/Response sequence
        3.2.1.1.3 Associated functional requirements

...

3.2.1.m Feature 1.m

3.2.1.m.1 Introduction/Purpose of feature

3.2.1.m.2 Stimulus/Response sequence

3.2.1.m.3 Associated functional requirements

3.2.2 User class 2

...

3.2.n User class n

3.3 Performance Requirements

3.4 Design Constraints

3.5 Software System Attributes

3.6 Other Requirements

We now give a brief description of each important term appearing in the SRS.

Purpose

1. Delineate the purpose of the SRS.
2. Specify the intended audience.

Scope

1. Name the software product(s) to be produced.
2. Explain what they will and will not do.
3. Describe the applications of the software, including benefits.
4. Ensure that the above is consistent with higher-level specifications (such as system requirement specification).

Definitions, Acronyms, and Abbreviations

Appendix may be given to explain the terms.

References

1. Give a completer list of all documents referenced elsewhere in the SRS.
2. Give titles, report number, date and publishing organization.
3. Specify the sources from which the references can be obtained.

Overview

1. Describe what the rest of the SRS contains.
2. Explain how the SRS is organized.

General Description

Describe factors that affect the product and its requirements, providing a background for the requirements of the software.

Product Perspective

Describe relationship with other products. If it is self-contained, it should be stated so. If, instead, it is part of a larger system, then relationship of the larger system functionality with the software requirements and interfaces between the system and the software should be stated. This subsection should include such interfaces between the system and the software as user interfaces, hardware interface, software interfaces, and communication interfaces.

User Interfaces

(*a*) State the logical feature of each interface, screen formats, page or window layouts, contents of reports or menus, and availability of programmable function keys.

(*b*) Optimize the interface with the user (for example, requirements for long/short error message, verifiable requirement such as a user learns to use the software within first 5 minutes, etc.).

Hardware Interfaces

They include configuration characteristics (such as number of ports and instruction sets), devices to be supported, and protocol (such as full screen support or line-by-line support).

Software Interfaces

They include data management system, operating system, mathematical package or interfaces with other application packages, such as accounts receivables, general ledger system. For each software package, give name, mnemonic, specification number, version number, and source. For each interface, give the purpose and define the interface in terms of message content and format.

Communication Interfaces

Specify interfaces to communications such as local network and protocols.

Product Functions

Provide a summary of the major high-level functions that the software will perform. It should be understandable and should use graphical means to depict relationships among various functions.

User Characteristics

Indicate the level of education, experience and expertise that a target user should have in order to make the full utilization of the software.

Constraints

Provide a general description of items that constrain the developer's options. They include regulatory policies, hardware limitations, application interfaces, parallel operations, audit functions, control functions, higher-order language requirements, signal handshake protocols, reliability requirements, criticality of the application, and safety and security considerations.

Assumptions and Dependencies

List changes in factors that can bring in changes in the design of the software. Thus changes in an assumed operating system environment can change the design of the software.

Specific Requirements

Detail out each requirement to a degree of detail such that not only designers and testers understand it clearly so as to pursue their own plan of action, but also users, system operators, and external system personnel understand it clearly. For each requirement specify the inputs, the process, and the outputs. The principles for writing this section are the following:

(*a*) State the requirements conforming to the desirable characteristics mentioned earlier.

(*b*) Cross-reference each requirement with earlier documents, if any.

(*c*) Ensure that each requirement is uniquely identifiable.

(*d*) Maximize readability of the document.

External Interfaces

Without repeating the interface description given earlier, give detailed description of all inputs and outputs from the software system. It should include the following content and format: (*a*) Name of item, (*b*) Description of purpose, (*c*) Source of input or destination of output, (*d*) Valid range, accuracy and/or tolerance, (*e*) Units of measure, (*f*) Timing, (*g*) Relationships to other inputs/outputs, (*h*) Screen formats/organization, (*i*) Window formats/organization, (*j*) Data formats, (*k*) Command formats, and (*l*) End messages.

Functional Requirements

Specify each function, with the help of '*shall*' statements, and define the actions that the software will take to accept and process the inputs and produce the outputs. The actions include: (*a*) Validity checks on the inputs, (*b*) Exact sequence of operations, (*c*) Responses to abnormal situations including overflow, communication facilities, and error handling and recovery, (*d*) Effect of parameters, and (*e*) Relationship of outputs to inputs including input/output sequences and formulas for input to output conversion.

Performance Requirements

Give static and dynamic performance requirements and express them in measurable terms. Static performance requirements, often written under a separate section entitled *capacity*, include: (*a*) Number of terminals to be supported, (*b*) Number of simultaneous users to be supported, and (*c*) Amount and type of information to be handled. Dynamic performance requirements include: (*a*) Number of transactions and tasks and (*b*) Amount of data to be processed within a specific period, for both normal and peak workload conditions.

Logical Database Requirements

Specify the logical requirements for any data to be placed into a database. They include: (*a*) Types of information used by various functions, (*b*) Frequency of use, (*c*) Accessing capabilities, (*d*) Data entities and their relationships, (*e*) Integrity constraints, and (*f*) Data retention requirements.

Design Constraints

Specify the design constraints imposed by other standards and hardware.

Standards Compliance

Specify the requirements derived from the existing standards regarding (*a*) Report format, (*b*) Data naming, (*c*) Accounting procedures, and (*d*) Audit tracing.

Software System Attributes

Specify the relevant software system attributes such as (*a*) reliability, (*b*) availability, (*c*) security, (*d*) maintainability, and (*e*) portability so that their achievement can be objectively verified.

Appendices

Include, as part of the appendices, (*a*) sample of input/output formats, (*b*) results of cost analysis studies, (*c*) results of user surveys, (*d*) supporting information for the benefit of the readers, (*e*) description of the problems to be solved by the user, and (*f*) special packaging instructions for the code and media, to meet security, export, initial loading, or other requirements.

10.5 VALIDATION OF REQUIREMENTS DOCUMENT

A requirements document needs to be validated to show that it actually defines the system that the client wants. Cost of inadequate specification can be very high. Usually the requirements are to be checked from both the customer's and the developer's point of view. The aspects to be checked from the customer's viewpoint are: validity, consistency, completeness, and realism (or realization). Those to be checked from a developer's viewpoint are: verifiability, comprehensibility, traceability (detecting the source when requirements evolve), and adaptability (the ability of the document to be changed without large-scale effects on other system requirements).

Boehm (1984) and many others have given different methods of validating software requirements. These are the following:

1. Reading by someone other than the author.
2. Constructing scenarios.
3. Requirements reviews for detecting incompleteness, inconsistency, and infeasibility.
4. Automated tools for checking consistency when requirements are written in a formal language.
5. Simulation that checks for critical non-functional requirement, such as 'time'. A requirements statement language (RSL) simulates each functional definition by automatically generating a system simulator in PASCAL.

Dunn (1984) has given a sample checklist with which requirements can be reviewed:

- Are all hardware resources defined?
- Have the response times of functions been specified?
- Have all the hardware external software and data interfaces been defined?
- Have all the functions required by the client been specified?
- Is each requirement testable?
- Is the initial system state defined?
- Are the responses to exceptional conditions specified?
- Does the requirement contain restrictions that can be controlled by the designer?
- Are possible future modifications specified?

10.6 IDENTIFYING AND MEASURING QUALITY IN SRS

Based on a survey of a number of papers on quality of SRS, Davis, *et al.* (1997) have listed 24 quality attributes for SRS (Table 10.1). They have suggested how to define and measure them in an SRS so as to evaluate the quality of the SRS. In what follows, we define and give quality measures of 12 of those quality attributes.

Assume the following:

n_r : number of requirements in the SRS

R : the set of all requirements

n_f : number of functional requirements in the SRS

R_f : the set of all functional requirements

n_{nf} : number of non-functional requirements in the SRS

R_{nf}: the set of all non-functional requirements

Thus the sum of all functional and non-functional requirements is the total number of requirements. Also, the union of the sets of functional and non-functional requirements is the set of all requirements:

$$n_r = n_f + n_{nf} \quad \text{and} \quad R = R_f \cup R_{nf}$$

We discuss below the metrics for a selected set of 12 quality attributes.

Table 10.1: Quality Attributes for an SRS

Unambiguous	Concise	Annotated by Version
Complete	Design Independent	Not Redundant
Correct	Traceable	At Right Level of Detail
Understandable	Modifiable	Precise
Verifiable	Electronically Stored	Reusable
Internally Consistent	Executable/Interpretable	Traced
Externally Consistent	Annotated by Relative Importance	Organized
Achievable	Annotated by Relative Stability	Cross-Referenced

Ambiguity

An SRS is unambiguous if and only if every requirement stated therein has only one possible interpretation. Ambiguity is a function of the background of the reader. Therefore, a way to measure ambiguity is by resorting to *review* of the specifications.

Let n_u be the number of unambiguous requirements for which all reviewers presented identical interpretations. The metric that can be used to measure the degree of unambiguity of an SRS is

$$Q_1 = \frac{n_u}{n_r}$$

Obviously, Q_1 ranges from 0 to 1. Because of the importance of unambiguity, the recommended importance weight of Q_1 is $W_1 = 1$.

Complete

An SRS is complete if an SRS includes everything that the software is supposed to do. Davis, *et al.* (1997) suggest that a requirement may or may not be included in the SRS and may or may not be fully known, understood or comprehended (perhaps because it is too abstract or poorly stated). Thus there are four possibilities:

1. Known and understood, and included in SRS
2. Known and understood, but not included in SRS
3. Known but not fully understood, and included in SRS
4. Known but not fully understood, and not included in SRS

We define the following:

n_A : Number of understood requirements included in the SRS

n_B : Number of understood requirements not included in the SRS

n_C : Number of known and non-understood requirements included in the SRS

n_D : Number of known and non-understood requirements not included in the SRS

The suggested metric then is

$$Q_2 = \frac{n_r}{n_A + n_B + n_C + n_D}$$

Considering that completeness is important but some requirements cannot be fully comprehended, the recommended weight for this metric is $W_2 = 0.7$.

Correct

An SRS is correct if every requirement in the SRS contributes to the satisfaction of some need. Thus only the users can know if a requirement is correct. The following metric reflects the percentage

$$Q_3 = \frac{n_{CO}}{n_r}$$

of requirements in the SRS that have been validated by the users to be correct. n_{CO} is the number of requirements in the SRS that have been validated by the user to be correct. Because of its criticality, the recommended weight for this measure is $W_3 = 1$.

Understandable

An SRS is understandable if all classes of SRS readers can easily comprehend the meaning of each requirement in the SRS. Two classes of readers are discernible: (1) the users, the customers and the project managers, and (2) the software developers and the testers. The former is happy with natural language specifications, whereas the latter likes to have formal specifications. Thus once again understandability of an SRS can be of four types:

1. High degree of understandability by developers and high degree of understandability by users.
2. High degree of understandability by developers and low degree of understandability by users.

3. Low degree of understandability by developers but high degree of understandability by users.
4. Low degree of understandability by developers and low degree of understandability by users.

We assume that the reviewers of SRS represent both parties.

If n_{ur} is the number of requirements which were thought to be understood by the reviewers, then the metric for this quality attribute is

$$Q_4 = \frac{n_{ur}}{n_r}$$

Because of its criticality to project success, a recommended weight for this metric is $W_4 = 1$.

Verifiable

An SRS is verifiable if every requirement can be verified within a reasonable time and cost. Unfortunately some requirements are difficult to verify due to ambiguity or due to exorbitant time and cost. If n_v is the number of requirements that can be verified within reasonable time and cost, a suitable metric is

$$Q_5 = \frac{n_v}{n_r}$$

Its recommended weight W_5 is 0.7.

Internally Consistent

An SRS is internally consistent if and only if no subsets of individual requirements stated therein conflict. Considering an SRS to be a deterministic FSM that maps inputs and states to outputs and states, if there are n_i inputs and n_s states, then there should be $(n_i \times n_s)$ unique functions. But if the SRS is internally inconsistent then the corresponding FSM will be non-deterministic, resulting in more than one output or state for the same input and state. Taking cue from this analogy, we define the metric for this quality attribute as

$$Q_6 = \frac{n_u - n_n}{n_r}$$

where, n_u is the number of actual unique functions in the SRS and n_n is the number of non-deterministic functions in the SRS. Recommended weight for this metric is $W_6 = 1$.

Externally Consistent

An externally consistent SRS does not have any requirement in conflict with baselined documents such as system-level requirements specifications, statements of work, white papers, an earlier version of SRS to which this new SRS must be upward compatible, and with other specifications with which this software will interface. If n_{EC} is the number of externally consistent requirements in the SRS, then the metric for this quality attribute is

$$Q_7 = \frac{n_{EC}}{n_r}$$

The recommended weight is $W_7 = 1$.

Achievable

An SRS is achievable if there is at least one design and implementation that can correctly implement all the requirements stated therein. Thus the quality metric Q_8 takes the value of 1 or 0 depending on if the requirements are implementable within the given resources. The weight recommended is $W_8 = 1$.

Concise

An SRS is concise if it is as short as possible without adversely affecting any other quality of the SRS. Size (number of pages) of an SRS depends on the number of requirements. One way to assess the conciseness of an SRS is to compare the ratio (size/number of requirements) of the SRS with those of the other SRSs developed by the firm for other projects in the past. Thus the metric could be

$$Q_9 = \frac{(\text{size}/n_r)_{\min}}{\text{size}/n_r}$$

where the numerator $(\text{size}/n_r)_{\min}$ is the minimum of this ratio for all the SRSs developed by the organization in the past and the denominator is the value of the ratio for this SRS. Considering that it is not very critical to project success, the recommended weight for this metric is $W_9 = 0.2$.

Design-Independent

An SRS should not contain any design features; thus it should be possible to have more than one system design for a design-independent SRS. A metric for this quality a' ...te is

$$Q_{10} = \frac{n_{Ri \cup Rd}}{n_{Ri}}$$

where, R_i is the set of design-independent requirements, R_d is t' ... ments, and n_{Ri} and $n_{Ri \cup Rd}$ are respectively the number of requirer ...

Because projects can succeed even if certain re ... recommended weight is $W_{10} = 0.5$.

Traceable

If each requirement is referenced uniqu ... arranged hierarchically), then the SRS is trace ... as: (*a*) numbering paragraphs hierarchical' ... unique number for each requirement, an ... used to extract the requirements. The ...

$$Q_{11} = \ldots$$

Since it is not critic ... this metric is $W_{11} = 0.5$.

Modifiable

An SSR is modifiable if its structure and style are such that any changes can be made easily, completely, and consistently (IEEE 84). Since table of contents and index enhance modifiability, the metric for this attribute is taken as

$$Q_{12} = \begin{cases} 1, \text{ if the table of contents and index are provided.} \\ 0, \text{ otherwise.} \end{cases}$$

The weight W_{12} for this metric is highly application dependent.

The quality metrics Q_1 through Q_{12} and the wieghts W_1 through W_{12} can each take a value within 0 to 1. So the overall quality of an SRS is

$$Q = \frac{\sum_{i=1}^{12} W_i Q_i}{\sum_{i=1}^{12} W_i}$$

The requirements analysis phase culminates with an SRS — a document that provides a baseline for the design phase activities to start. The next seven chapters discuss the concepts, tools, and techniques underlying software design.

REFERENCES

Behforooz, A. and F. J. Hudson (1996), Software Engineering Fundamentals, Oxford University Press, New York.

Boehm, B. (1984), Verifying and Validating Software Requirements and Design Specifications, IEEE Software, Vol. 1, No. 1, January, pp. 75–88.

Davis, A., S. Overmyer, K. Jordan, J. Caruso, F. Dandashi, A. Dinh, G. Kincaid, G. Ledeboer, P. Reynolds, P. Sitaram, A. Ta, and M. Theofanos (1997), Identifying and Measuring Quality in a Software Requirements Specifications, in Software Requirements Engineering, by Thayer and Dorfman (eds.), IEEE Computer Society, Los Alamitos, CA, 2nd Edition, pp. 164–175.

Dunn, R.H. (1984), Software Defect Removal, NY: McGraw-Hill.

Ghezzi, C.M. Jazayeri, D. Mandrioli (1991), Fundamentals of Software Engineering, Prentice-[illegible] India, Eastern Economy Edition.

[illegible] 84), IEEE Guide to Software Requirements Specifications, Standard 830–1984, New [illegible] Society Press.

[illegible] EE Recommended Practice for Software Requirements Specifications, in [illegible] by Thayer and Dorfman (eds.), Second Edition, IEEE Computer [illegible] 176–205.

DESIGN

11 Introduction to Software Design

After the analysis phase, the design phase begins. While requirements specify *what* the software is supposed to give, design specifies *how* to develop the system so that it is capable of giving what it is supposed to give. Design, therefore, is a creative process of transforming the problem into a solution.

Design is both a (transitive) verb and a noun. As a verb, it means to "*draw; to perform a plan; to contrive; ...*". It means "processes and techniques for carrying out design". As a noun, it means "*a plan or scheme formed in the mind, pattern, relationship of parts to the whole; ...*". It means "*notations for expressing or representing design*". In the context of software engineering, the term has interpretation both as a verb and as a noun. These definitions bring out several facets of design:

A. *Process.* It is an intellectual (creative) activity.

B. *Process and product.* It is concerned with breaking systems into parts and identifying the relationships between these parts.

C. *Product.* It is a plan, the structure of the system, its functionality, etc., in the sense of an architect's drawing to which a system will be built, and it also forms the basis for organizing and planning the remainder of the development process.

Another important facet of design is its "quality". Hence the fourth facet of design can be stated as under:

D. *Quality of design.* This constitutes the guidelines and procedures for carrying out the design verification and validation.

Design is important. Given below is a list of points signifying the importance of design:

1. Design provides the basic framework that guides how the program codes are to be written and how personnel are to be assigned to tasks.
2. Design errors outweigh coding errors. They take more time to detect and correct, and are therefore costlier, than coding. Table 11.1 makes a comparison between design and coding errors based on a study of 220 errors.
3. Design provides a basis for monitoring the progress and rewarding the developers.
4. A poorly designed software product is often unreliable, inflexible, inefficient, and not maintainable, because it is made up of a conglomeration of uncoordinated, poorly tested, and, sometimes, undocumented pieces.

5. The larger the system and the larger the number of developers involved, the more important the design becomes.

Table 11.1: Design and Coding Errors

	Design errors	Coding errors
Total	64%	36%
Average Diagnostic Time	3.1 hours	2.2 hours
Average Correction Time	4.0 hours	0.8 hour

11.1 GOALS OF GOOD SOFTWARE DESIGN

Goals of good software design are presented here under three heads. The first divides the goals as functional, nonfunctional, and legal. The second elaborates the design quality factors and attributes. And the third identifies the five most important software design goals.

11.1.1 Functional, Nonfunctional, and Legal Goals

Design goals may be classified as under:

1. *The Functional Objective:* Deliver the functionality required by the user.
2. *The Non-functional (Quality) Objectives.* These objectives may be:
   (*a*) *Directly quantifiable requirements*
      (*i*) *Performance parameters,* such as response times, throughput, down-time percentages.
      (*ii*) *Crudely quantifiable quality characteristics,* such as coupling and cohesion.
      (*iii*) *Difficult-to-quantify requirements,* such as safety and security (for high-integrity systems).
   (*b*) *Non-quantifiable requirements*
      (*i*) *User interface related attributes and quality attributes,* such as user-friendliness, robustness, and reliability.
      (*ii*) *Long-term behaviour related properties,* such as maintainability, modifiability, extensibility, and reusability.
3. *Legal objectives.*

11.1.2 Quality Factors and Attributes of Software Design

Design greatly affects software quality. It not only affects its correctness, but it also affects efficiency, reliability, portability, maintainability, reusability, and interoperability, among others. Software design is best described by its quality attributes. The quality attributes can be product-, process-, or design-oriented:

- *Product-oriented quality attributes* (Witt *et al.* 1994) are: Modularity, Portability, Malleability (adaptation to changing user requirements), and Conceptual integrity (adhering to a single concept).

- *Process-oriented quality attributes* are: Feasibility, Simplicity, Manageability, Quality, Reliability, and Productivity.
- *Design-oriented quality attributes* (Parnas and Weiss 1987) are: Structuredness (degree of consistency with the chosen design principles), Simplicity, Efficiency, Adequacy, Flexibility, Practicality, Implementability, and Degree of Standardization.

ISO (ISO 9126) has suggested six design quality factors each associated with a number of quality attributes (Fig. 11.1).

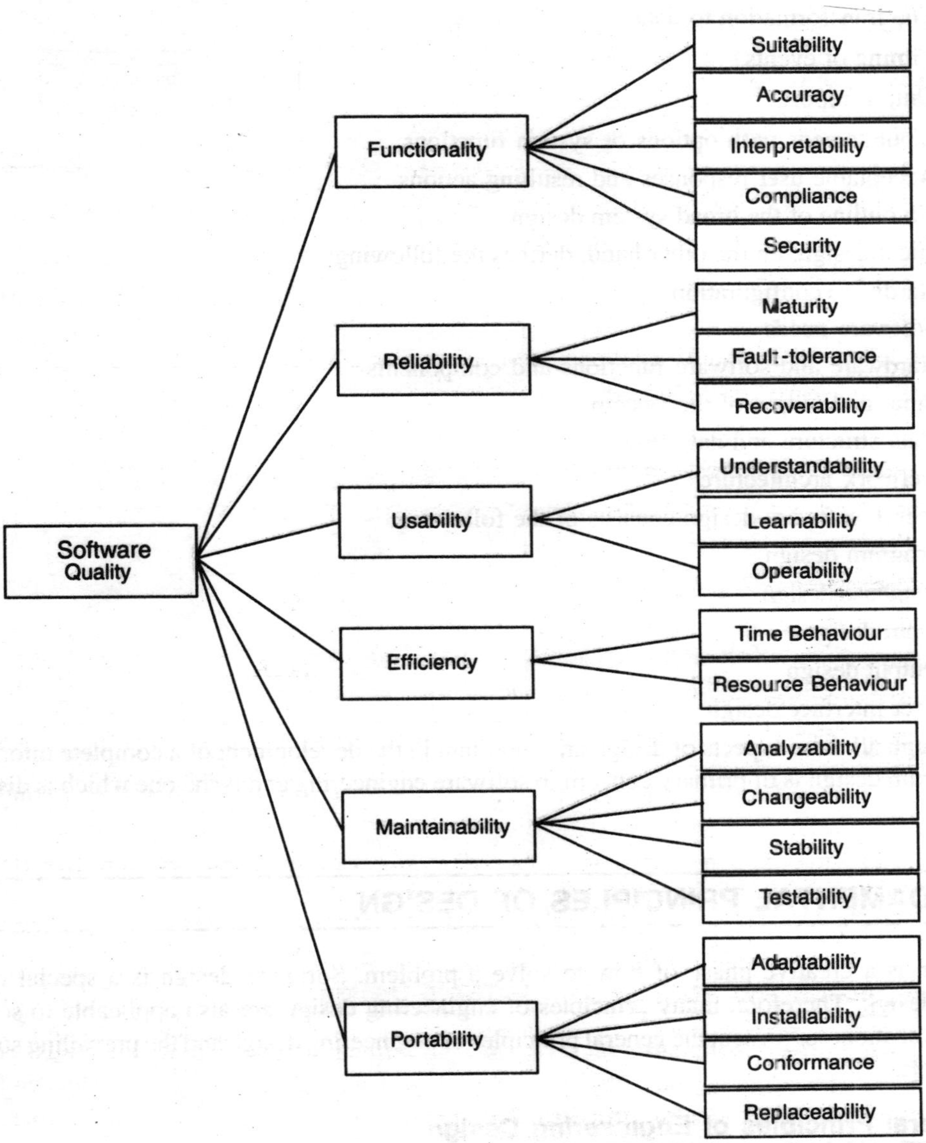

Fig. 11.1. ISO software quality model

11.2 CONCEPTUAL DESIGN AND TECHNICAL DESIGN

Pfleeger (2001) has distinguished between *conceptual design* and *technical design*. The conceptual design is concerned with the "What" of the design while the technical design is concerned with the "How" of the design. Written in customer-understandable language, linked to requirements document, and independent of implementation, the conceptual design defines the following:

- The source of data
- The transformation to data
- Timing of events
- Output report
- Input screens with options or system functions
- Acceptable user responses and resulting actions
- An outline of the broad system design

Technical design, on the other hand, defines the following:

- Hardware configuration
- Software needs
- Hardware and software functions and components
- Input and output of the system
- Data structure and data flow
- Network architecture

In general, software design consists of the following:

1. Program design
2. Database design
3. Input design
4. Output design
5. User interface design

Although all these aspects of design are important in the development of a complete information system, program design is of primary concern in software engineering and is the one which is discussed in this text.

11.3 FUNDAMENTAL PRINCIPLES OF DESIGN

Design is a creative phase of how to solve a problem. Software design is a special case of engineering design. Therefore, many principles of engineering design are also applicable to software design. In this section, we present the general principles of engineering design and the prevailing software design principles.

11.3.1 General Principles of Engineering Design

Mayall (1979) has proposed a set of ten axioms and has considered them as "principles". We state these principles with examples from the field of software design.

1. *The Principle of Totality:* Design requirements are always interrelated and must always be treated as such throughout the design task. Conflicting user requirements for a software product must be given due cognizance.
2. *The Principle of Time:* The features and characteristics of the products change as time passes. Command-line input-output has given way to graphic user interfaces for human-computer interaction.
3. *The Principle of Value:* The characteristics of products have different relative values depending upon the specific circumstances and times in which they may be used. A good program of yesteryears may not serve the users' (non-functional) requirements today.
4. *The Principle of Resources:* The design, manufacture, and life of all products and systems depend upon materials, tools, and skills upon which they are built. Development tools, human skills, and run-time support systems influence the quality of software design.
5. *The Principle of Synthesis:* Features of a product must combinedly satisfy its desired design quality characteristics with an acceptable relative importance for as long as we wish, bearing in mind the resources available to make and use it. The software design quality is greatly influenced by the time and effort deployed.
6. *The Principle of Iteration:* Evaluation is essential to design and is iterative in nature. It begins with the exploration of the need for the product, continues throughout the design and development stages, and extends to the user, whose reactions will often cause the iterative process to develop a new product.
7. *The Principle of Change:* Design is a process of change, an activity undertaken not only to meet changing circumstances, but also to bring about changes to those circumstances by the nature of the product it creates. Business process reengineering has become essential when new software products are adopted.
8. *The Principle of Relationships:*Design work cannot be undertaken effectively without established working relationships with all the activities concerned with the conception, manufacture, and marketing of products and, importantly, with the prospective user. That the user is central to a software product has been unequivocally accepted in software engineering discipline.
9. *The Principle of Competence:* The design team must have the ability to synthesize the desired product features with acceptable quality characteristics.
10. *The Principle of Service:* Design must satisfy everybody, and not just those for whom its products are directly intended. Maintainability, portability, reusability, etc., are other design features which do not directly concern the user but are important to design.

11.3.2 Software Design Principles

Based on the general principles of engineering design, software design principles have evolved over the years. These principles have provided the fundamental guidelines for software design. The principles, as stated here, have many overlapping concepts that will be obvious when we discuss them. The important principles are the following:

- Abstraction
- Divide-and-Conquer Concept
- Control Hierarchy

- Principle of Information Hiding
- Principle of Localization

Abstraction

Abstraction, in general, is the process of forming a general concept as separate from the consideration of particular instances. When applied to the process of software design, it permits one to concentrate on a problem at some level of generalization, considering the low level of details as irrelevant, while working with the concepts and terms that are familiar in the problem environment. Application of this concept has divided the field of design into two distinct but related levels of design:

(*a*) The architectural design

(*b*) The detailed design

During architectural design, we talk in terms of broad functions (high-level abstraction), and during detailed design, we talk in terms of procedures (low-level abstraction).

Architectural design has the following features:

- A high-level design is created where the general structure (architecture) of the system is determined.
- The system is decomposed into subsystems with interfaces properly defined.
- All the software requirements are allocated to the subsystems and are verified against the software specifications.
- An architectural design review is done and a design baseline is defined.

Detailed design is concerned with:

- Developing specific algorithms and data structures for each module (subsystem) defined in the architectural design.
- Allocating software requirements to the modules.
- Verifying against the requirements specifications and the architectural design used as the baseline.
- Defining the detailed design as the baseline.

In the recent years, a third level of design abstraction — *software architecture* — has evolved. It is a set of abstract, system-level designs, indicating architectural styles (the structure and organization) by which components and subsystems interact to form systems and which enable to design and analyze the properties of systems at the system level. We devote a full chapter to a discussion on software architecture.

Divide-and-Conquer Concept

According to this concept, a difficult problem should be solved by dividing it into a set of smaller, independent problems that are easier to understand and solve. This principle is used to simplify the programming process (functional decomposition) and the program (modularity). Two important considerations are made here:

- Multi-level, functional decomposition
- Modularity

Multi-level, functional decomposition

The *method of multi-level functional decomposition* is general and is applied to design in many fields of engineering. When applied to software design, the method is concerned with decomposing a function into sub-functions and sub-sub-functions at different levels. At each level, the system is described by the specifications of each component and their interactions i.e., by their functions and interface specifications.

In the field of software engineering, the process of hierarchical decomposition is known as '*stepwise refinement*' (Wirth 1971). Here, a hierarchy is developed by decomposing a macroscopic statement of function in a stepwise fashion until programming language statements are reached. Stepwise refinement forms the background of the *top-down design* and other *structured design methodologies,* discussed later in this chapter.

Modularity

The basic unit of decomposition in the software architecture is referred to as a *module.* All modules are integrated to satisfy problem requirements. A module is often composed of other modules, representing a hierarchical composition of modules. According to Myer (1978), modularity is the single attribute of software that allows a program to be intellectually manageable. DeMarco (1982) remarks that the principal approach to design is to determine a set of modules or components and intercomponent interfaces that satisfy a specified set of requirements. We call a design *modular* when a specific function is performed by exactly one component and when intercomponent inputs and outputs are well-defined. To specify a module, one has to specify its function and its interface with other modules.

While specifying the module function, the following points are always kept in mind:

(*a*) What the modules and the functions within the modules actually do is the primary (but not the only) source of information for detailed design and implementation.

(*b*) In defining the function of a module, the Parnas' principle of '*information hiding*' is applied. This principle asks the designer to hide inessential information, so that a module sees (gets) only the information needed by it, and nothing more. The principle guides the functional decomposition process and the design of the module interfaces. Hiding inessential information makes a system easier to understand and maintain.

The architectural definition of module interfaces deals with the following:

(*a*) Type and format of parameters passing to the module functions:
- Whether a numerical value is passed.
- Whether a variable name with its value is passed.
- Whether a variable name passed with one value is passed back to the calling module with a new value.

(*b*) Protocol governing the communication between the modules:
- Whether a calling module stops waiting for a value from the called module.
- Whether a calling module continues to work concurrently with the module which it calls.

Control Hierarchy

Merely defining the modules is not enough. It is also important to know the way the control is exercised among the modules. Usually, modules are connected in a hierarchical manner, with high-level modules mainly doing the control and coordination functions and the low-level modules mainly doing the computational work. This is discussed in more detail later in the section on Structured Design.

Principle of Information Hiding

The Principle of Information Hiding, as enunciated by Parnas (1972), requires that the modules be defined independently of each other so that they communicate with one another only for that information which is necessary to achieve the software function. The advantages of this principle are the following:

- Code development for the module is easy.
- Since the scope is limited, testing the module becomes easy.
- Any error that may creep into the code during modification will not propagate to other parts of the software.

Principle of Localization

This principle requires that all logically related items should be placed close to one another i.e., all logically related items should be grouped together physically. This principle applies both to data sets and process sets. Thus, both data sets (such as arrays and records) and program sets (such as subroutines and procedures) should ideally follow the principle of localization.

The following additional design principles are due to Witt *et al.* (1994) and Zhu (2005):

- ***Principle of Conceptual Integrity.*** This calls for uniform application of a limited number of design forms.
- ***Principle of Intellectual Control.*** It is achieved by recording designs as hierarchies of increasingly detailed abstractions.
- ***Principle of Visualization.*** This calls for giving visibility to a design with the help of diagrams, pictures, and figures.

11.4 DESIGN GUIDELINES

Braude (2004) identifies five important software goals and provides a set of design guidelines for achieving these goals. The five software goals are the following:

1. *Correctness.* Satisfying software requirements as specified in the SRS is correctness. This term is generally reserved for the detailed design. When used in the stage of design of architecture, it measures the sufficiency of the design to implement the software requirements.
2. *Robustness.* A design is robust if it is able to handle miscellaneous and unusual conditions such as bad data, user error, programmer error, and environmental conditions.
3. *Flexibility.* A design should be flexible to change according to changing requirements. Some of the changes are to handle (*a*) more volume of transactions, (*b*) new functionalities, and (*c*) changing functionalities.
4. *Reusability.* Quick creation of useful products with assured quality at minimal cost is referred to as reusability. Readymade windows and reusable classes, such as Java API, are examples of reusable components.Options for reusability are many: (*a*) object code, (*b*) classes in source code, (*c*) assemblies of related classes (such as Java.awt package), and (*d*) patterns of class assemblies.

5. *Efficiency.* Time and storage space required to give a solution determine the efficiency of a design. Usually, time-cost trade-offs are possible.

Below we discuss the guidelines for each of the five design goals.

11.4.1 Correctness

When used for meaning sufficiency, one has to use informal approaches that judge whether a given design is sufficient to implement the software requirements. It thus boils down to mean understandability (the ease of understanding the design), which, in turn, is facilitated by design modularity. Modularity is achieved in object-oriented design by defining classes or packages of classes. To achieve design correctness, modularization and interfaces to modules must be properly designed.

Formal approaches to achieving correctness are usually applied in the detailed design stage. It involves keeping the variable changes under tight control by specifying invariants which define the unchanging relationships among variable values. We give examples, based on object-oriented design, to illustrate the application of this guideline:

In class-level designs, class invariants for a class *Employee* can take the following forms for its variables:

- *name* has at most 20 alphabetic characters.
- *gender* is either M or F.
- *experience* > 5.

The operations of *Employee* have to check for the satisfaction of these invariants.

Modularization and Module Interfaces

Modularization is done in object-oriented applications at either the lower levels (classes) or the higher levels (packages). Classes should be chosen as under:

- Normally, *domain classes* are selected from a consideration of the use case and the sequence diagrams drawn during the object-oriented analysis.
- *Non-domain classes,* such as abstract and utility classes, are defined from design and implementation considerations. They are needed to generalize the domain classes, as we shall see soon.

When a class has many operations, it is better to group the methods into interfaces. Basically the operations are polymorphic and the class organization is like a gen-spec diagram (Fig. 11.2). Figure 11.2c is the UML notation for the interfaces.

Packages are an essential part of an application's architecture (Fig. 11.3). Together, they constitute the software architecture. An application may use even 10 packages. Unlike a class, a package cannot be instantiated. Therefore, to access the services of functions within a package, a client code interfaces with a class (that can have at most one object) of the package. This *singleton* class supports the interface. Note that the singleton class is stereotyped by enclosing its name within guillemets (a French notation for quotations).

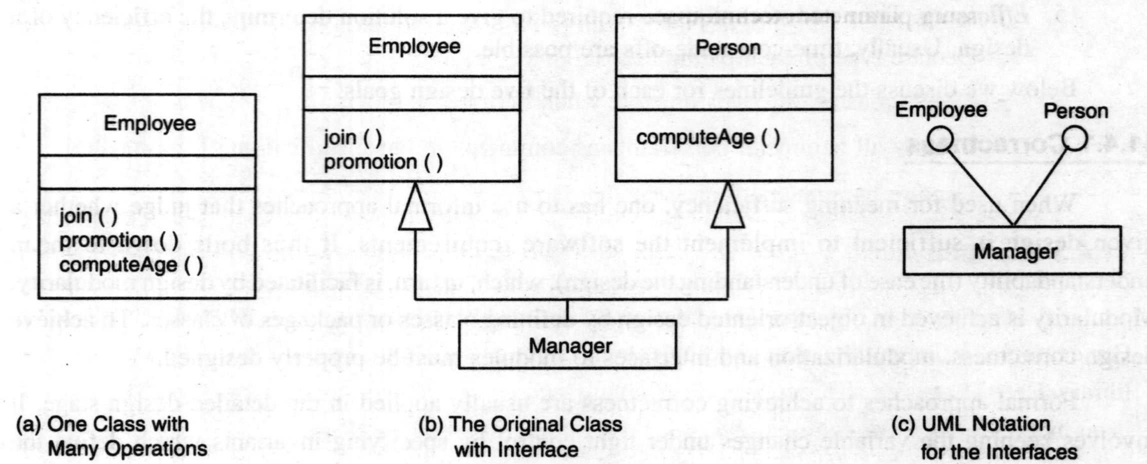

Fig. 11.2. Class interface

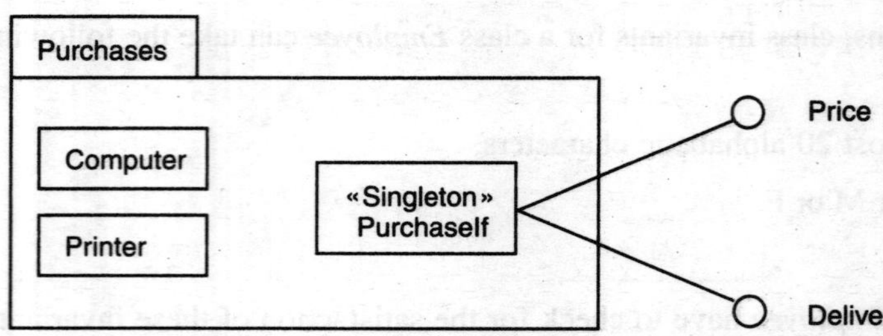

Fig. 11.3. Interfacing a package

Additional Guidelines for Achieving Correctness

Often, promoting attributes to the status of a class can improve the correctness (and flexibility) of an application. To increase the scope of application, *price,* otherwise an attribute of a *Product* class, can be made a class if its value changes with time as the cost of production changes.

Further, to make its application more general, an abstract class can be created and used as a base class. For example, a *worker* and a *manager* are each an *Employee* (base class).

11.4.2 Robustness

To withstand variations in environmental inputs, various age-old techniques are used. For example,

- Instead of aborting when a user enters an invalid account number, the program can prompt the user to try again.
- Carry out type verification (integer, string, etc.)
- Check against preconditions and invariants (*e.g., amountToWithdraw < balance*)
- Variables can be initialized.

- Passing parameters techniques:
  —Declare type of each parameter.
  —Check constraints on parameters when defining the method.
  —Specify all parameter constraints as comments in the specification of the method.
  —Capture parameters in classes.

11.4.3 Flexibility

Adding more of the same kind of functionality helps in handling more number of transactions. For example, a library may have its students as users and alumni can be added as new users of the library. Here *User* is an abstract base class having a *has-a* relationship with *Library* (Fig. 11.4). *Student* is an inherited class. *Alumnus* can be added as another inherited class.

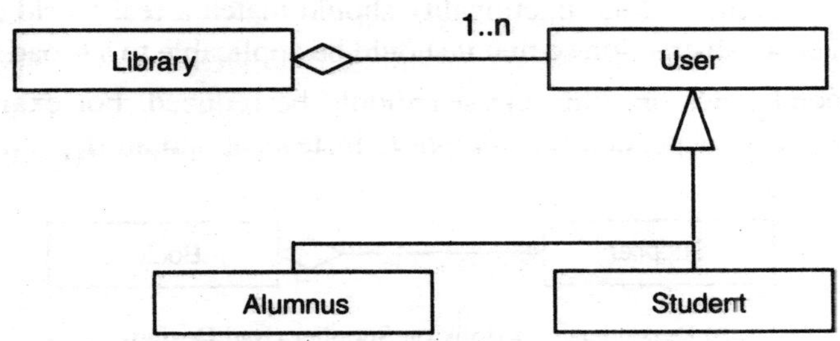

Fig. 11.4. Flexibility for additional transactions

Adding new functionalities is possible by

- adding a method to an existing set of related methods of a class (such as *computeRemaining Leave*) to an existing class *Leave* which may have such methods as *getLeaveDetails* and *computeLeaveTaken.*
- adding child classes with similar new methods within the scope of a base class (Fig. 11.5).
- adding design flexibility by design patterns. This is the subject of the Chapter XV which is discussed within the scope of object-oriented design.

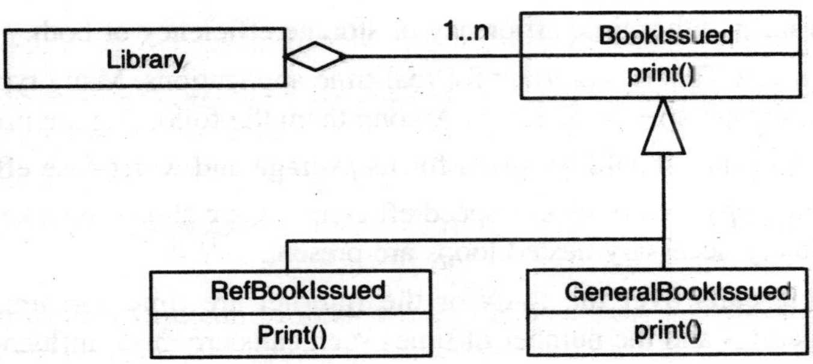

Fig. 11.5. Flexibility for additional function within the scope of a base class

11.4.4 Reusability

Methods, classes, and combination of classes can be reused:

- *Reusability of methods.* Reusability of a method is better if it is independent of its environment. Static methods are thus highly reusable. But they suffer from the fact that they have loose coupling with the classes containing them. They are thus less object-oriented. Certain guidelines for reusability of methods are the following:
  (*a*) Specify the method completely with preconditions, postconditions, and the like.
  (*b*) Avoid coupling with a class. Make it a static method if possible.
  (*c*) The method name should be self-explanatory.
  (*d*) The algorithm of the method should be available and easy to follow.
- *Reusability of class.* A class can be reusable if the following guidelines are followed:
  (*a*) The class should be completely defined.
  (*b*) The class name and its functionality should match a real-world concept. Or, the class should be an abstraction so that it should be applicable to a broad range of applications.
  (*c*) Its dependencies on other classes should be reduced. For example, the *Book* class should not be dependent on *Supplier;* instead, it should depend on *BookOrder* (Fig. 11.6).

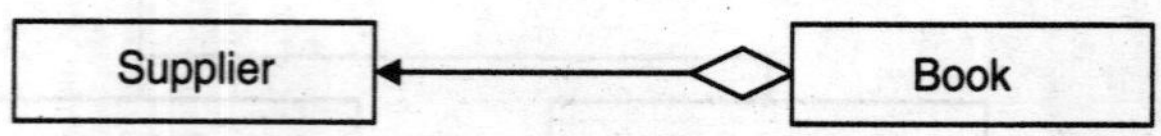

(*a*) Dependence of Book on Supplier (Bad Design)

(*b*) Dependence of Book on Supplier (Bad Design)

Fig. 11.6. Reusability of a class

- *Reusability of combination of classes.* Design patterns are especially designed to facilitate reusability of combination of classes. Here we show simple cases of getting reusability by alternatively using inheritance, aggregation, and dependency (Fig. 11.7). More about design patterns will be discussed in Chapter XV.

11.4.5 Efficiency

Efficiency can mean either time efficiency or storage efficiency or both.

- *Time Efficiency.* This is important for real-time applications. Many types of approaches are used for achieving speed efficiency. Among them the following are prominent:
  (*a*) The algorithm should be tested for its average and worst-case efficiency.
  (*b*) Nested loops greatly reduce speed efficiency. Care should be taken to see that only the absolutely necessary nested loops are present.
  (*c*) Remote calls over the LAN or the Internet are time consuming. The volume of transactions and the number of times such calls are made influence time efficiency.

(*d*) Sequence of function calls also reduces time efficiency.

- *Storage Efficiency.* To achieve storage efficiency, one should store only those data that are absolutely required and consider trading it off with the time required to obtain it after due processing.

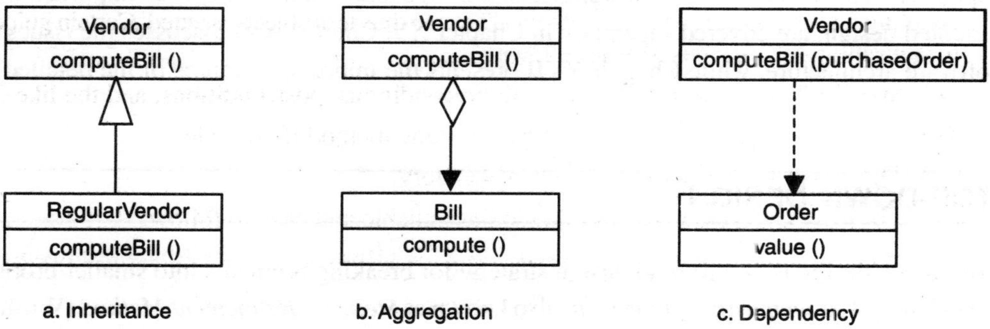

Fig. 11.7. Reusability of combination of classes-alternatives

In practice, one is usually confronted with the possibility of trading off one measure with another. For example, one may use extreme programming approach (that ensures the application at hand that is wanted) rather than go for flexible or reusable design.

11.5 DESIGN STRATEGIES AND METHODOLOGIES

Zhu (2005) suggests four software design strategies:

1. *Decompositional.* It is a top-down approach where stepwise refinement is done. Structured design approach is a good example of this strategy.
2. *Compositional.* Here entities and objects are classified, grouped, and interrelated by links. Jackson's structured programming and object-oriented design approaches are examples of this strategy.
3. *Template-based.* This strategy makes use of design reuse by instantiating design templates. Software architectures, styles, and design patterns are examples of this strategy.
4. *Evolutionary.* It is an incremental strategy.

There have been a number of methodological approaches to the design of software architecture during the past forty years. In this text we consider all these approaches so as to trace their evolution as well as know their application premises. These methodological approaches are the following:

1. Top-Down Design
2. Data-Structure-Oriented Design
   - Jackson Design Methodology
   - Warnier-Orr Design Methodology
3. Miller's Database-Oriented Design
4. Constantine and Yourdon's Dataflow-Oriented Structured Design
5. Object-Oriented Design

6. Design of Architecture

In the current chapter we shall discuss only the informal top-down design. In the next chapter (Chapter XII) we shall discuss the data-structure- and database-oriented designs. Dataflow-oriented design is covered in Chapter XIII whereas object-oriented design is covered in Chapter XIV and Chapter XV. Chapter XIV covers the basics of object-oriented design and design patterns, an important aspect in object-oriented design, are covered separately in Chapter XV. Chapter XVI discusses the issues related to the software architecture, while Chapter XVII presents the important features of the detailed design phase.

11.6 TOP-DOWN DESIGN

Top-down design is an informal design strategy for breaking problems into smaller problems. It follows a *functional decomposition approach,* also known as *Stepwise Refinement Method* (Wirth 1971). The approach begins with the most general function, breaks it down into sub-functions, and then repeats the process for each sub-function until all sub-functions are small enough and simple enough so that either they can be coded straightaway or they are obtainable off the shelf. The strategy is applicable to the design of a module, a program, a system, or even a data structure.

The process of top-down design can be divided into two parts:

Step 1: Define an initial design that is represented in terms of high-level procedural and data components.

Step 2-n: In steps, the procedural and data components are defined in more and more detail, following the stepwise refinement method.

The following guidelines are used to make design decisions:

- While breaking problems into parts, the components within each part should be logically related.
- Alternative designs are considered before adopting a particular design.

The following principles hold for the top-down approach:

- Input, function, and output should be specified for each module at the design step.
- Implementation details should not be addressed until late in the design process.
- At each level of the design, the function of a module should be explained by at most a single page of instructions or a single page diagram. At the top level, it should be possible to describe the overall design in approximately ten or fewer lines of instructions and/or calls to lower-level modules.
- Data should receive as much design attention as processing procedures because the interfaces between modules must be carefully specified.

The top-down design is documented in narrative form (pseudocode), graphic form (hierarchy chart), or a combination of the above. Alternatively, *Hierarchy plus Input-Process-Output (HIPO) diagrams* can be used to document the design. HIPO diagrams are proposed by IBM (1974) and were very popular at one time.

There are three kinds of HIPO diagrams:

1. Visual Table of Contents
2. Overview Diagrams
3. Detail Diagrams

A *visual table of contents* is the highest-level HIPO diagram. It shows the interrelationships among the modules, indicating how a system (program) is broken down in hierarchical manner into subsystems, programs, or program modules. *Overview HIPO diagrams* describe the input, the process, and the output of the top-level functional components, whereas *Detail HIPO diagrams* deal with those of the low-level functional components.

Detail diagrams give textual description of each process and identify the module name. These diagrams contain three boxes, one each for input, process, and output:

1. An *input box* shows the input data items that may be a file, a table, an array, or an individual program variable.
2. A *process box* contains the relevant sub-functions that are identified in the visual table of contents. It also contains the logic that governs the execution of the process steps.
3. An *output box* contains the output data produced by the process. The output data item may be a file, a table, a report, an error message, or a variable.

Top-down design helps to achieve the following objectives:

(*a*) Systematize the design process,

(*b*) Produce a modular program design, and

(*c*) Provide a framework for problem solving.

Top-down design is appropriate for the design of small, simple programs, but becomes too informal a strategy to guide the design process of large systems.

An example of Top-Down Design is presented in Fig. 11.8 through Fig. 11.10 for an Employee Payroll system.

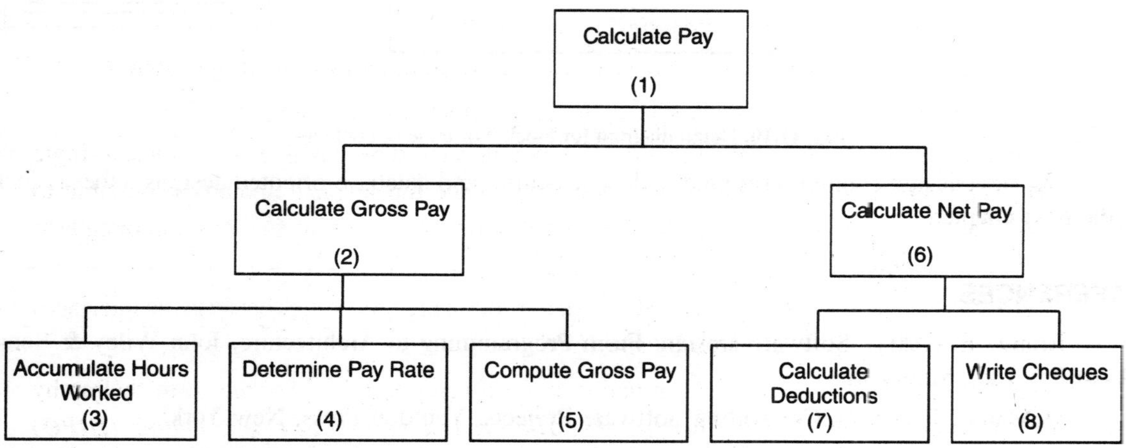

Fig. 11.8. Visual table of contents for calculating pay

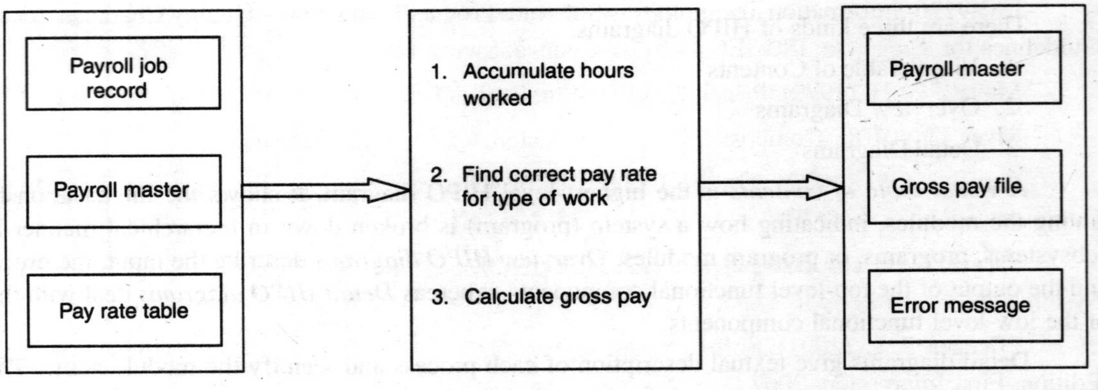

Fig. 11.9. Overview diagram for block 2 of table of contents

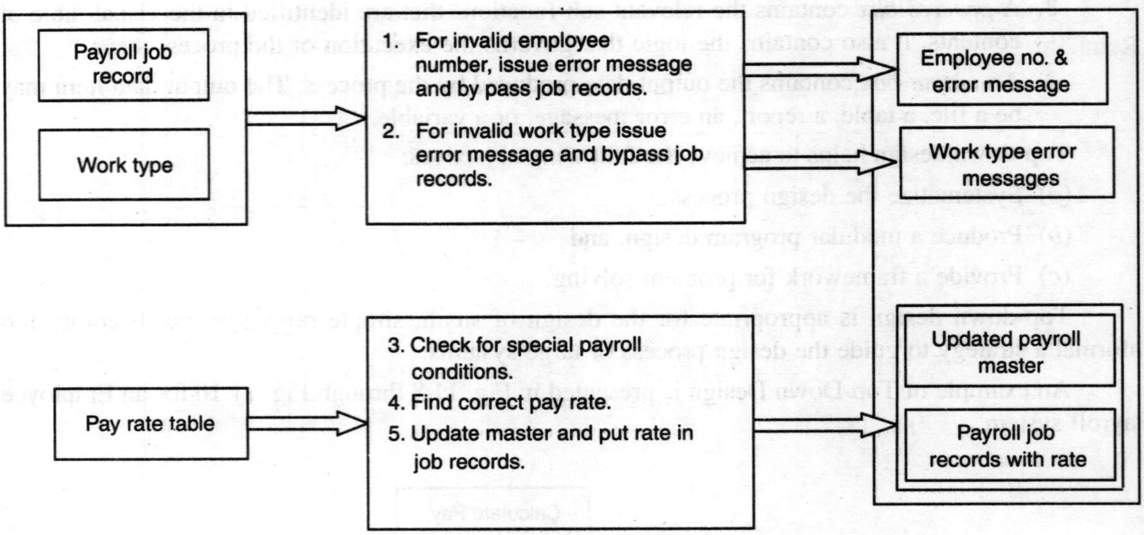

Fig. 11.10. Detail diagram for block 3 of table of contents

The next design evolution resulted in data-structure- and database-oriented designs—the subject of the next chapter.

REFERENCES

Braude E. (2004), Software Design: From Programming to Architecture, John Wiley & Sons (Asia) Pvt. Ltd., Singapore.

DeMarco, T. (1982), Controlling Software Projects, Yourdon Press, New York.

IBM (1974), HIPO: A Design Aid and Implementation Technique (GC20-1850), White Plains, IBM Corporation, New York.

ISO 9126: Information Technology—Software Product Evaluation—Quality Characteristics and Guidelines for Their Use, ISO/IEC IS 9126, Geneva, Switzerland.

Mayall, W. H. (1979), Principles in Design, Design Council, London.

Myer, G. (1978), Composite/Structured Design, Van Nostrand Reinhold.

Parnas, D. L. (1972), On the Criteria to be Used in Decomposing Systems into Modules, Communications of the ACM, vol. 15, no. 2, pp. 1053–1058.

Parnas, D. L. and D, M. Weiss (1987), Active Design Reviews: Principles and Practices, J. of Systems and Software, vol. 7, no. 4, pp. 259–265.

Pfleeger, S. L. (2001), Software Engineering: Theory and Practice, Pearson Education, Second Edition, First Impression, 2007.

Wirth, B. (1971), Program Development by Stepwise Refinement, Communications of the ACM, vol. 14, no. 4, pp. 221–227.

Witt, B., T. Baker and E. Merritt (1994), Software Architecture and Design, Van Nostrand Reinhold, New York.

Zhu, H. (2005), Software Design Methodology, Butterworth-Heinemann, Oxford.

12 Data-Oriented Software Design

In this chapter we shall discuss three data-oriented software design methods. These methods are oriented according to either the underlying data structures or the underlying data base structure. Accordingly they are grouped as under:

A. Data Structure-Oriented Design
 —Jackson Design Methodology
 —Warnier-Orr Design Methodology

B. Data Base-Oriented Design

12.1 JACKSON DESIGN METHODOLOGY

Developed by Jackson (1975), this methodology of designing program structure is based on an analysis of the data structure. The design process consists of first defining the structure of the data streams and then ordering the procedural logic (or operations) to fit the data structure. The design consists of four sequential steps:

1. *Data Step.* Each input and output data stream is completely and correctly specified as a *tree structure diagram.*
2. *Program Step.* All the data structures so produced are combined with the help of a *structure network diagram* into one hierarchical program structure. There has to be one-to-one correspondence (*consume-produce relationship*) between the *input data stream* and the *output data stream,* such that one instance of the input data stream is *consumed* (used) to produce one instance of the output data stream. A program structure encompassing corresponding input and output data structures is thereafter created.
3. *Operation Step.* A list of executable operations is now made that makes it possible to produce program output from the input. Each operation on the list is then allocated to a component of the program structure.
4. *Text Step.* The program structure is then transcribed into a *structure text* (a format version of pseudocode) adding conditional logic that governs selection and iteration structures.

Tree-structure diagrams show control constructs of sequence, selection, and iteration. The following guidelines help show these constructs in a tree-structure diagram:

- The *sequence* of the parts is from left to right. Each part occurs only once and in a specified manner. Figure 12.1 shows an example of a sequence component.
- The *selection* between two or more parts is shown by drawing a small circle in the upper right-hand corner of each of the components. Figure 12.2 shows a selection component.
- The *iteration* of a component is shown by an asterisk in the upper right-hand corner of the component. Figure 12.3 shows an iteration component.
- Both selection and iteration are low-level structures. The first level names the component and the second level lists the parts which are alternatives or which iterate.

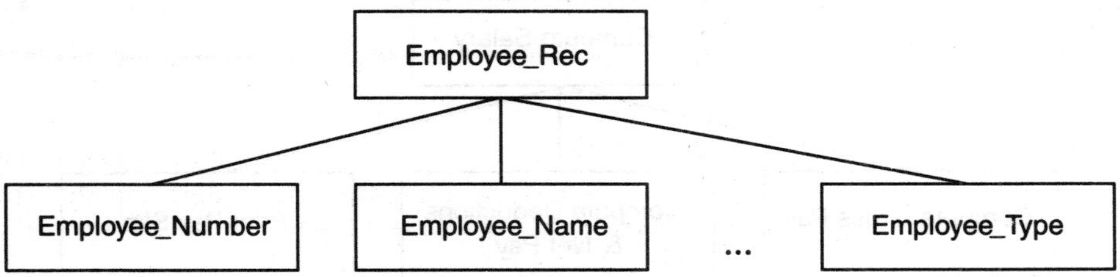

Fig. 12.1. Sequence in data structure diagram

They are called *data-structure diagram* when applied to depicting the structure of data and are called the *program-structure diagrams* when applied to depicting the structure of the programs. Figure 12.1 through Fig. 12.3 show examples of data-structure diagrams, whereas Fig. 12.4 through 12.6 show examples of program-structure diagrams.

A *system network diagram* is an overview diagram that shows how data streams enter and leave the programs (Fig. 12.7). The following symbols are used in a system network diagram:

- It uses circles for data streams and rectangles for programs.
- An arrow is used to depict relationships among data streams and programs.
- An arrow connects circle and a rectangle, not two circles or two rectangles.
- Each circle may have at most one arrow pointing towards it and one arrow pointing away from it.

Jackson methodology holds that if there is no clash between the structure of input file and that of the output file (so that there is a correspondence between the data structure diagram for the input file and that of the output file) then the program structure can be easily designed. The structure of the program also has a structure similar to that of the data structure because it consumes (gets) the input data file and produces the output file.

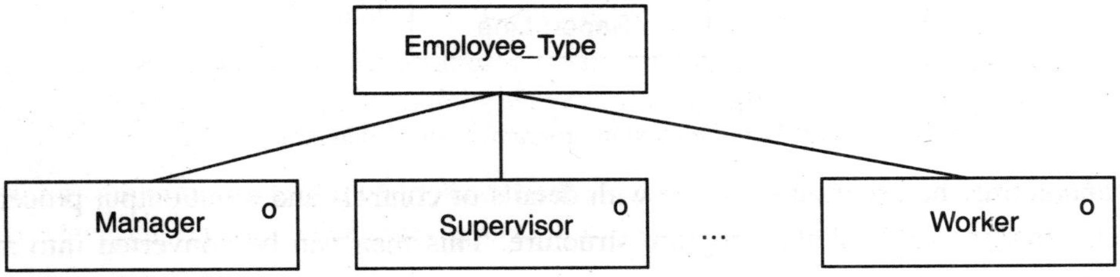

Fig. 12.2. Selection in data structure diagram

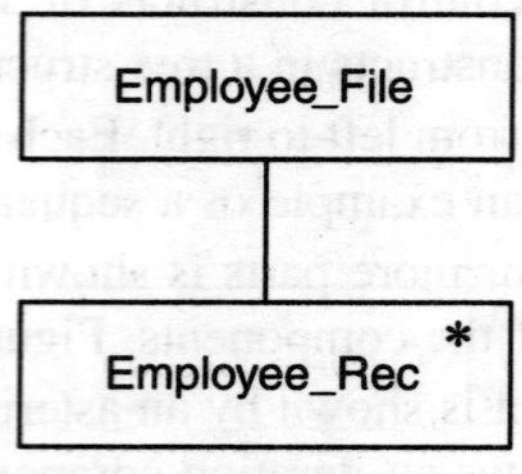

Fig. 12.3. Iteration in data structure diagram

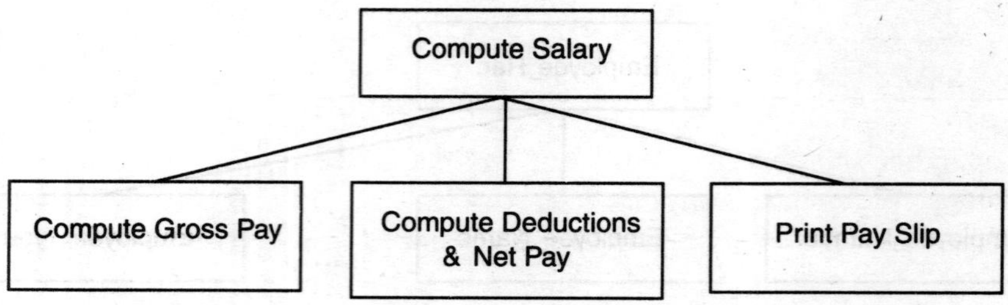

Fig. 12.4. Sequence in program structure diagram

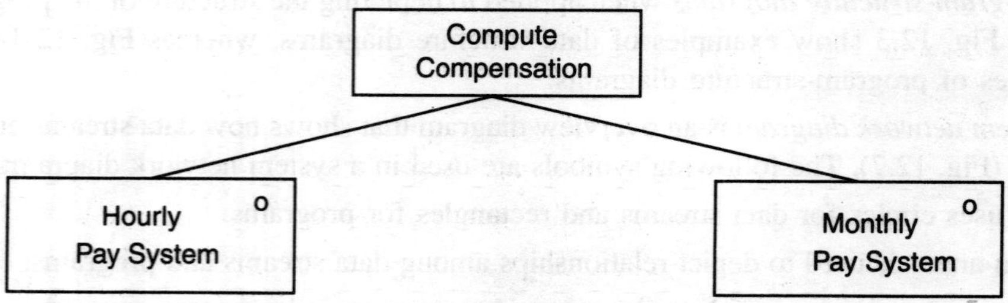

Fig. 12.5. Selection in program structure diagram

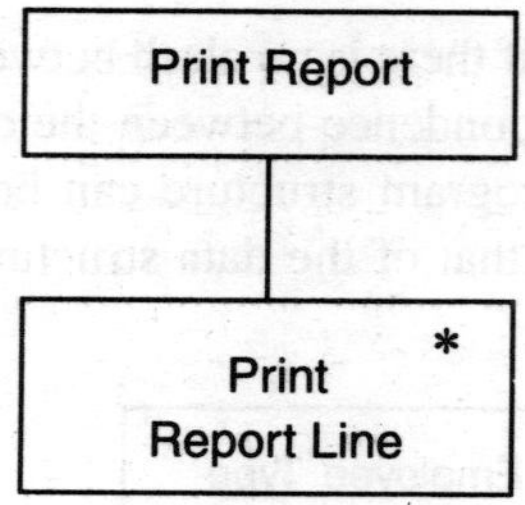

Fig. 12.6. Iteration in program structure diagram

By annotating the program structure with details of controls and input/output procedures, one gets a much broader vision of the program structure. This then can be converted into an English structure text version of the design.

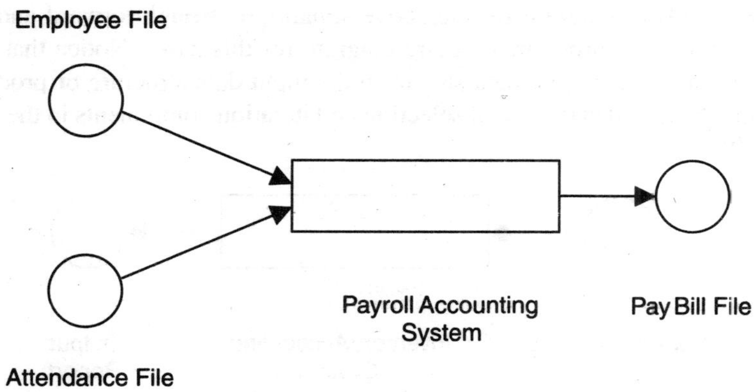

Fig. 12.7. System network diagram

We now apply the steps outlined at the beginning of this section to demonstrate the use of the Jackson methodology. We assume that we are interested to design the program for preparing a summary report on the status of inventory items after a series of receipts and withdrawals take place.

In the data step, we draw the tree-structure diagram of the input file and that of the output file. They are shown on the left-hand and the right-hand side of Fig. 12.8. Notice the horizontal lines joining, and indicating correspondence between, the blocks of the tree-structure diagrams for the input and the output files.

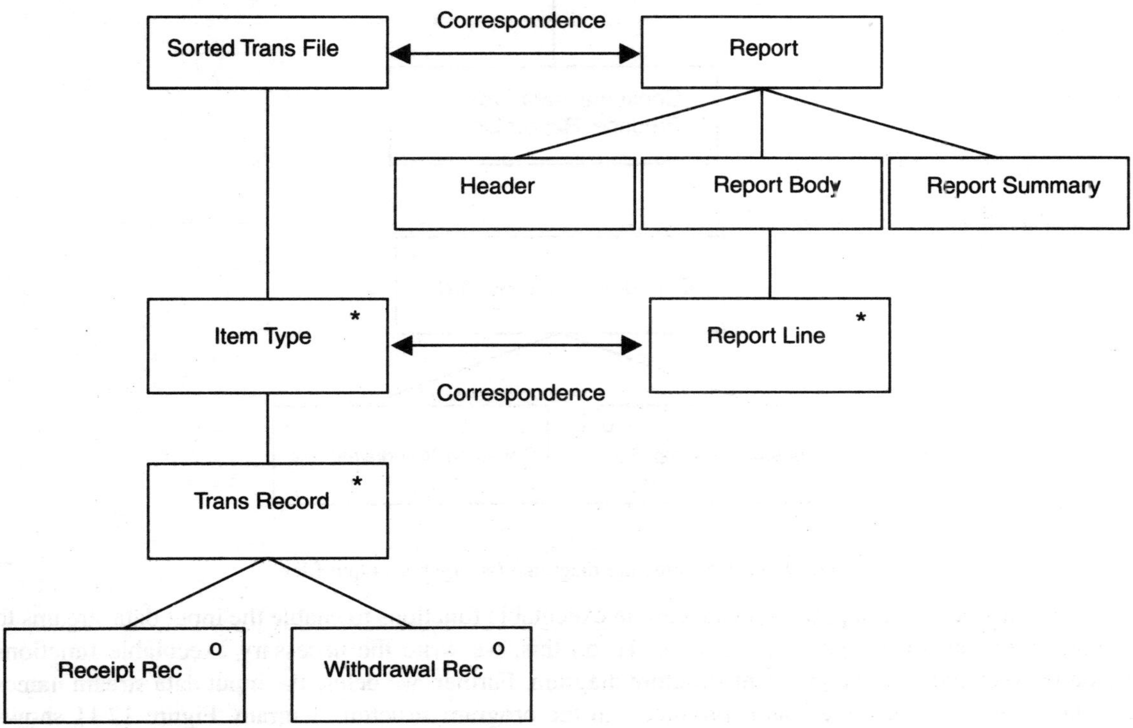

Fig. 12.8. Tree structure diagram for input and output files

The structure network diagram for the above situation is straightforward and is shown in Fig. 12.9. Figure 12.10 shows the program structure diagram for this case. Notice that each rectangle in Fig. 12.10 either consumes (uses) the data stream in the input data structure or produces the required output data structure. Notice also the use of selection and iteration components in the program structure diagram (Fig. 12.10).

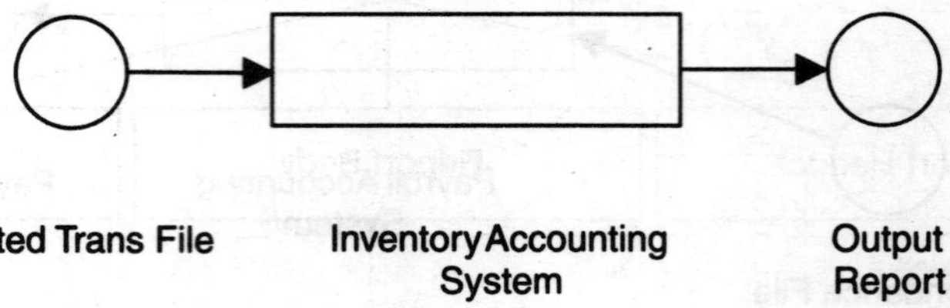

Fig. 12.9. System network diagram for the inventory problem

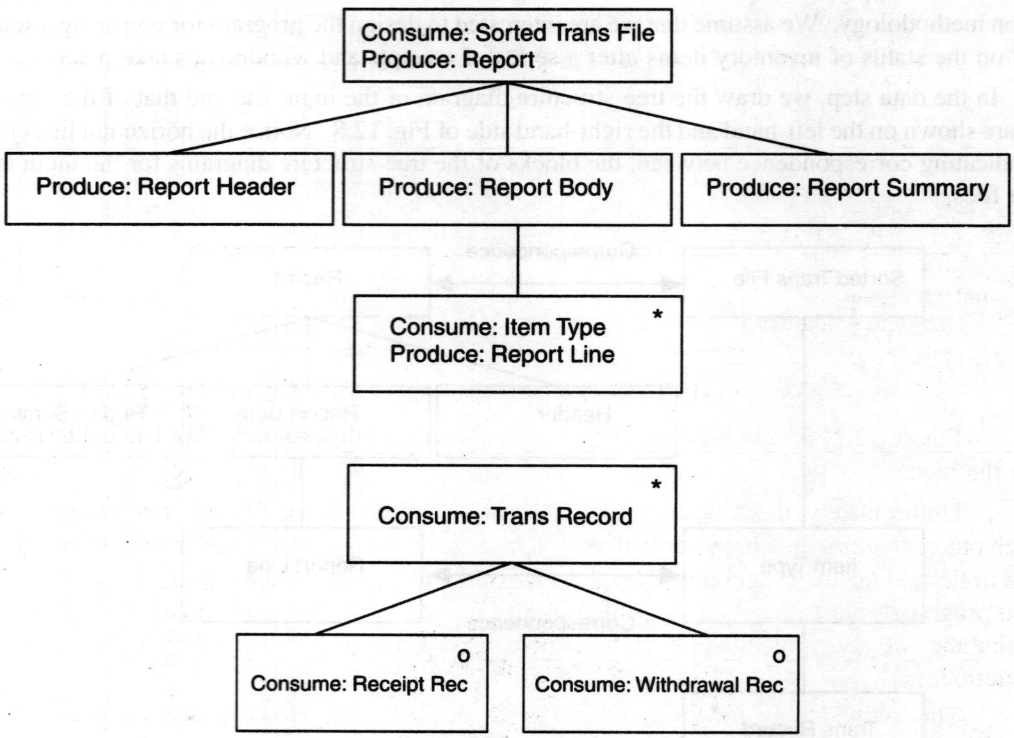

Fig. 12.10. Tree structure diagrams for input & output files

In the operation step, we allocate certain executable functions to enable the input data streams to be converted into the output data streams. To do this, we write the necessary executable functions beside the rectangles of the program structure diagram. Further, we delete the input data stream names and the keywords 'consumes' and 'produces' in the program structure diagram. Figure 12.11 shows the transformed program structure diagram.

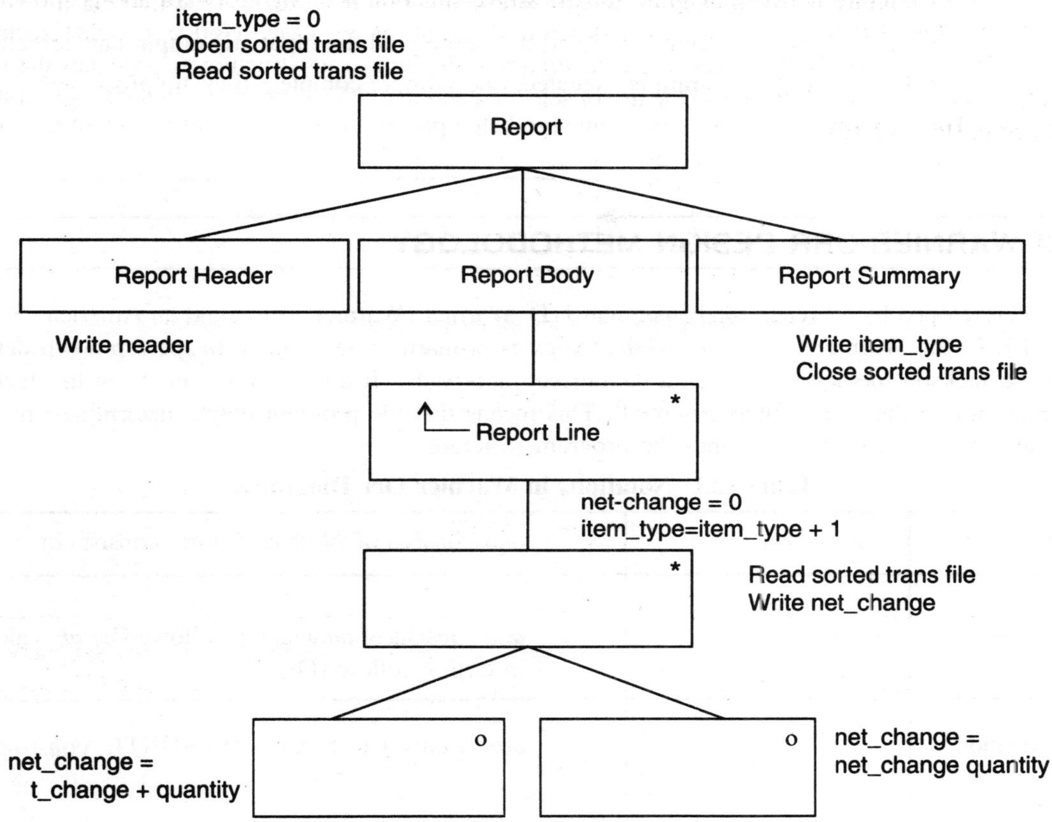

Fig. 12.11. Transformed program structure diagram

Figure 12.11 is now used to develop a pseudocode of the program. We leave this as an exercise for the reader.

Unfortunately, the data structures of the input and the output file may not perfectly match with each other, resulting in what is termed as *structure clash*. In the presence of such a structure clash, one has to first divide the program into two programs, define an intermediate data stream that connects the two programs (the data stream is written by the first program and read by the second program), and define the two data structures for the intermediate data stream (corresponding to each of the clashing structures).

This methodology, however, is weak in the areas of control logic design and design verification:

(*a*) Jackson held that the control logic is dictated by data structures, and, in fact, the condition logic governing loops and selection structures is added only during the last part of the last step of this design process.

(*b*) The methodology is applicable to a simple program that has the following properties:

- When the program is executed, nothing needs to be remembered from a previous execution.
- The program input and output data streams are sequential files.

- The data structures must be compatible and ordered with no structure clash.
- The program structure is ordered by merging all the input and output data structures.
- Each time the program is executed, one or more complete files are processed.

(*c*) The Jackson methodology is oriented to batch processing systems, but is effective even for online and data base systems.

12.2 WARNIER-ORR DESIGN METHODOLOGY

Developed by a French mathematician J. D. Warnier (Warnier, 1981) and an American K. Orr (Orr, 1977), the Warnier-Orr design methodology is primarily a refinement of the top-down design. Like the Jackson methodology, it is a data-driven approach. It differs, however, from the Jackson methodology in that it is 'output-oriented'. This means that the program output determines the data structure, which, in turn, determines the program structure.

Table 12.1: Notations in Warnier-Orr Diagrams

Hierarchy	aaa { bb { c	*aaa* consists of *bb* that, in turn, consists of *c*.
Sequence	aaa { aa aa aa	*aaa* consists of *aa* which is followed by *bb* which, in turn, is followed by *cc*.
Repetition	aaa (1, N) {	*aaa* occurs 1 to N times (DO UNTIL construct)
	aaa (N) {	*aaa* occurs 0 to N times (DO WHILE construct)
	aaa (10) {	*aaa* occurs ten times.
	aaa {	*aaa* occurs once.

Selection	{ bb {
	(0, 1)
	⊕
	cc {
	(0, 1)
		aaa consists of either *bb* (that occurs 0 or 1 time) or *cc* (that occurs 0 or 1 time) but *aaa* does not contain either *bb* or *cc*.

Concurrency	aaa { bb + c	*aaa* consists of both *bb* and *c*. The order of occurrence of *bb* and *c* is not important. They may also occur simultaneously.

The methodology extensively uses the Warnier-Orr diagrams. The various basic control structures and other ancillary structures are shown in diagrammatic forms. The various notations used in these diagrams are explained in Table 12.1.

Like Jackson diagrams, Warnier-Orr diagrams can represent both data structures and program structures. We now show some examples to illustrate the applications.

Figure 12.12 shows a Warnier-Orr diagram for a data structure. Here the *employee* file consists of *employee* records. Each *employee* record consists of fields (*employee number, name,* and *date of birth*) in sequence. Furthermore, *employee number* consists of sub-fields *year* and *serial number*, whereas *date of birth* consists of sub-fields *day, month,* and *year*.

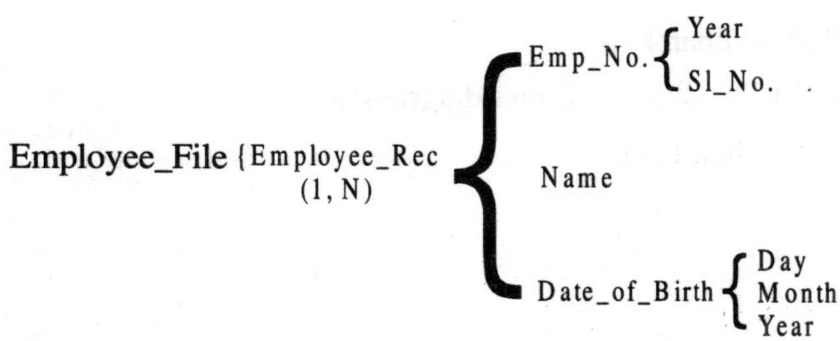

Fig. 12.12. An employee record

Figure 12.13 shows a Warnier-Orr diagram for a program structure. It shows that for each employee the program finds out if he is paid on a monthly salary basis or on a daily payment basis and accordingly finds the payment. This is a high-level design, however. One can develop such a diagram at the program level highlighting such elementary programming operations as reading a record, accumulating total, initializing variables, and printing a header.

Warnier-Orr design methodology follows six steps:

1. Define the program output in the form of a hierarchical data structure.
2. Define the logical data base, the data elements to produce the program outputs.
3. Perform event analysis, *i.e.,* define all the events that can affect (change) the data elements in the logical data base.
4. Develop the physical data base for the input data.
5. Design the logical program processing logic to produce the desired output.
6. Design the physical process, *e.g.,* add control logic and file-handling procedures.

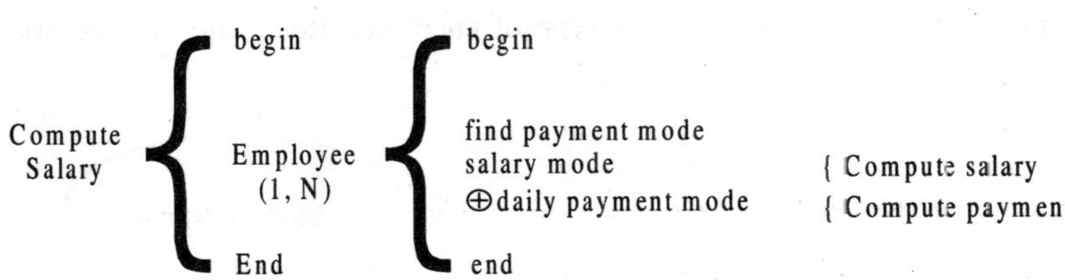

Fig. 12.13. Warnier-Orr diagram for a program structure

Once again, like Jackson methodology, Warnier-Orr methodology is applicable to simple, batch-processing type of applications. It becomes very complicated when applied to large, complex situations involving online, real-time applications.

12.3 DATABASE-ORIENTED DESIGN METHODOLOGY

Developed by Martin and McClure (1988), the database-oriented design methodology evolves around a data base where data are non-hierarchical in structure. This design makes use of the following tools, most of which are diagramming tools, like all the previous design methodologies:

1. Data Analysis diagram (or Bubble chart)
2. Entity-Relationship diagram (ER diagram, or Entity diagram)
3. Database Planning and Third-Normal Form
4. Data-Navigation diagram
5. Action diagram

12.3.1 Data Analysis Diagram

Data items form the most elemental form of data in a data base. This diagram provides a way of drawing and understanding the associations among the data items. The associations among different data-item types lead to what is called a *data model.* An understanding of the associations among data items in a data model is necessary to create records that are structured.

Associations among data items can be

1. one-to-one, or
2. one-to-many.

If a data-item type *A* has a *one-to-one association* with a data-item type *B*, then at any instant of time, each value of *A* is associated with one and only one value of *B*. This is also referred to as a one-to-one association from *A* to *B*. For example, for every value of student registration number (*Student_No.*) there is only one student name (*Student_Name*). The diagrammatic representation of this example is given in Fig. 12.14. As another example, consider that a student can register for many subjects. So *Student_No.* has a *one-to-many association* with *Subject_Name*. The diagrammatic representation of this example is shown in Fig. 12.15. Combining the two, we get Fig. 12.16 where both the associations are depicted. Note that the diagrams show the type of each data item, and not specific values or the instances of the data items.

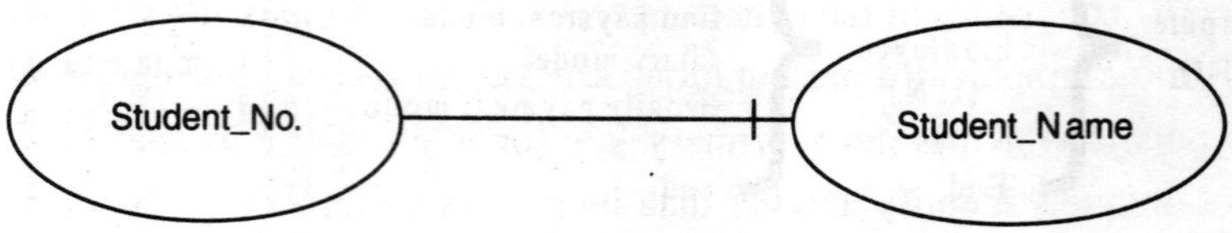

Fig. 12.14. One-to-one association

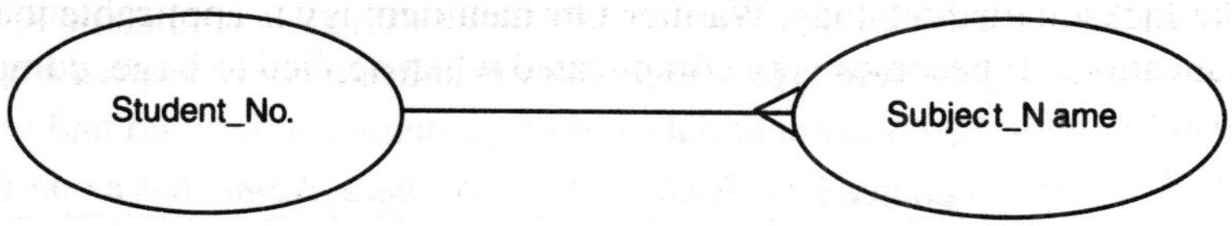

Fig. 12.15. One-to-many association

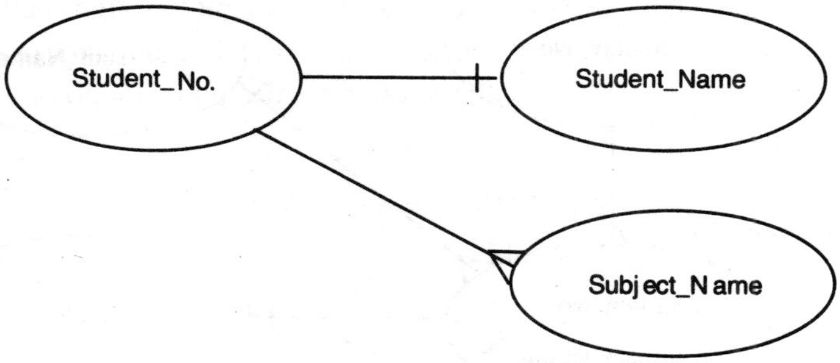

Fig. 12.16. Associations of student

Reverse associations are also possible. For example, one student name may be associated with more than one student number, while one subject may be associated with many students. The diagram showing the forward and the reverse associations is given in Fig. 12.17. Note, however, that often reverse associations are not of interest and are therefore not shown.

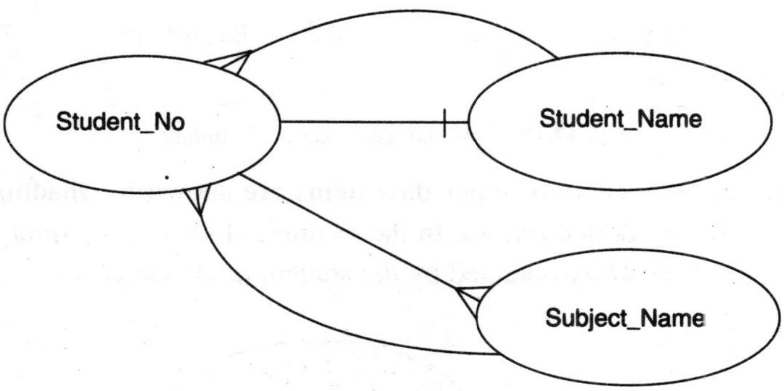

Fig. 12.17. Forward and reverse associations of student

The concept of primary key, (non-prime) attributes, and secondary key are important in data models. A *primary key* uniquely identifies many data items and is identified by a bubble with one or more one-to-one links leaving it. The names of the data-item types that are primary keys are underlined in the bubble charts (as also in the graphical representation of a logical record). A *non-prime attribute* (or simply, *attribute*) is a bubble which is not a primary key (or with no one-to-one links leaving it). A *secondary key* does not uniquely identify another data item, *i.e.*, it is one that is associated with many values of another data item. Thus, it is an attribute with at least one one-to-many associations leaving it.

Some data-item types cannot be identified by one data-item type. They require a primary key that is composed of more than one data-item type. Such a key is called a *concatenated key*. A concatenated key is shown as a bubble with the constituent data-item type names underlined and separated by a plus (+) sign. In Fig. 12.18, the concatenated key, *Student_No. + Subject_Name,* has a one-to-one association with *Mark* (that the student got in that subject).

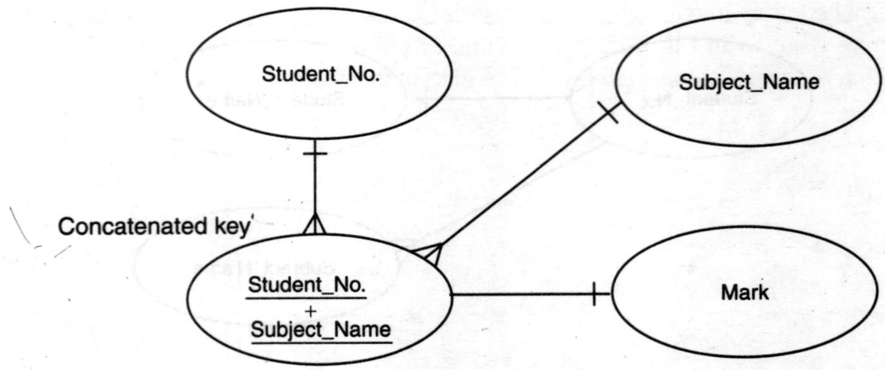

Fig. 12.18. Use of concatenated key

Certain data item types may be optional or derived. A student who may or may not take a subject indicates an *optional association.* This is indicated on the bubble chart by showing a small circle just before the crow's feet on the link joining the *Student_No. with the Subject_Name* (Fig. 12.19).

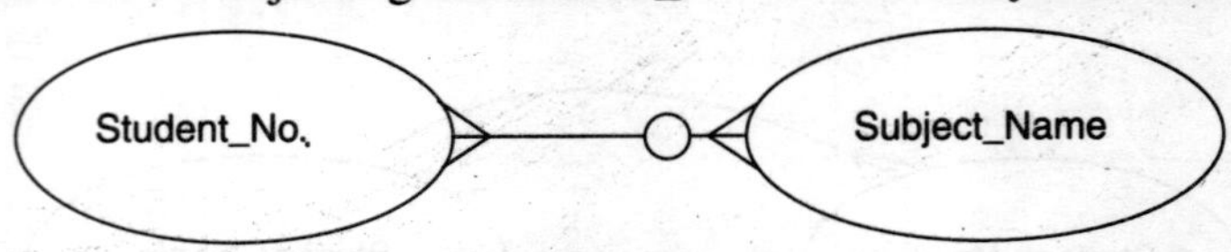

Fig. 12.19. Optional association of student

Data items that are derived from other data items are shown by shading the corresponding bubbles and by joining them by dotted arrows. In the example (Fig. 12.20), *Total_Mark* obtained by a student is obtained by summing *Mark* obtained by the student in all subjects.

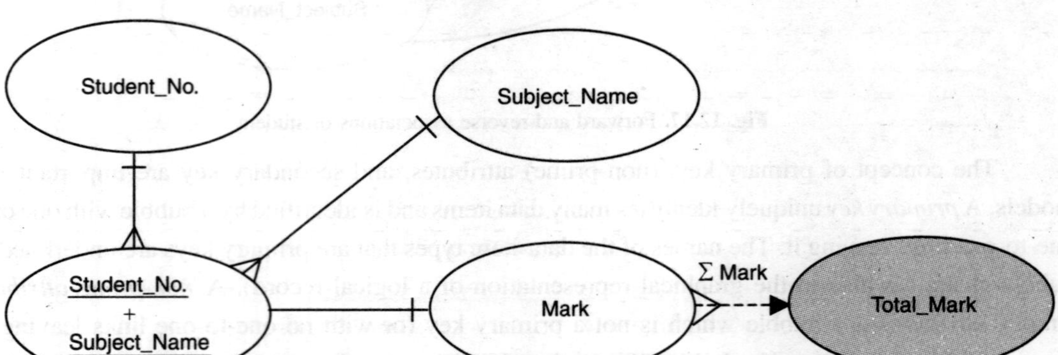

Fig. 12.20. Derived data items

12.3.2 Data Item Groups and Records

In a database environment, we extract several views of data from one overall database structure. Data analysis diagrams help us to group together data items that receive one-to-one links from a primary key. Such a group of data items is stable and is referred to as a *record*. We normally refer to a *logical record* as a group of data items that are uniquely identified by a primary key (by receiving one-to-one links), no matter where they may be physically stored. Consider the data analysis diagram (Fig. 12.21). Its record structure is given in Fig. 12.22. The name of the record is *STUDENT. Student_No.* is the primary key. *Student_name, Department*, etc., are data item types.

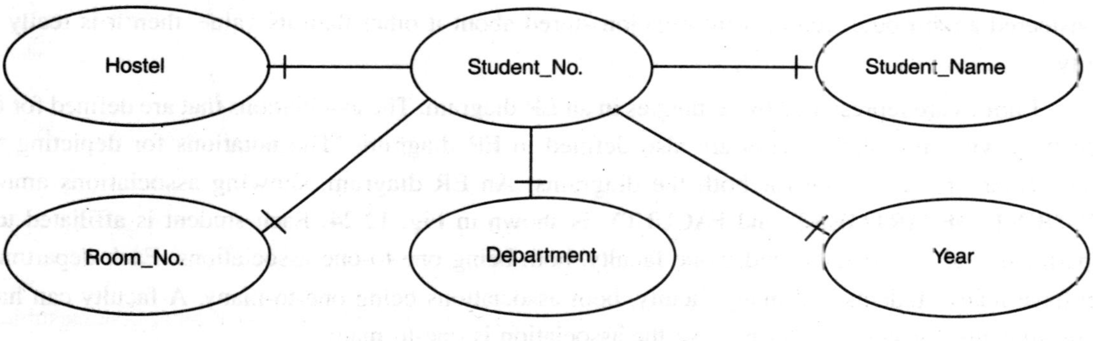

Fig. 12.21. Data analysis diagram for a student

STUDENT

Student_No.	Student_Name	Department	Year	Address	
				Hostel	Room_No.

Fig. 12.22. Student record

Figure 12.23 shows two records *CUSTOMER* and *PART* and a many-to-many relationship between them. The *CUSTOMER* record has the primary key *Customer_No.* and the *PART* record has the primary key *Part_No.*

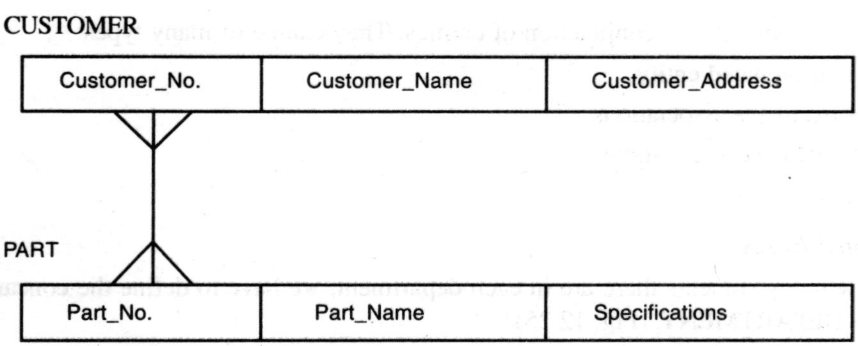

Fig. 12.23. Association between records

12.3.3 Entity-Relationship Diagram (or Entity Diagram)

Entity-relationship diagrams (ER diagrams) provide high-level overview of data that are used in strategic or top-down planning. An entity (or entity type) is something, real or abstract, about which we store data, by storing the values of its attributes. For example, *STUDENT* is an entity whose attributes are *Student_No. Name, Address, Sex,* and so on. Every specific occurrence is called an *entity instance.* For example, *Pramod Shastri* is an instance of the entity *STUDENT.*

We describe data in terms of *entities* and *attributes.* Information on entities is stored in multiple data-item types. Information on attributes is not stored in multiple data-item types. If a data-item type (considered an attribute) requires information stored about it other than its value, then it is really an entity.

Entities are represented by rectangles in an ER diagram. The associations that are defined for the data item types in bubble charts are also defined in ER diagrams. The notations for depicting the associations are also same for both the diagrams. An ER diagram, showing associations among STUDENT, DEPARTMENT, and FACULTY, is shown in Fig. 12.24. Each student is affiliated to a department and is registered under one faculty, both being one-to-one associations. Each department can have many students and many faculty, both associations being one-to-many. A faculty can have many students registered under him, so the association is one-to-many.

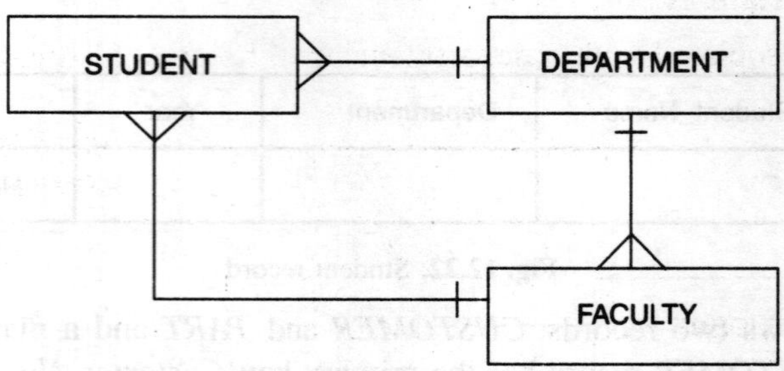

Fig. 12.24. Association among data-item types

Concatenated entities refer to conjunction of entities. They can be of many types:

1. Normal concatenated entity
2. Mutually exclusive associations
3. Mutually inclusive associations
4. Looped associations

Normal Concatenated Entity

To know how many students there are in each department, we have to define the concatenated entity STUDENT + DEPARTMENT. (Fig. 12.25).

Mutually exclusive associations

A student will be staying either in at the hostel or at home, but not at both (Fig. 12.26)

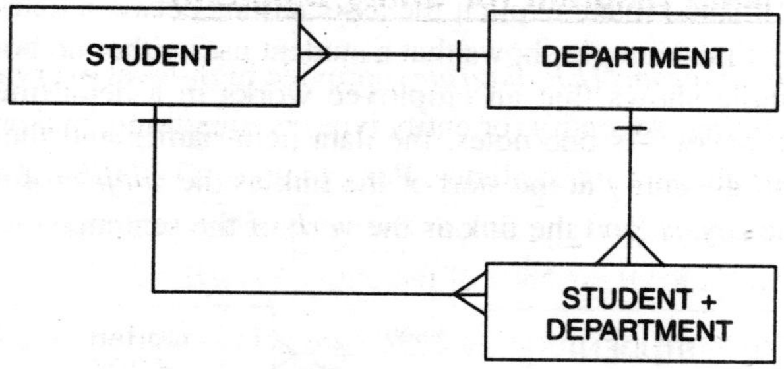

Fig. 12.25. Normal concatenated entity

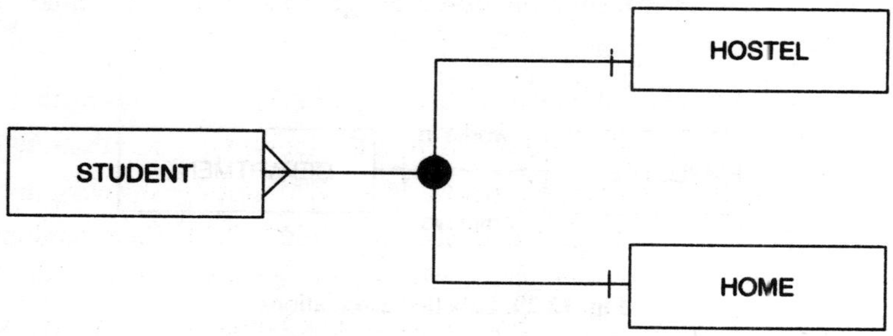

Fig. 12.26. Mutually exclusive associations

Mutually Inclusive Associations

If a student is associated with a department, then he must also be associated with a hostel (Fig. 12.27).

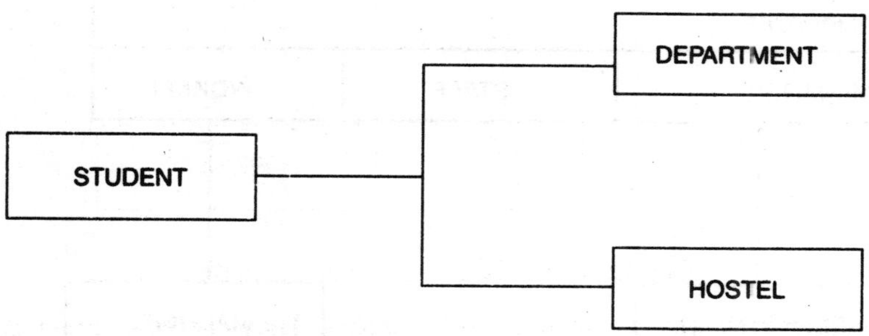

Fig. 12.27. Mutually inclusive associations

Looped Associations

Looped associations occur when occurrence of an entity is associated with other occurrences of the same type. For example, a subassembly may contain zero, one, or many subassemblies and may be contained in zero, one, or many subassemblies (Fig. 12.28).

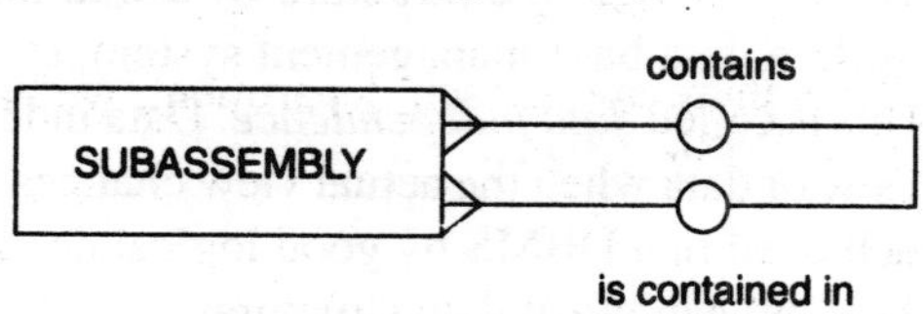

Fig. 12.28. Looped Associations

We may label the links to make explicit the associations between data-item types. Figure 12.29 shows two examples. The first example shows that a student uses either no book, or one book, or many books. The second example shows that an employee works in a department, and, conversely, the department employs employees. As one notes, the data item names and the label on the link should constitute a sentence, with the entity at the start of the link as the *subject* of the sentence, the entity to which the link goes as the *object*, and the link as the *verb* of the sentence.

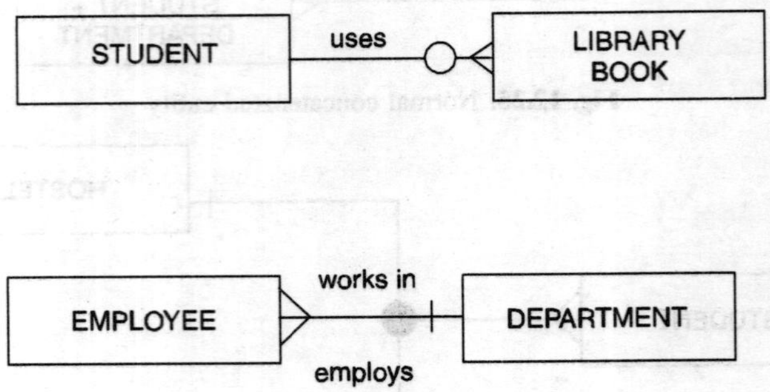

Fig. 12.29. Labelled associations

12.3.4 Entity Subtypes

It is often helpful to divide entity type into subtypes. Figure 12.30 gives an example where the EMPLOYEE is classified as MANAGER, STAFF, and WORKER.

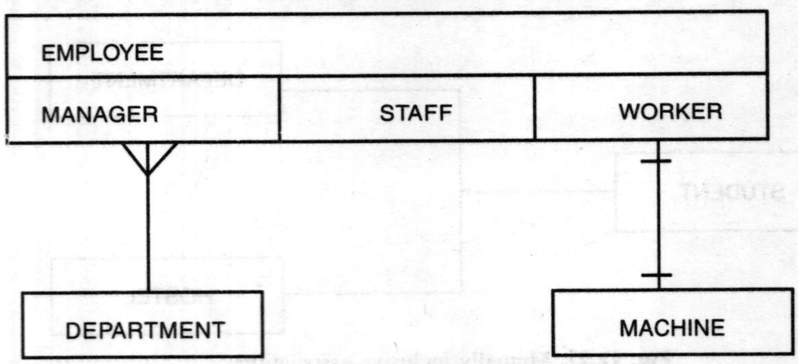

Fig. 12.30. Entity subtypes

12.3.5 Database Planning and Third Normal Form

Database systems are used to reduce redundancy and inconsistency and reduce maintenance problems. When users' requirements change, the structure of a traditional file changes, resulting in various changes in the programs. In a data base management system, changes in data structures do not result in changes in programs. This is called *data independence*. Data independence is achieved by being able to preserve the program's view of data when the actual view changes in either a logical or a physical manner. Data independence is achieved in a DBMS by good logical design of the data structures that is achieved by normalization of data and canonical data structures.

Normalization refers to the way data items are logically grouped into record structures. Third normal form is a grouping of data so designed as to avoid the anomalies and problems that can occur with data. To put data into third normal form, it is first put into the first normal form, then into the second normal form, and then into the third normal form.

First normal form refers to data that are organized into records such that they do not have repeating groups of data items. Such data in first normal form are, then, said to constitute *flat files* or *two-dimensional matrices of data items.*

An example of a record that contains repeating groups of data items is shown in Fig. 12.31. Here *subject number, name,* and *mark* repeat many times. Thus, the record is not in the first normal form and is not a flat, two-dimensional record. To put this into first-normal form, we put subject and mark in a separate record (Fig. 12.32). The Subject-Mark record has a concatenated key (*Student_No. + Subject_No.*). This key uniquely identifies the data in the record.

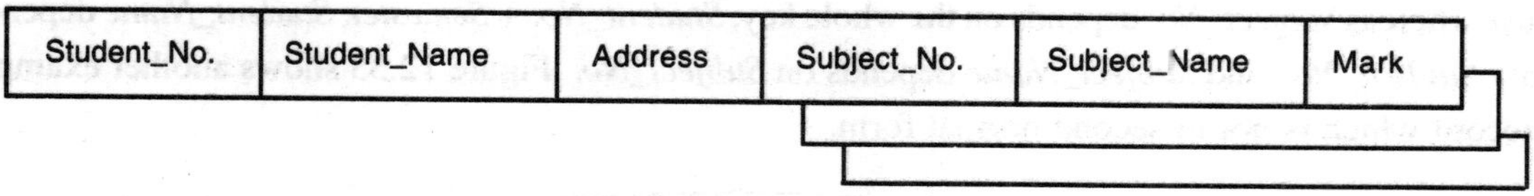

Fig. 12.31. Repeating group of data items in a record

SUBJECT

Student_No.	Student_Name	Address

SUBJECT-MARK

Student_No. + Subject_No.	Subject_No.	Subject_Name	Mark

Fig. 12.32. First-normal form

Once a record is in first normal form, it is now ready to be put in the *second normal form*. The concept of functional dependence of data items is important in understanding the second normal form. Therefore, to be able to understand the conversion of a record in first normal form to a second normal form, we must first understand the meaning of *functional dependency.*

In a record, if for every instance of a data item *A*, there is no more than one instance of data item *B*, then *A identifies B*, or *B* is *functionally dependent* on *A*. Such a functional dependency is shown by a line with a small crossbar on it. In Figure 12.33, *Student_Name* and *Project_Team* are functionally dependent on *Student_No.,* and *Project_Name* is functionally dependent on *Project_Team.*

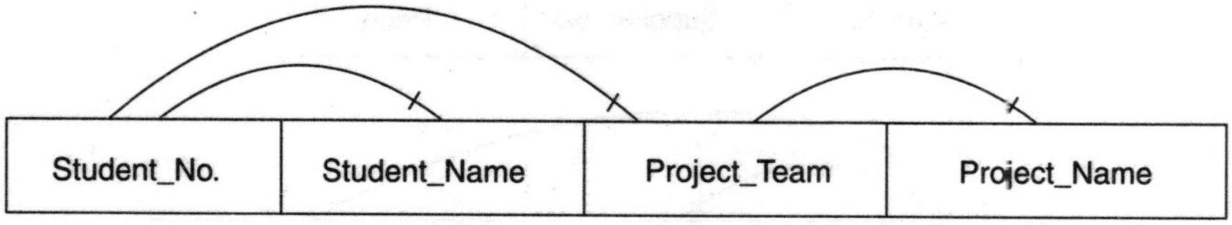

Fig. 12.33. Functional dependency

A data item may be functionally dependent on a group of items. In Figure 12.34, *Subject_No.* is shown to be functionally dependent on *Student_No.* and *Semester*, because a student registers for different subjects in different academic years.

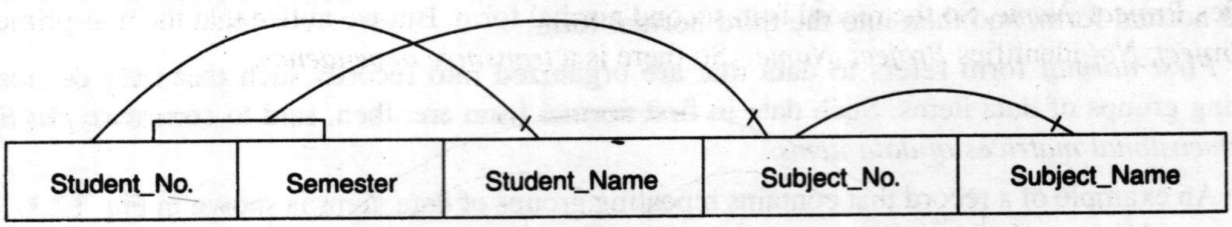

Fig. 12.34. Functional dependency on group of items

A record is said to be in second normal form if each attribute in a record is functionally dependent on the whole key of that record. The example given in Figure 12.34 is not in second normal form, because whereas *Subject_No.* depends on the whole key, *Student_No. + Semester, Student_Name* depends on only *Student_No.*, and *Subject_Name* depends on *Subject_No.* Figure 12.35 shows another example of a record which is not in second normal form.

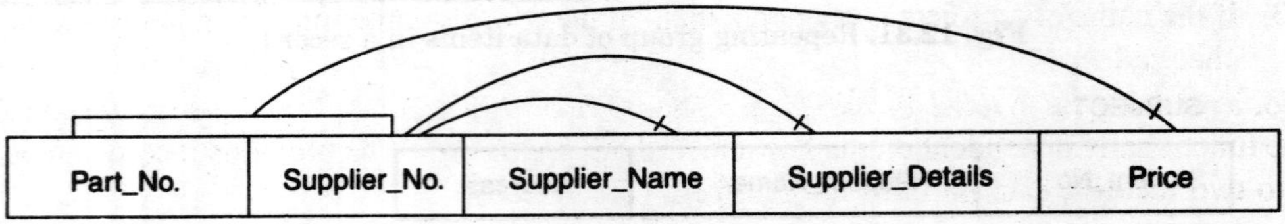

Fig. 12.35. A record not in second normal form

The difficulties that may be encountered in a data structure, which is not in second normal form, are the following:

(*a*) If a supplier does not supply a part, then his details cannot be entered.

(*b*) If a supplier does not make a supply, that record may be deleted. With that, the supplier details get lost.

(*c*) To update the supplier details, we must search for every record that contains that supplier as part of the key. It involves much redundant updating, if the suppler supplies many parts.

The record shown in Figure 12.35 can be split into two records, each in second normal form (Figure 12.36).

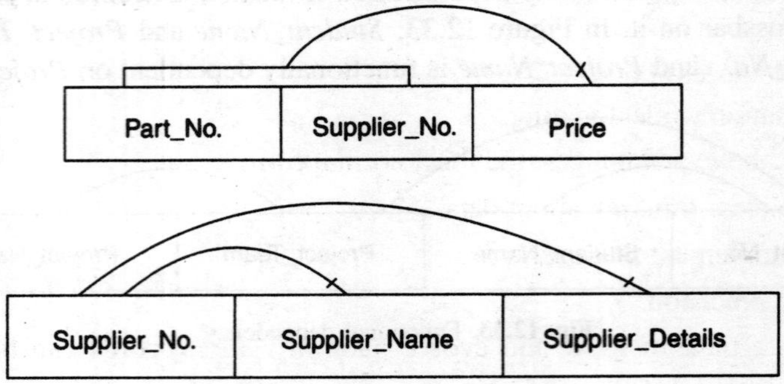

Fig. 12.36. Records in second normal form

A record in second normal form can have a *transitive dependency, i.e.,* it can have a non-prime data item that identifies other data items. Such a record can have a number of problems. Consider the example shown in Figure 12.37. We find here that *Student_No.* identifies *Project_No. Student_No.* also identifies *Project_Name.* So the record is in second normal form. But we notice that the non-prime data item *Project_No.* identifies *Project_Name*. So there is a *transitive dependency.*

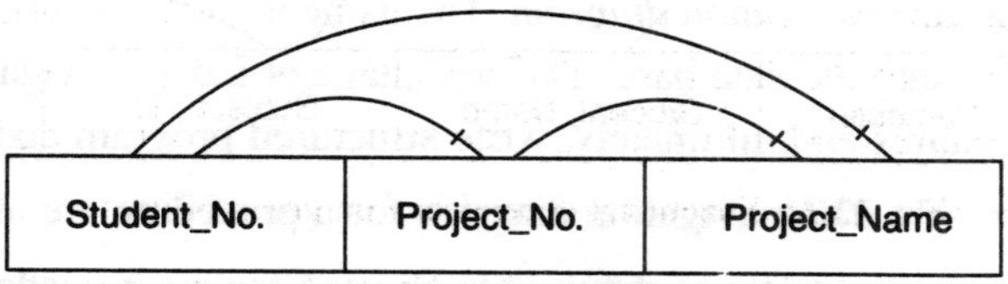

Fig. 12.37. Record with transitive dependency

Presence of transitive dependency can create certain difficulties. For example, in the above example, the following difficulties may be faced:

1. One cannot have *Project_No.* or *Project_Name* unless students are assigned a project.
2. If all students working on a project leave the project, then all these records will be deleted.
3. If the name of a project is changed, then all the records containing the names will have to be changed.

For a record to be in *third normal form* it should first be in second normal form and each attribute should be functionally dependent on the key and *nothing but the key.* The previous record can be broken down into two records, each in third normal form (Fig. 12.38).

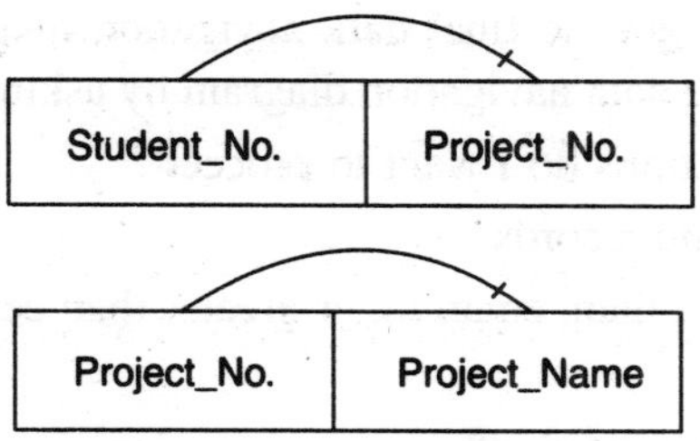

Fig. 12.38. Records in third normal form

The advantages of records in third normal form are:

(*a*) Less *value redundancy* (*i.e.,* the same value of data item is not repeated across the records).
(*b*) Less storage, although more number of records (since the number of data items in a record is less).
(*c*) Less time to access data.
(*d*) Less duplication while updating.

Apart from the above advantages, the third normal form

(*a*) Is an aid to clear thinking about data.
(*b*) Is easy to implement and use.
(*c*) Is an aid to precision.
(*d*) Helps a data base to grow and evolve naturally (*i.e.,* records can be added, deleted, or updated in a straightforward fashion).

12.3.6 Data Navigation Diagram

We have already seen that data in the third normal form are stable and that such data items have their properties that are independent of procedures. To create procedures with the help of a data model, one has to identify the sequence in which the records are accessed and overdraw it on the data model. The resultant diagram is a *data navigation diagram*. The name is such because it helps to visualize how a designer can navigate through the data base. The advantage of a data navigation diagram is that with this, one can design procedures and, ultimately, write structured program code.

The steps for drawing a data navigation diagram for a procedure are as follows:

1. Establish the main entity types required to be used for the procedure.
2. Find the neighbourhood of these entity types, *i.e.*, the entities that can be reached by these entities by traversing one link in the model.
3. Examine the data items in these records and eliminate the records from the neighbourhood that are not needed for the procedure.
4. Draw the subset data model needed for the procedure, in the form of an ER diagram.
5. Decide the sequence in which the records will be accessed.
6. Write the operations on this subset data model to get a rough sketch of the data navigation diagram.
7. This rough sketch is now annotated with details such as conditions, options, alternate paths, and error situations to get the final data navigation diagram. For annotation, we need to analyze each step in the data navigation diagram by asking three questions:
   (*a*) Under what conditions do I want to proceed?
   - Valid or invalid records?
   - Data item less than, equal to, or greater than certain value?
   - Errors?
   - Results of computation?
   - Matching data items in different records?

   (*b*) What do I want to do with, or to, the data?
   - Create, retrieve, update, or delete records?
   - Search, sort, project, or join relations?
   - Computations with the data?

   (*c*) What other operations accompany the data-base actions?
   - Print documents?
   - Data-entry screen usage?
   - Security checks?
   - Audit controls?
   - Execution of subroutines?
   - Triggering other transactions?

The data navigation diagram, thus annotated, is now ready for use for drawing the action diagram, which ultimately paves the way for code design.

12.3.7 An Example of Data Navigation Diagram

Consider a partial data model in third-order form (Figure 12.39) for a customer order processing system (Martin and McClure, 1988). The model depicts the situation where a customer places an order for a product with a wholesaler. If the product is available with the wholesaler, then an order line is created whereas if it is not available, then it is backordered. The main entities in Figure 12.39 are the following records:

CUSTOMER_ORDER
PRODUCT

The neighbourhood of these entities are the following records:

CUSTOMER_ORDER
- CUSTOMER
- ORDER_LINE
- BACKORDER

PRODUCT

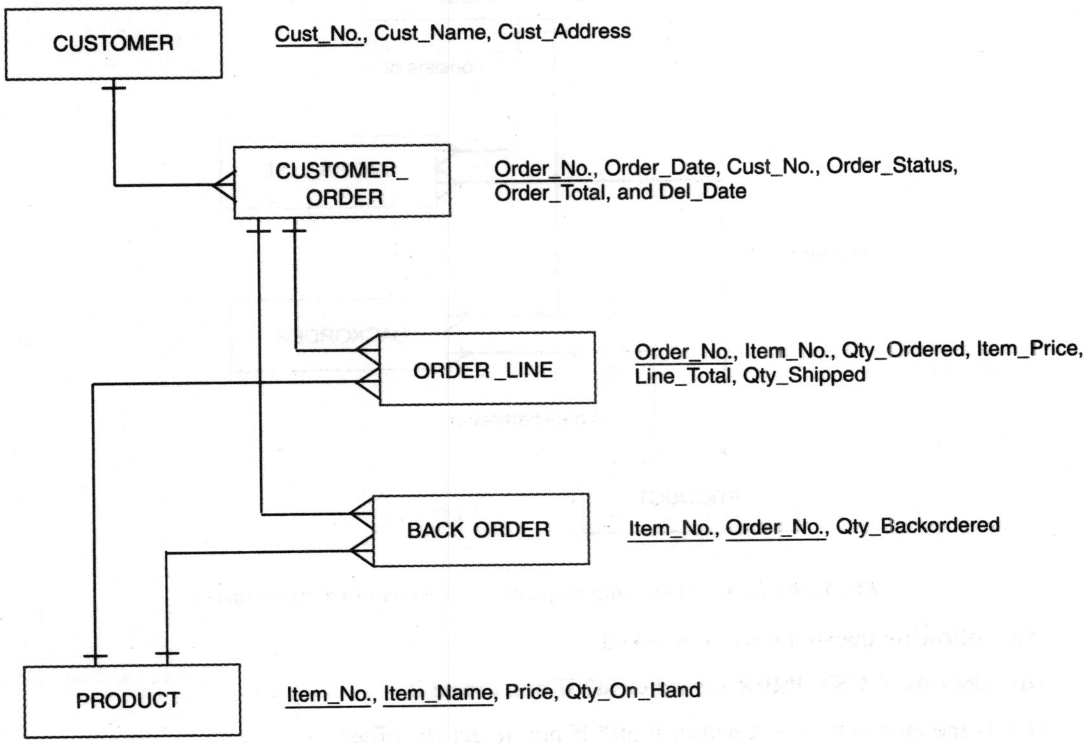

Fig. 12.39. Partial data model for customer order processing

Rough sequence in which the records will be accessed:

1. The CUSTOMER records will be inspected to see whether the customer's credit is good.
2. If the credit is good, a CUSTOMER_ORDER record is created.
3. For each product on the order, the PRODUCT record is inspected to see whether the stock is available.
4. If stock is available, an ORDER_LINE record is created, linked to the CUSTOMER_ORDER record, for each product on the order.
5. If stock is not available, a BACKORDER record is created.
6. The ORDER_RATE is updated.
7. When all items are processed, an order confirmation is printed, and the CUSTOMER_ORDER record is updated with Order_Status, Order_Total, and Del_Date.

Figure 12.40 is the entity-relationship diagram for Figure 12.39.

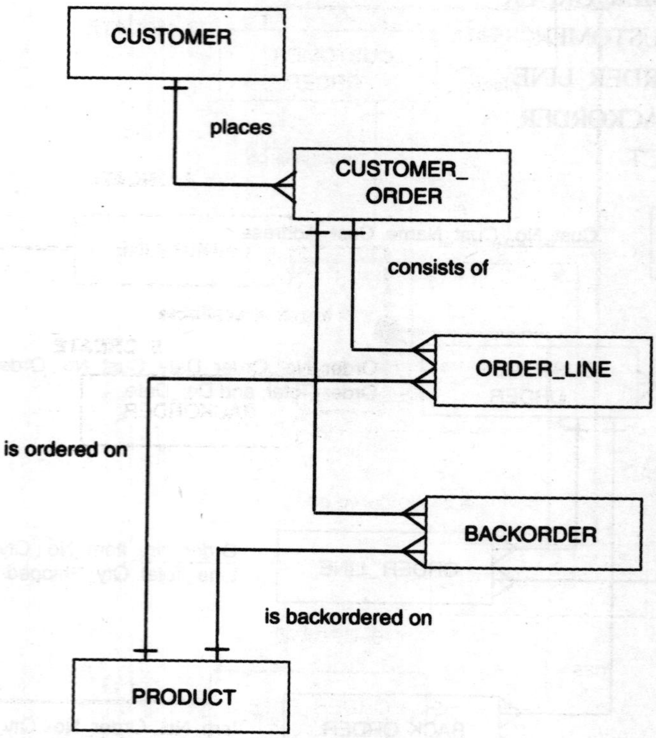

Fig. 12.40. Entity relationship diagram for customer order processing

The following questions are now asked:

(*a*) Does the CUSTOMER record exist? If not, create it.

(*b*) Is the customer credit within limit? If not, reject the order.

(*c*) Is this a valid product? If not, reject it.

(*d*) Is there sufficient product in stock? If not, place the order in backorder. If yes, an ORDER_LINE is created.

(*e*) Is the ORDER_LINE record processed? If yes, update the ORDER_RATE record.

(*f*) Finally, the CUSTOMER_ORDER record is updated.

These details are now shown on the rough sketch of the *data access map* (drawn with thick line), resulting in the *data navigation diagram* (12.41).

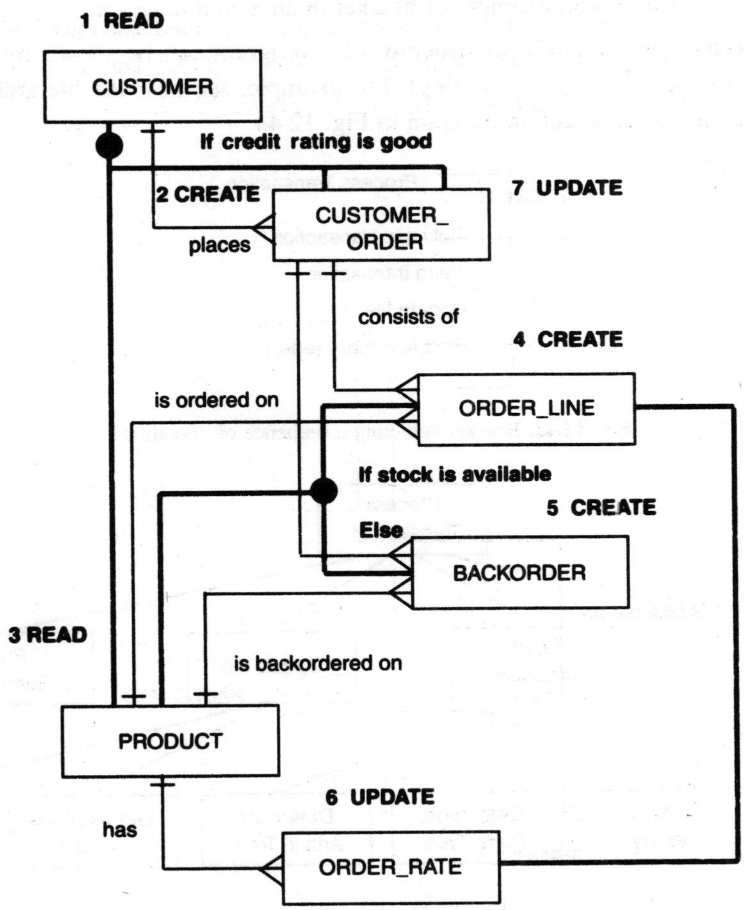

Fig. 12.41. Data navigation diagram

The data navigation diagram is now used to create the *action diagram* which can be expanded t find the logical procedure. We give below the basics of the action diagram before taking up the above mentioned case.

12.3.8 Action Diagram

Action diagrams simultaneously show (i) the overview of the program structures (like structure charts, HIPO, Jackson, and Warnier-Orr diagrams) and (ii) the detailed logic of the program (like flow chart, structured English, pseudocode, or Nassi-Shneiderman charts). The various notations used in action diagrams are as follows:

1. **Brackets.** Brackets are the basic building blocks of action diagram. A bracket encloses a sequence of operations, performed one after the other in a top-to-bottom sequence. A title may (or may not) appear on the top of the bracket. Any degree of detail can be included in the bracket. Other structures can be depicted by suitably modifying or editing the brackets. Figure 12.42 shows an example of bracket in an action diagram.
2. **Hierarchy.** The hierarchical structure of a program can be shown by drawing brackets within the bracket (*i.e.*, by nesting). For example, see how the hierarchy chart in Figure 12.43 is drawn as an action diagram in Fig. 12.44.

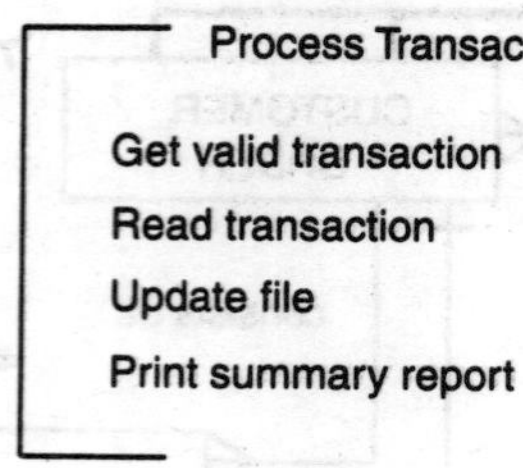

Fig. 12.42. Bracket depicting a sequence of operations

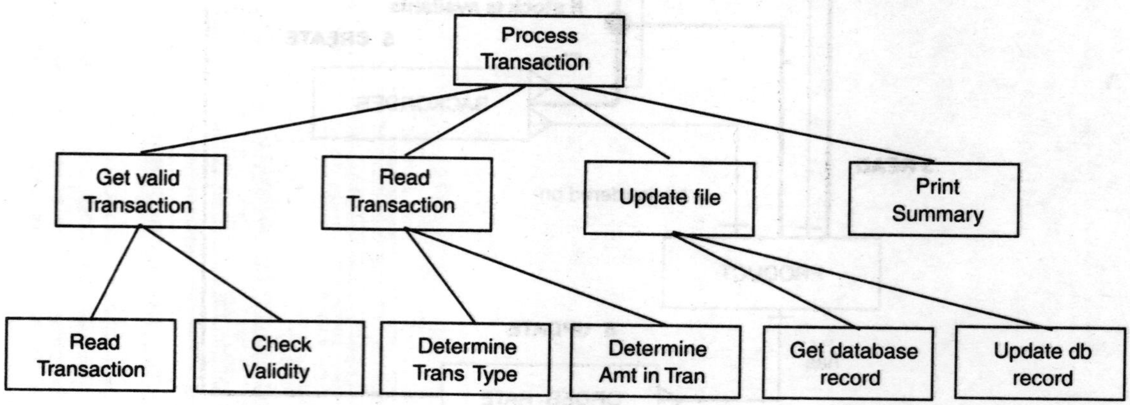

Fig. 12.43. Hierarchy chart

3. **Repetition (Looping).** A double horizontal line at the top of the bracket shows repetition of the operations included inside the bracket. Captions can appear at the top (for WHILE DO loop) or the bottom (for DO UNTIL loop) or at both places of the bracket. Examples are given in Fig. 12.45 through Fig. 12.48.

```
Process Transaction
    Get valid transaction
        Read transaction
        Check validity
    Read a transaction
        Determine transaction type
        Determine amount in transaction
    Update File
        Get DBF record
        Update DBF record
    Print Summary
```

Fig. 12.44. Action diagram for processing transaction

```
    Read A Transaction
        Determine transaction type
        Determine amount in transaction
```

Fig. 12.45. Repetition of operations

```
For Each Issue Transaction
        Get inventory record
        Subtract issue amount from stock to get new stock
```

Fig. 12.46. Repeat structure using FOR clause

```
Do While Issue Records Last
        Get inventory record
        Subtract issue amount from stock to get new stock
```

Fig. 12.47. Repeat structure using FOR clause

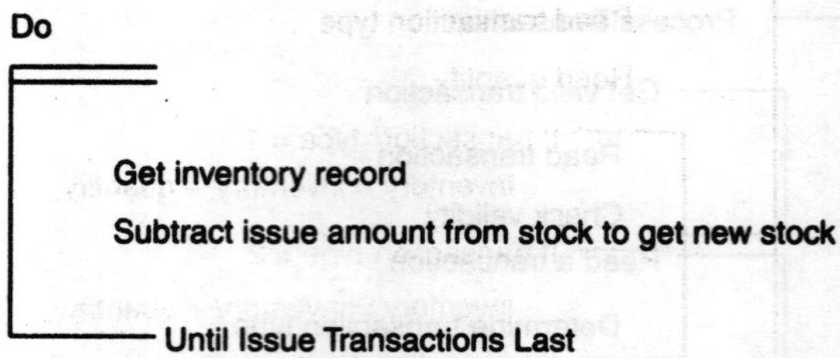

Fig. 12.48. Repeat structure using FOR clause

4. **Mutually Exclusive Selection.** When one of several processes is to be executed, a bracket with several divisions is used (Fig. 12.49).

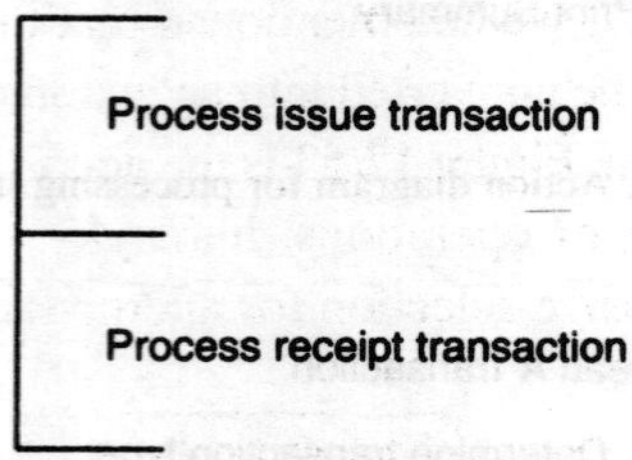

Fig. 12.49. Mutually exclusive selection

5. **Conditions.** Often, certain operations are executed only if certain conditions are satisfied. Here, the condition is written at the head of a bracket. ELSE clause may be used in cases of two mutually exclusive conditions. For a CASE structure, several conditions are partitioned. Examples are given in Fig. 12.50 through Fig. 12.52.

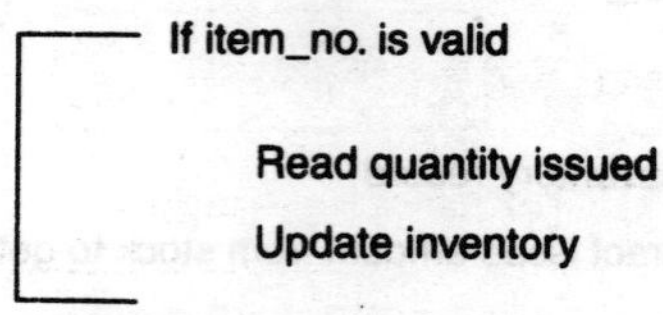

Fig. 12.50. Use of IF clause

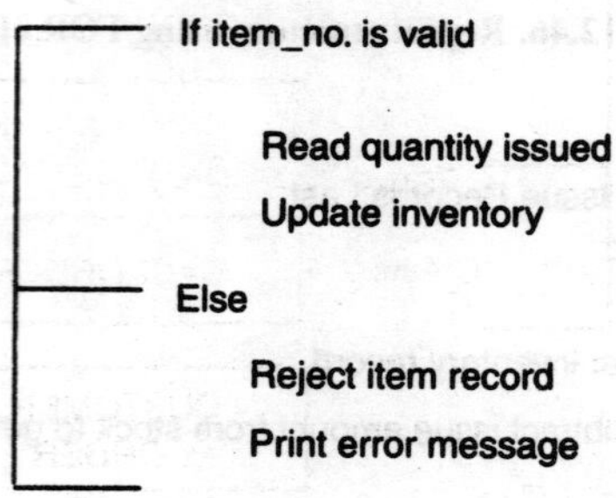

Fig. 12.51. Use of IF-Else clause

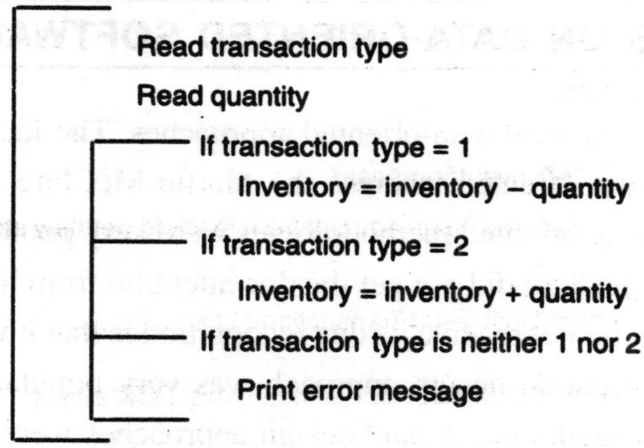

Fig. 12.52. Multiple IF clauses

At the end of the section 12.3.7, we had mentioned that the data navigation diagram developed for customer ordering processing can be converted into an action diagram. We are now armed with the skills of developing the action diagram. Figure 12.53 is the action diagram for the case. Note the use of brackets for indicating the sequence of operations, hierarchy for hierarchical structures, repetition structures for looping, mutually exclusive selection for alternative operations, and conditions.

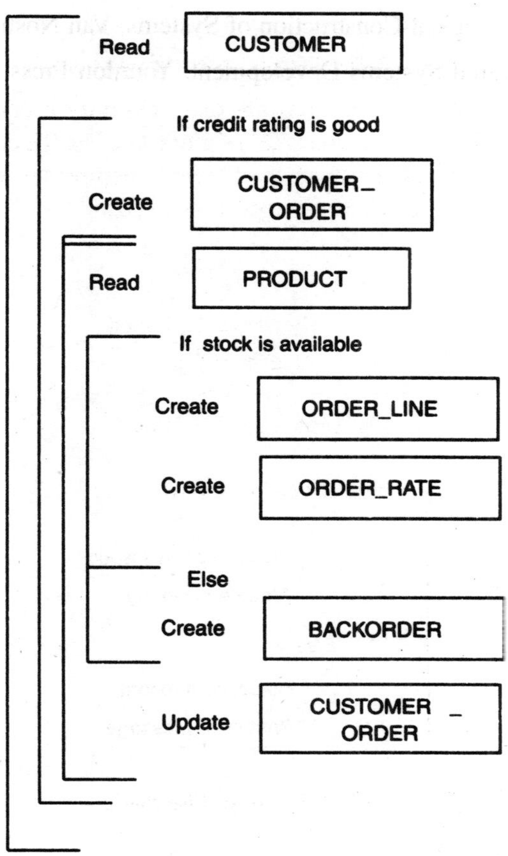

Fig. 12.53. Action diagram for customer order processing

12.4 FINAL REMARKS ON DATA-ORIENTED SOFTWARE DESIGN

This chapter dealt with classical data-oriented approaches. The Jackson and Warnier-Orr design methodologies are data structure oriented whereas the Martin-McClure design approach is data-base oriented. While the data structure oriented methodologies were very popular at one time, the data base-oriented approach of Martin-McClure did not get the due attention from the software designers. One of the reasons why this approach did not receive its due recognition is that it was developed during the mid and late eighties when the structured design approach was very popular among the software design community and the object-oriented analysis and design approaches were making strong headway. We take up these two design approaches in the next two chapters.

REFERENCES

Jackson, M. A. (1975), Principles of Program Design, Academic Press, New York.

Martin, J. and C. McClure (1988), Structured Techniques: The Basis for CASE, Revised Edition, Prentice Hall, Englewood Cliffs, New Jersey.

Warnier, J. D. (1981), Logical Construction of Systems, Van Nostrand Reinhold, New York.

Orr, K. (1977), Structured Systems Development, Yourdon Press, Inc, New York.

13

Structured Design

Some of the brilliant concepts on program design and modularization have come from Yourdon and Constantine (1979). Following the tradition of structured programming, they called their approach to program design as *structured design*. The design approach is a refinement of the top-down design with the principle of modularity at its core. The specific topics that we are going to discuss here are the following:

(1) Structure Chart
(2) Coupling
(3) Cohesion
(4) Structured Design Guidelines
(5) Strategies of Structured Design

13.1 STRUCTURE CHART

A structure chart is a graphic representation of the organization of the program structure in the form of a hierarchy of modules. Modules performing high-level tasks are placed in the upper levels of the hierarchy, whereas those performing low-level detailed tasks appear at the lower levels. They are represented by rectangles. Module names are so selected as to explain the primary tasks the modules perform.

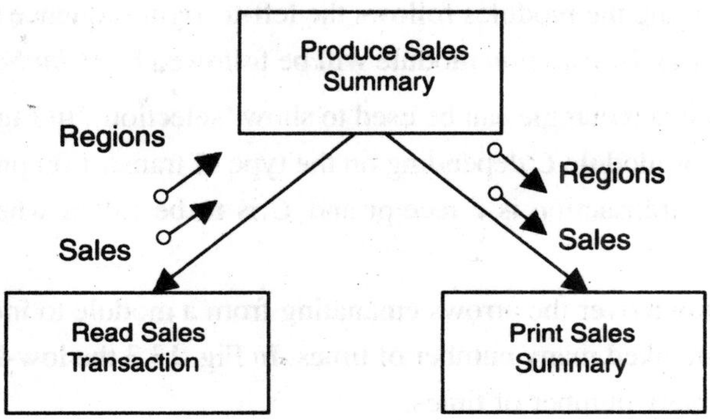

Fig. 13.1. A structure chart

Figure 13.1 shows a structure chart of a program that prints the region-wise sales summary. As shown in the figure, the top module is called *Produce Sales Summary*. It first calls the low-level module *Read Sales Transaction* and extracts the data on region-wise data. After the execution of this module, it then calls the next low-level module *Print Sales Summary* while passing the region-wise data to this module for facilitating printing the summary report.

The tree-like structure of the structure chart starts with only one module (the *root*) at the top of the chart. Arrow from one module *A* to another module *B* represents that *A* invokes, or calls, *B* at the time of execution. Control is always passed back to the invoking module. Therefore, whenever a program finishes executing, control returns to the root.

If a module *A* invokes module *B*, then *B* cannot also invoke *A*. Also, a module cannot invoke itself. A module can invoke several subordinate modules. The order in which the subordinate modules are invoked is not shown in the chart. A module that has no subordinate modules is called a *leaf*. A module may be invoked by more than one module. Such an invoked module is called *common module*.

When module *A* invokes module *B*, information transfer can take place in either direction (*i.e.*, from and to *A*). This information can be of two forms:

— data (denoted by an arrow with an open circle o——›)

— control (denoted by an arrow with a closed circle ●——›)

Whereas data have the usual connotation of carrying the values of variables and parameters that are required to solve the problem, controls are data that are used by the programs to direct execution flow (such as end-of-file switch or error flag).

In Fig. 13.1, data on regions and corresponding sales are passed on to the top module when the *Read Sales Transaction* module is executed. Later, when the top module calls the *Print Summary Report* module, the data on regions and sales are passed on to it. The data are required for the problem at hand and so the arrow with open circle symbol is used for the data flow. No control flow exists in this diagram.

A structure chart normally does not show the important program structures: sequence, selection, and iteration. Sometimes, the following rules are followed:

(1) Sequence of executing the modules follows the left-to-right sequence of the blocks. Thus, in Fig. 13.1, *Read Sales Transaction* module will be followed by *Print Sales Summary* module.

(2) A black diamond in a rectangle can be used to show 'selection'. In Fig. 13.2, the top module *A* calls module *B* or module *C* depending on the type of transaction processed. May be, *B* is to be called if the transaction is a receipt and *C* is to be called when the transaction is a payment.

(3) An arc may be drawn over the arrows emanating from a module to indicate that lower-level modules will be invoked many number of times. In Fig. 13.3 the low-level modules *B* and *C* will be invoked many number of times.

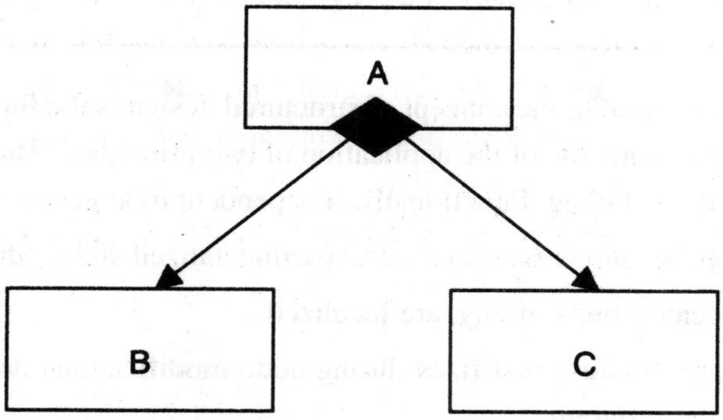

Fig. 13.2. Depicting selection in a structure chart

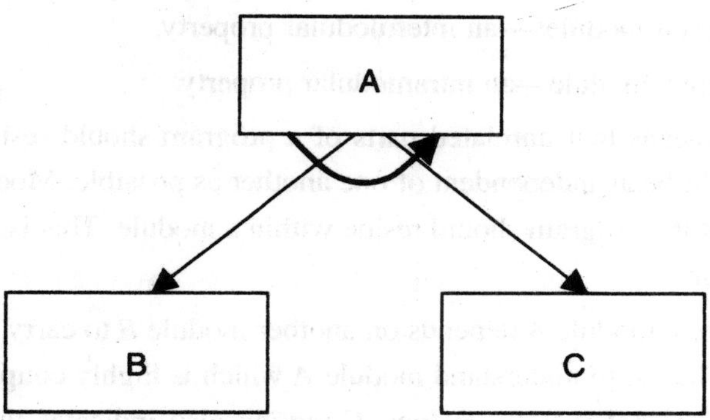

Fig. 13.3. Depicting iteration in a structure chart

A structure chart can have more than two levels. Fig. 13.4 shows a three-level structure chart. Notice that *A* and *B* have two immediate subordinates each, with *E* as a common module that both *B* and *C* can call. The module *F* with two vertical double lines is a stored library routine. Naturally, *F* has to be a leaf module with no offspring of its own.

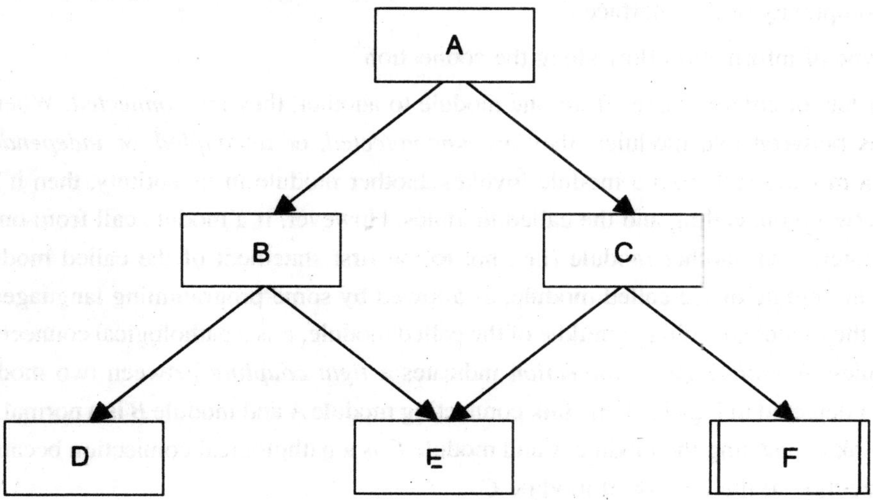

Fig. 13.4. A three-level structure chart

13.2 COUPLING

A principle which is central to the concept of structured design is the functional independence of modules. This principle is an outcome of the application of two principles: The principle of abstraction and the principle of information hiding. Functionally, independent modules are:

(*a*) Easy to develop, because a function is compartmentalized and module interfaces are simple.

(*b*) Easy to test, because bugs, if any, are localized.

(*c*) Easy to maintain, because bad fixes during code modifications do not propagate errors to other parts of the program.

Module independence is measured using two qualitative criteria:

(1) *Coupling* between modules—an intermodular property,

(2) *Cohesion* within a module—an intramodular property.

Module coupling means that unrelated parts of a program should reside in different modules. That is, the modules should be as independent of one another as possible. Module cohesion means that highly interrelated parts of the program should reside within a module. That is, a module should ideally focus on only one function.

In general, the more a module *A* depends on another module *B* to carry out its own function, the more *A* is coupled to *B*. That is, to understand module *A* which is highly coupled with another module *B*, we must know more of what module *B* does. Coupling also indicates the probability that while coding, debugging, or modifying a module, a programmer will have to understand the function of another module.

There are three factors that influence coupling between two modules:

(1) Types of connections

(2) Complexity of the interface

(3) Type of information flow along the connection

When data or control passes from one module to another, they are *connected*. When no data or control passes between two modules, they are *unconnected,* or *uncoupled*, or *independent* of each other. When a module call from a module invokes another module in its entirety, then it is a *normal connection* between the calling and the called modules. However, if a module call from one module is made to the interior of another module (i.e., not to the first statement of the called module but to a statement in the middle of the called module, as allowed by some programming languages), invoking only a part of the module residing in middle of the called module, it is a pathological connection between the two modules. A *pathological connection* indicates a *tight coupling* between two modules. In the structure chart depicted in Fig. 13.5, the link connecting module *A* and module *B* is a normal connection, whereas the link connecting the module *A* and module *C* is a pathological connection because *A* directs control of execution to the interior of module *C*.

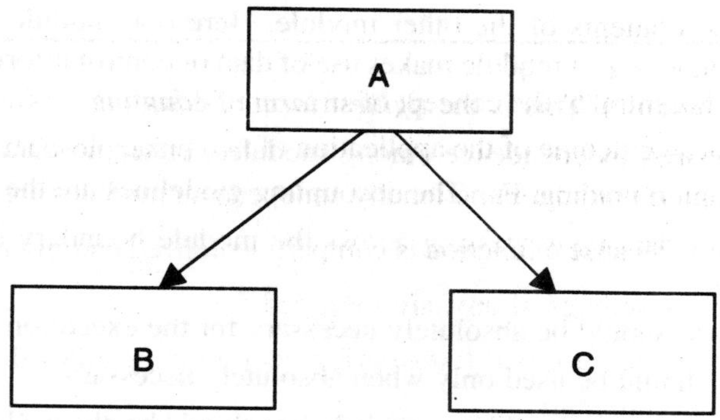

Fig. 13.5. Normal and pathological connections

Complexity of the modular interface is represented by the number of data types (not the volume of data) passing between two modules. This is usually given by the number of arguments in a calling statement. The higher the number of data types passing across two module boundaries, the tighter is the coupling.

Information flow along a connection can be a flow of data or control or of both data and control. Data are those which are operated upon, manipulated, or changed by a piece of program, whereas control, which is also passed like a data variable, governs the sequence of operations on or manipulations of other data. A control may be a flag (such as end-of-file information) or a branch address controlling the execution sequence in the activating module.

Coupling between modules can be of five types:

1. Data (or input-output) coupling
2. Stamp coupling
3. Control coupling
4. Common coupling
5. Content coupling

Data (input-output) coupling is the minimal or the best form of coupling between two modules. It provides output data from the called module that serves as input data to the calling module. Data are passed in the form of an elementary data item or an array, all of which are used in the receiving module. This is the *loosest and the best type of coupling* between two modules.

Stamp coupling exists between two modules when composite data items are passed to the called module, whereas many elementary data items present in the composite data may not be used by the receiving module.

Control coupling exists between two modules when data passed from one module directs the order of instruction execution in the receiving module. Whereas normally a pathological connection is always associated with the flow of control, even a normal connection may also be associated with the flow of control.

Common coupling refers to connection among modules that use globally defined variables (such as variables appearing in COMMON statements in Fortran programs). This form of coupling is tighter than the previously defined coupling types.

Content coupling occurs between two modules when the contents of one module, or a part of them, are included in the contents of the other module. Here one module refers to or changes the internals of the other module (*e.g.*, a module makes use of data or control information maintained within the boundary of another module). This is the *tightest form of coupling.*

To achieve the desired independence among modules, either no data or only elementary data items should pass across their boundaries. The decoupling guidelines are the following:

- The number of data types passing across the module boundary should be reduced to the minimum.
- The data passed should be absolutely necessary for the execution of the receiving module.
- Control flags should be used only when absolutely necessary.
- Global data definitions should be avoided; data should be always localized.
- Content coupling should be completely eliminated from the design.

13.3 COHESION

Cohesion is an intramodular property and measures the strength of relationships among the elements within a module. A module that focuses on doing one function contains elements that are strongly interrelated; hence the module is highly cohesive. On the other hand, a module that does too many functions has elements that are not very strongly related and has low cohesion.

Yourdon and Constantine propose seven levels of cohesion:

1. Functional
2. Sequential
3. Communicational
4. Procedural
5. Temporal
6. Logical
7. Coincidental

Functional cohesion is the strongest and is the most desirable form of cohesion while coincidental cohesion is the weakest and is the least desirable. In general, the first three forms of cohesion, namely functional, sequential, and communicational, are acceptable whereas the last three, namely temporal, logical, and coincidental cohesion, are not.

A functionally cohesive module does only one function, is fully describable in a simple sentence, and contains elements that are necessary and essential to carry out the module function. Modules that carry out matrix inversion or reads a master record or finds out economic order quantity are each functionally cohesive.

Sequential cohesion results in a module when it performs multiple functions such that the output of one function is used as the input to another. Thus a module that computes economic order quantity and then prepares purchase requisition is sequentially cohesive.

Communicational cohesion occurs in a module when it performs multiple functions but uses the same common data to perform these functions. Thus a module that uses sales data to update inventory status and forecasts sale has communicational cohesion.

Functional, sequential, and communicational cohesions in modules can be identified with the help of data flow diagrams. Figure 13.6 is a data flow diagram that shows four processes — read sales, forecast sales, update inventory, and plan production. Suppose, in the program design, we define four modules each with each of the functions given in the data flow diagram, then the cohesion in each of the modules is functional. If, however, we define a module that reads sales and forecasts sales then that module will have sequential cohesion. Suppose we define a module that forecasts sales and uses the forecast values to plan production, then the module is also sequential. Suppose we define a module that simultaneously updates inventory and forecasts sales, then both these functions use the common data on sales, thus this module will have communicational cohesion (Figure 13.7).

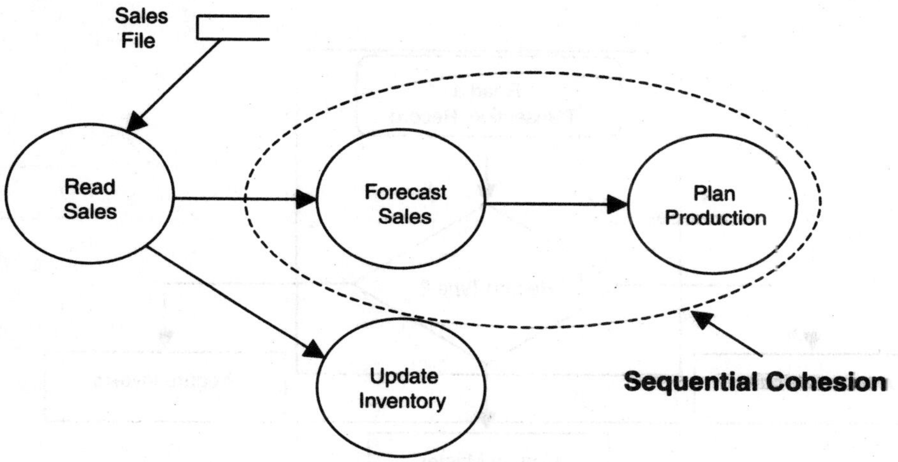

Fig. 13.6. Sequential cohesion

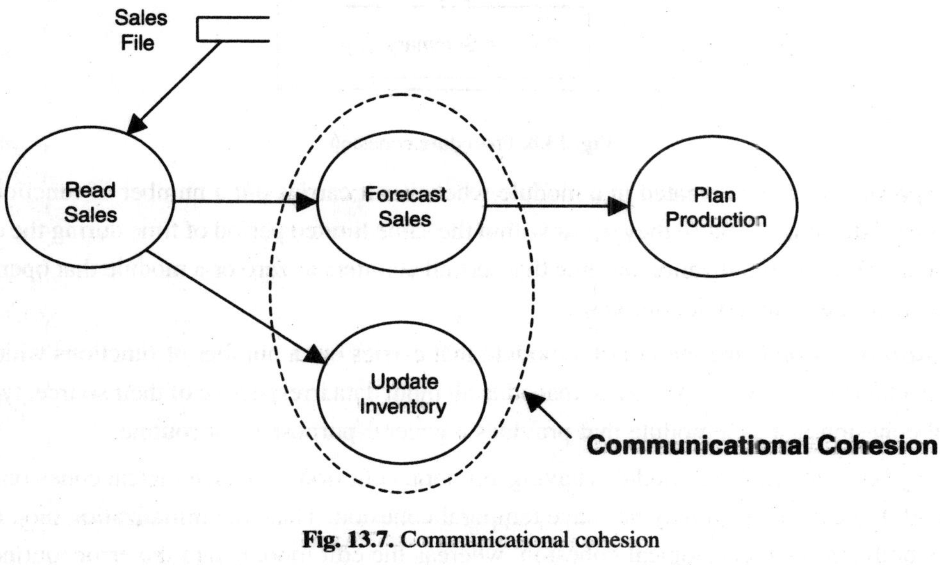

Fig. 13.7. Communicational cohesion

Procedural cohesion exists in a module when its elements are derived from procedural thinking that results from program flow charts and other such procedures that make use of structured programming constructs such as sequence, iteration, and selection. For example, Fig. 13.8 shows a program flow chart depicting processing of sales and receipt transactions. One may define modules *A*, *B*, *C*, and *D* depending on the proximity of control flows. Here the modules are said to be have procedural cohesion. In procedural thinking, it is likely that the tasks required to carry out a function are distributed among many modules, thus making it difficult to understand the module behaviour or to maintain a module in case of a failure.

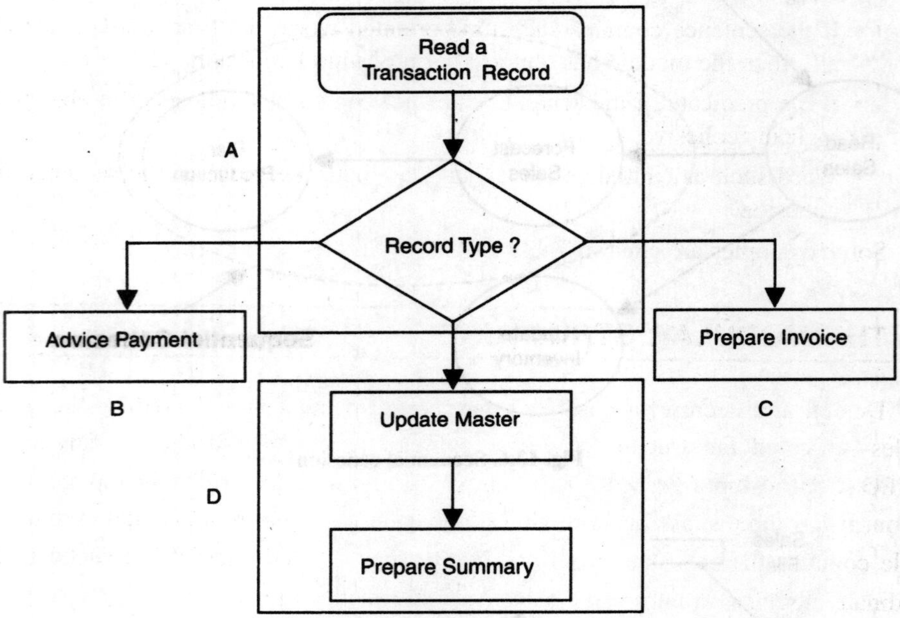

Fig. 13.8. Procedure cohesion

Temporal cohesion is created in a module whenever it carries out a number of functions and its elements are related only because they occur within the same limited period of time during the execution of the module. Thus an initialization module that sets all counters to zero or a module that opens all files at the same time has a temporal cohesion.

Logical cohesion is the feature of a module that carries out a number of functions which appear logically similar to one another. A module that edits all input data irrespective of their source, type or use, has logical cohesion just as a module that provides a general-purpose error routine.

It may be mentioned that modules having temporal cohesion also have logical cohesion, whereas modules with logical cohesion may not have temporal cohesion. Thus, the initialization module, stated earlier, has both temporal and logical cohesion, whereas the edit module and the error routine module have logical cohesion only.

Coincidental cohesion exists in a module when the elements have little or no relationship. Such cohesion often appears when modularization is made after code is written. Oft-repeating segments of code are often defined as module. A module may be formed with 50 lines of code bunched out of a program. Coincidental cohesion must be avoided at any cost. Usually, the function of such a module cannot be described coherently in a text form.

The type of cohesion in a module can be determined by examining the word description of the function of the module. To do so, first, the module's function is described fully and accurately in a single simple sentence. The following guidelines can be applied thereafter (Yourdon and Constantine, 1979):

- If the sentence is compound or contains more than one verb, then the module is less than functional; it may be sequential, communicational, or logical.
- If the sentence contains such time-oriented words as 'first', 'next', 'after', 'then', or 'for all', then the module has temporal or procedural cohesion.
- If the predicate of the sentence does not contain a single specific objective, the module is logically cohesive.
- Word such as 'initialize', 'cleanup', or 'housekeeping' in the sentence implies temporal cohesion.

Some examples are cited in Table 13.1.

13.4 THE MODULAR STRUCTURE

Design architecture, according to structured design, is reflected by the organization of the modules—the modular structure. The most aggregative modular structure of any program is based on the CIPO (Control-Input-Process-Output) model (Figure 13.9) in which the top module does the control function. It has three subordinate modules, one each for input, process, and output. Here the control module contains the call statements and coordinates the activities of the subordinate modules. The subordinate modules, in turn, carry out the actual functions required.

Table 13.1: Type of Cohesion from Word Description

Sentence describing module function	Type of cohesion
Reads 'hours worked' data and computes daily wage. Using 'hours worked' data, prints time sheet, and computes daily wage.	Sequential Communicational
First, reads 'daily hours worked' data, then computes 'monthly hours worked', then computes the monthly wage, and finally prints the pay slip.	Procedural
Initializes all counters to zero.	Temporal
Edit all input data.	Logical

In the structure chart in Fig. 13.9, each subordinate module is loaded with massive functions to carry out. It is both possible and desirable that the subordinate modules should have their own subordinate modules so that each of them can factor their functions and distribute them among their subordinates. Figure 13.10 is one such structure chart where the subordinate modules have their own subordinates.

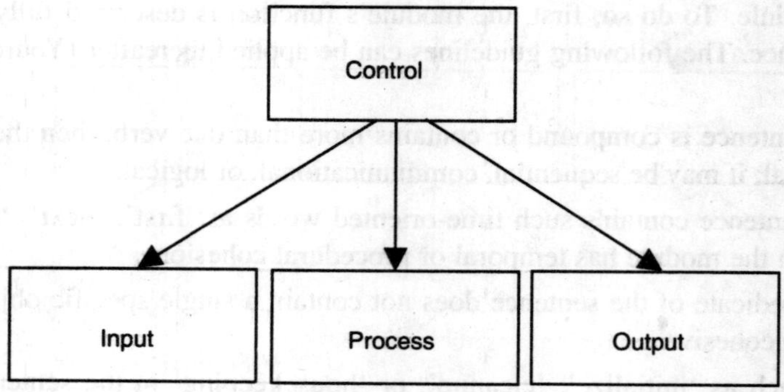

Fig. 13.9. The CIPO modular structure of a program

13.5 CONCEPTS UNDERSTANDING THE CONTROL HIERARCHY

Concepts underlying the control hierarchy are the following:

(*a*) Subordinate and superordinate

(*b*) Visibility and connectivity

(*c*) Afferent, efferent, transform, and coordinate flow

(*d*) Depth and width

(*e*) Fan-in and fan-out

(*f*) Scope of control and scope of effect

If module *A* invokes another module *B*, then module *A* is the *superordinate* of *B* and *B* is the *subordinate* of *A*.

Representing flow of data that pass explicitly from one module to another module makes the control more *visible*. Similarly, showing the flow of control with the use of links joining one module with another shows the way the modules are *connected* with one another.

Afferent and *efferent flows* derive their names from the afferent and efferent neurons in the brain. Afferent neurons carry sensory data from different parts of the body to the brain, whereas efferent neurons carry motor signals from the brain to different parts of the body. Afferent flow and efferent flow in a structure chart have similar meanings. When a module receives information from a subordinate module and passes it upward to a super-ordinate module then an afferent flow takes place. Figure 13.11 gives examples of afferent flow, efferent flow, transform flow, and coordinate flow, and the corresponding modules. Usually, afferent modules occur in the input side of a structure chart whereas efferent modules are present in the output side of the structure chart. Transform and coordinate flows occur in the middle processing portion of the structure chart.

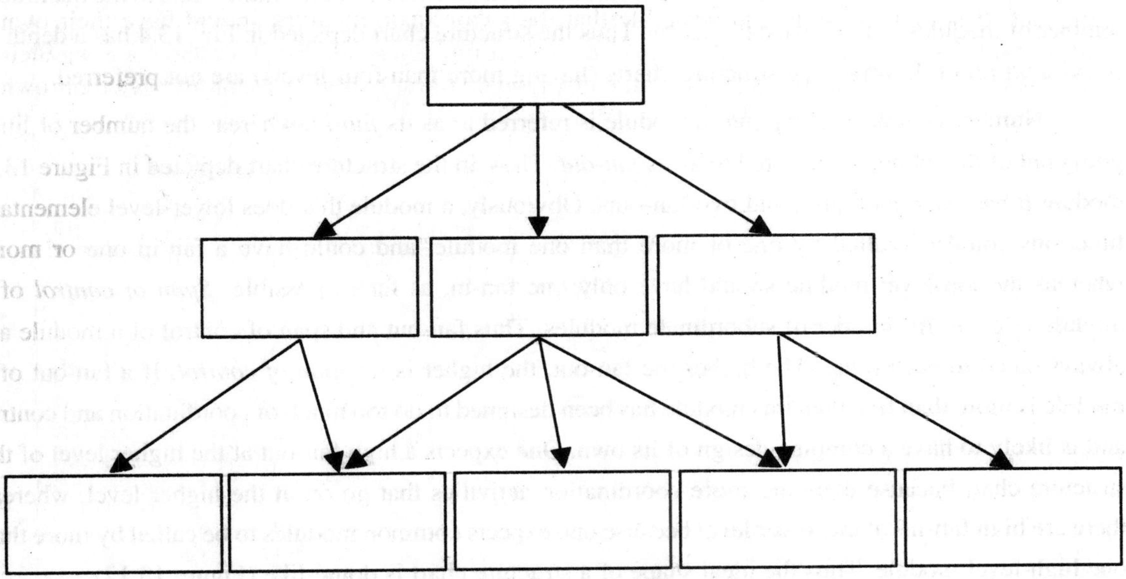

Fig. 13.10. Multi-level modular structure of a program

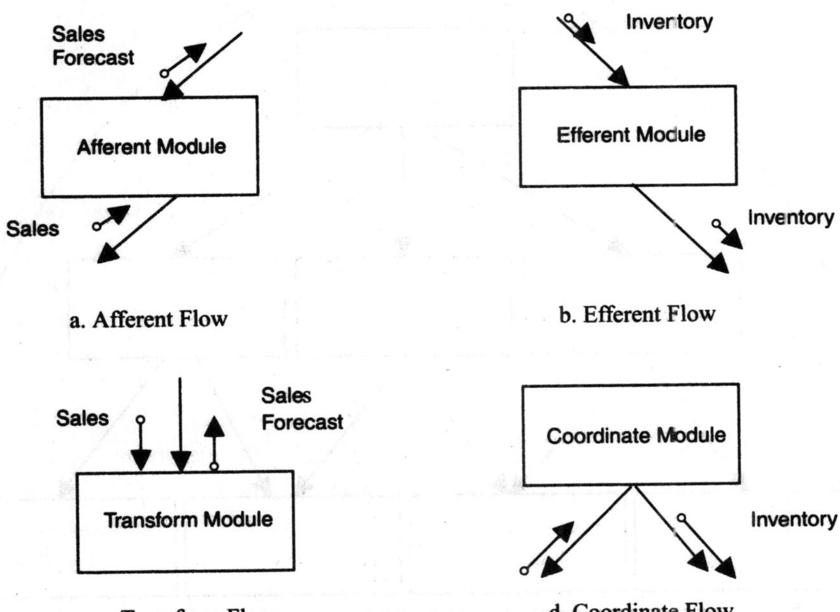

Fig. 13.11. Afferent, efferent, transform and coordinate flows

Depth refers to the number of levels of hierarchy in a structure chart. *Width* refers to the maximum number of modules in the lowest hierarchy. Thus the structure chart depicted in Fig. 13.4 has a depth of 3 and a width of 3. Very deep structure charts (having more than four levels) are not preferred.

Number of links coming into a module is referred to as its *fan-in*, whereas the number of links going out of the module is referred to as its *fan-out*. Thus, in the structure chart depicted in Figure 13.4, module *B* has only one fan-in and two fan-outs. Obviously, a module that does lower-level elementary functions could be called by one or more than one module, and could have a fan-in one or more, whereas the top-level module should have only one fan-in, as far as possible. *Span of control* of a module refers to its number of subordinate modules. Thus fan-out and span of control of a module are always equal to each other. The higher the fan-out, the higher is its *span of control*. If a fan-out of a module is more than five then this module has been designed to do too much of coordination and control and is likely to have a complex design of its own. One expects a high fan-out at the higher level of the structure chart because there are more coordination activities that go on at the higher level, whereas there are high fan-ins at the lower level because one expects common modules to be called by more than one high-level module. Thus the ideal shape of a structure chart is dome-like (Figure 13.12).

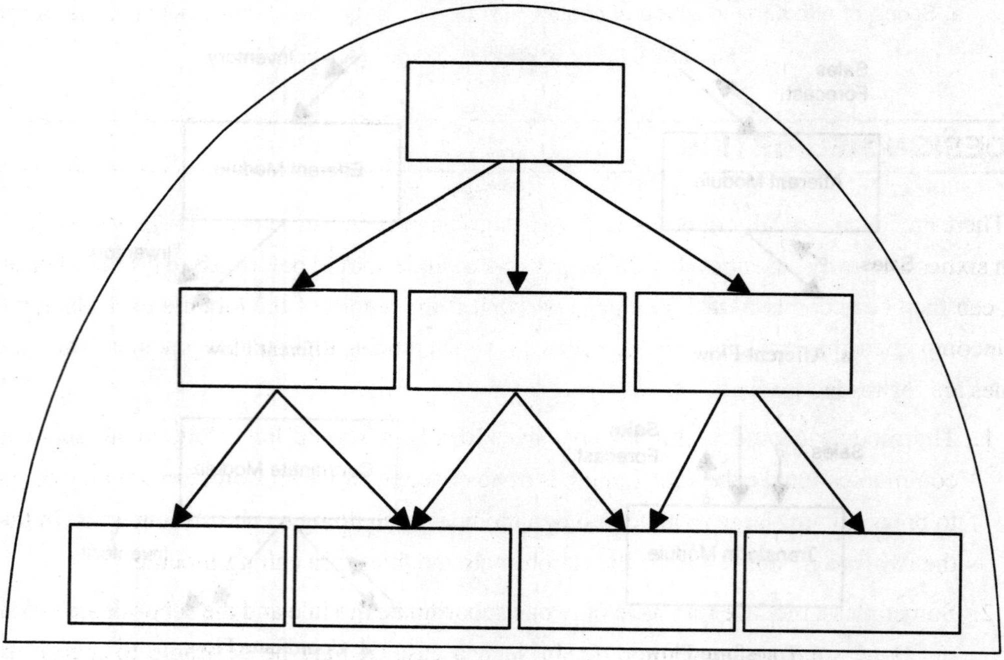

Fig. 13.12. Dome-like structure of a structure chart

Scope of control of a module *A* refers to all the modules that are subordinates to the module *i.e.*, to all the modules that can be reached by traversing through the links joining them to the module *A*. *Scope of effect* of module *A*, on the other hand, refers to all the modules which get affected by a decision made in the module *A*. In the structure chart depicted in Fig. 13.13a, the scope of control of *A* is the set of modules *B, C, D, E,* and *F*; that of *B* is the modules *D* and *E*; and so on. If a decision made in *D* in Fig. 13.13a affects the module *D* and *E* (the shaded modules), then the scope of effect of *D* includes the modules *D* and *E*. In Fig. 13.13b, the scope of effect of a decision taken at *B* consists of modules *B, D,* and *E* (the shaded modules) because a decision taken at *B* affects modules *B, D,* and *E.*

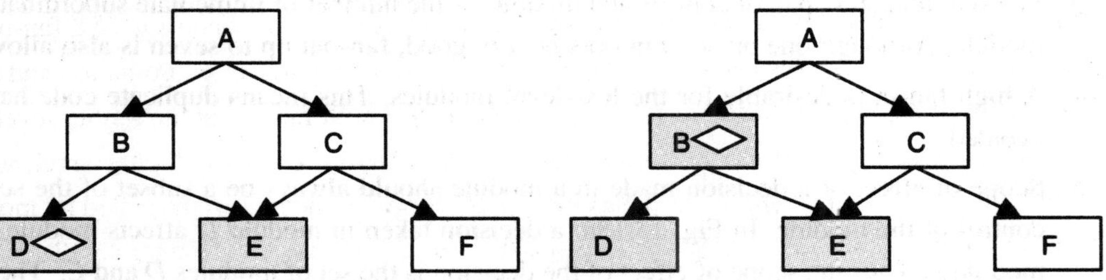

a. Scope of effect not in scope of control b. Scope of effect not in scope of control

Fig. 13.13. Scope of effect vs. scope of control

13.6 DESIGN HEURISTICS

There are no analytically rigorous tools of designing program structures. There was a widespread belief in sixties and early seventies that the length of a module should be limited to 50 lines because the module can then be accommodated on a page and that if the length of the module exceeds that then it will be incomprehensible. Structured design does not attach much weight to this practice. The following guidelines are forwarded instead:

1. The module should be highly cohesive. Ideally it should have functional, sequential or communicational cohesion. Length is of no concern. However, sometimes it may be possible to break down a large module into two modules each doing some sub-functions. In that case the two sub-modules will be the subordinate modules of a calling module.
2. Sometimes a module may have only one subordinate module and the subordinate module has only one super-ordinate module. In such a case, it may be desirable to merge the two together (Figure 13.14).

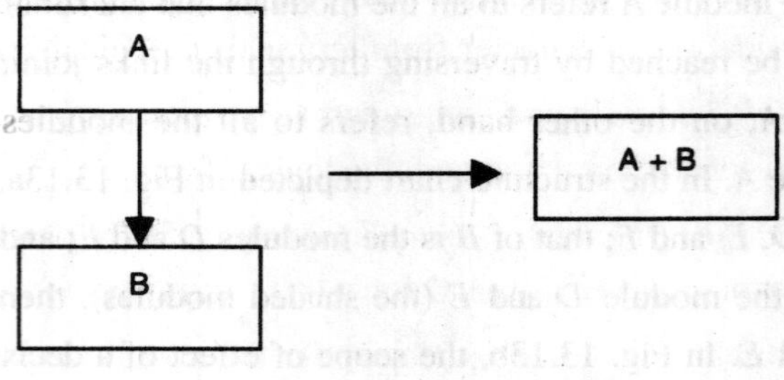

Fig. 13.14. Upward merging of modules

3. Fan-out indicates span of control of a module — the number of immediate subordinates of a module. Although one or two fan-outs is very good, fan-out up to seven is also allowed.
4. A high fan-in is desirable for the low-level modules. This means duplicate code has been avoided.
5. Scope of effect of a decision made in a module should always be a subset of the scope of control of the module. In Fig. 13.13*a*, a decision taken in module *D* affects module *D* and module *E*. Thus the scope of effect of the decision is the set of modules *D* and *E*. The scope of control of the module where this decision is taken consists of only the module *D* itself. Thus the scope of effect of the decision is not a subset of the scope of control. This is thus not a good design. An alternative design is given in Fig. 13.13*b* where the decision resides in the module *B*. One can see that now the principle holds. Thus the design depicted in Fig. 13.13*b* is better than that in Fig. 13.13*a*.

13.7 STRATEGIES OF STRUCTURED DESIGN

Structured design recommends two strategies for program design:

1. Transform analysis (Transform-centered design)
2. Transaction analysis (Transaction-centered design)

The former starts with an examination of the data flow diagram where data items undergo various types of transformation while the latter is best applied to situations dealing with multiple transaction processing. We discuss them in some detail below.

13.7.1 Transform Analysis

Transform analysis consists of five broad steps:

1. To start with, a level-2 or a level-3 data flow diagram of the problem is considered so that the processes represent elementary functions.
2. The data flow diagram is divided into three parts:

(*a*) The *input part* (*the afferent branch*) that includes processes that transform input data from physical (*e.g.*, character from terminal) to logical form (*e.g.*, internal table).

(*b*) The *logical* (*internal*) processing part (*central transform*) that converts input data in the logical form to output data in the logical form.

(*c*) The *output part* (*the efferent branch*) that transforms output data in logical form (*e.g.*, internal error code) to physical form (*e.g.*, error report).

3. A high-level structure chart is developed for the complete system with the *main module* calling the *inflow controller* (*the afferent*) *module*, the *transform flow controller module*, and the *outflow controller* (*the efferent*) *module*. This is called the *first-level factoring*. Figure 13.15 shows the high-level structure chart for this scheme.

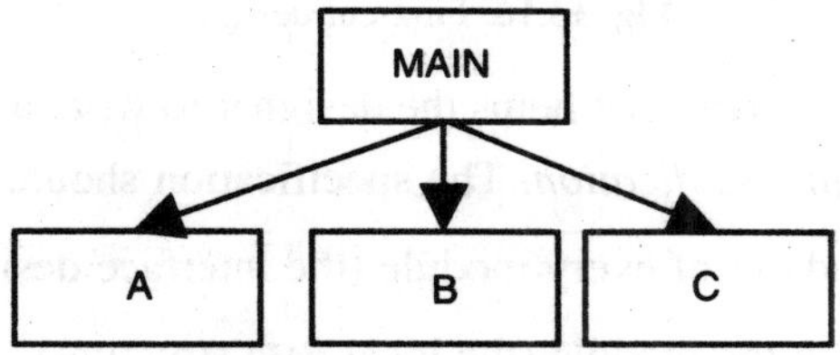

Fig. 13.15. First-level factoring

When activated, the main module carries out the entire task of the system by calling upon the subordinate modules. *A* is the input controller module which, when activated, will enable the subordinate afferent modules to send the input data streams to flow towards the main module. *C* is the output controller module which, when activated, will likewise enable its subordinate modules to receive output data streams from the main module and output them as desired. *B* is the transform flow controller which, when activated, will receive the input streams from the main module, pass them down to its subordinate modules, receive their output data streams, and pass them up to the main module for subsequent processing and outputting by the efferent modules.

4. The high-level structure chart is now factored again (*the second level factoring*) to obtain the *first-cut design*. The second-level factoring is done by mapping individual transforms (bubbles) in the data flow diagram into appropriate modules within the program structure. A rule that is helpful during the process of second-level factoring is to ensure that the processes appearing in the afferent flow in the data flow diagram form themselves into modules that form the lowest-level in the structure chart sending data upwards to the main module, and the processes appearing in the efferent flow in the data flow diagram form themselves into modules that also appear at the lowest-level of the structure chart and receive data from the main module downwards. Figure 13.16 shows the first-cut design.

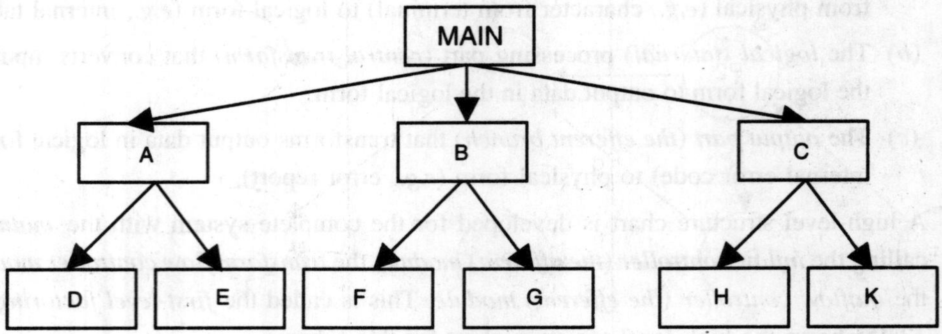

Fig. 13.16. First-cut design

The first-cut design is important as it helps the designer to write a brief processing narrative that forms the *first-generation design specification.* The specification should include

(*a*) the data into and out of every module (the interface design),

(*b*) the data stored in the module (the local data structure),

(*c*) a procedural narrative (major tasks and decisions), and

(*d*) special restrictions and features.

5. The first-cut design is now refined by using design heuristics for improved software quality. The design heuristics are the following:

(*a*) Apply the concepts of module independence. That is, the modules should be so designed as to be highly cohesive and loosely coupled.

(*b*) Minimize high fan-out, and strive for fan-in as depth increases, so that the overall shape of the structure chart is dome-like.

(*c*) Avoid pathological connections by avoiding flow of control and by having only single-entry, single-exit modules.

(*d*) Keep scope of effect of a module within the scope of control of that module.

We take a hypothetical data flow diagram (Figure 13.17) to illustrate the transform analysis strategy for program design. It is a data flow diagram with elementary functions. It contains 11 processes, two data stores, and 21 data flows. The two vertical lines divide the data flow diagram into three parts, the afferent part, the central transform, and the efferent part.

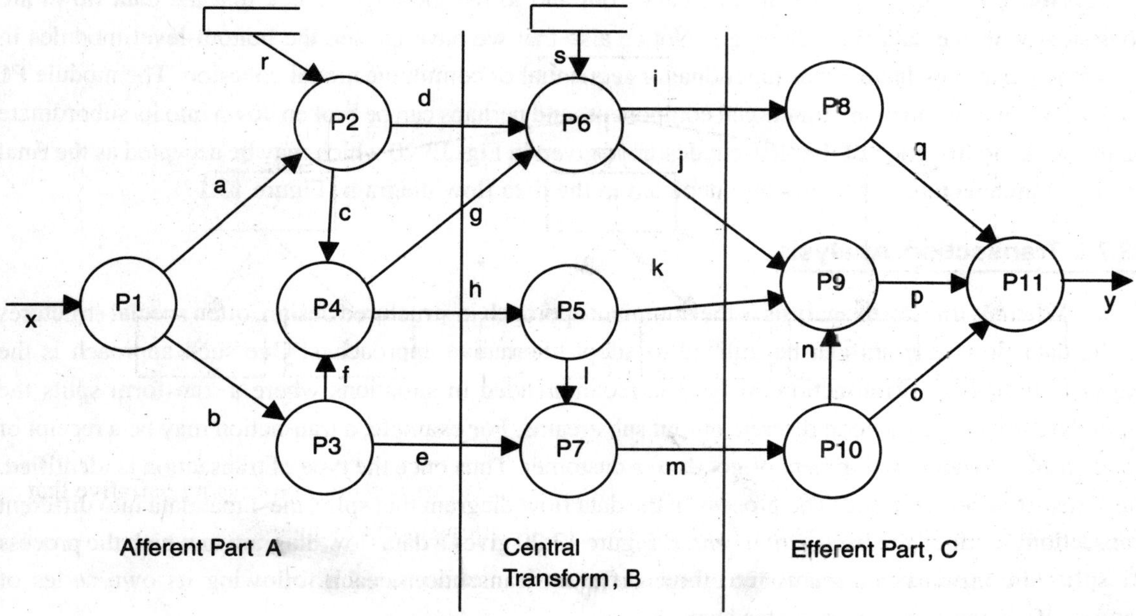

Fig. 13.17. DFD with elementary functions

Figure 13.18 is the structure chart showing the first-level structuring of the data flow diagram. Here module *A* represents the functions to be done by processes P1 through P4. Module *B* does the functions P5 through P7, and module *C* does the functions P8 though P13.

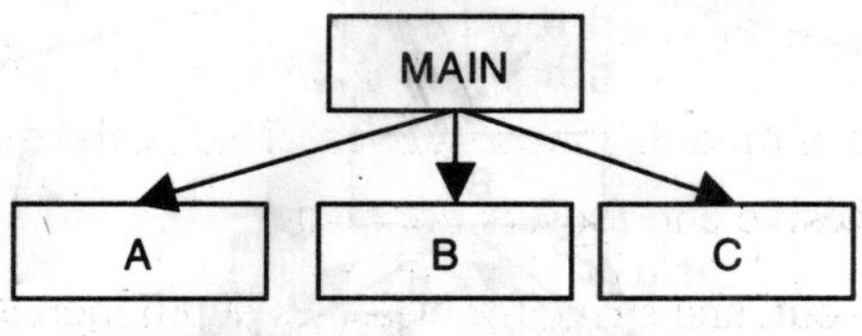

Fig. 13.18. First-level factoring

We now carry out a second-order factoring and define subordinate modules for *A*, *B*, and *C*. To do this, we look at the functions of various processes of the data flow diagram which each of these modules is supposed to carry out.

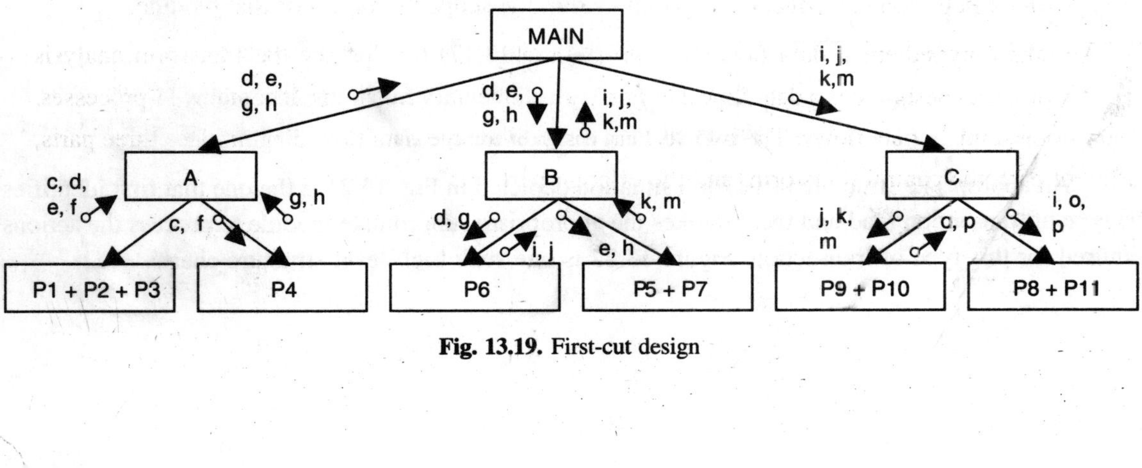

Fig. 13.19. First-cut design

Notice in Fig. 13.19 the flow of data from and to the modules. Check that the data flows are consistent with the data flow diagrams. Notice also that we have chosen the bottom-level modules in such a way that they have either functional or sequential or communicational cohesion. The module P1 + P2 + P3 contains too many functional components and perhaps can be broken down into its subordinate modules. A modification of the first-cut design is given in Fig. 13.20 which may be accepted as the final design of architecture of the problem depicted in the data flow diagram (Figure 13.17).

13.7.2 Transaction Analysis

Whereas transform analysis is the dominant approach in structured design, often special structures of the data flow diagram can be utilized to adopt alternative approaches. One such approach is the transaction analysis. Transaction analysis is recommended in situations where a transform splits the input data stream into several discrete output substreams. For example, a transaction may be a receipt of goods from a vendor or shipment of goods to a customer. Thus once the type of transaction is identified, the series of actions is fixed. The process in the data flow diagram that splits the input data into different transactions is called the *transaction center*. Figure 13.20 gives a data flow diagram in which the process P1 splits the input data streams into three different transactions, each following its own series of actions. P1 is the transaction center here.

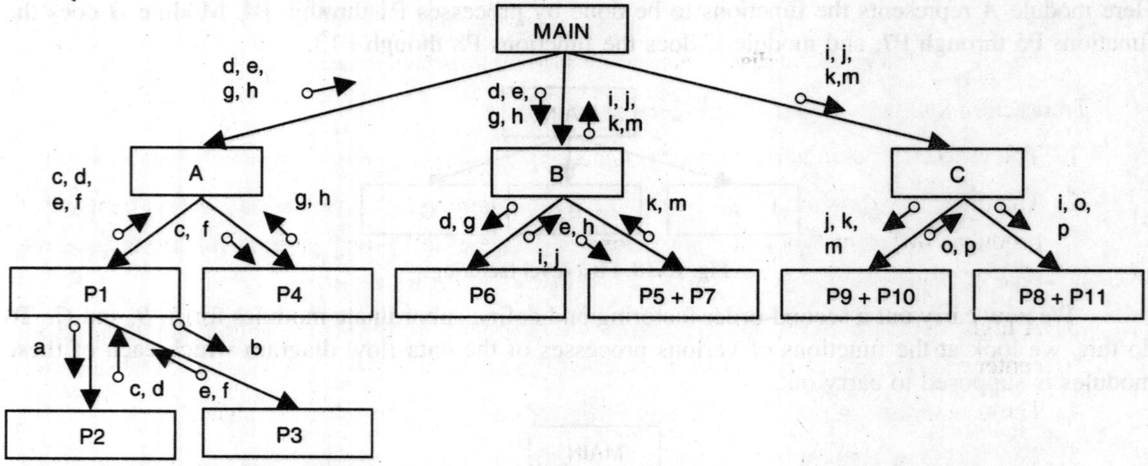

Fig. 13.20. Final design of architecture

An appropriate structure chart for a situation depicted in Fig. 13.21 is the one that first identifies the type of transaction read and then invokes the appropriate subordinate module to process the actions required for this type of transaction. Figure 13.22 is one such high-level structure chart.

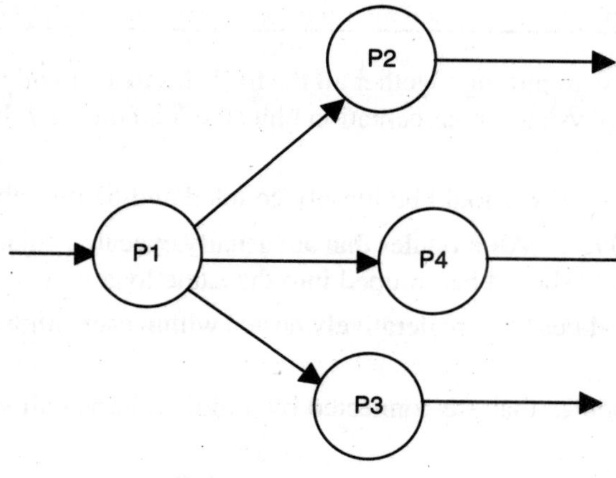

Fig. 13.21. Transaction center in a DFD

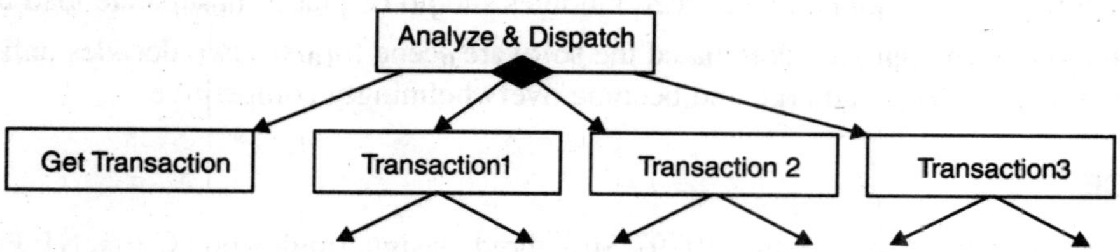

Fig. 13.22. High-level structure chart for transaction analysis

Transaction analysis consists of five steps:

1. The problem specifications are examined and transaction sources are identified.
2. The data flow diagram (level 2 or level 3) is examined to locate the transaction center that produces different types of transactions and locate and group various functions for each type of transaction.
3. A high-level structure chart is created, where the top level is occupied by the transaction-center module that calls various transaction modules, each for a specific type of transaction.
4. The transaction modules are factored to build the complete structure chart.
5. The 'first-cut' program structure is now refined using the design heuristics for improved software quality.

In practice, often a combination strategy is used. This strategy combines the features of transform analysis and transaction analysis. For example, when transform analysis alone cannot identify a reasonable central transform, transaction analysis is used to break the system (or program) into subsystems. Similarly, during a transaction analysis, if defining the root module as at transaction center makes it too complex, several transaction centers can be identified.

13.8 PACKAGING

Packaging is the process of putting together all the modules that should be brought into computer memory and executed as the physical implementation unit (the load unit) by the operating system. The packaging rules are as follows:

(*a*) Packages (*the load units*) should be loosely coupled and be functionally cohesive.

(*b*) *Adjacency (Basic) rule:* All modules that are usually executed adjacently (one after another) or use the same data should be grouped into the same load unit.

(*c*) *Iteration rule:* Modules that are iteratively nested within each other should be included in the same load unit.

(*d*) *Volume rule:* Modules that are connected by a high volume call should be included in the same load unit.

(*e*) *Time-interval rule:* Modules that are executed within a short time of each other should be placed in the same load unit.

(*f*) *Isolation rule:* Optionally executed modules should be placed in separate load units.

Structured design approach dominated the software scene for over two decades until the object-oriented approaches started to emerge and become overwhelmingly competitive.

REFERENCE

Yourdon, E. and. L. Constantine (1979), Structured Design, Englewood Cliffs, NJ: Prentice Hall, Inc.

14

Object-Oriented Design

14.1 INTRODUCTION

Emergence of object-oriented analysis and design methods has grown prominently during the past decade. We have already devoted two chapters (Chapter 8 and Chapter 9) to object-oriented analysis. In the current chapter, we discuss how objects interact to do a particular task. We also introduce elementary concepts of design patterns and their use in object-oriented design. The next chapter is devoted entirely to more advanced design patterns.

We give in Table 14.1 the activities and supporting tools carried out during object-oriented design.

Table 14.1: Activities and Tools in Object-Oriented Design

Sl. No.	Major steps/Substeps of OOA	Useful tools/Approaches for the step
1.	Make high-level implementation plan with regard to inputs and outputs.	Real use case User-interface storyboard
2.	Plan task fulfillment by associating objects. Plan object interactions. Decide the level of visibility.	Sequence diagram, Collaboration diagram
3.	Determine class relationships. Identify classes, attributes, types, and operations. Add associations and navigability. Add dependency relationships.	Static structure diagram Design class diagram Class hierarchy diagram Principles of object-oriented design
4.	Assign responsibilities to objects.	GRASP patterns
5.	Address information system architecture issues.	GRASP patterns

14.2 HIGH-LEVEL IMPLEMENTATION PLAN FOR INPUTS AND OUTPUTS

Design transforms requirements into plan for implementation. The first design step is to identify actual inputs and the corresponding actual outputs. A real use case is very useful here. A real use case considers the implementation details particularly with regard to the actual inputs to and actual outputs from the system. User-interface storyboards are normally used to consider the low-level interaction with the windows objects (widgets). We consider the case of *Borrow Books* presented earlier in Chapter 9. A relevant user-interface storyboard for this case is shown in Fig. 14.1 and the corresponding real use case is given in Fig. 14.2.

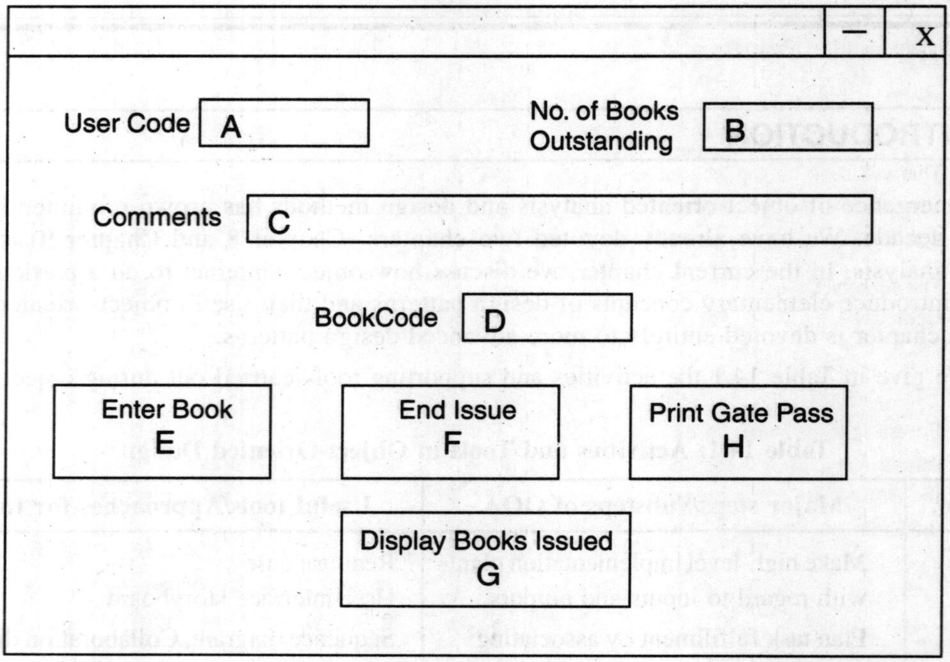

Fig. 14.1. User-interface storyboard

14.3 OBJECT INTERACTIONS

Different objects interact to accomplish a task. The principle of assigning responsibility to particular objects will be discussed later in the text. In this section we only discuss the use of interaction diagrams in depicting the flow of messages among objects to accomplish a task. Two types of interaction diagrams are in use:

1. Sequence Diagram
2. Collaboration Diagram

A sequence diagram is similar to a system sequence diagram, discussed earlier, with a difference that various objects participating in fulfilling a task replace the system object. An example is given in Fig. 14.3 to illustrate a sequence diagram. This example shows how the system operation message (due to the event created when the Library Assistant presses the *enterBook* button E) induces flow of internal

Use Case: Borrow Books

Actors: User, Library Asst.

Purpose: This use case describes the actor actions and system responses when a user borrows a book from the Library.

Overview: A valid user is allowed to borrow books provided he has not exceeded the maximum number of books to be borrowed. His borrowed-book record is updated and a gate pass is issued to the user.

Type: Primary and Real

Typical Course of Events

Actor Action	System Response
1. This use case begins when a User arrives at the Counter with books to borrow.	
2. The Library Asst. scans the User Code.	3. Displays the User Code in A and the number of books outstanding against the User in B.
4. For each of the books to be issued, the Library Asst. scans the Book Code and presses the Enter Book button E.	5. Displays the Book Code in D and updates the books issued and displays the total number of books issued in B. Displays "No more books can be issued." in C if the number of books issued equals the maximum number allowed.
6. The Library Asst. presses the End Issue button on completion of the issue of books.	
7. If required, the Library Asst. presses the Displays Books Issued button G.	8. Displays the details of all the books issued in a separate window.
9. The Library Asst. presses the Print Gate Pass button H.	10. Prints separate Gate Passes for each of the books issued.

Fig. 14.2. Real use case for borrow books

messages from objects to objects. This externally created message is sent to an instance of LLIS which sends the same *enterBook* message to an instance of *IssueOfBooks*. In turn, the *IssueOfBooks* object creates an instance of *IssuedBook*.

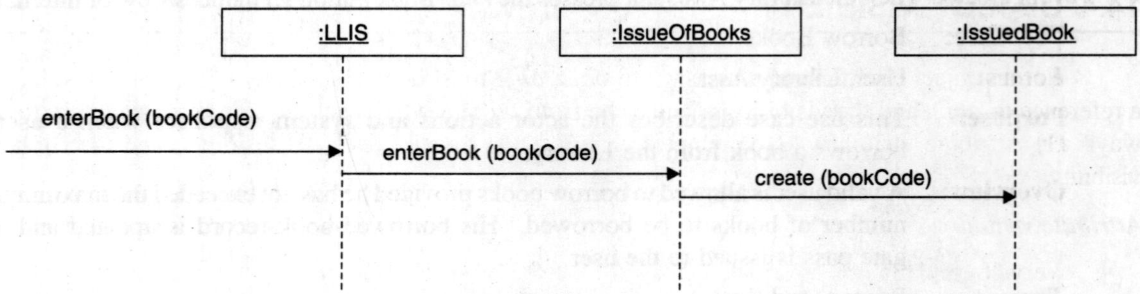

Fig. 14.3. Sequence diagram

A *collaboration diagram*, on the other hand, shows the flow of messages in a graph or network format, which is, in fact, the format adopted in this book. The line joining two objects indicates a link between two objects. Messages flow along the links. Directions of flow of messages are shown by means of arrows. Parameters of the messages appear within parentheses. Thus *bookCode* is the message parameter. Often the parameter type can be indicated; for example,

enterBook (bookCode: Integer)

The complete UML syntax for a message is:

Return := message (parameter: parameter type): return type

The example illustrated in the sequence diagram is now shown in the collaboration diagram (Figure 14.4).

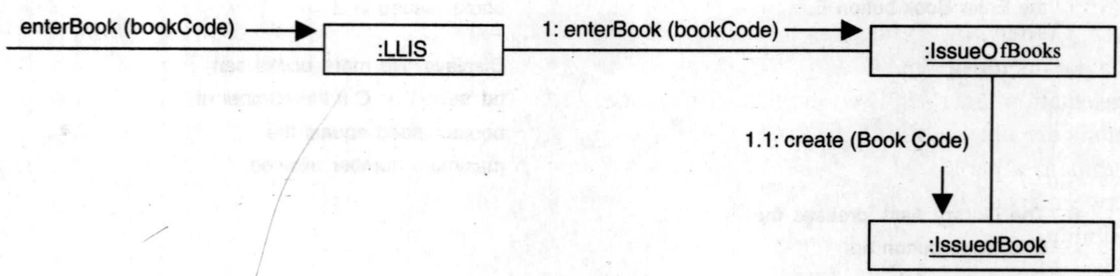

Fig. 14.4. Collaboration diagram

Many messages can flow in one link. In such cases, they are numbered to indicate their sequential ordering.

Often, same messages are repeatedly sent. In such cases, an asterisk (*) is shown after the sequence number. If the number of times a message is sent is known in advance, then it may also be indicated after the asterisk.

We know that messages are numbered to show their sequence of occurrence. We also know that upon receiving a message, an object, in turn, can send multiple messages to different objects. These subsequent messages can be numbered to indicate that they are created as a result of receiving an earlier message.

14.4 OBJECT VISIBILITY

For an object *obj1* to send a message to *obj2*, *obj2* must be visible to *obj1*, *i.e.*, *obj1* must have a reference to *obj2*, and the visibility is said to be from *obj1* to *obj2*. Visibility can be achieved in four ways: (1) Attribute visibility, (2) Parameter visibility, (3) Locally declared visibility, and (4) Global visibility.

Attribute visibility

Very common in object-oriented design, this form of visibility arises when *obj2* is an attribute of *obj1*. In Fig. 14.5, *issuedBooks* is an attribute in the class *IssueOfBooks*. Thus to execute *enterBook* (*bookCode*), the *IssueOfBooks* object sends the message *create* (*bookCode*) to the *IssuedBooks* object. The following Java instruction holds:

issuedBook.create (bookCode)

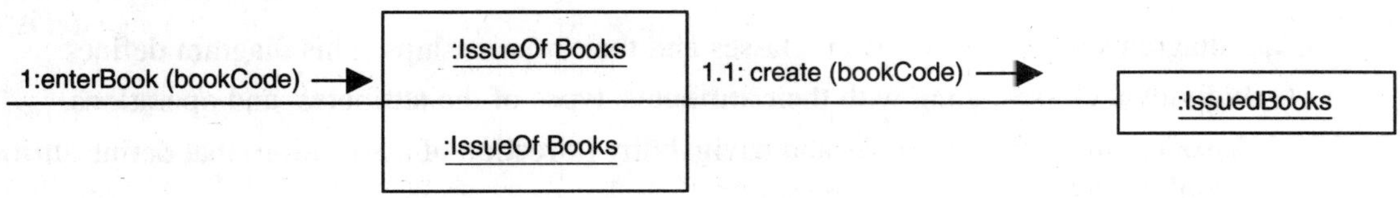

Fig. 14.5. Attribute visibility

The attribute visibility is a relatively permanent form of visibility since the visibility remains in vogue as long as the two objects continue to exist.

Parameter Visibility

When *obj1* defines another object *obj2* as a parameter in its message to *obj3*, *i.e.*, *obj2* is passed as a parameter to a method of *obj3*, then *obj3* has a parameter visibility to *obj2*. In Fig. 14.6, when the presentation layer sends an *enterBook* message, *LLIS* first sends a message to *BookDetails*. The book details are obtained in the form of *details*, an instance of the class *BookDetails*. *LLIS* thereafter uses *details* as a parameter in its *haveIssueLine* message to the *Issue* object. The dependency relationship between *Issue* and *BookDetails* objects is shown by a broken arrow. This is an instance of parameter visibility.

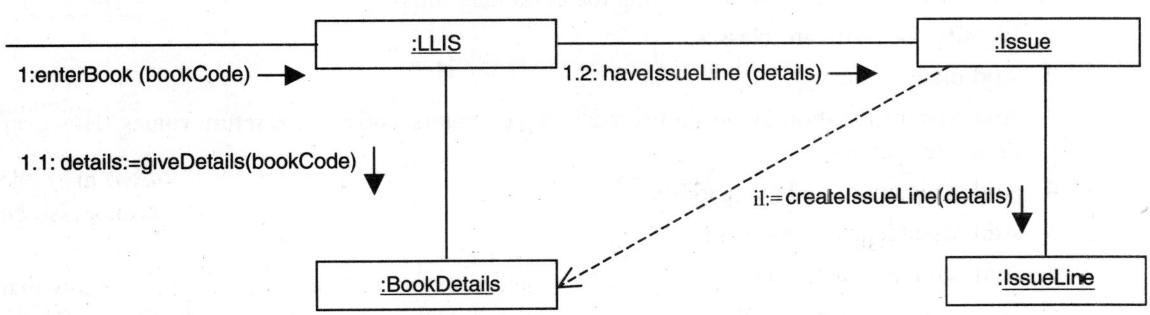

Fig. 14.6. Parameter visibility

Usually, parameter visibility is converted into attribute visibility. For example, when the *Issue* object sends a message to create the *IssueLine* object, then *details* is passed to the initializing method where the parameter is assigned to an attribute.

Locally Declared Visibility

Here *obj2* is declared as a local object within a method of *obj1*. Thus, in Fig. 14.6, *BookDetails* (an object) is assigned to a local variable *details*. Also when a new instance is created, it can be assigned to a local variable. In Fig. 14.6, the new instance *IssueLine* is assigned to a local variable *il*.

The locally declared visibility is relatively temporary, because it persists only within the scope of a method.

Global Visibility

Sometimes *obj2* is assigned to a global variable. Not very common, this is a case of relatively permanent visibility.

14.5 CLASS DIAGRAMS

Class diagrams depict the software classes and their relationships. This diagram defines

1. Individual classes along with their attributes, types of the attributes, and operations,
2. Associations between classes and navigability (direction of association) that define attribute visibility, and
3. Dependency relationships that define non-attribute visibility.

Class diagrams are similar to the static structure diagram (or the conceptual model). But there are a number of differences among the two:

1. The former is a design tool whereas the latter is an analysis tool.
2. The former defines software classes whereas the latter deals with domain-level concepts.
3. Operations are defined in the former, whereas they are absent in the latter.
4. Navigability arrows indicate the direction of visibility between two design classes, whereas they are absent in the latter.
5. Dependency relationships are indicated in the class diagrams whereas they are absent in the latter.

The following steps are used in drawing the class diagrams:

1. Identify the software classes.
2. Add method names.
3. Add type information for attributes, method parameters, and method return values. However these are optional.
4. Add associations and navigability.
5. Add dependency relationships.
6. Add reference attributes.

Identify the software classes

Conceptual models and collaboration diagrams are very useful to identify the software classes. Certain domain-level concepts, such as Library Assistant, are excluded, since they are not software entities.

Add method names

A study of collaboration diagram is very useful at this stage. A message to an object *B* in the collaboration diagram means that the class *B* must define an operation named after the message. Thus, from the collaboration diagram (Figure 14.7) we can say that the *enterBook* method must be defined in the class *IssueOfBooks*.

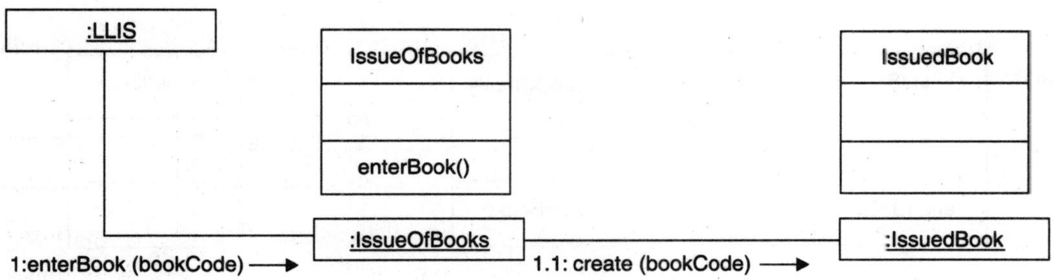

Fig. 14.7. Adding method names

We note that the following are not depicted as class operations:

1. create (such as *new*)
2. access methods (such as *get* or *set*)
3. send message to multi-objects (such as *find*).

Add type information

Type information may be optionally given for attributes, method parameters, and method return values. Thus, for example, *bookCode*, a parameter in the *enterBook* method (Figure 14.8), is defined as an integer. The return value for this method is void. A second method *total* returns a value which is defined as a quantity.

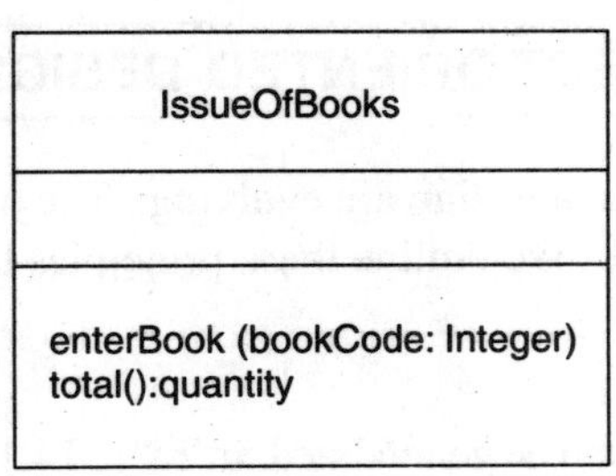

Fig. 14.8. Adding type information

Add associations and navigability

Conceptual models and the collaboration diagrams help in defining the *associations* among the software classes. These associations may be adorned with an open arrow from the source class to the target class whenever there is a necessity for unidirectional navigation from the former to the latter (Figure 14.9). Navigability indicates visibility (usually attribute visibility) from the source class to the target class.

Recall that 'needs to know' was the main principle while deciding the associations between concepts in the conceptual diagram. That principle still holds for deciding the associations among classes. However, since we are dealing with software classes, we need to also define class associations (1) whenever a class *A* creates an instance of class *B* and (2) whenever *A* needs to maintain a connection to *B*.

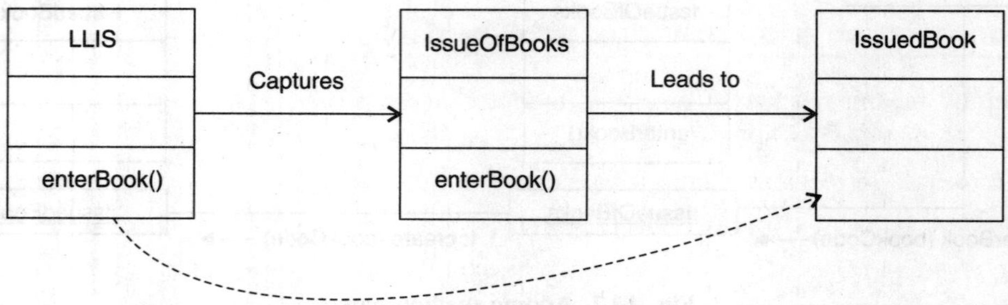

Fig. 14.9. Adding associations, navigability and dependency relationships—A class diagram

Add dependency relationships

Whereas attribute visibility is shown by a firm arrow, all other types of visibility are shown by dashed arrows. For example, the class diagram (Figure 14.9) has a dependency relationship between *LLIS* and *IssuedBook* if the number of books issued is returned to *LLIS* via the *IssueOfBooks*.

Add reference attributes

Whenever a class *A* sends a message to a class *B*, a named instance *b* of the class *B* becomes an attribute of *A*. The named instance is called the reference attribute. It is often shown near the target end of the arrow in the class diagram. Sometimes it is also implied and not shown in the diagram.

14.6 PRINCIPLES OF OBJECT-ORIENTED DESIGN

The principles of object-oriented design are evolving. The ones presented by Page-Jones (2000) are very fundamental and very novel. We outline these principles here.

14.6.1 Encapsulation

The concept of encapsulation can be generalized. In Table 14.1, packages and software components indicate higher-level encapsulation. *Class cohesion* refers to the degree of relatedness (single-mindedness) of a set of operations (and attributes) to meet the purpose of the class. *Class coupling* is a measure of number of connections between the classes.

Table 14.1: Meanings of Encapsulation

Encapsulation	Examples	Within-encapsulation property	Across-encapsulation property
Level-0	Line of code	Structured Programming	Fan-out
Level-1	Function, Procedure (single operation)	Cohesion	Coupling
Level-2	Class and Object (multiple operations)	Class Cohesion	Class Coupling

14.6.2 Connascence and Encapsulation Boundary

Literally meaning "having been born together" in Latin, *connascence* between two software elements means that two elements *A* and *B* are so related that when one changes the other has to change to maintain overall correctness. Connascence can be either static or dynamic. Examples of static and dynamic connascence are given in Table 14.2 and Table 14.3 respectively.

Negative connascence (or *contranascence*) exists in the case of multiple inheritance because features of two superclasses that are inherited by the subclass must have different names.

Connascence offers three guidelines for improving maintainability:

1. Minimize overall connascence (contranascence) by breaking the system into encapsulated elements.
2. Minimize any remaining connascence that crosses encapsulation boundaries.
3. Maximize the connascence within encapsulation boundaries.

Table 14.2: Types of Static Connascence and Examples

Type of connascence	Example
Name	A class uses an inherited variable of its superclass.
Type	If A is defined as an integer, then only integer value is accepted whenever it is used.
Convention	The class Transaction has instances that can be either Sale or Receipt. The code has to have statements like *if* Transaction is Sale then ....
Algorithm	The algorithm used for generating the check digit must be used for checking it.
Position	The sequence of arguments in the sender object's message and that in the target object must be the same.

Table 14.3: Types of Dynamic Connascence and Examples

Type of connascence	Example
Execution	Initializing a variable before using it.
Timing	A multimedia projector can be switched on a minimum of 2 minutes after it is switched off.
Value	Locations of corner points of a square are constrained by geometrical relationships.
Identity	If Sales Report (obj1) points to December spreadsheet, then the Salesmen Commission must also point to December spreadsheet.

These three guidelines point to keeping like things together and unlike things apart. Three basic principles of object orientation emerge from these guidelines:

Principle 1: Define encapsulated classes.

Principle 2: An operation of a class should not refer to a variable within another class.

Principle 3: A class operation should make use of its own variable to execute a function.

The friend function of C++ violates Principle 2 because it allows an operation of a class to refer to the private variables of objects of another class. Similarly, when a subclass inherits the programming variable within its superclass, it also violates Principle 3.

Classes can belong to four domains: (1) Foundation domain, (2) Architecture domain, (3) Business domain, and (4) Application domain. Table 14.4 gives the classes belonging to the domains and also gives examples of these classes.

Table 14.4: Domain, Class, and Examples

Domain	Type of application	Class	Examples
Foundation	Many applications, many industries, and many computers	Fundamental	Integer, Boolean, Character
		Structural	Stack, Queue, Binary Tree
		Semantic	Date, Time, Money, Point
Architectural	Many applications, many industries, and one computer	Machine-communication	Port, Remote Machine
		Database-manipulation	Transaction, Backup
		Human interface	Window, CommandButton
Business	Many applications and one industry	Attribute	BankBalance, BodyTemp
		Role	Supplier, Student
		Relationship	ThesisGuidance,
Application	Single or small number of related applications	Event-recognizer	ProgressMonitor
		Event-manager	SheduleStartOfWork

Foundation domain classes are the most reusable while the application domain classes are the least reusable. The knowledge of how far a class is away from the foundation class is quite useful. This can be known if we find the classes that this class refers to either directly or indirectly. In Fig. 14.10, class *A's direct class-reference set* consists of classes *B*, *C*, and *M*, whereas the *indirect class-reference set* (that is defined to include the direct class-reference set also) consists of all the classes (excepting *A*).

Encumbrance is defined as the number of classes in a class-reference set. Thus *A*'s direct encumbrance is 3, whereas its indirect encumbrance is 12. The classes *H* through *M* appearing as leaf nodes are the fundamental classes. Notice that the root class *A* has a direct reference to a fundamental class *M*.

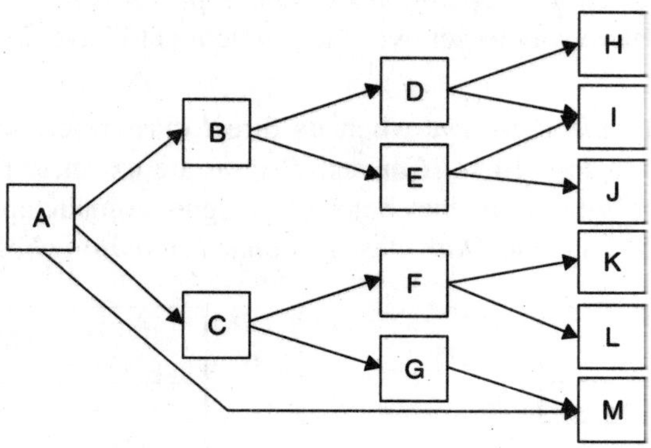

Fig. 14.10. Class reference set of class A

Based on the above, the guiding principles can be set as under:

Principle 4 : High-level classes should have high indirect encumbrance. If one finds a high-level class with low encumbrance, then most likely, the designer has built it directly using foundation classes, rather than reusing class libraries.

Principle 5 : A low-domain class should have low indirect encumbrance. If such a class has a high indirect encumbrance, then most likely the class is doing too many functions and has low cohesion.

The *Law of Demeter* (after the name of a project entitled *Demeter*) provides a guiding principle to limit the direct encumbrance by limiting the size of the *direct class-reference set*.

Principle 6 : It states that the target of an operation of an object must be limited to the following:

a. The object itself.

b. The object referred to by an argument within the operation's signature.

c. An object referred to by a variable of the object (*The strong law of Demeter*) or by a variable inherited from its superclass (*The weak law of Demeter*). The strong law is preferred because it does not permit the operation of an object to refer to the internal variable of another object.

d. An object created by the operation.

e. An object referred to by a global variable.

14.6.3 Class Cohesion

Class cohesion is a measure of the relatedness of operations and attributes of a class. A class can have (1) mixed-instance cohesion, (2) mixed domain cohesion, and (3) mixed-role cohesion, all of which make the class less cohesive. *Mixed-instance cohesion* is present in the class if one or more features are absent in one or more of the class's objects. Consider a class *Transaction* whose objects are named *Sale* and *Receipt*. Naturally, the objects have different features. An operation *Sale.makePayment* does not make sense just as it is for an operation *Receipt.prepareInvoice*. Here *Transaction* has mixed-instance cohesion. An alternative way to get over the problem is to have *Sale* and *Receipt* as subclasses of *Transaction*.

A class has *mixed-domain cohesion* when its direct class-reference set contains an extrinsic class of a different domain. In Fig. 14.11, *Car* and *Person* are extrinsic to *Date* in that they can be defined independent of *Date*. Furthermore, they belong to a higher domain (application domain) compared to *Date* (foundation domain). Thus the *Date* class has *mixed-domain cohesion*.

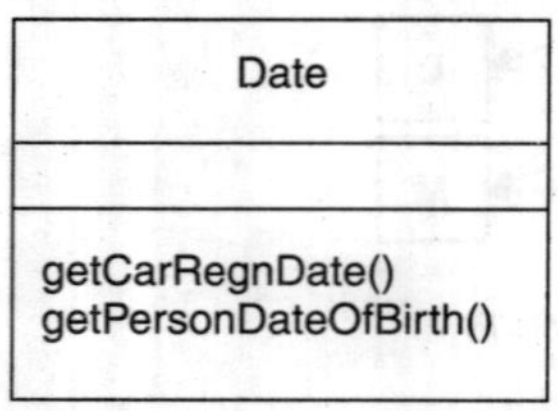

Fig. 14.11. Mixed-domain cohesion

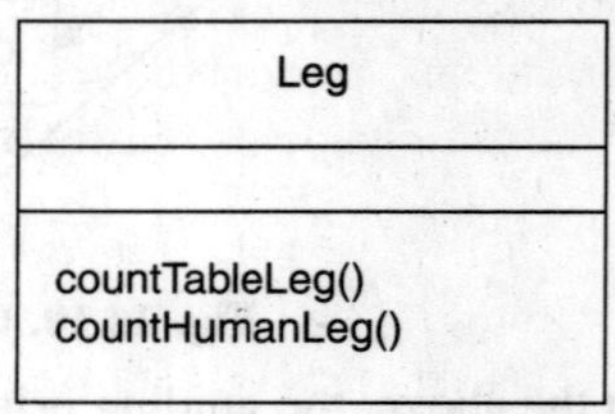

Fig. 14.12. Mixed role cohesion

A class *A* has *mixed-role cohesion* when it contains an element that has a direct class-reference set with an extrinsic class that lies in the same domain as *A*. In Fig. 14.12, *Leg* refers to *Table* and *Human* both belonging to the same domain as *Leg*, but they are extrinsic to *Leg* because they can be defined with no notion of *Leg*. Here, *Leg* has a mixed-role cohesion.

The mixed-instance cohesion is the most serious problem and the mixed-role cohesion is the least serious problem. The principle that has evolved out of the above-made discussion is:

Principle 7: Mixed-class cohesion should be absent in the design.

14.6.4 State Space and Behaviour

A class occupies different *states* depending on the values its attributes take. The collection of permissible values of the attributes constitutes the *state space* of the class. Thus, for example, the state space of a class may be a straight line, a rectangle, a parallelopiped, or an n-dimensional convex set depending on the number of attributes defined in the class.

As we know, a class can inherit attributes of its superclass but it can define additional attributes of its own. In Fig. 14.13, *ResidentialBuilding* and *CommercialBuilding* inherit the attribute *noOfFloors* from their superclass *Building*. Additionally, *ResidentialBuilding* defines a new attribute *area*; *CommercialBuilding*, on the other hand, does not. The state space of *ResidentialBuilding* is a rectangle

(Figure 14.14a), whereas it is a straight line for *Building* as well as for *CommercialBuilding* (Figure 14.14b).

Two principles apply to subclasses:

Principle 8 : The state space of a class constructed with only the inherited attributes is always a subset of the state space of its superclass.

In Fig. 14.13, the state space of *CommercialBuilding* is the same as that for *Building*.

Principle 9: A class satisfies the condition imposed by the class invariant defined for its superclass.

Suppose that the invariant for *Building* is that *noOfFloors must be less than or equal to 20.* Then the two subclasses must satisfy this condition.

14.6.5 Type Conformance and Closed Behaviour

To ensure that class hierarchies are well designed, they should be built in type hierarchies. A *type* is an abstract or external view of a class and can be implemented as several classes. A class, thus, is an implementation of a type and implies an internal design of the class. Type is defined by (1) the purpose of the class, (2) the class invariant, (3) the attributes of the class, (4) the operations of the class, and (5) the operations' preconditions, postconditions, definitions, and signatures. In a *type hierarchy*, thus, a *subtype* conforms to all the characteristics of its supertype.

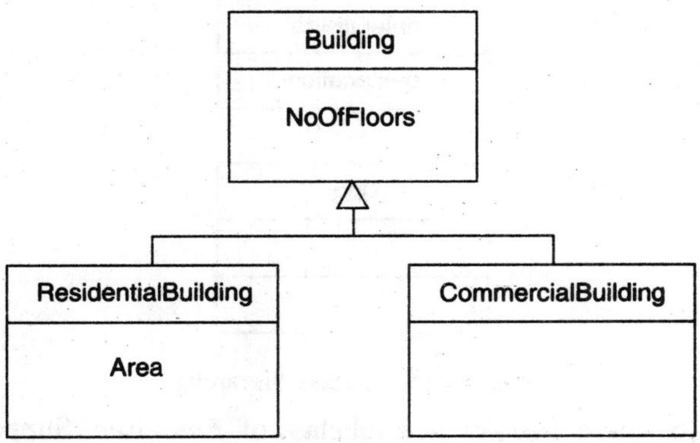

Fig. 14.13. Hierarchical structure

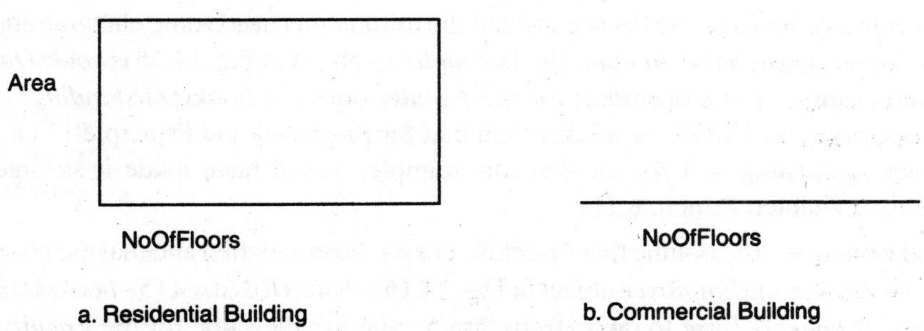

Fig. 14.14. State space

A class *A* inherits operations and attributes of class *B* and thus qualifies to be a subclass of a class *B* but that does not make *A* automatically a subtype of *B*. To be a subtype of *B*, an object of *A* can substitute any object of *B* in any context. A class *Circle* is a subtype of class *Ellipse*, where the major and minor axes are equal. Thus *Circle* can be presented as an example of an *Ellipse* at any time. An *EquilateralTriangle* is similarly a subtype of *Triangle* with all its sides equal.

Consider the class hierarchy shown in Fig. 14.15. Here *Dog* is a subclass of *Person* and inherits the *dateOfBirth* attribute and *getLocation* operation. That does not make *Dog* a subtype of *Person*.

Two principles emerge out of the above-made discussion:

Principle 10 : Ensure that the invariant of a class is at least as strong as that of its superclass.

Principle 11 : Ensure that the following three operations are met on the operations:

a. Every operation of the superclass has a corresponding operation in the subclass with the same name and signature.

b. Every operation's precondition is no stronger than the corresponding operation in the superclass (*The Principle of Contravariance*).

c. Every operation's postcondition is at least as strong as the corresponding operation in the superclass (*The Principle of Covariance*).

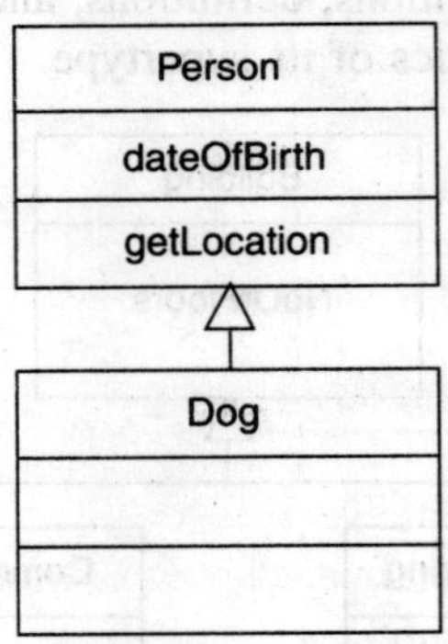

Fig. 14.15. A class hierarchy

Consider Fig. 14.16 where *Faculty* is a subclass of *Employee*. Suppose that the invariant of *Employee* is *yearsOfService* > 1 and that of *Faculty* is *yearsOfService* > 0, then the invariant of the latter is stronger than that of the former. So Principle 10 is satisfied.

Principle 11a is pretty obvious, but the second and the third points need some elaboration. Assume that the precondition for the operation *borrowBook* in the *Employee* object in Fig. 14.16 is *booksOutstanding* < 5, whereas the precondition of this operation for the *Faculty* object is *booksOutstanding* < 10. The precondition of the operation for *Faculty* is weaker than that for *Employee* and Principle 11a is satisfied. A precondition *booksOutstanding* < 3 *for faculty*, for example, would have made it stronger for the subclass and would have violated Principle 11a.

To understand Principle 11b, assume that Principle 11a has been satisfied and that the postcondition of the operation *borrowBook* in the *Employee* object in Fig. 14.16 is *booksToIssue* < (5 - *booksOutstanding*) resulting in the values of *booksToIssue* to range from 0 to 5, whereas the same for the *Faculty* object is *booksToIssue* < (10 - *booksOutstanding*) with the values of *booksToIssue* to range from 0 to 10. Here the postcondition for *Faculty* is weaker than that for *Employee* and Principle 11b is violated.

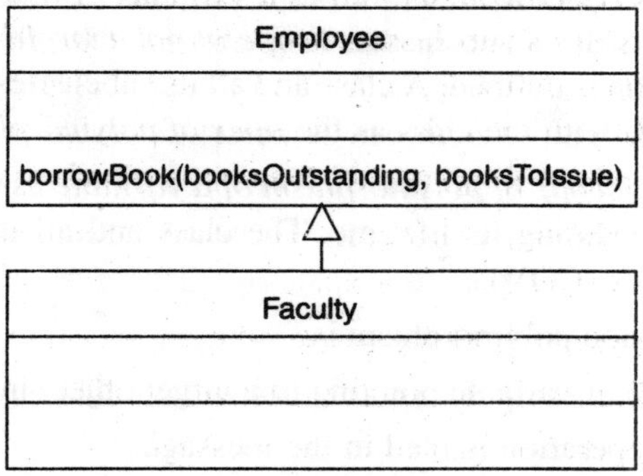

Fig. 14.16. Class hierarchy diagram for employee and faculty

The legal (and illegal) preconditions and postconditions can therefore be depicted as in Fig. 14.17.

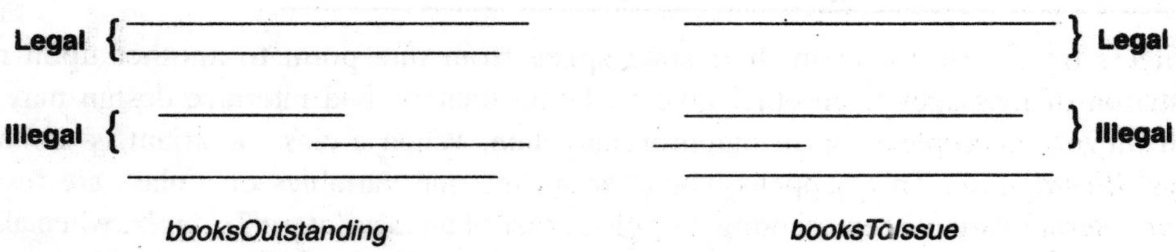

Fig. 14.17. Legal and illegal pre- and post-conditions

14.6.6 The Principle of Closed Behaviour

The principle of closed behaviour (Principle 12) states the following:

Principle 12 : An operation in a subclass, including the one inherited from its superclass, must satisfy its own invariant, when executed.

To understand the principle, consider the case of *Motorcycle* inheriting an operation *addWheel* from *Vehicle*. After the operation is executed, the object of *Motorcycle* no more retains its basic property. The operation, therefore, needs to be *overridden* to ensure that the object does not lose its basic property. Better still, the operation was not inherited in the first place, or *Motorcycle* was a subclass of *TwoWheelers* instead.

This principle is very useful in *modifier* operations, whereas the principle of type conformance is useful for *accessor* (or *query*) operations.

14.6.7 Inheritance – Problems

Sometimes inheritance causes problems. Consider a case where *Pen* is a subclass of *HollowCylinder*. Whereas *findInternalVolume*, an operation in *Cylinder*, makes perfect meaning when inherited by *Pen*, another operation *reduceDiameter* in *Cylinder* is meaningless for *Pen*, needing the operation to be overridden.

Polymorphism allows an operation, as well as a variable, of a superclass to be used in the same name, but differently, in objects of its subclasses. *Scope of polymorphism of an operation* is the set of classes upon which the operation is defined. A class and all its subclasses who inherit the operation form a *cone of polymorphism* (COP) with the class as the *apex of polymorphism* (AOP).

Similarly, we define the *scope of polymorphism of a variable* as the set of classes whose objects are referred to by the variable during its lifetime. The class and all its subclasses referred to by the variable form a *cone of variable* (COV).

A principle that helps good polymorphism is:

Principle 13 : The cone of variable pointing to a target object in a message must lie within the cone of operation named in the message.

To understand the principle, consider Fig. 14.18. COV of *HouseholdGoods* is the set of all classes including itself, but COP of the operation *lock* of the class *HouseholdGoods* does not include the subclass *Chair*. Here COV is not a subset of COP and thus violates the Principle 13.

14.6.8 Class-Interface Design – State Space and Behaviour

Objects of a class move in their state space from one point to another upon receipt and implementation of messages from other objects. Unfortunately, bad interface design may move it to occupy an illegal, incomplete, or an inappropriate state. When a class invariant is violated, a class occupies an *illegal state*. This happens when certain internal variables of a class are revealed. For example, an internal variable representing a single corner of an *EquilateralTriangle*, when allowed to be accessed and moved, violates the invariance property of the *EquilateralTriangle*, class, resulting in a triangle that is no more equilateral.

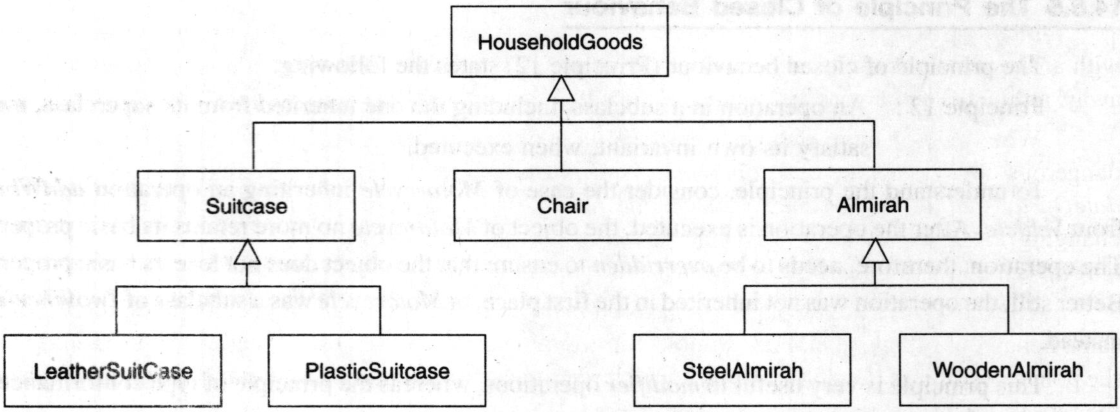

Fig. 14.18. Polymorphism, COP, and COV

When legal states cannot be reached at all, it indicates design flaws. For example, a poor design of *Triangle* does not allow creation of an *IsoscelesTriangle*. This indicates a class-interface design with *incomplete class*.

Inappropriate states of a class are those that are not formally part of an object's class abstraction, but are wrongly offered to the outside object. For example, the first element in a *Queue* should be visible and not its intermediate elements.

A class interface has the *ideal states* if it allows the class objects to occupy only its legal states.

While moving from one state to another in response to a message, an object displays a behaviour. The interface of a class supports ideal behaviour when it enforces the following three properties which also form the Principle 14.

Principle 14:

1. An object must move from a legal state only to another legal state.
2. The object's movement from one state to another conforms to the prescribed (legal) behaviour of the object's class.
3. There should be only one way to use the interface to get a piece of behaviour.

Unfortunately, bad class-interface design may yield behaviour that is far from ideal. Such a piece of behaviour can be illegal, dangerous, irrelevant, incomplete, awkward, or replicated. *Illegal behaviour* results due to a design of a *Student* object who can move from a state of *unregistered* to the state of *appearedExam* without being in a state of *registered.*

A class interface yields *dangerous behaviour* when multiple messages are required to carry out a single piece of object behaviour with the object moving to illegal states because of one or more messages. For example, assume that the state of *Payment* object is *approved.* But because cash is not sufficient to make the payment, negative cash balance results. To correct this situation, the state of *Payment* should be *deferred.* Two messages may carry out this state change:

1. A message sets the amount to be paid as a negative number, an illegal state.
2. The second message makes the payment, *i.e.*, brings back the state of *Payment* to a positive value and sets its state to *deferred.*

A class interface may result in an *irrelevant behaviour* if no state change of an object occurs — perhaps the object just passes message to another object.

Incomplete behaviour results when a legal state transition of an object is undefined — a problem with analysis. For example, a *Patient* object in an *admitted* state cannot be in a *discharged* state right away, although such a possibility may be a reality.

When two or more messages carry out a single legal behavour (but with no illegal state as in dangerous behaviour), the class interface displays an *awkward behaviour*. For example, to change the *dateOfPayment* of the *Payment* object, one needs the services of two messages, the first message changing the *made* state of *Payment* to the *approved* state and the second message changing its *dateOfPayment* and bringing the *Payment* back to *made* state.

The class interface displays a *replicated behaviour* when more than one operation results in the same behaviour of an object. For example, the coordinates of a vertex of a triangle are specified by both the polar coordinates (angle and radius) and by rectilinear coordinates (x- and y-axis) in order to enhance the reusability of the class *Triangle*.

14.6.9 Mix-in Class

A *mix-in class* is an abstract class that can be reused and that helps a business class to be cohesive. In Fig. 14.19, *Travel* is an abstract class that helps *TravellingSalesman* to be cohesive. *Travel* is then a mix-in class. This leads to Principle 15.

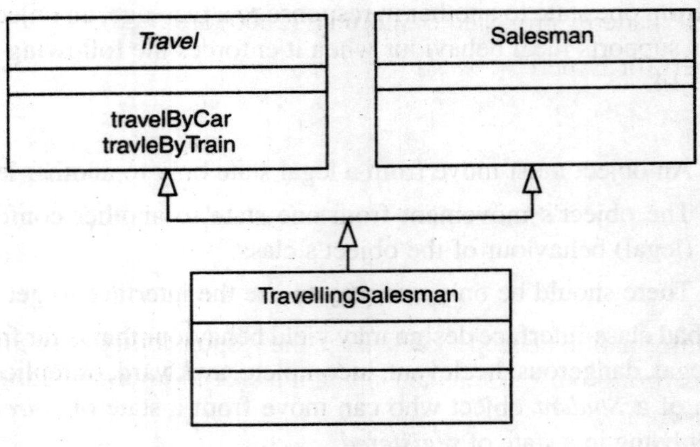

Fig. 14.19. A mix-in class

Principle 15 : Design abstract mix-in classes that can be used along with business classes to create combination classes, via inheritance, enhance cohesion, encumbrance, and reusability of the business classes.

14.6.10 Operation Cohesion

An operation can be designed to do more than one function. In that case it is not cohesive. There are two possibilities: (1) Alternate Cohesion and (2) Multiple Cohesion. *Alternate cohesion* exists in an operation when more than one function are stuffed into one operation A flag passed as a parameter in the operation indicates the particular function to be executed. *Multiple cohesion*, on the other hand, means that it is stuffed with many functions and that it carries out all the functions when executed. Ideally, an operation should be *functionally cohesive* (a term and a concept borrowed from structured design) meaning that ideally an operation should carry out a single piece of behaviour. This leads to Principle 16.

Principle 16 : An operation should be functionally cohesive by being dedicated to a single piece of behaviour.

Whereas an operation name with an "or" word indicates an alternate cohesion and that with an "and" word a multiple cohesion, the name of a functional cohesive operation contains neither the word "or" not the word "and".

14.7 ASSIGNMENT OF RESPONSIBILITIES OF OBJECTS

Recall that when a system operation is involved, a contract specifies, assuming the system to be a black box, what responsibilities the operation is called upon to discharge and what post-conditions (state changes) it will lead to.

Larman (2000) suggests GRASP patterns that help assigning responsibilities to objects in order to execute the system operation. GRASP is an acronym for General Responsibility Assignment Software Patterns. There are five basic GRASP patterns and several advanced GRASP patterns.

14.7.1 The Basic GRASP Patterns

The five basic GRASP patterns proposed by Larman (2000) are:

1. Information Expert (or Expert)
2. Creator
3. High Cohesion
4. Low Coupling
5. Controller

The Expert Pattern

A class that has the information needed to discharge the responsibility is an *information expert.* Thus the responsibility of carrying out the relevant operation has to be assigned to that class. This principle is alternatively known as

- Place responsibilities with data.
- That which knows, does.
- Do it myself.
- Put services with the attributes they work on.
- Animation (meaning that objects are 'alive' or 'animate'; they can take on responsibilities and do things.).

In the collaboration diagram (Figure 14.20), we see that to carry out a system operation *printGatePass*, the responsibilities are assigned to two information experts. The experts and the assigned responsibilities are the following:

Design Expert	Responsibility
GatePass	Prints Gate Pass
IssuedBook	Stores details of currently issued books

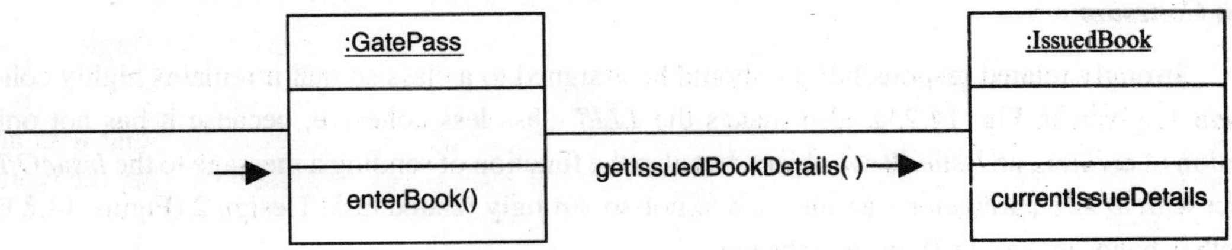

Fig. 14.20. The information experts

The Creator Pattern

Creator helps in assigning the responsibility of creating instances of a class. For example, a class *B* is given the responsibility of creating the *A* objects if

- *B* aggregates *A* (a whole-part relationship: chair-seat).
- *B* contains *A* (*Sale* contains *SaleLine*)
- *B* records instances of *A*.

- *B* uses *A* objects.
- *B* has the initializing data that get passed to *A* when it is created. Thus, *B* is an Expert with respect to the creation of *A*.

In Fig. 14.21, *IssueOfBooks* contains a number of *IssuedBook* objects. Therefore, *IssueOfBooks* should have the responsibility of creating *IssuedBook* instances.

Fig. 14.21. The creator pattern

Passage of initializing data from a class *B* to a class *A* when *A* is created is another example of the creator pattern. During processing of sales transactions, a *Sale* object knows the *total amount*. Thus, when a *Payment* object is created, then the *total amount* can be passed to the *Payment* object. Thus the *Sale* object should have the responsibility of creating a *Payment* object. Figure 14.22 shows the collaboration diagram for this example.

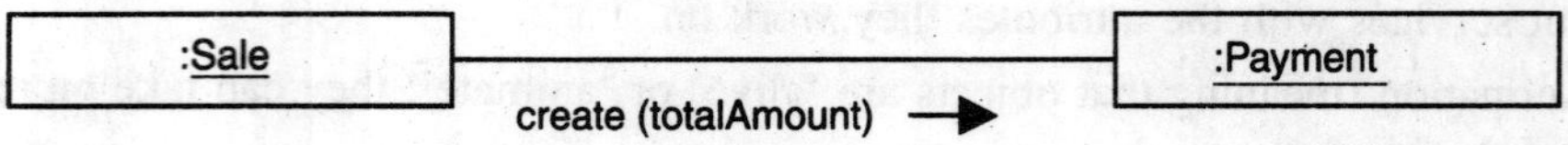

Fig. 14.22. The creator pattern

Low Coupling

Responsibility should be so assigned as to ensure low coupling between classes. Figure 14.23 shows two designs. In design 1 (Figure 14.23a), *LLIS* creates the *IssuedBook* object and passes the named object *ib* as a parameter to the *IssueOfBooks* object. It is an example of high coupling between *LLIS* and *IssuedBook*. In design 2 (Figure 14.23b), such coupling is absent. Hence design 2 is better.

High Cohesion

Strongly related responsibilities should be assigned to a class so that it remains highly cohesive. Design 1, given in Fig. 14.23a, also makes the *LLIS* class less cohesive, because it has not only the function of creating an *IssuedBook* object, but also the function of sending a message to the *IssueOfBooks* object with *ib* as a parameter – an instance of not-so-strongly related task. Design 2 (Figure 14.23b), on the other hand, makes *LLIS* more cohesive.

We may mention here that the well-established module-related principles of coupling and cohesion are valid in the context of object-oriented analysis and design. Classes are the modules that must contain highly cohesive operations. Highly cohesive modules generally result in low intermodular coupling and vice-versa.

The Controller Pattern

A controller class handles a system event message (such as *borrowBook* and *returnBook*). There are three ways in which one can select a *controller* (Figure 14.24):

(1) Façade Controller

(2) Role Controller

(3) Use-Case Controller

A *façade controller* is one that represents the overall 'system'. In the Library example, the class *LLIS* itself can handle the system events and system operations (for example *borrowBook*). In that case *LLIS* is a façade controller.

We could, on the other hand, define a class *User* and then assign it the responsibility of handling the system operation *borrowBook*. *User*, then, is a *role controller*.

Lastly, we could define a class *borrowBook*, named after the use case *Borrow Books*, which could handle the system operation *borrowBook*. The class *Borrow Book*, then, represents a *use case controller*.

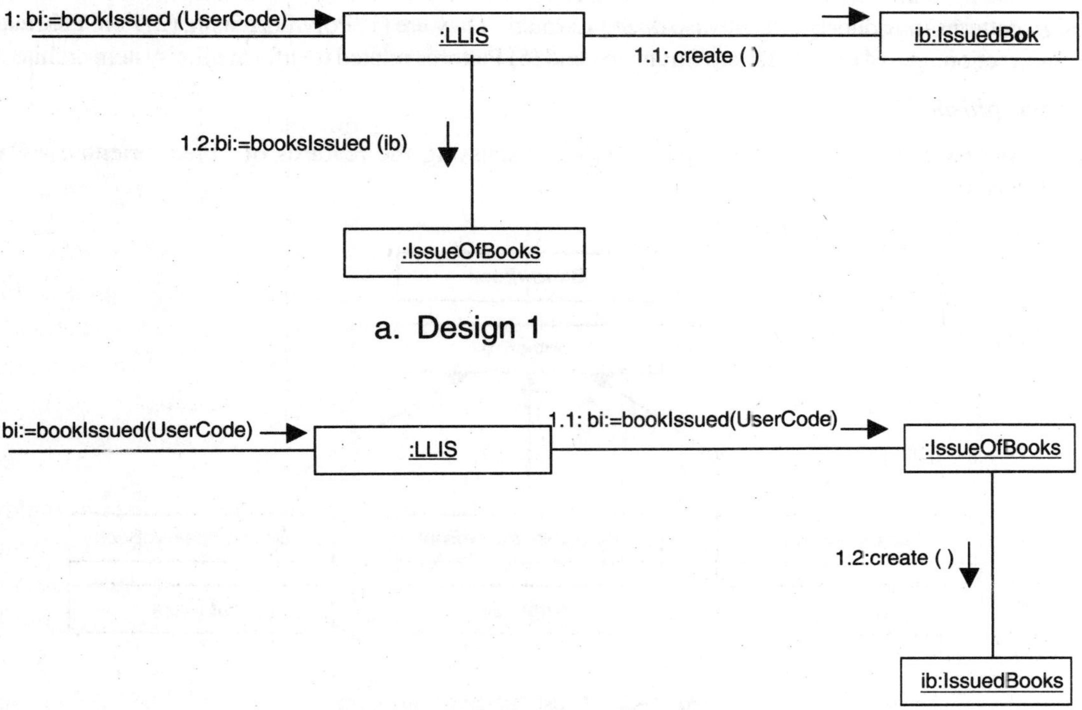

Fig. 14.23. Low coupling and high cohesion

Whereas a façade controller is preferred when there are small number of system operations, use-case controllers are preferred when the system operations are too many. Classes that are highly loaded with large number of system operations are called *bloated controllers* and are undesirable.

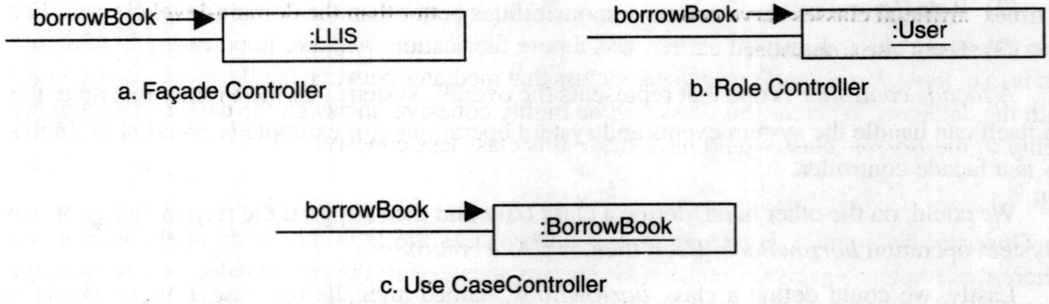

Fig. 14.24. Controller patterns

14.7.2 Other GRASP Patterns

We have already discussed five basic GRASP patterns proposed by Larman (2000). A few more design patterns introduced here are also due to Larman. They are (1) Polymorphism, (2) Pure Fabrication, (3) Indirection, and (4) Don't Talk to Strangers, and (5) Patterns related to information system architecture.

Polymorphism

We have discussed polymorphism while discussing the features of object oriented software development.

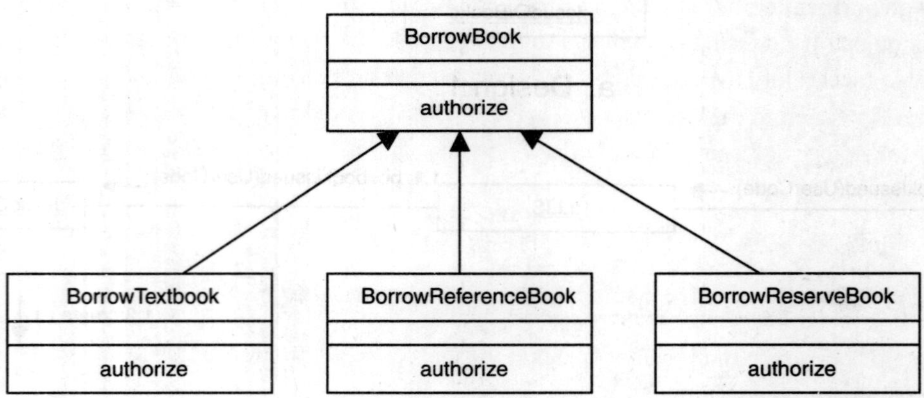

Fig. 14.25. Class hierarchy diagram

In the example shown in Fig. 14.25, the method *authorize* in case of *BorrowTextbook* means verifying if the book is on demand by any other user, whereas it is verifying a permission from the Assistant Librarian (Circulation) in case of *BorrowReserveBook*, it is verifying permission from the Assistant Librarian (Reference) in case of *BorrowReferenceBook*. Thus, while implementing the method, *authorize* is used in different ways. Any other subclass of *BorrowBook* such as *BorrowDonatedBook* could be added with the same method name without any difficulty.

Pure Fabrication

At times, artificial classes serve certain responsibilities better than the domain-level classes. For example, an *Observer* class, discussed earlier, was a pure fabrication. Another good example of a pure fabrication is to define a *PersistentStorageBroker* class that mediates between the *Borrow/Return/Renew* classes with the database. Whereas this class will be highly cohesive, to assign the database interfacing responsibility to the *Borrow* class would have made this class less cohesive.

Indirection

An *Observer* class and a *PersistentStorageBroker* class are both examples of the indirection pattern where the domain objects do not directly communicate with the presentation and the storage layer objects; they communicate indirectly with the help of intermediaries.

Don't Talk to Strangers

This pattern states that within a method defined on an object, messages should only be sent to the following objects:

(1) The same object of which it is a part.

(2) A parameter of the method.

(3) An attribute of the object.

(4) An element of a collection which is an attribute of the same object.

(5) An object created within the method.

Suppose we want to know the number of books issued to a library user. Design 1, given in Fig. 14.23a, violates the principle of *Don't Talk* to Strangers, because the *LLIS* object has no knowledge of the *IssuedBooks* object. It first sends a message to the *IssuedBooks* object which sends the reference of the *IssueOfBooks* object. Only then does the *LLIS* send the message to the *IssuedBooks* object to know the number of books issued to the user. Design 2 (Fig. 14.23b), on the other hand, does not violate this principle. *LLIS* sends the message to *IssueOfBooks* object, which, in turn, sends a second message to *IssuedBooks* object.

We discuss the patterns related to information system architecture in the next section.

14.7.3 Patterns Related to Information System Architecture

Following the principle of division of labour, the architecture for information system is normally designed in three tiers or layers (Figure 14.26):

(1) The Presentation layer at the top that contains the user interface,

(2) The Application (or Domain) layer, and

(3) The Storage layer.

The *presentation layer* contains windows applets and reports; the *application layer* contains the main logic of the application; and the *storage layer* contains the database. A (logical) three-tier architecture can be physically deployed in two alternative configurations: (1) Client computer holding the presentation and application tiers, and server holding the storage tier, (2) Client computer holding the presentation tier, application server holding the application tier, and the data server holding the storage.

An advantage of the three-tier architecture over the traditionally used two-tier architecture is the greater amount of cohesion among the elements of a particular tier in the former. This makes it possible to (1) reuse the individual components of application logic, (2) physically place various tiers on various physical computing nodes thus increasing the performance of the system, and (3) assign the development work of the components to individual team members in a very logical manner.

Application layer is often divided into two layers: (1) The Domain layer and (2) The Services layer. The *domain layer* contains the objects pertaining to the primary functions of the applications whereas the *services layer* contains objects that are responsible for functions such as database interactions, reporting, communications, security, and so on. The services layer can be further divided into two more layers, one giving the *high-level services* and the other giving the *low-level services*. The high-level services include such functions as report generation, database interfacing, security, and inter-process communications, whereas the low-level services include such functions as file input/output, windows manipulation. Whereas the high-level services are normally written by application developers, the low-level services are provided by standard language libraries or obtained from third-party vendors.

The elements within a layer are said to be horizontally separated or *partitioned*. Thus, for example, the domain layer for a library application can be partitioned into *Borrow*, *Return*, *Renew*, and so on.

One can use the concept of packaging for the three-tier architecture (Figure 14.26). The details of each package in each layer can be further shown as partitions. It is natural for an element within a partition of a layer to collaborate with other elements of the same partition. Thus, objects within the *Borrow* package collaborate with one another. It is also quite all right if objects within a partition of a layer collaborate with objects within another partition of the same layer. Thus, the objects within the *Renew* package collaborate with the objects of the *Borrow* and *Return* packages.

Often, however, there is a necessity to collaborate with objects of the adjacent layers. For example, when the *BookCode* button is pressed in the *Borrow* mode, the book must be shown as issued to the user. Here the presentation layer must collaborate with the domain layer. Or, when a book is issued to a user, the details of books issued to the user are to be displayed on the monitor, requiring a domain layer object to collaborate with the windows object.

Since a system event is generated in the presentation layer and since we often make use of windows objects in handling various operations involving the user interface, there is a possibility to assign windows objects the responsibility of handling system events. However, such a practice is not good. The system events should be handled by objects that are defined in the application (or domain) layer. Reusability increases, as also the ability to run the system off-line, when the system events are handled in the application layer.

The Model-View Separation Pattern

Inter-layer collaborations require visibility among objects contained in different layers. Allowing direct visibility among objects lying in different layers, unfortunately, make them less cohesive and less reusable. Further, independent development of the two sets of objects and responding to requirement changes become difficult. It is therefore desirable that the domain objects (The *Model*) and windows objects (The *View*) should not directly collaborate with each other. Whereas the presentation objects sending messages to the domain objects are sometimes acceptable, the domain objects sending messages to the presentation objects is considered a bad design.

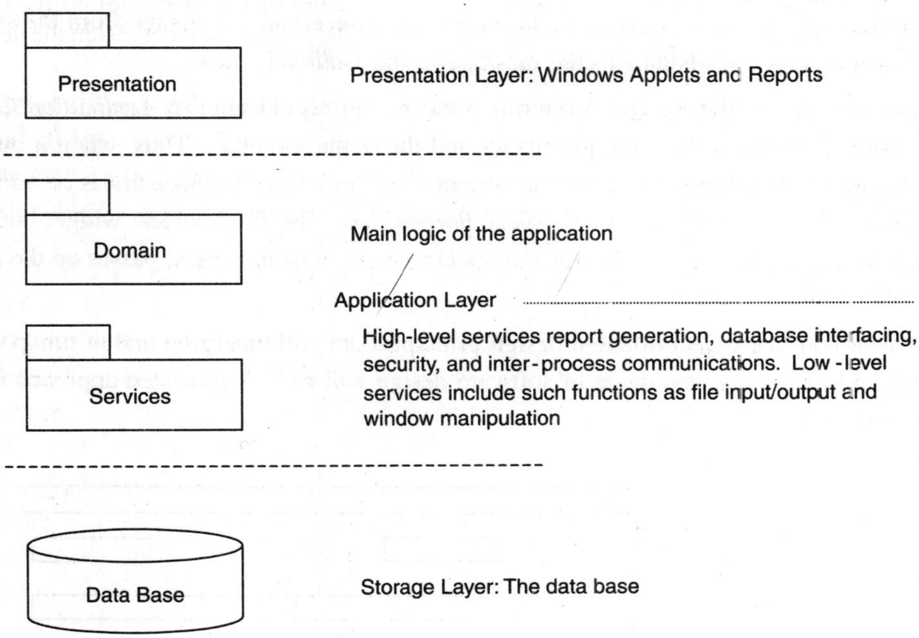

Fig. 14.26. The three-tier architecture

Normally, widgets follow a *pull-from above* practice to send messages to domain objects, retrieve information, and display them. This practice, however, is inadequate to continuously display information on the status of a dynamically changing system. It requires a *push-from-below* practice. However, keeping in view the restriction imposed by the *Model-View Separation* pattern, the domain layer should only indirectly communicate with the presentation layer. Indirect communication is made possible by following the *Publish-Subscribe* pattern.

The Publish-Subscribe Pattern

Also called the *Observer*, this pattern proposes the use of an intermediate *EventManager* class that enables event notification by a publisher class in the domain layer to the interested subscriber classes that reside in the presentation layer. The pattern requires the following steps:

1. The subscriber class passes a subscribe message to the *EventManager*. The message has the subscriber name, the method name, and the attributes of interest as the parameters.
2. Whenever an event takes place it is represented as a simple string or an instance of an event class.
3. The publisher class publishes the occurrence of the event by sending a *signalEvent* message to the *EventManager*.
4. Upon receiving the message, the *EventManager* identifies all the interested subscriber classes and notifies them by sending a message to each one of them.

As an alternative, often the subscriber name, the method name, and the attributes of interest (given in step 1 above) are encapsulated in a *Callback* class. In order to subscribe, a subscriber class sends an instance of this class to the *EventManager*. Upon receiving a message from the subscription class, the *EventManager* sends an execute message to the *Callback* class.

Implementation of the *Publish-Subscribe pattern* requires defining an *Application Coordinator* class that mediates between the windows object and the domain objects. Thus, when a button *Enter Button* is pressed by the Library Assistant, the system event *Borrow* takes place that is communicated as a *borrowABook* message to the windows object *BorrowView*. The *BorrowView* widget then forwards this message to the application coordinator *BorrowDocument*, which, in turn, passes on the message to *LLIS* controller (Figure 14.27).

We must add that object-oriented design principles are still emerging and at this point of time there is clear indication that this mode of software design will be a deep-rooted approach in software design for years to come.

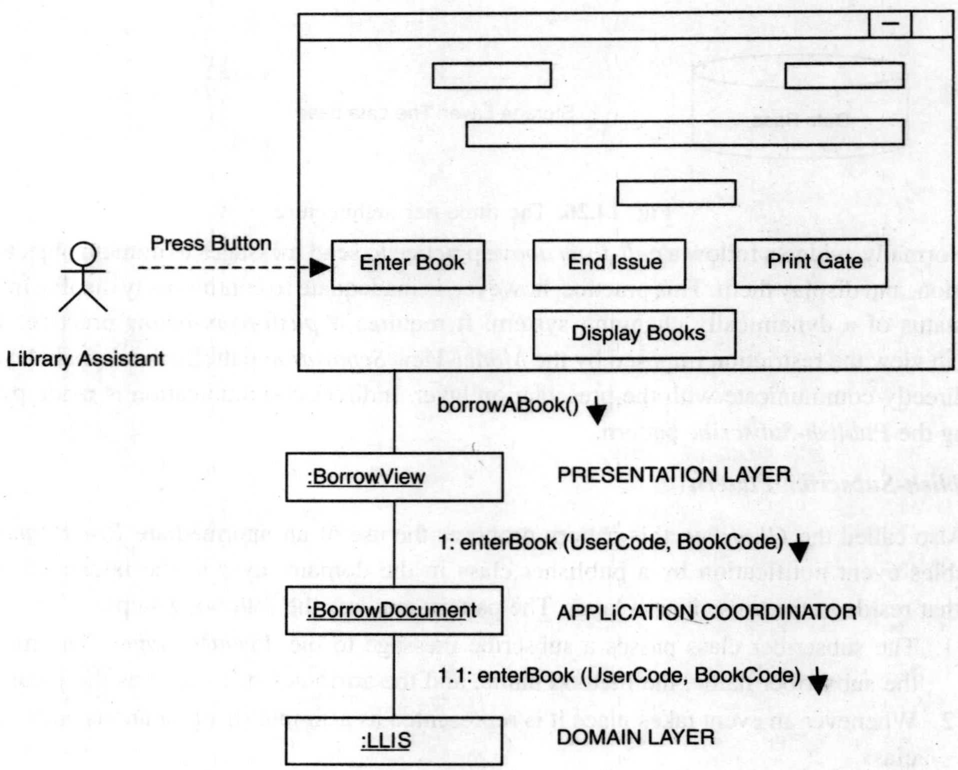

Fig. 14.27. Application in publish-subscribe pattern

REFERENCES

Gamma, E., R. Helm, R. Johnson and J. Vlissides (1995), Design Patterns, Addison-Wesley, Reading, MA.s

Larman, C. (2000), Applying UML and Patterns: An Introduction to Object-oriented Analysis and Design, Addison-Wesley, Pearson Education, Inc., Low Price Edition.

Page-Jones, M. (2000), Fundamentals of Object-oriented Design in UML, Addison-Wesley, Reading, Massachussetts.

15 Design Patterns

Reusability is one of the primary advantages of object-oriented approaches to software development. It is made easier when design patterns—recurring patterns of classes and communicating objects that solve specific design problems—are recognized, standardized, documented, and catalogued. Design patterns make the tasks of designing new systems easy, improve documentation of maintenance of existing systems, and help less experienced designers in their design task.

The credit of coining the term "design pattern" goes to the famous building architect Christopher Alexander (Alexander *et al.* 1977, Alexander 1979). Describing a pattern language for architecture for towns, buildings, rooms, gardens, and so on, he said, "A pattern describes a problem which occurs over and over again in our environment, and then describes the core of the solution to that problem, in such a way that you can use this solution a million times over, without ever doing it the same way twice." Following Alexander, Gamma *et al.* (1995) define a pattern to be "the solution to a recurring problem in a particular context, applicable not only to architecture but to software design as well."

Following the idea that patterns repeat themselves, Riehle and Zullighoven (1996) state that three types of patterns are discernible:

- Conceptual patterns
- Design patterns
- Programming patterns

Conceptual patterns describe the concepts, terms, beliefs, and values of the application domain using the domain-level language, easily understandable by the users. They help to understand the domain and the tasks, and provide a platform to debate and negotiate, thus providing a kind of "world view". Metaphors are used here as understandable "mental pictures" to support taking a step from the current situation to the design of the future system."

Design pattern is one whose form is described by means of software design constructs, for example, objects, classes, inheritance, aggregation, and user relationships. Applicable to the whole scale of software design, ranging from software architecture issues to micro-architectures, this definition shows a close connection between design patterns and frameworks. A framework incorporates and instantiates design patterns in order to "enforce" the reuse of design in a constructive way. Design patterns should fit or complement the conceptual model.

Programming patterns are technical artifacts needed in the software construction phase. Its form is described by the programming language constructs, such as sequence, selection, and iteration.

We discuss only the design patterns in this chapter. According to Riehle and Zullighoven (1996), design patterns can be described in three forms:

- The Alexandrian form (Alexander 1979)
- The Catalog form (Gamma *et al*. 1995)
- The General form (Riehle and Zullighoven, 1996).

The Alexandrian form of presentation consists generally of three sections, *Problem*, *Context*, and *Solution*, and is used mainly to guide users to generate solutions for the described problems. The Catalog form uses *templates* tailored to describe specific design patterns and *instantiate* solutions to specific design problems. The General form consists of two sections, *Context* and *Pattern*, and is used to either generate solutions or instantiate specifics.

We discuss the catalog form because it is well suited for object-oriented design, the order of the day. Gamma *et al.* (1995), the originators of this form of presentation and fondly called the Gang of Four, proposed 23 design patterns. In this chapter, we follow Braude's approach (Braude, 2004) to discuss 18 of these design patterns.

Design patterns introduce reusability of a very high order and therefore make the task of object-oriented design much simpler. We devote the present chapter to an elaborate discussion on design patterns because of their importance in object-oriented design. We first review the traditional approaches to reusability and then introduce the basic principles of design patterns before presenting the important standard design patterns.

15.1 TRADITIONAL APPROACHES TO REUSABILITY

Recall that an object operation's signature specifies its name, the parameters it passes, and the return value. The set of all signatures defined by an object's operations is called the interface to the object, which indicates the set of requests that can be directed to the object. Gamma *et al.* (1995) summarize the traditional approaches to reusability as under.

The traditional method of reusability resorts to class inheritance, where the functionality in the parent class is reused by the child classes. The degree of usability increases many times when polymorphism is allowed. Polymorphism becomes quite effective when subclasses inherit from an abstract class and can add or override operations that they inherit from their abstract class. In this way all subclasses can respond to requests made to the interface of the abstract class. This has the advantages that clients interface only with the abstract class and do not have to know the specific objects that execute their requests, not even with the classes that implement these objects. This leads to the overriding principle:

"Program to an interface, not an implementation."

It means that the client should interface with the abstract class and should not declare variables to be instances of concrete classes.

Reusing functionality by inheritance is often called *white-box reuse* in contrast to reusing by composition which is called *black-box reuse*. *Composition* here refers to an interacting set of objects that together deliver a specific functionality (generally of complex nature). The internals of the objects are not visible whereas the object interfaces are. Furthermore, inheritance is defined during compilation time and any change in the implementation of the super-class affects the implementation of the subclass — a case of breaking of encapsulation. However, inheritance from abstract classes overcomes the problem of interdependency. Object composition, on the other hand, is defined at runtime. Here objects are generally implementation independent, class encapsulation is not disturbed, and the objects are interface connected. This leads to the second principle of reuse:

"Favour object composition over class inheritance."

Two common forms of composition used in classical object-oriented practices are:

1. Delegation
2. Parameterized interfaces.

In delegation, a request from a client is passed on to other objects using the association principle. In parameterized interface techniques, on the other hand, parameters are supplied to the point of use. Thus, for example, a type "integer" is supplied as a parameter to the list class to indicate the type of elements it contains. Templates in C++ provide an example of the use of the parameterized interface technique.

15.2 PRINCIPLES OF DESIGN PATTERNS

The main principles underlying the operation of design patterns are two:

1. Delegation (or Indirection, a term used in machine language)
2. Recursion

Delegation is at work when a design pattern replaces direct operation calls by delegated calls to separate operations of an abstract class which, in turn, calls the desired operation of other concrete classes during runtime. In Fig. 15.1, the *client* calls the operation *getPriceOfCar()* of the interface class *Car.* This operation delegates its responsibility to the operation *price()* of an abstract base class (*CarType*) whose subordinate classes are *Maruti800* and *Alto*. At runtime, only object of either *Maruti800* or the *Alto* class will be instantiated and the corresponding price will be obtained. Notice the advantages of delegation: (1) Behaviours are composed at runtime; and (2) The way they are composed can be changed at will (*e.g.*, we could get price of Maruti800 or Alto).

Recursion is at work when part of the design pattern uses itself. In Fig. 15.2, the *Client* calls the method *print()* of the abstract class *Player*. The *print()* method of *Team* prints the team name and then calls the *print()* method in each of the *Player* objects in the aggregate. The *print()* method of *IndividualPlayer* prints the name of each player in that team. This process is repeated for each team.

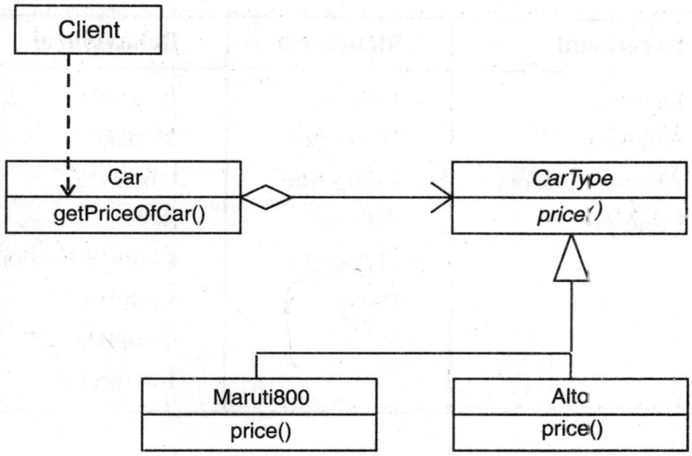

Fig. 15.1. Delegation principle applied to design patterns

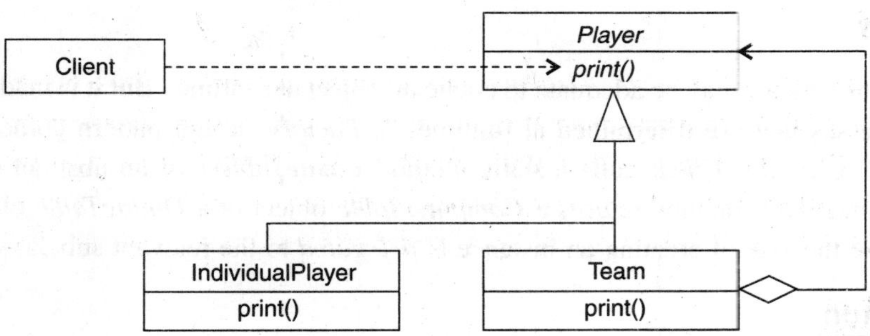

Fig. 15.2. Recursion principle applied to design patterns

15.3 CATEGORIES AND BASIC PRINCIPLES OF DESIGN PATTERNS

As stated earlier, Gamma, *et al.* (1995) gave a catalog of 23 design patterns which they grouped into three categories. We select 18 of them and present them (the categories and their constituent design patterns) in Table 15.1.

Creational design patterns abstract the instantiation process and help creating several collections of objects from a single block of code. Whereas many versions of the collection are created at runtime, often only a single instance of an object is created. *Structural design patterns* help to arrange collection of objects in forms such as linked list or trees. *Behavioural design patterns* help to capture specific kinds of behaviour among a collection of objects.

Table 15.1: Categories of Design Patterns

Creational	Structural	Behavioural
Factory	Façade	Iterator
Singleton	Decorator	Mediator
Abstract Factory	Composite	Observer
Prototype	Adapter	State
	Flyweight	Chain of Responsibility
	Proxy	Command
		Template
		Interpreter

15.4 CREATIONAL DESIGN PATTERNS

15.4.1 Factory

Using a constructor may be adequate to create an object at runtime. But it is inadequate to create objects of subclasses that are determined at runtime. A *Factory* design pattern comes handy in that situation. In Fig. 15.3, the *Client* calls a static method *createTable()* of an abstract class *Table*. At runtime, the *createTable()* method returns a *ComputerTable* object or a *DiningTable* object as the case may be. Note that the task of creating an instance is *delegated* to the relevant subclass at runtime.

15.4.2 Singleton

The purpose of a *singleton* design pattern is to ensure that there is exactly one instance of a class and to obtain it from anywhere in the application. For example, during a web application, it is required for a profiler to have only one instance of a user at runtime. Figure 15.4 shows the design pattern. The *User* class defines its constructor as private to itself so that its object can be created by only its own methods. Further, it defines its single instance as a static attribute so that it can be instantiated only once. The *User* class defines a *public* static accessor *getSingleUser* method which the *Client* accesses.

Singleton is a special class of Factory. Thus, the principle of delegation works here as well.

15.4.3 Abstract Factory

The purpose of an *abstract factory* is to provide an interface to create families of related or dependent objects at runtime without specifying their concrete objects, with the help of one piece of code. This is done by creating an *abstract factory* class containing a factory operation for each class in the family.

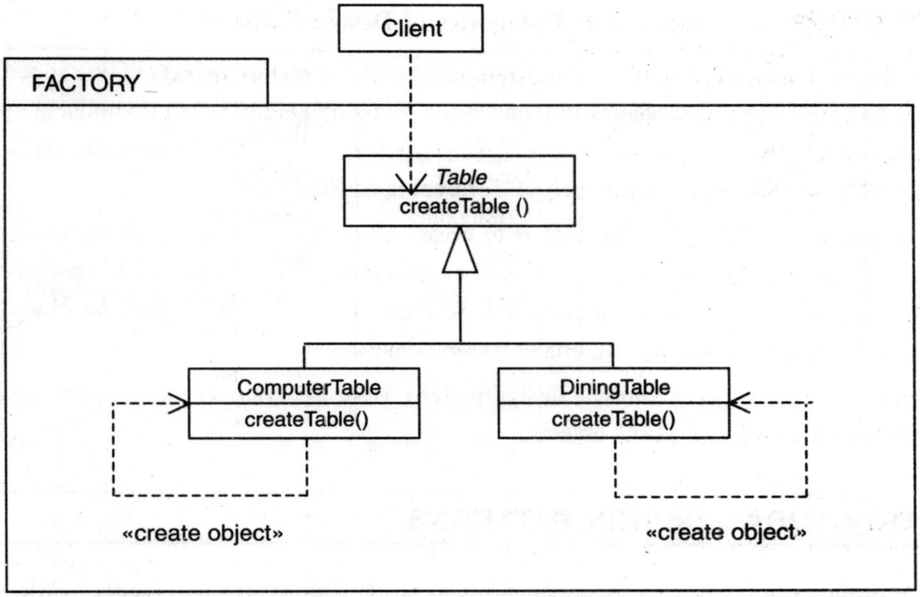

Fig. 15.3. Delegation principle applied to Factory

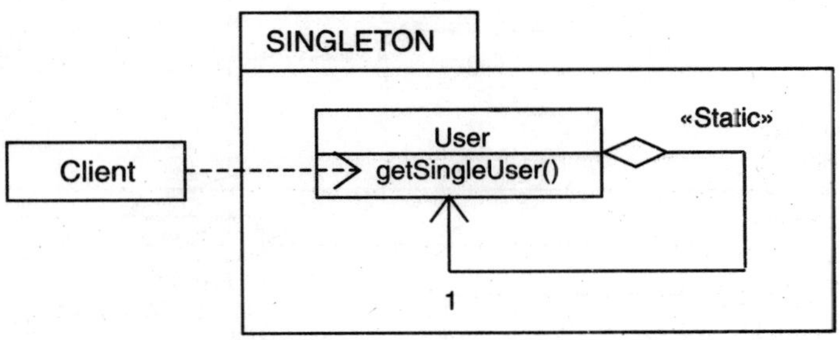

Fig. 15.4. The Singleton design pattern

The *Client* specifies the member of the family about which information is required. Suppose it is the *print( )* operation of the *Group* class. *AbstractFactory* class is the base class for the family of member classes. It has all the factory operations. Acting on the *delegation* form, it produces the objects of a single member class.

Figure 15.5 shows a class diagram of how the *AbstractFactory* pattern functions. *Group* consists of *Part1* and *Part2* objects. As the *client* makes a call to *Group* to print the *Part1Type1* objects, it sets the *AbstractFactory* class through its attribute and calls its *getPart1Object* — a virtual operation. In reality, it calls the *getPart1Object* operation of *Type1Factory* which returns the *Part1Type1* objects. Similarly, the client can print the *Type2* parts.

15.4.4 Prototype

As we have seen, the *Abstract Factory* pattern helps to produce objects in one specified type. A client often has the need to get objects in many types by being able to select component specifications of each type and mix them. For example, a computer-type requires such of its components as a computer, a printer, a UPS, a table, and a chair, each of different specifications.

The purpose of a *Prototype* pattern is to create a set of almost identical objects whose type is determined at runtime. The purpose is achieved by assuming that a prototype instance is known and cloning it whenever a new instance is needed. It is in the *delegation* form, with the *clone( )* operation delegating its task of constructing the object to the constructor.

Figure 15.6 shows the *Prototype* design pattern. Here the *createGroup()* operation constructs a Group object from *Part1* and *Part2* objects.

15.5 STRUCTURAL DESIGN PATTERNS

It is often required in various applications to work with aggregate objects. *Structural design patterns* help to build aggregate objects from elementary objects (the *static* viewpoint) and to do operations with the aggregate objects (the *dynamic* viewpoint).

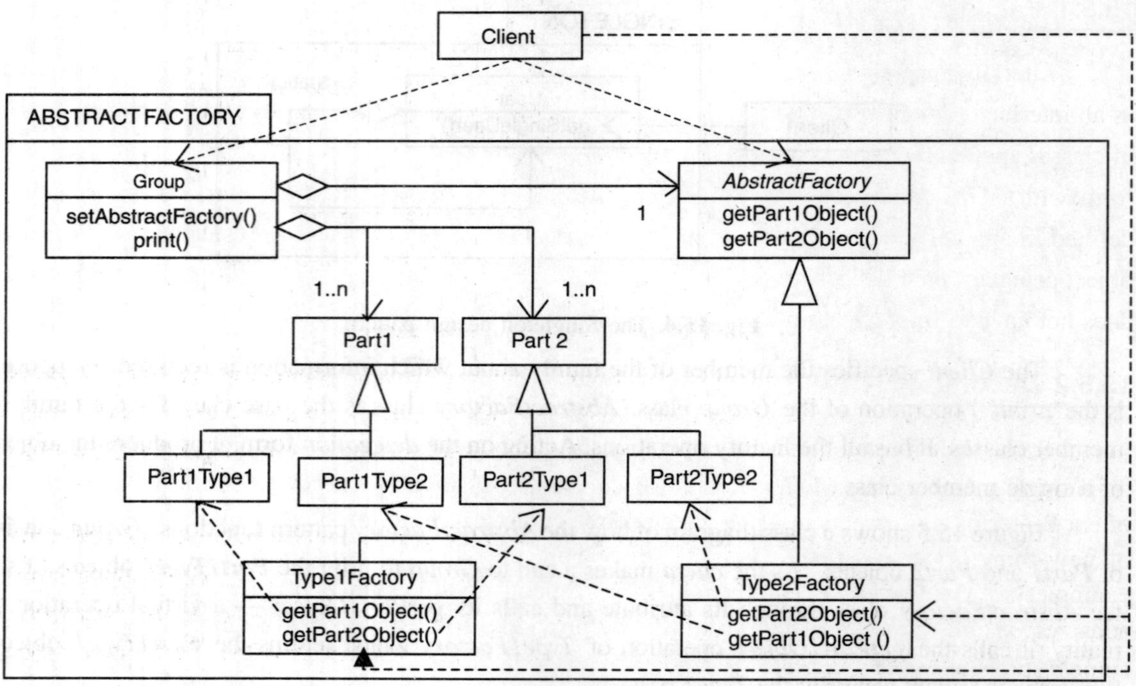

Fig. 15.5. Abstract factory

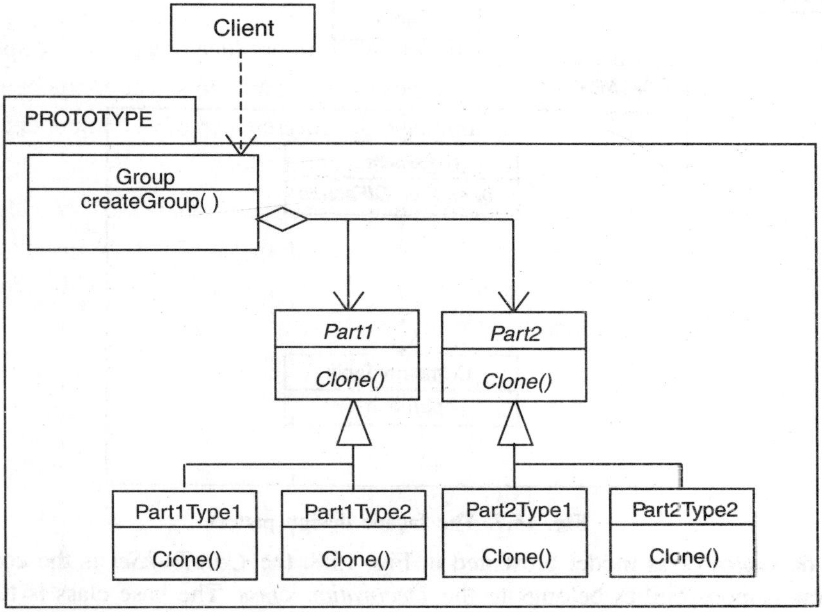

Fig. 15.6. Prototype

15.5.1 Façade

Literally meaning face or front view of a building (also meaning false or artificial), a *Façade* acts as an interface for a client who requires the service of an operation of a package (containing a number of classes and number of operations). For example, assume that an application is developed in modular form, with each module developed by a different team. A module may require the service of an operation defined in another module. This is achieved by defining the *Façade* class as a singleton. The *façade* object delegates the *client* request to the relevant classes internal to the package (Fig. 15.7). The client does not have to refer to the internal classes.

15.5.2 Decorator

Sometimes it is required to use an operation only at runtime. An example is the operation of diagnosing a new disease when the pathological data are analyzed. A second example is the operation of encountering new papers in a pre-selected area while searching for them in a website. The addition of new things is called '*decorating*' a set of core objects. The core objects in the above-stated examples are the disease set and the paper set, respectively. In essence, the *decorator* design pattern adds *responsibility* to an object at runtime, by providing for a linked list of objects, each capturing some responsibility.

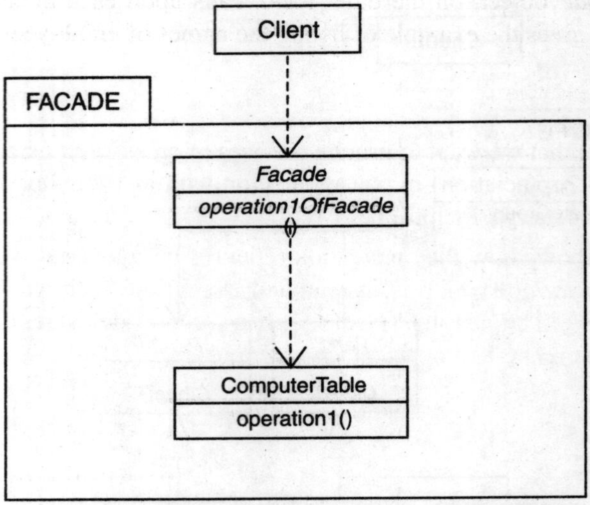

Fig. 15.7. The façade design pattern

In the decorator class model presented in Fig. 15.8, the *CoreTaskSet* is the core class and the addition of new responsibilities belongs to the *Decoration* class. The base class is the *TaskSet* class which acts as an interface (a collection of method prototypes) with the client. Any *TaskSet* object which is not a *CoreTaskSet* instance aggregates another *TaskSet* object in a *recursive* manner.

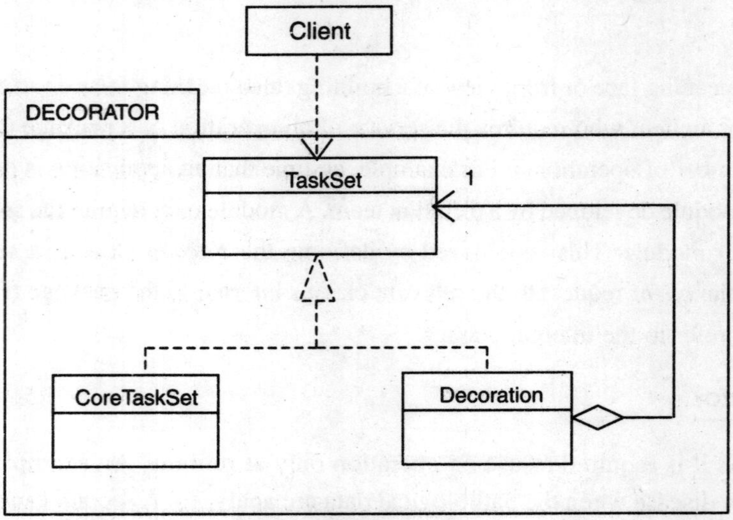

Fig. 15.8. Decorator

15.5.3 Composite

The purpose of this pattern is to represent a *tree* of objects, such as an organization chart (i.e., a hierarchy of employees in an organization) where non-leaf nodes will have other nodes in their next level. The pattern uses both a *gen-spec* structure and an *aggregation* structure. It is also *recursive* in nature. Figure 15.9 shows the general structure of this pattern. Here the *Client* calls upon the *Component* object for a service. The service rendered by the *Component* is straightforward if it is a *LeafNode* object. A *NonLeafNode* object, on the other hand, calls upon each of its descendants to provide the service. Figure 15.10 gives the example of listing the names of employees in an organization.

15.5.4 Adapter

It is quite often that we want to use the services of an existing external object (such as an object that computes annual depreciation) in our application with as little modification to our application as possible. An *adapter* pattern is helpful here.

Figure 15.11 shows how the application (client) first interfaces with the abstract method of an abstract class (*Depreciation*) which is instantiated at runtime with an object of a concrete subclass (*DepreciationAdapter*). The adapter (*DepreciationAdapter*) delegates the services required by the application to the existing system object (*DepreciationValue*).

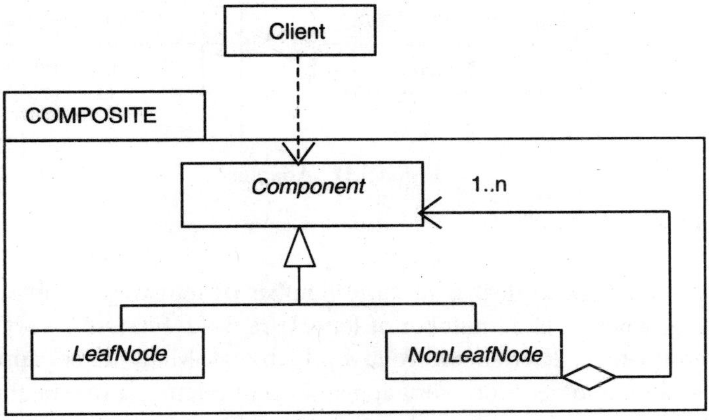

Fig. 15.9. Composite

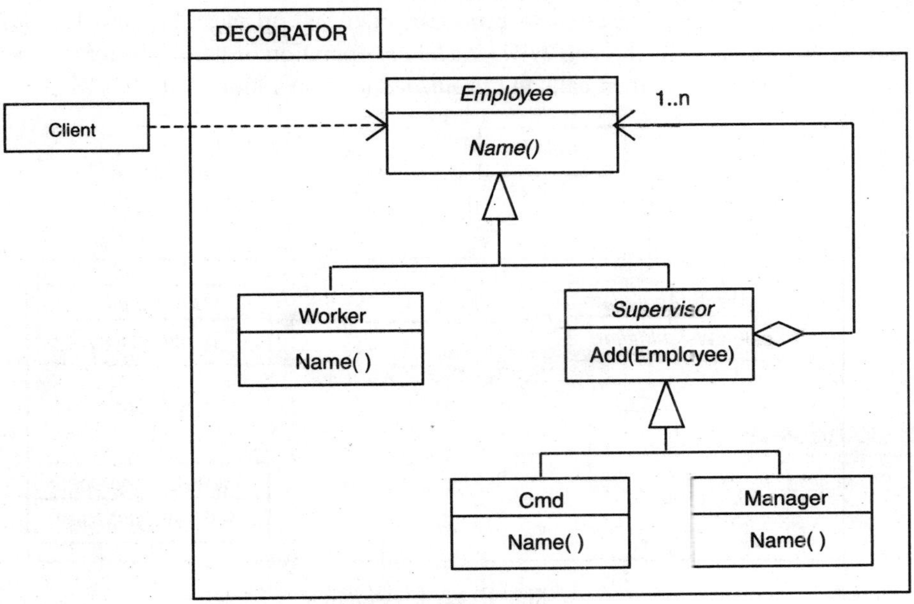

Fig. 15.10. Organization chart

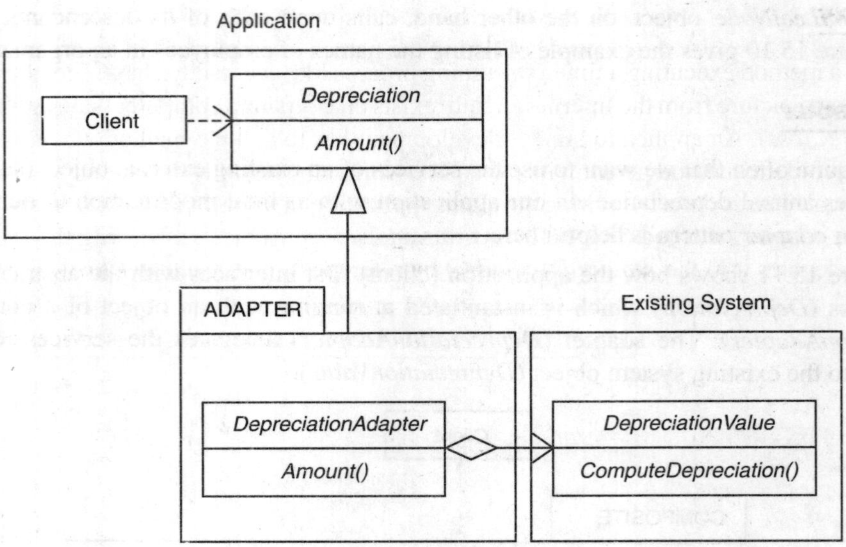

Fig. 15.11. Adapter

15.5.5 Flyweight

Applications often need to deal with large number of indistinguishable objects. A case arises during text processing, where a large number of letters are used. First, it is very space-inefficient and, second, we must know which letter should follow which one. Many letters appear a large number of times. Instead of defining an object for every appearance of a letter, a flywheel pattern considers each unique letter as an object and arranges them in a linked list. That means that the objects are shared to be distinguished by their positions. These shared objects are called "flyweights".

In Fig. 15.12, a *Client* interested to print the letter "a" on page 10, line 10, and position 20 (defined here as "*location*" calls the *getFlyWeight(letter)* operation of the *FlyWeightAggregate* class by setting *Letter* to "a". The Client then calls the *print(location)* operation of the *FlyWeight*.

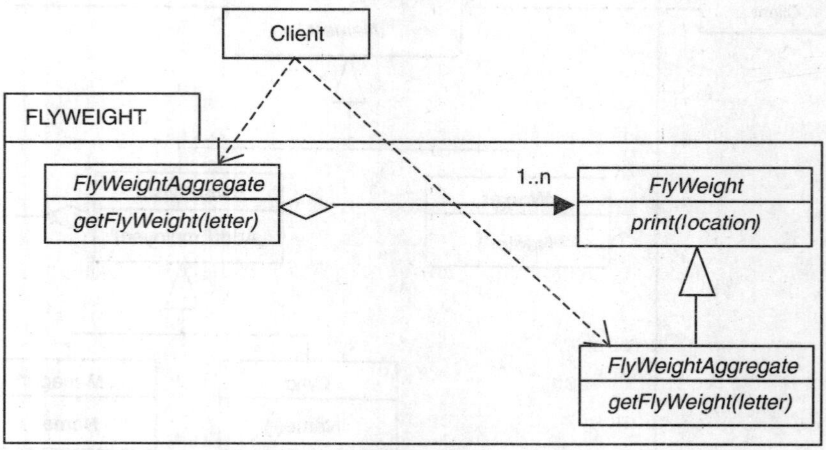

Fig. 15.12. Flyweight

15.5.6 Proxy

Often a method executing a time-consuming process like accessing a large file, drawing graphics, or downloading a picture from the Internet already exists on a separate computer (say, as *requiredMethod ( )* in *SeparateClass*). An application under development has to call the method whenever its service is required. To avoid the method perform its expensive work unnecessarily, a way out is to call the method as if it were local. This is done by writing the client application in terms of an abstract class *SeparateClass* containing the required method (Fig. 5.13). At runtime, a *Proxy* object, inheriting the method from the *BaseClass*, delegates it to the *requiredMethod ( )* by referencing the *SeparateClass*.

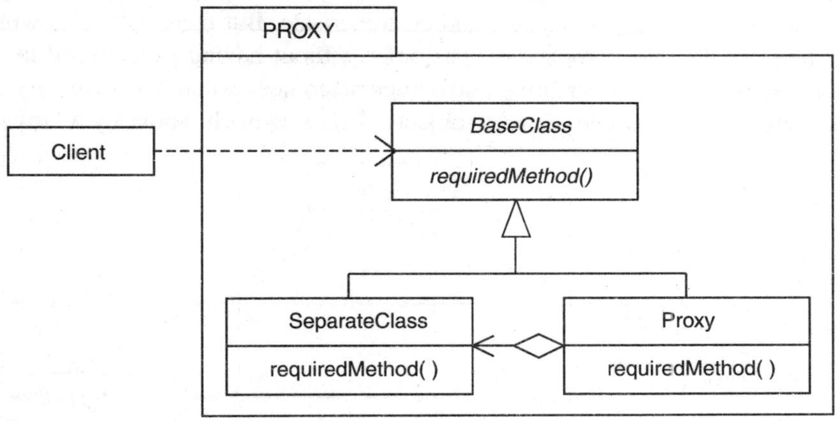

Fig. 15.13. Proxy

15.6 BEHAVIOURAL DESIGN PATTERNS

Behavioural design patterns encapsulate behaviour of multiple objects, thus enabling their use at runtime, coding them efficiently, or using them in other applications.

15.6.1 Iterator

Applications often require doing a service for each member of an aggregate, such as mailing a letter to each employee. The design for this service is similar to that of a *for* loop, with its control structure defining the way in which each member has to be visited and its body defining the operations to be performed on each member.

The ways a member of an aggregate is visited can be many: alphabetically, on a seniority basis, on the basis of years of services, and so on. Accordingly, various *iterators* can be specified. The purpose of *iteration* is to access each element of an *aggregate* sequentially without exposing its underlying representation.

As we know, iteration requires

(*i*) specifying the first element,

(*ii*) getting the first element of the aggregate,

(*iii*) incrementing or finding the next element, and

(*iv*) exiting the loop upon reaching a termination condition.

The *Iterator* design pattern defines an *Iterator* interface that encapsulates all these functions. The *Aggregate* can have a *getItertator( )* method that returns the *ConcreteIterator* object for the purpose wanted (*e.g.*, on seniority basis for years of service). The *Client* references the *ConcreteIterator* for its services which, in turn, gives the details required on each *Element* of the *ConcreteAggregate*. The *Iterator* class model is shown in Fig. 15.14.

15.6.2 Mediator

To improve reusability, coupling among classes should be as low as possible, *i.e.*, their reference to other classes should be as low as possible. For example, we often come across pairs of related classes such as worker/employer, item/sale, and customer/sale. But there may be a worker without an employer, an item not for sale, a (potential) customer without having participated in a sale. Directly relating them is not good. *Mediators* bring about such references whenever necessary and obviate the need for direct referencing between concrete objects. This is brought about by a "third-party" class.

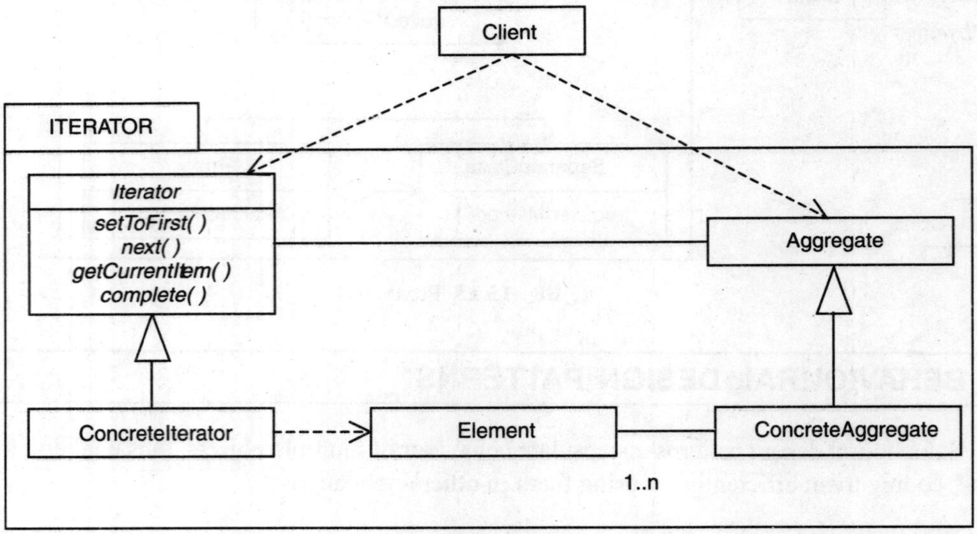

Fig. 15.14. Iterator

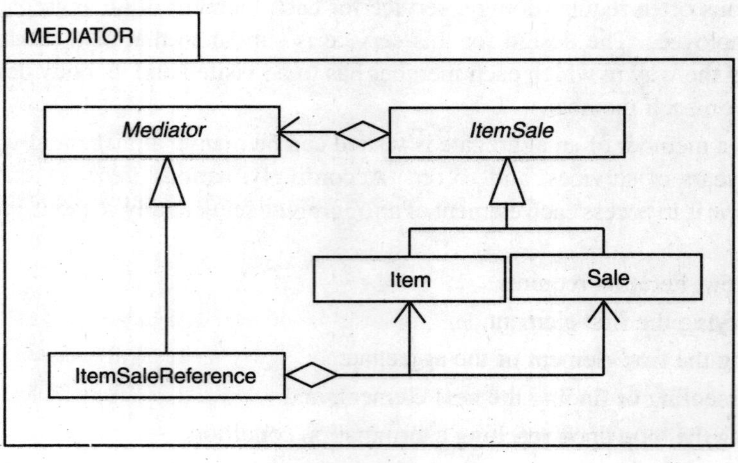

Fig. 15.15. Mediator

In Fig. 15.15, reference (interaction) between *Item* and *Sale* objects is brought about by *ItemSaleReference* (created at runtime). *ItemSale* references *Mediator*, ensuring that interacting objects need not know each other.

15.6.3 Observer

When data change, clients' functions using the data also change. For example, as production takes place, the figures for daily production, inventory, production cost, and machine utilization, etc., have to be updated. This is achieved by a single observer object aggregating the set of affected client objects, calling a method with a fixed name on each member.

In Fig. 15.16, the *Client* asks a known *Interface* object to notify the observers who are subclasses of a single abstract class named *Observer*, with the help of *notify( )* function. The *notify( )* method calls the *update( )* function on each *ConcreteObserver* object that it aggregates through its parent abstract class *Observer*.

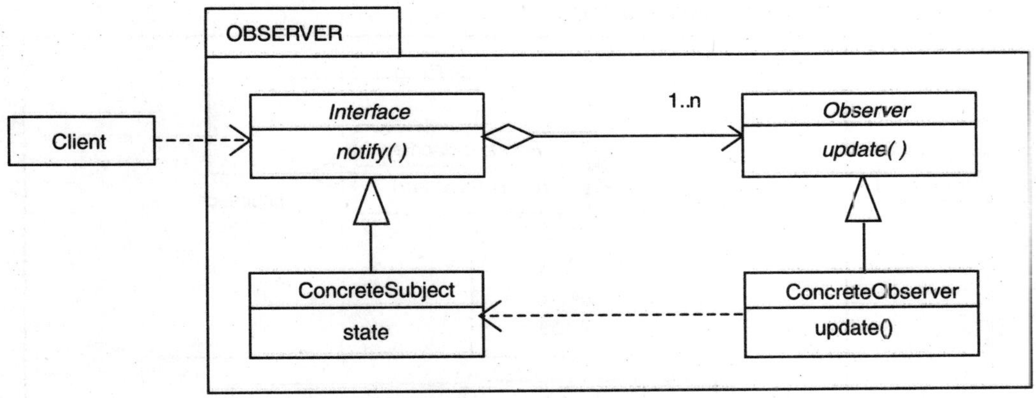

Fig. 15.16. Observer

15.6.4 State

An object behaves according to the state it occupies. Thus, for example, all event-driven systems respond to externally occurring events that change their states. To make this happen, a state design pattern aggregates a *state* object and d*elegates* behavour to it.

In Fig. 15.17, the *act( )* function will be executed according to the state of the object *Target*. *State* is an attribute of the class *Target*. The client does not need to know the state of *Target* object.

15.6.5 Chain of Responsibility

Often, a collection of objects, rather than a single object, discharge the functionality required by a client, without the client knowing which objects are actually discharging it. An example can be cited when a customer sends his product complaint to a single entry point in the company. Many persons, one after another, do their part, to handle the complaint.

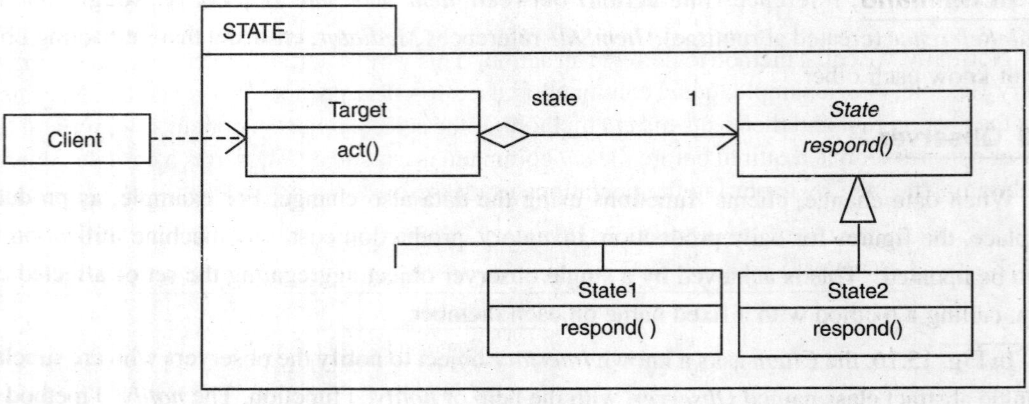

Fig. 15.17. State

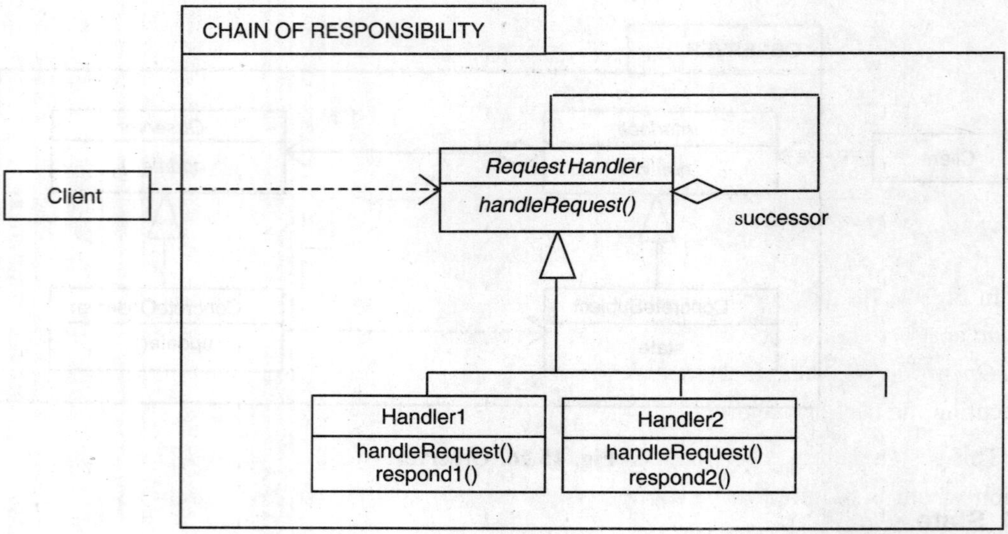

Fig. 15.18. Chain of Responsibility

In Fig. 15.18, the *Client* requests functionality from a single *RequestHandler* object. The object performs that part of the function for which it is responsible. Thereafter it passes the request on to the successor object of the collection.

Design patterns for *Decorator* and *Chain of Responsibility* are similar in many ways. But there are differences, however. The former statically strings multiple objects; the latter dynamically shows functionality among them. Also, aggregation in the former is a normal whole-part aggregation, whereas it is a self aggregation in the latter.

15.6.6 Command

Normally, we call a method to perform an action. This way of getting an action done is sometimes not very flexible. For example, a *cut* command is used to cut a portion of a text file. For this, one selects the portion first and then calls the *cut* method. If the selected portion contains figures and tables, then user confirmation is required before the *cut* command is executed. Thus, it is a complex operation. It can be implemented by capturing the operations as classes.

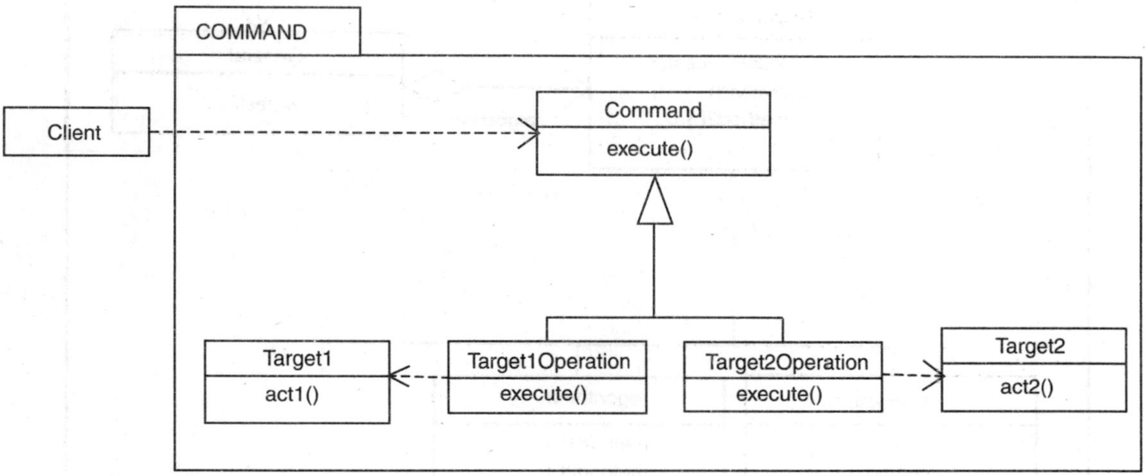

Fig. 15.19. Command

In Fig. 15.19, the *Client*, interested to execute *act1( )* operation of *Target1*, interfaces with the *command* abstract class — a base class that has an *execute( )* method. At runtime, the control passes to *Target1Operation* class that makes the necessary checks before delegating the control to *Target1* class for executing the *act1( )* operation.

This design pattern is very helpful in carrying out *undo* operations where a precondition is that an operation which is required to be reversed with the help of the *undo* operation has to be executed previously.

15.6.7 Template

The *Template* pattern is used to take care of problems associated with multiple variations of an algorithm. Here a base class is used for the algorithm. It uses subordinate classes to take care of the variations in this algorithm.

In Fig. 15.20, the *client* interfaces with a class *General* calling its *request( )* method. It passes control to *workOnRequest( )* method of *TemplateAlgorithm* abstract class. At runtime, the *TemplateAlgorithm* passes on the control to the appropriate algorithm *Algorithm1* and *Algorithm2*, etc., to execute the appropriate variation in the algorithm required, using their needed methods *method1* or *method2*, etc.

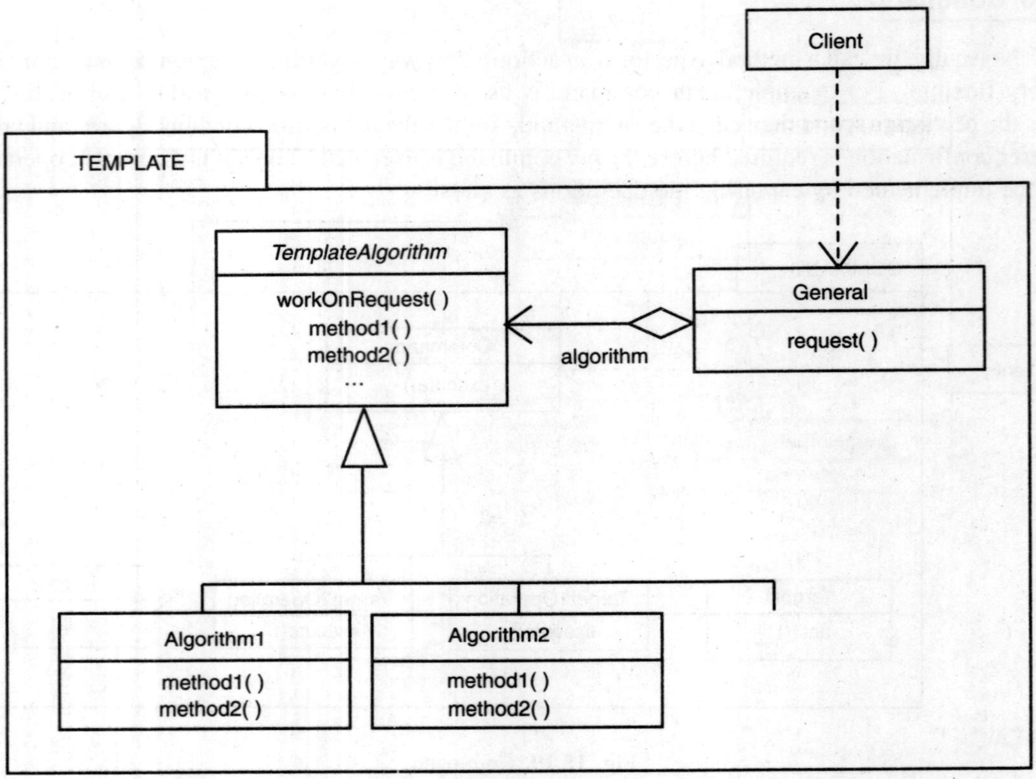

Fig. 15.20. Template

15.6.8 Interpreter

As the name indicates, an *interpreter* design pattern performs useful functionality on *expressions* (written in *a grammar) that are already parsed into a tree of objects. Based on the principle of* recursion in view of the presence of subexpressions in an expression, this pattern passes the function of interpretation to the aggregated object.

In Fig. 15.21, the Client calls the *interpret( )* operation of the abstract class *Expression*. This class can be either a *TerminalSubexpression* or a *NonTerminalSubexpression*. In case of the latter, the aggregate *Expression* class executes its own operation *interpret( )* to recursively carry out the function.

In this chapter, we present only a few selected design patterns from the ones proposed by Gamma *et al*. Design patterns have proliferated over the years and we hope to see a large number of them in the future.

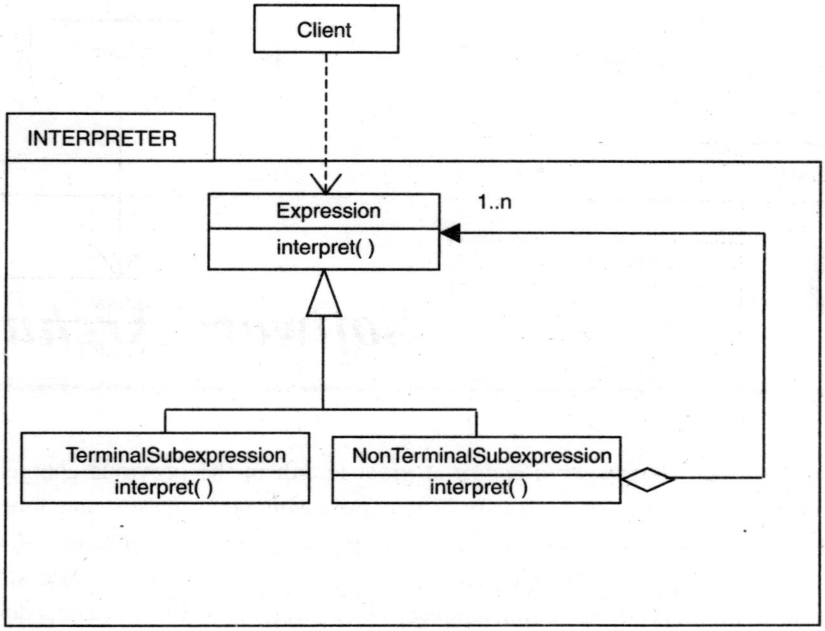

Fig. 15.21 Interpreter

REFERENCES

Alexander, C. (1999), The Timeliness Way of Building, NY: Oxford University Press.

Alexander, C., S. Ishikawa, and M. Silverstein (1977), A Pattern Language, NY: Oxford University Press.

Braude, E. J. (2004), Software Design: From Programming to Architecture, John Wiley & Sons (Asia) Pte. Ltd., Singapore.

Gamma, E., R. Helm, R. Johnson, and J. Vlissides (1995), Design Patterns: Elements of Reusable Object-oriented Software, MA: Addison-Wesley Publishing Company, International Student Edition.

Riehle, D. and H. Zullighoren (1996), Understanding and Using Patterns in Software Development, in Software Engineering, Volume 1: The Development Process, R. H. Thayer and M. Dorfman (eds.), IEEE Computer Society, Wiley Interscience, Second Edition, pp. 225 – 238.

16 Software Architecture

We have discussed *design architecture* at great length in the previous chapters. It basically characterizes the internal structure of a software system, prescribing how the software functions specified in SRS are to be implemented. *Software architecture* differs from design architecture in that the former focuses on the overall approach the designer takes to go about designing the software. It is compared to adopting an approach or a style of designing a house. The overall approach could be a design suitable to a rural setting, or a temple architecture, or a modern style. Within the overall approach selected, the architect can decide on the design architecture that is concerned with where to have the rooms for meeting the required functions. Once this design architecture is fixed, the *detailed design* of dimensions and strengths of pillars, etc., is done. Software architecture is concerned with deciding the overall approach to (*style* of) software design.

16.1 CONCEPTS UNDERLYING SOFTWARE ARCHITECTURE

Oxford English Dictionary defines *architecture* as "the art of science of building, especially the art or practice of designing edifices for human use taking both aesthetic and practical factors into account." It also means "a style of building, a mode, manner, or style of construction or organization, and structure."

The concept of architecture in the field of computer science is quite old, dating back to the origin of computers. The von Neumann computer hardware architecture (Fig.16.1), with the basic theme of stored program and sequential execution of instructions, has dominated the design of computer hardware design until recently.

The von Neumann architecture allows only sequential execution of instructions – a shortcoming, which has been overcome in recent years with evolution of architectures of many forms:

1. *Single-Instruction Multiple Dataflow (SIMD) architecture with shared memory* which works with parallel computers that are interconnected in a network and share a common memory.
2. *SIMD architecture without shared memory* which basically is a set of processing units each with local memory that are connected with interconnection network.

3. *Multiple-Instruction Multiple Dataflow (MIMD) architecture with shared memory* which are a set of processing units each with local memory that are not only interconnected in a network but that access shared memory across the network.
4. *MIMD architecture without shared memory.*

Without delving into the details of these architectures we know how the hardware components are interconnected once the architecture is specified. Software architecture has a similar meaning. It indicates the basic design philosophy made early in the design phase and provides an intellectually comprehensible model of how the software components are connected to effect the software development process.

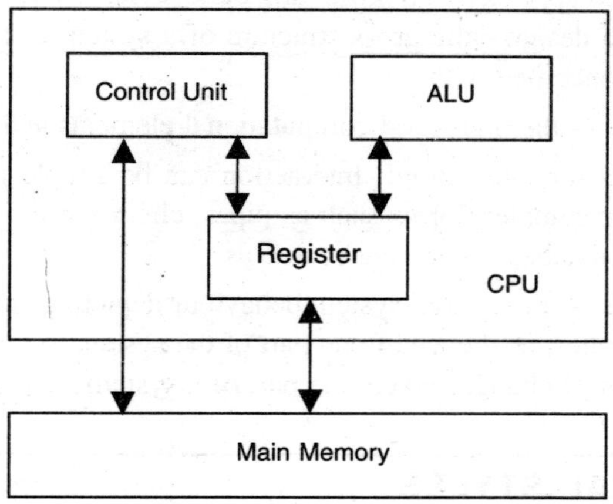

Fig. 16.1. von Neumann architecture

In November 1995, the *IEEE Software* journal celebrated software architecture as an identifiable discipline and the first international software architecture workshop was held. But, even today, there is no accepted definition of the term *software architecture.* According to Kruchtren *et al.* (2006), software architecture involves the following two concepts.

- The structure and organization by which system components and subsystems interact to form systems.
- The properties of systems that can be best designed and analyzed at the system level.

Perry and Wolf (1992) have suggested the following:

{elements, forms, rationale} = software architecture

Three *elements* comprise the structure of software architecture:

1. *Data elements.* They consist of information needed for processing by a processing element.
2. *Processing elements — the components.* They transform inputs into outputs.
3. *Connecting elements — the connectors.* They connect different pieces of architecture.

Forms are the repeating patterns and consist of (i) *relationships* among the elements, (ii) *properties* that constrain the choice of the architectural elements, and (iii) *weights* that represent the importance of the relationship or property to express the preference among a number of choices among alternative.

Rationale is the reasoning behind the architecture.

An early attempt towards cataloging and explaining various common patterns was made by Bushmann *et al.* (1996). According to Shaw and Garlan (1996), software architecture involves the description of elements from which systems are built, the interactions among those elements, patterns that guide their composition, and the constraints on these patterns. Bass *et al.* (1998) look upon software architecture as the structure or structures of the system, which comprise software components, the externally visible properties of those components, and the relationships among them. Tracing its historicity, Shaw and Clements (2006) have given a record of various achievements at different times that have paved the way for software architecture to its present state.

Monroe *et al.* (2003) have elaborated the functions of software architecture, architectural style, and the role of object-oriented approach to representing these styles. Architectural designs focus on the architectural level of system design—the gross structure of a system as a composition of interacting parts. They are primarily concerned with

1. System structure — the high-level computational elements and their interactions.
2. Rich abstractions for interaction. Interaction can be simple procedure calls, shared data variable, or other complex forms such as pipes, client-server interactions, event-broadcast connection, and database accessing protocols.
3. Global properties — the overall system behaviour depicting such system-level problems as end-to-end data rates, resilience of one part of the system to failure in another, and system-wide propagation of changes when one part of a system such as platform is modified.

16.2 ARCHITECTURAL STYLES

Architectural descriptions use idiomatic terms such as client-server systems, layered systems, and blackboard organizations. Such architectural idioms convey informal meaning and understanding of the architectural descriptions and represent specific *architectural styles*. *An architectural style* characterizes a family of systems that are related by shared structural and semantic properties. It provides a specialized design language for a specific class of systems. Style provides the following:

- Vocabulary of design elements, such as pipes, filters, servers, databases.
- Design rules or constraints that specify specific compositional rules or patterns for specific situations. For example, a client-server organization must be an *n-to-one* relationship.
- Semantic interpretation, with the design elements having well-defined meanings.
- Analysis such as schedulability analysis for real-time processing, deadlock detection for client-server message passing, etc.

Software architecture provides the ability to reuse design, reuse code, understand a system's organization easily, achieve interoperability by standardized styles (such as CORBA, OSI – Open Systems Interconnection Protocol), and make style-specific specialized analysis for throughput, freedom from deadlock, etc.

Design patterns and architectural styles are closely related:

- Architectural styles can be viewed as kinds of patterns — or perhaps more accurately as pattern languages providing architects with a vocabulary and framework with which they can build design patterns to solve specific problems.

- For a given style there may exist a set of idiomatic uses — architectural design patterns (or sub-styles) to work within a specific architectural style.

Recent advances in the design of software architecture have resulted in many families of architectural styles. We follow Peters and Pedrycz (2000) to highlight the characteristics of six such styles :

1. Data-Flow architecture
2. Call-and-Return architecture
3. Independent-Process architecture
4. Virtual-Machine architecture
5. Repository architecture
6. Domain-Specific architecture

16.3 DATA-FLOW ARCHITECTURE

Used principally in application domains where data processing plays a central role, *data flow architecture* consists of a series of transformations on streams of input data. It is suitable for systems such as those encountered in the following situations:

- Batch processing (jobs executed in sequence)
- Cryptographic systems (secret mapping of streams of characters in a text)
- Pipelining (processing at various stations like assembly lines in manufacturing)
- Process control (computing a response to error between the output and a reference input)

We shall discuss pipelining in some detail because this concept will be used in discussions on other architectural styles.

Pipelining

Modeled along the principle of assembly lines in manufacturing, *pipelining* is a process of bringing about a temporal parallelism in the processing of various operations at the same time by various processing elements (components) that are joined by connecting elements (connectors). The processing elements are generally called *filters* that transform streams of typed input data to produce streams of typed output data. The streams of data are carried by connecting elements that are also known as *pipes*. Pipes generally allow unidirectional flow and describe (1) binary relationship between two filters and (2) a data transfer protocol. Thus, it has one input channel called *left channel*, and one output channel called *right channel* (Fig. 16.2).

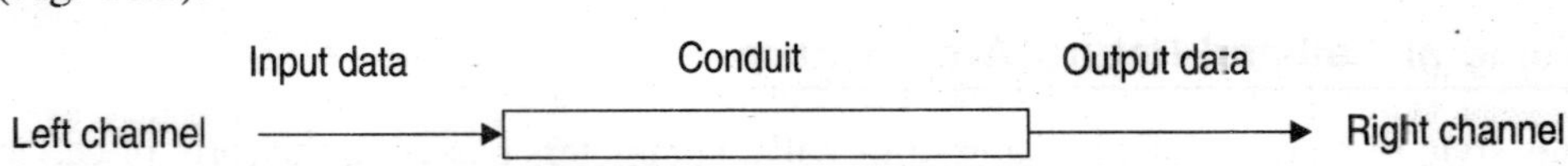

Fig. 16.2. Architecture of a pipe

Formal specifications can be used to describe the semantics of the design elements for use in pipes and filters, along with a set of constraints to specify the way the design elements are to be composed to build systems in the pipe-and-filter style. Unix shell programming provides a facility for pipelining. For example, using the Unix symbol "|", we can specify the architecture of a design that carries out operations like "sort", "process", and "display" in sequence:

sort | process | display

Here, the symbol "|" between two filters indicates a pipe that carries the output data from the preceding filter and delivers it as the input data to the succeeding filter. Figure 16.3 shows a pipeline for the above.

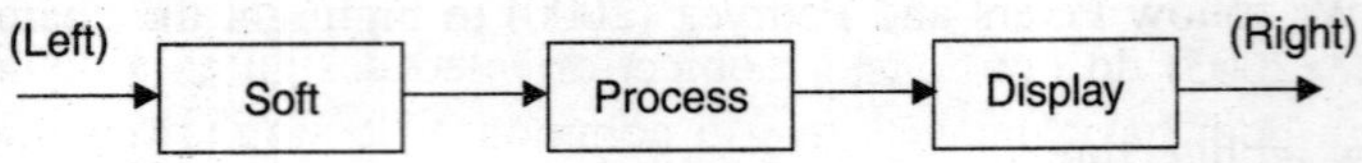

Fig. 16.3. A pipeline

We can make the following observations on the pipe-and-filter architectural style:

- The specifications for this style define (1) the protocol for data transmission through the pipe, (2) the sequencing behaviour of the pipe, and (3) the various interfaces that the pipe can provide to its attached filters.
- Both pipes and filters have multiple, well-defined interfaces, *i.e.,* they allow the services to only specific entities (not to any other arbitrary entity),
- Backed by a rich notion of connector semantics built into the style definition, one can evaluate emergent system-wide properties such as freedom from deadlock, throughput rate, and potential system bottlenecks with the help of queuing theory analysis and simulation modelling.

Pipelining is good for compiling a program where filters are in a linear sequence: lexical analysis, parsing, semantic analysis, and code generation which are required in program compilation. This form of software architecture, however, suffers from the following drawbacks (Pfleeger, 2001):

- Pipelining is good for batch processing but is not good for handling interactive applications.
- When two data streams are related, the system must maintain a correspondence between them.
- Making filters independent of one another is a complex task.

16.4 CALL-AND-RETURN ARCHITECTURES

Supported by the classical and the modern programming paradigms, this architectural style has dominated the software architecture scene for the past three decades. A number of sub-types of architecture are used in practice:

1. General call-and-return architecture
2. Object-oriented architecture
3. Layered architecture

16.4.1 General Call-and-Return Architecture

This style is characterized by subroutine calls, parameters passed in the form of call arguments, fixed entry and exit to subroutines, and by access to global data. When the architecture has a hierarchical structure, it is called the *main-program-and-subroutine with shared data sub-type* of the call-and-return architecture. Here coupling and cohesion are the main considerations.

16.4.2 Object-Oriented Architecture

We have devoted considerable amount of space and time in the previous chapters to discuss object-oriented analysis and design. As we know, objects encapsulate data and behaviour and provide explicit interfaces to other objects; and a message abstraction connects the objects. A drawback of this architecture is that one object must know the identity of other objects in order to interact. Thus, changing the identity of an object requires all other components to be modified if they invoke the changed object.

Monroe *et al.* (2003) do not consider object-oriented design as a distinct style of software architecture, although both have many things in common. The similarities and differences are the following:

- Object-oriented design allows public methods to be accessed by any other object, not just a specialized set of objects.
- Object-oriented design, like software architecture, allows evolution of design patterns that permit design reusability. But software architecture involves a much richer collection of abstractions than those provided by the former. Further, software architecture allows system-level analyses on data-flow characteristics, freedom from deadlock, etc., which are not possible in OOD.
- An architectural style may have a number of idiomatic uses, each idiom acting as a micro-architecture (*architectural pattern*). The framework within each pattern provides a design language with vocabulary and framework with which design patterns can be built to solve specific problems.
- Whereas design patterns focus on solving smaller, more specific problems within a given style (or in multiple styles), architectural styles provide a language and framework for describing families of well-formed software architectures.

16.4.3 Layered Architecture

Appropriate in the master-slave environment, this architecture is based on the principle of hierarchical organization. Designed as a hierarchy of client-server processes, each layer in a layered architecture acts as a server to the layers below it (by making subroutine calls) and as a client to the layers above it by executing the calls received from them. The design includes protocols that explain how each pair of layers will interact. In some layered architecture, the visibility is limited to adjacent layers only.

This architecture is used in database systems, operating systems, file security, and computer-to-computer communication systems, among many others. In an operating system, for example, the user layer provides tools, editors, compilers, and application packages that are visible to the users, whereas the supervisor layer provides an interface between users and inner layers of the operating system. In a file-security system, the innermost layer is for file encryption and decryption, the next two layers are for file-level interface and key management, and the outermost layer is for authentication.

The difficulty associated with this architecture is that it is not always easy to decompose a system into layers. Further, the system performance may suffer due to the need for additional coordination among the layers.

16.5 INDEPENDENT -PROCESS ARCHITECTURE

In this architecture, components communicate through messages that are passed to named or unnamed components. This architecture is suitable for independent processes in distributed/parallel processing systems. The architecture uses the concept of pipelining for communicating the input signals as well as the output results of each filter. This style has various sub-styles:

- Communicating process model
- Event-based implicit invocation systems
- Multi-agent systems

16.5.1 Communicating Processes

Communicating processes (Hoare 1978, 1985) use the pipelining principle to pass messages from an input port through the output port to the monitor (Fig. 16.4). Hoare's specification language CSP (Communicating Sequential Processes) is well suited for specifying such pipeline message flows.

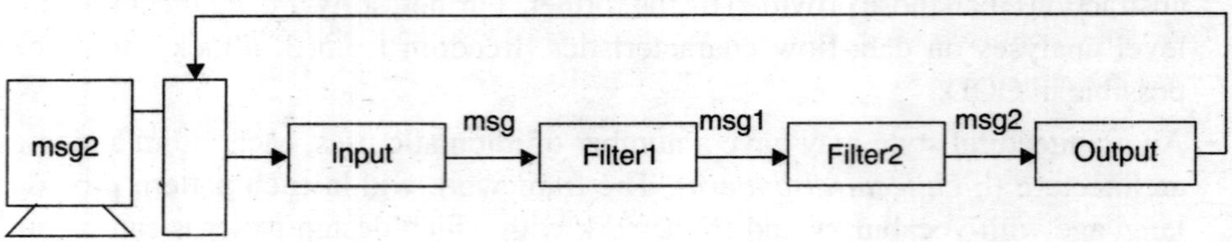

Fig. 16.4. A pipeline process

Communications can be synchronous (processes engage in communications all the time) or asynchronous. Communication can also be *point-to-point* (messages are received by one specific process), *broadcasted* (messages are received by all processes) or *group-broadcasted* (messages are received by a group of processes). The client-server architecture may be considered a subtype of the communicating process style of architecture.

16.5.2 Event-Based Implicit Invocation Systems

Here components announce (*publish*) the data that they wish to share with other unnamed components. This announcement is called an *event*. Other components register their interest (*subscribe*). A message manager (*event handler*) distributes data to the registered components. Examples of this architecture are database management systems and GUI systems that separate presentation of data from applications.

16.5.3 Agent Architecture

An *agent* is a complete, independent information processing system, with its own input/output ports, memory, and processing capability. It receives inputs from a network of channels connected to other agents and the environment, processes various classes of inputs in a predefined manner and produces a set of outputs, and sends them to other agents (*i.e.*, cooperate with other agents in a network) or to environment (*i.e.*, function in isolation). When used in a real-time system, the tasks performed by an agent are time constrained (*i.e.*, the duration for each task is limited). A *coordinator agent* receives a message over a channel from the environment specifying a task to perform and the maximum acceptable duration and passes it on to an agent to perform the task.

The task is represented by

- The deliverables,

- A set of quality-of-product (QoP) standards represented by the QoP transition, and
- A timer represented by the clock transition.

Multi-agent systems are quite effective. They use concepts of distributed artificial intelligence using a collection of cooperating agents with varying capabilities. An agent can be either *cognitive* (capable of drawing inference and making decisions) or *reactive* (react to input in a limited way). Each agent in a multi-agent system performs its tasks independent of other agents and they are thus *orthogonal* to each other. Statecharts are a very convenient means of specifying the requirements of a multi-agent system. Multi-agent systems support modularity, parallelism, flexibility, extensibility, and reusability.

16.6 VIRTUAL-MACHINE ARCHITECTURE

A virtual machine is a software architecture that has the capabilities of an actual machine. Virtual machines are usually layers of software built on the top of an actual machine which a user does not see; the user sees, instead, the software interface for a virtual machine. An oft-repeated example is a distributed computer system (working on a collection of networked machines) that appears like a uniprocessor to the users. Thus, the distributed system is a virtual uniprocessor. Three subtypes of this architecture are discussed below.

16.6.1 Interpreter architecture

Interpreter architecture converts pseudocodes into actual executable code. A common example of this architecture is Java that runs on top of Java virtual machine, thus allowing Java programs to be platform independent. Analogous to the computer hardware architecture, this architecture has four main components:

- Interpretation of each instruction of the program (analogous to execution of the program instructions run on a computer)
- Storage of the data (analogous to the memory of a computer)
- The interpretation engine (analogous to the CPU of the computer)
- Storage of the internal state (analogous to the registers of the computer)

16.6.2 Intelligent System Architectures

An intelligent system architecture is a collection of structures that fetch (sense) da[illegible], process them, and act (actuates) on the results. After sensing the data, a structure can do two types of functions:

1. Cognitive function. Like humans, it can plan, monitor, and control, constituting a virtual reasoning system.
2. Physical function. It senses data and reacts — a perception-action virtual machine.

Naturally, a bi-directional pipeline architecture is required to allow information flow between the physical and the cognitive competence modules. A statechart configuration (Fig. 16.5) is helpful in showing an abstract model of an intelligent system architecture showing three architectural styles:

1. Layering (physical and cognitive modules that act like a filter)
2. Pipelining (with bi-directional pipeline flows)
3. Virtual machine (the physical and cognitive virtual machines)

16.6.3 Chemical Abstract Machine (CHAM) Architecture

Introduced by Bouldol (1992) and popularized by Inverardi and Wolf (1995), this type of architecture uses concepts of chemistry in explaining its design principles. The equivalence between the concepts underlying chemistry and those underlying this architecture are given in Table 16.1.

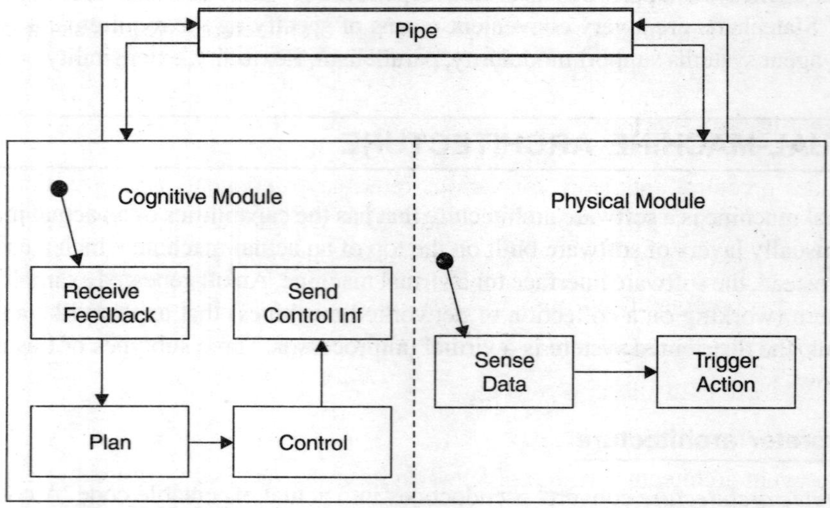

Fig. 16.5. Adaptive intelligent system architecture

Table 16.1: Concepts of Chemistry and CHAM Architecture

Concepts of chemistry	Concepts of CHAM architecture
Molecule	Set of processing elements {I, P, O}
Atom	Each element of a processing element
Solution (Collection of molecules)	Software architecture (Collection of processing elements)
Reaction rule	Transformation rule

Reactions between molecules and solutions of molecules are governed by reaction law, chemical law, absorption law, and extraction law. A *reaction law* leads to formation of new molecules that replace old molecules; a *chemical law* specifies that combination of two solutions leads to combination of two different solutions; an *absorption law* specifies emergence of a new solution on account of combination of two solutions; and an *extraction law* specifies that when two solutions combine, it leads to removal of one of these two solutions. Various notations are used to indicate the application of these laws in the specification of this architecture. Readers are advised to read Inverardi and Wolf (1995) for details.

16.7 REPOSITORY ARCHITECTURE

Used in various forms of information management systems, this architecture is characterized by a central data store and a set of components that operate on data to store, retrieve, and update. Reuse library systems, database systems, web hypertext environment, archival systems, and knowledge-based systems (also called blackboards) are examples of this architecture. We discuss a couple of these systems here.

16.7.1 Reuse Library System

It includes a central data store for various reusable components and operations. The reusable components could be SyRS, SRS, prototype, source code, designs, architectures, test plans, test suites, maintenance plans, and documentation. Various operations required here are:

- Classify components according to keywords.
- Catalog them alphabetically.
- Install them in the library.
- Retrieve them.

A multi-agent architecture with a pipeline architecture that helps communication is well-suited here. However, there is no cognitive function, making layering inappropriate in this case.

16.7.2 Blackboard Architecture

In a traditional database, the shared data is a *passive repository* and the input streams trigger process execution, whereas a *blackboard* is an *active repository* because it notifies subscribers when data of interest change. In a blackboard architecture, the central store controls triggering of processes.

This architecture is helpful for knowledge-based systems, for example in speech recognition. Three principal components make up this architecture (Fig. 16.6):

1. *Blackboard.* This is a repository of problem-solving state data arranged in an application-dependent hierarchy, which stores designs, intentions, and actions as assertions, becomes conditions for actions by Knowledge Source Activation (KSA), and provides communication and cooperation between designers. It helps the designers to detect conflicts and guides evolution of the design scheme by identifying constraints (timing, resource) and dependencies.
2. *Knowledge sources.* These are processes which specify specific actions to be taken for specific conditions defined by the changing states of the blackboard. This is a virtual designer.
3. *Control.* It monitors information in the blackboard. It makes strategic plans for solving problems. It also evaluates the plans, schedules the implementation of the plan, and chooses the appropriate action.

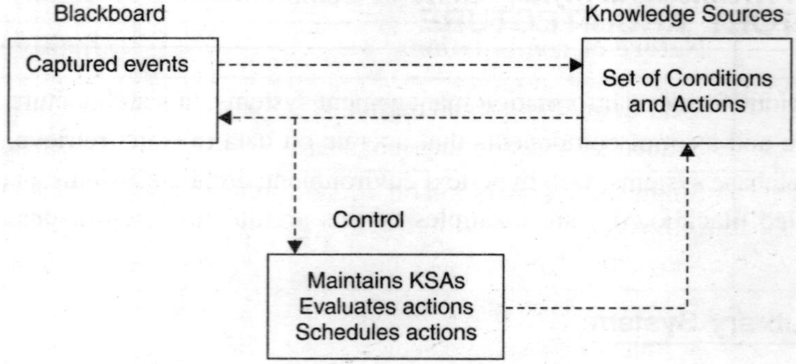

Fig. 16.6. Blackboard architecture

16.8 DOMAIN-SPECIFIC ARCHITECTURE

Tailored to the needs of a specific application domain, these architectures differ greatly and are generally rooted in the domain-level expertise. Examples of these architectures are the following:

- Process control
- Neural-based software architecture
- Genetic-based software architecture

Process-control architecture is characterized by three components: (1) Data elements that include the process variables (input, control variable, and the output variables), the set points (the reference values of the output variables), and the sensors, (2) Computational elements (the control algorithm), and (3) Control loop scheme (open loop, closed loop and feedforward).

Neural computing is the underlying principle of *Neural-based software architecture* while genetic algorithm is the underlying principle of *Genetic-based software architecture*. One naturally has to master the relevant principles before developing these architectures.

16.9 CHOICE OF AN ARCHITECTURAL STYLE

The nature of computations required to solve a given problem and the quality attributes of interest govern the choice of an architectural style. Table 16.2 (adapted from Zhu 2005) gives the nature of computations and quality attributes for the architectural styles.

In practice, most software systems do not follow any particular architectural style, rather they combine different styles to solve a design problem. Shaw (1998) identifies three ways to combine architectural styles. They are the following:

1. Hierarchical heterogeneous style
2. Simultaneous heterogeneous style
3. Locationally heterogeneous style

Table 16.2: Architectural Styles, Nature of Computations, and Quality Attributes

Architecture	Nature of computations	Quality attributes
Data Flow	Well-defined input and output. Sequential transformation of input.	Integratability, Reusability
Batch-sequential	Single output operation on a single collection of input. Sequential processing of input.	Reusability Modifiability
Pipe-and-filter	Transformation of continuous streams of data. Simultaneous transformation of available data elements.	Scalability Response to input element before the whole stream of data becomes available.
Call-and-Return	Fixed order of computation	Modifiability, Integratability, Reusability
Object-oriented	Computations restricted to fixed number of operations for each element of a set of entities.	Reusability, Modifiability
Layered	Division of computational tasks between application-specific and platform-specific layers.	Portability, Reusability
Independent-Process	Independent computations on a network of computer systems.	Modifiability Performance
Communicating	Message passing as an interaction mechanism.	Modifiability, Performance
Event-base implicit invocation	Computations triggered by a collection of events.	Flexibility, Scalability, Modifiability
Agent	Computations performed by interacting information processing systems.	Reusability, Performance, Modularity
Virtual Machine		Portability
Interpreter	Computation on data controlled by internal state.	Portability
Intelligent system	Both cognitive and reactive forms of computation.	Portability
CHAM	Computations mimic laws of chemistry.	Portability
Repository	Computation on highly structured data. Order of computation governed by query requests.	Scalability Modifiability
Reuse library	Computation on passive data acquisition, storage, change of forms, and retrieval.	Scalability Modifiability
Blackboard	Computation on active data control.	Scalability, Modifiability

Hierarchical heterogeneous style is characterized by one overall style adopted for the design with another style adopted for a subset of the design. For example, the interpreter may be followed as the overall architectural style to design the Java virtual machine whereas the interpretation engine of the virtual machine may follow the general call-and-return architecture.

Simultaneous heterogeneous style is characterized by a number of architectural styles for different components of the design. For example, in layered (client-server) architecture, each client may be designed as following independent-process architecture style.

Sometimes no clear-cut style can be identified in a design. Different architectural styles are observed when design is viewed differently. In such cases, the design is said to have adopted a *locationally heterogeneous architecture style*. This happens because (1) sharp differences do not exist in architectural styles; (2) the catalog of architectural styles is not exhaustive as on today; (3) different architectural styles are adopted when a software design evolves over time, and (4) software design may have poor integrity (harmony, symmetry, and predictability).

16.10 EVALUATION OF SOFTWARE ARCHITECTURAL STYLES

Scenario-based analysis is very useful in evaluation of software architectural styles. A scenario is a set of situations of common characteristics between stakeholders and a system. Common characteristics reflect (1) the specific set of participating stakeholders, (2) a specific operational condition under which the interactions take place, and (3) a specific purpose for which stakeholders interact with the system (Zhu, 2005).

Scenarios are commonly developed in object-oriented analysis in the form of use cases to elicit users' functional requirements where stakeholders are the end-users. In the design of architectural styles they involve a variety of stakeholders such as a programmer and a maintainer, and are used to analyze non-functional requirements that include performance, reusability, and modifiability.

Scenarios can be generic or concrete. In a *generic scenario*, stakeholders, conditions, and purposes are abstract whereas a *concrete scenario* has concrete instances for all these conditions.

Scenarios are written in text form. Examples of scenarios for evaluating modifiability to meet a changed functional requirement and for performance of a software system are given below.

Scenario 1

The income tax is computed as 20% of the amount that results by subtracting Rs.1,00,000/- from the net income.

Scenario 2

A maximum of 10,000 persons are likely to browse the company website at the same time during 10:00 and 12:00.

16.10.1 The Software Architecture Analysis Method

Software Architecture Analysis Method (SAAM) is developed at Carnegie-Mellon University (Clements *et al.*, 2002) to evaluate the suitability of architectural styles for meeting specific design requirements. The method, when used to evaluate modifiability, consists of the following six activities:

1. Developing scenarios.
2. Describing candidate architectures.
3. Singling out indirect scenarios that the architectures do not support directly and hence need modification to support the scenarios.
4. Evaluating indirect scenarios in terms of specific architectural modifications and the costs of such modifications.
5. Assessing the extent of interaction of multiple scenarios because they all require modification to the same set of software components.
6. Evaluate the architectures by a weighted-average method. In this method, each scenario is evaluated in terms of the fraction of components in the system that need change to accommodate the demand of the scenario, and each scenario is assigned a weight that represents the likelihood (probability) that the scenario will happen. The architectural style that ranks the highest in terms of the lowest weighted average value is the preferred architectural style for the design.

In Table 16.3 we compare the pipe-and-filter and object-oriented architectures for the scenarios corresponding to modifiability in a hypothetical example. The object-oriented architecture is preferred because of its lower weighted average value of modification effort (= 0.245).

Table 16.3: Evaluation of Architectures

Scenario			Modification effort	
Number	**Description**	**Weight**	**Pipe-and-filter**	**Object-oriented**
1.	To carry out real-time operations.	0.40	2/5	3/10
2.	To operate in 100M ethernet.	0.25	3/5	2/10
3.	To use in Windows 2000 operating system.	0.15	1/5	1/10
4.	To accept text input files.	0.10	2/5	4/10
5.	To make use of COTS components.	0.10	1/5	2/10
	Overall		0.37	0.245

16.10.2 The Architecture Trade-Off Analysis Method

Software Architecture Analysis Method is geared to evaluate architectural designs for single quality attribute. *Architecture Trade-Off Analysis Method* (ATAM) was developed by SEI (Clements *et al.*, 2002) to evaluate architectural designs for multiple quality attributes, some of which may be conflicting in nature. The steps for applying ATAM are the following:

1. Present the ATAM before all the stakeholders.
2. Present the business goals, system overview, and motivation for the evaluation exercise.
3. Present the architectural styles (designs).
4. Identify the architectural design decisions to be taken on the architectural styles.

5. Generate *quality attribute utility tree*. The evaluation team (consisting of architects and project leaders, etc.) is engaged in developing the tree. Here, the root node represents the overall "goodness criterion" of the system. The second level of the utility tree represents the quality attributes such as modifiability, reusability, performance, and so on. The children of each quality attribute, spanning the third level of the tree, represent the refinements for each quality attribute (such as new product categories and changed COTS for modifiability). The fourth level of the tree specifies a concrete scenario for each quality attribute refinement. Each scenario is now rated, in a scale of 0 to 10, for (1) its importance to the success of the system and (2) the degree of difficulty in achieving the scenario.

   Figure 16.7 shows a utility tree. Only two quality attributes and three scenarios are considered here. The two numbers appearing within brackets for each scenario indicate the ratings subjectively done by the stakeholders.

6. Analyze the architectural design decisions to reflect on how they realize the important quality requirements. This calls for identifying sensitivity points, trade-off points, risks, and non-risks.

   Sensitivity points and *trade-off points* are key design decisions. A sensitivity point helps in achieving a desired quality attribute. For example, "Backup CPUs improve performance" is a sensitivity point. A trade-off point, on the other hand, affects more than one quality attribute, often in a conflicting manner, thus requiring a trade-off between them. For example, "Backup CPUs improve performance but increase cost" is a trade-off point.

   Risks are potentially problematic architectural decisions. Not specifying specific functions of agents in agent-based architecture for an e-auction system is risky. *Non-risks* are good design decisions. But they hold under certain assumptions. These assumptions must be documented and checked for their validity.

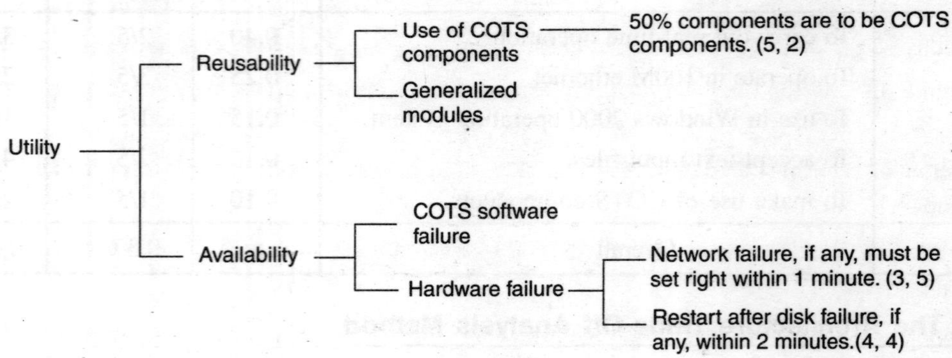

Fig. 16.7. Utility tree

7. Brainstorm and prioritize scenarios. Here the participating stakeholders brainstorm to generate use-case scenarios for functional requirements, growth scenarios to visualize changes in required functionalities, and exploratory scenarios for the extreme forms of growth. The scenarios are now prioritized and compared with those in the utility tree in Step 5. Note that in Step 5 the same task was carried by the evaluation team and it is now carried out by the participating stakeholders.

8. Analyze the architectural design decisions. The evaluation team uses the scenarios generated in Step 7 in the utility tree to examine the design decisions.
9. Present the results. The report summarizing the results include all that was discussed above and also include the *risk themes* — sets of interrelated risks, each set with common underlying concern or system deficiency. These themes help assessing the adopted architectural design with respect to the specified business goals.

16.11 FINAL REMARKS

Software architecture is a recent development but is seen by many as very important. In this chapter, we have given an outline of the works that have been reported in the literature. Recent developments that are likely to affect the field of software architecture are listed below:

- Development platforms (such as J2EE, .NET, Websphere) provide precooked architectures.
- Application layer interchange standards, such as XML, have a significant impact on architectures.
- Scripting languages (like Perl) also affect the way we construct systems.
- Open source software is strongly affecting the practice.
- A large number of Architecture Description languages (ADL) have been developed some of which are ACME, Unicon, Koala, and UML.

REFERENCES

Bass, L., P. Clements and R. Kazman (1998), Software Architecture in Practice, Addison Wesley.

Booch, G. (2006), On Architecture, IEEE Software, vol. 23, no. 2, March-April, pp. 16–17.

Bouldol, G. (1992), The Chemical Abstract Machine, Theoretical Computer Science, vol. 96, pp. 217–248.

Bushmann, *et al.* (1996), Pattern-oriented Software Architecture – A System of Patterns, John Wiley & Sons.

Clements, P., R. Kazman and M. Klein (2002), Evaluating Software Architectures – Methods and Case Studies, Addison Wesley.

Hoare, C. A. R. (1978), Communicating Sequential Processes, Communications of the ACM, vol. 21, no. 8, pp. 66–67.

Hoare, C. A. R. (1985), Communicating Sequential Processes, Prentice-Hall, Englewood Cliffs, NJ.

Inverardi, P. and A. L. Wolf (1995), Formal Specification and Analysis of Software Architectures Using the Chemical Abstract Machine, IEEE Transactions on Software Engineering, vol. 21, no. 4, pp. 373–386.

Kruchten, P., H. Obbink and J. Stafford (2006), The Past, Present and Future of Software Architecture, IEEE Software, vol. 23, no. 2, March-April, pp. 22–30.

Monroe, R. T., A. Kompanek, R. Melton and D, Garlan (2003), Architectural Styles, Design Patterns and Objects in Software Engineering, in Software Engineering, Volume 1: The Development Process, R.H. Thayer and M. Dorfman (eds.), IEEE Computer Society, Wiley Interscience, Second Edition, pp. 239–248.

Perry, De. E. and A. L. Wolf (1992), Foundations for the Study of Software Architecture, ACM Software Engineering Notes, vol. 17, no. 4, pp. 40–52.

Peters J. F. and W. Pedrycz (2000), Software Engineering: An Engineering Approach, John Wiley & Sons (Asia) Pte. Ltd., Singapore.

Pfleeger, S. L. (2001), Software Engineering: Theory and Practice, Pearson Education, Second Edition, First Impression, 2007.

Shaw, M. (1998), Moving Quality to Architecture, in Software Architecture in Practice, by L. Bass, P. Clements, and R. Kazman, Addison Wesley.

Shaw, M. and D. Garlan (1996), Software Architecture: Perspectives on an Emerging Discipline, Prentice-Hall.

Shaw, M. and P. Clements (2006), The Golden Age of Software Architecture, IEEE Software, Vol. 23, No. 2, pp. 31–39.

Zhu, H. (2005), Software Design Methodology, Oxford: Butterworth-Heinemann.

DETAILED DESIGN AND CODING

17 Detailed Design

Detailed design is concerned with specifying the algorithms and the procedures for implementing the design of architecture. The selection of the algorithms depends on the knowledge and the skill level of the designers. Outlining these in understandable ways in the form of detailed design documentation with good component names and their interfaces is what we shall mainly focus in this chapter.

17.1 NAMING DESIGN COMPONENTS AND SPECIFYING THE INTERFACES

Christensen (2002) has given a set of guidelines for naming the design components:

1. The name of a component (such as a procedure, function, module, or object) should reflect its function. It should make sense in the context of the problem domain.
2. The name should be unique.
3. It should be reasonably short and yet be meaningful.
4. Company guidelines (*e.g.*, *nxt* for *next* and *val* for *value*) should be used if they exist.

Interfaces provide links between the design components and help evaluating the extent of coupling between them. To specify a component interface, one has to specify two types of items: inputs and outputs, occasionally an item taking the role of both. Object-oriented languages have *private* interfaces and methods. Often, a maximum of five or seven items are allowed in an interface in order to limit the use of unrelated items to find a place in the interface.

17.2 DETAILED DESIGN DOCUMENTATION TOOLS

Detailed design documentation is important because this is the one that a programmer will use in code development. Also, this is used by the testers for developing the unit test cases. We discuss the following tools that are popularly used in detailed design documentation.

1. Program Flow Chart
2. Structured Programming Constructs
3. Nassi-Shneiderman Diagram
4. Program Design Language

17.2.1 Program Flow Chart (Logic Chart)

The most primitive, yet the most popular, graphical technique is the *program flow chart* (or *logic chart*). It shows the flow of logic (control) of the detailed design. Typical symbols used in such a chart are given in Fig. 17.1. An example of a program flow chart is already given earlier.

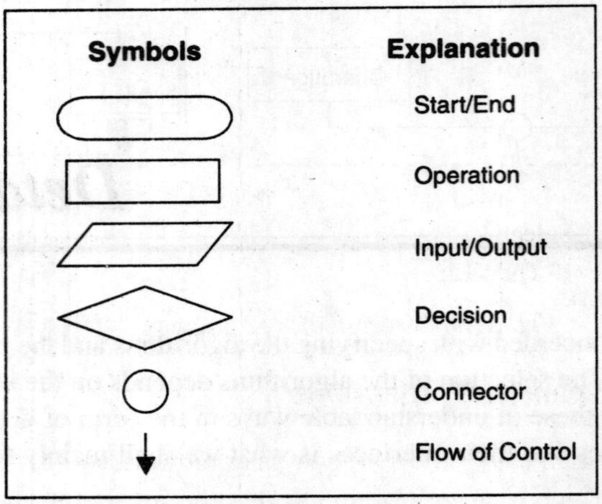

Fig. 17.1. Symbols used for program flow chart

17.2.2 Structured Programming Constructs

Excessive GOTO statements lead to flows of control that lack proper structure and make the code difficult to understand, test, debug, and maintain. Dijkstra (1965 and 1976) forwarded the now-famous three basic *constructs of structured programming: sequence, repetition,* and *selection*. Figure 17.2 gives the flow chart representations of these structures. Note that here the repetition and the selection constructs have two variants each.

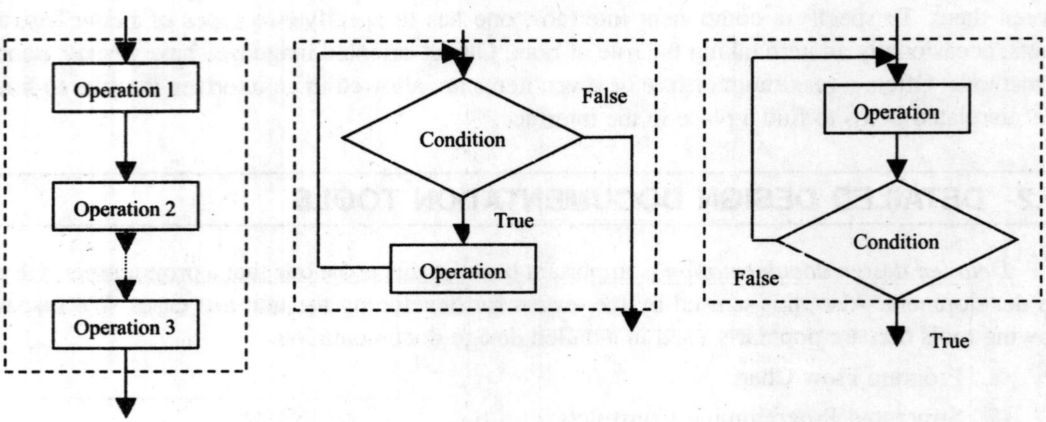

(*a*) Sequence

(*b*) Repeat-While (Post-Test Loop)

(*c*) Repeat-Until (Pre-Test Loop)

(Fig. 17.2. cont.)

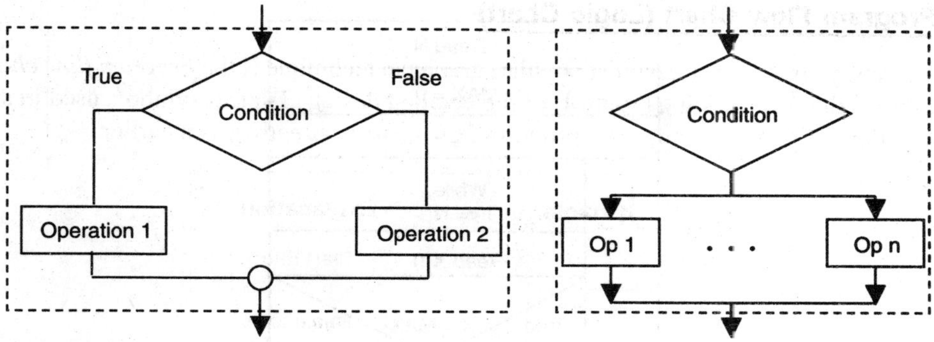

(*d*) Selection (If-Then-Else)   (*e*) Selection (Case)

Fig. 17.2. Structured programming constructs

17.2.3 Nassi-Shneiderman (N-S) Diagrams

Nassi and Shneiderman (1973) developed a diagram for documenting code that uses structured programming constructs. The box-diagram symbols used in the *Nassi-Shneiderman (N-S) diagrams* are given in Figure 17.3.

Figure 17.4 shows an N-S diagram for finding the maximum of N given numbers.

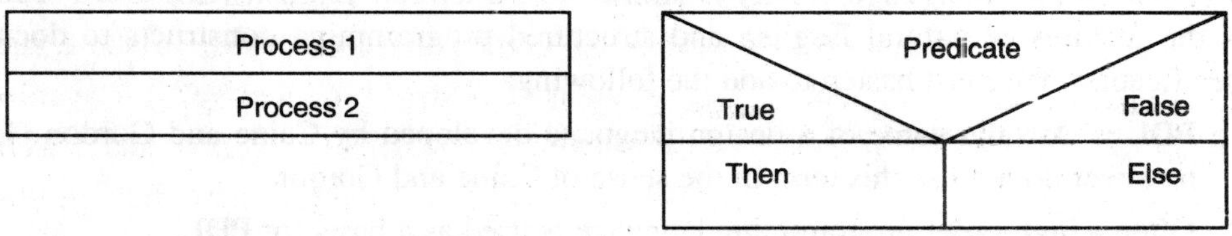

(*a*) Sequence   (*b*) Selection

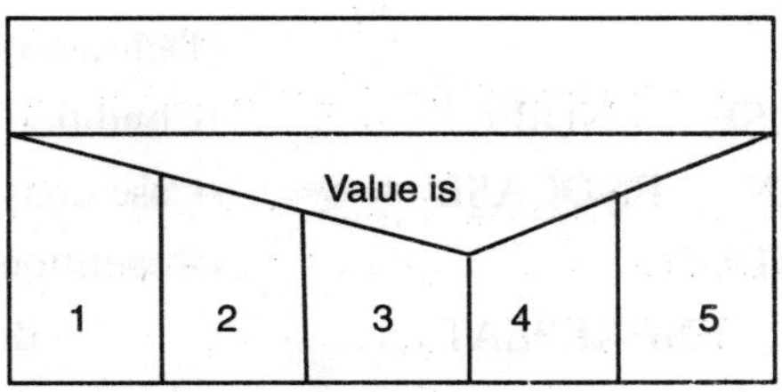

(*c*) Case

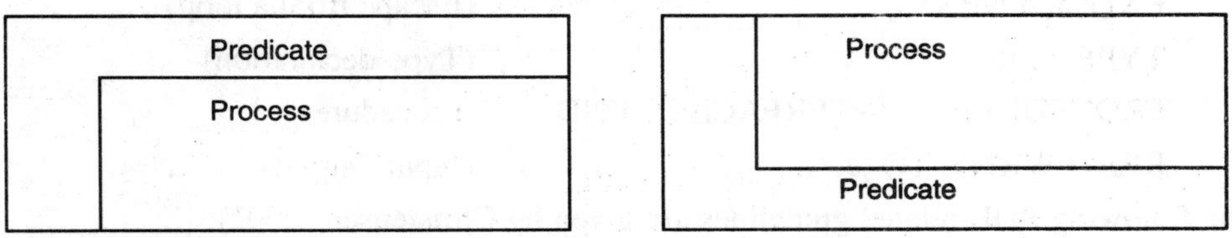

(*d*) Repeat -While   (*e*) Repeat - Until

Fig. 17.3. Symbols in Nassi-Shneiderman diagram

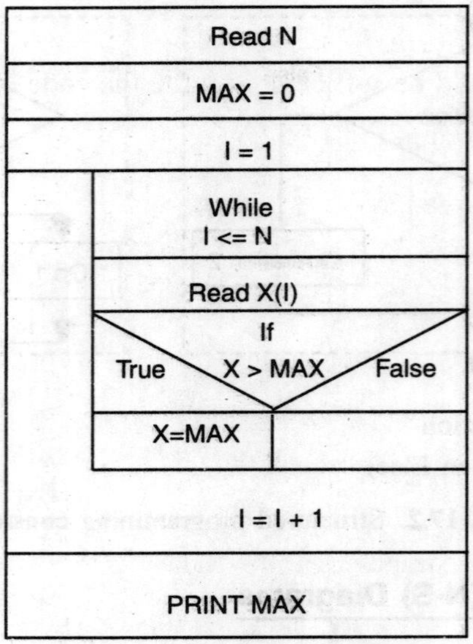

Fig. 17.4. Diagram for finding the maximum number

17.2.4 Program Design Language

Program Design Language (PDL) is similar to Structured English (SE) and Pseudocode. It combines the features of natural English and structured programming constructs to document the design specification. We must hasten to add the following:

1. PDL is also the name of a design language developed by Caine and Gordon (1975). We however do not use this term in the sense of Caine and Gordon.
2. Often a high-order programming language is used as a basis for PDL.

PDL includes various keywords such as

BEGIN … END	(Delimiters for block-structuring)
IF … THEN … ELSE …ENDIF	(Condition construct)
CASE OF …WHEN … ENDCASE	(Case construct)
DO WHILE … ENDDO	(Repetition construct)
REPEAT UNTIL … ENDREPEAT	(- do -)
FOR … ENDFOR	(- do -)
EXIT and NEXT	(Escape from a loop)
TYPE … IS …	(Type declaration)
PROCEDURE … INTERFACE … END	(Procedures)
READ/WRITE TO …	(Input/Output)

The following PDL-related guidelines are given by Christensen (2002):

1. The PDL description of a software component is mainly for the purpose of communication. Therefore, it should have no ambiguity associated with it.

2. Programming language syntax should not be used on a one-to-one basis in the PDL description of a component.
3. PDL description should be sufficient to write the code directly.

An example of PDL is given in Fig.17.5.

```
BEGIN Determine Employee Pay
    FOR each employee
        Get employee type
        IF employee type is temporary
            THEN follow wage rate table
                Get hours worked
                Compute monthly wage earned
            ELSE compute monthly salary
        ENDIF
        BEGIN Print Salary Slip
            CASE of employees
                When employee type is temporary
                WRITE TO printer
                    'Name', 'Hours Worked', 'Wage Rate', 'Total Wage'
                When employee type is permanent
                WRITE TO printer
                    'Name', 'Basic pay', 'DA', 'Deductions', Net Pay'
            ENDCASE
        END
    ENDFOR
END
```

Fig. 17.5. Example of a PDL description of a software component

17.2.5 Documentation of Detailed Design

Detailed design of a software component should be always documented because the design can undergo many changes. Every software firm has its own design documentation standard. Every such design documentation normally has the following details:

> Project name, Component name, Purpose, Modification history, Input parameters, Output parameters, Global variables accessed, Constants used, Hardware and operating system dependencies, Assumptions, Internal data description, Description of the algorithm using a documentation tool, Date, and Author.

The detailed design documentation is usually inserted into the project configuration control system. In addition, a copy of the detailed design documentation of a component (unit) is maintained as *unit development folder* (UDF) that forms the working guide for the individual component developer.

17.3 DESIGN REVIEW

Design documentation helps in carrying out a peer review of the design. Here, a team of four to six individuals review the design of a set of interrelated software components over a period of one to two hours. The review team usually follows a checklist and examines the component designs for the following:

- Correct specification and use of inputs and outputs
- Simplicity of the algorithm
- Cohesion of the component
- Coupling of the component with the rest of the system
- Naming of the component
- Protection of the component from bad inputs and bad internally generated data
- Validation of the pointers
- Allocation and release of dynamic memory
- Changeability of code when developed
- Testability of code when developed
- Error-handling procedures
- Numerical accuracy of computation

The review team writes down their recommendations that are used by the component designers to revise the designs before the actual coding work starts.

The detailed design of a software component paves the way to coding — the subject of the next chapter.

REFERENCES

Caine, S. and K. Gordon (1975), PDL—A Tool for Software Design, in Proceedings of National Computer Conference, AFIPS Press, pp. 271–276.

Christensen, M. (2002), Software Construction: Implementing and Testing the Design, in Software Engineering Volume 1: The Development Process, R. J. Thayer and M. Dorfman (eds.), pp. 377–410, IEEE Compute Society, Second Edition, Wiley Interscience, N. J.

Dijkstra, E. (1965), Programming Considered as a Human Activity, Proceedings of 1965 IFIP Congress, North-Holland Publishing Company.

Dijkstra, E. (1976), Structured Programming in Software Engineering, Concepts and Techniques, J. Buxton *et al.* (eds.), Van Nostrand Reinhold.

Nassi, I. and B. Shneiderman (1973), Flowchart Techniques for Structured Programming, SIGPLAN Notices, Vol. 8, ACM, pp. 12–26.

18 Coding

After user requirements are identified, software requirements specified, architectural design finalized, and detailed design made (and the user-interface and the database design completed which are not covered in this book), the software construction begins. Construction includes coding, unit testing, integration, and product testing. In this chapter, we discuss coding while we discuss other construction-related activities in the five subsequent chapters.

Coding is defined as translating a low-level (or detailed-level) software design into a language capable of operating a computing machine. We do not attempt to cover any computer programming language in any detail. Rather, we discuss different things: the criteria for selecting a language, guidelines for coding and code writing, and program documentation.

18.1 SELECTING A LANGUAGE

McConnell (1993) suggests several criteria to evaluate programming languages and provides a table of "Best and Worst" languages (Table 18.1).

Table 18.1: The Best and the Worst Languages

Criterion	Best language	Worst language
Structured data	Ada, C/C++, Pascal	Assembler, Basic
Quick-and-dirty application	Basic	Pascal, Ada, Assembler
Fast execution	Assembler, C/C++	Interpreted languages
Mathematical calculation	Fortran	Pascal
Easy-to-maintain	Pascal, Ada	C, Fortran
Dynamic memory use	Pascal, C/C++	Basic
Limited-memory environments	Basic, Assembler, C/C++	Fortran
Real-time program	Ada, Assembler, C/C++	Basic, Fortran
String manipulation	Basic, Pascal	C/C++

The table is only suggestive. Available development and execution environments tend to influence the programming language selected. The other consideration is the memory utilization, as affected by the length of the object code that depends on the vendor's tool set.

Bell *et al.* (2002) suggest that a programming language should:

- Be well matched to application area of the proposed project.
- Be clear and simple and display a high degree of orthogonality.
- Have a syntax that is consistent and natural, and that promotes the readability of programs.
- Provide a small but powerful set of control abstractions.
- Provide an adequate set of primitive data abstractions.
- Support strong typing.
- Provide support for scoping and information hiding.
- Provide high-level support for functional and data abstraction.
- Provide a clear separation for the specification and the implementation of program modules
- Support separate compilation.

We now discuss some terms in the above-mentioned guidelines.

- A language is *clear* when it is devoid of ambiguity and vagueness — a property that boosts programmer's confidence and helps good communication.
- For a language to be *simple* it should have small number of features, requiring small size reference manual to describe it.
- *Orthogonality* of a programming language indicates the ability of the language to combine language features freely, enabling a programmer to make generalizations. Pascal, for example, can write Booleans but cannot read them, thus displaying a lack of orthogonality. And, a function returning values of any type rather than values of only scalar type displays good orthogonality.
- Many studies have confirmed the need of good language syntax:
  - — Using semi-colon as a terminator results in less number of mistakes than using it as a separator.
  - — Missing END statement in a BEGIN … END pair and missing a closing bracket in a bracketing convention are quite common syntax errors.
  - — Use of *endif* and *endwhile* statements results in fewer syntax errors.
  - — Program layout with indentation and blank lines help readability and understandability.
  - — Limitation on size of object identifiers in a program (such as 6 characters in Fortran) hinders the expressiveness of meaning.
- *Control abstractions* refer to the structured programming constructs (sequence, selection, and repetition).
- A *data type* is a set of data objects and a set of operations applicable to all objects of that type. When a programmer explicitly defines the type of the object then he/she is using a typed language (for example, Fortran, Cobol, C, and Ada). A language is *strongly-typed* if it is possible to check, at compilation time, whether the operations to be performed on a program object are consistent with the object type. Type inconsistency indicates an illegal operation. Pascal and Ada are strongly-typed languages. Some languages (Lisp and APL) allow changing the data type at run time. This is called *dynamic typing*. While stongly typed languages result

in clear, reliable, and portable codes, dynamic typing provides increased flexibility but must be used with extreme care.

- Whereas *primitive data types* include Boolean, Character, Integer, Real, etc., aggregating data abstractions lead to *structured data types* such as arrays and records. Whereas arrays contain data objects of the same type, records contain data objects (fields) of differing types.
- *Scoping* indicates the boundary within which the use of a variable name is permitted. Whereas BASIC takes all variables as *global* (meaning that the name can be referenced anywhere in the program), all variables in Fortran are *local*, unless defined in a COMMON block, and Ada and Pascal are *block-structured language* allowing use of names in a block (program, procedure or function).
- *Functional and data abstraction* lead to modularity. Conventional programming languages support functional abstraction, whereas object-oriented languages support both functional and data abstractions.

18.2 GUIDELINES FOR CODING

No matter what programming language is used for implementing the design into code, coding should follow certain guidelines with respect to control structures, algorithms, and data structures (Pfleeger 2001). These guidelines are summarized below.

18.2.1 Guidelines with respect to Control Structures

1. Preserve the control structures planned during architecture and design.
2. Follow the top-down philosophy while writing the code so that the code can be easily understood.
3. Avoid clumsy control flow structures where control flow moves in haphazard ways.
4. Use structured programming constructs wherever possible. The various guidelines with respect to each of the three basic constructs are as under:

   (*a*) Sequential Code

   — It should read naturally from top to bottom.
   — Adjacent lines should be related to one another.
   — Lines and data items referenced should have clear dependencies between them.
   — Code with low cohesion should be broken down into blocks to make each of them functionally cohesive.

   (*b*) Conditional Code

   — The logic should be simple.
   — The most likely case of an *if* statement should be put in the *then* block with the less likely case in the *else* block.
   — Common code in the two blocks of an *if-then-else* construct can be moved out so that it appears only once.
   — In case of nested *if-then-else* constructs, one may consider using a *case* statement or breaking up the nesting between modules.
   — One may consider using a *case* or *switch* statement if there are a lot of sequential *ifs*.

— The case selectors in *case* statements should be sequenced according to their frequency of occurrence.

— If the condition being tested is complex, consisting of several variables, one may consider writing a separate function to evaluate the condition.

(*c*) **Looping Constructs**

— *For* loops are a natural choice when traversing simple *lists* and *arrays* with simple exit conditions.

— Considering that *while-do* loops may never execute whereas *do-while* loops execute at least once, their use should be examined carefully to ensure that their use is correctly made.

— Termination condition should be natural and well understood.

— Infinite loops or illegal memory access should be avoided by using safety flags.

— The exit (or continuation) condition for *while-do* and *do-while* loops should be either simple or written as a separate function.

— The code within a loop should have strong cohesion.

5. The program should be made modular. Macros, procedures, subroutines, methods, and inheritance should be used to hide details.
6. The program should be made a little more general in application so that it can be applied to a more general situation, keeping in mind that making a program very general makes it more costly and its performance may drop.

18.2.2 Guideline with respect to Algorithms

Often design specifies the type of algorithm to be followed. The programmer decides how to implement the same. The programmer usually attaches high priority to performance of the code. Unfortunately, high performance is invariably accompanied by more coding effort, more testing effort, and more complex piece of code. A trade-off is therefore necessary between these factors in order to decide the desired level of performance.

18.2.3 Guidelines with respect to Data Structures

Data should be formatted and stored to permit straightforward data management and manipulation. Thus, relationships among data, if established, should be used instead of reading each data separately. This is an example of a recursive data structure.

18.2.4 Additional Guidelines

1. Input and output functions should be included in separate modules so that they can be easily tested and any incompatibilities with the hardware and software facilities can be detected.
2. Writing pseudocode before actually coding reduces coding time and inherent faults. Effort should be made to write pseudocode and get it approved by designers if it deviates from the design already made in the design phase.
3. During the initial code writing phase certain problems may surface that may be related to design errors. Therefore the design should be throughly examined to faults.
4. If the programmer is using reusable components, then care should be taken to understand all the details of the component (including their functions, interface variables, etc.) so that they can be included in the program.

5. If instead the programmer is producing reusable components, then he/she has to take care to ensure that it is general enough to be applicable to a wide field of situations.
6. Company standards regarding coding should be followed.

The *most overriding programming guideline,* however, is the conformance of coding to the design, so that one can go back and forth between design and coding.

18.3 CODE WRITING

While code is supposed to translate the internal design of the components, an important consideration while code writing is the requirements of the post-coding phases of testing, deployment, and maintenance of code. To satisfy these requirements, structured programming constructs (sequence, selection, and iteration) must be used, comments must be added, and the code must be properly laid out.

Guidelines with regard to comments and code layout, given by Christensen (2002), are the following:

Comments should

— not replicate the code.

— indicate what the code is trying to do, that is, the intent of the code should be clear.

— not be interspersed and interwoven with the code too densely. Doing so makes it hard to find the code and follow its logic.

— be simple and helpful.

The developers should use the following while laying out the code:

- Blank lines should be provided between consecutive blocks of code to visually break the code up so that readers can find things easily, much like paragraphing in normal writing.
- Indentation should be given to program statements to highlight control structures.
- Blank space should be provided to highlight terms in expressions, so that one does not strain eyes trying to read them.
- Format should be consistent. The reader should not be kept guessing as to what the style of coding is.
- Declarations should be placed at the beginning of the component, not in the middle.

There is no hard and fast guideline with regard to the length of a piece of code (module). However, as a general rule, it should be less than 100 lines of code (Christensen, 2002). Many prefer to keep it within 60 lines of code so that it can be accommodated within a page.

18.4 PROGRAM DOCUMENTATION

Program documentation is a set of written materials that describe what a program does and how it does it. It can be both internal and external documentation. Meant for programmers, *internal documentation* gives textual, summary information about the program in the source code itself so that the code can be fairly understood if it is read through with care. *External documentation,* on the other hand, is meant for mostly non-programmers and tends to be very elaborate.

18.4.1 Internal Documentation

Internal documentation consists of comments at various places of a piece of code.

1. Every component and module should start with a *header comment block* giving details of name of the component, name of the programmer, dates of development and revision, if any, what the component does, how it fits with the overall design, how it is to be invoked, the calling sequence, the key data structures, and the algorithm used.
2. The code can be broken down into sections and paragraphs. Each section (and paragraph) can be explained as to its purpose and the way it is met.
3. Comments should be written as and when code is written rather than after the code is developed.
4. Comments should also be given regarding the type and source of data used and the type of data generated when statements are executed.
5. Variable and parameter names should be meaningful and self-explanatory.
6. Indentation and spacing should be provided to help to understand the control flow very easily.

18.4.2 External Documentation

External documentation gives the details of the source code. It is used by designers, testers, and maintenance personnel, and by those who like to revise the code later. It consists of

1. A description of the problem addressed by the component in relation to the overall problem being considered.
2. The time and condition of invocation of the component.
3. Description of each algorithm with diagrams, equations, and references, etc.
4. Manner in which special cases are handled.
5. Data flow diagrams and data dictionaries and/or details of objects and classes.

The constructed code requires testing — the subject of the next five chapters.

REFERENCES

Bell, D., I. Morrey and J. Pugh (2002), The Programming Language, in Software Engineering Volume 1: The Development Process, R. J. Thayer and M. Dorfman (eds), pp. 377–410, IEEE Compute Society, Second Edition, Wiley Interscience, N. J.

Christensen, M. (2002), Software Construction: Implementing and Testing the Design, in Software Engineering Volume 1: The Development Process, R. J. Thayer and M. Dorfman (eds.), pp. 377–410, IEEE Compute Society, Second Edition, Wiley Interscience, N. J.

McConnell, S. (1993), Code Complete, Microsoft Press, Redmond, Washington.

Pfleeger, S. L. (2001), Software Engineering: Theory and Practice, Pearson Education, Inc., Second Edition.

TESTING

19

Overview of Software Testing

"To err is human; to find the bug, divine", thus wrote Dunn (1984). Software code — a product of human brainwork and the final product of the effort spent on requirements and design — is also likely to contain defects and therefore may not meet the user requirements. It is necessary to detect software defects, locate bugs, and remove them. Testing is the process of detecting software defects.

Software defects are introduced in all phases of software development — requirements, design, and coding. Therefore, testing should be carried out in all the phases. It thus has its own lifecycle and coexists with the software development lifecycle. We recall that the waterfall model has a specific phase assigned to testing and is possibly the main reason why this aspect of the model has been subjected to much criticism.

In this chapter we shall introduce various concepts intrinsic to testing and give an overview of the testing process applied to all phases of software development. We shall also introduce the unit testing in some detail. In the next four chapters, we shall discuss various techniques applied to test the code at the module (unit) level and at higher levels. The first three of these chapters deal with important techniques applied to test the code at the module (unit) level, and the next chapter deals with integration and higher-level testing. Considering the emergence of object-orientation as the principal way of software development in recent years, we have also discussed object-oriented testing, but the discussion is splintered in all the four chapters.

19.1 INTRODUCTION TO TESTING

There are many definitions of testing. We give here two definitions:

Myers (1979): Testing is the "process of executing a program with the intent of finding errors."

Hetzel (1988): Testing is the "process of establishing confidence that a program or system is what it is supposed to do."

We adopt the definition given by Hetzel because it is more pervasive in the sense that it includes tests that require both executing and not executing a program and that it includes both the program and the software system.

In the past, software developers did not take testing very seriously. Mosley (1993) aptly summarizes the attitude by stating five commonly held *myths about software testing*:

1. Testing is easy.
2. Anyone can do testing.
3. No training or prior expertise is required.
4. Errors are just bad luck.
5. Development of automation will eliminate the need to test.

Over the years that attitude has changed and, as we shall see in this and the next few chapters, testing is based on strong analytical foundations and is a serious field of study.

19.1.1 Software Defects

A *software defect* is a variance from a desired product attribute. They can appear in (1) the code, (2) the supporting manuals, and (3) the documentation. Defects can occur due to:

1. Variance of the software product from its specifications
2. Variance of the software product from customer/user requirement

Even if a product meets its defined specifications stated in the SRS, it may not meet the user requirements. This can happen when the user requirements are not correctly captured in the SRS.

Defects can belong to one of the following three categories:

1. Wrong:	Incorrect implementation of product specification gives rise to this category of defects (*Error due to Omission*).
2. Extra:	Incorporation of a feature that does not appear on software specification (*Error due to Commission*).
3. Missing:	Absence of a product specification feature or of a requirement that was expressed by the customer/user late in the development phase (*Error due to Ignorance*).

Defects are introduced into the system mainly due to miscommunication (incomplete user requirements and unclear design and code specifications), changing user requirements, adding new features when the software is underway, software complexity (windows-type interfaces, client-server and distributed applications, data communications, enormous relational databases, size of applications, and the use of object-oriented techniques), unrealistic schedule and resulting time pressure (on the developer when schedule is not met), poor documentation, inadequate testing, and human error.

Defects are introduced in various software development phases. Although not exhaustive, a list of causes of defects is given below:

Requirement:	Wrong specification of requirements by users
	Misunderstood user requirements
	Incorrect recording of requirements
	Indifference to initial system state
	Unquantified throughput rates or response times

Design:	Misinterpretation of requirements specifications
	Wrong design specifications
	Wrong program specifications such as incorrect analysis of computational error and infinite loops
	Inadequate memory and execution time reserves
Coding and Unit Testing:	Programming defects such as unreachable statements, undefined variables, inconsistency with design, and mismatched procedure parameters
	Erroneous unit tests
	Infusion of defects during error correction
Integration Testing:	Erroneous integration tests
	Infusion of defects during error correction
Operation:	Wrong data entry

19.1.2 Error, Defect, Bug, Failure, and Problem – A Glossary of Terms

In the literature on software quality, terms, such as error, fault, bug, defect and failure, are used very extensively. Although they are often used interchangeably, they have definite meanings. IEEE has defined error and fault, and others have defined related terms such as defect, problem, and failure:

Error: A conceptual, syntactic, or clerical discrepancy that results in one or more faults in the software. A synonym of error is *mistake*. Examples of errors are requirements errors, design errors, and coding errors. Coding errors are also called *bugs*.

Fault: A specific manifestation of an error is fault. More precisely, fault is the representation (*i.e.*, the mode of expression) of an error. It is a discrepancy in the software that can impair its ability to function as intended. The manifestation can be in the form of data flow diagram, hierarchy chart, or the source code. An error may be the cause of several faults. Faults can be grouped as *faults of commission* or *faults of omission.* While software testing helps detecting the first group of faults, they are not very effective in detecting the second group of faults.

Failure: A software failure occurs when a fault in the computer program is evoked by some input data, resulting in the computer program not correctly computing the requirement function in an exact manner (Lloyd and Lipow, 1977).

Thus the causal 3-tuple:

Errors create faults that cause failures (Dunn, 1984).

Defect: A defect is either a fault or a discrepancy between code and documentation that compromises testing or produces adverse effects in installation, modification, maintenance, or testing (Dunn, 1984). Another definition due to Fagan (1976) is that "a defect is an instance in which a requirement is not satisfied."

Humphrey (1989) differentiates among errors, defects, bugs, failures and problems. Wrong identification of user requirements and wrong implementation of a user requirement are human *errors.*

Such errors result in software *defects*. A defect may not always result in software faults. For example, defects like a wrong comment line or wrong documentation does not result in programming faults. When encountered or manifested during testing or operation, they are called software *faults*. The encountered faults in a program are called *program bugs*. Thus, if there is an expression *c/x*, a defect exists, but only when *x* takes value equal to zero, is a bug encountered. While some defects never cause any program fault, a single defect may cause many bugs. Bugs result in system *failure*. System failures are also caused by failure of the hardware, communication network, and the like. Such failures lead to *problems* that the user encounters. Problems also occur due to misuse or misunderstanding at the user end.

A cause-effect chain (Fig. 19.1) depicts the flow of causality among these concepts.

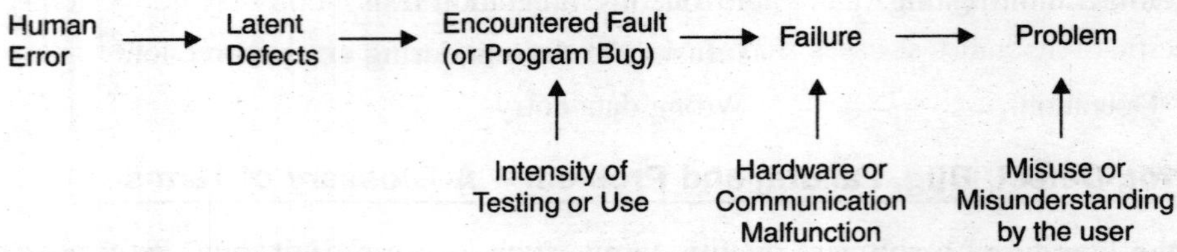

Fig. 19.1. Cause-effect chain of a software problem

19.1.3 Errors of Commission and Omission in Testing

It quite often happens that what is desired to be developed into a program is not developed, whereas the program is developed to deliver things that do not appear in the requirements specifications. Similarly, test cases may be developed that are divorced somewhat from the required specifications and also from the developed program. These relationships among required specification, actual program specification, and test cases give rise to the problems of errors of commission and errors of omission. Figure 19.2 shows the relationships in a set theoretic framework (Jorgensen, 2002). In Fig. 19.2, we define the following:

S: Specification required

P: Program developed

T: Test cases developed

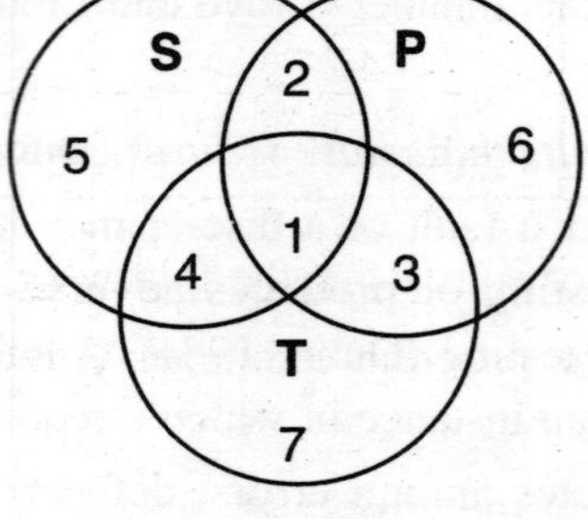

Fig. 19.2. Specifications, program and test cases – Venn diagram representation

Table 19.1 interprets various regions, 1 through 7, defined in Fig. 19.2. The regions have the following interpretations:

1. Desired specifications that are programmed and tested.
2. Desired specifications that are programmed but cannot be tested.
3. Extra functionality in the program being tested.
4. Desired specifications that are not programmed but for which test cases are designed.
5. Desired specifications that are neither programmed nor tested.
6. Extra functionality that are not tested.
7. Test cases that cover neither the desired nor the actual specifications.

It is assumed in Fig. 19.2 and Table 19.1 that a developed program may not perfectly match the desired specifications and test cases may deviate from both the desired specifications and the actual program specifications.

19.1.4 Lifecycle Testing

A traditional view is that testing is done after the code is developed. The waterfall model of software development also proposes the testing phase to follow the coding phase. Many studies have indicated that "*the later in the lifecycle that an error is discovered, the more costly is the error.*" Thus, when a design fault is detected in the testing phase, the cost of removing that defect is much higher than if it was detected in the coding phase.

Table 19.1: Types of Behaviour due to Errors of Commission and Omission

	Tested	**Untested**
Specified Behaviour	$1 \cup 4$ $(S \cap T)$	$2 \cup 5$ $(S - S \cap T)$
Unspecified Behaviour	$3 \cup 7$ $(T - S \cap T)$	7 $(T - (P \cap T) - (S \cap T - S \cap P \cap T))$
Programmed Behaviour	$1 \cup 3$ $(P \cap T)$	$2 \cup 6$ $(P - P \cap T)$
Unprogrammed Behaviour	$4 \cup 7$ $(T - P \cap T)$	5 $(S - (S \cap P) - (S \cap P - S \cap P \cap T)$

The cost of discovering a defect consists of the following:

(*a*) The cost of developing the program erroneously, including cost of wrong specification, coding and documenting.

(*b*) The cost of testing to detect the error.

(*c*) The cost of removing the defects and adding correct specification, code, and documentation.

(*d*) The cost of retesting the system to determine that the defect and all the preceding defects that had been removed are no more present.

In view of the above, testing in all phases of system development lifecycle is necessary. This approach is called the *lifecycle testing*. In this text we shall cover various approaches that are used in life cycle testing of software products.

19.1.5 Axioms and Paradigms of Testing

Myers (1976) gives the following axioms that are generally true for testing:

- A good test is one that has a high probability of detecting a previously undiscovered defect, not one that shows that the program works correctly.
- One of the most difficult problems in testing is to know when to stop.
- It is impossible to test your own program.
- A necessary part of every test case is the description of the expected output.
- Avoid non-reproducible or on-the-fly testing.
- Write test cases for invalid as well as valid input conditions.
- Thoroughly inspect the results of each test.
- As the number of detected defects in a piece of software increases, the probability of the existence of more undetected defects also increases.
- Assign your best programmers to testing.
- Ensure that testability is a key objective in your software design.
- The design of a system should be such that each module is integrated into the system only once.
- Never alter the program to make testing easier (unless it is a permanent change).
- Testing, like almost every other activity, must start with objectives.

Myers' idea of testing that "finding error is the main purpose of testing" is termed often as representing a destructive frame of mind. In this respect it is worthwhile to introduce the five historical paradigms of software testing as conceived by Gelperin (1987). The five paradigms are the following:

1. *Debugging Oriented.* Testing is not distinguished from debugging (the process of diagnosing the precise nature of a fault and correcting it).
2. *Demonstration Oriented.* Prove that the software works.
3. *Destruction Oriented.* Find errors after construction during implementation. This is the dominant view at the present.
4. *Evaluation Oriented.* Find errors in requirement specifications, designs, and code.
5. *Prevention Oriented.* Prevent errors in requirement specifications, designs, and code.

Mosley (1993) is of the opinion that combining features of (3), (4), and (5) is the best approach for effective software testing.

19.2 DEVELOPING TEST STRATEGIES AND TACTICS

Software testing presents a problem in economics. Generally, more the number of tests more will be the number of defects detected. DeMarco (1982) gives a very pessimistic picture when he says that no amount of testing can remove more than 50% of defects. Therefore, the pertinent question is not whether all the defects have been detected, but whether the program is sufficiently good to stop testing. To make the testing process both effective and economical, it is necessary to develop certain strategies and tactics.

Perry (2001) is of the opinion that the objective of testing is to reduce the *risks* inherent in software systems. According to him, a risk is a condition that can result in a loss and that the concern about a risk is related to the probability that a loss will occur. He suggests that testing can reduce that probability of loss to an acceptable level. Risks can be broadly divided into two types:

1. Strategic Risks
2. Tactical Risks

19.2.1 The Strategic Risks

There are 15 types of *strategic risks* (Table 19.2) that define the *test factors*. Perry (2001) suggests that a test strategy should be developed for every software product. Such a strategy should essentially rest on a *risk analysis*. A risk analysis requires the following:

- Key users, customers and the test team jointly select and rank the test factors that are relevant for a particular software product under development.
- They brainstorm to identify the specific risks or concerns for each test factor that they think the software may face, and rank them as high, medium, or low.
- They decide the development phase with which these risks should be associated.
- They decide the test strategy to address each concern.

Thus, if the test factor "correctness" for a payroll accounting system is ranked high, then the specific concerns could be:

Is the gross pay correctly calculated?

Are the deductions correctly made?

Both the concerns may be rated high. Let us consider the second concern. The team may decide the test strategies given in Table 19.3 with respect to this concern. Note that the test strategies are distributed in various phases.

Table 19.2: Strategic Risks and Test Factors

Strategic risk	Test factor	Explanation
Incorrect results will be produced.	Correctness	Data should be entered, read, and processed correctly, and the results should be outputted correctly.
Unauthorized transactions will be accepted by the system.	Authorization	Data and its processing logic must be authorized by the management.
Computer file integrity will be lost.	File integrity	Data entered will be returned unaltered.
Processing cannot be reconstructed.	Audit trail	Save the supporting evidential matter to substantiate the processing.
Continuity of processing will be lost.	Continuity of processing	Ensure backup information for recovery in case of system failure.
Service provided to the user will degrade to an unacceptable level.	Service levels	Desired results should be available within an acceptable time frame.
Security of the system will be compromised.	Access control	The system should be secured against unintentional and unauthorized uses.
Processing will not comply with organizational policy or governmental regulation.	Compliance	The system should be designed as per the organization's strategy, policies, procedures, and standards.
The system will not give correct results for an extended period of time.	Reliability	The system should continue to function correctly for a long time.
System will be difficult to use.	Ease of use	Effort required to learn, operate, prepare data and interpret output should be small.
Programs will not be maintainable.	Maintainability	Effort to locate and fix a software defect should be small.
System will not be portable to other hardware and software.	Portability	Effort to transfer a program to another hardware/software environment should be small.
System will not be able to interconnect with other computer systems.	Coupling	Effort to interconnect components within the system and with other systems should be small.
Performance level will be unacceptable.	Performance	The extent of computing resources used should be small.
System will be difficult to operate.	Ease of operations	Effort to integrate the system with the operating environment and to operate the system should be small.

Table 19.3: Test Strategies for the Test Factor "Are the Deductions Correctly Made?"

Phase	Test strategy
Requirement	Check that all forms of non-tax deductions are considered. Ensure that for each such case, the pertinent set of rules for each deduction is correctly specified. Ensure that the current tax rules are noted and specified.
Design	Check that the programs correctly depict the requirement specifications with respect to each deduction.
Coding	Verify that the codes correctly calculate the deductions.
Testing	Develop test cases for each deduction.
Operation & Maintenance	Update the rules for deduction as and when they change.

19.2.2 The Test Tactics

To carry out lifecycle testing, the test team studies the test strategies formulated and develops test plans (or tactics) *in parallel* with the development of the software. Specific tactics can be of four types in two groups:

Group I:	1. Verification	2. Validation
Group II:	3. Functional Testing (Black-Box Testing)	4. Structural Testing (White-Box Testing)

The review and test stages of the quality lifecycle constitute the scope of *verification and validation* (V & V) of a software product. In these stages, software defects are identified and communicated back for rectification.

Verification is the process of determining whether the output product at the end of a particular lifecycle phase follows logically from the baseline product at the earlier phase. That is, the former echoes the intentions of the immediately preceding phase. *Validation*, on the other hand, is the process of determining whether the output product at the end of a particular lifecycle phase will lead to the achievement of the software requirements specifications. Boehm (1981) succinctly summarizes the differences between the two thus:

Verification: Are we building the product right?

Validation: Are we building the right product?

Thus, the overall goal of verification and validation is quality assurance. It is achieved by

1. Conscious search for defects.
2. Feedback to software engineers for rework and correction of defects.
3. Feedback to management for fixing baselines.
4. Providing visibility to design and code.
5. Providing confidence to the management regarding the quality and the program of the software.

Verification usually consists of non-executing type of reviews and inspection. Here the internal details are checked. Requirement review, design review, code walkthrough, and code inspection do not need to execute the components but require checking of internal details. These are therefore said to use verification techniques. *Validation*, on the other hand, requires execution of a component which can be done with the knowledge of the input to the component and its desired output, and does not require the knowledge of the internal details of the component.

Functional testing, also called *black-box testing*, is concerned with *what* the component does. It is carried out to test the accuracy of the functionality of the component, without using the knowledge of the internal logic of the component being tested. On the other hand, *structural testing*, also called *white-box testing*, is concerned with *how* the component works. It uses the knowledge of the internal (structural) details of the component being tested, in planning the test cases.

On the basis of the above-made statements, we can say the following:

"*Functional tests use validation techniques and structural tests use verification techniques*."

19.2.3 The Tactical Risks

Strategic risks discussed earlier are high-level business risks. Tactical risks, on the other hand, are the subsets of the strategic risks. These are identified by the test team in the light of the strategic risks that are identified by the users/customers and a few members of the test team.

Tactical risks can be divided into three types: (1) Structural risks, (2) Technical risks, and (3) Size risks. The *structural risks* are associated with the application and methods that are used to build the application. They include the following:

- Changes in the area of business and the existing system
- Staffing pattern and project organization
- Skill of the members of the development and the test team
- Experience of the project team in the application area
- Degree of control by project management and effectiveness of team communications
- Status and quality of documentation
- Availability of special test facilities
- Plan for maintenance and operational problems
- User approval of project specifications
- User status, attitude, IT knowledge, and experience in the application area and commitment
- Adequacy of configuration management
- Standards and guidelines followed during project development

The *technical risks* are associated with the technology in building and operating the system. They include:

- Plan for hardware and software failure
- Required system availability
- Dependence on data from external systems
- Provision of input data control procedures
- Suitability of, and familiarity of the team members with, the selected hardware, operating system, programming language, and operating environment

- Margin of tolerable error
- Type of test tools used

The *size risks* include:

- Relative ranking of the project on the basis of total effort spent on development
- Project implementation time
- Number of interconnecting systems
- Number of transaction types
- Number of output types
- Percentage of project resources allocated to system testing

Identifying these risks and weighing them for their importance help to find the critical risk areas and to develop test plan by allocating more resources to them.

19.3 THE TEST PLAN

A test plan describes how testing will be accomplished on a software product, together with the resources and schedule needed. Mosley (1993) suggests that every software organization should develop its own test plan. A test plan usually consists of a number of documents:

1. *A comprehensive* (*or master*) *test plan* that gives an overview of the tests.
2. Several *mini-test plans* for Unit Testing, Integration Testing, System Testing, and Regression Testing.

Perry (2001) suggests that test plans be developed at two levels — one at the system level (the system test plan) and the other at the unit level (the unit test plan). Whereas a system test plan gives a roadmap followed in conducting tests, a unit test plan gives guidelines as to how to conduct tests at a unit level.

A *system test plan* includes the following:

1. General Information
   (*a*) Summary of the functions of the software and the tests.
   (*b*) Environment and pretest background.
   (*c*) Test objectives.
   (*d*) Expected defect rates.
   (*e*) References to project request authorization and project-related documents.
2. Plan
   (*a*) Software description of inputs, outputs, and functions
   (*b*) Test team composition and assignments.
   (*c*) Milestones.
   (*d*) Budgets.
   (*e*) Testing (System checkpoint where the software will be tested)
   (*f*) Schedule of events including resources allocated, volume and frequency of the input, and familiarization and training, etc.

(*g*) Requirement of such resources like equipment, software, and personnel.

(*h*) Testing materials such as system documentation, software, test inputs, test documentation, and test tools.

(*i*) Test training.

(*j*) Testing (System checkpoint where the second and subsequent testing of the software like (e) above).

3. Specifications and Evaluation

(*a*) Specifications of business documentation, structural functions, test/function relationships, and test progression.

(*b*) Methods regarding methodology, test tools, extent of testing, method of recording the test results, and constraints due to such test conditions as interfaces, equipment, personnel, and databases.

A *unit test plan* includes the following:

1. Plan

1. Unit description with the help of flowchart, input, outputs, and functions to be tested.
1. Milestones
1. Budget
1. General method or strategy for the test
1. List of functions not to be tested
1. Test constraints involving interfaces, equipment, personnel, and databases.

2. Business and Structural Function Testing

3. Business functional requirements
3. Structural functions
3. Test descriptions
3. Expected test results which will validate the correctness of the unit functions
3. Test number cross-reference between the system test identifiers and the unit test identifiers.

3. Interface Test Descriptions

(*a*) List of interfaces in the unit

(*b*) Test description for evaluating the interfaces

(*c*) Expected test results

(*d*) Test number cross-reference between the system test identifiers and the interface test identifiers.

4. Test Progression. (The system of tests to be performed obtained from the system test plan).

19.4 THE PROCESS OF LIFECYCLE TESTING

Defect-free software is what everyone dreams for. Although never achievable, the software team always aims to achieve that. Testing during the entire process of software development can substantially reduce the *latent errors* which may surface only during implementation. Such lifecycle testing requires that just as the development team designs and constructs the software to deliver the software requirements, the test team plans and executes the tests to uncover the software defects.

Perry (2001) suggests that lifecycle testing should follow an 11-step procedure:

1. Assess development plan and status.
2. Develop the test plan.
3. Test software requirements.
4. Test software design.
5. Conduct program phase testing.
6. Execute and record results.
7. Conduct acceptance tests.
8. Report test results.
9. Test software installation.
10. Test software changes.
11. Evaluate test effectiveness.

Below we highlight the basic characteristics of each of the above-mentioned steps.

19.4.1 Assessing Development Plan and Status

Quite often, estimate of the development effort, and therefore of the testing effort, is far short of the actual need. Similarly, the planned schedule of the project may be too ambitious and therefore any testing and manpower schedule made on the basis of the project schedule is very likely to be wrong. Although the step of assessing the project development and monitoring plan is skipped in many organizations, it is recommended that this should form the first step in software testing.

19.4.2 Developing Test Plan

Careful preparation of a test plan, often taking one-third of the total test effort, is a prerequisite for effective testing. Four tasks are done while preparing the Test Plan:

1. *Form the Test Team.* The Team can be formed in four ways:
   (*i*) Internal IT Team. The project team members become members of the test team. Although the team, so formed, has a cost advantage, it lacks independent view and cannot always challenge project assumptions.
   (*ii*) External IT Test Team. Here members are drawn from the testing group in the quality assurance group of the IT department. This approach is costly but an independent view is obtained here.

(*iii*) Non-IT Test Team. Here members of the test team are users, auditors, and consultants who do not belong to the information services department. This approach is costly but gives an independent view of testing.

(*iv*) Combination Test Team. Here members are with a variety of background. The team has multiple skills, but the approach is costly.

2. *Build the Test Plan*. Building the test plan requires developing a *test matrix* and planning the schedules, milestones, and resources needed to execute the plan. In the test matrix, rows indicate the software modules and columns indicate tests to be conducted. The appropriate cell entries are tick-marked. Preparation of this matrix requires first deciding the evaluation criterion for each module.

19.4.3 Requirements Phase Testing

As we already know, correctly specified requirements form the basis of developing good software. It is necessary that requirements are tested. In requirements phase testing, a *risk team* with a user as one of its members identifies the risks and specifies the corresponding control objectives. The test team assesses the requirements phase test factors. A *walkthrough team* (with a user as one of its members) conducts a requirements walkthrough (review) and discusses the requirements for their accuracy and completeness. Here users normally take the responsibility of requirements phase testing.

19.4.4 Design Phase Testing

The project leader or an experienced member of the test team rates the degree of risks (Low, Medium, High) associated with each project attribute. For example, if the number of transaction types exceeds 25 and the number of output reports exceeds 20, it can be considered as a high-risk project attribute. The risks help in identifying the test factors and defining controls that reduce the risks to acceptable level. A design review team then conducts a *formal, structured design review*. The team usually has members who were part of the project team; it also has members who are not. In case a project team member is included in the *review team*, then he is not given the task of reviewing a specific design made by him.

A *design review* is carried out for both the business system design and the computer system design, often in two rounds of review. In the first round, the systemic issues of interfaces, major inputs and outputs, organization and system control, and conversion plans, etc., are reviewed, while in the second round, database-related processes (storage, update, and retrieval), hardware/software configuration, system-level testing procedures, function-related processes, error-handling procedure, etc., are reviewed. Usually, the review team ticks a Yes/No/NA column in a checklist.

19.4.5 Program Phase Testing

The main work in this phase is to verify that the code performs in accordance with program specification. *Code verification* is a form of static testing. The testing involves the following tasks:

1. *Desk-debug the program*. Here its programmer verifies (i) the completeness and correctness of the program by checking for its compliance with the company standards, (ii) structured mismatch (unused variables, undefined variables, etc.), and (iii) functional (operational) inconsistency (data scarcity, error-handling procedure, etc.).

2. *Perform test factor analysis.* The test team identifies program phase test factors like data integrity control, file-integrity control, audit trail, security, and other design factors like correctness, ease of use, etc.

3. *Conduct a program peer review.* A *peer review team*, consisting of three to six members, conducts a review of flowchart, source code, processing of sample transactions, or program specifications, and the like.

19.4.6 Execution of Tests

This step evaluates the software in its executable mode. The tasks done are primarily of three types:

1. *Build test data.* Here test transactions are created representing the actual operating conditions. Generating test data for exhaustive testing is uneconomical, even impossible. Various structured methods based on data flow and control flow analysis are available to judiciously generate test data to capture important operating conditions. Usually, a test file should have transactions that contain both valid data that reflect normal operating conditions and invalid data that reflect abnormal conditions. These test data are now put on basic source documents. Usually, a test file is created that stores both valid data (from its current master file) and invalid data (simulated input data). The team predetermines the result from each of the test transactions.

2. *Execute tests.* Tests can be of various types. They are given in Table 19.4.

3. *Record test result.*

Table 19.4: Types of Execution Tests

Manual regression and functional testing (Reliability)	Functional testing (Correctness)
Compliance testing (Authorization)	Manual support testing (Ease of use)
File testing (File integrity)	Inspections (Maintainability)
File testing (Audit trail)	Disaster testing (Portability)
Recovery testing (Continuity of testing)	Functional and regression testing (Coupling)
Stress testing (Service level)	
Compliance testing (Security)	Compliance testing (Performance)
Testing compliance with methodology (compliance)	Operations testing (Ease of operation)

19.4.7 Conducting Acceptance Test

Acceptance testing helps a buyer to determine whether the software fulfils the functional and non-functional objectives specified in the SRS. This has four tasks:

1. *Define acceptance criteria.* The acceptance criteria are usually specified in the SRS and can be broadly divided into four types (Table 19.5).

2. *Develop an acceptance plan.* Developed in consultation with the users, the plan documents the criteria, the appropriate tests to be carried out for the purpose, and the pass/fail criteria.

3. *Conduct acceptance test and reviews.* This involves reviews of both interim and partially developed products and testing of the software system. Testing of the software system involves deciding the operating conditions. Use cases can be used to generate test cases. The input values and conditions associated with the actors described in the use cases help in generating the test cases.

4. *Reach an acceptance decision.* Here the developers and users reach a contractual agreement on the acceptance criteria. Once the user unconditionally accepts the software system, the project is complete.

19.4.8 Reporting Test Results

Reviews, inspections, and test executions lead to surfacing of hidden defects. The nature of defects, their locations, severity levels, and origins are normally collected, stored, and analyzed. The analysis can take various forms, from plotting Pareto charts and making time-series analysis to developing causal models in order to prevent occurrence of future problems.

Table 19.5: Acceptance Criteria Specified in the SRS

Functionality	Internal consistency of documents and code, traceability of functionality, correctness of logic, functional evaluation and testing, preservation of functionality in the operating environment.
Performance	Correct simulation and instrumentation tools, performance analysis in the operating conditions.
Interface Quality	Interface documentation, integration test plans, operational environment interface testing.
Overall Software Quality	Quality metrics, acceptance criteria, adequacy of documentation, quality criteria for operational testing.

19.4.9 Testing Software Installation

Testing software installation involves testing the software before its actual installation. It may be a new system or a changed version of software. A sample of the tests done for the new software is the following:

- Files converted from old to new files have to be tested for integrity.
- The output files should be tested for their integrity, for example by means of control totals.
- Processes and changes, if any, are to be recorded on a special installation trail in order to revert back to the old position if there is a need.
- Procedures for security during the installation phase should be laid down.
- Dissemination of the user's manual and training material should be verified.
- Complete documentation for both the developed software and its maintenance should be ensured.

- In case the software has to operate in more than one operating environment, the documentation regarding potential change and operating characteristics is to be ensured to facilitate portability.
- If the new system needs to interface with one or more software systems, then a coordination notification need to be given to ensure that all such systems become operational at the same time.

Testing changed version of software requires (i) testing the adequacy of restart/recovery plan, (ii) verifying that the correct change has been entered into production, and (iii) verifying that the unneeded versions have been deleted. Restart involves the computer operations to begin from known integrity and recovery is required when the integrity of the system is violated. Testing the following is required for a changed version of software:

- Addition of a new function.
- Change of job control.
- Additional use of utility programs.
- Change in computer programs.
- Change in operating documentations.
- Introduction of a new or revised form.

19.4.10 Testing Software Changes

Software maintenance requires extensive testing of changes and training of users. The main tasks here are (*i*) testing a change, (*ii*) testing a change control process, and (*iii*) testing that training materials and sessions are actually prepared and training imparted.

Testing a change involves (*i*) developing or updating the test plan where elements to be tested are stated and (*ii*) developing/updating test data. Elements to be tested include (*i*) transactions with erroneous data, (*ii*) unauthorized transactions, (*iii*) too early entry of transactions, (*iv*) too late entry of transactions, (*v*) transactions not corresponding to the master data, and (*vi*) transactions with larger-than-anticipated values in the fields.

Testing a change control process involves (*i*) identifying the part of the system which will be impacted by the change, (*ii*) documenting changes needed on each data (such as length, value, consistency, and accuracy of data), and (*iii*) documenting changes needed in each process. The parts are normally identified by reviewing system and program documentation and interviewing users, operators, and system support personnel.

Developing the training materials involves (*i*) making a list of required training materials, (*ii*) developing a training plan work paper, (*iii*) preparing training materials, and (*iv*) coordinating the conduct of training programmes.

19.4.11 Evaluating Test Effectiveness

The objective of this step is to evaluate the testing process. Evaluation of the testing process requires identifying the good and the bad test practices, need for new tools, and identifying economic ways of conducting the tests. The ultimate criterion for evaluation is of course the number and frequency of user complaints. However, other interim evaluation criteria can be set by defining *testing metrics.* Testing metrics range from "time a user has spent in testing" to "total number of defects uncovered" and from "the extent of coverage criteria satisfied" to "total testing effort".

19.5 SOFTWARE TESTING TECHNIQUES

A *testing technique* describes the process of conducting a test. There are two ways in which the testing techniques can be categorized:

1. On the basis of execution
   - 1.1 Static testing
   - 1.2 Symbolic testing
   - 1.3 Dynamic testing
2. On the basis of level of application
   - 1.1 System testing techniques
   - 1.2 Unit testing techniques

Static testing of program is done without executing the program. It is typically done by a compiler which checks for syntax errors and control flow errors such as unreachable code. Other types of static analysis can find out data anomaly such as a variable that is used but never defined before or a variable that is defined but never used afterwards.

Symbolic testing is carried out by providing symbolic inputs to the software and executing the code by symbolically evaluating the program variables. Since the normal form of program execution using input data is not done here, often symbolic testing is considered as a form of static testing.

Dynamic testing requires execution of the program using input data. Here the usual approach is to select the input data values such that desired control paths are executed. Since there can be infinite number of control paths in a program, dynamic test cases are designed to satisfy a minimal number of conditions that indicate the extent of control paths or alternative criteria that are covered in the test cases.

System testing is carried out for the entire application and verifies that the product — an assemblage of components — works as a cohesive whole to satisfy the user requirements. *Unit testing*, on the other hand, carries out tests at the component (unit) level.

Whether at system or at unit level, testing techniques can be either structural or functional. As discussed earlier, structural tests consider the internal logic of the system (or unit) whereas functional tests consider the input to and output of the system (or unit).

Structural system tests are conducted to ensure that the system is able to meet various exigencies when implemented. The tests are designed to check the ability of the software to (1) handle more-than-normal volume of transactions (stress testing), (2) meet the performance criteria with regard to response time to a query, process turnaround time, degree of use of hardware, and so on (performance testing), (3) continue operations after the system stops due to external reason (recovery testing), and (4) guard against leakage and loss (security testing). The tests are also geared to ensure that operator manuals and operator training are adequate (operations testing) and that the standards and procedures are followed during software development (compliance testing).

Functional system tests are designed to ensure that the system (1) is able to function correctly over a continuous period of time (requirements testing), (2) retains all its good aspects after modifying it in order to remove a defect (regression testing), (3) is able to properly process incorrect transactions and conditions (error-handling testing), (4) is supported by well-tested manual support documents (manual-support testing), (5) is able to interface with other systems (inter-system testing), (6) has satisfied the internal controls with regard to data validation, file integrity, etc. (control testing), and (7) is run in parallel with the existing system to ensure that the two outputs are same (parallel testing).

We shall discuss system testing — both structural and functional — in detail in Chapter 23. In the next section we discuss unit testing in some detail.

19.6 UNIT TESTING

Usually, a "unit" denotes a module; but it can also be a single statement or a set of coupled subroutines, as long as the defined unit denotes a meaningful whole. Unit tests ensure that the unit possesses the desired features as stated in the specification.

As shown in Fig. 19.3, a unit test case provides the input parameter values and also provides the expected results when the code is executed. The unit test is carried out to verify the results of the module against the expected results.

Typically, programmers themselves carry out these tests, as they have the required detailed knowledge of the internal program design and code. Programmers may select their own test cases or use the test cases developed previously by the test team.

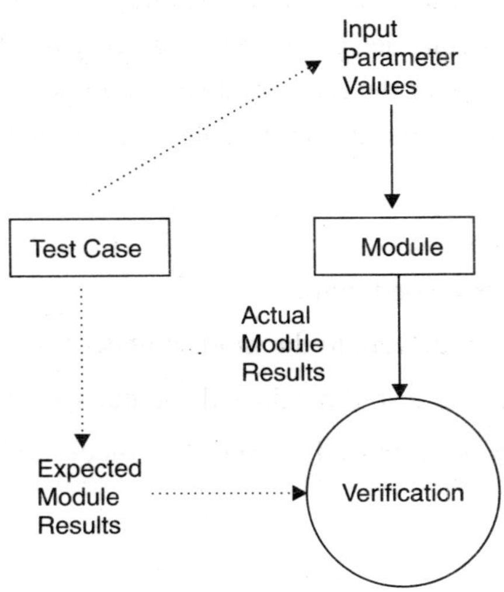

Fig. 19.3. The unit test

results in the expected outputs. Here test data are developed from the design specification documents. There are two categories of functional testing:

- Testing independent of the specification techniques
- Testing dependent on the specification techniques

Testing Independent of the Specification Techniques

These techniques can assume two forms:

- Testing based on the interface
- Testing based on the function to be computed

Testing based on the interface may be of three types:

(*a*) Input domain testing

(*b*) Equivalence partitioning

(*c*) Syntax checking.

Input domain testing. It involves choosing input data that covers the extremes of the input domain, including those in the mid-range.

Equivalence partitioning. It involves partitioning all inputs into classes that receive equivalent treatment. Thus it results in identifying a finite set of functions and their associated input and output domains.

Syntax checking. It helps in locating incorrectly formatted data by using a broad spectrum of test data.

Testing based on the function to be computed can assume two forms:

- Special-value testing
- Output domain coverage

Special-Value Testing. While equivalence testing results in identifying functions and associated input and output, in *special-value testing*, one selects special values of these input data, taking advantage of the special features of the function, if any.

Output Domain Coverage. In this type of testing, one selects input data in such a manner that the whole range of output data is spanned. This, of course, requires knowledge of the function.

Testing dependent on the specification techniques

Structural properties of a specification can guide the testing process. It can take four forms:

- Algebraic
- Axiomatic
- State machines
- Decision tables

Algebraic testing. It requires expressing the properties of data abstraction by means of axioms or rewrite rules. While testing, each axiom can be compiled into a procedure which is then run by a driver program. The procedure indicates whether the axiom is satisfied.

Axiomatic testing. It requires use of predicate calculus as a specification language. Some have suggested a relationship between predicate calculus specifications and path testing.

State machine testing. It requires the use of state machines with finite number of nodes as program specifications. Testing can be used to decide whether the program is equivalent to its specification.

Decision tables. It represents equivalence partitioning, each row suggesting significant test data. Cause-effect graphs provide a systematic means of translating English specifications into decision tables, from which test data can be generated.

19.6.4 Structural (White-Box) Testing and Analysis Techniques

White box tests (alternatively also known as Structural Tests, Logic-Driven Tests, or Testing in the Large) are those that make use of the internal logic of the module. Thus, they take an *internal perspective*. These tests are so framed that they cover the code statements, branches, paths, and conditions. Once again, the test cases can be prohibitively large, and one therefore applies some logic to limit the number of test cases to a manageable value. In this type of testing, test data are developed from the source code. They can have two forms:

Structural analysis

Structural testing

Structural Analysis

Here programs are analyzed, but not executed. They can be done in three ways:

(*a*) Complexity measures

(*b*) Data flow analysis

(*c*) Symbolic execution

Complexity Measures. The higher the value of the complexity measure of the program, the higher should be the testing effort.

Data Flow Analysis. A flow graph representation of a program (annotated with information about variable definitions, references, and indefiniteness) can help in anomaly detection and test data generation. The former include defining a variable twice with no intervening reference, referencing a variable that is undefined, and undefining a variable that has not been referenced since its last definition. Test data can be generated to explicit relationship between points where variables are defined and points where they are used.

Symbolic Execution. Here the input to the program under interpretation is symbolic. One follows the execution path of the program and determines the output which is also symbolic. While the symbolic output can be used to prove the correctness of a program with respect to its specification, the path condition can be used to generate test data to exercise the desired path.

Structural Testing

It is a dynamic technique where test data are selected to cover various characteristics of the code. Testing can take various forms:

operations, or associations. An association is unnecessary if it has redundant information or if no operation uses a path. An association is wrong if the role names are too broad or narrow for their placement.

Jacobson *et al.* (1992) point out that inheritance creates difficulties in testing. An operation inherited from a superclass can be executed by the inheriting subclass. Although such an operation may have been tested in the superclass, it should be tested once again in the subclass also because the context may have changed here. Thus, when a change is brought about in the operation in a superclass, the changed operation needs to be tested in not only the superclass but also the subclass which inherits it. To test the subclass with the inherited operation, one normally flattens the subclass, *i.e.*, a *flattened class* is defined to contain the inherited operation also. Thus the economics of object orientation is lost. Further, it should be noted that the flattened class does not form part of the system which is delivered to the customer.

Procedure-oriented software considers a "unit" as the smallest software components which are developed by no more than one developer and which can be independently compiled and executed. When this guideline is followed for object-oriented development, object-oriented units can be either methods or classes. When methods are considered as units, then unit testing is like traditional unit testing discussed earlier. This, however, makes the task of integration difficult because the methods within a class are to be first integrated (intra-class testing) before attempting the integration at the class and the higher levels. Considering classes as units makes integration easy. Class as a unit is most appropriate when inheritance is absent.

19.8 LEVELS OF TESTING

The importance of lifecycle testing has been already emphasized earlier. As software gets developed following different software development lifecycle phases, tests are carried out in a reverse manner as shown in Fig. 19.8. Accordingly, different types of tests are carried out at different levels. These are

1. *Unit (or Module) tests*. They verify single programs or modules. These are typically conducted in isolated or special test environments.
2. *Integration tests*. They verify the interfaces between system parts (modules, components, and subsystems).
3. *System tests*. They verify and/or validate the system against the initial objectives.
4. *Acceptance (or Validation) tests*. They validate the system or program against the user requirements.

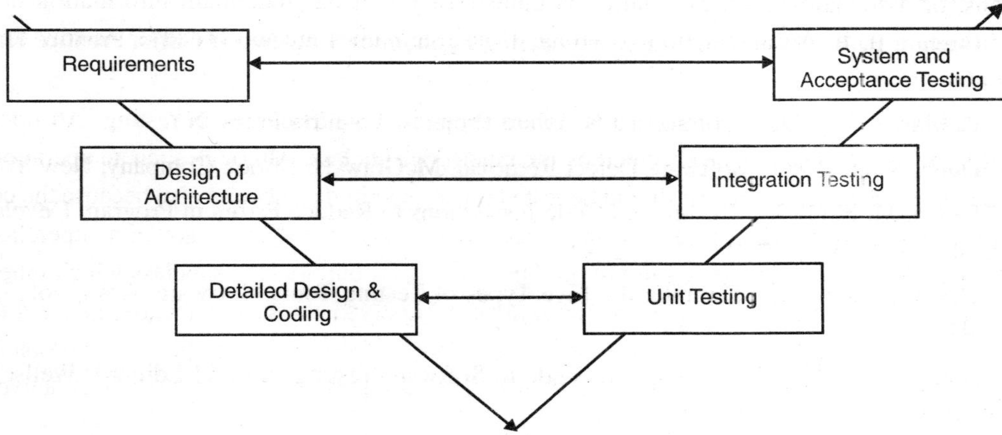

Fig. 19.8. Levels of testing

19.9 MISCELLANEOUS TESTS

Before we end this chapter, we would like to say that a number of other tests have been proposed and used in practice. Below we highlight their properties in brief.

End-to-end testing. Similar to system testing, it involves testing of a complete application environment in a situation that mimics real-world use, such as interacting with a database, using network communications, or interacting with other hardware, applications, or systems if appropriate.

Sanity testing. It is an initial testing effort to determine if a new software version is performing well enough to accept it for a major testing effort. For example, if the new software is crashing the system every 5 minutes or destroying databases, the software may not be in a 'sane' enough condition to warrant further testing in its current state.

Usability testing. It tests the 'user-friendliness' of the software. User interviews and surveys and video recording of user sessions are used for this type of testing.

Compatibility testing. It tests how well software performs in a particular hardware/software/operating system/network environment.

Comparison testing. This testing is useful in comparing software weaknesses and strengths with available competing products.

Mutation testing. By deliberately introducing bugs in the code and retesting with the original test data/cases to determine if the bugs are detected, the test determines if a set of test data or test cases is useful.

REFERENCES

Boehm, B. W. (1981), Software Engineering Economics, Englewood Cliffs, Prentice Hall, Inc., NJ.

DeMarco, T. (1982), Controlling Software Projects, Yourdon Press, NY.

Dunn, R. H. (1984), Software Defect Removal, McGraw-Hill Book Company, New York.

Fagan, M. E. (1976), Design and Code Inspections to Reduce Errors in Program Development, IBM System J. 15(3), 182–211.

Gelperin, D. (1987), Defining the Five Types of Testing Tools, Software News, vol. 7, No. 9, pp. 42–47.

Hetzel, W. (1988), The Complete Guide to Software Testing (Second Edition), Wellsely, MA: QED Information Sciences.

Humphrey W.S. (1989), Managing the Software Process, Reading, MA: Addison-Wesley.

Jacobson, I., M. Christenson, P. Jonsson, and G. Övergaard (1992), Object-oriented Software Engineering: A Use Case Driven Approach, Addison-Wesley, Reading, Massachusetts.

Jorgensen, P. C. (2002), Software Testing—A Craftsman's Approach, Second Edition, Boca Raton: CRC Press.

Lloyd, D. K. and M. Lipow (1977), Reliability, Management, Methods, and Mathematics, Second Edition, Published by the Authors, Redondo Beach, California.

Mosley, D. J. (1993), The Handbook of MIS Application Software Testing, Yourdon Press, Prentice-Hall, Englewood Cliffs, New Jersey.

Myers, G. J. (1976), Software Reliability: Principles and Practices, Wiley, NY.

Myers, G. J. (1979), The Art of Software Testing, Wiley-Interscience, NY.

Perry, W. E. (2001), Effective Methods for Software Testing, Second Edition, John Wiley & Sons (Asia) Pte Ltd., Singapore.

Rumbaugh, J., M. Blaha, W. Premerlani, F. Eddy and W. Lorenson (1991), Object-oriented Modeling and Design, Englewood Cliffs, Prentice-Hall, NJ.

20 Static Testing

Testing is fundamental to the success of a software system. Although it is a field of active research, it lacks a strong theoretical rigour and a comprehensive theory. One reason for the absence of a theory of testing is that there are quite a few testing-related problems that are inherently undecidable (unsolvable). In this chapter we shall first discuss certain fundamental problems of testing that elude solution and then cover static and symbolic testing.

20.1 FUNDAMENTAL PROBLEMS OF DECIDABILITY

A problem is said to be undecidable (or unsolvable) if it can be proved that no algorithm exists for its solution (White 1981). The following problems have been proved to be undecidable in the context of testing:

1. *The test selection problem.* It states that although we know that a reliable test set exists for each program, no algorithmic method exists for constructing such a set for an arbitrary program (Howden, 1976).
2. *The path feasibility problem.* It states that although we know the predicate inequalities, and therefore the path conditions, along a path, we may not be able to solve the set of inequalities, and thus an input data point may not exist which will actually execute the control path Davis (1973).
3. *The code reachability problems.* The following problems are undecidable (Weyker, 1979a, 1979b):
   (*a*) Will a *given* statement ever be exercised by any input data?
   (*b*) Will a *given branch* ever be exercised by any input data?
   (*c*) Will a *given control path* ever be exercised by any input data?
   (*d*) Will *every statement* in a program be exercised by some input data?
   (*e*) Will *every branch* in the program be exercised by some input data?
   (*f*) Will *every control path* in the program be exercised by some input data?

Fundamental Theorem of Testing

We use the notations by White (1981) to state the fundamental theorem of testing that was originally stated by Goodenough and Gerhart (1975). We first define various terms: a program, a correct program, a test selection criterion, a test selected by the criterion, an ideal test, a successful test, and a consistent criterion.

- A *program* P is a function whose input domain is the set D and output domain is R such that on input $d \in D$, it produces (if it terminates) output $P(d) \in R$.
- P is a *correct program* on the input d if $P(d)$ satisfies the output requirement for P.
- A *test selection criterion* C specifies conditions which must be fulfilled by a test where a test T is a subset of the input domain (*i.e.*, $T \subseteq D$).
- A *test selected by the criterion* C is a set of inputs which satisfies these conditions.
- An *ideal test* for P consists of test data $T = t_i$ such that there exists an input $d \in D$ for which an incorrect output is produced if and only if there is some $t_i \in T$ for which $P(t_i)$ is incorrect.
- A *successful test* on P is one if P is correct for every element of T.
- A criterion C is consistent if when two test sets T_1 and T_2 satisfy C, T_1 is successful if and only if T_2 is successful.

We are now in a position to define the fundamental theorem of testing:

If there exists a consistent, complete test selection criterion C for P, and if a test T satisfying criterion C is successful, then P is correct. (Goodenough and Gerhart, 1975).

20.2 CONVENTIONAL STATIC TESTING FOR COMPUTER PROGRAMS

Static testing of computer program is done without executing the program. It is typically done by a compiler which checks for syntax errors and control flow errors such as unreachable code. Other types of static analysis can find out data anomaly such as a variable that is used but never defined before or a variable that is defined but never used afterwards. In this chapter we give insights into some of the fundamental aspects of static testing.

The programming language itself provides the greatest avenue for static testing. It checks whether the program has adhered to the language definitions. Such consistency checks are normally carried out during translation (parsing). Although all errors found during static testing can be found during dynamic testing, in the absence of static testing, the program execution becomes less reliable and less efficient.

Program entities are: variables and subprograms. Accordingly, the programming language provides three basic types of checks (Ghezzi, 1981):

1. Variable manipulation checking,
2. Subprogram manipulation checking, and
3. Intermodule checking.

20.2.1 Variable Manipulation Checking

A variable has attributes like name, type, scope, life-time, and value. *Type* specifies the set of operations that can be legally applied to the variable. A variable that is declared as integer can take integer values 0, 1, 2, etc., but cannot be compared with a binary variable that takes TRUE or FALSE value. During static binding of values during compilation this check can be done easily. The same check can also be done during run time (dynamic binding) but it requires saving the type information that makes execution less efficient.

Scope is the range of program instructions over which the variable is known, and thus manipulatable. In case of static scope binding, the program structure defines the scope of a variable. In dynamic scope binding, a declaration for a variable extends its effect over all the instructions executed after the declaration until a new declaration of a variable with the same name is encountered. Naturally, static testing is not possible here; further, it produces rather obscure programs.

Lifetime is the interval of time when a storage area is bound to a variable.

20.2.2 Subprogram Manipulation Checking

A subprogram has attributes like name, scope, parameters of a certain type, and certain parameter passing conventions. A subprogram is usually called within the scope of its declaration and actual parameters must be consistent in number and type with the subprogram declaration. Usually, compilers execute this consistency check.

20.2.3 Inter-module Checking

Often variables are passed from one module to another. Usually, traditional language compilers do not check the consistency of the imported variables to a module. The interconnection between two separately compiled modules is done by the system-provided linkage editors. The untested inconsistency, if any, causes run-time errors. Object-oriented language compilers, however, compile the module interfaces. Therefore, inter-module consistency checking is done statically during compilation time.

As discussed above, compilers carry out consistency checks; however, they are generally unable to remove many other errors and anomalies that can be checked before program execution. One common anomaly occurs when a variable, initialized once, is initialized once again before use. Data flow analysis and symbolic execution can detect these errors.

20.3 DATA FLOW ANALYSIS

Two rules that specify expected sequences of execution for any given program variable are the following (Osterweil *et al.*, 1981):

1. A *reference* must be preceded by a *definition*, without an intervening *undefinition*. If a variable is not initialized, then this rule is violated. Other reasons may be: misspelling of variables, misplacing statements, and faulty subprogram statements. A violation of this rule leads to an error.
2. A definition must be followed by a reference, before another definition or undefinition. A programmer may forget that a variable is already defined or that such a variable will not be used later. Violation of this rule leads to the *problem of 'dead' variable definition* and to waste of time, but not to an erroneous result.

Certain compilers can perform a linear scan and detect the violation of Rule 1. Certain other compilers assign arbitrary initial values and can detect the problem during execution. However, in many complex problems both approaches do not succeed. Data flow analysis provides a way to find the violation of both the rules.

20.3.1 Events and Sequences of Usage of Variables

Data flow analysis uses program flow graph to identify the definition, reference, and undefinition events of variable values. We thus need to first understand these terms. We follow the definitions given by Osterweil *et al.* (1981).

When the execution of a statement requires that the value of a variable is obtained from memory, the variable is said to be *referenced* in the statement. When the execution of a statement assigns a value to a variable, we say that the variable is *defined* in the statement. The following examples show variables that are defined and/or referenced.

A = B + C	:	*A* is defined whereas *B* and *C* are referenced.
J = J + 1	:	*J* is both referenced and defined.
X (I) = B + 1.0	:	*X* (*I*) is defined, while *I* and *B* are referenced.

In the following pseudocode of a segment of a program code, *K* is both defined and referenced within the *For* loop; but after the loop operation is complete and the control goes out of the loop, *X is undefined.*

```
For K = 1 to 20
    X = X + Y (K)
EndFor
Write ...
```

Similarly, when a subprogram is entered or exited, all local variables will be undefined.

For the purpose of drawing the equivalent flow graph of a program, we shall use the convention of showing a statement or a segment of statement by a node. We shall also use a node to show the undefinition of a variable. Also we shall treat all array variables to be represented by only one variable and represent it by a node. Thus the variables *Y* (*K*), *K* = 1, 20 will be treated as one variable *Y* (although it is an unsatisfactory practice) and will appear as a node in the flow graph.

To represent the sequence of actions that take place on a variable of a program, we use the abbreviations *r*, *d*, and *u* for reference, define, and undefine, respectively, and define the sequence in a left-right order corresponding to the sequence of occurrence of the actions. The sequences of actions on various variables are *A*: *dr*, *B*: *rrd*, *C*: *rr*, and *D*: *d* in the following program segment:

```
A = B + C
B = B – 5
D = A * C
```

The sequences *dr*, *rrd*, etc., are also called *path expressions*. Often *p* and *p′* are used to indicate arbitrary sequence of actions on a variable prior to and after the sequence of variable of interest in a program segment. Thus the above-mentioned sequences could be expressed as *pdrp′*, *prrdp′*, *prrp′*, and *pdp′*. As discussed earlier, the following sequences do not make sense and are therefore *anomalous*:

pddp′: Define a variable and again define it before referencing.

pdup′: Define a variable and then undefine it before referencing.

purp′: Undefine a variable and then reference it.

We use an approach, generally followed in the field of global program optimization, to handle the *live variable problem* and the *availability problem.* We represent a program in the form of a flow graph. Certain actions take place on the variables at each node. The actions can be of four types: define, reference, undefine, or no action. We can define a variable at each node to belong to three sets according to the following definitions:

gen (n): The variable is defined at node *n*.

kill (n): The variable is either referenced or undefined at node *n*.

null (n): No action takes place on the variable at node *n*.

When we focus on a control path of a program, we can trace the actions that take place on a program variable *A* at each node of the control path following the abbreviations below:

$A \in$ gen (n) (abbreviated as *g*) when *A* is defined at the node *n*.

$A \in$ kill (n) (abbreviated as *k*) when *A* is either referenced or undefined at the node *n*.

$A \in$ null (n) (abbreviated as *l*) when no action takes place on *A* at the node *n*.

Path expressions for a program variable on any path can now be denoted conveniently by using the symbols *g*, *k*, and *l* (instead of *d*, *r*, and *u*). We take an example to illustrate the idea. We take the problem of finding the maximum of *N* numbers. The pseudocode and the program flow graph for this problem are given in Fig. 20.1 and the actions taken on program variables at each program nodes are tabulated in Table 20.1.

Program flow graphs are taken up very elaborately in the chapter on White-Box Testing (Chapter 22). It suffices here to say that a computer program can be represented in the form of a directed graph. Here nodes represent program statements and arrows (branches) represent flow of control. A *path* is a sequence of nodes from the start node to the end node. An *independent* path contains at least one more branch that does not appear in any other independent path.

We can identify three independent paths in the flow graph represented in Fig. 20.1:

p_1: a-b-c-d-e-f-g-h-d-i

p_2: a-b-c-d-i

p_3: a-b-c-d-e-f-h-d-i

The *path expression* for a variable can be found out by finding out, from Table 20.1, the type of action taken on variable *X* at each of the nodes appearing in the path. For example, the path expression for the variable *X* in path p_1: *a-b-c-d-e-f-g-h-d-i* in the program *P* is denoted by $P(p_1; X)$ and is given by (*lllgkklll*). Whenever we traverse a loop, we indicate it by putting the actions within brackets followed by an asterisk. For example, $P(p_1; X)$ = *llll*(*gkkll*)**l*.

```
a. Read N
b. MAX = 0
c. I = 1
d. While I <= N
e.    Read X(I)
f.     If X > MAX
g.        THEN MAX = X
h.    I = I + 1
i. PRINT MAX
```

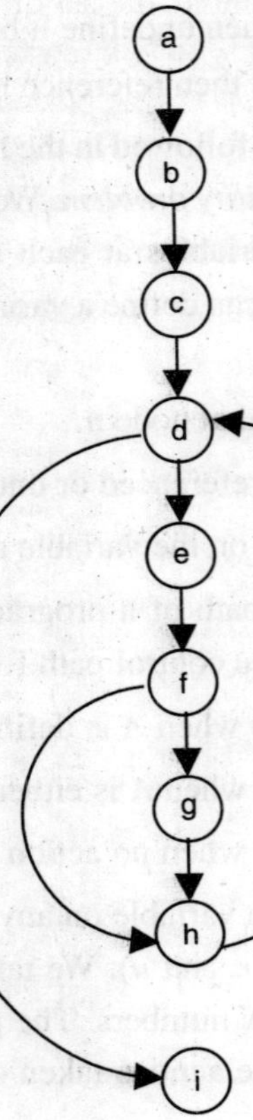

Fig. 20.1. Pseudocode and program flow graph

Table 20.1: Actions Taken on Program Variables at Program Nodes

Node (n)	gen, g	kill, k	null, l	Live	Avail
a	N		MAX, I, X	MAX, I, X	
b	MAX		N, I, X	I, X	N
c	I		N, MAX, X	X	N, MAX
d		I, N	MAX, X	X	N, MAX, I
e	X		N, MAX, I	I	MAX
f		X, MAX	N, I	I	X, MAX
g		X, MAX	N, I	I	
h	I	I	N, MAX, X		
i		MAX	N, I, X		

We can also denote the set of path expressions for any variable on the set of all paths leaving or entering any node. In the above example, the set of path expressions for *MAX* leaving node *e* is given by $P\ (e \rightarrow;\ MAX)$ and is given by *kkllk* + *kllk* (corresponding to subpaths: *f-g-h-d-i* and *f-h-d-i*). Note that we have not considered the actions taking place at node *e*. Similarly, the set of path expressions for *I* entering node *g*, $P(\rightarrow g;\ I)$, is given by *llgkll* + *llgkll kgkl* (corresponding to subpaths: *a-b-c-d-e-f-g* and *a-b-c-d-e-f-h-d-e-g*). Note that we have not considered the actions taking place at the node *g*. Also note that *I* is both killed and generated at node *h*.

Notice that a variable in the null set at a node is merely waiting for getting referenced or redefined. Thus the following equivalence relations are evident:

$$lg \rightarrow g,\ lk \rightarrow k,\ gl \rightarrow g,\ kl \rightarrow k,\ ll \rightarrow l,\ l + l \rightarrow l.$$

Two path expressions are equivalent due to the above relations. Thus,

$$lkg + kgll + lkkgl \equiv kg + kgl + kkg$$

20.3.2 The Live Variable Problem and the Availability Problem

We now introduce two more concepts:

- A variable *X* belongs to a set *live* (*n*) if and only if on some path from *n* the first 'action' on *X*, other than null, is *g*. Thus $X \in$ *live* (*n*) if and only if $P\ (n \rightarrow;\ X) \equiv gp + p'$, where, as before, *p* and *p′* indicate arbitrary sequence of actions on *X*.
- A variable *X* belongs to a set *avail* (*n*) if and only if the last 'action' on *X*, other than null, on all paths entering the node *n* is *g*. Thus $X \in$ *avail* (*n*) if and only if $P\ (\rightarrow n;\ X) \equiv pg$.

The *live variable problem* is concerned with finding the elements of *live* (*n*) for every *n*. And the *availability problem* is concerned with finding the elements of *avail* (*n*) for every *n*. We have indicated the sets *live* (*n*) and the *avail* (*n*) for every node *n* in the example given above.

It is expected that if a variable is defined at a node, it should not be contained in the live set at that node. Conversely, a data flow anomaly problem exists if a variable *A* is defined at a node *n* (*i.e.*, $P\ (n;\ A) = g$) and it is once again defined in some path leaving the node (*i.e.*, $P\ (\rightarrow n;\ A) = gp + p'$) because $P(n\ ;\ A)\ P(\rightarrow n;\ A) \equiv ggp + p''$. Many algorithms (such as Heck and Ullman 1972) exist that do not explicitly derive path expressions and yet solve the live variable and the availability problems.

Based on the discussion made above, Rapps and Weyuker (1985) have given the concepts of define/use path (*du-path*) and Define/Use Testing and have defined a set of data flow metrics. The metrics set subsumes the metrics set initially given by Miller (1977). We take them up later in Chapter 22.

20.4 SLICE-BASED ANALYSIS

A variant of data flow analysis is slice-based analysis. A *program slice* $S(V, n)$ is basically a set of statements of the program *P* that contributes (or affects) the set of variables *V* at statement *n*. The set of statements need not appear physically before the statement *n*. The contribution of the slice can take place in various ways (Jorgensen, 2002):

P-use:	Used in a predicate (decision)
C-use:	Used in computation
O-use:	Use for output

L-use: Used for location (pointers, subscripts)

I-use: Used for iteration (internal counters, loop indices)

P- and *C-use* statements are included in the *slices*. *If the statement n defines a variable then the slice contains the statement n, but if it is a C-use* node, then it is not included. The *O-*, *L-*, and *I-use* statements are not included in the slice. Usually, a slice is defined in terms of the node numbers representing the statements. We take up slice-based analysis in detail in Chapter 22.

20.5 SYMBOLIC EVALUATION METHODS

Recall that a control flow graph may contain both executable and non-executable paths. *Path domain* corresponding to a path is the set of all input values for which that path could be executed. Thus, the path domain of a non-executable path must be empty. Execution of a path performs a *path computation* that transforms the input values to give the output values.

Symbolic evaluation methods do not carry out the numeric execution on the input data along an execution path. Instead, they monitor the manipulations performed on the input values. Computations are represented as *algebraic expressions* over the input data, thus maintaining the relationships between the input data and the resulting values. Normal executions, on the other hand, compute numeric values but lose information on the way they were derived.

There are three basic methods of symbolic evaluation (Clarke and Richardson, 1981):

1. *Symbolic execution.* It describes data dependencies for a path in a program.
2. *Dynamic symbolic evaluation.* It produces traces of data dependencies for a specific input data.
3. *Global symbolic evaluation.* It represents data dependencies for all paths in a program.

We now describe each method in some detail.

20.5.1 Symbolic Execution

Here a path is given or selected on the basis of a coverage criterion and the method represents the input values in terms of symbolic names, performs the path computations by interpreting the program statements along the path, maintains the symbolic values of all variables, and finds the branch conditions and the path condition as expressions in terms of the symbolic names.

At the start, the symbolic values of variables are initialized at the start node of the program flow graph:

— Input parameters are assigned symbolic names.

— Variables that are initialized before execution are assigned the corresponding constant values.

— All other variables are assigned the undefined values "?".

Usually, variable names are written in upper case whereas symbolic names and input parameter names are written in lower case.

At a time when a statement or path is interpreted, if a variable is referenced, then it is replaced by its current symbolic value. Thus both branch predicates and *path computations* (symbolic values of output parameters) contain expressions in symbolic variables only. The conjunction of the symbolic values of the branch predicates defines the path domain and is referred to as the *path condition*. Only the output values satisfying the path condition can cause the execution of the path.

The interpretations of all the statements in path p_1 defined for Fig. 20.1 are given in Table 20.2.

Table 20.2: Interpretations of Statements in Path p_1

Statement or edge	Interpreted branch predicate	Interpreted assignments
a		N = n
b		MAX = 0
c		I = 1
d	i <= n	
e		X (I) = x (i)
f	x(i) > max	
g		MAX = x (i)
h		I = I + 1
i		

The *path condition* for this path is given by $i <= n$ and $x(i) > max$. And the *path computation* of this path is given by $MAX = x(i)$.

Several techniques are used for symbolic execution implementation, two popular ones being *Forward Expansion* and *Backward Substitution*. Forward expansion is intuitively appealing and is the interpretation technique used above. Symbolic evaluators using this technique usually employ an algebraic technique to determine the consistency of the path condition. Here the symbolic evaluator system first translates the source code into an intermediate form of binary expression, each containing an operator and two operands. During forward expansion, the binary expressions of the interpreted statements are used to form an acyclic directed graph, called the *computation graph*, which maintains the symbolic values of the variables.

In backward substitution, the path is traversed backward from the end node to the start node. This technique was proposed to find the path condition rather than the path computation. During backward traversal of the path, all branch predicates are recorded. Whenever an assignment to a variable is referenced, the assignment expression is substituted for all occurrences of that variable in the recorded branch predicates. Thus, suppose a branch predicate $X \geq 10$ was encountered and recorded. Thereafter the assignment statement $X = Y + 5$ was encountered. Then the branch predicate is taken as $Y + 5 \geq 10$. Symbolic names are assigned only when the start node is reached.

Not all paths are executable. It is desirable to determine whether or not the path condition is consistent. Two popular techniques are used for this purpose:

1. The axiomatic technique of predicate calculus that employs a theorem-proving system.
2. The algebraic technique of gradient hill-climbing algorithm or linear programming that treats the path condition as a system of constraints. In the linear programming method, for example, a solution (test data) is found when the path condition is determined to be consistent. Davis (1973) has proven that solution of arbitrary system of constraints is unsolvable.

In symbolic execution, a non-executable path is recognized by examining for inconsistency by incrementally interpreting the branch predicate at each branch and representing the path condition for the partial path traversed at any time in the forward expansion. Thus, a branch predicate $X > 5$ with another branch predicate $X = 5$ following it along the path is inconsistent. Some symbolic evaluation systems switch over to an alternate branch, and thus to an alternate path, as soon as an inconsistent path condition is detected.

Symbolic execution has applications in validation and documentation, test data generation, and error detection. It provides a concise functional representation of the output for the entire path domain. Suppose a statement $Y = X * 2$ is wrongly written as $Y = X + 2$, an error is not detected if X is taken as 2. This is called *coincidental correctness.* Symbolic execution does not allow coincidental correctness, *i.e.*, it does not allow an output to be correct while the path computation is wrong. This is often interpreted as *symbolic testing*.

Symbolic execution checks the predefined user condition for consistency. A non-constant divisor is maintained and reported as a potential source of error. Whenever the symbolic execution system encounters such a predefined user condition, it executes expressions for them and conjoins them to the path condition.

Symbolic execution also helps verifying user-created assertions that must be true at designated points in the program. Usually, the complement of the assertion is conjoined to the path condition. If the resulting path condition is consistent, then the assertion is invalid while it is valid if the resulting path condition is inconsistent.

Because a path condition can be constructed for each path, symbolic execution makes it possible to generate test data. Thus, for example, while normal execution that gives numerical value may not detect a possible run-time error (such as division by zero) unless such an instance actually occurs, symbolic execution can detect this possibility — a case of detection of program error.

Test data generation by algebraic technique is facilitated by examining both path computation and path condition (*error-sensitive testing strategies*). A form of domain testing (a subject of next chapter) is done by examining boundary points of the predicate. Most symbolic execution systems allow interactive path detection and allow the user to 'walkthrough' the program, statement by statement. Here one can observe how the path condition and path computation evolve — a means of debugging.

Although a path may be predefined by the user for symbolic execution, most symbolic execution support systems help indicating the paths to be evaluated based on the choice of a criterion by the user. Often, statement, branch, and path coverage criteria are used to select a set of paths. In *statement coverage* each statement of the program occurs at least once on one of the selected paths. Testing a program on a set of paths satisfying this criterion is called *statement testing*. In *branch coverage* each branch predicate occurs at least once on one of the selected paths and testing such a set of paths is called *branch testing*. In *path coverage*, all paths are selected — referred to as *path testing. Path coverage implies branch coverage whereas branch coverage implies statement coverage.*

Path coverage is often impossible because it involves selection of all feasible combinations of branch predicates, requiring sometimes an infinite number of paths involving loop iterations. Symbolic execution systems usually bind loop iteration between a minimum and a maximum value.

20.5.2 Dynamic Symbolic Evaluation

Whereas in symbolic execution paths to be evaluated are predefined by the user or selected on the basis of statement, branch, and path coverage criteria, in dynamic symbolic evaluation, the paths to be evaluated are determined on the basis of the test data and symbolic representations of the path computation are found out. Usually, this is carried out along with normal execution in a dynamic testing system. Forward expansion is the method used to symbolically represent the computation of each executed path. Throughout the execution, dynamic evaluation maintains the symbolic values of all variables as well as their actual computed values, and symbolic values are represented as algebraic expressions which are maintained internally as a computation graph like that for symbolic execution. The graph, however, is augmented by including the actual value for each node. A tree structure is usually used to depict dynamic symbolic values. Here the path condition is true but is not necessary to check for path condition consistency. Run-time error, if any, will be created. Examination of path condition can uncover errors.

The primary use of dynamic symbolic evaluation is program debugging. In case of an error, the computation tree can be examined to isolate the cause of the error.

The dynamic testing system usually maintains an execution profile that contains such information as number of times each statement was executed, number of times each edge was traversed, the minimum and maximum number of times each loop was traversed, the minimum and maximum values assigned to variables, and the path that was executed. Such statement execution counts, edge traversal counts, and paths executed help in determining whether the program is tested sufficiently in terms of statement, branch, or path coverage strategies. The responsibility of achieving this coverage, however, falls on the user.

20.5.3 Global Symbolic Evaluation

Global symbolic evaluation uses symbolic representation of all variables and develops case expressions for all paths. Similar to symbolic execution, global symbolic evaluation represents all variables in a path as algebraic expressions and maintains them as a computation graph. Interpretation of the path computation is also similar to symbolic execution, the difference being that here all partial paths reaching a particular node are evaluated and a case expression, composed for path conditions for a partial path, is maintained at each node for each partial path reaching the node as also the symbolic values of all the variables computed along that partial path.

Global symbolic evaluation uses a *loop analysis technique* for each loop to create a closed-form loop expression. Inner loops are analyzed before outer loops. An analyzed loop can be replaced by the resulting loop expression and can be evaluated as a single node in the program flow graph. Thus, at any time, there is only one backward branch in the control flow graph. Loop analysis is done by identifying two cases:

1. The first iteration of the loops where the recurrence relations and the loop exit condition depend on the values of the variables at entry to the loop.
2. All subsequent iterations, where the recurrent relations and the loop exit conditions are considered.

We take a simple case to illustrate the use of loop analysis. The *While-Do* loop shown in Fig. 20.2 can be represented as case statements. Note that *loop-exit conditions* (*lec*) for the first and the *K*-th iteration are given in the form of two cases.

21 Black-Box Testing

We have already introduced black-box testing earlier. It is alternatively known as *functional testing*. Here the program output is taken as a *function* of input variables, thus the name functional testing. Before we describe some practical ways of carrying out black-box testing, it is useful to make a general discussion on domain testing strategy.

21.1 THE DOMAIN TESTING STRATEGY

Recall that *predicates* define the flow of control in *selection* constructs. A *simple predicate* is linear in variables $v_1, v_2, \ldots, v_n$ if it is of the form

$A_1v_1 + A_2v_2 + \ldots + A_nv_n$ ROP k

Here A_i's and k are constants and *ROP* denotes *relational operators* (<, >, =, ≤, ≥, ≠).

A *compound predicate* results when more than one *simple predicate* are encountered either in a branch or in a path. A compound predicate is linear when its simple constituent predicates are linear. When we replace program variables by input variables, we get an equivalent constraint called *predicate interpretation*.

Input space domain is defined as a set of input data points satisfying a path condition, consisting of a conjunction of predicates along the path. It is partitioned into a set of domains. Each domain corresponds to a particular executable path and corresponds to the input data points which cause the path to be executed.

We consider a simple predicate. The predicate can be an equality (=), an inequality (≤, ≥), or a non-equality (≠). Whereas the relational operators (<, >, ≠) give rise to *open border segment* in the input space domain, the relational operators (=, ≤, ≥) give rise to *closed border segments*.

The domain testing strategy helps to detect errors in the domain border. Test points are generated for each border segment to determine

1. border operator error due to the use of an incorrect relational operator in the corresponding predicate and
2. error in the position of the border when one or more incorrect coefficients are computed for the particular predicate interpretation.

We consider two-dimensional linear inequalities forming predicates. We consider two types of test points:

1. ON test point that lies on the given border.
2. OFF test point that lies a small distance E from the border and lies on the open side of the given border.

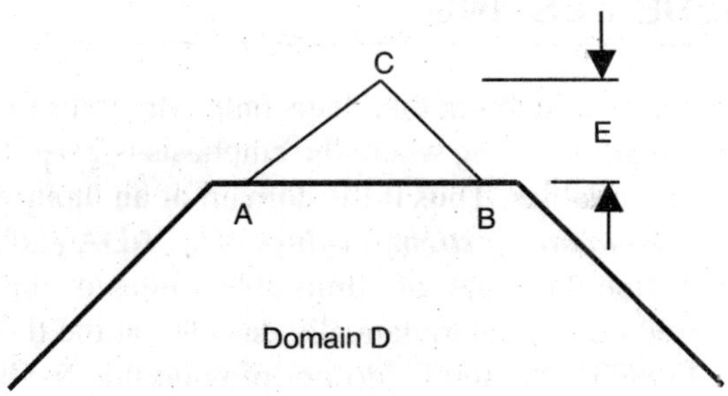

Fig. 21.1. ON-OFF-ON test points

The thick line in Fig. 21.1 defines the closed borders for a compound predicate. These borders together constitute a convex set that satisfy all input domain points in *D*. We consider only one simple predicate and define two ON test points *A* and *B* lying on the border and define one OFF test point *C* lying outside the adjacent domain. Note that the sequence is ON-OFF-ON, *i.e.*, the point *C* does not satisfy only one predicate (in this case the predicate on whose border point *A* and *B* lie) but satisfies all others. Thus, a projection from *C* on the border containing points *A* and *B* will be lying within the two points *A* and *B*.

White *et al.* (1981) have shown, under a set of assumptions, that test points considered in this way will reliably detect domain error due to boundary shifts. That is, if the resultant outputs are correct, then the given border is correct. On the other hand, if any of the test points leads to an incorrect output, then there is an error. The set of assumptions are the following:

1. Coincidental correctness does not occur for any test case.
2. A missing path error is not associated with the path being tested.
3. Each border is produced by a simple predicate.
4. The path corresponding to each adjacent domain computes a function which is different from that for the path being tested.
5. The given border is linear.
6. The input space is continuous rather than discrete.

If the linear predicates give rise to *P* number of borders then we need a maximum of 3**P* number of test points for this domain. We can of course share the test points between the adjacent borders, *i.e.*, take corner points — points of intersection of adjacent borders. Thus the number of test points can be reduced to 2**P*. The number of test points can be further reduced if we share test points between adjacent domains.

When we encounter *N*-dimensional inequalities, then we choose *N* linearly independent ON test points and one OFF test point that should satisfy all other borders excepting the one containing the ON test points. Thus, it requires *N*+1 test points for each border, and the maximum number of test points equals (*N*+1)**P*. By sharing test points between the adjacent borders and between adjacent domains we can of course reduce the number of required test cases.

In general, if equality and non-equality predicates are also present, then we need *N*+3 test points with 3 OFF test points and resulting in a maximum of (*N*+3)**P* test points for *P* borders.

In this chapter, we shall discuss three important black-box techniques in more detail. They are: Boundary-value testing, Equivalence-class testing, and Decision Table-based testing.

21.2 BOUNDARY-VALUE TESTING

A program can be defined as a function that maps input variables to output variables. Boundary-value testing is basically *input-domain testing* where the emphasis is given to testing the program output for *boundary values* of the input variables. Thus if the domain of an input variable x is $[x_{min}, x_{max}]$, then x_{min} and x_{max} constitute the two *boundary (extreme) values* of x. ADA and PASCAL are strongly typed languages and can explicitly define the range of admissible values of input variables. Thus, an input variable value outside the desired range is automatically detected at the time of compilation. But other languages, such as COBOL, FORTRAN, and C, do not provide this facility. Programs written in this latter class of languages are good candidates for boundary-value testing.

Usually, a program with two input variables is a good case to illustrate the intricate points of boundary value testing. Figure 21.2 shows two input variables $x_1 \in [x_{1min}, x_{1max}]$, and $x_2 \in [x_{2min}, x_{2max}]$. Thus x_{1min}, x_{1max}, x_{2min}, and x_{2max} are the admissible boundary values. The rectangle shows the input space—the entire set of feasible values of the two input variables.

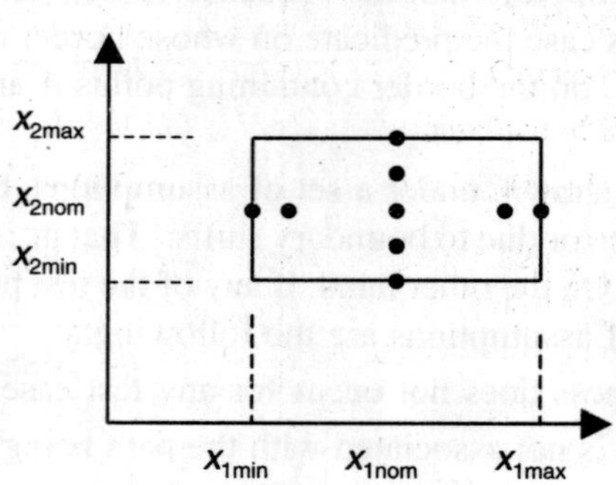

Fig. 21.2. The input domain

Dots in Fig. 21.2 indicate the test cases. They indicate

Points on the boundary:

$(x_{1min}, x_{2nom}), (x_{1nom}, x_{2mmax}), (x_{1max}, x_{2nom}), (x_{1nom}, x_{2min})$

Points near the boundary and within the input space:

$(x_{1min+}, x_{2nom}), (x_{1nom}, x_{2max-}), (x_{1max-}, x_{2nom}), (x_{1nom}, x_{2min+})$

Nominal Point:

(x_{1nom}, x_{2nom})

In the specification of the above-mentioned test cases, the subscripts with minus and plus signs indicate values that are respectively a little lower or higher than the values with which they are associated. The test cases are selected such that we hold one variable at its boundary value and take the other at its nominal value. We then take cases that are adjacent to the selected cases. We also take one interior point. Thus there are nine test cases (= 4 × 2 +1).

When defining the test cases with n input variables, one variable is kept at its nominal value while all other variables are allowed to take their extreme values. In this case there will be $(4n + 1)$ test cases.

There are at least four variations of the basic boundary-value analysis presented above. They are:

1. Robustness Testing
2. Worst-Case Testing
3. Special Value Testing
4. Random Testing

Robustness testing allows a test case with an invalid input variable value outside the valid range. That is, max+ and min- values of variables are also allowed in selecting the test cases. An error message should be the expected output of a program when it is subjected to such a test case. A program, written in a strongly typed language, however, shows run-time error and aborts when the program encounters an input variable value falling outside its valid range. Figure 21.3 shows the case for such a test.

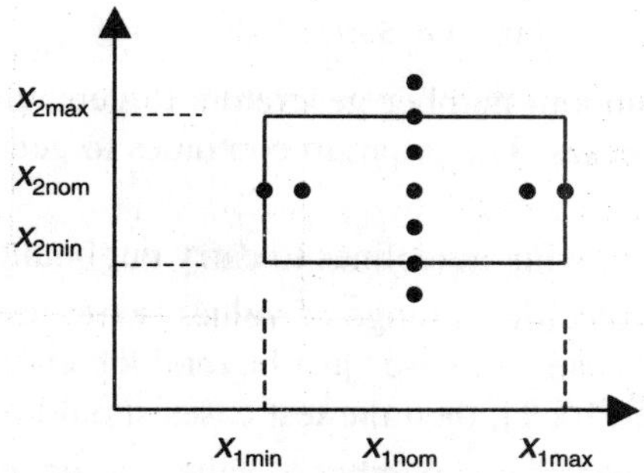

Fig. 21.3. Robustness testing

Worst-case testing defines test cases so as to test situations when all the variable values simultaneously take their extreme values (Fig. 21.4(*a*)). ***Robust worst-case testing*** defines test cases that consider input variable values to lie outside their valid ranges (Fig. 21.4(*b*)). Both types of testing are shown for the case of two input variables. Note that they involve 25 and 49 test cases respectively.

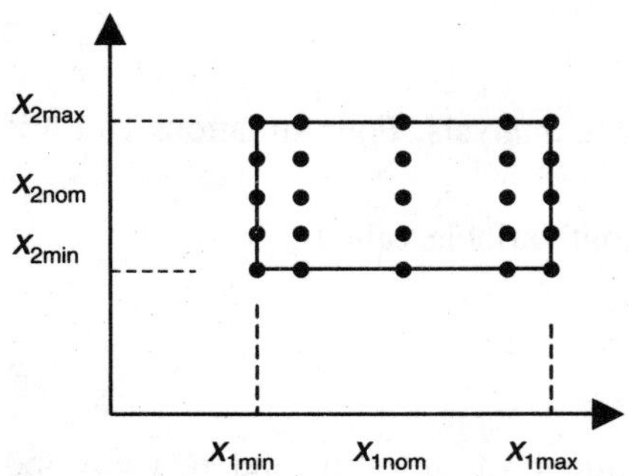

Fig. 21.4(*a*) Worst-case testing

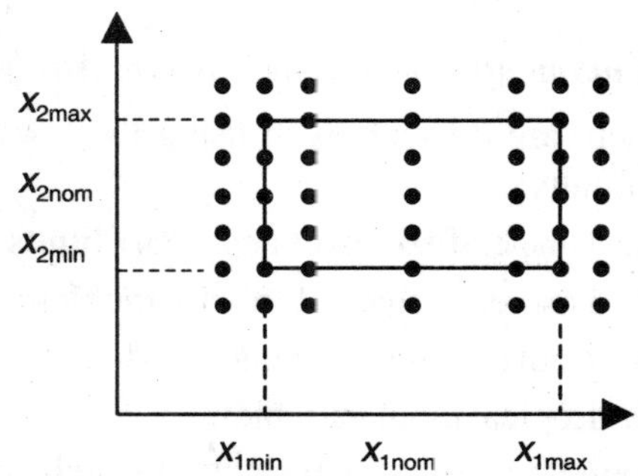

Fig. 21.4(*b*) Robust worst-case testing

Special value testing refers to boundary value analysis when a tester uses domain-level knowledge to define test cases. Take the following example. A wholesaler sells refrigerators of two capacities and sells them at prices of Rs. 10,000/- and Rs. 15,000/- respectively. He usually gives a discount of 5%. But if the total sales price equals or exceeds Rs. 60,000/-, then he gives a discount of 8%. The tester is aware of the discount policy of the wholesaler. Figure 21.5 shows how test cases can be defined in the presence of this domain knowledge.

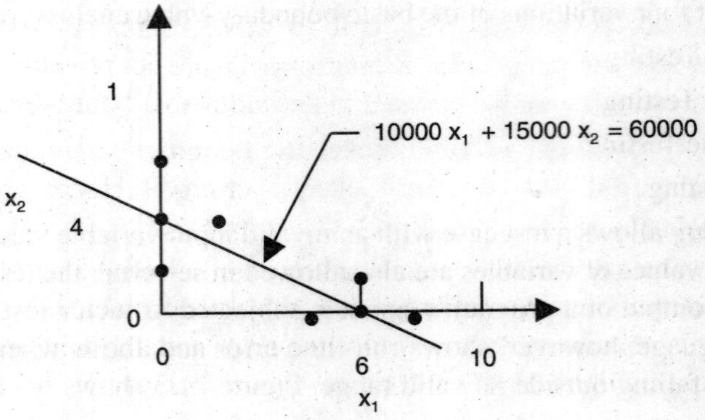

Fig. 21.5. Special-value testing

Random testing allows random number generators to generate the input values for test cases. This avoids bias in defining test cases. The program continues to generate such test cases until at least one of each output occurs.

Myers (1979) gives the following guidelines to carry out boundary-value analysis:

1. If an input condition specifies a range of values, write test cases for the ends of the range, and invalid input test cases for cases just beyond the ends. For example, if the range of a variable is specified as [0, 1], then the test cases should be 0, 1, – 0.1, and 1.1.
2. If an input condition specifies a number of values, write test cases for the minimum and the maximum number of values, and one beneath and one beyond the values. For example, if a file can contain 1 to 100 records, then the test cases should be 1, 100, 0, and 101 records.
3. Use guideline 1 for each output condition.
4. Use guideline 2 for each output condition.
5. If the input and the output of a program is an ordered set (*e.g.*, a sequential file, linear list, table), focus attention on the first and the last elements of the set.

Critical Comments on Boundary-Value Analysis

There are difficulties in using the boundary-value analysis. Four situations can arise that can create difficulty:

1. Unspecified lower and upper limits of the input variable values,
2. Discrete values of input variables,
3. Boolean input variables, and
4. Logical input variables.

Boundary-value analysis works well when the input variables are independent and ranges of values of these variables are defined. In many cases neither holds. For example, pressure and temperature are interrelated, just as year, month and date. The maximum or minimum temperature and pressure to which an instrument will be subjected when in use may not be correctly anticipated in advance and they cannot be defined in the program. In situations where lower and upper limits of input variable values are not specified, the tester should either study the context and assume plausible values or force the designers to specify the values.

When an input variable value is discrete, *min+* indicates the next-to-minimum (*i.e.* the second lowest) value and *max–* indicates the second highest value.

When an input variable is Boolean (*e.g., true* or *false*), boundary test cases can be defined without difficulty; but their adjacent points and the interior point are not possible to define. By the by, we shall see later that Boolean variables are best treated in decision table-based testing.

The presence of a logical input variable makes the boundary-value analysis most difficult to apply. Thus, for example, payment may be in cash, cheque, or credit. Handling this in boundary value analysis is not straightforward.

At least two other problems surround boundary value testing. First, it is not complete in the sense that it is not output oriented. Although Myers suggested developing test cases from the consideration of valid and invalid outputs, it is not always easy to develop them in actual conditions. Second, in boundary value analysis many test cases will be highly redundant.

21.3 EQUIVALENCE CLASS TESTING

In equivalence class testing, the input (or output) space is divided into mutually exclusive and collectively exhaustive partitions, called *equivalence classes*. The term 'equivalence' is derived from the assumption that a test of a representative value of each class is equivalent to a test of any other value in that class, *i.e.*, if one test case in a class detects an error, all other test cases in that class would be expected to find the same error. The converse is also true (Myers, 1979).

To define the equivalence classes, one has to first divide the range of each variable into intervals. The equivalence classes are then defined by considering all the combinations of these intervals. Test cases are thereafter defined for judiciously chosen equivalence classes.

Four forms of equivalence class testing are used (Jorgensen, 2002):

1. Weak Normal Equivalence Class Testing
2. Strong Normal Equivalence Class Testing
3. Weak Robust Equivalence Class Testing
4. Strong Robust Equivalence Class Testing

Weak normal equivalent class testing defines the minimum number of test cases that cover all the intervals of the input variable values (Fig. 21.6). It makes a single-fault assumption.

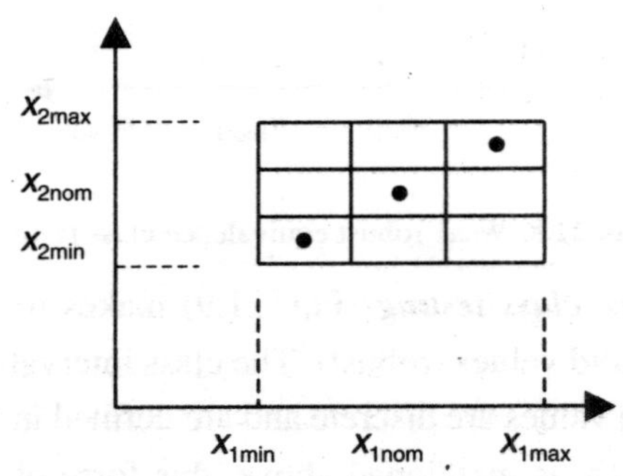

Fig. 21.6. Weak normal equivalence class testing

Strong normal equivalence class testing (Fig. 21.7) is based on a multiple-fault assumption. Here a test case is selected from each element of the Cartesian product of the equivalence classes. In this sense it is complete.

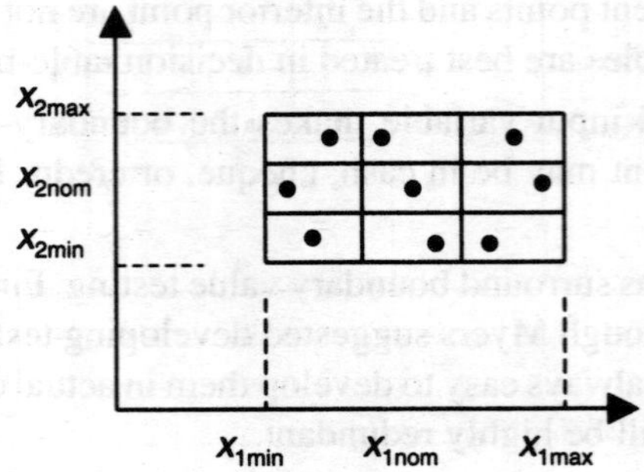

Fig. 21.7. Strong normal equivalence class testing

Weak robust equivalence class testing considers both valid and invalid inputs (Fig. 21.8). For all valid inputs it uses the procedure of weak normal equivalence testing, choosing one value from each valid class, whereas for all invalid inputs it defines test cases such that a test case contains one invalid value of a variable and all valid values of the remaining variables. It is weak because it makes single-fault assumption, and it is robust because it considers invalid values. This is the traditional form of equivalence class testing.

One faces two types of difficulty while working with this form of testing. One, the output for an invalid test case may not be defined in the specifications. Two, the strongly typed languages obviate the need for checking for invalid values.

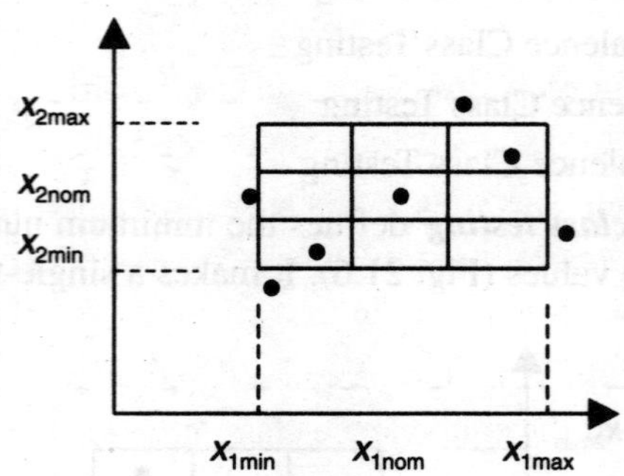

Fig. 21.8. Weak robust equivalence class testing

Strong robust equivalence class testing (Fig. 21.9) makes multiple-fault assumption (strong) and considers both valid and invalid values (robust). The class intervals in this form of testing need not be equal. In fact, if the input data values are discrete and are defined in intervals, then equivalence class testing is easy to apply. However, as mentioned above, this form of testing (as also boundary value analysis) has lost much of its importance with the advent of strongly typed languages.

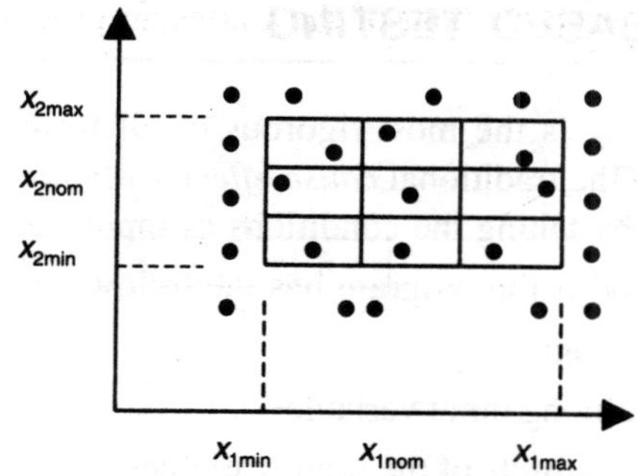

Fig. 21.9. Strong robust equivalence class testing

Myers (1979) suggests the following procedure to identify equivalence classes:

1. Find input conditions from the design specifications.
2. Partition each input condition into two or more groups. While doing this, identify *valid equivalence classes* that represent admissible input values and *invalid equivalence classes* that represent erroneous input values.
   (*a*) If an input condition specifies a *range* of values (*e.g.*, "student strength can vary from 50 to 100"), then one valid equivalence class is (50 ≤ student strength ≤ 100), and the two invalid classes are (student strength < 50) and (student strength > 100).
   (*b*) If an input condition specifies a *number* of values (*e.g.*, "Up to 50 characters form a name"), then one valid equivalence class and two invalid classes (zero number of characters and more than 50 characters) are formed.
   (*c*) If an input condition specifies a set of input values and the program handles each input value differently (*e.g.*, "product type can be refrigerator or TV"), then one valid equivalence class for each input value and one invalid equivalence class (*e.g.*, "microwave oven") are defined.
   (*d*) If an input condition specifies a "must be" situation (*e.g.*, "Name must start with an alphabet"), then one valid equivalence class (the first character is a letter) and one invalid equivalence class (*e.g.*, the first character is a numeral) are defined.
   (*e*) If there is a possibility that the program handles the elements in an equivalence class differently, then split the equivalence class into smaller equivalence classes.
3. Assign a unique number to each equivalence class.
4. Write a test case to cover as many uncovered valid equivalence classes as possible and continue writing new test cases until all the valid equivalent classes are covered.
5. Write test cases to cover all the invalid equivalence classes such that each test case covers only one invalid equivalent class.

The main virtues of equivalence class testing are that it is able to reduce redundancy which is normally associated with boundary value testing and it can be either input oriented or output oriented, thus providing the much needed completeness of testing.

21.4 DECISION TABLE-BASED TESTING

Decision table-based testing is the most rigorous of all forms of black-box testing. They are based on the concepts underlying the traditional *cause-effect graphing* and *decision tableau* techniques. Here the test cases are designed by taking the conditions as inputs and the actions as outputs.

This form of testing is good if the program has the following characteristics:

- Prominent *if-then-else* logic
- Logical relationships among input variables
- Calculations involving subsets of the input variables
- Cause-and-effect relationships between and inputs and outputs
- High cyclomatic complexity

We consider the case of Library Requisition (discussed in Chapter 4). The decision table for the case is given in Fig. 21.10.

Conditions	**Decision Rules**			
	1	2	3	4
Textbook?	Y	Y	N	N
Funds Available?	Y	N	Y	N
Actions				
Buy.	X		X	
Waitlist for Next Year.		X		
Return the Reco to the HOD.				X

Fig. 21.10. Decision table for library requisition

The test cases and the corresponding expected outputs are obvious and are given in Table 21.1.

Table 21.1: Text Cases and Expected Output in Decision Table-Based Testing

Sl. No.	Test case	Expected output
1.	Textbook: Yes, and Funds Available: Yes	Buy.
2.	Textbook: Yes, and Funds Available: No	Waitlist for Next Year.
3.	Textbook: No, and Funds Available: Yes	Buy.
4.	Textbook: No, and Funds Available: No	Return the Reco to the HOD.

21. 5 BLACK-BOX TESTING IN OBJECT-ORIENTED TESTING

As mentioned in Chapter 19, when methods are used as units then we need a driver and stub classes (that can be instantiated) to conduct unit testing. When classes are used as units, then *state-*

based testing appears to be very appropriate. Recall that the state of an object is defined by the values that the attributes defined in that object take. In state-based testing the test requires selecting combinations of attribute values giving rise to special states and special object behaviour. Usually, equivalent sets are defined such that combination of attribute values in a particular equivalent set gives rise to similar object behaviour.

21.6 FINAL COMMENTS ON BLACK-BOX TESTING

Boundary value testing considers the ranges of input values. The number of test cases can be very high. It considers neither the data dependencies nor the logic dependencies. Equivalence class testing considers the internal values of the input variables and thus the data dependencies among them. It is based on the philosophy that equivalence classes get similar treatment from the program. It reduces the number of test cases. Decision table-based testing considers both the data and the logic dependencies among the input variables. It is the most rigorous of all the black-box testing methods. It is associated with the least number of test cases compared to boundary value and equivalence-class testing. In terms of effort, however, it is the most demanding whereas the boundary-value testing is the least demanding.

Jorgensen (2002) suggests the following guidelines to select the type of testing method in a particular case:

- If the variables refer to physical quantities, boundary-value testing and equivalence class testing are preferred.
- If the variables are independent, boundary-value testing and equivalence class testing are preferred.
- If the variables are dependent, decision table-based testing is preferred.
- If the single-fault assumption is warranted, boundary-value analysis and robustness testing are preferred.
- If the multiple-fault assumption is warranted, worst-case testing, robust worst-case testing, and decision-table testing are preferred.
- If the program contains significant exception handling, robustness testing and decision table testing are preferred.
- If the variables refer to logical quantities, equivalence-class testing and decision-table testing are preferred.

REFERENCES

Jorgensen, P. C. (2002), Software Testing—A Craftsman's Approach, Second Edition, Boca Raton: CRC Press.

Myers, G. J. (1979), The Art of Software Testing, John Wiley, NY.

White, L. J., E. I. Cohen and S. J. Zeil (1981), Domain Strategy for Computer Program Testing, in Computer Program Testing, B. Chandrasekaran and S. Radicchi (eds.), North-Holland, pp. 103–113, New York.

A *path* between two nodes n_i and n_j is the set of adjacent nodes (or edges) in sequence starting from node n_i and ending on n_j. Thus, in Fig 22.1, there are two paths between the nodes n_1 and $n : n_1 - n_4 - n_6$ and $n_1 - n_2 - n_6$.

Paths have nodes that are connected. Thus nodes n_i and n_j are connected if they are in the same path. The nodes n_1 and n_6 are connected as also the nodes n_2 and n_6 in the path $n_1 - n_2 - n_6$.

The maximum set of connected nodes constitutes a *component* of a graph. Unconnected nodes belong to different components of a graph. The graph in Fig. 22.1 contains two components: $C_1 = \{n_1, n_2, n_3, n_4, n_5, n_6\}$and $C_2 = \{n_7\}$.

A graph can be condensed to contain only *parts* with no edges between them. The two parts $C_1 = \{n_1, \ldots, n_6\}$ and $C_2 = \{n_7\}$ of Fig. 22.1 are shown in the *condensation graph* (Fig. 22.2). An important use of a condensation graph is that each part of the graph can be tested independently.

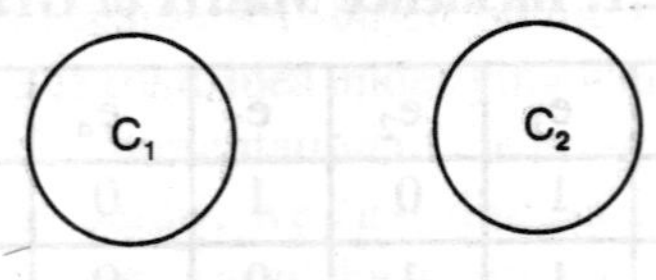

Fig. 22.2. A condensation graph of Fig. 22.1

Cyclomatic complexity number of a graph (McCabe 1976) is given by

$$\gamma(G) = e - n + p$$

where, e: the number of edges, n: the number of nodes, and p: the number of parts

Cyclomatic complexity number is an important characteristic of a graph and is very useful in white-box testing. We shall say more about it later when we discuss basis path testing.

22.1.1 Directed Graphs

A *directed graph* (also known as *digraph*) also contains nodes and edges. But here every edge is defined from a node to another node, rather than between two nodes. That is, an edge shows a direction from a node to another. Some authors call edges in directed graphs as *arcs*. We continue to use the word "edge" for directed graphs also. We define an edge e_k as an ordered pair of nodes $<n_i, n_j>$, indicating that the edge is directed from the node n_i to n_j. Figure 22.3 is a directed graph which can be symbolically defined as:

$$G = (N, E)$$

$$N = \{n_1, \ldots, n_7\}$$

$$E = \{e_1, \ldots, e_5\} = \{<n_1, n_2>, <n_2, n_3>, <n_1, n_4>, <n_4, n_5>, <n_4, n_6>, <n_2, n_6>\}$$

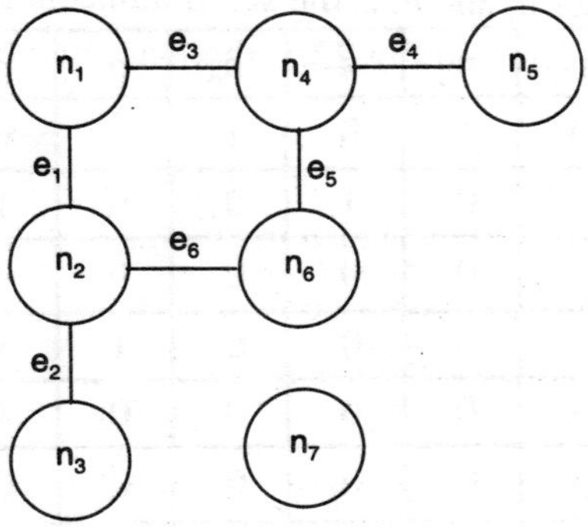

Fig. 22.3. A directed graph

Indegree of a node is the number of distinct edges that terminate at the node. *Outdegree* of a node is the number of distinct edges that emanate from the node. The indegrees and the outdegrees of various nodes in the graph of Fig. 22.3 are indicated in Table 22.3.

Table 22.3: Indegree and Outdegree of Nodes of a Graph

i	1	2	3	4	5	6	7
Indeg (n_i)	0	1	1	1	1	2	0
Outdeg (n_i)	2	2	0	2	0	0	0

We are now in a position to define a *source* node, a *sink* node, a *transfer* (or *internal*) node, and an *isolated* node:

Source node: Indegree = 0.

Sink node: Outdegree = 0.

Transfer node: Indegree ≠ 0; Outdegree ≠ 0.

Isolated node: Indegree = 0; Outdegree = 0.
That is, an isolated node is a node that is both a source node and a sink node.

The *adjacency matrix* of a directed graph has nodes in both rows and columns such that the *ij*th element is 1 if an edge exists from the *i*th node to the *j*th node, otherwise it is 0. The row sum corresponding to a node indicates its outdegree, while the column sum corresponding to a node indicates its indegree. The adjacency matrix for the graph in Fig. 22.3 is given in Table 22.4. Verify that indegree (n_1) = 0 while outdegree (n_1) = 2.

A (directed) *path* is a sequence of edges joined from head to tail, *i.e.*, the end node of an edge is the start node of the next edge. A *cycle* is a path that begins and ends at the same node. A (*directed*) *semipath* is a sequence of edges such that at least one adjacent pair of edges, e_i and e_j share either a common start node or a common end node.

Table 22.4: The Adjacency Matrix of Graph in Fig. 22.3

	n_1	n_2	n_3	n_4	n_5	n_6	n_7
n_1	0	1	0	1	0	0	0
n_2	0	0	1	0	0	1	0
n_3	0	0	0	0	0	0	0
n_4	0	0	0	0	1	1	0
n_5	0	0	0	0	0	0	0
n_6	0	0	0	0	0	0	0
n_7	0	0	0	0	0	0	0

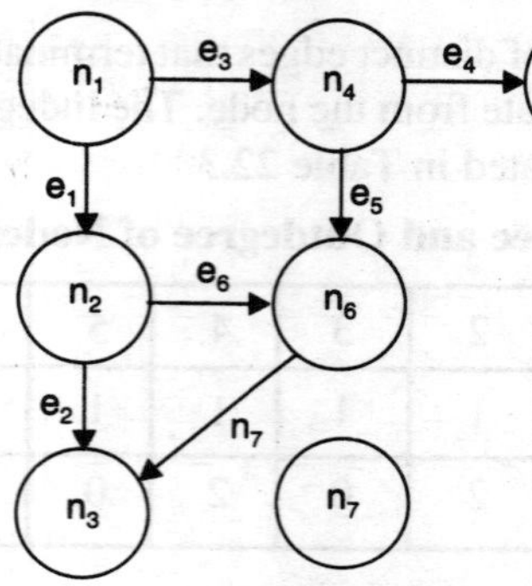

Fig. 22.4. A directed graph with a cycle

In Fig. 22.4, there is a path from n_1 to n_5, two paths from n_1 to n_6 ($n_1 - n_4 - n_6$ and $n_1 - n_2 - n_6$), a semipath between n_5 and n_6 (because n_4 is the common start node), a semipath between n_2 and n_4 (because they share a common start node n_1, or because they share a common end node n_6), and a cycle containing nodes n_2, n_6, and n_3. Notice that with the presence of a cycle the number of execution paths can be indefinitely large.

The *reachability matrix* of a graph is a matrix with nodes in both rows and columns whose *ij*th element is 1 if a path exists from n_i to n_j and is 0 otherwise. The reachability matrix of the graph in Fig. 22.3 is given in Table 22.5.

Table 22.5: The Reachability Matrix of Graph in Fig. 22.3

	n_1	n_2	n_3	n_4	n_5	n_6	n_7
n_1	0	1	1	1	1	1	0
n_2	0	0	1	0	0	1	0
n_3	0	1	0	0	0	1	0
n_4	0	0	1	0	1	1	0
n_5	0	0	0	0	0	0	0
n_6	0	1	1	0	0	0	0
n_7	0	0	0	0	0	0	0

The concept of connectedness introduced earlier can be extended for directed graphs in the following ways:

The nodes n_i and n_j are

0-*connected* if and only if no path exists between them;

1-*connected* if and only if a semipath, but no path, exists between them;

2-*connected* if and only if a path exists between them; and

3- *connected* if and only if a path goes from n_i to n_j and a path goes from n_j to n_i.

In the graph in Fig. 22.4, for example, n_1 and n_7 are 0-connected; n_5 and n_6 are 1-connected; n_1 and n_5 are 2-connected; and n_2 to n_3 are 3-connected.

A *strong component* of a directed graph is a maximal set of 3-connected nodes. In the graph in Fig. 22.4, the nodes n_2, n_6, and n_3 form a strong component and n_7 alone forms another strong component. Calling these strong components S_1 and S_2 we can represent the graph in Fig. 22.4 as a condensation graph (Fig. 22.5). Such a condensation graph is also called a *directed cyclic graph.* Notice that the number of execution paths of such a graph is drastically reduced.

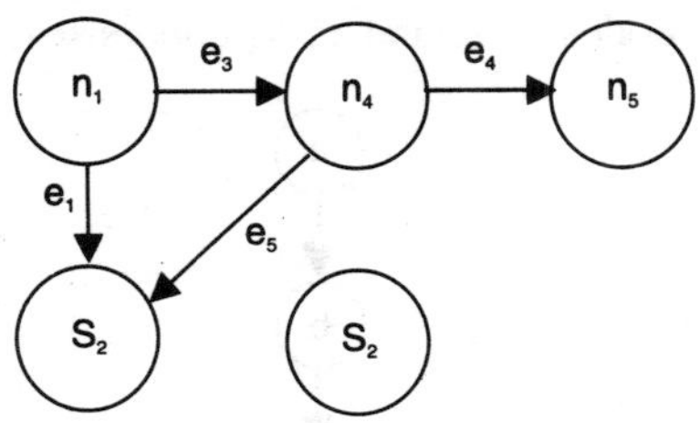

Fig. 22.5. Condensation graph for Fig. 22.4

At the end of the discussion on graph theory, we define subgraph, partial graph, and tree. A *subgraph,* G_S, of the graph G, contains a subset of nodes N and subset of edges E. A *partial graph,* G_P, contains all nodes in N but only a subset of E. A *tree,* G_T, is a partial graph which is connected but with no cycles.

22.1.2 Program Flow Graph

Application of graph theory to computer programming dates back to 1960 (Karp 1960). A program written in imperative programming language can be represented in a *program flow graph* (or *program graph* or *control graph*) where nodes represent statements or statement segments and edges represent flow of control. Thus a program flow graph is a graphical representation of flow of control from one statement to another in a program. A computer program has to have only one entry point but may have more than one exit point. In testing, program flow graph is very useful because it shows the execution paths from the start of a program to the end of the program, each of which can be exercised by a test case.

Two contiguous statements (*sequence*) are shown in Fig. 22.6*a*; an *if-then-else* statement is shown in Fig. 22.6*b*; a *repeat-while* loop is shown in Fig. 22.6*c*; and a *repeat-until* loop is shown as in Fig. 22.6*d*.

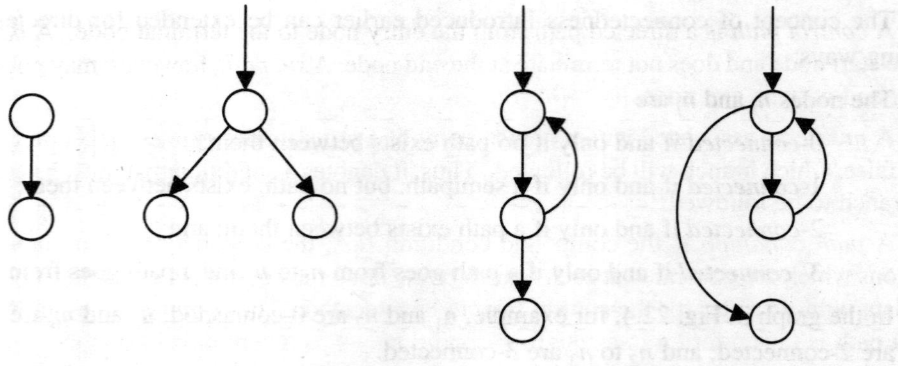

(*a*) Sequence (*b*) If-then-else (*c*) Repeat-while (*d*) Repeat-until

Fig. 22.6. Flow graph representation of basic program structures

Figure 22.7*a* gives a program logic (in the form of structured English) of a program that finds the maximum of a given set of *N* non-negative numbers and prints it; Figure 22.7*b* is its program flow graph; and Figure 22.7*c* is its condensation graph, where each sequence of statements is condensed into one node. Note that S_1 condenses nodes *a*, *b*, and *c*; S_3 condenses nodes *e* and *f*, while S_4 condenses nodes *g* and *h* of Fig. 22.7*b*.

a. Read N
b. MAX = 0
c. I = 1
d. While I <= N
e. Read X(I)
f. If X(I) > MAX
g. THEN MAX = X(I)
h. I = I + 1
i. PRINT MAX

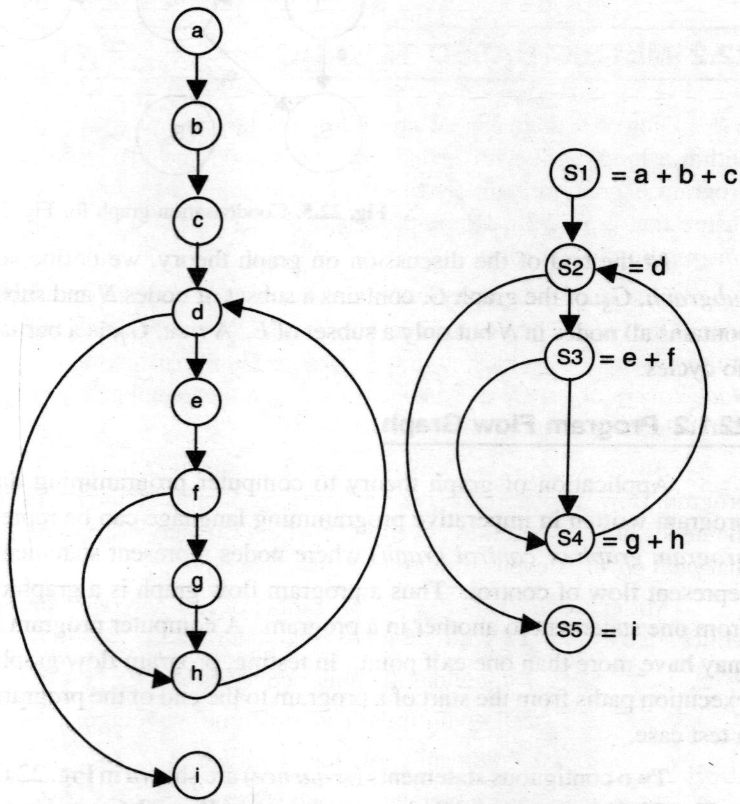

(*a*) Program Logic (*b*) Program Flow Graph (*c*) Condensation Graph

Fig. 22.7. The problem of finding the maximum of a set of numbers

A *control path* is a directed path from the entry node to the terminal node. A *partial path* starts with the start node and does not terminate at the end node. A *subpath*, however, may not start with a start node or end with an end node.

A *predicate* associated with a branch point of a program determines, depending on whether it is true or false, which branch will be followed. Thus, it denotes a condition that must be either true or false for a branch to be followed.

A *path condition* is the compound condition (*i.e.*, the conjunction of the individual predicate conditions which are generated at each branch point along the control path) that must be satisfied by the input data point in order for the control path to be executed. The conjunction of all branch predicates along a path is thus referred to as the path condition. A path condition, therefore, consists of a *set of constraints*, one for each predicate encountered on the path. Each constraint can be expressed as a program variable, and, in turn, as a function of input variables.

Depending on the input values, a path condition may or may not be satisfied. When satisfied, a control path becomes an *execution path*; otherwise the path is infeasible and is not used for testing. A control flow graph contains all paths — both executable and non-executable.

We shall discuss three forms of white-box testing. They are: (1) Metric-based testing, (2) Basis path testing, and (3) Data flow testing.

22.2 METRIC-BASED TESTING

Note that there can be a prohibitively large number of execution paths considering that the nodes within a loop can be traversed more than once and that each such loop traversal can lead to a new program execution path. Because it is impossible to generate test cases for all execution paths or to ensure that a program is completely error-free, usually we evaluate the extent to which a program is *covered* by the test cases.

One important objective of testing is to ensure that all parts of the program are tested at least once. One natural choice is to ensure that all statements are exercised at least once. Since the statements are represented by nodes, naturally, one would think that the tests should cover all the program nodes. *Node cover* (or *vertex* or *statement cover*) is thus a subgraph G' of the program flow graph G that is connected and contains all the nodes of G.

An *edge cover* is, however, a more general concept. An edge cover is a subgraph G'' of the program flow graph G that is connected and contains all the edges of G'. Note that G'' has to contain all the nodes of G. Therefore, an edge cover is also, and is stronger than, a node cover. We shall soon see that *path cover* is even stronger than the edge cover.

Miller (1977) has suggested a number of *test-coverage metrics*. Jorgensen (2002) has augmented Miller's list to give the following coverage metrics:

- C_0: Statement (or node) coverage
- C_1: DD-path (predicate outcome) coverage
- C_1p: Predicate-Outcome coverage
- C_2: C1 coverage + Loop coverage
- C_d: C1 coverage + Every dependent pair of DD-paths
- C_{MCC}: Multiple-condition coverage

p_1 = 1-6

p_2 = 1-2-3-4-5-6

p_3 = 1-2-7-5-6

p_4 = 1-2-7-5-2-3-4-5-6

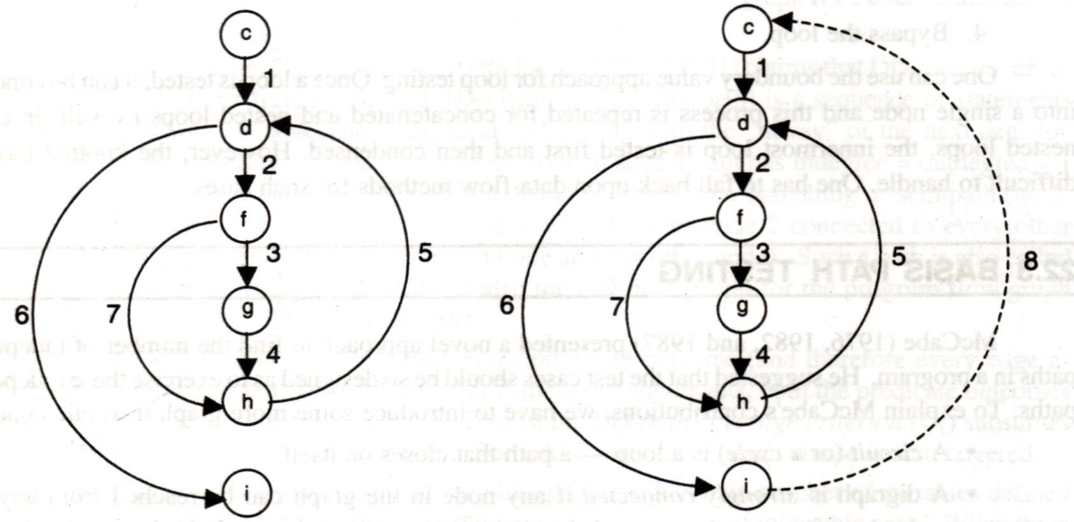

(a) Not Strongly Connected Program Flow Graph *(b)* Strongly Connected Program Flow Graph

Fig. 22.9. Program flow graphs without and with a phantom arc

Table 22.6 shows a *path-edge traversal matrix* for Fig. 22.9*a* whose entries indicate the number of times an edge is traversed in a path. The row entries (for a path) in the matrix help to define the corresponding vector. Thus the vectors associated with the paths are:

$$p_1 = (1\ 0\ 0\ 0\ 0\ 1\ 0),\ p_2 = (1\ 1\ 1\ 1\ 1\ 1\ 0),$$

$$p_3 = (1\ 1\ 0\ 0\ 1\ 1\ 1),\ p_4 = (1\ 2\ 1\ 1\ 2\ 1\ 1)$$

Using the basic knowledge of linear algebra, one can see that the vectors associated with the paths p_1, p_2, p_3 are independent. That means that any one of them cannot be expressed as linear combination of the other vectors. However, the vector p_4 can be expressed as a linear combination of the other three vectors. One can check that

$$p_4 = p_2 + p_3 - p_1$$

One could have defined p_1, p_2, and p_4 as linearly independent vectors and could express p_3 as a dependent vector, instead. Thus, whereas the set of linearly independent vectors is not unique, the number in the set is fixed. In our example, the maximum number of linearly independent vectors is three. These linearly independent vectors form a *basis*. *Basis path testing* derives its name from the concept of *basis* discussed here.

Table 22.6: Path-Edge Traversal Matrix

Path \ Edge	1	2	3	4	5	6	7
p_1	1	0	0	0	0	1	0
p_2	1	1	1	1	1	1	0
p_3	1	1	0	0	1	1	1
p_4	1	2	1	1	2	1	1

One can give a physical interpretation of independence of paths. One can observe that each independent path consists of at least one edge that is not present in any path defined as independent. For example, suppose we assume p_1 as an independent path to start with. When we consider path p_2 as independent, we see that it has the edges 2, 3, 4, and 5 which were not present in path p_1. Similarly, the path p_3 has the edge 7 which was not present in either of the previous two independent paths and hence qualifies to be an independent path. However, when we consider path p_4, we find that the path contains no edge that is not contained in the other paths. Hence, this path is not a linearly independent path.

If we associate a vector with each cycle in a program, we can extend the concept of independence to cycles as well. An *independent cycle* (also called *mesh* or *face*) is a loop with a minimum number of branches in a planar program flow graph (one which can be drawn on a sheet of paper with no branches crossing). McCabe considered the strongly connected planar graph such as the one in Fig. 22.9*b* and showed that the maximum number of independent paths in such a graph equals the maximum number of linearly independent cycles. In Fig. 22.9*b*, the independent cycles are given by

1 - 6 - 8, 2 - 3 - 4 - 5, and 2 - 7 - 5

A fourth cycle, 1 - 2 - 7 - 5 - 6 - 8, is also visible, but this cycle is not independent as it does not contain any edge that is not defined in the three cycles defined earlier. Therefore, the fourth cycle is not independent. McCabe defines the number of independent cycles in a planar program flow graph as its *cyclomatic complexity number* $\gamma(G)$. The word "cyclomatic" derives its name from the word "cycle". Incidentally, $\gamma(G)$, the maximum number of linearly independent cycles in a strongly connected program flow graph equals the maximum number of linearly independent paths in the program flow graph.

There are other methods to arrive at the value of $\gamma(G)$ of a program flow graph. We mention them here.

Formula-based method

$$\gamma(G) = m - n + p$$

where, m = number of edges, n = number of nodes, and p = number of parts in the graph. Usually, program flow chart contains only one part and so $p = 1$ for such a graph. Note that often a program flow graph is not strongly connected. To make it strongly connected, one adds a phantom arc and hence the number of edges increases by 1. Considering Fig. 22.9*a* (a program flow graph without a phantom arc), we see that $m = 7$ and $n = 6$. We take $p = 1$ and get $\gamma(G) = 7 - 6 + 2 = 3$. If, on the other hand, we consider Fig. 22.9*b* (a strongly connected program flow graph with the addition of a phantom arc), then we have $m = 8$, and $n = 6$, $p = 1$, and $\gamma(G) = 3$.

The Tree Method

The cyclomatic complexity number, γ (*G*), of a strongly connected non-directed graph *G* equals the minimum number of edges that must be removed from *G* to form a *tree*. Figure 22.9*b* is redrawn as a non-directed graph in Figure 22.10*a*. Three edges, 5, 7, and 8, can be removed from Figure 22.10*a* to yield a tree (Figure 22.10*b*).

The Branch Point Method

γ (*G*) equals the number of branch points (predicate nodes) in a strongly connected graph plus 1. In Fig. 22.9*b*, branching takes place at two nodes, *d* and *f*. Hence the number of predicate nodes is 2 and γ (*G*) equals 3 (= 2 + 1).

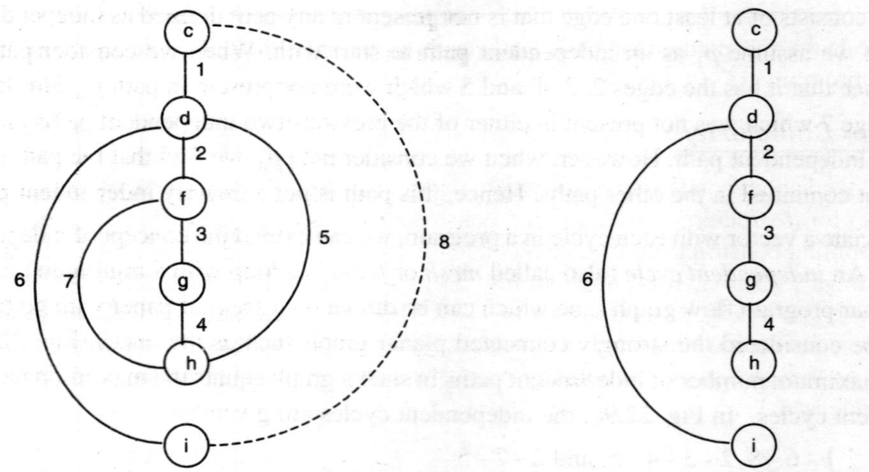

(*a*) Strongly Connected Undirected Graph (*b*) Tree Formed with Edges 5, 7, and 8 Removed

Fig. 22.10. Tree method of computing cyclomatic complexity number

22.3.2 Procedure for Generating Independent Paths

McCabe has recommended an algorithmic procedure to generate the independent paths. The procedure has the following steps:

1. Choose a path (the *baseline path*) with as many decision nodes as possible.
2. Retrace the path and flip each decision (*i.e.*, when a node of outdegree ≥ 2 is reached, a different edge is taken).

Applying the procedure in Fig. 22.9*a*, we get the baseline path 1 - 2 - 3 - 4 - 5 - 6 (step 1); flipping at node *d* we get the path 1 - 6 (step 2); and flipping at node *f* we get the path 1 - 2 - 7 - 5 - 6 (step 2).

22.3.3 Defining Paths and Test Cases

We now select the data values that will force the execution of these paths. The choice of the following data values will exercise the independent paths:

$N = 2$ with numbers $X(1) = 7$ and $X(2) = 8$ will exercise the baseline path 1 - 2 - 3 - 4 - 5 - 6.

$N = 0$ with no numbers given will exercise the path 1-6.

$N = 2$ with numbers $X(1) = 7$ and $X(2) = 6$ will exercise the path 1 - 2 - 7 - 5 - 6.

The test cases are specified in Table 22.7.

Table 22.7: Test Cases for the Maximum-Number-Finding Problem

Path	Input values	Expected output
p_1 (1-6)	N = 0 (The input record is empty with no data value)	MAX = 0
p_2 (1-2-3-4-4-5-6)	N = 2, X(1) = 7, X(2) = 8	MAX = 8
p_3 (1-2-7-5-6)	N = 2, X(1) = 7, X(2) = 6	MAX = 7

Before we leave the method of basis path testing, we should shed some light on "essential complexity" of a program.

22.3.4 Essential Complexity

We have talked about condensed graph where nodes in sequence could be condensed. Branching and repetition also form structured programming constructs. Suppose a program is written with only structured programming constructs and we also condense the branching and repetition constructs, then the program will have $\gamma(G) = 1$. It is shown in Fig. 22.11 for the graph in Fig. 22.7*b*. We see that the final condensation graph in Fig. 22.11*c* has a $\gamma(G) = 1$. Thus, the cyclomatic complexity number of a program graph with structured programming constructs, which is condensed, is always 1. *Essential complexity* refers to the cyclomatic complexity number of a program where structured programming constructs are condensed.

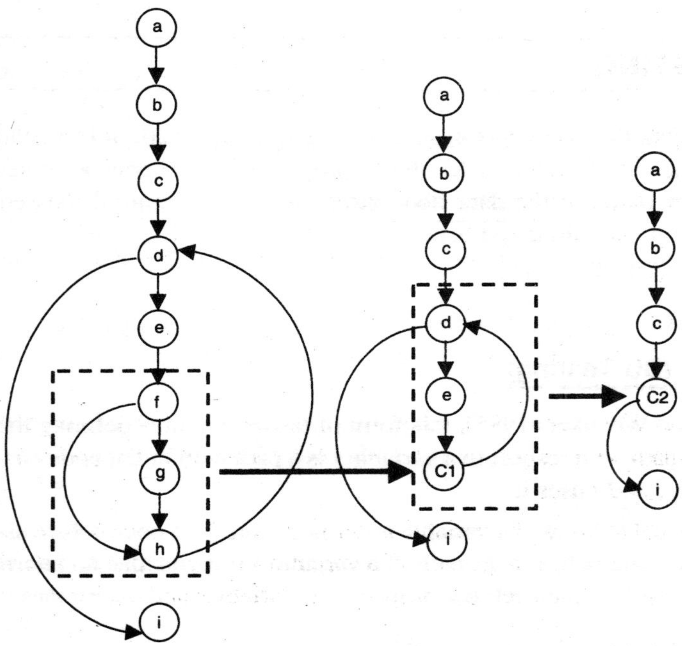

(*a*) The Original Graph (*b*) Condensing the Branching Structure (*c*) Condensing the Repetition Structure

Fig. 22.11. Graph after condensing the structured programming constructs

In practice, however, a program may contain many "unstructures" (a term used by McCabe 1982) such as those given in Fig. 22.12. In the presence of such unstructures, the essential complexity will be always more than 1.

In general, basis path testing is good if $\gamma(G) \le 10$. If $\gamma(G) > 10$, then the program is highly error prone. Two options are available for such programs:

1. If essential complexity > 1, then remove the unstructures.
2. Carry out more number of testing than what the basis path testing suggests.

In any case, it is clear that $\gamma(G)$ provides only a lower bound for number of tests to be carried out. More details are given by Shooman (1983).

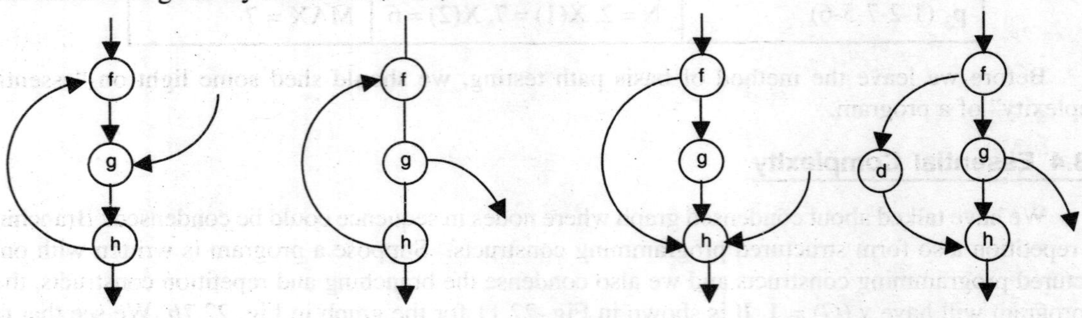

Fig. 22.12. Unstructures in program flow graphs

22.4 DATA FLOW TESTING

We have already used data flow concepts in static testing in Chapter 20. It is essentially a form of structured testing because one uses the internal details of a program. The material presented in Chapter 20 provides the foundation for much of the data flow-based structured testing discussed here. Two popular forms of data flow testing are discussed here:

1. Define/Use Testing (DU Testing)
2. Slice-Based Testing

22.4.1 Define/Use Testing (DU Testing)

Developed by Rapps and Weyuker (1985), this form of testing requires defining the *definition-use* paths (the *du-paths*). A du-path with respect to a variable *v* is a path with initial node *i* and final node *j*, such that *i* defines the variable and *j* uses it.

Since we are also interested to know if a variable is defined more than once before use, we define a *du-clear path* (*dc-path*). A dc-clear path is a du-path of a variable *v* if it contains no internal node that defines the variable. Given a program, one finds out du-paths for variables and determines whether they are definition-clear.

We draw Fig. 22.7 once again, and name it Fig. 22.13, to find out the du-paths for various variables and to check whether they are du-clear. Recall that Fig. 22.13*c* — the condensation graph for the program (Fig. 22.13*b*) to find the maximum of a set of non-negative numbers — is also the DD-path graph for the problem. Recall also that each node of this graph represents a DD-path. For example, the node S1 in Fig. 22.13*b* indicates the DD-path *a-b-c*.

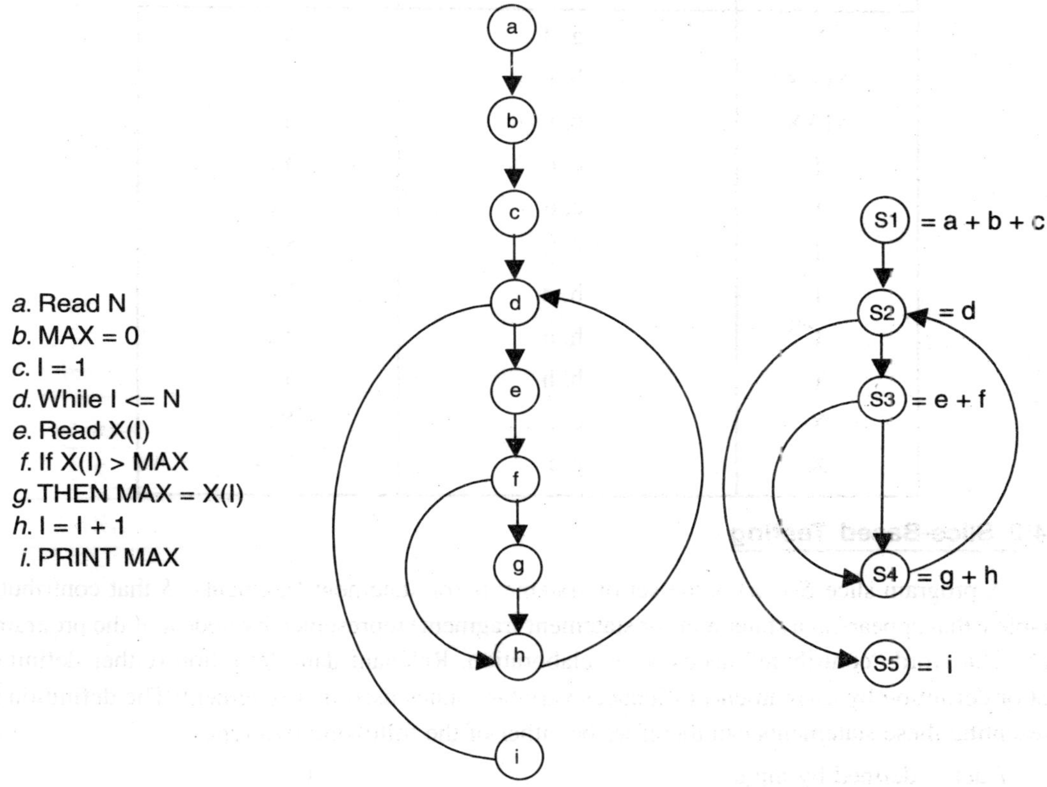

(*a*) Program Logic (*b*) Program Flow Graph (*c*) Condensation Graph

Fig. 22.13. The problem of finding the maximum of a set of numbers

Table 22.8 gives the nodes where each variable used in the program is defined and used. Table 22.9 gives the du-paths for each variable and writes whether each path is du-clear. That all the du-paths are du-clear is itself a good test of the correctness of the program. Note that in constructing Table 22.8 and Table 22.9 we have made use of the code given in Fig. 22.13*a*.

Define/Use testing provides intermediate metrics between the two extremes: All-paths coverage and All-nodes coverage.

Table 22.8: Define/Use Nodes for Variables

Variable	Defined at nodes	Used at nodes
N	a	d
MAX	b	f, i
I	c, h	d, e, h
X	e, g	f

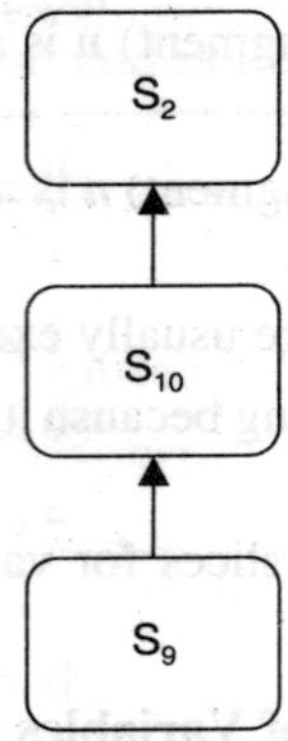

Fig. 22.14. Lattice of slices on MAX

Slices help to trace the definition and use of particular variables. It is also possible to code, compile, and test slices individually. Although slice-based testing is still evolving, it appears to provide a novel way of testing programs.

22.5 WHITE-BOX OBJECT-ORIENTED TESTING

As indicated earlier, white-box object-oriented tests can be performed considering either methods or classes as units. When methods are used as units, program flow graphs are useful aids for generating test cases. Testing with classes as units is preferred when very little inheritance occurs and when there is a good amount of internal messaging (*i.e.*, when the class is high on cohesion). Statechart representation of class behaviour is quite helpful here in generating test cases. The coverage metrics can be every event, or every state, or every transition.

REFERENCES

Jorgensen, P. C. (2002), Software Testing: A Craftsman's Approach, Boca Raton: CRC Press, Second Edition.

Karp, R. M. (1960), A Note on the Application of Graph Theory to Digital Computer Programming, Information and Control, vol. 3, pp. 179–190.

McCabe, T. J. (1976), A Complexity Metric, IEEE Trans. on Software Engineering, SE-2, 4, pp. 308–320.

McCabe, T. J. (1982), Structural Testing: A Software Testing Methodology Using the Cyclomatic Complexity Metric, National Bureau of Standards (Now NIST), Special Publication 500–599, Washington, D.C.

McCabe, T. J. (1987), Structural Testing: A Software Testing Methodology Using the Cyclomatic Complexity Metric, McCabe and Associates, Baltimore.

Miller, E. F. (1977), Tutorial: Program Testing Techniques, COPSAC '77 IEEE Computer Society.

Miller, E. F., Jr. (1991), Automated Software Testing: A Technical perspective, American Programmer, vol. 4, no. 4, April, pp. 38–43.

Rapps, S. and Weyuker, E. J. (1985), Selecting Software Test Data Using Data Flow Information, IEEE Transactions on Software Engineering, vol. SE-11, no. 4, pp. 367–375.

Shooman, M. L. (1983), Software Engineering: Design, Reliability and Management, McGraw-Hill International Edition, Singapore.

23 Integration and Higher-level Testing

After the detailed discussion on unit testing in the last four chapters, we take up the higher-level testing in this chapter. We cover integration testing, application system testing, and system-level testing in this chapter. In integration testing, one tests whether the tested units, when integrated, yields the desired behaviour. In the application system testing, one tests whether the application yields the correct response to inputs provided externally. In the system-level testing, one tests whether the application responds in a predictable manner to inputs from its environment that consist of hardware, communication channel, personnel, and procedures.

23.1 INTEGRATION TESTING

Recall that integration testing corresponds to the preliminary design of a program. In the preliminary design of a program, various modules, along with their individual functions, are identified and their interfaces are specified. In the structured design approach, the output of the preliminary design phase is the structure chart that shows the modules of a program and their interfaces. During integration testing, various unit-tested modules are integrated and tested in order to ensure that module interfaces are compatible with one another in such a way that desired outputs are obtained.

Jorgensen (2002) suggests three forms of integration testing:

1. Decomposition-Based Integration testing.
2. Call Graph-Based Integration testing.
3. MM Path-Based Integration testing.

23.1.1 Decomposition-Based Integration

This classical form of integration testing uses the control hierarchy (structure chart) of the program. It consists of the following classical testing methods:

1. Big-Bang Integration
2. Incremental Integration
   a. Top-Down Integration
      – Depth-first
      – Breadth-first
   b. Bottom-Up Integration

The *big-bang method* basically means testing the complete software with all the modules combined. This is the worst form of carrying out an integration test. Here a lot of errors surface simultaneously at one time and it is almost impossible to find out their causes. Thus, it is not at all advisable to adopt a big-bang approach to integration testing.

Incremental Integration

Here two unit-tested modules are combined and tested, to start with. The surfacing errors, if any, are less in number and are rather easy to detect and remove. Thereafter, another module is combined with this combination of modules. These combination modules are tested, and the process continues till all modules are integrated. The following is a list of advantages of incremental integration:

- Mismatching errors and errors due to inter-modular assumptions are less in number and hence easy to detect and remove.
- Debugging is easy.
- Tested programs are tested again and again, thereby enhancing the confidence of the model builder.

Top-Down Integration

Top-down integration is a form of incremental approach where the modules are combined from the top (the main control module) downwards according to their position in the control hierarchy (such as a structure chart), and tested. Thus, to start with, the main module is integrated with one of its immediate subordinate modules.

Choice of the subordinate modules can follow either a *depth-first* or a *breadth-first* strategy. In the former, the subordinate modules are integrated one after another. Thus it results in a vertical integration. In the latter strategy, the modules that appear in the same hierarchical level are integrated first, resulting in a horizontal integration.

Figure 23.1 shows a structure chart. Data is read by module M_4 and the results are printed by modules M_7. Data passing among modules are shown in the structure chart.

In a top-down approach, there is no need to have a fictitious driver module. But it requires the use of stubs in the place of lower level modules. The functions of stubs are to (1) receive data from the modules under test and (2) pass test case data to the modules under test.

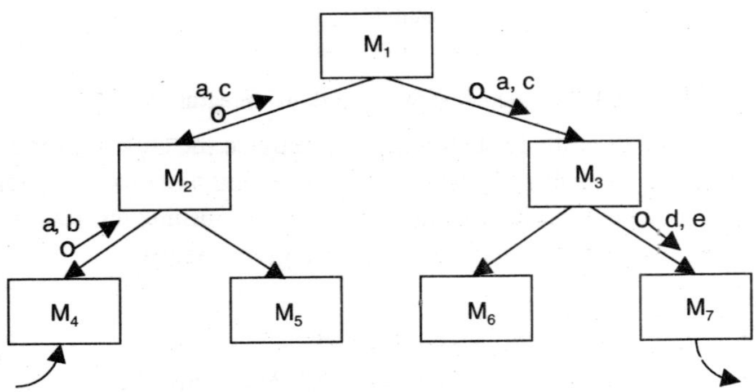

Fig. 23.1. Top-down integration of modules

To actually implement the top-down, breadth-first strategy, one has to first test the topmost (main) module M_1 by using stubs for modules M_2 and M_3 (Fig. 23.2). The function of the stub M_2, when called by module M_1, is to pass data *a* and *c* to M_1. The main module must pass these data to the stub M_3. The function of stub M_3, when called by M_1, is to receive data *a* and *c* (and possibly display an OK message).

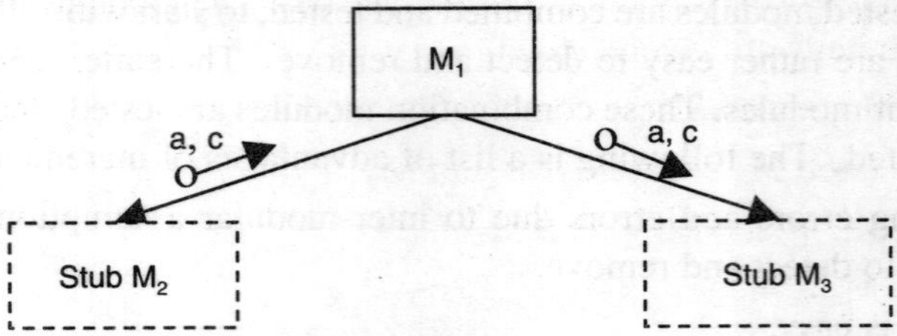

Fig. 23.2. The first step in top-down strategy-testing of the top (Main) module

The second step in the top-down strategy is to replace one of the stubs by the actual module. We need to add stubs for the subordinate modules of the replacing module. Let us assume that we replace stub M_2 by the actual module M_2. Notice in Fig. 23.1 that the modules M_4 and M_5 are the low-level modules as far as the module M_2 is concerned. We thus need to have the stubs for modules M_4 and M_5. Figure 23.3 shows the second step. The main module M_1 calls module M_2 which, in turn, calls stub M_4 and stub M_5. Stub M_4 passes data *a* and *b* to module M_2 which passes data *b* to stub M_5. Stub M_5 passes data *d* to module M_2. The module now processes these data and passes data *a* and *c* to the main module M_1.

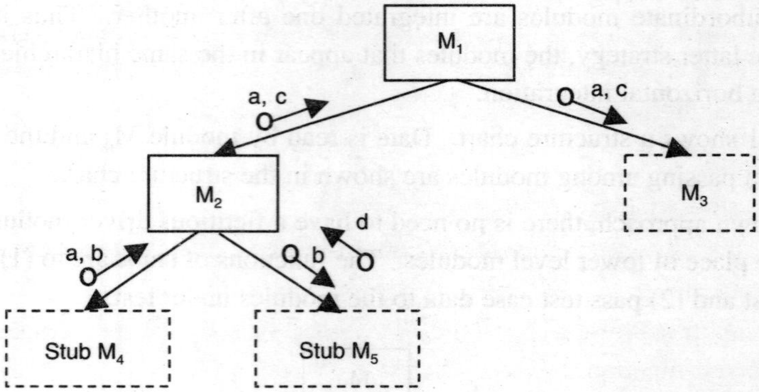

Fig. 23.3. The second step in top-down integration of modules

In the third step of the breadth-first strategy, we replace the stub M_3 by the actual module M_3 and add stubs for its subordinate modules M_6 and M_7 and proceed as before. Needless to say that next we substitute the stub M_4 by its actual module M_4 and test it, then continue with this process for the remaining stubs. The modules to be integrated in various steps are given below:

- M_1 + stub M_2 + stub M_3
- $M_1 + M_2$ + (stub M_4 + stub M_5) + stub M_3
- $M_1 + M_2$ + stub M_4 + stub M_5 + M_3 + (stub M_6 + stub M_7)
- $M_1 + M_2 + M_4$ + stub M_5 + M_3 + stub M_6 + stub M_7
- $M_1 + M_2 + M_4 + M_5 + M_3$ + stub M_6 + stub M_7

- $M_1 + M_2 + M_4 + M_5 + M_3 + M_6$ + stub M_7
- $M_1 + M_2 + M_4 + M_5 + M_3 + M_6 + M_7$

In the depth-first strategy, the third step is to replace stub M_4 by its actual module M_4. The successive steps will involve replacing stub M_5 by its actual module M_5, replacing stub M_3 by the actual module M_3 (while adding stubs for its subordinate modules M_6 and M_7), replacing stub M_6 by the actual modules M_6, and replacing stub M_7 by the actual module M_7. The modules to be integrated in various steps in the depth-first strategy are given below:

- M_1 + stub M_2 + stub M_3
- $M_1 + M_2$ + (stub M_4 + stub M_5) + stub M_3
- $M_1 + M_2 + M_4$ + stub M_5 + stub M_3
- $M_1 + M_2 + M_4 + M_5$ + stub M_3
- $M_1 + M_2 + M_4 + M_5 + M_3$ + (stub M_6 + stub M_7)
- $M_1 + M_2 + M_4 + M_5 + M_3 + M_6$ + stub M_7
- $M_1 + M_2 + M_4 + M_5 + M_3 + M_6 + M_7$

As one may notice, stubs play important role in top-down strategy. However, the design of a stub can be quite complicated because it involves passing a test case to the module being tested. In case the stub represents an output module, then the output of the stub is the result of the test being conducted for examination. Thus, when module M_1 is tested, the results are to be outputted through the stub M_3.

Often, more than one test case is required for testing a module. In such a case, multiple versions of a stub are required. An alternative is for the stub to read data for test cases from an external file and return them to the module during the call operation.

Another problem with the use of stubs is faced while testing an output module. When testing M_3 while following the breadth-first strategy, for example, test case data are to be inputted through stub M_4 with many intervening modules separating the two modules.

Bottom-Up Integration

A bottom-up strategy (Myers, 1979) consists of

(*a*) Testing, one by one, the terminal, bottom-level modules that do not call any subordinate modules.

(*b*) Combining these low-level modules into *clusters* (or *builds*) that together perform a specific software sub-function.

(*c*) Using drivers to coordinate test case input and output.

(*d*) Testing the clusters.

(*e*) Continuing with the similar testing operations while moving upward in the structure chart.

In Fig. 23.4, D_1 and D_2 are driver modules and cluster 1 consists of modules M_4 and M_5, whereas cluster 2 consists of modules M_6 and M_7. When the testing of these modules is complete, the drivers are removed, and they are thereafter integrated with the module immediately at their top. That is, cluster 1 is interfaced with module M_2 and the new cluster is tested with a new driver, whereas cluster 2 forms a new cluster with M_3 and is tested with the help of a new driver. This process continues till all the modules are integrated and tested.

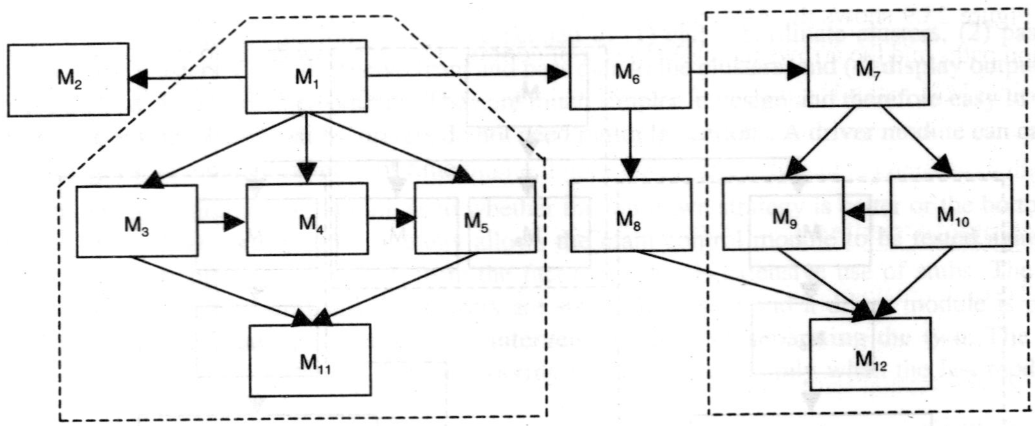

Fig. 23.7. Neighbourhood integration of modules in call graph

23.1.3 MM Path-Based Integration

A *module-to-module path* (*MM path*)) describes a sequence of model execution paths that include transfer of control (via call statements or messages) from one module to another. A *module execution path* is the sequence of statements in a module that are exercised during program execution before the control is transferred to another module. Figure 23.8 shows three modules A, B, and C, with nodes representing program statements and edges showing transfer of control. The series of thick lines indicate an MM path (in a program written in procedural language). The module execution paths (MEPs) in various modules are:

MEP(A, 1): <1, 3>; MEP(A, 2): <4, 5>; MEP(A, 3): <1, 3, 4, 5>; MEP(A, 4): <1, 2, 4, 5>; MEP(B, 1): <1, 2, 4>; MEP(B, 2): <5, 6>; MEP(B, 3): <1, 2, 4, 5, 6>; MEP(B, 4): <1, 2, 3, 5, 6>; MEP(C, 1): <1, 2, 3, 4>.

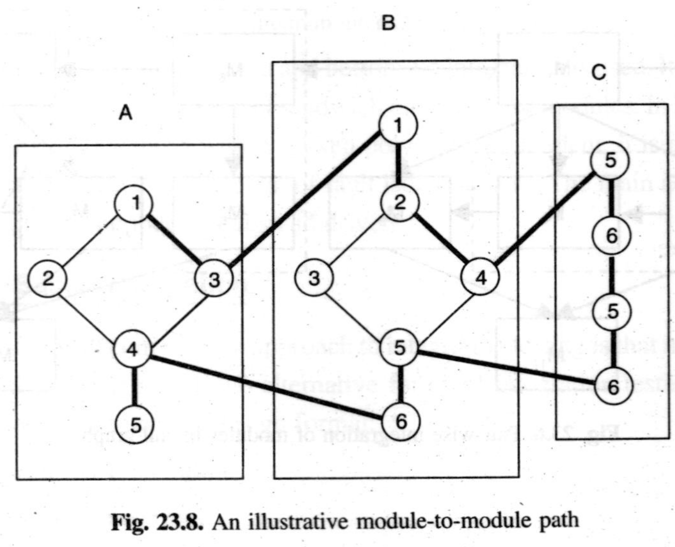

Fig. 23.8. An illustrative module-to-module path

Figure 23.9 shows the MM path graph for the above problem. The nodes indicate the module execution paths and the arrows indicate transfer of control. One can now develop test cases to exercise the possible MM paths.The merits of this method are: (1) the absence of stubs and drivers and (2) its applicability to object-oriented testing. The demerits are: (1) the additional effort necessary to draw an MM path graph and (2) the difficulty in isolating the faults.

23.1.4 Object-Oriented Integration Testing

Three alternative ways of integration testing can be visualized:

1. Integration testing based on UML diagrams.
2. Integration testing based on MM paths.
3. Integration testing based on data flows.

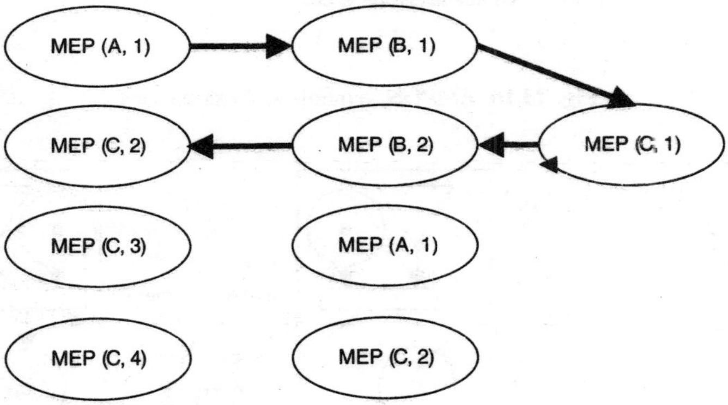

Fig. 23.9. MM path graph for the case in Fig. 23.8

The (UML-based) collaboration and sequence diagrams are the easiest means for integration testing of object-oriented software. The former permits both pair-wise and neighbourhood integration of classes. Two adjacent classes (between which messages flow) can be pair-wise integration tested with other supporting classes acting as stubs. Neighbourhood integration is not restricted to only two adjacent classes. A class and all its adjacent classes can be integration tested with one test case. Classes, two edges away, can be integrated later.

A sequence diagram shows various method execution-time paths. One can design a test case by following a specific execution-time path.

In object-oriented testing, MM path is the *Method/Message path.* It starts with a method, includes all methods that are invoked by the sequence of messages (including and the methods that are internal to a class) that are sent to carry them out, includes the return paths, and ends with a method that does not need any more messages to be sent. One can thus design test cases to invoke an MM path for an operation/method. Such a starting operation/method could preferably be a system operation/method. Note that integration testing based on Method/Message path is independent of whether the unit testing was carried out with units as methods or classes.

Data flow-based integration testing is possible for object-oriented software. Jorgensen (2002) proposes *event- and message-driven Petri nets* (EMDPN) by defining new symbols given in Fig. 23.10. A Petri net with the extended set of symbols allows representation of class inheritance and define/use paths (du paths) similar to code in procedural language. Figure 23.11 shows an alternating sequence of data places and message execution paths representing class inheritance.

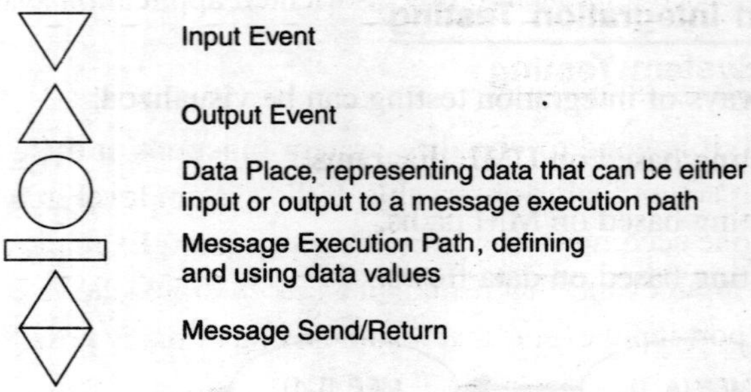

Fig. 23.10. EMPDN symbols and exlanations

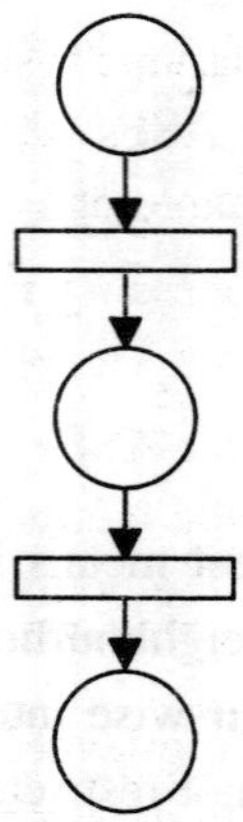

Fig. 23.11. Inheritance in EMPDN

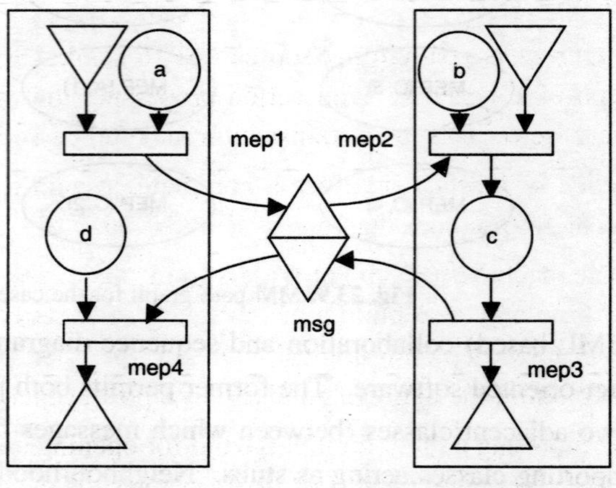

Fig. 23.12. Data flow by messaging

One can now define a define/use path (du path) in such an EMPDN. For example, Fig. 23.12 shows messages being passed from one object to another. Assuming that *mep*1 is a define node that defines a data that is passed on by *mep*2, modified by *mep*3, and used by *mep*4. The du paths are given by

du 1 = <mep1, mep2, c, mep3, mep4>

du 2 = <mep3, mep4>

Following the ideas given earlier, one can check whether the path is definition clear. In the above example, du 1 is not definition clear (because the data is redefined by *mep*3 before being used) whereas du 2 is. Further, one can design test cases accordingly.

23.2 APPLICATION SYSTEM TESTING

In application system testing we test the application for its performance and conformance to requirement specifications. So we test the software from a functional rather than a structural viewpoint. Therefore, testing is less formal. In what follows, we shall discuss a thread-based system testing and indicate its use in an FSM-based approach to object-oriented application system testing.

23.2.1 Thread-Based System Testing

At the system level, it is good to visualize system functions at their atomic levels. An *atomic system function* (*ASF*) is an action that is observable at the system level in terms of port input and port output events with at least one accompanying stimulus-repair pair. Examples of atomic system function are: entry of a digit (a port input event) that results in a screen digit echo (a port output event) and entry of an employee number (a port input event) that results in one of many possible outcomes (a port output event).

An ASF graph of a system is a directed graph in which nodes are ASFs and edges represent sequential flows. Data entry is an example of a *source ASF* whereas termination of a session is an example of *sink ASF*.

A *system thread* is a path from a source ASF to a sink ASF (a sequence of atomic system functions) in the ASF graph of a system. Transaction processing that involves several ASFs, such as entering employee number, selecting type of transaction to be processed, etc., is an example of a system thread.

A *sequence of threads* involves a complete session that involves processing more than one transaction, and therefore more than one system thread.

Finite state machines (FSMs) provide a good way to graphically portray the ASFs and the system testing threads. One may also build a hierarchy of finite state machines (like the hierarchy of DFDs), with the top-level FSM depicting logical events (rather than port events) and the bottom-level FSMs progressively exploding the aggregated nodes into port events.

Consider inputting a three-digit password for opening an application. A top-level FSM is shown in Fig. 23.13. A second-level FSM (Fig. 23.14) shows the details of entering the password three times. Figure 23.15 shows a third-level FSM for port-level entry of each digit of the password.

Thus, we see that finite state machines can be constructed at different levels. Accordingly, threads can be identified and test cases can be constructed at different levels. It is good to proceed from bottom level FSM upward.

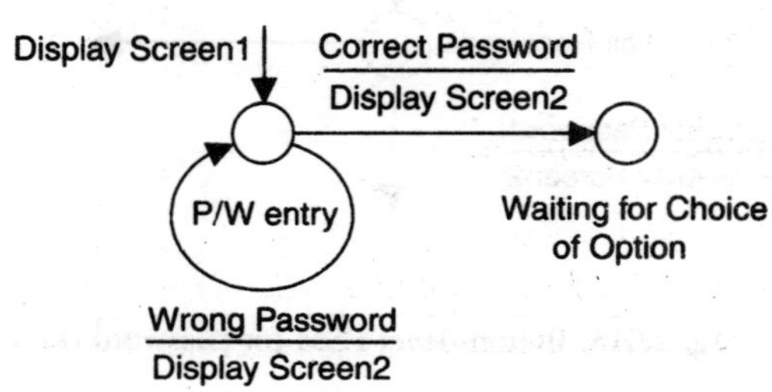

Fig. 23.13. Top-level FSM for password entry

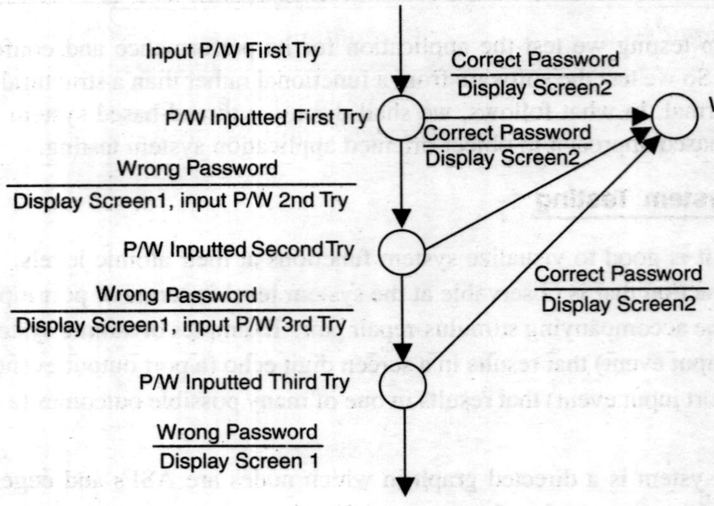

Fig. 23.14. Top-level FSM for password entry

An example of a thread path for the correct entry of a password in the second try depicted in the FSM in Fig. 23.14 and Fig. 23.15 is given in Table 23.1.

We have four thread paths for the case of password entry as tabulated in Table 23.2. These paths help in constructing the test cases.

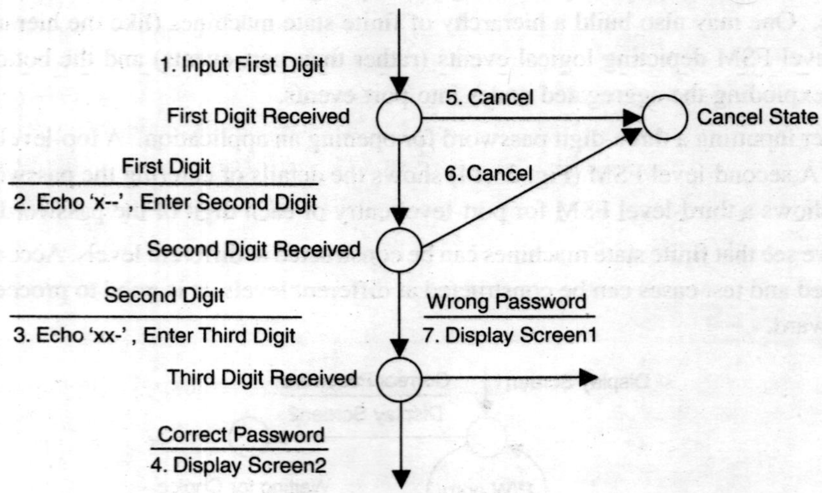

Fig. 23.15. Bottom-level FSM for password entry

Table 23.1: Port-Event Sequence in the Second Try

Port input event	Port output event
	Screen 1, displays '---'
P Entered	Screen 1, displays 'x–'
Q Entered	Screen 1, displays 'xx-'
J Entered	Screen 1, displays 'xxx'
(Wrong Password)	
(Second Try)	Screen 1, displays '---'
P Entered	Screen 1, displays 'x–'
K Entered	Screen 1, displays 'xx-'
J Entered	Screen 1, displays 'xxx'
(Correct Password)	Screen 2 appears

Table 23.2: Thread Paths in Fig. 23.15

Input event sequence (Thread)	Transition path
PKJ	1, 2, 3, 4
$P_{\underline{C}}$	1, 5
$PK_{\underline{C}}$	1, 2, 6
PLJ	1, 2, 3, 7

23.2.2 Object-Oriented Application System Testing

Real use cases developed during the phase of requirements analysis in the case of object-oriented application system testing provide useful information on the input events, system responses, and postconditions. Such information can be used to construct finite state machines for applications developed in object-oriented approach. Once the finite state machines are developed, threads and test cases can be developed.

23.3 SYSTEM TESTING

As indicated in Chapter 19, system tests can be grouped as structural system tests and functional system tests. We discuss them in detail here.

23.3.1 Structural System Testing Techniques

Software does not perform in isolation. It works in an environment that has hardware, persons, and procedures. Tested and otherwise good software may face many problems while operating in a particular environment. Although a software developer is not entirely responsible to look at these anticipated problems, it is desirable that the developer takes steps to see that many of these problems do not occur. Structural system testing techniques can be of many types (Perry, 2001):

- Stress testing
- Performance (or Execution) testing
- Recovery testing
- Operations testing
- Compliance testing
- Security testing

Stress Tests

Often, during implementation, software has to handle abnormally high volume of transactions and data, and input of large numerical values and large complex queries to a database system, etc. Unless anticipated, these situations can stress the system and can adversely affect the software performance in the form of slow communication, low processing rate due to non-availability of enough disk space, system overflow due to insufficient storage space for tables, queues, and internal storage facilities, and the like. Stress tests require running the software with abnormally high volumes of transactions. Such transactions may be

- a subset of past transactions,
- generated by test-data generators, or
- created by the testers.

Very important for on-line applications (where volume of transactions is uncertain), it can also be used for batch processing. Unfortunately, the test preparation and execution time in such cases is very high. In a batch processing system, the batch size can be increased whereas in an online system, the number of transactions should be inputted at an above-normal pace.

Stress tests are required when the volume of transactions the software can handle cannot be estimated very easily.

Performance (or Execution) Tests

Performance (or Execution) tests help to determine the level of system efficiency during the implementation of the software. In particular, the following items are tested:

- Response time to on-line user requests.
- Transaction processing turnaround time.
- Optimum use of hardware and software.
- Design performance.

These tests can be carried out

- On the entire software or a part thereof.
- Using the actual system or its simulation model.
- In any of the following ways:
  - Using hardware and software monitoring.
  - Simulating the function of the system or the intended part of the system.
  - Creating a quick rough-cut program (or prototype) to evaluate the approximate performance of a completed system.

Performance tests should be carried out before the complete software is developed so that early information is available on the system performance and necessary modification, if any, can be made.

Recovery Tests

Often, software failure occurs during operation. Such a disaster can take place due to a variety of reasons: manual operations, loss of communication lines, power failure, hardware or operating system failure, loss of data integrity, operator error, or even application system failure. Recovery is the ability to restart the software operation after a disaster strikes such that no data is lost. A recovery test evaluates the software for its ability to restart operations. Specifically, the test evaluates the adequacy of

- The backup data,
- The security of the storage location of the backup data,
- The documentation of the recovery procedures,
- The training of recovery personnel, and
- The availability of the recovery tools.

Usually, judgment and checklist are used for evaluation. Often, however, disasters are simulated, by inducing a failure into the system. Inducing single failure at a time is considered better than inducing multiple failures, because it is easy to pinpoint a cause for the former.

Usually, a failure is induced in one of the application programs by inserting a special instruction to look for a transaction code. When that code is identified, an abnormal program termination takes place. Usually, computer operators and clerical personnel are involved in recovery testing, just as they would be in a real-life disaster. An estimate of loss due to failure to recover within various time spans, (5, 10 minutes, etc.) helps to decide the extent of resources that one should put in recovery testing.

Recovery tests are preferred whenever the application requires continuity of service.

Operations Test

Normal operating personnel execute application software using the stated procedures and documentation. Operations tests verify that these operating personnel can execute the software without difficulty. Operations tests ensure that

- The operator instruction documentation is complete.
- Necessary support mechanisms, such as job control language, are prepared.
- The file labeling and protection procedures function properly.
- Operator training is adequate.
- Operating staff can operate the system using the documentation.

Operations testing activities involve evaluation of the operational requirements delineated in the requirements phase, operating procedures included in the design phase, and their actual realization in the coding and delivery phases. These tests are to be carried out obviously prior to the implementation of the software.

Compliance Tests

Compliance tests are used to ensure that the standards, procedures, and guidelines were adhered to during the software development process, and the system documentation is reasonable and complete.

The standards could be company, industry, or ISO standards. The best way to carry out these tests is by peer review or inspection process of an SRS, or design documentation, a test plan, a piece of code, or the software documentation. Noncompliance could mean that the company standards are (*a*) not fully developed, or (*b*) poorly developed, or (*c*) not adequately publicized, or (*d*) not followed rigorously.

Compliance testing helps in reducing software errors, reducing cost of change in composition of software development team, and in enhancing maintainability.

Security Tests

In a multiple-user environment, it is difficult to secure the confidentiality of information. Unauthorized users can play foul with the system, often leading to data loss, entry of erroneous data, and even to leakage of vital information to competitors. Security tests evaluate the adequacy of protective procedures and countermeasures. They take various forms:

- Defining the resources that need protection.
- Evaluating the adequacy of security measures.
- Assessing the risks involved in case of security lapse.
- Defining access to parts of the software according to user needs.
- Testing that the designed secured measures are properly implemented.

Security tests are important when application resources are of significant value to the organization. These tests are carried out both before and after the software is implemented.

23.3.2 Functional System Testing Techiniques

Functional testing techniques are applied to the entire product and are concerned with what the assembled product does. They can be the following:

- Requirements testing technique
- Regression testing technique
- Error-handling testing technique
- Manual-support testing technique
- Inter-system testing technique
- Control testing technique
- Parallel testing technique

Requirements Testing Technique

Requirements testing helps to verify that the system can perform its function correctly and over a continuous period of time (reliably). For this, it verifies if the following conditions are satisfied:

(*a*) All the primary user requirements are implemented.

(*b*) Security user needs (those of database administrator, internal auditors, controller, security officer, record retention, etc.) are included.

(*c*) Application system processes information as per government regulations.

(*d*) Application system processes accounting information as per the generally accepted accounting procedures.

Usually, test conditions are created here directly from user requirements.

Regression Testing Technique

It assures that all aspects of an application system remain functional after testing and consequent introduction of a change. Here one tests if

(*a*) System documentation remains current after a change.

(*b*) System test data and test conditions remain current.

(*c*) Previously tested functions perform correctly after the introduction of changes.

It involves (*a*) rerunning previously conducted tests, (*b*) reviewing previously prepared manual procedures, and (*c*) taking a printout from a data dictionary to ensure that the documentation for data elements that have been changed is correct.

Error-handling Testing Technique

It determines the ability of the application system to properly process incorrect transactions and conditions. Often a brainstorming exercise is conducted among a group (consisting of experienced IT staff, users, auditors, etc.) to list the probable unexpected conditions. On the basis of this list, a set of test transactions is created. The error-handling cycle includes the following functions:

(*a*) Introduce errors or create error conditions,

(*b*) Recognize the error conditions,

(*c*) Correct the errors, and

(*d*) Reenter the corrected error condition in another cycle.

Manual-support Testing Technique

Preparing data and using processed data are usually manual. The manual support tests ensure that (*a*) manual-support procedures are documented and completed; (*b*) the responsibility for providing the manual support is assigned; (*c*) the manual-support people are adequately trained; and (*d*) the manual support and the automated segment are properly interfaced. To conduct the test, (*a*) the expected form of the data may be given to the input persons for inputting them into the system, and (*b*) the output reports may be given to users for taking necessary action.

Inter-System Testing

Often the application system under consideration is connected with other systems, where either data or control or both pass from one system to another. Here one particular difficulty is that these systems are under the control of various authorities.

Control Testing

These tests ensure that processing is done so that desired management intents (the system of internal controls) with regard to data validation, file integrity, audit trail, backup and recovery, and documentation are satisfied. These tests ensure (*a*) accurate and complete data, (*b*) authorized transactions, and (*c*) maintenance of an adequate audit trail.

Parallel Testing

Here the same input data is run through two versions of the same application. It can be applied to a complete application or to a segment only. It ensures that the new application delivers the same result as that delivered by the old application.

Acceptance (or Validation) Test

After the integration test, the software is ready as a package. Before delivery to the customer, however, acceptance tests are carried out. They have the following characteristics:

- The tests are carried out with the actual data that an end user uses.
- Black-box strategy is followed during these tests.
- The comparison of the test results is made with those given in the software requirement specification. That is why this test is also called a validation test also.

The test has two forms:

2. Alpha Test

2. Beta Test

The customers conduct both the tests. But, whereas they carry out the alpha tests at the developer's site in the presence of the developer, they carry out the beta tests at their own site in the absence of the developer. Alpha tests may use test data that often only mimic real data, while the beta tests invariably use actual data. Further, minor design changes may still be made as a result of alpha tests, whereas beta tests normally reveal bugs related to coding.

As and when problems are reported after beta tests, the developer modifies the software accordingly. Before releasing the software to the customers, however, the management carefully audits and ensures that all the software elements are developed and catalogued, so as to properly support the maintenance phase of the software.

REFERENCES

Jorgensen, P. C. (2002), Software Testing A Craftsman's Approach, Boca Raton: CRC Press, Second Edition.

Mosley, D. J. (1993), The Handbook of MIS Application Software Testing, Yourdon Press, Prentice-Hall, Englewood Cliffs, New Jersey.

Myers, G. J. (1979), The Art of Software Testing, Wiley-Interscience, NY.

Perry, W. E. (2001), Effective Methods for Software Testing, John Wiley & Sons (Asia) Pte Ltd., Singapore, Second Edition.

BEYOND DEVELOPMENT

24

Beyond Development

Beyond development lies the world of administrators, operators, and users. The software is now to be deployed to reap success in terms of achieving the desired functionalities. Normally the developers are eager to see their efforts brought to fruition, while the users cling on to their old systems and procedures. Many good software systems do not see the light of the day purely because of stiff user resistance. Ensuring smooth software deployment primarily requires user involvement right from the day the project is conceptualized and throughout all phases of software development. Capturing user requirements in the phase of requirements analysis, planning for maintainability and modifiability in the design phase, emphasizing usability in the coding and unit testing phase, and integration and system testing in the integration phase reflect the ways the project managers generally address the software deployment concerns and issues.

Deployment gives rise to many issues, in particular the issues related to delivery and installation, maintenance, and evolution of software. This chapter is devoted to highlight some of the important features of these three post-development issues.

24.1 SOFTWARE DELIVERY AND INSTALLATION

24.1.1 Planning and Scheduling

Planning for delivery and installation requires planning for procurement of hardware, software, and skilled manpower, preparing the documentation and manuals, and planning for training. Scheduling for delivery and installation, on the other hand, requires the preparation of a timetable for putting the system in place vis-à-vis the existing system. One-shot installation of the new system as a replacement of the existing system is never desirable because of the shock it creates in the environment and the likelihood of appearance of residual errors that can bring the system to disrepute and can embolden the sympathizers of the existing system to openly challenge the prudence of adopting the new system. Such an opposition is sure to disrupt the physical operating system of the organization that the information system strives to serve.

It is desirable that the new software is installed while the old system is still in operation. It means that both systems operate simultaneously. Although this arrangement involves redundancy, it does not disrupt the physical operating system while enhancing the credibility of the new system and helping to plan to phase out the old system.

An alternative method of smooth migration to the new system is to install the modules of the new system one at a time while the old system is still in operation. A variant of this method is that the corresponding module of the old system is phased out when its replacement is fully operational. This alternative is the least disruptive, boosts confidence in the new system, and makes the transition to the new system very smooth.

Figure 24.1 shows the three alternative conversion plans discussed above.

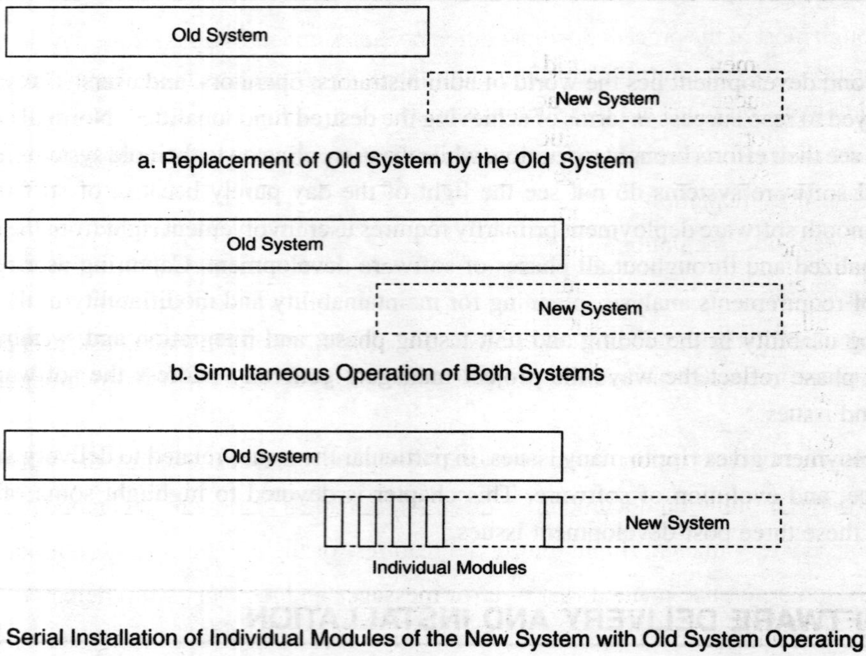

Fig. 24.1. Alternative modes of installation of new system

24.1.2 Documentation and Manuals

Recall that the definition of "software" includes "documentation." Every software development phase culminates with a product and its related documentation. While efforts have been made by different institutions to develop documentation guidelines and standards, the philosophy underlying these guidelines is the ease with which another software professional, totally unrelated with the development details of the software, can understand the way the product was developed, and work further upon the product with the help of the documentation.

Sommerville (2005) puts documentation into two classes:

1. Process documentation
2. Product documentation

Process documentation is made for effective management of the process of software development. It may fall into five categories:

1. Plans, estimates, and schedules
2. Reports
3. Standards followed
4. Working papers
5. Memos and electronic mail messages

Although most of the process documentation becomes unnecessary after the development process, a few may be needed even after the development process. Working papers on design options and future versions and conversion plans are two such examples.

Product documentation describes the delivered software product. It falls into two categories:

1. User documentation
2. System documentation

User Documentation

User documentation caters to the user needs. Because users vary in their needs, user documentation has to be different for each type of user. Sommerville (2005) divides the user documentation into five types:

1. Functional description of the system (overview of services given by the software)
2. System installation document (or installation manual or how to get started)
3. Introductory manual (highlighting the features for the normal operation mode)
4. System reference manual (list of error messages and recovery from defects)
5. System administrator's guide (on how to operate and maintain the system)

Software manuals provide a form of user documentation that can be used as ready references to carry out an activity with regard to the piece of software in place. They are developed for various types of user and can take the following forms:

1. Installation manual (or system installation document)
2. Training manual
3. Operator's manual
4. User's manual

An *installation manual* is oriented towards the need of a system administrator whose task is to successfully install the software for use. Naturally, such a manual must clearly mention the essential features with respect to the software. The features include the hardware specifications, the speed of network connectivity, the operating system, the database requirements, and the special compilers and packages needed, etc.

Training manuals are used as aid to train the administrators and operators.

An *operator's manual* is needed to operate the system. It highlights the role of the operator in taking back-ups, providing user assistance from time to time, taking appropriate overflow and security measures, analyzing job history, and generating status and summary reports for managers.

A user's manual is geared towards the need of the users. It should be organized according to various user functionalities. It should be lucid and straightforward to allow easy navigation through the software. Conditions for alternative paths during navigation should be clearly mentioned with examples. Each input screen layout, with definition and example for each data entry, must be included in the manual. The types of analysis and results should be described in the manual with examples. Software generated reports can be many. The purpose of a report, the way it can be generated, the report format, and most importantly, the analysis of such a report are of paramount importance to a user. A user's manual must include all of the above to be a meaningful guide for a user.

IEEE Standard 1063-2001 provides a template for developing a software user's manual.

System Documentation

System documentation includes all the documents—the requirements specifications, the design architectures, the component functionalities and interfaces, the program listings, the test plan, and even the maintenance guide. All documentation must be updated as changes are implemented; otherwise they get outdated very soon and lose their utility.

24.2 SOFTWARE MAINTENANCE

In the initial chapters of this text, we have indicated that a significant fraction (40%–80%) of the software lifecycle cost occurs in the software maintenance phase. Unfortunately, neither the practice of software maintenance is well understood nor the theory of software maintenance is well developed. We make an attempt to only give the salient features of the maintenance activities.

Maintenance refers to the post-delivery activities and involves modifying the code and the associated documentation in order to eliminate the effect of residual errors that come to surface during use. IEEE defines software maintenance as:

> Modifying a software system or component after delivery to correct faults, improve performance, and new capabilities, or adapt to a changed environment. (IEEE Std 610.12-1991).

Maintenance activities have been categorized as

Corrective maintenance:	Identification and removal of discovered faults
Adaptive maintenance:	Response to changes in software environment
Perfective (or evolutive) maintenance:	Changes as a result of user request to improve software performance or functionality

Emergency maintenance: Unscheduled corrective maintenance to keep a system operational

Preventive maintenance: Changes to detect and correct latent faults

A widely held belief about maintenance is that majority of them is corrective. Studies (*e.g.*, by Pigosky, 1997; Lientz and Swanson, 1980) indicate that over 80% of the maintenance activities are adaptive or perfective rather than corrective, emergency, or preventive.

24.2.1 Phases of Software Maintenance

IEEE Standard 1219-1998 identifies seven maintenance phases, each associated with input, process, output, and control. The seven phases are the following:

1. Problem/modification identification, classification, and prioritization
2. Analysis
3. Design
4. Implementation
5. Regression/system testing
6. Acceptance testing
7. Delivery

Given below are the input, process, output, and control for each of these phases.

Problem/modification identification, classification, and prioritization

Input	The modification request
Process	Each request is given an identification number, classified (corrective, adaptive, etc.) analyzed to accept or reject, estimated for resource requirement, and scheduled for implementation.
Control	The request is put in the repository.
Output	The validated request and the process details.

Analysis

Input	The validated request, project/system document, and repository information.
Process	Conduct feasibility analysis and detailed analysis.
Control	Conduct technical review, verify test strategy, re-document, and identify safety and security issues.
Output	Feasibility report, detailed analysis report, updated requirement, preliminary modification list, implementation plan. and test strategy.

Design

Input	Project/system document, source code databases, and analysis phase output.
Process	Create test cases and revise requirements and implementation plan.
Control	Software inspection/review and verify design.
Output	Revised modification list, revised detail analyses, revised implementation plan, and updated design baseline and test plans.

Implementation

Input	Source code, product/system document, results of design phase.
Process	Code, unit test, and test-readiness review.
Control	Inspect/review, verify configuration control and design traceability.
Output	Updated software and associated documentation at design, test, user, and training levels, and report on test-readiness review.

Regression/system testing

Input	Updated software documentation, report on test-readiness review, and updated system.
Process	Functional test, interface testing, regression testing, test-readiness review.
Control	Configuration control of code, program listing, modification report, and tests.
Output	Tested system test reports.

Acceptance testing

Input	Test-readiness review report, fully integrated system, acceptance test (plan, cases, and procedures).
Process	Acceptance test and interoperability test.
Control	Acceptance test, functional audit, and establish baseline.
Output	New system baseline acceptance test report.

Delivery

Input	Tested/accepted system.
Process	Physical configuration audit, install, and training.
Control	Physical configuration audit and version description document.
Output	Physical configuration audit report and version description document.

24.2.2 Technical Aspects of Software Maintenance

Certain aspects of maintenance that make it different from development are the following (Bennett 2005):

Impact analysis

Traceability

Legacy system analysis

Reverse engineering

Unique to maintenance, *impact analysis* is concerned with identifying, in the maintenance analysis phase, the modules or components that are affected by the changes to be carried out as a result of the modification request. While the primary impact of a change will be on one such module or component, more than one module or component may also experience cascaded (or ripple) impacts. The *ripple effect propagation* phenomenon is one that shows the effect of a change in one module or component along the software life cycle on another.

Traceability is a degree to which a relationship can be established between two or more products of the development process, especially products having a predecessor-successor or master-subordinate relationship to one another (IEEE, 1991). It helps to detect the ripple effects and carry out impact analysis. Attempts at achieving high traceability have met with some success at the code level by resorting to static analysis, whereas those made at design and specification level by deriving executable code from formal specifications and deriving formal specifications from executable code have met with limited success.

A *legacy system* is characterized by the following:

1. The system was developed many years ago, and got modified very frequently to meet the changing needs.
2. It is usually based on an old technology, being written in old languages.
3. Often the system supports huge database.
4. Although not one member of the original development team may be around, the system may need the support of a very large team to maintain it.

Naturally, such a system becomes inefficient, although it still retains its usefulness. Replacing it by a new one is expensive and may disrupt the organization's work. Various approaches are used in practice (Bennett 2005) to address the problem:

1. Subcontract the maintenance work.
2. Replace it with a package.
3. Re-implement from scratch.
4. Discard and discontinue.
5. Freeze maintenance and phase in a new system.
6. Encapsulate the old system and use it as a server to the new.
7. Reverse engineer and develop a new suite.

Changes in the legacy systems, leading to code restructuring, should evolve, not degrade, the system. A few examples of ways to carryout such changes are the following (Bennett, 2005):

— Control flow restructuring to remove unstructured, "spaghetti" code

— Using parameterized procedures in place of monolithic code

— Identifying modules and abstract data types

— Removing dead code and redundant variables

— Simplifying common and global variables

In a generic sense, *reverse engineering* is the process of identifying a system's components and their interrelationships and creating a representation in another form or at a higher level of abstraction. According to IEEE glossary, reverse engineering is the process of extracting software system information (including documentation) from source code. Quite often, documentation of existing systems is not comprehensive. For maintenance, it becomes necessary to comprehend the existing systems, and thus there exists a need for reverse engineering.

Considering the importance of reverse engineering, we devote the next section to this topic and devote the section after that to an allied area.

24.2.3 Reverse Engineering

Chikofsky and Cross (1990), in their taxonomy on reverse engineering and design recovery, have defined *reverse engineering* to be "analyzing a subject system to identify its current components and their dependencies, and to extract and create systems abstractions and design information." Mostly used for reengineering legacy systems, the reverse engineering tools are also used whenever there is a desire to make the existing information systems web based.

Reverse engineering can be of two types (Müller *et al.* (2000):

1. Code reverse engineering
2. Data reverse engineering

Historically, reverse engineering always meant *code reverse engineering*. Code provides the most reliable source of knowing the business rule, particularly in the absence of good documentation. However, over time, codes undergo many changes, persons responsible for developing and modifying the code leave, and the basic architecture gets forgotten. A *big-bang reverse engineering,* if tried at that time, may not be very easy. It is, therefore, desired that *continuous program understanding* be undertaken so as to trace a business rule from a piece of code (reverse engineering) and translate a change in the business rule by bringing about a change in the software component (*forward engineering*). Furthermore, to ensure that reverse engineering is carried out in a systematic manner, every component should be designed with a specific real system responsibility in view, so that reverse engineering, as well as forward engineering, becomes an effective practical proposition.

An under-utilized approach, *data reverse engineering*, aims at unfolding the information stored and how they can be used. Traditional division of work between the database developers and the software developers is the main reason for neglecting this line of thought in reverse engineering. However, migration of traditional information systems into object-oriented and web-based platforms, the increased used of data warehousing techniques, and the necessity of extracting important data relationships with the help of data mining techniques have made it necessary to comprehend the data structure of a legacy system and has opened up the possibility of adopting data reverse engineering.

The data reverse engineering process is highly human intensive. It requires (*a*) analyzing data to unearth the underlying structure, (*b*) developing a logical data model, and (*c*) abstracting either an entity-relationship diagram or an object-oriented model. An iterative process of refining the logical model with the help of domain experts is usually necessary. Often, available documentation, however outdated it may be, provides a lot of information to refine the logical model and gain knowledge about the legacy system.

Reverse engineering tools can be broadly divided into three categories: (1) unaided browsing, (2) leveraging corporate knowledge, and (3) using computer-aided tools. When a software engineer browses through the code to understand the logic, it is a case of *unaided browsing*; and when he interviews with informed individuals, he is *leveraging corporate knowledge*. *Computer-aided tools* help the software engineers to develop high-level information (such as program flow graph, data flow graph, control structure diagram, call graph, and design architecture) from low-level artifacts such as source code. Today many reverse engineering tools are available commercially, but their use rate is low.

Unfortunately, reverse engineering is not a topic that is taught in many computer science courses, unlike in many engineering science courses where maintenance engineering is a well-recognized discipline.

24.2.4 Software Reengineering

A piece of software undergoes many changes during its lifetime. Such changes bring in a lot of disorder in its structure. To make the structure understandable and for greater maintainability of code, it is often desirable to reengineer the software. Thus, reengineering is not required to enhance the software functionality. However, often one takes the opportunity of adding additional functionality while reengineering the software.

Software reengineering has four objectives (Sneed, 1995):

1. Improve maintainability
2. Migrate (*e.g.,* from a mainframe to a Unix server)
3. Achieve greater reliability
4. Prepare for functional enhancements

The process of reengineering involves reverse engineering to understand the existing software structure followed by forward engineering to bring in the required structural changes.

Reengineering means different things to different people. When applied at a process level, it is *business process reengineering*. Here the way a business is carried out and the process supporting it undergo a change. The change, however, could be so great that it may call for software reengineering to adapt to the change in the business process. For example, when the business practice of selling on payment basis gives way to selling on credit, the software may have to reflect these changes. This is software modification at the module level. Sometimes, however, the changes could be very radical to call for software reengineering at a larger scale.

When applied at a data level, reengineering is referred to as *data reengineering*. It involves restructuring existing databases, where the data remaining the same, the form may change (for example, from hierarchical to relational).

Sometimes modules of an abandoned software system are reengineered for the sole purpose of reusability. This is called *recycling*. In contrast to software reengineering which retains the business solution but changes the technical architecture, recycling abandons the business solution but largely retains the technical architecture.

Justifying a reengineering project is the most challenging issue. The greatest advantage of reengineering is being able to reduce maintenance cost and enhance quality and reliability. Unfortunately, it is difficult to test whether these objectives can be achieved. It is also difficult to assess the utility of reengineering projects and compare them with the cost of reengineering.

24.2.5 Software Configuration Management

The concepts underlying software configuration management evolved during the 1980s as a "discipline of identifying the configuration of a system at discrete points in time for the purpose of systematically controlling changes to the configuration and maintaining the integrity and traceability of the configuration throughout the system life cycle" (Bersoff, 2005; p. 10). It provides a "means through which the integrity and traceability of the software system are recorded, communicated, and controlled during both development and maintenance." (Thayer and Dorfman, 2005; p. 7).

Integrity of a software product refers to the intrinsic set of product attributes that fulfill the user needs and meet the performance criteria, schedule, and cost expectations. *Traceability,* on the other hand, refers to the ability to be able to trace and unearth the past development details of a system. This is made possible by documenting, in a very structured way, every important milestone in the development and maintenance stages of a software system.

As in hardware configuration management, software configuration management can be said to have four components:

- Identification
- Control
- Status accounting
- Auditing

Software configuration identification consists of (1) labeling (or naming) the baseline software components and their updates as they evolve over time and (2) maintaining a history of their development as they get firmed up. The software components may be the intermediate and the final products (such as specification documents, design documents, source code, executable code, test cases, test plans, user documentation, data elements, and the like) and supporting environmental elements (such as compilers, programming tools, test beds, operating systems, and the like). The *baselines* are the developed components, and the updates are the changes in the baselines.

The labeling mechanism consists of first identifying and labeling the most elementary software components, called the *software configuration items*. Such items may exist in their baseline forms and in their updates over time. When threaded together and reviewed, they give a history of development of the system and help to judge the product integrity. Software configuration management can be thus seen as a set of interrelated software configuration items. Often, the interrelations among the historically developed baselines and their updates are depicted in the form of a tree (Fig. 24.2). Labeling usually requires uniquely naming an item by specifying the version number and the level of change made to the item.

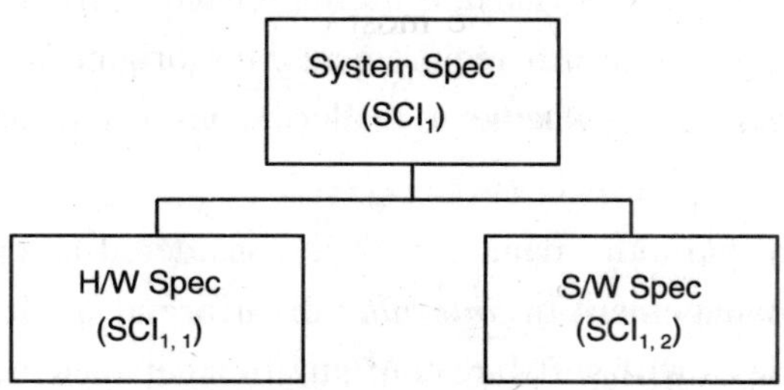

Fig. 24.2. Evolution of software component items

Maintaining configuration items requires building libraries for storing the identified baselines of specifications, code, design, test cases, and so on in physical storages, such as file folders and magnetic media, with proper specification so that accessing and retrieving them are easy.

Software configuration control is concerned with managing the changes (updates) to the software configuration items. Management of change involves three basic steps:

1. Documenting the proposed change (*i.e.,* specifying the desired change in the appropriate administrative form and supporting materials). A document, often called the *Engineering Change Proposal*, is used for this purpose. It has details of who initiates the changes, what the proposed changes are, which baselines and which versions of the configuration items are to be changed, and what the cost and schedule impacts are.
2. Getting the change proposal reviewed, evaluated and approved (or disapproved) by an authorized body. Such a body is often called the *Configuration Control Board* that consists of just one member or may consist of members from all organizational units affected by, and interested in, the proposed change. Evaluation requires determining the impact of the changes on the deliverables and on the schedule and cost of implementing the changes.
3. Following a set procedure to monitor and control the change implementation process. For example, an approved procedure that demands all change proposals to be archived requires that a proposal, which is rejected by the Configuration Control Board, has to be stored for future reference.

Software Configuration Status Accounting is the process of tracking and reporting all stored configuration items that are formally identified and controlled. Because of large amount of data input and output requirement, it is generally supported by automated tools, such as *program support libraries* (PSLs) that help storing collected data and outputting reports on the desired history of stored configuration items. At the minimum, the data, required to be tracked and reported, include the initial approved version, the status of requested change, and the implementation status of approved change.

Software Configuration Auditing is intended to enhance visibility and traceability. It helps the management to visualize the status of the software, trace each requirement originally defined in the requirements specification document to a specific configuration item (traceability), and thereby check the product integrity. Visibility, thus obtained, is useful in many ways. It helps to monitor the progress of the project, know whether extraneous requirements, not originally included in the requirements document, are also developed, decide whether to reallocate physical resources, and evaluate the impact of a change request.

Often software configuration management is considered as either *external* (or formal or baseline) configuration management or *internal* (or informal or developmental) configuration management. The former deals with software configuration between the developer and the customer (or the user) and is relevant for post-delivery operation and maintenance, whereas the latter deals with software configuration during the period of development.

IEEE Std. 828-1998 provides a template for developing a software configuration management plan.